MW00365671

WORD AND FAITH

WORD
AND FAITH

GERHARD EBELING

SCM PRESS LTD

Translated by James W. Leitch from the German
Wort und Glaube
J. C. B. Mohr (Paul Siebeck) Tübingen, 1960

All rights reserved. No part of this publication may be reproduced,
stored in a retrieval system, or transmitted, in any form or by any
means, electronic, mechanical, photocopying, recording or otherwise, without the prior permission of the publisher, SCM Press Ltd.

English translation © SCM Press Ltd 1963

334 01803 X

First published in English 1963
by SCM Press Ltd
26–30 Tottenham Road, London N1 4BZ
Second impression 1984

Printed in Great Britain at
The Camelot Press, Southampton

To my friends
Hanns Rückert and Ernst Fuchs

CONTENTS

PREFACE TO ENGLISH EDITION

THE publisher has asked me for a few introductory remarks which would facilitate the English-speaking reader's approach to this volume of essays, and in answer to this request I would attempt a definition of my own position. That of course is not to be done by drawing a plan of past and present theological schools and persuasions and pointing my place in it. Labelling people by means of party names and slogans is certainly convenient, yet it seldom serves towards clarity. Rather, I would mention a few standpoints influencing my work, yet not as if they were my own special concerns but because I think that every evangelical theologian could claim to regard them as essential.

We can give expression to our own theological aim only by trying to say what it is that counts in present-day theological work as a whole. Our own theology must be nothing else but a contemporary attempt to answer for theology as such. Answering for something implies, as does the concept of witness, two things: staking our *person*, in dedication to the *matter* concerned. Hence it can never be a question of forcing our own theology on to others and making it a law to them, but only of offering our own limited and transitory services as the means of making others free to observe their theological responsibility for themselves.

Now it seems to me eminently important to expose ourselves to the tension between different factors which on a superficial view are at loggerheads with each other, and yet on proper consideration belong so inseparably together that to lose their togetherness would be to lose what theology itself stands for. The fact that the enduring of tensions is thereby required of the theologian as *conditio sine qua non* of his calling, should not appear strange to anyone.

To take our bearings from the *theology of the Reformers* and at the same time to take *modern thought* seriously seems to be incompatible, or possible only by means of sorry compromises. For me, however, my vocation as a theologian stands or falls with the opposite view. For we can be evangelical theologians neither without the Reformers' understanding of the Gospel nor without thinking within the field of present-day experience of reality. That is why my efforts move in both directions: they are concerned on the one hand with the interpretation of Reformation theology, above all the theology of Luther (cf.

the essays 'On the Doctrine of the *Triplex Usus Legis* in the Theology
of the Reformation', 'Reflexions on the Doctrine of the Law', or 'The
Necessity of the Doctrine of the Two Kingdoms'), which was also the
focal point of my earlier activities as a church historian; and on the
other hand I am concerned with the grasp of the modern understanding of reality (e.g. 'Theology and Reality', or 'The World as
History'). Neither factor of course is indisputably established, but both
require exposition and clarification. Hence it can neither be a case of
refurbishing the theology of the Reformers, nor can it be a question of
regarding modern thought as a criterion which stands beyond question
and to which we must blindly bow. My experience and conviction as
a theological thinker is this: that there is no need to construct a supplementary and artificial bond between what belongs to the Reformation and to the modern age. Rather, both come properly to light
only in mutual encounter, and thus when they are considered together.
To that extent the first essay, 'The Significance of the Critical Historical Method for Church and Theology in Protestantism', is a
pointer for the whole, though only the beginning of a task that has a
long way to go.

As regards method, the thing is to stand up to the tension between
the historical and dogmatic approaches and their different ways of
working. The conflict between historical and dogmatic theology
threatens to tear theology apart today and so have it ruined by its own
inner contradiction. My transition from the discipline of church history to that of systematic theology was not meant, however, as a change
of front in this internal theological warfare, but as the resolve to observe the responsibilities of the historian and the dogmatician in one
person, and thus to take upon myself what is after all really expected
of every theological student. The assurance that that was a hopeful
undertaking was provided by insight into the hermeneutic problem, in
which the historical and dogmatic tasks ultimately appear as mere
aspects of one single process of understanding. The hermeneutic problem has therefore been decisive for my work form the start (cf. my
dissertation, *Evangelische Evangelienauslegung: Eine Untersuchung zu
Luthers Hermeneutik*, 1942, 2nd ed. 1962; in the present volume
cf. especially the essay, 'Word of God and Hermeneutics'). The
concentration on the hermeneutic question corresponds to Reformation theology's adoption of the *Sola Scriptura*, but includes
also the acceptance of the obligations which that involves for
a conscientious treatment of the text of holy scripture (on this point

cf. among others the essay 'The Meaning of "Biblical Theology" ').

The hermeneutic task consists for theology in nothing else but in understanding the *Gospel* as addressed to *contemporary man*. Whoever does not expose himself to the tension that entails, betrays both—the Gospel and contemporary man alike. That would also be the case if we attempted to resolve the tension by means of an apologetic that tones it down and renders it harmless (cf. 'The "Non-religious Interpretation of Biblical Concepts" ', or 'Faith and Unbelief in Conflict about Reality'). Rather, it is of the nature of the Gospel itself to seek out man at the point where he actually stands. It is only when we follow this movement of the Gospel right into the situation of godlessness that the depth of the Gospel is disclosed (here belong especially essays like 'Jesus and Faith', 'Rudimentary Reflexions on Speaking Responsibly of God', 'Worldly Talk of God', and 'Theological Reflexions on Conscience'). Theology, understood as hermeneutics, draws the conclusion which the nature of the Gospel implies for the nature of theology.

The tension—so much lamented today because it is not rightly understood and hence not faced up to either—between *theology and proclamation* is the vital factor in the task to which I see myself committed. In both cases—for theology and proclamation alike—the dependence on each other, the inability to disregard each other, makes things not easier but harder. Yet the study of theology is rightly pursued precisely when the fact of its being done with an eye to the proclamation makes the task really difficult and the responsibility really great; and likewise, the proclamation is preserved by right theology from losing its weight through our failing to keep in mind from first to last how incomparable is the task and responsibility of proclamation, and hence perhaps making it too easy for ourselves.

The aim of the following essays is therefore, to give encouragement to endure the tensions as I have just sketched them in their promising aspect. The resulting themes, for all their variety, are so closely entwined with each other that the most sensible arrangement of the studies is in chronological order. The one which consequently chances to come at the end completely accords in substance with the aim of the whole: it serves as an 'Introduction to the Study of Theology', and thus points beyond itself as leading on to the proclamation.

I wish to thank Dr James Leitch for the care with which he has performed the difficult task of translation.

GERHARD EBELING

Zürich, 17th February 1963

TRANSLATOR'S NOTE

A GOOD translation should require no extensive introduction. But there are one or two points to which the reader's attention should perhaps be drawn here:

Professor Ebeling's intense interest in words and language leads to a number of word-plays which can often be indicated only by noting the relevant German words in brackets, and to the coining of some new terms and phrases for which see p. 294 note 1. It also leads to difficulties with the English convention, of distinguishing 'Word' and 'word'. I have usually observed the convention, but the reader would be well to regard it as a difference only in print and make no mental distinction. German printers of course observe no distinction. And with Professor Ebeling it is a fundamental point that a word is precisely the same in its 'word-quality' whether it is spoken by God or by man.

I have normally tried to distinguish between *geschichtlich* and *historisch* by using 'historic' and 'historical' respectively (see p. 28 note 2) —which I subsequently learned to be the regular practice also e.g. in the American series 'New Frontiers in Theology'. Yet it proved hardly possible to maintain this throughout. It applies (with rare exceptions) to chs. I, V-XI, XVI, XVIII. But in chs. III, IV, XII, XV, XVII, 'historical' (except on pp. 129 and 383) invariably represents *geschichtlich*, while in ch. XIV it has been used indiscriminately for both the German terms, though the different senses should be reasonably clear from the context. A terminological distinction in English is admittedly somewhat arbitrary—and indeed I have felt bound to reverse it with the nouns, rendering *Geschichtlichkeit* by 'historicalness' (though I should now prefer 'historicality') and keeping 'historicity' for *Historizität*.

Quotations from Bonhoeffer's *Ethics* and his *Letters and Papers from Prison* have been taken from the official English translations (in the latter case sometimes with slight alterations). All other quotations have been independently translated, and references to the official translations kindly supplied later by the SCM Press.

In the final revision for the press, the translation of ch. XI was carefully compared with an earlier, unpublished translation by Professor Robert W. Funk of Drew University. I wish to thank him for so readily allowing the adoption of some of his renderings and the inclusion of his references to English translations of Latin works quoted. I am also grateful to Professor James S. Robinson of Claremont for many helpful suggestions, especially in connexion with the same chapter.

JAMES W. LEITCH

Bathgate, 22nd February 1963

PREFACE

THE studies here gathered together from a decade are steps on my way towards systematic theology and in it. If they let it be seen that I have not been marking time, then the advance I have made implies both a confession that there is much I would put differently today from before, and also a readiness to continue being a learner in the language school of faith. I have kept, I hope, to my basic theme—that of upholding the Reformers' concentration on Word and faith as a responsible doctrine of theological principles today. *Neque enim deus . . . aliter cum hominibus unquam egit aut agit quam verbo promissionis. Rursus, nec nos cum deo unquam agere aliter possumus quam fide in verbum promissionis eius* (Luther, *De captivitate Babylonica ecclesiae*, 1520, praeludium, *WA* 6, p. 516.30-32).

All the papers without exception were originally delivered orally. Those on pp. 282 ff, 354 ff, 363 ff and 374 ff were intended for a wider audience. In the case of those which have already been published in the *Zeitschrift für Theologie und Kirche* or elsewhere, I have tacitly improved a few stylistic shortcomings, but made no material alterations. I have added only exceptionally a later note, marked as such. That I have refrained from expanding the essays in the light of the present state of the discussion accords with the character of this publication, as does also the arrangement in order of date.

My gratitude to Hanns Rückert and Ernst Fuchs, to which the dedication of this volume gives expression, is too extensive to allow of detailed comment. Yet I must mention the unforgettable period of our work together in Tübingen, above all in the joint tutorials on Luther's exposition of Paul. Many, like us, felt that time to be a hopeful one. In spite of the ensuing geographical separation we have kept together, and rejoice in the continued good progress of what was then begun.

Finally, I would thank the publisher, Hans Georg Siebeck, for the close co-operation to which this collection of essays testifies in more ways than one, and also Thomas Bonhoeffer for the improvements he so selflessly suggested over and above the normal assistance with the work of correction.

GERHARD EBELING

Zürich, 23rd July 1960

ABBREVIATIONS

ADB	*Allgemeine Deutsche Biographie*
BKW	Bible Key Words (ETs of articles in *TWNT*)
CR	*Corpus Reformatorum*
CSEL	*Corpus Scriptorum Ecclesiasticorum Latinorum*
E	D. Bonhoeffer, *Ethik*, ed. E. Bethge, Munich 1949, 4th ed. 1958; ET, *Ethics*, SCM Press 1955
EKL	*Evangelisches Kirchenlexikon*
EvTh	*Evangelische Theologie*
FRLANT	Forschungen zur Religion und Literatur des Alten und Neuen Testaments
GCS	*Die Griechischen christlichen Schriftsteller der ersten drei Jahrhunderte*
KuD	*Kerygma und Dogma*
LTK	*Lexikon für Theologie und Kirche*
RAC	*Reallexikon für Antike und Christentum*
RGG	*Religion in Geschichte und Gegenwart*
SGV	Sammlung gemeinverständlicher Vorträge und Schriften auf dem Gebiet der Theologie- und Religionsgeschichte
SynT	R. Bultmann, *The History of the Synoptic Tradition* (ET by John Marsh), Oxford 1963
TLZ	*Theologische Literaturzeitung*
TR	*Theologische Rundschau*
TWNT	*Theologisches Wörterbuch zum Neuen Testament*
WA	Complete Works of Luther, *Weimarer Ausgabe*
WE	D. Bonhoeffer, *Widerstand und Ergebung: Briefe und Aufzeichnungen aus der Haft*, ed. E. Bethge, Munich 1951, 8th ed. 1958; ET, *Letters and Papers from Prison* (in USA, *The Prisoner for God*), 1953, revised ed. 1956
ZA(N)W	*Zeitschrift für die alt(neu) testamentliche Wissenschaft*
ZTK	*Zeitschrift für Theologie und Kirche*

I

THE SIGNIFICANCE
OF THE CRITICAL HISTORICAL METHOD
FOR CHURCH AND THEOLOGY
IN PROTESTANTISM[*][1]

I

PROTESTANT theology has for the last thirty years been marked by a
passionate renunciation of Neo-Protestantism, i.e. of the development
that took place in the churches of the Reformation from about the
middle of the seventeenth century under the influence of the modern
spirit. The aversion applies equally to the entire changing pattern of
theological thinking and its results in the Church in the period of the
Enlightenment, of Idealism, of Romanticism and of Liberalism. Indeed,
it includes also the whole of Pietism, as a phenomenon sprung from the
same roots, and even turns likewise against early Protestant Orthodoxy
in so far as it is held to have already paved the way for the false developments of later days. Instead of this a radical return to the theology of the
Reformers is sought.

In regard to this basic tendency in contemporary Protestant theology
the question arises whether, or in what sense, such a renunciation of the
theological work of the last two or three centuries and a radical return

---

* *ZTK* 47 (1950), pp. 1-46.
[1] The essay is based on a paper which in October 1949 introduced a discussion
on the proposed joint undertaking among the members of the editorial circle
[of the *ZTK*]. To the ensuing debate I owe various suggestions which have been
taken into account in revising the paper. Yet it has retained the character of a
purely private work of the author, and, in spite of the far-reaching agreement
that has been achieved in principle, it must not by any means be regarded as
expressing the common policy of all the associates responsible for the Journal.
The range and difficulty of the questions raised forbid any attempt to see in the
remarks that follow more than a provisional contribution for discussion. I have
resolved to publish it only in the hope of thereby stimulating a debate which may
lead us to greater clarity, and in which also many subsidiary problems that are
here of necessity only fleetingly touched on can be expounded separately and in
detail.

to the theology of the Reformers is possible at all. Without discussing
this question in detail, general historical considerations make it possible
to say one thing right away: a mere refurbishing and repetition of the
theology of the Reformers is as utterly impossible as the by-passing of
the intervening history with its alterations in the statement of the problems and its new presentations of them. Even a theology which is ever so
closely oriented towards the theology of the Reformers will be compelled
to differ from it considerably, as surely as disregard of the historical
difference between the sixteenth and twentieth centuries turns out in
the end to be nothing but a piece of self-deception. If the change that
has taken place between the age of the Reformation and ourselves may
be provisionally characterized by saying that the rise of the critical
historical method is one at least of the decisive features of so-called
Neo-protestantism, then the question boils down to this: what is the
relationship between the return to the theology of the Reformers which
is now demanded and practised and the critical historical method which
has meantime attained increasing, and in the second half of the nineteenth century wellnigh undisputed, dominance in theology?

It is true that in contemporary theological literature there are occasionally statements to be found which advocate the fundamental rejection of the critical historical method.

That is surely nowhere done more bluntly than by the teacher of
philosophy at the Kirchliche Hochschule Berlin, Dr Erwin Reisner,
in his essay on *Offenbarungsglaube und historische Wissenschaft* (published in the Kirchliche Hochschule Berlin's series *Der Anfang*, vol. 3,
1947). In it he says: 'To recognize and accept revelation means quite
simply, to capitulate to it unconditionally, to surrender everything that
belongs to the nature of the godless world and its godless history and
makes it a perverse world and perverse history. The man who has once
grasped what it means to be a sinner has no option but to let go of the
whole superstition that calls itself science, above all historical science'
(p. 14). Commenting on a sentence from Berdyaev, Reisner asserts
'that the "Christian philosophy of history", i.e. simply revelation's
understanding of history, unmasks not only the failure of history but
also that of secular scientific historical research' (p. 17). And he goes
on: 'Till now—at least in the last two centuries—the truth of revelation has been subordinated to the judgment of historical science. It
was considered right, often in fact even obligatory, to subject the
sacred traditions to rational criticism and measure them by the standards which the autonomous mind had set up for its own purposes.
Even theology itself, especially the theology of the more recent Protestant schools, has displayed and for the most part still displays this
questionable scientific ambition. One could often almost say: it finds

vindication at the bar of science more important than vindication before God. That is called human autonomy. This fruit of the enjoyment of the forbidden fruit of the tree of knowledge arrogates to itself the right and the power to decide on the truth or falsehood of the Word of God. The rational science that rests on the foundation of the pre-scientific decision to be "as God" seeks—and this is an extremely clever trick of the devil's—to abrogate the very revelation by means of which that pre-scientific decision has to be unmasked in the first place and then disputed. There is a whole list of very telling, and in fact seemingly thoroughly obvious, arguments in favour of this procedure. It is alleged, for example, that scientific criticism is justified because the Word of God has assumed the form of a servant—that is to say, because it has humbled itself and presented itself in a guise which bears all the marks of human, all-too-human weakness and is for that very reason also subject to human criticism. Thus critical historical science (it is said) has not the slightest wish to impugn the Word of God itself, but is concerned only with a thorough examination of the human word in which it is clothed. With that the impious treatment of scripture goes the length of assuming the mask of peculiar piety. The alleged intention is to analyse the servant-form in order to bring to light the glorious form behind it. But is that itself not a dreadful piece of presumption? If God reveals himself to man under the veil of the servant-form, then he thereby brings man under judgment, because owing to his unfitness for God he could not bear the glorious form. Thus the servant-form of God in his revelation shows me my own true form: *ecce homo*! I am here subjected to the criticism of God. How should it be possible now to turn the tables by making myself the judge and critic of the Word that here confronts me, for all its servant-form? This servant-form does not in fact confer any rights on me at all: quite the contrary, it takes clean out of my hands every right to make any autonomous judgment. The real call of today—and this can never be impressed urgently enough upon theology and theologians—is to make a turn of 180 degrees and bring historical science, especially in so far as it has gained a dominant position within theology itself, under the judgment of revelation and mark it plainly as an erroneous path leading to falsehood. It is not at all a case of "demythologizing" the New Testament, or any other part of the scriptures: it is a case of "de-historizing" theology' (pp. 17 ff).

Reisner's effort to uphold the authoritative character of the word of scripture (identified with revelation) over against the despotism of historical criticism coincides with the concern shown by the Greifswald teacher Dr Helmut Echternach in a study on the limits of theology and the authority of the Word under the title *Es stehet geschrieben* (appearing as volume 14 of the Furche Studies edited by Hanns Lilje, Berlin 1937). He sets in the forefront of his study the thesis: 'The biblical text that is binding for church and theology and therefore verbally immune from error is for us the German translation of Martin Luther in the form prescribed to the church as text and canon' (p. 9). Any reader who thinks at first that he has not rightly understood, or that the author is only using a paradoxical statement to induce him to read further, will learn to think again when he meets another no less astonishing thesis: 'An exegesis which does not agree with the confessional statements of the Lutheran Evangelical Church, is from the start also false' (p. 80). That Echternach really means the tomfoolery of his opening thesis seriously, is perfectly clear from his reflexions on the problem of textual revision of the Luther Bible: 'Whoever ventures the outrageous attempt at textual revision puts himself . . . *extra ecclesiam*' (p. 72). True, Echternach himself raises the objection that the Luther text used in the church today is itself the product of a revision. To that too, however, he finds an answer worthy of his basic thesis. Return to the original Luther text would of course also be textual revision. But the fact is: 'The text that now happens to be valid must remain' (p. 73). 'The fact that in the Evangelical Church of Germany a revision could come about at all—and the 1911 one at that!—was not only the ever-new result of Genesis 11. Over and above that, it was the issue of a special divine wrath that hung over this church. We have to bear the 1911 Bible as a punishment' (p. 73). If one takes the trouble, in spite of these samples, to examine the elaborations of such an ingeniously tricked-out theology of catastrophe in search of their point, then what comes to light is again the attempt to safeguard the real objectivity of the Word of God in its absurdity and contradictoriness against the 'boring-through tendency' (as Echternach calls it) of modern critical exegesis, which seeks the content of revelation somehow or other behind the text and so becomes its master, instead of letting it stand over against us as the hard, indissoluble, offence-giving thing it is and so 'experiencing the pounding and shattering of theology upon the rocks of truth' (p. 10). When Echternach describes pressing back to the original text as already a stirring of the 'boring-through tendency' (p. 72) and talks of boring through to inanity as a necessary result of the development of the concept of scripture in the last 200 years (p. 32), when he considers the search for the original meaning of the text to be an illusion and defines the task of exegesis as merely ascertaining what the text has to say to us today (p. 75), so as thereby to rule out in principle all questions of analysis (p. 76), then we are certainly surprised to hear again in the end that 'naturally' that is not by any means to say the work of philological historical science is meaningless. The examples, however, which he then provides of the process of opening up the depths of the Luther text by comparing it with the different meaning of the original text as ascertained by critical historical means, prove to be cheap pieces of dextrous harmonizing. Theology, of which Echternach says that in every age it is the shock-troops of antichrist (p. 40), here changes again after all into a massive bulwark of ecclesiastical positivism and traditionalism. If Echternach complains that Karl Barth's correct starting-point in the concept of revelation is thwarted by the philologically analysed concept of scripture, which is nowhere expressed with such fundamental sharpness as in Barth (p. 34), he nevertheless praises Barth on the other hand for the fact that in his case the thwarting takes place only theoretically in the concept of scripture, but not however in his exegesis (p. 36)—so that Echternach in spite of his preceding criticism can describe Barth as the only contemporary theologian whose theology is free of any element of construction (p. 67).

As a final example of disregard of the critical historical method, particularly noteworthy because of the eminence of its author, we would cite a statement to be found in Hans Asmussen's preparatory study for the World Council of Churches conference in Amsterdam with the title *Gesetz und Evangelium* (appearing in the academic series *Lebendige Wissenschaft* edited by Professor von Campenhausen, vol. 3, Stuttgart 1947). Asmussen wishes to take Isaiah 40-66 as an illustration of the free and unconditional proclamation of grace, i.e. of our venturing to testify to deliverance before the necessity for a deliverance arises on our horizon at all. Already in 1944, he says, at a Bible-study retreat for Württemberg ministers, he had 'laid great stress on the preacher's having clear ideas regarding the authorship of these chapters' (p. 32). What Asmussen understands by these 'clear ideas' is disclosed in the following sentences: 'For about 150 years it has been taken for one of the most elementary marks of theological education to ascribe the section Isaiah 40-66 to a different author from the author of the first 39 chapters. The common conviction is, that these 26 chapters [I count 27 chapters!] did not arise until after the event they presuppose. It is thought that the prophet did not proclaim the message "Comfort ye, comfort ye my people" until after the release from Babylonian captivity had become a thing of the past. I have never considered this hypothesis correct. It has ultimately no scientific grounds, but is dogmatically conditioned throughout. It rests chiefly on observation of the fact that the name Cyrus appears in these 26 chapters. It is considered self-evident that either God did not yet know that the liberator of his people would be called Cyrus, or else that God was not in a position, or was not of a mind, to reveal this name to his prophet. For that reason, in the preparation for the Bible Study in the autumn of 1944, I earnestly prayed for the renunciation of this pet theory. This is not merely a literary question. It is rather one where a central part of our proclamation is at stake. If we take the 26 chapters of the prophet Isaiah quite simply as having been spoken 150 years before the events they refer to, then and not till then do we appreciate the weight of the glad tidings they bring' (pp. 32 f). This primitive dogmatical way of arguing, which incidentally does not even reveal precise acquaintance with the *communis opinio* of Old Testament research which it attacks, does not only in this one case evade the labour of good clean exegesis, but tacitly includes a fundamental rejection of the critical historical method.

Examples of such radical disregard of the principles of historical method in the more recent Protestant theological literature could, it is true, be multiplied—especially from the field of Old Testament exegesis —yet they really form exceptions in the picture as a whole. We might ask whether troubling ourselves with them is not already doing them too much honour—or rather, whether pointing them out in public is not sufficient to make them impossible on their own showing. Of course, the fact that the publications cited are not obscure cases but that each of them, both through the name of the author and through the place of publication is intimately associated with the official Evangelical Church, must be a warning against taking their appearance all too lightly. We must ask ourselves if we are not here face to face with certain symptoms of a much more deep-seated sore in theology and the church, i.e. if it is not the case that here a widespread theological current, whose consequences are commonly veiled, suddenly emerges with all the clarity one could wish.

For that reason we must first of all very much widen the scope of our observations and reflexions, and seek to grasp a few characteristic features of the theological and ecclesiastical situation in which we find ourselves. For the question of the critical historical method is far from being a formal, technical problem of methodology: it is a question which, from the historical and the factual point of view, touches on the deepest foundations and the most difficult interconnexions of theological thinking and of the church situation.

To interpret one's own age by setting it in its wider historical context is, owing to the all too short distance from the object, always a very risky and easily contested undertaking, to which the historian in particular has an understandable aversion. Yet to refrain entirely from doing so would—apart from our being really quite unable to help making ourselves some sort of picture of the history of our own times—be all the more noxious for the fact that reflexion of this kind, however defective it may be, constitutes a necessary element in responsible examination of our own position and action in the present. This sort of contemplation of the history of the times can on occasion become a not immaterial kind of direct participation in the events of the times.

There is likely to be general agreement that the end of the First World War forms a milestone also in the history of the church and of theology. However much the general political and intellectual upheaval may have contributed to that, and however little fundamental changes took place at first in strictly ecclesiastical circles, there is still no mistaking the fact that since the beginning of the twenties a new power has arisen in the

Protestant world which has remarkable driving-force and moves in a direction of its own.

It is characteristic of the nature of Protestantism that this new factor has proceeded from theology and has remained confined, in the first instance at least, to the work of the theologians. Authors and works so far apart to our way of thinking today as Rudolf Otto with his book on the Holy, Karl Barth with his Romans, Karl Holl with his collection of Luther Essays, Wilhelm Lütgert with his work on the Religion of German Idealism and its End, Emil Brunner with his Schleiermacher book *Die Mystik und das Wort*, Friedrich Gogarten with his controversy with cultural idealism in *Illusionen*, Rudolf Bultmann with his book on Jesus—they all form, in that more or less accidental chronological order, a chain of effective impulses towards a thoroughgoing new orientation of theological thinking. The right to join their names together like that at all certainly rests above all merely on the fact that at roughly the same time and in relative independence of each other they threw theology into a ferment. And yet surely more than that can be said of their mutual affinity, be it ever so limited. Even the one still most strongly indebted to the nineteenth century in his method and his way of thinking, Rudolf Otto, certainly also had his share in contributing from the religious-historical standpoint towards the unsettling of a popular theological liberalism, and in his own way likewise towards the pointing up of elements grown unfamiliar in the Reformers' faith. For the consciousness of being unable simply to continue on the nineteenth century's line of theological development, and of being called to subject church and theology to a thoroughgoing critical revision that takes its bearings from the Reformation, is the basic tendency that has established itself since the end of the First World War with surprising speed and power of appeal. The fact that the theological and ecclesiastical party formations of left and right inherited from the nineteenth century have been broken through and are felt over a wide front to have been left behind, is the clearest sign of the change that has come over the situation. From now on one can hardly find another notable theological work that is not touched somehow or other by this change of situation. And yet it is very difficult to give more precise substance to the common factor which comes to expression here. Even the 'dialectic theology' group, which to begin with rose up as a unity from among the multiplicity of forces participating in the upheaval, broke apart after only a short decade to become apparently irreconcilable opponents, although at first a specific common impulse had unquestionably been present and had proved itself the most effective in comparison with the motive forces at work alongside it. The premature split in the circle, which had its voice in the journal *Zwischen den Zeiten*, must not be interpreted as a sign of weakness, but rather as a result of the swift successes which accelerated the internal development, but therewith also the differentiation and complication of the problems. Yet no sharply definable groupings have resulted from this process. Only the immediate entourage of Karl Barth —though his actual influence extends far beyond it and indisputably sounds the dominant note in the present theological situation—forms a more or less firmly outlined unity. This state of affairs must not, however, prevent us from seeing that even the most violently conflicting standpoints of today possess a wide measure of agreement in their reaction against the nineteenth century. And this assertion again, though now almost a commonplace of theology, must not create any illusions about the fact that the relation of contemporary theology to that of the nineteenth century is really not after all simply one of radical breach, but there exist on the contrary manifold lines of communication which amid all the emphasizing of the contrast are all too easily forgotten. Examples that readily come to mind are Wilhelm Herrmann or Martin Kähler or the Neo-Lutheranism of the nineteenth century. It is a real question, however, whether the relationship to the nineteenth century does not require to be more carefully considered and reviewed also at *the* very points on which there is today a widespread conviction of having reached a final judgment. Bultmann's formulation of the problem certainly points most sharply in that direction. Yet from a great variety of other quarters, too, the question forces itself ever more clearly upon us, whether the practice of all too quickly dismissing the problems which the theology of the nineteenth century wrestled with is not the increasingly discernible weakness of the theological situation today.

This sketch, so far confined to a formal outline, will have to be filled in in the light of the essential theological problems. But before I proceed to that, it is necessary to touch on one more matter which came to be of considerable significance for the present theological and ecclesiastical situation. The commencement of the theological change after the First World War coincided with the task of reorganizing the Evangelical Church in Germany, occasioned by the collapse of the political system with which the Evangelical Church constitution in the form of the system of church government by the civil princes had been closely linked since the Reformation. This external impulse in the year 1918 of course only brought to its close a development which had already been going on in theory and practice since the beginning of the nineteenth century. Thus it is no wonder that the solution of the constitutional problem was in essence determined by the nineteenth-century beginnings. The theological change that was just in its initial stages came too late to carry any weight at all in the reorganizing of the Evangelical Church. Rather it took its effect in church life only slowly in the course of the twenties, on the one hand through inward renewal of the preaching and on the other through growing criticism of the structure of the Evangelical Church with its nineteenth-century features.

The turbulent political upheaval in the year 1933, however, prevented the process of church renewal from ripening quietly. The tremendous task which arose for German Protestantism with the coming to a head simultaneously of the ecclesiastical and the political crisis naturally brought with it the possibility of a comprehensive consideration of all the problems of evangelical doctrine and evangelical life that had long been waiting for clarification. The story of the church struggle with its dual front inwards and outwards contains a veritably inexhaustible supply of theological illustrations of the formulation and multiplication of concrete problems. When we speak of the 'experiences of the church struggle', we must of course beware of isolating individual aspects. We must rather look soberly at the whole complex and keep in view among the so-called 'experiences' primarily also all the variations on the theme of failure. It would be false to draw a line under what has happened and let it pass into oblivion. But it would be equally false to complete the urgently needed assimilation of the experiences of the church struggle while remaining rigidly in the battle order of the day, and to maintain the poisonous atmosphere that made clarification so tremendously difficult. For although here and there church existence was liberatingly reduced to essentials and its basic elements laid bare and given completely new life, yet at the same time there came also the temptation to safeguard this position by barring the doors to the outside world, and thereby to leave aside the problems which arose from the debate with the historical heritage of Protestantism. The result could therefore hardly fail to be that the reorganization of the church after 1945 only restored a shabby and in many respects unsatisfactory framework in which the struggle for church renewal must now go on. Starting from this position can be fruitful only when we succeed thereby in freeing the whole range of our field of vision. That, however, can only happen when a theology without blinkers maintains its indispensable critical function in the church. But that again depends on whether theology musters up the necessary measure of self-criticism in reviewing its own history.

II

That changes in the history of theology always display close relations to contemporary variations in the history of thought in general, will appear out of place only to those who dream of the ideal of a *theologia perennis*, i.e. who fail to realize that the pursuit of theology is subject as such to the historicalness of existence and that theology, precisely in so far as it is not free speculation but is bound to a definite *traditio*, which for the Protestant mind means to holy scripture, is an ever new attempt at exposition, i.e. at translation. Thus theology, in so far as it remains true to its task, of its very nature moves with the times, i.e. it accepts the language, thought-forms and approach of the present. Now of course I need only recall the expression 'conforming to the times', which acquired such an ominous tone in the early days of the church struggle, in order to bring before us the full complexity of the problem here involved. Indeed it could actually be said that the question as to the rightness and limits of theology's conforming to the times is really the basic problem of the theological situation today. It is of course an acute question in every age and demands renewed clarification from every generation. For indeed it belongs, as we have said, to the very nature of the theologian's work. But today the question is of greater urgency, and must be set in the centre of the discussion, because the present dominant tendency in theology arose as a reaction against so-called Neo-Protestantism, i.e. against a period in the history of theology in which the motto of conformity to the times was trumps and obviously led to the severest crises in church and theology. For that reason the question as to the rightness and limits of theology's conforming to the times has grown all the more urgent the more we—for the most part certainly with very good reason—contemplate the mistaken developments of two centuries and are therefore inclined in the sharpness of our contradiction of them to overlook the question itself altogether. For it is surely a case of mistaking the problem as such when we suppose that the question of theology's conforming to the times can be met simply by demanding its conformity to scripture, or to the confessions, as if that were an end of the matter. For of course the very concept of conformity to scripture or confession contains itself the problem of exposition and therewith the problem of conformity to the times. And it contributes just as little towards clarification when we suppose that the problem can be eliminated by calling upon the fact that in virtue of the object it represents theology is at all times necessarily out of conformity with the times. For of course the whole point is precisely, how this lack of conformity with the times is attested at a given juncture in the history of thought. And that brings us again to the problem which we are trying to indicate by the concept of conformity to the times.

That obviously brings us to the basic methodological problem of theology. If a moment ago I called the question as to the rightness and limits of theology's conformity to the times the basic problem of the theological situation today, I could now also adopt a more general formulation: it is the problem of method that in the theological situation today has entered an extremely topical and critical stage. And this could again be formulated still more precisely by saying that the question of hermeneutics forms the focal point of the theological problems of today. A brief glance at the individual theological disciplines can elucidate this assertion. That Old Testament and New Testament scholars come up against the problem of hermeneutics in a special way, is obvious at once. But the same is true also of the discipline of church history—here, indeed, in two respects: first in so far as it is likewise continually concerned with the interpretation of sources, but then also and above all because of course the process of exposition of scripture that goes on in the history of the church presents the hermeneutical problem in its full compass, and thus the question of a theological grasp of the nature of church history opens straight into the basic problem of hermeneutics. The difficult problem of theology's systematic method can be properly solved only when it is likewise set in the light of the question of hermeneutics. For resting on the exposition of scripture and the history of theology, dogmatics has the task of bringing the church's teaching into contact and discussion with contemporary principles of thought, there to submit it to critical sifting and present it in its full inner coherence. Thus here the struggle for the momentarily required translation of the kerygma is brought to its issue in the most comprehensive way— whereby, however, the hermeneutical question in its basic methodological significance is also momentarily brought to a decision. And it is likewise plain that for so-called practical theology, above all in its teaching on sermon, instruction and pastoral care, the hermeneutic question presents the one central problem underlying all questions of detail, in so far as the *applicatio* must not stand unrelated and all on its own alongside the *explicatio*. More particularly also in the study of missions, with its difficult questions (so highly instructive for theological work as a whole) of translating the biblical message into the languages of totally different civilizations, the hermeneutic problem proves to be of fundamental significance. In view of the importance which thus attaches to the hermeneutic question it is necessary to trace out somewhat more closely its inner structure in the theological realm.

Christianity[1] stands or falls with the tie that binds it to its unique historical[2] origin. That means first of all: Christianity is a historic

---

[1] The theologian rightly has qualms about employing this designation, as also with the general concepts 'Protestantism' and 'Catholicism'. Instead of expressing the claim to revelation, as could properly be done only by the term 'church', these concepts smoothe away the peculiarity of the church and fit it into the realm of spiritual and religious development—to do which presupposes not only modern ways of thinking but also the rise of the confessional problem in the West since the sixteenth century. Both, of course, stand in close historical connexion with each other. For the moment the absolute validity of the one Catholic Church was in fact broken and mutually contradictory ways of understanding revelation stood over against each other, there inevitably arose the necessity to provide, irrespective of the question of truth, a neutral designation for the total phenomenon of Christianity, sprung from the same historical root but now separated into opposing parts. Since the Reformation it is impossible to employ 'church' as an unequivocal historical category and assume the identity of its dogmatic and historical meaning. The fact of the confessional division, which can of course be shown to have had a vigorous part in the genesis of modern thinking and the modern consciousness of history, does not release the theologian from the dilemma in which the empirical categories of history and the systematic categories of dogmatics cannot be made simply to coincide. Whoever faces up to the full weight of the confessional problem—it could be shown that that can be done only on Protestant ground—cannot evade the use of categories whose employment requires, from the dogmatic point of view, at least to be corrected. To shirk this difficulty would mean failing to grasp the situation in which theology has in fact been placed since the Reformation and not just since about the middle of the seventeenth century.
Incidentally, in thus referring to the significance which the confessional split has for the method and language of theology we must, at least in the form of a passing reference, ward off the mistaken view that from the purely dogmatic standpoint the confessional problem really did not arise until the sixteenth century. The *una sancta ecclesia catholica* in demonstrable and undisputed unity is a thing which never existed in history. To that extent the confessional problem is as old as Christianity itself. The special significance of the sixteenth century for the confessional problem is merely that here for the first time since Constantine within the same political area (namely, the West, or to put it more precisely, the Empire) mutually opposing churches and views of revelation were accorded public and legal recognition. This political event, which has its basis in intellectual conditions that can certainly no longer be set aside, has come to be of revolutionary significance also for the history of the church and of theology.
[2] For the understanding of what follows, it should be noted that German has two not entirely interchangeable words for 'historical': *historisch* and *geschichtlich*. The distinction may be roughly expressed by saying that *geschichtlich* means belonging to the succession of events, while *historisch* means accessible to, or connected with, the methods of scientific historical research. I have tried here

phenomenon. It derives from a definite historical past and therefore stands in historical relation to that past. But the proposition that Christianity stands or falls with the tie that binds it to its unique historical origin means much more than that. It contains an assertion which is paradoxical in comparison with all other phenomena in history. For it not only means that the historical origin of Christianity has the peculiarity of a *primum movens* at the beginning of a process of development in history, but it ascribes to this historical origin once and for all abiding, normative, absolute significance for the whole historic phenomenon of Christianity in its entirety. That is, the historical origin of Christianity is assigned the character of revelation. It is thereby withdrawn from the relativity and transience of all historic events. It forms a realm which is once and for all defined, distinguished from all the other phenomena of history—a judgment which finds expression in the fixing of the canon of holy scripture.

The bearing of that of course does not become plain until what is claimed to be revelation is more closely defined. What counts as revelation is not so much (I am purposely expressing myself vaguely, in order to leave room for the multiplicity of ways of understanding revelation that meet us in the history of Christianity) or at least not in the first instance holy scripture. For what counts as revelation is not so much, or at least not in the first instance, the disclosure and communication of general timeless truths. On the contrary, revelation is primarily and properly a definite event—namely, the event attested in holy scripture —which again, to define it still more closely and state its absolute peculiarity, is the appearance of Jesus Christ. To this event, then—the event of revelation in the most proper sense, and the one in which at the same time the historical origin of Christianity is concentrated— there belongs once and for all abiding, normative, absolute significance. The event in question is one which, although it is attested as a unique historical event and as such belongs to a definitely fixed past, nevertheless does not become a thing of the past but has a constant present quality. The historical Jesus of Nazareth is proclaimed as the present Lord exalted to the right hand of God, the work wrought in his suffering, dying and rising again is proclaimed as the salvation that is wrought for all time and therefore always present.

These sentences, which have attempted to outline first of all in a purely descriptive way, and therefore as broadly and neutrally as pos-

---

(as far as possible) to use 'historic' (sometimes 'in history') for the former and 'historical' for the latter.—*Translator.*

sible, what for Christianity is the constitutive understanding of its origin and nature, have a very profound bearing on the hermeneutic question. If to begin with we disregard for a moment all the problems which have arisen in this respect since the dawning of modern times, then the result is the following picture of the ancient and medieval church's view, over against which we shall set point for point the position of the Reformers and the early Protestants.[1]

1. The question arises as to what are the ontological categories under which the event of revelation is to be comprehended. In this the two tendencies of fully preserving both its historicity and its revelational character have both had to be respected to the full. The ancient church attempted to do that by applying at one and the same time both physical and metaphysical, historical and metahistorical categories to the event of revelation. That found its classic outcome in the formulae of the Christological dogma, in the thought of the history of redemption, and also in the practice that became a model for all later dogmatics of combining the trinitarian and the redemptive-history structure in the Credo. With that a canon of exposition was set up which exercised the function of a bulwark, on the one hand to secure for the event of revelation its place in the world and its history, but on the other hand to isolate it at the same time from the world and its history. For the event of revelation so interpreted was in fact after all from the ontological point of view an event *sui generis* and therefore in principal inviolable. But precisely this attempt at an ontological interpretation of the event of revelation offered the possibility of linking up with a previous general metaphysical view, as taken over from Greek philosophy, surmounting it to be sure, but allowing its validity in principle and so reconciling natural thought and supernatural revelation.

The Reformation upset this ontological interpretation of the event of revelation, but did not in principle surrender it. It is true that in shifting the accent from the metaphysical categories to the personalistic redemptive-history categories it destroyed the scholastic system, but for all that it still allowed a metaphysical and metahistorical common sense that

---

[1] This in itself points at once to the intermingling of the confessional and the hermeneutic problems. It is on a different understanding of the relation between church (or revelation) and history that the confessions part company. To realize this seems to me to provide standpoints that are essential for the carrying out of any study of the confessions that is to succeed in reaching beyond a purely polemic, or merely static and descriptive, presentation and achieving a theological grasp of the confessional problem as such. I must here content myself with this pointer.

remained within the framework of the traditional way of thinking. The revolutionary new element in its understanding of revelation was gained without departing from the traditional general principles of thought—a circumstance which again and again presents us with great difficulties in interpreting the theology of the Reformers, as could be shown for example with Luther's doctrine of the two kingdoms. The revival of a modified scholasticism in early Protestant Orthodoxy is the historical proof of how easy it was to overlook, or not take at all seriously, the doubts the Reformers had cast on the ontological interpretation of the event of revelation. Thus the Reformation certainly altered radically the objective understanding of the meaning of the event of revelation, but not the general speculative presuppositions in which the event of revelation had become embedded and anchored by church tradition.

2. Bound up with the ontological interpretation of the event of revelation is the view of holy scripture. If revelation from the ontological point of view is an event *sui generis*, if by means of metaphysical and metahistorical categories a separate place is thus provided for it in the world and its history, then there belongs to it a certain definable sphere in which it shines and which is illumined by it in a special way. Then there is a *historia sacra* which exists alongside secular history and is to be assessed by different standards from it. Then too, however, the witness to this *historia sacra* is a literary genus of a wholly peculiar kind, in fact holy scripture. Since it is the sole way of approach to the revelation, it even comes to take the place of revelation. As communication of revelation it must be ontologically the same in kind as the event of revelation itself. The Christological dogma of the two natures is mirrored again in the doctrine of scripture. It, too, is of human and divine nature at the same time. It, too, stands in spite of its human nature so to speak outside the context of original sin. It is infallible. To the dogma of incarnation there corresponds the dogma of verbal inspiration. This duplication of the miracle of revelation inevitably brings with it an extension and multiplication of the content of revelation. The quality of revelation now belongs to every single communication in the Bible as such. Its picture of the world and of history supplies the unquestioned basis of the Christian world view.

This idea of scripture, which in the ancient and medieval church in spite of its validity in principle was nevertheless (for reasons to be discussed under our next point) not the only determining factor in the understanding of revelation, was again deeply shaken at the Reformation but in practice not subjected to thoroughgoing critical revision. The

concentration of the scripture testimony upon Jesus Christ as *the* Word
of God and the differentiation of law and Gospel as a rule for the
exposition of scripture set up an extraordinarily critical canon within
the canon. The preponderance, it is true, which in the opposition to the
Catholic understanding of revelation was now accorded exclusively to
scripture had at once the result that this sole surviving foundation amid
the great collapse of authorities was brought into agreement after all
with the traditional views by being safeguarded also in theory as an
unassailable realm *sui generis*, while the critical pressure of the material
principle was taken up and balanced out by the formal principle and the
doctrine of verbal inspiration received an intensification and a funda-
mentalistic significance that were hitherto unknown.

3. The understanding of revelation and the concept of scripture are
the presuppositions which lead to the heart of the hermeneutic question,
to the problem of how revelation becomes a present actuality. Since the
uniqueness, completeness and historicity of revelation is maintained
in principle, the relation to revelation is essentially of a historical kind.
Revelation's claim to validity for the present is made room for by
recognizing its content as unalterable truth. To that extent the distance
in history from revelation is not seen as a hindrance to its significance
for the present. Literal historical exegesis is therefore recognized as the
foundation of the church's exposition of scripture. Nevertheless the
possibilities of conflict between the literal meaning and the requirements
arising from the application to the present are not entirely excluded.
They are indeed reduced to a minimum by the fact that the particular
expositor shares the Bible's picture of the world and of history from the
start, naively and without conflict, as a presupposition that has become
a traditional heritage of civilization. For the rest, however, any difficulties that may arise are cleared away by harmonizing, circumvented
by an eclectic use of scripture, or explained with the help of a church
tradition of doctrine that amplifies and develops revelation. Special, but
yet supplementary rather than decisive, significance attaches to the
method of using allegorical interpretation to turn to good account those
passages also which are unproductive or offensive when it comes to
relating them to the present.

Yet these remarks on the technical aspect of the exposition of scripture
bring us only to the beginning of what has to be said on the question of
how revelation becomes a present actuality. If the identification of holy
scripture and revelation is taken as the starting point, then the present
actualization is effected by means of the binding force of the doctrinal

and moral teaching derived from scripture, that is, via the law which finds its realization in the present life of the church and of the individual believer. But that already leads to certain difficulties for the actualization. Thus, for example, specific instructions of Jesus to his disciples that were conditioned by the situation are not susceptible of direct and general realization in the present. In this case the actualization can be achieved by imitative reconstruction of an exceptional situation, by assimilation of the present to the past. This procedure, which in the medieval sects, for example, became a danger to the church but was domesticated in monasticism, could be termed the method of actualization by imitative historizing. In the case of the doctrinal teachings, especially in so far as they affect the event of revelation, the aim of actualization can at the least be supported by the method of actualization by contemplative historizing. We transpose ourselves into the past so as thereby to become contemporaneous with it. Promoting contemplation of the event in the mind's eye, meditative entering into the experience, intensified into sharing in it as if we were there ourselves, representation in mime, but also repetition of the course of the events of revelation in the ordering of the Christian year, or immediate actualization of the past event by means of relics or pilgrimages to sites of the sacred history— all these are phenomena that must be seen in their conjunction with the basic hermeneutic problem of the present actualization of past revelation.

But while in the actualization by imitative historizing and by contemplative historizing we have to do with methods in which the emphasis lies on the activity proceeding from man in the present, the Roman Catholic Church has always put the principal accent on those ways of actualizing revelation in which the revealing reality actively actualizes itself. As an intermediate form we must mention mystical actualization, which indeed historically often stands in closest connexion with the actualization by contemplative historizing. In mystical actualization, in which human activity and passivity hang peculiarly in the balance, direct contact with the revealing reality is provided in the sense of immediate experience, so that the time factor is excluded altogether. The encounter takes place in timeless eternity. That itself, it is true, points towards the fact that in mystical actualization the element of being related to the revelation in history all too easily vanishes altogether, the church's concept of revelation is lost, and hence too holy scripture as a means of helping towards the actualization disappears. Indeed, with the pure form of mysticism there can be no more talk at all of the hermeneutic problem of actualization.

While the relation to the church's understanding of revelation and redemption here recedes, to say the least, entirely into the background, it is preserved in the case of another form in which it is now, also exclusively, the self-actualization of the revealing reality that is maintained. I should like to call this form realistic metaphysical actualization. If a moment ago in connexion with the actualization by contemplative historizing I mentioned relics, then there was only half a right to do so at that point. For—if I may put it so for once—the hermeneutic relevance of relics lies not so much in the fact that they stimulate the contemplative historizing actualization as rather in the fact that in them the unique past event of revelation is itself present. Relics do not only remind us of the past, nor are they present merely as dead remains of the past, but in them the saving power that derives from the unique historical saving event is still abidingly alive and present in direct continuity. Relics mediate, precisely by representing in the crassest way the historicity of the event of revelation, the immediate entry to the realm of the past distinguished by revelation. True, only so to speak to a tiny corner of that realm. But all the same, here actualization takes place without the detour via the literary testimony to the past in holy scripture. Here the past is directly present. Relics are of course only a special case of what I mean by realistic metaphysical actualization. The whole history of redemption indeed, although past in the historical sense, is in the realistic metaphysical sense present in the form of its outstanding representatives, the patriarchs, prophets, apostles and saints including Mary the Queen of Heaven. To them we have access not only in historic remembrance but as immediate contemporaries. We can turn to them for intercession and help, and they intervene actively in the events of the present. Sometimes, indeed, it even happens that the veil that hides from ordinary eyes this heavenly transfiguration of the historical past is lifted for a moment, say through an apparition of the Virgin. Let it not be said that that has nothing to do with the hermeneutic problem. Only think what it means for our relation to the Bible story when we believe in its historical figures at the same time as existing in the real metaphysical present!

But all that is of secondary importance compared with what Catholicism considers the central thing: the way the event of revelation actualizes itself, in sacramental actualization. Let us confine ourselves here to the sacrament in which the relation to the historically unique event of revelation, the decisive thing for the hermeneutic problem, is most clearly expressed: the sacrifice of the Mass. It is a false picture of the

Catholic position when the repeatedly celebrated sacrifice of the Mass
is understood as an amplificatory repetition of the sacrifice once for all
on Golgotha. It is not that an infinite number of momentarily present
sacrifices take their place alongside the one historical one, but the one
historical sacrifice is sacramentally present in the many. And present,
too, apart from any symbolical or spiritualistic interpretation: objectively, even *extra usum sacramenti*, in the transubstantiated host. The
hermeneutic problem of the present actualization of the historically
unique event is here solved in such a radical way that a hermeneutic
question in the narrower sense really no longer exists at all. For the
question that arises primarily in regard to the exposition of scripture—
the question how far what is therein attested as the event of revelation
has decisive significance for the present—is taken out of the context of
scripture exposition and answered by the objective event of the sacrament. The real actualization of the event of revelation does not at all
take place via scripture and its exposition in the sermon, but solely via
the sacrament. For through scripture exposition the revelation always
becomes present only as law, solely in the sacrament on the other hand
as grace.

Yet now there is still one final step we must take if we wish to have a
reasonably complete grasp of the solution found by the Catholic system
to the question of the present actuality of the historically unique event
of revelation. The crown and consummation is the actualization through
a spiritual institution. At this stage, too, the tension between the historical and the present is grandiosely reconciled. The institution of the
Roman Church, existing in unbroken episcopal succession from the days
of the apostles to the present, is the continuing mystical body of Christ
with the *Vicarius Christi* at its head. It possesses the *Charisma veritatis*,
culminating in the infallible teaching office of the pope. It is the abiding
representation of the incarnation. The revelation once for all in history
has entered for all time into history. The perfect tense of the event of
revelation is swallowed up by the continuous present of the church.

The revolution which the Reformation produced in the complex of
questions just sketched is so tremendous that it could be said: the
antithesis between Catholicism and Protestantism rests on the different
understanding of the present actualization of the historical ἅπαξ (once-
for-all-ness) of revelation. The Reformation achieves the tremendous
feat of reducing everything to this, that the historical ἅπαξ of revelation
becomes present in faith alone. The *sola fide* of the Reformation is
directed not only against justification by works and thereby against a

legalistic exposition of scripture, not only against mysticism and against multiplication of the revealing reality in the form of saints and against materialization of the revealing reality in the form of sacred objects. But the *sola fide* has undoubtedly also an anti-sacramental and an anti-clerical point. To the *sola fide* there corresponds *solus Christus*. Revelation and the present are separated from each other in such a way that only *one* bridge remains: the Word alone—and indeed, lest any mis-understanding should arise, the Word interpreted as salvation *sola gratia, sola fide*. All other bridges have been broken up. The whole system of Catholicism has thereby collapsed. There is no such thing as a simple, matter-of-fact presence of revelation. But the actualization of revelation, understood as the self-actualization of Christ, takes place in each individual case through the Word—*sola fide, sola gratia*. We will not dwell on the dearness of the price paid for this change in the under-standing of the present actualization of the ἄπαξ of revelation. Humanly speaking the price was a frightful impoverishment of religious life and an alarming surrender of religious safeguards. We will only ask what was thereby gained in regard to the question that concerns us here. For one thing: the re-establishment of the ἄπαξ in all its stringency and exclusiveness, and therewith the purification of the content of revelation from amplifications, additions and adulterations. And for another: the assurance of salvation that lies in the *pro me*. For the actualization as Catholicism understands it is such in and for itself. The question of appropriation remains the great point of uncertainty. Whereas Christ's becoming present in faith as the Reformers understand it takes place *pro me*. The question of appropriation can no longer be separated from it at all.

This revolution brought about by the Reformers had far-reaching consequences for theology's method. First of all this: that theology acquired growing significance for the church. In the clerical church of the sacrament, theology, however vast may be the resources expended on it, is a peripheral matter. Whereas in the church of the Word, theo-logy serves the preaching which is the source of faith. Moreover: theo-logy becomes primarily exegesis. And historical exegesis at that, which breaks through the accumulated rubble of tradition to the original text. Further—as is already indicated by the last remark—theology becomes critical theology. For the Reformation, that certainly does not yet mean critical historical theology in today's sense, though there do exist notable first steps in that direction. Rather, the criticism takes its start from scripture as its centre, and to begin with becomes predominantly criticism of tradition. And finally: for theology in the Reformers' sense the hermeneutic question acquires fundamental significance, and that precisely to the extent that it is theology of the Word. In the hermeneutic question is concentrated the whole problematical nature of theology whose full weight Protestantism has to bear. For it possesses no church tradition alongside scripture to relieve the problems set by the exposition of scripture. And it has no infallible teaching office over it, but enjoys the freedom of having to bear its own responsibility for its work, bound solely to the scriptures. And the very question as to what that bond implies is again part of the hermeneutic problem.

But now, this sketch of the Reformers' position is—it must be openly admitted—from the historical point of view a stylized one. I do not mean we have not caught its essential features. But that is not everything. The situation in detail is essentially more complicated. The relation to Catholicism is not exhausted by the plain, antithetical statements I have employed. The Reformers' exposition of scripture, too, presupposed as self-evident the validity of the biblical picture of the world and of history. It, too, finds in metaphysical reality a bridge that joins past and present. The church of the Word also has sacraments. It, too, has an ordered ministry. It, too, takes over a part of the primitive church tradition. It, too, exists in historical continuity. That leads to a further element in the structure of the hermeneutic problem.

4. I began by saying that Christianity stands or falls with the tie that binds it to its unique historical origin. From that there arose the problems, first of the ontological interpretation of the event of revelation, secondly of the view of the testimony to this event of revelation, i.e. of holy scripture, and then thirdly of the present actualization of the event of revelation. But now there is still a fourth problem that presents itself —namely, the problem of the historic character of the present actualization of the event of revelation. Christianity is, in spite of the tie that binds it to its unique historical origin—which bond actualizes itself when the event of revelation becomes present, and is thus not only a postulate but a bond that again and again rises in actual fact—Christianity, I say, is for all that not a phenomenon that abides always identical and unchanged, but it exists in history, i.e. it is subject to the march of time. It can never simply remain precisely the same as it was at the start; for then it would not exist in history at all. But how, then, can it remain identical with itself in the absolute sense presupposed by the statement that Christianity stands or falls with the tie that binds it to its unique historical origin?—'in an absolute sense', because this

unique historical origin claims to be revelation in the utterly absolute sense. It is of course the basic structure of all historic being that it exists in the dialectic of constancy and change. Mutation can take place only in a thing that remains identical with itself. To the essence of the historic there belong not only the several variations of each new moment, but at the same time also continuity of being, not only change but also tradition. But now, does not transience likewise belong to the nature of historic existence? Is it not only the transitory, the relative that can vary? Christianity, however, makes the claim to exist in history as something absolute, intransitory. But what, then, is the relation of the historic mutation to the identity of the absolute?

To this problem, which is presented to us by the simple fact of the history of the church and of theology, a solution has been sought in the formula that here the divine and the human, the eternal and the temporal, exist side by side. The human and temporal element is said to be the changing forms, the divine and eternal one the content that abides identical and unchanged. But to formulate it that way really only describes the problem here presented—and that, too, by applying the categories of form and content in a highly questionable way. For the distinction of form and content suggests the idea that the content can be separated from the form. But how can e.g. the content of a theological statement be separated from its form? That is in fact precisely the difficulty—that the content can be had only in a particular form. If it were desired to separate e.g. the content of the Credo from its particular form, then that could really only be done in a new form. There is certainly a problem here that presses for the making of a distinction. But it seems to me the proper distinction here is not one of form and content, but of word and exposition. The problem of how the church exists amid the mutations of history and yet is bound absolutely to its unique historical origin, constantly changing and yet remaining identical with itself, is thereby set in the light of the hermeneutic question. I consider the category of exposition the only proper one for coming to grips with the question of the nature of the history of church and theology. For the category of exposition embraces the historic character of the present actualization of the event of revelation.

How does the Roman Catholic Church now come to terms with the fact of mutations in the history of church and theology? Again in a compelling way. As extension of the incarnation the church is, like the incarnation, ontologically a phenomenon *sui generis*. It is divine and human at once, not however in the sense of the distinction between form and content but by way of a juxtaposition of concrete, historically de-monstrable factors of divine and human origin—which of course in practice are not always easy to distinguish from each other. But in principle the distinction is certainly maintained—in dogmatics for ex-ample between infallible statements *de fide* and discussible *opiniones*, or in ecclesiastical law between *ius divinum* and *ius humanum*. That leaves room for both things: there is a changing element and an unchanging one. The unchanging element exists in the history of the church from the beginning in unbroken continuity. The changing element varies according to the particular circumstances. To that extent all historic mutations affect the church only on the periphery. And even the chang-ing element is, thanks to the principle of tradition, generally of astonish-ing stability. At bottom, however, the church goes through no historic changes. To be sure, the truth contained in it from the beginning can pass through stages of successive unfolding. Thus new dogmas can be proclaimed by the infallible teaching office of the church. But this pro-cess is not mutation, not change, but only generic growth. In this peculiar combination and interpenetration of the historic and the supra-historic the Roman church has in history an astounding stability and elasticity at the same time.

The Reformation broke with the presuppositions of this way of look-ing at church history and thereby surrendered also the historical advan-tages of this view. It knows no divine church law that can be defined and established as such. It knows no infallible ecclesiastical decisions on doctrine either. It knows no demonstrable institutional guarantee for the continuous existence of the church in history. In the distinction between the visible and the invisible church this lack of any guarantee for the church in history finds its crystallization. Church history presents itself as the story of apostasy, in which there shine a few scattered *testes veritatis*, until at last the Gospel was discovered anew at the Reformation. As a result of the Reformation the problem of the relation between church and history arose in an entirely new way. But in the Reformation itself this problem was not sufficiently worked out. That, if I am not mistaken, becomes specially clear at two points.

For one thing, in the relation between the Reformation and early Christianity. The rediscovery of the right understanding of the Gospel, the recourse to scripture alone, and the abandonment of all interpolated human precepts in the doctrine and order of the church only too easily suggested the idea that the Reformation was simply a reduction of the church's history to its historical origin. Certainly the one thing Luther can least of all be reproached with is a legalistic biblicism. And yet it is a simple fact that the Reformation was not sufficiently aware of its own distance from early Christianity. For that reason there was no reflexion upon the question of the historic mutations of Christianity. We could also say: the Reformation was not critical enough of itself. That can be seen from the fact that the question whether its theology conformed to scripture was one it was all too ready to answer directly in the affirmative, without seeing the distance that necessarily and rightly separates the interpreter's exposition and assimilation of a text from its original historical meaning, to say nothing of direct errors of interpretation. And thus the question of what was to be the future relation to the Reformer's theology and their exposition of scripture was also one that was not worked out clearly enough. The idea all too soon arose that the theology of the Reformers was of conclusive significance, at least in so far as it had crystallized itself in the Confessions, that the only task now still remaining for theology was to preserve this newly formed church tradition and expound the scriptures in its light. It was not sufficiently clearly realized that post-reformation theology must not be simply Reformed scholasticism, and that Reformed scholasticism in spite of its attempts at most loyal conservation is by no means identical with Reformation theology. It was therefore inevitable that one day the time should come when a mere conservation of Reformation theology was obviously no longer enough, when changed days with their changes in thought and language brought home to Protestant theology that it was obliged to use the means of the present and face the problems of the present in studying theology and expounding scripture.

The other point at which it becomes clear that the problem of the relation between church and history which arose as a result of the Reformation was not sufficiently worked out by the Reformation, is the question of church order, i.e. of the church's shape in history. It may have been entirely right that in this respect Lutheranism did not set to work with a purist's biblicism, and in spite of the breakthrough to the New Testament left standing much of the heritage of early catholic tradition. But it was not really clearly realized what that implies for the fundamental problem of the relation between church and history. Likewise the path towards the system of church government by the civil princes may have been wholly unavoidable, and in sixteenth-century Germany even entirely right. But again it was not realized plainly enough that such time-conditioned solutions must not be preserved indefinitely. And if in Lutheranism a certain magnanimity and indifference towards the so-called outward forms of the church justified that procedure, then at any rate the vindication of it by the argument about the neutrality of the form compared with the content is a sign that not enough attention was paid to the question of the historic character of the church.

III

The development of the hermeneutic problem as a whole in all its general theological implications, but in the first instance without regard to the special questions of today, must be kept in view if we wish to assess the significance of the rise of the critical historical method. For the comparison of the Catholic position with that of the Reformers has shown how deeply the revolution of the sixteenth century affects the whole hermeneutic problem, yet how little on the other hand the Reformation itself was in a position to subject the questions that thereby arose, or was interested in subjecting them, to a comprehensive examination in respect of their methodological and material consequences. It would be short-sighted to make that a reproach to the Reformation. For the full effects of the Reformation on the history of thought could in the nature of the case develop only gradually. And the very fact that the theology of the Reformers was so deeply entwined in their medieval heritage proves that the upheaval of the Reformation primarily came not from without, from the general changes in the history of thought at the close of the Middle Ages, but from within, from the understanding of revelation allowing as far as possible the validity of the accepted principles of thought. But for that very reason it would likewise be short-sighted to seal up the testimony of the Reformation within what was, rightly understood, a traditional situation that could not possibly be preserved. There has doubtless been much mischief caused by the idea of permanent reformation. Nevertheless it must be taken seriously in two respects. Firstly, in so far as the Word of God must be left free to assert itself in an unflinchingly critical manner against distortions and fixations. But secondly—and on closer inspection this is included in the first—in so far as theology and preaching should be free to make a translation into whatever language is required at the moment and to refuse to be satisfied with correct, archaizing repetition of 'pure doctrine'. And this very task of carrying on the heritage of the Reformation in a way that genuinely moves with the times necessarily led to the point where in regard to the general principles of thought certain problems that had very rightly remained untouched at the Reformation arose and demanded a decision such as was not to be gained from the utterances of the Reformers and from the Confessions. To these problems that necessarily emerged sooner or later there belonged, however, first and foremost the hermeneutic problem, which as a result of the Reformation had already in actual fact—though how far that was recognized is another question—been made central and set on a new theological basis, but only hesitatingly come to grips with in all its implications.

The question therefore now arises, what the appearance of the critical historical method implies for the complex of problems we have described, and what connexion it has with the basic principle from which the Reformers set out and which inevitably made clarification of the whole hermeneutic problem a necessary step towards further progress. From all the many viewpoints that here force themselves on the mind I can select only a few.

1. It leads only to obscuring the nature of the problem when the critical historical method is held to be a purely formal scientific technique, entirely free of presuppositions, whose application to the historical objects in the theological realm provokes no conflicts and does no hurt to the dogmatic structure. Even though it will prove in a higher sense to be correct that the critical historical method does not destroy the truth of the Christian faith, yet we certainly must not make light of the difficulties that here arise. For historical criticism is more than lively historical interest. Even the early and medieval churches concerned themselves more or less with history and the study of its sources, and therefore also always provided a certain measure of criticism where legends and falsifications of history were concerned. At the close of the Middle Ages, the Renaissance and Humanism put new life into the historical, and therewith also the critical, sense. And the Reformation, however exclusively guided by essentially theological interests, arrived at surprisingly sharp and accurate verdicts on many individual historical questions. The demands of confessional apologetics and polemics then intensified the study of history in both camps under the discipline of keeping a sharp eye on each other. And yet that was all merely accompaniment, but was not of revolutionary significance for the church's teaching and the generally recognized traditional picture of the world and of history. It was not what we know today as the critical historical method. For the latter is not concerned with the greatest possible refinement of the philological methods, but with subjecting the tradition to critical examination on the basis of new principles of thought. The critical historical method first arose out of the intellectual revolution of modern times. It is—not just, say, where it oversteps its legitimate

limits, but by its very nature—bound up with criticism of content. In its concern with the past and its interpretation of the sources of the past it cannot simply set aside the understanding of reality as that has been acquired by the modern mind. It is therefore closely coupled with the advance of the sciences and with the development of philosophy. Certainly, it is thereby in danger of becoming uncritical in the other direction, of succumbing to the influences of what is modern for the moment and of employing improper standards in its historical criticism. But even where men have recognized this danger, they have not seen themselves compelled to abandon in principle the path they have taken, but only to be the more careful and the more critical of themselves in repeatedly testing also the appropriateness of their own presuppositions.

2. In order to grasp the nature of the critical historical method it is thus necessary to take account of the intellectual change in the modern age. In doing so we can set aside the vexed question advanced (with at all events extraordinarily fruitful results) by Dilthey and Troeltsch—the question of the historical roots of the modern age and the precise time at which it began. It is doubtless correct that the great breach in the dam took place only in the seventeenth and eighteenth centuries. And this, too, is certain—nor indeed is it fundamentally denied by Troeltsch's usually roughly-quoted thesis—that the Reformation has its place among the antecedents of the change in question, while on the other hand the view which is not only repeatedly advocated by Catholicism and the Eastern Church but also proudly championed in much of Neo-Protestantism, and according to which the modern outlook is directly or even exclusively descended from the Reformation, is certainly false. We naturally cannot enter either into the endless question of the inner development and change in modern thought itself. We must confine ourselves to the question whether there is a common factor that fundamentally and irrevocably marks off the modern age as a whole from all preceding Western history, and in what that common factor consists.

First of all a negative point: in the modern age the Christian faith has forfeited the self-evident validity that was ascribed to it in Western history for more than a millennium. It is no longer accorded any formal authority that stands *extra controversiam*. Self-evident universal validity is now possessed only by what man as such with his rational and empirical faculties can know, perceive, prove and control. That, however, leads to a positive point: in the modern age there exists on a previously unknown scale a realm of new self-evident assumptions whose validity even the

Christian cannot evade—and that not even when they stand in contradiction to the sort of views which before the dawn of the modern age belonged to the self-evident assumptions of the Christian world-view. But from this realm of the new self-evident assumptions we have now to distinguish the dimension of the problematical which is everywhere latent within it. It would be a serious mistake to suppose that modern thinking knows only the realm of the self-evident and that therefore one of the consequences of modern thinking would be to deny the dimension of the problematical altogether. It is quite true that the history of modern thought is full of examples to show that the attempt at such a denial has repeatedly been made, that the realm of the self-evident has thus been posited as absolute. But all these attempts prove to be illegitimate extension of the realm of the self-evident into the dimension of the problematical. The course of the history of modern thought, with its infinite variety of absolute systems succeeding and excluding each other, itself refutes the possibility of eliminating the dimension of the problematical, or expanding the realm of the self-evident to cover it.

But now, the usefulness of this distinction between the self-evident and the problematical depends upon how it is possible to define them over against each other. It is not a case of distinguishing separate spheres of being or of reality. It is rather a case of an epistemological distinction. And with the introduction of this distinction it must not be held that the boundary can be certainly determined once and for all. For the realm of the self-evident manifestly changes in the course of history, and it would betray an unhistorical way of thinking if we were to consider the present self-evident assumptions as finally and unchangeably established. The boundaries between the self-evident and the problematical are much rather open, fluid boundaries. That, however, does not exclude the possibility that in the realm of the self-evident, verdicts and critical corrections can be arrived at that are universally binding and changes in thought made that can never be unmade again. I am aware of the great difficulty of the questions I am touching here, and the utter impossibility of mastering them in this short compass. Yet I consider it important to recognize and come to grips with the task here characterized. For the clarification of the question how far the self-evident assumptions are legitimate self-evident assumptions or illegitimate ones has a decisive bearing on our methods of exposition in general and hence on our methods in theological work in particular.

If I may just venture one closer definition merely by way of a suggestion, then the fundamental change never again to be unmade which came over the self-evident assumptions with the dawn of the modern age seems to me to consist legitimately in the following: First in a restriction, namely in the elimination of all metaphysical statements from the realm of the self-evident. And then in an extension, namely in the relative autonomy of science and of social life. 'Relative autonomy' is intended to mean that here, while respecting the proximity of the problematical and refraining from absolutism, i.e. refraining from taking the non-self-evident as self-evident—or we could also say, in a state of aporia where metaphysics is concerned—men can after all attain to an understanding that is universally binding. Or to put it more concretely: it is a legitimate self-evident assumption of the modern age, never again to be unmade, that neither the church nor any world-view that supposes itself absolute may impugn the relative autonomy of science and of social life. That the modern age is in actual fact full of repeated attempts to do that after all in one form or another, that in the modern age the self-evident assumption in question is thus not everywhere recognized and treated as self-evident, merely makes clear that in the so-called self-evident assumptions we have not to do with automatisms but with claims to validity.

If the changed intellectual situation by which the modern age is dominated is worked out in the way I have tried at least to indicate, then the view must surely become untenable which sees the rise of the modern age as essentially revolt from the Christian faith, or something in the nature of a second Fall. The designation of the Enlightenment as the age of consummate sinfulness derives, as is well known, from Fichte, and in his case arises from a view that could hardly be agreeable to those who as Christians adopt the same judgment with regard not only to the Enlightenment but to the whole modern age and would dearly love to undo this Fall by means of a radical de-secularization of scientific and public life. Quite apart from the fact that even these fundamental opponents of the modern age are for the most part completely unable to avoid its self-evident assumptions and, when it comes right down to it, have no wish to avoid them either, and when in actual fact they do it, really only do it in illegitimate and inwardly false, or at least badly thought-out and inconsistent ways—quite apart from that, there is another thing that must be taken much more seriously: is this basic structure of the modern mind not something that is entirely in accordance with the Christian faith? Is it not of the essence of that faith that it is not found a place in the realm of the self-evident but for the natural man as such belongs entirely in the dimension of the problematical?

Can it do any harm to the Christian faith if it can no longer be confused
with a particular view of the world or a particular social or political plan
for the shaping of the world, if faith can no longer pledge itself to take
the place of responsible thinking, and if, as against any hybridizing
tendencies, the world is discovered again in all its worldliness, i.e. is
secularized? Indeed, is it not entirely in accordance with the Christian
faith if in the undoubtedly existing tendency of the modern mind to take
the realm of its own self-evident assumptions and—illegitimately and in
violation of these self-evident assumptions—make it absolute, the godlessness of the world comes more plainly to light than when it clothes
itself with the semblance of Christianity? And can there be anything
more foolish than seeking to make capital for the Christian faith out of
these tendencies to absolutism by pressing them into the service of the
Christian cause and trying, say, to take advantage of such reactionary
aspects of the modern age as e.g. the cry for authority from a world
weary of thinking and of responsibility? Could the remarkable situation
not indeed arise that the Christian faith is obliged, is perhaps even the
only thing still able, to put up an energetic defence of the self-evident
assumptions which the modern age brought into being but has itself
denied, such as freedom of research, tolerance, etc.? Certainly, the relation to the basic structure of thought in the modern age is the decisive
point for the understanding of the Christian faith. Here a deep gulf
becomes visible between Catholicism and Protestantism.

3. What now is the inner connexion between the critical historical
method and the modern mind's principles of thought? They made it
possible, because only with the collapse of traditional Western metaphysics, i.e. with the loss of its self-evident character, did men become
fully aware of the historic character of existence. For it was only when
the absoluteness of the hitherto dominant picture of the world and of
history disappeared, when to prove a thing traditional was no longer to
prove it true, when not only particular phenomena in history but history
itself ceased in principle to have unconditionally binding and materially
decisive authority as such, when men therefore discovered the fact of
historic change, of the time-conditioned character of each event and of
our distance from it in history—it was only then that there came the
freedom, but also the sheer necessity, to regard historical events in their
pure historicity, i.e. objectively, from the distance. Only then came the
extraordinary sharpening of the critical eye for the question of dependability and genuineness of sources, for cases of historical dependence,
interconnexion and change. In short: only then could the whole appar-

atus of historical research, as it has become a matter of course for us today, be fully developed.

But that is surely not yet all that can be said. The really decisive and revolutionary thing about the critical historical method came from the fact that the modern historian sees himself compelled to take the sources of the past and set them, too, in the light of the new self-evident assumptions. Not that he foists these new self-evident assumptions on to the witnesses of the past, as if they had been self-evident assumptions also for them, but he does examine the factual content of their testimony on the basis of these self-evident assumptions. Thus he will not accept the truth e.g. of statements which presuppose the Ptolemaic picture of the world, not even when for the rest the source has a high degree of historical dependability. The modern historian is rightly convinced that he knows certain things better. The fact that for the modern age all that is metaphysical and metahistorical has entered the dimension of the problematical is also a thing the modern historian cannot simply put out of his mind when reading sources which presuppose the self-evident character of the metaphysical and metahistorical. He cannot, for example, accept the self-evident validity of statements which introduce metaphysical beings in the sense of the older picture of the world as internal factors in the world and its history—just as of course he himself also oversteps the boundaries of scientific method if for his own part he tries to explain something historically problematical by means of metaphysical statements, i.e. to render it self-evident. He is therefore also unable to take over the recognition of a special *historia sacra* or *scriptura sacra* in the ontological sense as a self-evident intellectual presupposition influencing his method of research. He deals with all historic and literary phenomena of the past by the same method, *viz.*—the critical historical method, which can certainly undergo infinite modifications according to the nature of the particular historical object, but which cannot be put fundamentally out of currency by any historical object.

In the circumstances in history in which the intellectual transition to the modern age took place, it was natural that theology was more especially affected by the awakening of the historical consciousness and that the battle very soon became hottest in the realm of scripture exposition. And the most amazing thing about the history of theology in modern times is, that it was above all the theologians themselves who dauntlessly and inexorably employed the critical historical method and in the field of research into Old and New Testament, Church History and the History of Dogma made way for startlingly new and unforsakable insights, yet—with very few exceptions—did not feel that gave them reason to turn their backs on the business of theology proper.

But let us first leave out of account for the moment the effects of the critical historical method in the realm of theology. In the so-called secular realm, too, there came with the beginning of the modern age a tremendous upsurge of historical science, which, if at first variously hampered by the Enlightenment and by Idealism, presently came in the nineteenth century to dominate intellectual life. On the one hand it brought lasting achievements in the illumination of the past, yet on the other hand there arose unmistakable dangers in this process of historization. If at first the danger was more that of doing violence to history, whether by failing to maintain the necessary measure of self-criticism and making hasty judgments according to the limited standards of the present, or by venturing to systematize the course of history in ruthless disregard of the historically unique and contingent, or by heroification and glorification of particular epochs of the past, yet it was not long before the tables were turned and the present was in danger of being violated by history. The historian of the late nineteenth century, in which this development reached its peak, dragged all norms and values into a boundless relativism that made manifest the serious crisis into which the modern mind had found its way. It would be an illusion to hold that this crisis with its characteristic historism has been overcome. For all the many anti-historical reactions that have appeared are unserviceable attempts to settle the problem it has brought. Nevertheless, especially since Dilthey's labours on the problem of the understanding of history, and as a direct result of them, new and promising ways have been adopted to ward off the danger of historism without surrendering the stringency of the critical historical method and evading the tasks it prescribes. The view has gained ground that a purely objective attitude to history, which takes the methods of natural science as its ideal and is content to establish how things once were, simply does not do justice to the task of understanding history and is also feasible only within very definite limits—that history then has nothing at all to say to us and the result is only an amassing of dead material instead of a living, personal encounter with history.

In this situation it would, of course, be disastrous in the extreme if that were to give rise to a bifocal concern with history—if on the one hand professional historical science were to restrict itself to a formal, technical use of the critical historical method, while on the other hand attempts were made, quite apart from strictly methodical study of that

kind, to explain the meaning of historic events and bring them vividly
to life. Rather, everything depends on the critical historical method
being freed from this mistaken curtailment to a mere technical tool and
being understood in such a way as to include in itself the whole of the
hermeneutic process. That does not imply the slightest prejudice to the
stringent methods of historical research and their technical application.
On the contrary, the very process of taking the historical source in all its
historicity (and that means in its distance from the present) and making
it luminous by means of a critical examination that penetrates to the
uttermost limits of its explicability, and thereby at the same time also
critically correcting the prejudices of the expositor himself and making
clear to him the historical conditionedness of his own preconceptions—
that very process creates the necessary basis for a genuine encounter
with the text, and thereby also for the possibility of having it speak to us.
Then the transformation and interpretation of historic events in order
to illumine our own existence ceases to be arbitrarily and naively reading things into the source. Rather, the way is now open to genuinely
historic, personal encounter and discussion, whereby the interpreter
remains aware of the fact that the actualization he has achieved is a
transformation of the historical—a transformation in which the historical
distance is constantly kept in view and remains a critical corrective of
the understanding of history. And then again it can happen, in accordance with the well-known principle of the hermeneutic circle, that the
understanding which achieves the actualization becomes the key to seeing specific matters of historical fact for the first time in their distinct-
iveness and peculiarity, and thus also to applying properly the technical
methods of historical research. Modern historical science is unquestionably still a long way from being able to take the critical historical method
as it here appears in the wide context of the hermeneutic problem and
provide in satisfying categories an exposition of it that is theoretically
unobjectionable. For that it depends on the co-operation of philosophy,
which in its turn can make progress on the problem of hermeneutic
methods only in closest touch with historical science.

4. Theology, too, is affected by the existence of all these still unclarified problems in regard to the critical historical method. As historical theology in the nineteenth century it passed through the same
successes, difficulties and dangers as secular historical science. It does
not find itself the happy possessor of its own, specifically theological
method of fulfilling the hermeneutic task. So far as it has to do with the
understanding of history, it knows no difference at all in its method

from the tasks that are prescribed to so-called secular historical science. It has no expository method of its own at its disposal—no 'spiritual' method, or whatever it may be called—that differs as a method from the way in which, say, a text of Plato is to be interpreted. In regard to the tasks and problems of the critical historical method theology has therefore in actual fact no option but to take its place along with historical science and philosophy in what is essentially the same struggle to discover the nature and correct employment of the critical historical method. Only in one respect, it is true, is theology in a special case: in so far as it is doubly affected by the problems that here arise—first in the general form of how genuine knowledge and understanding of history is possible, but then also on the particular point of what the consequences of the modern attitude to history are for matters so closely related to history and bound up with history as the proclamation and teaching of the church. Is there not a danger that with the emancipation of the critical historical method the very substance of theology, the revelation in history, will come to be destroyed? It would imply failure to grasp the theological situation in which we find ourselves if I were to try in what follows to provide solutions for the whole vast array of problems whose treatment is precisely the onerous task this Journal seeks to serve. I can therefore only try to provide a few pointers to indicate the nature of the problems.

(*a*) I have already pointed out that here Catholicism and Protestantism are radically opposed. One need only observe the way Roman Catholicism has concentrated and consolidated its theological forces since the beginning of the nineteenth century—its uncompromising attitude of opposition to the spirit of the times and its transition from the defensive to the offensive both inwardly and outwardly—in order to find it a sore trial how very different is the picture of church and theology presented by modern Protestantism: countless splits in all directions, progressive dissolution not only of its unity but also of its dogmatic substance, such infection by modern thought as apparently leads to internal sepsis, and where the attempt is made to defend or re-vitalize the old, the unseasonable, the distinctive and indispensable, there we find a defensive attitude towards the outside opponent that savours of anxiety, grimness or despair, while the courage, indeed the sheer brazen audacity of which modern Protestantism has certainly no lack is devoted to ever new onslaughts of criticism within the camp and is more inexorable than the enemies of Christianity in ruthlessly questioning the foundations of the Protestant Church and of its theology.

It is a decision of fundamental importance what attitude we take to this, what judgment we pass on the respective paths of Catholicism and Protestantism today. Are we to look enviously and longingly towards Catholicism and say: there the Christian cause has been championed more purely and decisively, and better maintained? Must we be ashamed of the history of modern Protestantism and confess: here the cause of Christianity has been betrayed, or at the very least men have been carelessly playing with fire? And must the conclusion be: what Protestantism in the nineteenth century failed to do and what, if there is anything at all still to be salvaged, must now be made good as quickly and thoroughly as possible is, *mutatis mutandis* likewise the preparation of a *Syllabus errorum*, the establishment of a final, absolute doctrinal authority, of an antimodernist oath and of an ecclesiastically authorized standard Thomist theology? Or must we assent to the other possibility—namely, to expose ourselves relentlessly to the vulnerability, the insecurity and the dangers, to refuse to let our ties with the thought of the day be broken, not to wait until criticism comes from an opponent's side and then be the more inflexible in rejecting all criticism, but to go ahead with the critical examination of our foundations, to let everything burn that will burn and without reservations await what proves itself unburnable, genuine, true—and to adopt this attitude at the risk that much that seemed established may begin to rock, that indeed some things may even be temporarily considered shaky which upon ever new examination then prove to be stable after all, that thus many mistakes and errors are made, much asserted and much taken back again, that our path takes us through serious crises, bitter struggles, bewildering debates and the results are apparently weakness and collapse? And to increase the difficulty of the decision that faces us here: it is not by any means as if Catholicism in all this had become a dead, stagnant pool, whereas Protestantism had provided proof that it alone has power and life and a future. If we sought to judge by outward success, then the history of the modern age has surely rather justified Catholicism. The fact is, that through the developments of modern times the opposition between Catholicism and Protestantism has become a degree sharper, that to the old confessional distinctions of the sixteenth century there has been added still another new element of separation, whose basis was of course already given in the Reformation itself—namely, a fundamentally different attitude to the spirit of the modern age.

Not as if the position of Protestantism in this respect were a wholly unified one. It is no wonder that the decisive question which has arisen has taken root within Protestantism itself and now the two tendencies struggle together within it: either to take a path that runs at least parallel to that of Catholicism—in other words, the path of restoration, of concentration and of remaining as immune from the modern spirit as possible—or to assent to the path to which Protestantism has been led by an inner necessity, i.e. the path into vulnerability, into the fires of criticism. And it is likewise no wonder that between these two extremes there has arisen an abundance of attempts at mediation. But whatever position we may adopt, the simple fact has emerged that Protestantism of any shade is completely unable to evade the emancipation of historical criticism which distinguishes it from Catholicism,[1] that it

[1] In view of the more recent and the latest papal pronouncements on the problem of hermeneutics, it could certainly be asked whether and how far the problem of the critical historical method still stands to divide the confessions. If we consider only the notorious decisions of the papal Bible Commission in the heyday of the struggle against modernism under Pius X, then more especially the encyclical *Divino afflante spiritu* of 1943 (*Acta Apostolicae Sedis* 35 [1943], 297-325—the most important parts of it are in Denzinger, *Enchiridion Symbolorum, editio 26*, Freiburg 1947, No. 2292/4) and the new 1945 translation of the Psalms with its independence of the Vulgate and its downright revolutionary flavour (cf. *TLZ* 73 [1948], 203-208) make it appear as if Catholicism had undergone a thoroughgoing change of heart in regard to hermeneutics. And indeed it is in fact surprising how far the Roman Church goes to meet the demands of historical exegesis and actually draws the logical conclusion of supplanting the Vulgate even in liturgical use by newer translations.

That in expounding scripture a certain amount of weight must be given to the original Hebrew and Greek text alongside the Vulgate, had of course never been denied in theory. The assertion of the *Tridentinum*, 'ut haec ipsa vetus et vulgata editio, quae longo tot saeculorum usu in ipsa Ecclesia probata est, in publicis lectionibus, disputationibus, praedicationibus et expositionibus pro authentica habeatur, et quod nemo illam reicere quovis praetextu audeat vel praesumat' (Denz. 785), could not indeed be otherwise understood than in the sense of a dogmatic authenticity of the Vulgate text. That however means: in the case of a conflict with the original text, the Vulgate text was in practice recognized as the exegetical norm. Even when Leo XIII in 1893 in the Encyclical *Providentissimus Deus* described the knowledge of the original languages as necessary for a philologically unobjectionable Bible exegesis, he was still of the same opinion as always: that the primary meaning of the Hebrew and Greek original is well apparent from the Vulgate, and the original text has only to be referred to in case of doubt (Denz. 1941).

Yet the above-mentioned Encyclical of Pius XII, *Divino afflante spiritu*, goes beyond that. If it seeks to escape the noose of the *Tridentinum* by saying that the authenticity of the Vulgate there asserted is not really understood in a critical, but in a juridical sense, yet this distinction is of no importance as long as the dogmatic authenticity of the Vulgate is maintained ('. . . *quo quidem usu demonstratur eamdem, prout intellexit et intelligit Ecclesia, in rebus fidei ac morum ab omni prorsus esse errore immunem; ita ut, ipsa Ecclesia testante et confirmante, in disputationibus, lectionibus concionibusque tuto ac sine errandi periculo proferri possit* . . .' Act. Ap. Sed. 35, 309, Denz. 2292). This interpretation of the

cannot take the road via *Syllabus errorum*, infallible authority on doctrine, anti-modernist oath and standard church theology, and that the
only question is how the task of criticism is to be properly carried out

---

Tridentinum, it is true, deviates quite plainly from its original meaning, in that
what Trent declared in the form of a strict order regarding the use of the
Vulgate, is weakened by Pius XII into a mere possibility (*possit!*)—whereby,
however, the appearance of a contradiction is avoided by explicitly maintaining
the infallibility of the Vulgate *in rebus fidei ac morum*. And yet the loosening of
the attitude to the Vulgate heralds a greater freedom in the use of historical
methods of exposition. That comes to expression in the following way of formulating the guiding principle of hermeneutics: '*Linguarum antiquarum cognitione
et criticae artis subsidiis egregie instructus, exegeta catholicus ad illud accedat munus,
quod ex omnibus ei impositis summum est, ut nempe germanam ipsam Sacrorum
Librorum sententiam reperiat atque exponat. Quo in opere exsequendo ante oculos
habeant interpretes sibi illud omnium maximum curandum esse, ut clare dispiciant
ac definiant, quis sit verborum biblicorum sensus, quem litteralem vocant. Hanc
litteralem verborum significationem omni cum diligentia per linguorum cognitionem
iidem eruant, ope adhibita contextus, comparationisque cum assimilibus locis; quae
quidem omnia in profanorum quoque scriptorum interpretatione in auxilium vocari
solent, ut auctoris mens luculenter patescat*' (*Act. Ap. Sed.* 35, 310, Denz. 2293).
    The means of discovering this *sensus litteralis* are further expounded in
hermeneutic rules of the most noteworthy kind. As *summa interpretandi norma*
is laid down the task of ascertaining what the author intended to say. That,
however, involves above all paying attention to the historical distance, whose
result is, particularly with writings which appeared in the Orient many centuries
ago, that they arose under literary laws completely different from those we are
accustomed to today. Consequently special value has to be assigned to research
into literary types. Only then shall we begin to understand much that to us today
appears offensive or even erroneous, yet when historically treated reveals itself
as only a time-conditioned manner of speaking. In such accommodation to the
language of a particular day we can see at once the condescension of God,
exactly parallel to the incarnation of the Word of God. For that reason careful
exegesis involves not only grammatical and philological, but also historical,
archaeological and ethnological examination. That of course is not meant to
imply any alteration in the basic principles of Catholic hermeneutics. Bible
exegetes must at the same time bear in mind that here they have to do with the
divinely inspired Word, and must therefore pay no less attention to the elucidations and explanations of the church's teaching office and the fathers, and
thereby to the viewpoint of the *analogia fidei*. They must therefore beware of
the mistake of many commentaries—namely, of confining themselves to philological, historical or archaeological explanations. The exposition should rather
aim above all at bringing out the theological content. That is the only way to
silence those who complain that the biblical commentaries offer nothing that
contributes to edification, and who therefore have recourse to some kind of
spiritual or mystical interpretation. The emphasis on the *sensus litteralis* is not
indeed meant to rule out entirely the recognition of a *sensus spiritualis*. But such
a meaning exists only where God as the Author of holy scripture intended it and
where we have plain evidence of that intention in scripture itself. The *sensus
spiritualis* must therefore be applied with all due care and reserve.
    We cannot too strongly recommend anyone who wishes to go further into the
hermeneutic problem to make a thorough study of this latest official Catholic

and what the result of it proves to be. Without making light of the
difficulties that here arise, it must nevertheless be said that Protestantism
has decided in principle for the critical historical method and there-

---

pronouncement on the question of scripture exposition. There is much truth in
it which one could only v·ish every Protestant theologian would also take to
heart. It is certainly not to ...he glory of Protestantism today that in comparison
with much that can be heard from the Protestant side on these questions, the
pope's pronouncement appears decidedly progressive from the scientific point
of view, and that the opinion of at least the average Protestant theologian on the
question of the critical historical method essentially coincides with the attitude
adopted in the Encyclical and it therefore suddenly causes some embarrassment
to determine correctly the point at which the Catholic and Protestant views of
the hermeneutic problem part company. Compare only the main points:—On
both sides recognition of historical, archaeological and philological methods as
means of assisting towards exegesis, yet only within the limits of apologetic
purposes and under appeal to the not yet clearly and methodically thought-out
viewpoint of the *analogia fidei*. But also on both sides a certain surfeit of 'merely'
historical commentaries and therefore an insistence on theological exegesis, on
exegetical work that can be turned to practical account. On both sides the danger
of slipping into uncontrollable spiritual exegesis and, even where that danger is
recognized, no escaping from the dualism between merely historical and properly theological exposition. What actually is the real significance of critical
historical exposition, in so far as it is not merely something that can be made
serviceable for apologetic purposes, remains on both sides unexplained. On both
sides there has been precious little penetration of the real hermeneutic problem,
in spite of the apparently progressive acceptance of historical exegesis as an
auxiliary discipline that simply happens to be necessary and in certain respects
useful. On both sides the standpoint is fundamentally the rather harmless one
of a supra-naturalism such as was already adopted in Protestant theology about
150 years ago in defence against, but also in partial accommodation to, the
problems presented to theology by modern historical thinking.

It is necessary to bring out these points so sharply because there is a danger
that in face of the modern Catholic view of the method of scripture exposition,
Protestant theology should feel itself suddenly disarmed because it has no longer
to do with the crasser form of antimodernism but with the Catholic counterpart
of its own average outlook. Only a Protestant theology which, in face of Catholic
exegesis and the way it is bound to the norm of tradition, has better weapons
than merely an exegesis that is also bound to tradition, albeit the tradition of the
Reformers—hence only a Protestant theology which takes seriously the full
weight of the hermeneutic problem, and does not rest content with a dualism in
exegesis but thinks through the question of the critical historical method in such
a way that that method itself becomes identical with so-called theological exegesis
—only a Protestant theology of that kind will recognize that agreement between
the confessions on the subject of scripture exposition has at bottom not been
brought a single step nearer even by the seemingly so amazing Encyclical of 1943.
The debate has only become vastly more difficult. And as Protestants we can
only be thankful for that. It could be asked why the Roman Church is now able
to be so magnanimous both in regard to the text of the Vulgate and also in regard
to the problems of historical exposition of scripture. The reason is undoubtedly
that she is so sure of her position, resting as it does on the power of tradition—
ultimately, too, a tradition which is present in the pope himself—that she no

with for the dangerous path just described. And in that it has made the right decision. Indeed, I venture to assert that the Protestantism of the nineteenth century, by deciding in principle for the critical historical method, maintained and confirmed over against Roman Catholicism in a different situation the decision of the Reformers in the sixteenth century. That of course is not to say that wherever in the history of modern Protestant theology the motto of the critical historical method has been most loudly proclaimed and most radically applied, there men have also really been nearest to the Reformation in every respect. But what it certainly does mean is, that wherever they made way for the critical historical method and, however grievous their errors, took it seriously as their task, there, if certainly often in a very paradoxical way, they were really asserting the fundamental principle of the Reformers in the intellectual situation of the modern age.

(*b*) The proof that must be provided for the assertion that assent to the critical historical method has essentially a deep inner connexion with the Reformers' doctrine of justification leads to far-reaching questions in historical and systematic theology. To expound it fully will still require many detailed examinations of individual aspects of the theology of the Reformation and the history of modern Protestant theology. To that end a resumption and continuation of the work of Dilthey and Troeltsch on the historic relation between the Reformation and the rise of the modern spirit is urgently needed. The historical facts are, as far as the directly demonstrable historical connexions are concerned, manifestly very complicated. If the Reformation is taken as a historic whole,

---

longer feels she has any serious danger to fear from the side of critical historical exposition of scripture, at least within the limits in which she allows it. Inasmuch as the absolute authority of the church is assured, it is possible to give more latitude to scripture exposition. The extreme intensifying of the church's authority has the remarkable, but not incomprehensible, result of permitting a certain extension of freedom within the church. To put any other interpretation on the latest pronouncements on this point would to my mind be an illusion. I can perceive in them no trace of an indication that the Roman Church has any inclination to turn aside from the path whose direction is unequivocally laid down by the Tridentine and Vatican Decrees. Any individual concessions that may be made to the critical historical method are therefore based on a premise which from the start takes the critical sting out of the hermeneutic problem, *viz.* —*ut in rebus fidei ac morum ad aedificationem doctrinae christianae pertinentium is pro vero sensu sacrae Scripturae habendus sit, quem tenuit ac tenet sancta mater Ecclesia, cuius est iudicare de vero sensu et interpretatione Scripturarum sanctarum; atque ideo nemini licere contra hunc sensum aut etiam contra unanimem consensum Patrum ipsam Scripturam sacram interpretari* (*Vaticanum, Constitutio dogmatica de fide catholica,* cap. 2, Denz. 1788).

then there will certainly again and again be facts to notice that dialectically balance each other. The Reformation had both an extraordinarily
revolutionary effect on the course of thought, and on the other hand
was undoubtedly also a strongly retarding factor in the general intellectual transition from the Middle Ages to modern times. Yet not only
its positive, but also its critical relations with the humanism which more
especially paved the way for the modern age must be taken into account
as well in assessing the inner connexions that exist between the Reformation and the rise of modern historical thinking. And it could be asked
how far it is not precisely a result of the Reformation heritage when the
historical thinking of modern times, after a phase of rather strong dependence on the objectivistic thinking of humanism, goes on to a comprehensive solution of the hermeneutic problem from the standpoint of
a critical historical method that is understood far more deeply than in
merely technical ways.

However, operating with the Reformation as a historical whole will certainly not in itself enable us to solve the problem in question. Only
critical reflexion on the decisive basic principle from which the Reformers set out can help us to perceive whether and in what way there
exist in the complex dynamic field of the Reformation as a whole definite
essential inner connexions with the critical historical method of modern
times. That they do exist should already be clear from the above arguments, which have demonstrated all along the line the hermeneutic
relevance of the Reformers' theology as contrasted with the Catholic
position. The *sola fide* of the Reformation doctrine of justification both
contains a rejection of any existing ways of ensuring present actualization, whether ontological, sacramental or hierarchical, and also positively
includes an understanding of actualization in the sense of genuinely
historic, personal encounter. If this encounter with the historic revelation takes place solely in hearing the Word, then the shattering of all
historical assurances that supposedly render the decision of faith superfluous is completely in line with the struggle against the saving significance of good works or against understanding the working of the sacrament in the sense of the *opus operatum*. The *sola fide* destroys all secretly
docetic views of revelation which evade the historicalness of revelation by making it a history *sui generis*, a sacred area from which the
critical historical method must be anxiously debarred. In the Reformers'
view, both revelation and faith are discovered in their genuine historicalness, and that quite definitely means that faith is exposed to all the
vulnerability and ambiguity of the historical. Only in that way and only

for that reason can genuine encounter with the historic revelation be attained in faith and only in faith.

As everywhere in Reformation theology, so also here in regard to the relation to history, the assent to lack of guarantees is merely the reverse side of the certainty of salvation *sola fide*. And thus we are justified in asking whether a theology which evades the claims of the critical historical method has still any idea at all of the genuine meaning of the Reformers' doctrine of justification, even when the formulae of the sixteenth century are repeated with the utmost correctness. The objection that of course at the time of the Reformation and in early Protestant Orthodoxy the Reformers' doctrine of justification was presented and maintained without knowledge of the critical historical method, merely betrays the basic error of a traditionalism that believes itself relieved by the Reformers' theology from responsible theological labour of its own. On closer inspection, however, it is plain that alongside the fundamental relation between the Reformers' doctrine of justification and the critical historical method, the theology of the Reformation itself also broached an abundance of problems involving content with which the critical historical method has to do. One need only think of the at least latent criticism to which the Greek categories of thought in early church dogma were subjected, or the quite obvious internal criticism of content applied to the interpretation of the New Testament. The heritage of the Reformation with its obligations would be poorly preserved if the attempt were made to shirk the same problems as soon as they are posed anew— admittedly in the sharper form of historical reflexion—by the critical historical method. Precisely for the sake of keeping the heritage of the Reformation intact, we shall have to come to grips with many problems that are already heralded in the Reformers' theology itself, and to set about them, as befits the changed intellectual situation, by new and different methods from what were used at the Reformation.

(c) But now, in spite of the emphasis on the essential inner connexion between the Reformers' doctrine of justification and the critical historical method, there can of course be no denying the fact that the evolution of modern Protestant theology is full of unsolved difficulties. And these must be borne in mind if the call to adopt the critical historical method is not to be misunderstood as involving uncritical acceptance of all the painful errors manifested by the history of Neo-Protestant theology, but is rather to be understood as a demand for critical discussion of the history of Protestant theology in the sense of duly measuring it against the basic principles of the Reformers. The chief theological

difficulty, which every effort must be made to overcome, is the fatal
isolation of the historical disciplines from systematic theology and from
the life of the church. For the historical disciplines much will here
depend on whether work is continued not only on fearless pursuit of
individual researches committed solely to the discovery of truth, but
also on the hermeneutic problem by which the historical disciplines are
drawn into the wider context of theological work as a whole. It is vital
to clarify the manner in which what was above called genuinely historic,
personal encounter with the text takes effect in the realm of theological
study of the Old and New Testaments and of Church History and the
History of Theology in ways that can be methodically grasped—in other
words, to clarify the theological relevance of critical historical work on
these texts and events. This is a most vital task, both that we may avoid
the caricature of a research that is content with discussing minute matters of detail and also that we may escape the false path of a pseudo-
theological exposition that spares itself all the trouble of detailed historical
examination and makes the text a springboard for its own thoughts.
We shall therefore have to strive to secure recognition of the theological
bearing of historical work, not by by-passing critical historical examination nor in disconnected supplementation of it, but through the very
act of carrying it out.

Whether and how far it is possible to fix general norms for setting
limits to the improper employment of the critical historical method in
the realm of theology, is a question that assuredly requires very careful
consideration. Yet at the same time we must here primarily bear in
mind the fact that unceasing critical self-correction belongs to the nature
of the critical historical method, so that precisely with questions of
historical criticism an over-hasty censorship of doctrine is most readily
liable to cause only the greater harm by limiting freedom in matters of
teaching and research and thereby cutting off the possibility of genuine
critical self-correction. When we survey the course of historical theology
in the nineteenth century, then we must realize what a decisive share
the critical historical method had not so much in producing as rather
in overcoming dogmatic aberrations in the Enlightenment, Idealism,
Romanticism and Liberalism. Instead of everything succumbing step
by step to dissolution at the hands of the critics, as was feared, the
critical historical method actually taught a new regard for facts to which
the dominant theology was paying no attention at all. One need only
think, say, of the extraordinary theological significance of the eschatological view of the preaching of Jesus, or the stimulus that came from

the questions raised by the religious-historical or form-critical methods.

The task of even beginning to explore on any wide scale the real theological relevance of the tremendous work of critical historical theology in the nineteenth century is one in which nineteenth-century theology undoubtedly failed and which now, in the general antipathy towards the nineteenth century, threatens to be entirely forgotten. Systematic theology must therefore be required not only to respect the results of critical historical research—even on that point there is still much to be desired —but also to take up fully and completely into its own approach the outlook of the critical historical method. The trouble is—and it is plainly manifest in the history of modern theology—that Protestant dogmatics since the days of the Enlightenment has not succeeded in really squaring up to this task. It is not historical, but systematic theology that makes plain the crisis which has arisen in Protestant theology. To be sure, critical historical theology has also contributed to it in manifold ways. Yet the primary source of the trouble has not at all been its coming, as it often enough did and does, to mistaken conclusions in what are really uncritical ways. The trouble has been above all that its champions have either supposed that systematic theology could and must be abolished altogether, or else considered themselves in a position to produce a doctrine of the Christian Faith as a direct result of their critical historical labours, whether in the form of reducing everything to the life and teaching of Jesus or of progressively bringing to light the advances that have taken place in the history of church and theology itself. The fact that it is precisely in systematic theology that the problems arise with such sharpness points to a real aporia on the part of Protestantism. It will at all events be unable, if it rightly understands its own nature, to develop a dogmatics that is structurally identical with Catholic dogmatics. .Yet what the shape of Protestant dogmatics should be and what method it should go by is still an entirely open question—one which Schleiermacher certainly perceived with a clarity hardly ever to be attained again later, even if he, too, failed to solve it. If systematic theology takes up into its own approach the whole outlook of the critical historical method, then the result will be not only that it will achieve the critical destruction of all supposed assurances, but above all that it will be kept strictly to its proper concern—namely, the historic revelation in Jesus Christ— in full awareness of the historicalness of its own systematic theological labours.

And finally, the proclamation of the church—and the form of church order is also closely connected with that—must be required to take the work of historical criticism seriously. It is a real question whether the widespread frightful lameness and staleness of the church's message, her powerlessness to speak to the men of today, and likewise the lack of credibility that attaches to the church as such are not very largely connected with its fear of letting the work of critical historical theology bear fruit in the proper way and its failure to take sufficient account of the nature of the hermeneutic problem, which is acutely concentrated in the act of preaching. For critical historical theology is not identical with liberal theology. It is, however, the indispensable means of reminding the church of the freedom rooted in the *iustificatio impii*.

(*d*) We turn again in conclusion to the situation of today. The period since the first World War is marked by a movement of concentration in church and theology, introduced by new theological reflexion on the heart of the Christian kerygma and strengthened by the period of testing in the church struggle—a movement of concentration which found confessional expression in the Theological Declaration of Barmen. Something has happened there which no one can go back on and presumably only few wish to go back on either. But precisely when we know ourselves committed to what has happened, the commitment will have to consist in resolutely combatting the partly manifest and partly veiled dangers it immediately brings: we are committed not to a reactionary movement of opposition, but to watchful concern for the purity of the Gospel message. The dangers of a movement of concentration are by its very nature those of one-sidedness, foreshortening and isolation, of striving for security and impregnability, of seeking to avoid conflict and testing. To trace out these dangers concretely in detail would require a carefully differentiated analysis of the theological and ecclesiastical forces involved, extraordinarily different and conflicting as they were in spite of their common participation in the movement of concentration. Yet certain main tendencies stand out in various degrees: a new theological dogmatism and traditionalistic confessionalism, a clericalism and sacramentalism, an over-simplification through insistence on pietistic edification or else through catchword theology, radicalism, confessional rhetoric, etc. The critical historical method is certainly recognized in principle, except by a few outsiders. But in practice it is widely felt in ecclesiastical and theological circles to be really a tedious nuisance. Its results may perhaps be noted, but then they are left aside after all instead of being worked through. And where the critical historical method is seriously applied today, it remains a matter for the individual historical disciplines, and does not have an effect on theology as a whole, still less on the church—or when there is any visible sign of consequences of such a kind, it is pronounced to be rationalism and liberalism, or even rouses the cry of heresy. The path which theology has to tread in this situation for the church's sake is certainly full of unsolved problems, but there is no doubt as to the direction it must take.

II

ON THE DOCTRINE
OF THE *TRIPLEX USUS LEGIS* IN THE
THEOLOGY OF THE REFORMATION*

The doctrine of the *triplex usus legis* originated with Melanchthon. It meets us for the first time in the 1535 edition which introduces the *secunda aetas* of the *Loci*.[1] Luther on the other hand always spoke only of a *duplex usus legis*.

This statement applies first of all solely in a terminological sense, and even in that respect it requires closer definition.

The only two passages that testify to the appearance of the *triplex usus legis* in Luther must for different reasons both be rejected. Werner Elert has rightly pointed out that the conclusion of the second Antinomian Disputation of 12th January 1538, which does not indeed contain the expression *triplex usus legis* but does develop its theological content, is a later interpolation that depends on the *secunda aetas* of Melanchthon's *Loci*.[2] The exposition of Gal. 3.23-29 in the *Weihnachtspostille* of

---

* *TLZ* 75 (1950), pp. 235-246.   [1] *CR* 21, pp. 405 f.

[2] W. Elert, 'Eine theologische Fälschung zur Lehre vom tertius usus legis', in *Zeitschr. für Religions- und Geistesgeschichte*, ed. H.-J. Schoeps, 1 (1948), pp. 168-170; W. Elert, *Zwischen Gnade und Ungnade*, Munich 1948, pp. 161 ff. The conviction that the section in question (*WA* 39/1, p. 485.16-24) is spurious is one I, too, had reached before knowing of Elert's work, when I was dealing with the Antinomian Disputations in a seminar in the summer semester of 1948.

Elert's analysis of the findings of textual criticism requires correction. That the second Antinomian Disputation has come down to us in nine MSS cannot be concluded from *WA* 39/1, p. 418, since the ninth MS there cited is only a fragment of the Second Disputation (cf. *WA* 39/1, pp. 466-76) and is thus of no account as a textual witness to the conclusion of the Disputation. As a ninth MS of the whole Disputation we must, of course, add Codex Hamb. 74 (*WA* 39/2, pp. XXX f), whose variant readings are supplied later in *WA* 39/2, pp. 419-25. Of these nine witnesses to the text, it is not only two that give the disputed paragraph, as Elert says, but three, viz.—Monac. 940 as well as Helmst. 722 and Aug. 67. From the point of view of textual criticism it must now be noted that it is not only from p. 485.16 on that the MSS exhibit wide divergencies. The shortened form (Helmst. 688b) which Hermelink prints as Type B ends already with Argument XXVIII (p. 483.28). Hamb. 74, which is independent of this Type B but like it also a shortened form, ends at p. 485.7 (cf. *WA* 39/2, p.

1522,[1] on the other hand, does in fact contain the expression 'three-fold use of the law', which Bucer in his Latin translation of 1525 renders literally as *triplex usus legis*.[2] But that is a different thing from the later

[1] *WA* 10/1.1, pp. 449 ff.
[2] *Op. cit.*, pp. 456.8 f; 457.14, with the corresponding notes.

---

425 at bottom). With this Helmst. 722 also agrees, though this particular Codex then appends after all the section on the *triplex usus legis* (p. 485.16-24). Thus in this MS p. 485.9-16 is missing, while it alone has 'D. Martinus Lutherus' after p. 485.7. That could indicate (we could of course be certain only after a study of the original MS itself) that here the Disputation ends, so that what follows would be marked as an appendix added by the scribe (as a supposed summary of the results of the Disputation). Of the remaining six MSS, five end at p. 485.16 (Goth. 264, Helmst. 773, Monac. 940, Pal. 1827 and Rig. 242). Only one MS, *viz.*—Aug. 67—has the whole text of p. 485.9-24 supplied by Hermelink, while Codex Monac. 940, which also testifies to p. 485.16-24, gives this section in a totally different place, *viz.*—after Argument XXVII.

Thus at all events the text of p. 485.9-24 as supplied by Hermelink is untenable, since only one witness testifies to it as a whole. But as for the specially important passage p. 485.16-24, its spuriousness is already shown by the mere fact that although it is given by three MSS, yet it stands each time in a different context: in Monac. 940 inserted into Argument XXVII, in Helmst. 722 following p. 485.8, in Aug. 67 following p. 485.16. But now, it is a further striking fact that this paragraph, given three times but each time in a different place, apparently exhibits no variant readings within itself (provided we may suppose that the text-critical apparatus at this point is complete—as indeed this whole analysis must unfortunately depend solely on the facts given by the editor of *WA* 39). This fact, striking as it is in a MS tradition so extraordinarily rich in variants as that of the Antinomian Disputations, could be a sure sign that the three textual witnesses are using the same source—that we have thus an interpolation here which goes back to one and the same origin.

Since the relationship of mutual dependence between the MSS is so complicated and has not yet been clarified, it is very difficult, if not impossible, to penetrate any nearer to the originator of the interpolation. Elert's argument that the writer of the MS Helmst. 722, Israel Alectriander, cannot himself have witnessed the Disputation, is of no importance, since all the MSS we have of the Disputations are only secondary copies and thus none of them was written immediately by an eye-witness. The MS which is presumably the oldest, Helmst. 773, at all events does not contain the interpolation. The MS Helmst. 722, dated 1553, will presumably be somewhat older than Monac. 940, the writer of which is likewise known by name: Johann Spon of Augsburg, who studied at Wittenberg 1553-1557 (*WA* 39/2, p. XXI). Nevertheless it is not possible to designate Monac. 940 directly as a copy of Helmst. 722, since Monac. 940 in particular everywhere exhibits variants of its own. The composition of Codex Aug. 67 is certainly akin to that of Monac. 940, but a direct relation of dependence cannot be ascertained here either, and just as little between Aug. 67 and Helmst. 722. Thus it seems to me to be proved that Israel Alectriander cannot be the forger. How the interpolation came into the three MSS could at best be explained if we undertook the task—as laborious as it is on the whole unpromising—of solving the text-critical riddle which the MS tradition of the Antinomian Disputations so far poses. But in order to do that a new examination of the original codices would be indispensable.

doctrine of the *triplex usus legis*. The threefold use of the law which Luther speaks of here, bears solely on the question of fulfilling the law. Some do not keep it at all, others only externally, a third group both inwardly and outwardly.[1] And Luther expressly describes this third method in a way that excludes the *tertius usus legis* as Melanchthon understands it: 'Whoever seeks to preach the law rightly must observe these three distinctions, so as on no account to preach the law to the third group as if they could be saved thereby; for that would be corruption.'[2] 'Here is no Moses, but Jesus Christ, who leads by faith and fulfils all that is commanded by Moses; here are those unto whom there is no law.'[3] And likewise the *secundus usus legis* (*theologicus*) is not being maintained in this passage, since with the second group of people he is thinking of 'hypocrites' who only keep the law outwardly and refuse to look deeper into it and perceive that righteousness of that kind is nothing.[4] Explicit mention is made only of the *primus usus legis* which forces an outward righteousness on the insolent despisers of the law,[5] while the transition from the second to the third category of men is ascribed to the preaching of the Gospel.[6] But now it must be noted that this distinction of a threefold use of the law is only inserted by Luther in the form of a parenthesis in a context where the real topic is as plainly as may be the *duplex usus legis*, in the sense that there are said to be 'two things for which the law is necessary and good, and which God expects of it', *viz.*—'the one, that it should keep us in check and force us to a better nature outwardly . . . the other, that man should perceive through the law how false and wrong his heart is. . . . And should thus be humbled, creep to the Cross, sigh after Christ and long for his grace. . . .'[7] In regard to *this* distinction, too, he speaks of use of the law,[8] even if by way of variation he also employs other terms like 'benefit' or 'fruit'.[9] Our conclusion therefore is, that the formula 'threefold use of the law' is indeed found in Luther for the first time, yet it only expresses a passing thought and is then dropped again, while at the same time the doctrine of a twofold use of the law is

---

[1] Pp. 456.10-458.13.   [2] P. 457.2-5.   [3] P. 458.8-11.   [4] Pp. 457.17-458.7.
[5] 'But to the first group it should thus be preached: to them it is given, that they may leave their insolent life and be preserved under its discipline' (*op. cit.,* p. 457.5-7).
[6] 'Yet it is not enough that they are thus preserved and kept by the law, but they for their part must also learn to keep the law, so then we must go further and preach over and above the law also the Gospel in which the grace of Christ is given to keep the law' (p. 457.7-10).
[7] *Op. cit.,* pp. 454.8-455.14, as also the whole paragraph pp. 449.14-455.23 and 458.17-468.8.
[8] Pp. 460.17; 461.13; 463.4; 467.22.   [9] P. 460.1, 4 f, 11.

already established in essence and still awaits only its final conceptual formulation.

If in Melanchthon's case, too, we confine ourselves in the first instance strictly to the use of terms, then although in substance the *triplex usus legis* is plainly expounded in the 1535 edition of the *Loci*, yet that expression is not yet used there. In the new section that was inserted in the *Loci* of 1535 and given the title *De usu legis* he speaks of the *primum*, *secundum* and *tertium officium legis*, and in individual cases occasionally also of the *usus legis*.[1] But it is not till later that we find in Melanchthon along with increasingly frequent employment of the concept *usus* also the comprehensive formula *triplex usus legis*. I came across that expression for the first time (this naturally has to be marked as a merely provisional conclusion) in the *Catechesis puerilis* of the year 1540,[2] as also in the *Loci* itself in the edition of 1543 which stands at the beginning of the *tertia aetas*.[3] The final form of the stock phrase, however, is later in appearing than the doctrinal content of the *triplex usus legis* presented as early as the mid-thirties.

In order to shed more light on the origin of the distinction of different *usus legis*, I set down a few further observations on the linguistic facts. The situation in Melanchthon is as follows:— In the first edition of the *Loci* in 1521, the doctrine of the law is discussed without the expression *usus legis* assuming any importance. It occurs in all only twice in the later meaning, without being employed as a definite theological category.[4] There is thus no mention of different *usus legis*—not, at least, thus clearly conceived. But there is no other corresponding terminology

---

[1] *CR* 21, pp. 405 f. In the exposition of the *secundum officium legis* he says at one point: '. . . *hunc usum non habet Lex in hominibus securis*', and at the end of the whole section: '*Haec satis sit hic admonuisse de legis usu seu officiis. Nam cum de iustificatione dicimus, de secundo usu legis iterum dicendum erit. Tertius usus repetetur in loco de operibus; item, de abrogatione legis*' (p. 406). He had already once used the phrase: '*ut . . . de usu legis divinae recte iudicare possimus*' (p. 390).

[2] I had it before me in the first edition produced by Joh. Brenz (*Halae Sueuorum ex officina Petri Brubacchii Anno 1540*). The section *De usu legis* agrees verbatim with the edition of 1558 printed in *CR* 23, pp. 118 ff (the passage in question is pp. 176 f).

[3] The section *De usu legis* in the edition of 1543 has already verbally the same form as in the edition of 1559 printed in *CR* 21, pp. 601 ff (the passage in question is pp. 716-719).

[4] I quote it according to the edition of Plitt-Kolde (4th ed. 1925). As far as I can see, the concept *usus legis* occurs only twice—in the section *de vi legis* (pp. 149-58): '*Quid igitur lex? id est, si non profuit ad parandam iustitiam, quaeso, quis eius fuit usus?*' (p. 154), and in the section *de abrogatione legis*: '*Estque decalogi usus in mortificanda carne . . .*' (p. 220). On p. 214 we find the phrase *lege uti* in the normal secular sense.

either, which would express the distinction made in the later *usus legis* doctrine.[1] Only the difference between *carnalis* and *spiritualis intellectus legis* points in that direction, but it is not worked out into a positive evaluation of the former in the sense of the later so-called *usus politicus*.[2] There is essentially no change in that in the various editions of the *prima aetas* of the *Loci*.[3] In 1527 the *duplex usus legis* is in substance clearly taught in the *Visitation Articles*, but the concept *usus legis* is not employed. He speaks only of the two *effectus legis*.[4] The

[1] *Vis legis* relates solely to what was later called the *secundus usus legis* (pp. 149 ff), and so likewise do the concepts *opus legis* (pp. 151, 155, 156, 157), *officium legis* (p. 157), *sententia legis* (p. 156).

[2] Plitt-Kolde, pp. 149-53. It is naturally not Melanchthon's intention to deny the fact of what was later meant by the *politicus usus legis*. But in the first edition of the *Loci* he has no interest in this aspect of the doctrine of the law. It is significant that the two Bible proof-texts which are later his stock quotations in support of the *primus usus legis* are never cited in the *Loci* of 1521, viz.—Gal. 3.24 (*lex pedagogus noster*) and I Tim. 1.9 (*lex iniustis posita*). From I Tim. 1.9 he cites only once the negative statement: *Iusto non est lex posita* (p. 206).

[3] In two editions of the *Loci*—those of 1523 and 1525—theses are appended at the end *de duplici iustitia regimineque corporali et spirituali* (CR 21, pp. 227-30). That gave the *Loci* a wider reference in regard to the problem of *iustitia civilis*, yet without thereby formulating expressly the doctrine of the *duplex usus legis*. The lectures which Melanchthon held on the *Loci communes* in 1533, and which paved the way for the revised version of 1535, unfortunately exist only in the form of fragmentary students' notes (CR 21; 253-332). Precisely in the section *de lege Dei* the MS shows a break (CR 21; 296), so that we cannot establish whether Melanchthon presented a *locus de usu legis divinae* already in 1533 and whether it already had the form it had in 1535. This much at any rate can be gathered from the notes: that the concept *usus legis* is occasionally employed (p. 283), that Melanchthon strongly emphasizes what according to the sense, though of course without using the expression, is the *usus politicus* and also employs in this context the two scripture passages I Tim. 1.9 and Gal. 3.24 (pp. 279 f), and that he has in mind, likewise according to the sense, a *tertius usus legis* (p. 283).

[4] CR 26, p. 28. It is a mystery to me why G. Th. Strobel, who edited the *Articuli de quibus egerunt per visitatores in regione Saxoniae* again in 1776 after it had long been forgotten, had the conclusion printed in smaller type (from the second paragraph of the second last section *de libero arbitrio* onwards, and consequently also the last section *de lege* which concerns us here). He gives no reason for it—neither in his extensive historical introduction nor in the text-critical apparatus. The edition prepared by Bindseil in CR 26 gives no explanation of it either. An original copy of the edition of 1527 has unfortunately not been available to me.

In the *Instructions for Visitors of the parochial Clergy* published in 1528 (CR 26, pp. 29-96—I quote it according to the edition of Hans Lietzmann in *Kleine Texte für Vorlesungen und Übungen* No. 87, Bonn 1912), the section *de lege* is missing, and with it also the sharp distinction of the two *causae* for the sake of which the law is to be preached. Instead, in the section 'On the Ten Commandments' (*op. cit.*, pp. 8 f) the two *effectus legis* are summed up in one (p. 8.20 f), and from that another reason for the preaching of the law is then distinguished in the sense

Augsburg Apology likewise does not contain the concept *usus legis*.[1]
It is not until Melanchthon's *Commentary on Romans* that we come
across this terminology. Yet just here the change in the use of terms is
highly instructive. The earliest form of Melanchthon's exposition of
Romans is found in the *Annotationes in epistolam Pauli ad Romanos unam
et ad Corinthios duas*, which on the basis of students' notes and without
Melanchthon's knowledge was printed by Luther in 1522 and then in
1527 translated into German by Johann Agricola. Because Melanchthon
later disapproved this work and sought to replace it by the *Commentarii
in epistolam Pauli ad Romanos* of 1532, this early work of Melanchthon's
has foolishly not been taken up into the *Corpus Reformatorum*.[2] Between
the *Annotationes* and the *Commentarii*, however, there lies the *Dispositio
orationis in epistola Pauli ad Romanos*, which first appeared in 1529.
The facts are now as follows:— The early *Annotationes* reflect entirely
the theological attitude of the *Loci* of 1521. The concept *usus legis* plays
no part in it. But the substance of the later distinction between different
usus legis is not worked out either.[3] In the *Dispositio orationis* of

---

[1] In the *Apology* Melanchthon naturally teaches in substance the later *primus
usus legis* (*Die Bekenntnisschriften der evang.-luth. Kirche*, Göttingen 1930, p.
164.37 ff, where also Gal. 3.24 and I Tim. 1.9 are quoted) and the *secundus usus
legis* (to provide specific evidence of that is not necessary), but also gives indications of the *tertius usus legis* (p. 197.18 ff).   [2] Cf. *CR* 15, pp. 441 f.
[3] I have examined the two Strassburg editions of 1523 and 1525, which agree
verbatim with each other. It is significant that here Gal. 3.24, contrary to its later
exposition by Melanchthon, is quoted exclusively in order to prove the working
of the law in the sense of the *usus theologicus*: '*Ideo legem dedit . . . ut cognosce-
tur peccatum. . . . Sic ait Gala. 3. Lex pedagogus noster fuit in Christum, ut ex fide
iustificemur*' (on Rom. 4.15, *op. cit.*, 25a). On Rom. 5.20 (*op. cit.*, 30a) we find
the following sentences, which are characteristic of this early stage of Melanchthon's exposition of Romans: '*Cum mortem et propagationem peccati pertractasset,
quaeri potuit: Nunquid Lex ad tollendum fecerit? Nam vulgo putant legibus
coherceri peccatum. Huic quaestioni commode respondet, et quae supra diximus de
legis natura, eadem huc revocanda sunt. Nam ut supra Paulus ait: per legem esse
cognitionem peccati, legem iram operari, legis opus iram esse, ita in eandem sententiam
ait: Legem obiter intrasse, id est, ita introisse, ut maneret peccatum, immo, ut
augesceret, quia conscientia peccati adest, manente peccato, nec tollit peccatum, sed
multo magis auget. . . . Non quod lex proprie sit aucti peccati causa. Nam proprium
illius opus est ostendere peccatum, ostensionem sequitur incrementum peccati. Porro
nisi Lex esset, conscientia non esset; nisi conscientia esset, peccatum non cognosceretur;
Nisi cognosceretur, non humiliaremur, atque ita gratiam non desideraremus.*' The
whole exposition is aimed at the distinction of law and Gospel: '*Duplex iustitia
est. Altera quae est ex lege. . . . Altera est fidei iustitia*' (*op. cit.*, 56a). '*Duplex est
homo: Vetus et novus, seu carnalis et spiritualis*' (*op. cit.*, 31a).

---

of the later *tertius usus legis*: 'Therefore the ten commandments should once
more (!) be diligently preached, for in them all good works are comprised'
(p. 9.22 f).

1529[1] the concept *usus legis* does indeed occasionally occur,[2] and over and above that we find very plainly the doctrine of the two *officia legis* in the sense of the *duplex usus* doctrine, though not indeed in these terms[3]— very much as at the end of the *Visitation Articles*. In the *Commentarii*, which from 1532 on appeared in numerous editions of which the earliest I have had access to was unfortunately only that of 1540,[4] the doctrine of the *duplex usus legis* occurs in two places, and now indeed precisely in these terms.[5] Since, however, Melanchthon had already, in substance at all events, advanced the *triplex usus legis* in the *Loci* of 1535, it is to be presumed that the observations on the *duplex usus legis* were already contained in the first edition of 1532. The completely revised edition of 1556, which also bears the changed title *Enarratio epistolae Pauli ad Romanos*, then supplants the *duplex usus* doctrine by the doctrine of the *triplex usus legis*.[6]

[1] I have used the edition *Haganoae apud Johannem Secerium Anno MDXXX*, which in addition to the *Dispositio* contains notes by Agricola on the Epistle to Titus and an *Enarratio* by Luther on the 82nd Psalm. The final edition of the *Dispositio*, published in 1539, is printed in *CR* 5, pp. 443 ff.

[2] E.g. *op. cit.*, 53a f: *Accedit brevissima occupatio de usu legis. Necesse est enim lectori non stulto in mentem venire hanc quaestionem: Quod si legis opera non iustificant, cur igitur lata est lex? Videtur extreme absurdum, legem ferre, si legis opera non iustificant. Paulus respondet, et novam ac inauditam mundo sententiam ponit: Lex lata est, ut per eam cognoscatur peccatum, ut arguat peccatum, non ut aboleat....*

[3] *Op. cit.*, 61b f. The edition of 1539 is verbally the same.

[4] Published in Strassburg in September 1540. *CR* 15, pp. 493 ff prints the edition of 1544, which however agrees with that of 1540. On the relation of the 1540 edition to the first edition of 1532 the title page says: *Commentarii ... iam denuo hoc anno MDXL recogniti et locupleti*, and in *CR* 15, p. 494 the second edition (1540) is designated *multo locupletior*. I regret the more that it was not possible for me at the time to compare it with the edition of 1532. [*Addendum:* In the Commentary of 1532 Melanchthon discussed the *duplex usus legis* explicitly in commenting on Rom. 3.20, and in substance on Rom. 5.12 ff; yet the wording does not agree with the edition of 1540. On the other hand, the conjecture made in the following note is correct.]

[5] On Rom. 3.20 (*op. cit.* 198 = *CR* 15, p. 585) and on Rom. 5.12 ff (*op. cit.* 286–291 = *CR* 15, pp. 631 ff). The extensive treatment of the *usus politicus*, of the four reasons for its necessity and of the three aspects of the *paedagogia* was included in similar form in the *secunda aetas* of the *Loci* from 1541 on, viz.—in the section *De peccatis actualibus* (*CR* 21, p. 386)—and is found in the *tertia aetas* of the *Loci* in the section *De usu legis* (cf. above p. 65 note 3, *CR* 21, p. 717). I consider it unlikely that this detailed grounding of the *primus usus legis* is already to be found in the 1532 Commentary on Romans.

[6] I had before me the Wittenberg edition of 1556. *CR* 15, pp. 797 ff prints that of 1561. The section in question is the same in both editions. As in the *Commentarii* of 1540, the *usus* doctrine is here likewise discussed as such in commenting on Rom. 3.20—but now in the form of the *triplex usus legis* (*CR* 15, pp. 854 f).

The situation in Melanchthon may thus be summed up as follows:—
Only from 1527 on do we find a sharply worked out distinction of two
aspects of the preaching of the law, whereby to be sure it is not till the
beginning of the thirties that he uses the terminology *duplex usus legis,*
but then goes over to the doctrine of the *triplex usus legis,* in substance
in the mid-thirties at the latest, and in 1540 also in these terms. Indeed,
it could even be shown that as early as 1528 in the *Instructions for Visitors*
and in the *Augsburg Apology* Melanchthon touches on the idea of a
tertius usus legis.[1] Thus the *duplex usus legis,* clearly conceived in *these*
terms, was advanced by Melanchthon only for a very short time, and
even then contrary to his own real intentions. The only place I have
come across it is, as I have said, the *Commentary on Romans* in the
edition of 1540, where I presume it only remains as a relic of the edition
of the year 1532, although Melanchthon in 1540 was already teaching
the doctrine of the *triplex usus.* When Ragnar Bring asserts: 'While he
(Melanchthon) had originally spoken only of a *duplex usus legis,* from
that edition on (*viz.*—the *Loci* of 1535) he constantly spoke of the *triplex
usus legis*',[2] then that is to say the least a very sweeping judgment which
in many respects requires to be corrected and more exactly defined. It
may be seen particularly from these observations on Melanchthon's use
of terms how much we need both a textual edition that takes account of
all the editions published in Melanchthon's lifetime, and also a careful
and detailed examination of his theological development.

What, now, can we discover about the employment of the concept
usus legis in Luther? In that respect the development of the use of terms
in his theology can be most strikingly seen by comparing the *Commentary
on Galatians* of 1519 with that of 1535, or with the students' notes of
1531 on which it is founded. In 1519 Luther develops his doctrine of
the law without employing the expression *usus legis.*[3] In 1531/1535,[4] on

---

[1] See above, p. 66 note 4 and p. 67 note 1.

[2] Ragnar Bring, *Gesetz und Evangelium und der dritte Brauch des Gesetzes in
der lutherischen Theologie.* Separate reprint from *Zur Theologie Luthers. Aus der
Arbeit der Luther-Agricola-Gesellschaft in Finland* I, Helsinki 1943, p. 48.

[3] We do twice find the expression *lege uti* in preparation for, and also in the
same sense as, the later substantial phrase *usus legis:* WA 2, p. 500.12-14 and
p. 527.17-19. These passages would lead to the conclusion that there is only one
legitimate *usus legis, viz.*—the *usus theologicus.* Where Luther speaks of the mere
discipline of the law, he immediately sets that in closest connexion with the
working of the law in the *usus theologicus:* WA 2, p. 527.26-32. The remark on
pp. 466.19-26 and 498.10-13 could be heralding the thought of a *tertius usus
legis.* But on closer inspection precisely this last passage shows how far Luther
is from the thought of the *tertius usus legis* in Melanchthon's sense. For the pur-

(*Footnote* 4, *see p.* 70)

the other hand, the employment of the term *usus legis* is extraordinarily frequent[1]—and it has even been developed into the distinction of a two-fold *usus legis* which Luther, as Rörer's notes on the lectures show, almost without exception termed *usus civilis* and *usus theologicus*,[2] whereas the printed versions of 1535 and particularly of 1538, which were not supervised by Luther himself, more often replace the adjective *civilis* by *politicus*.[3] Moreover, a comparison between the MS of the printed editions brings to light in the latter something of the disciple's tendency towards polished formulae.[4] How little Luther himself standardizes, can be seen from the extraordinarily rare occurrence of the formula *duplex usus legis*,[5] the wealth of descriptions in verbal form[6] and of parallel

---

[1] Understandably enough especially on Gal. 3.19 ff (*WA* 40/1, pp. 473-547).

[2] E.g. *WA* 40/1, pp. 429.10 f; 519.11 f; 520.4 f; 530.16 f; 534.4. Further the expression *usus civilis* e.g. p. 530.18, 21, *sensus civilis* pp. 479.5; 480.8, *usus theologicus* pp. 499.6; 501.6. For the distinction see further the sentence: '*In religione loquimur aliter de rebus quam in politia*' (p. 176.13).

[3] An example of the admittedly only slight shift in the manner of expression: —MS (1531): *hunc locum potestis intelligere sive Civiliter sive Theologice. . . .* (p. 429.10 f); printed version (1535): *Itaque dixi hunc locum Mosi intelligi dupliciter, Civiliter et Theologice. Est enim lex lata ad duplicem usum: Primum ad cohercendos rudes et malos. . . . Is est Politicus legis usus. . . .* (p. 429.28 ff); printed version (1538): *Cum autem duplex sit usus legis, Politicus et Spiritualis. . . .* (p. 429, variant reading for line 27). A further example of the supplanting of *civilis* by *politicus* in 1535: p. 528.6; in 1538: p. 520, variant reading for line 18.

[4] I merely indicate this impression, without illustrating it by detailed examples, since that would require a very thorough examination. It must then also be borne in mind that the literary expansion of the abbreviated students' notes naturally resulted in a certain watering down. For the rest, as far as I can see, the printed version of 1535 shows no essential shift in the use of the terms *uti* and *usus* as compared with the notes, and a comparison with the printed version of 1538 would not provide any results of that kind either.

[5] *WA* 40/1, p. 491.1 f. The reference there made to an earlier statement applies merely to the distinction which had already been repeatedly made in substance. The expression *duplex legis* does not, to the best of my knowledge, occur elsewhere in the MS. The printed version of 1535 has it also e.g. on pp. 429.29; 479.17. In the printed version of 1538 the latter passage is also further emphasized by the addition of the heading *De duplici legis usu*.

[6] I mention only examples of joining the verb *uti* with *lex*:—*si recte utaris* (p. 489.10), *ut legitime quis utatur* (p. 508.10), *tantum legitime utaris* (p. 522.10), *isto opere et officio legis recte uti* (p. 531.19), *si contritus, bene utere contritione et*

---

pose of tracing out the use of the term *usus legis* it is worth noting the single occurrence of the phrase *usus evangelii*: *WA* 2, p. 479.16-18. The phrase *duplex lex* (*op. cit.*, pp. 498 ff) means the difference between *lex spiritus et fidei* and *lex literae et operum* in the sense of the *lex impleta* and the *lex non impleta*, and thus refers to the distinction of law and Gospel, but not to that of a *duplex usus legis*.

[4] *WA* 40, Pts. 1 and 2. The variants in the printed version of 1538 are noted in the text-critical apparatus. In the Erlangen edition J. C. Irmischer printed the 1538 form.

concepts to *usus legis*,[1] as also from the fact that the absolute centre of gravity is located in the *usus theologicus*, which really alone deserves to be called *usus legis*.[2] And indeed Luther's whole employment of this term *usus legis* must be seen in the context of his usage of *usus* and *uti* in general, for the study of which the 1531/1535 *Commentary on Galatians* offers particularly rich material. *Uti* and *usus* is for Luther the category of existential relation to an object. '*In usu rerum, non in rebus ipsis vis sita est.*'[3] Only where the *usus* is concerned are we in the correct, vital relation to the object. Only *in usu* is the understanding first put to the test: '*quando ventum ad usum, rem, vitam, affectum*'[4]—a list of four concepts in whose inseparable conjunction with each other one could more or less sum up the whole of Luther's ontology. The structure of Luther's thought, of which that is a mere indication, is naturally not bound to the employment of a concept like *usus*. That is clear from the striking fact that in the *Antinomian Disputations*, which stand so near in time to

[1] E.g. *officium legis* (pp. 481.4; 483.6; 484.2, 7, 8; 485.3; 489.2, 8); *opus et officium legis* (p. 531.19); *lex in suo ultimato opere* (p. 508.9 f); *finis legis* (p. 533.12); *ultimatus finis legis* (p. 506.4); *finis legis, tempus, modus legis* (p. 504.10); *natura legis, usus et vis* (p. 534.1). It should also be noticed that Luther is always well aware of the antonym of *usus*: *ex usu legis faciunt abusum* (p. 533.3 f); *incipit tractare de lege et de usu et abusu legis* (p. 530.8, also p. 531.9-13).

[2] E.g. *verus usus* (pp. 511.11; 530.22; 532.7); *optimus usus* (pp. 509.8 f; 530.15); *sanctus usus* (p. 480.3); *usus necessarius* (p. 535.8); *verum officium legis et proprius usus* (p. 481.4); *legis usus proprius et absolutus* (p. 482.3); *optimus et perfectissimus usus* (p. 490.5); *legitimus usus* (p. 509.1). The relation to the *usus civilis* can, it is true, be expressed in the comparative form: *usus civilis est utcunque bona, melior Theologicus* (p. 534.4). The *usus civilis* is *infimus usus* (p. 530.17). Whereas in the *usus theologicus* the law is *in maximo suo usu* (p. 509.4). Yet it can also be said again of the *usus theologicus* absolutely: 'That is *usus legis*' (pp. 483.1; 530.20; 533.8); '*tum usus legis*' (p. 489.12); '*ibi lex est in suo usu*' (p. 525.1).

[3] *WA* 40/1, p. 174.25 f. The MS has only, 'it lies *in usu rerum*' (p. 174.10).

[4] *WA* 40/1, p. 251.3. '*Papa etiam dicit legem et gratiam distincta et tamen in ipso usu contrarium dicit*' (p. 251.4 f). '... *nullus Anabaptista, Schwermerus intelligit distinctionem gratiae et legis, quia iudicio rerum et usu convincuntur*' (p. 252.6 f). '*Videri quidem volunt se quoque Evangelium et fidem Christi pure docere ut nos, Sed quando venitur ad usum, sunt doctores legis ...*' (p. 252.19 f, printed version of 1535). '*Ideo disce, ut usu discas*' (p. 251.9). '... *retinentes tantum in speciem verbum et nomen Christi, usu autem et revera prorsus negantes Christum et verbum ipsius*' (p. 255.23-25, printed version of 1535). '*Istam distinctionem assuesce usu practicare, ipsa vita*' (p. 261.6 f; in the printed version of 1535: '*Istam distinctionem discamus non tantum verbis, sed usu, vita et ipsis vivis affectibus practicare*', p. 261.24 f). '... *distinctionem illam valere non in syllaba et litera, sed in usu et corde*' (p. 263.9 f; in the printed version of 1535: '... *sed in usu rerum*', p. 263.27). '*Res distinctae; sic usus rerum*' (p. 478.3).

---

malleo (p. 490.2 f), *sic posse uti lege, quod faciat Christum sitire* (p. 509.9), *deus ... utitur hoc effectu legis in bonum usum* (p. 517.12).

the *Commentary on Galatians* and in their subject-matter are so closely
akin to it, the term passes very much into the background, both in its
general application and in its special conjunction with *lex*.[1] When we
turn from the 1531/1535 *Commentary on Galatians* to the *Antinomian
Disputations*, it is not indeed so very surprising that here we meet the
lecture-room formula *duplex usus legis* once only.[2] What rather strikes
us above all is, that Luther is not in danger of taking the manifold
problems of the doctrine of the law and pressing them into an *usus legis*
terminology that hardens into a rigid scholastic schema. In the very
absence here of the concept *usus legis* the knowledge of the true meaning
of the concept *usus legis* is kept alive.

Yet before I turn to the question what the expression *usus legis* really
means, I wish to try to bridge the gap between the two Commentaries
on Galatians of 1519 and 1531/1535. A starting-point is provided by the
passage discussed at the beginning from the *Weihnachtspostille* of 1522
with its still fluctuating employment of the expression 'use of the law'.
Soon after that, in February 1523, Luther begins his course of sermons
on the Decalogue with the assertion that the commandments of God
are given *ad duplicem usum*, and goes on with the sheer joy of a new
discovery to discuss one commandment after another from this standpoint.[3] When we recall that from the year 1519 on Luther finds in the
question of 'benefit and use' applied to the work of Christ,[4] to the Sacraments,[5] and to the Word of Scripture[6] the method and means of bringing

---

[1] Employment of *usus* or *uti* in general: *WA* 39/1, pp. 546.9; 401.9, 22, 24 f.
Theologically important: *fidei usus* (p. 495.9), *usus Christi* (p. 546.15 f). In conjunction with *lex*: *usus legis* (pp. 442.18; 497.24; 500.9), *necessarius usus* (p. 382.7 f),
verus usus legis (p. 421.28), *salutaris usus* (p. 446.3), *duplex usus legis* (p. 441.2 f),
Paulus . . . utitur . . . officio legis (p. 543.12 f), *evangelium . . . utitur lege* (pp.
426.22 f; 446.28; 542.16), *tam diabolus, quam Christus utitur lege* (p. 426.32).
Here belongs also: *hae quatuor viae ad poenitentiam, quibus Deus plerumque utitur*
(p. 580. 14 f).
   It is noteworthy that in the six lists of theses against the Antinomians (*WA*
39/1, pp. 345-58) *usus legis* never occurs, nor indeed do the words *usus* and *uti*
at all.
   [2] *WA* 39/1, p. 441.2 f.
   [3] See especially *WA* 11, pp. 31.6-23; 31.30-32.4; 32.5 f; 36.2 f. From the
point of view of content the early stage of the *duplex usus legis* doctrine is
unmistakable in these passages.
   [4] In the Sermon on Consideration of the Sacred Passion of Christ (1519),
WA 2, p. 138.16-19.
   [5] In the Sermon on Preparing for Death (1519), *WA* 2, p. 692.22-24; 695.3-12.
In the Sermon on the highly revered Sacrament of the Holy True Body of Christ
and on Brotherhood (1519), *WA* 2, p. 742.10-14. Specially important is the
controversy with the understanding of the Sacrament as *opus operatum*, pp.
(Footnote 6, see p. 73)

about the application of the Reformation's basic discovery to the whole field of theology, then that confirms the conjecture that in the section of the *Weihnachtspostille* referred to we find ourselves very near the original source of the term *usus legis*.[1]

For *'usus legis'* seems to me to be in fact a theological concept coined by Luther. So far as I am aware, the term is to be found neither in Augustine,[2] where one would soonest expect it, nor in the scholastics either.[3] Although in I Tim. 1.8—*Scimus autem quia bonus est lex, si quis ea legitime utatur*—the way is already prepared for the phrase, yet it was Luther who first gave it a significance that goes far beyond the sense of the New Testament passage. Not as if it had been under the stimulus of

[1] By that I naturally do not mean that Luther employed the formula 'use of the law' for the first time in the exposition of Gal. 3.23-29 in the *Weihnachtspostille*. It is also found e.g. already in the exposition of Gal. 4.1-7 that comes just before it (*WA* 10/1.1, p. 337.22), but not yet in conjunction with the distinction of a twofold use of the law, although that is referred to in substance (*op. cit.*, p. 344.18-21). To establish with absolute certainty when the term *usus legis* first appeared in Luther, I should require to go through again the whole of Luther's writings before 1522—a work I could not undertake for this paper.

[2] Whether Augustine's distinction in the doctrine of the sacraments between *habere* and *utiliter habere* had any effect on Luther's phrase about the use of the sacrament, seems to me questionable to say the least. Augustine does not to my knowledge employ the expression *usus sacramenti*. The phrase *lege uti* is taken over by Augustine from I Tim. 1.8. But it remains bound in his writings to the quotation of that passage, and does not become a theological *terminus technicus*. Cf. *De spiritu et litera* 10, 16 (*CSEL* 60, pp. 168 f), *De natura et gratia* 69, 83 (*CSEL* 60, p. 297).

[3] The concept *uti* is discussed in distinction to *frui*—e.g. Gabriel Biel, *Coll. in IV libros sententiarum*, lib. I dist. 1 qu. 1. See also M. F. Garcia, *Lexicon Scholasticum* 1910, p. 296. For the question we are concerned with, the discussions of concepts are wholly unfruitful. On Biel's concept of the law, see *Coll.*, lib. III dist. 37 and 40.

751.29-752.11. It was not beside the point when Melanchthon in 1521 summed up the significance of Luther as follows: 'If you ask what benefit Luther is to the church, you have it here in sum. He has taught a right manner of repentance and shown the right use of the sacrament: the consciences of many bear me out in that' (A Verdict of the Theologians in Paris on the Teaching of Dr Luther—A Counter-verdict of Dr Luther—A Defence of Dr Luther against the same Parisian Verdict by Philip Melanchthon, *WA* 8, p. 311.31-34).

[6] For the term *usus historiae* see my book, *Evangelische Evangelienauslegung: Eine Untersuchung zu Luthers Hermeneutik*, Munich 1942, pp. 424 ff, 86 f, 219, 232. The supplanting of the expression *sacramentaliter* in the hermeneutic sense as a term for the present significance of the history of Christ by the formula that the history of Christ must be understood as a 'gift' or 'present' begins with the *Weihnachtspostille*, and with that the way is paved at once for the terminology *usus* (or *fructus*) *historiae*. The concept *usus* in conjunction with the distinction of law and Gospel is employed in an interesting way as a hermeneutic category in *De servo arbitrio*, *WA* 18, p. 682.10-25.

I Tim. 1.8—which, incidentally, he quotes in the *Weihnachtspostille* passage referred to[1]—that Luther formed the concept *usus legis*.[2] Its roots lie far deeper, not even merely in the category of 'benefit and use' already employed earlier, but—*with* that category—in the Reformed understanding of justification *sola fide* and the distinction of law and Gospel; and from that again we cannot sever the question of scripture exposition, which is of course recalled by the close proximity of the concepts *sensus legis* and *usus legis*. The distinction of a *usus legis* that is specifically *duplex* is also prepared for in the doctrine of justification and the distinction of law and Gospel. But it is no accident that this aspect of the doctrine of the law, i.e. the relative validity of the *iustitia civilis* that has been stripped of its *opinio iustitiae* in the absolute sense, does not become acute for Luther till the beginning of the twenties. The further development of his use of terms was then, if I am not mistaken, that it was only in the lectures on Galatians in 1531 that he started to employ the terminology *usus legis* more intensively as a theological category—which then apparently struck an echo in Melanchthon in that he likewise took over the category, first of all, it is true, in dependence on Luther as *duplex usus legis*, yet very soon adapting the concept borrowed from Luther to suit the intentions of his own doctrine of the law and remodelling it into the scholastic schema of the *triplex usus*. If Melanchthon already deviated from Luther in making the term *usus legis* into a polished formula, then we must go on to ask whether his defining the *primus usus legis* as *usus paedagogicus* on the basis of Gal. 3.24 and on top of that his addition of a *tertius usus legis* does not make it clear that he neither held fast to a differentiated *usus legis* doctrine rooted exclus-

---

[1] *WA* 10/1, 1; p. 456.21 f.

[2] Entirely on the same lines as Augustine, and demonstrably due to him, is the employment of I Tim. 1.8 in the first course of lectures on the Psalms (1513/15), cf. Adolf Hamel, *Der junge Luther und Augustin* I, Gütersloh 1934, p. 129, note 3. Luther quotes I Tim. 1.8 also in the first course of lectures on Galatians (1516/17), without at that stage drawing any conclusions from it for the terminology of his doctrine of the law: *WA* 57, pp. 43.19 f (comment on Gal. 5.23) and 72.1-4 (note on Gal. 2.18). The latter passage is noteworthy all the same—for one thing because of the formal exposition of *uti* in the light of the distinction between 'thing in itself' and dealing with things, and secondly owing to the intrinsic interpretation (negatively formulated, it is true) of the meaning of *lege legitime uti*. That Luther is aware later of the connexion of his concept *usus legis* with I Tim. 1.8, is shown e.g. by the following passages from the large *Commentary on Galatians* (lecture notes of 1531): '... *quia lex in suo ultimato opere humiliat et praeparat, ut legittime quis utatur*' (*WA* 40/1, p. 508.9 f); '*Bene factum est, recte geritur, quod sic confusus es, tantum legittime utaris. Usus autem in futuram fidem*' (*op. cit.*, p. 522.9 f). In both cases the editor has failed to realize that he has to do with quotation from I Tim. 1.8.

ively in the distinction of law and Gospel, nor even adhered to the genuine meaning of the phrase *usus legis*.

For what does *usus legis* really mean? Who is the subject of this *uti*? God as the author of law? Or man, to whom the law applies? Or the man who preaches the law? Strangely enough, this question has never been discussed in Protestant theology. Yet understandably enough at the same time, under the domination of Melanchthon's faded version of the *usus legis* concept in which *usus* is merely the formal comprehensive term for the different angles on what the law is good for.

On the other hand, the same question appears in a very different light when we probe into Luther's doctrine of the law. The fundamental difference from Melanchthon can be shown already in his concept of law. Law for Luther is not a revealed statutory norm to which man then adopts this attitude or that, but law is for Luther an existentialist[1] category which sums up the theological interpretation of man's being as it in fact is. Law is therefore not an idea or an aggregate of principles, but the reality of fallen man. '*Haec tria, lex, peccatum, mors sunt inseperabilia.*'[2] The preaching of the law therefore merely uncovers '*illas res, quae iam existunt in natura humana*'.[3] To say, '*lex requiritur . . .*', is senseless. '*Nam lex iam adest*, is already there. *Lex prius adest in facto.*'[4] '*Lex enim nulla nostra necessitate, sed de facto iam invitis nobis adest. . . .*'[5] Just as senseless therefore is the demand, '*legem esse abolendam et e concionibus Ecclesiae tollendam.*'[6] '*Quare non potest in universum tolli lex. Nam etiamsi tollas has litteras: LEX, quae facillime deleri possunt, tamen manet chirographum inustum cordibus nostris, quod nos damnat et exercet.*'[7] To speak of the law does not mean to speak '*τεχνικῶς sive materialiter . . . seu grammatice*'[8] of the law, but '*de natura et vi et effectu legis*'.[9] *Lex* is not *lex vacua seu quiescens* or the *lex impleta*, but by *lex* must always be understood the *lex non impleta*, and that means, the *lex accusans, reos agens, exactrix* and *efficax.*[10] The eternal duration of the law even *in futura vita* is valid only *ut res, non ut lex.*[11]

If this relationship to existence is thus expressed already in Luther's very concept of law, then from the standpoint of justification *sola gratia sola fide* there can be *one* and only one *legitimus usus legis*, namely, as *paedagogus in Christum*. The subject of this *usus legis* cannot be man.

---

[1] Cf. my note, p. 331 below, note 1.—*Translator.*   [2] *WA* 39/1, p. 354.24.
[3] P. 361.30.   [4] P. 477.7.   [5] P. 353.37 f.   [6] P. 348.9 f.
[7] Pp. 456.18-457.1.   [8] P. 455.13 f.   [9] *Ibid.*
[10] Pp. 433.1-435.13. I shall enter more deeply into the interpretation of this difficult passage in the work I am planning on the Antinomian Disputations.
[11] P. 413.17 f.

For then of course the *lex* itself would be *necessaria ad iustificationem.* Like man, the *lex* is also only the material, not the efficient cause of justification.[1] The paradoxical necessity of the preaching of the law with a view to justification consists in the fact that the *lex non est necessaria, sed impossibilis ad iustificationem.*[2] For: '*Lex occidit per impossibilitatem suam.*'[3] But in this its proper function the law does not *per sese* become a *paedagogus in Christum*, but: '*Evangelium facit ex lege paedagogum in Christum.*'[4] That decides the question of the *usus legis*, whose subject is either Christ or the devil. For '*tam diabolus, quam Christus utitur lege in terrendis hominibus, sed fines sunt dissimillimi et prorsus contrarii.*'[5] To that extent it could of course also be said that faith alone is the subject of the *uti lege*, because here both the *finalis praesumptio* and also the *finalis dubitatio*[6] are ruled out. For the right *usus legis* is, to allow the law neither to be asserted as a means to justification nor as an objection to justification.

But now, what connexion has the doctrine of the *duplex usus legis* with all this? It would be completely misunderstood if the *usus civilis* were isolated from the *usus theologicus* in such a way as to stand so to speak on its own feet—in other words, if it were forgotten that it is only from the standpoint of the doctrine of justification that it is possible to speak at all of a *civilis usus legis* and of a *iustitia civilis*, i.e. of a *iustitia* that is not bound up with the illusion of being *iustitia coram Deo*. For when the *impii* are forced to an outward righteousness by the law in the sense of the *usus civilis*, then the law is in actual fact misused after all by the *impii* to produce an *opinio iustitiae*. True, the law is certainly there at work in the *usus civilis*, but of all people the *impius* does not understand it that way. Only the believer is able to use the law in the *usus civilis* in such a way that the result is not at the same time an *abusus legis*. To that extent the knowledge of the *usus theologicus* precedes the knowledge of the *usus civilis*. Yet it is not without good reason that in regard to the actual, practical working of the law the *usus civilis* is put first, before the *usus theologicus*. '*Omnium quidem est lex, sed non est omnium sensus legis.*'[7] I do not know what ground Werner Elert has for his assertion that the original order was, first use: *usus theologicus*, second use: *usus politicus*, and that it was Melanchthon who first put the latter in front.[8] In Luther also, when the two come together the *usus civilis* is always put first, whereas it is a peculiarity of Calvin that from the start

---

[1] Pp. 447.3-448.7.   [2] P. 348.11 f.   [3] P. 383.22.   [4] P. 446.22 f.
[5] P. 426.32 f.   [6] P. 428.19 f.   [7] P. 406.1 f.
[8] *Zeitschr. für Religions- und Geistesgeschichte* I (1948), p. 168.

he puts the *usus theologicus* in the first place and the *usus politicus* second.[1]
What causes Melanchthon to go astray is not merely his connecting the
usus politicus with Gal. 3.24 at all, but the fact that he applies Gal. 3.24
exclusively to the *usus politicus* and therefore calls it *usus paedagogicus* as
well. For with Luther both the *usus civilis* and the *usus theologicus* are
alike provided for in Gal. 3.24, in so far as it is the same law that is at
work in the *coercere delicta* and in the *ostendere delicta*. 'Nec politica aut
naturalis lex est quidquam, nisi sit damnans et terrens peccatores.'[2] Although
from the theological standpoint the *usus politicus* and *usus theologicus*
have to be sharply distinguished, yet in the *preaching* of the law they
are most closely interwoven, in so far as the preacher's aim is always
that the law should be understood at the same time in both its *usus
politicus* and *usus theologicus*. For it is surely to the same men that the
law applies in both *usus*, and not as if there were a category of some
kind of completely hardboiled sinners for whom the *usus civilis* alone is
appropriate, while the *usus theologicus* is for another category of—sinners
to be described I know not how.

And yet—Luther does distinguish very clearly from each other two
groups of men to whom the law has to be preached in different ways:
the *impii* and the *pii*. What does he mean when he makes the following
distinction: 'Est enim necessarium et utile officium legis perpetuo, tum
propter duros terrendos, tum etiam pios admonendos'?[3] Or: 'Quare impii
obtundendi sunt legis lumine, ut tandem perterrefacti discant Christum quaerere, et piis est etiam docenda lex monendi et cohortandi causa, ut in pugna
et concertatione permaneant.'[4] Is this a distinction in the sense of the
duplex usus legis? Obviously not! For it is specifically also to the *impii*
that the law is preached *ut tandem perterrefacti discant Christum quaerere*.
One could sooner ask: Is this a distinction between the *secundus* and a
tertius usus legis? But that does not tally either! For Luther emphasizes
again and again that the law has to be preached to the *pii* not *in quantum
iusti* but *in quantum peccatores*—which, however, means in the *usus theologicus*. So it is thus a case of a distinction in the execution of the
preaching of the law within the *usus theologicus*. Those who deny that
Luther taught a *tertius usus legis* in Melanchthon's sense always overlook
the fact that Luther does indeed differentiate between the effects which
the law in the *usus theologicus* has on the *impius* and on the *pius*, and
between the ways in which it has to be preached to the one and to the

---

[1] In the *Institutio* of 1536: *Calvini opera*, ed. P. Barth, I, pp. 61 f. In the
Institutio of 1559: *op. cit.* III, pp. 332 ff.
[2] *WA* 39/1, p. 358.28 f.   [3] P. 399.4 f.   [4] P. 513.4-6.

other.[1] Here the distinction of law and Gospel encroaches on the doctrine of the *usus legis*. Here Luther can make such surprising remarks as: '*Sic christianis quidem docetur lex, sed cum aliqua praerogativa.*'[2] '*Lex iam valde mitigata per iustificationem.* . . . *Ante iustificationem regnat et terret omnes, quos tangit. Sed non sic docenda lex piis, ut arguat, damnet, sed ut hortetur ad bonum.* . . . *Itaque lex illis mollienda est et quasi exhortationis loco docenda.*'[3] Here the doctrine of the *usus legis* acquires homiletic and pastoral relevance, so that it could even be said that the preacher becomes the subject of the *uti lege* in *recte secare verbum dei*—not, however, in the manner of different *usus legis*, but in the concrete distinction and interrelation of law and Gospel.

In what I have said in the last part of my remarks on the theological interpretation of the *usus legis* doctrine, I have purposely kept exclusively to the Antinomian Disputations. For it seems to me that for the interpretation of Luther it is urgently necessary to take a clearly defined textual complex and there trace out the interconnexions of thought to the very last shades of meaning. I hope to be able to do that presently in a larger work on the Antinomian Disputations.[4] In this paper I have had to confine myself to presenting a few observations on the problem of the distinction of different *usus legis* in the theology of the Reformation.

[1] This problem is not done sufficient justice to either in the work by Lennart Pinomaa, *Der existentielle Charakter der Theologie Luthers* (*Annales Academiae scientiarum Fennicae* XLVII, Helsinki 1940), although it is touched upon on pp. 173 f. See further pp. 155-195 on Luther's doctrine of the law.

[2] *WA* 39/1, p. 513.8 f.   [3] Pp. 474.8-475.6.

[4] For that reason I have here added very little documentation from the Antinomian Disputations.

III

THE MEANING
OF 'BIBLICAL THEOLOGY'*[1]

I

My contribution to the general theme of the conference is to set a question-mark against the concept of 'biblical theology'—not with the purpose of rejecting it *a priori*, but in order to inquire into its meaning, i.e. to disclose the problems that are contained in the concept 'biblical theology'. The main point of my observations will therefore lie not so much in answering as in formulating the question: What is 'biblical theology'? For much is achieved if theologians of widely differing standpoints come to an understanding with each other regarding the precise nature of a problem. That is a prerequisite for any fruitful co-operation towards solving it.

'Biblical theology' is at all events not an unequivocal idea. It can mean either 'the theology contained in the Bible, the theology of the Bible itself', or 'the theology that accords with the Bible, scriptural theology'. Both possible meanings bristle with a host of problems. To comprehend these rightly, we must consider as our basic problem the relation between these two possible meanings of 'biblical theology'. William Wrede, it is true, was of another opinion. In his book *Über Aufgabe und Methode der sogenannten Neutestamentlichen Theologie* (1897) he did indeed notice this distinction of meaning, but only to set it aside as uninteresting and of no importance. 'The name "biblical theology" ', says Wrede, 'originally means not a theology which the Bible has, but the theology which

* Published in English in *Journal of Theological Studies* VI, 1955, pp. 210-25. Also in *On the Authority of the Bible: Some Recent Studies* by L. Hodgson, C. F. Evans, J. Burnaby, G. Ebeling and D. E. Nineham, London 1960, pp. 49-67.
(The original English version, itself apparently also a translation, has here been carefully revised in the light of the German text as published in 1960, and several changes have been made. The division into numbered sections has also been taken over from that source, along with one or two minor additions to the text and four new footnotes.—*Translator*.)

[1] A paper read at the conference of the Society for the Study of Theology at Oxford on 30th March 1955.

has biblical character and is drawn from the Bible. For us that is a matter of indifference.'[1] I would hold that for us it cannot by any means be a matter of indifference. For here we touch the real root of the problem: What is 'biblical theology'? In the latter sense 'biblical theology' is a normative concept, in the former sense it is a historical concept. In the one case 'biblical theology' means theology of the right kind, in the other a specific historic form of theology. In the one case the concept 'biblical theology' relates to the essence of theology as such, in the other case only to a particular department of theology, a specific theological discipline. In the one case 'biblical theology' is the concern of the dogmatic theologian, in the other of the historical theologian. Even if we take these contrasts as a merely provisional characterization, yet it is clear that we cannot be content only to distinguish the two meanings of 'biblical theology'. Rather, the burning question arises: What is the connexion between them and where does the one pass over into the other? What is the relation between dogmatic and historical theology? And what about the relation between theology and the Bible in view of the juxtaposition of a dogmatic and a historical concern with holy scripture?

If we first consider the phrase 'biblical theology' as such, without regard to its origin and the changes in the way it has been understood, then by starting from naive presuppositions we could propose for the sake of argument two opposing views. First, the phrase appears to be a tautology. For theology (we presuppose that it is Christian theology) surely must be in agreement with the Bible if it is to be Christian theology at all. This principle also holds good for Roman Catholic theology. In spite of the fact that tradition ranks as an independent source of revelation beside scripture, in Roman Catholic thought it is *a priori* impossible that the relation between the two should be one of contradiction. Admittedly, in this case the designation 'biblical theology' would not be an adequate definition of the nature of theology; but nevertheless the accusation of an unbiblical theology contradicting holy scripture meets with a decided denial from the Roman Catholic side. The point in dispute within Christian theology is not the general *fact* but the *way* in which theology is related to the Bible. Only when the latter is more narrowly defined could the phrase 'biblical theology' become a serviceable formula. But now, we could also (as I have said, for the sake of argument) hold the opposite opinion: the phrase 'biblical theology' appears to be a contradiction in terms. For either the Bible itself is

---

[1] *Op. cit.*, p. 79.

theology in its content. How then can its normative, revelatory character be reconciled with the fact that the Bible does not absolve us from the task of studying theology for ourselves? Or else the Bible is, at least in its content proper, not theology. Then does not theology necessarily mean a departure from the Bible, a transformation of its content into something which is not strictly in accord with the Bible? If the formula 'biblical theology' is to be meaningful, we should have to explain the grounds on which the contradictory character of this tension disappears.

It will, however, be advisable not to continue this line of argument, but to seek help in the history of the concept 'biblical theology'. Certainly, the history of the concept will not simply absolve us from thinking for ourselves. For if it enables us to trace the historical changes through which the idea has hitherto passed, yet it does not provide us with our decision, but only with the material for our decision. Let no one say, however, that the concepts are a matter of relative indifference, and that we should rather concentrate solely on the thing itself. The history of a concept is never merely a matter of purely formal questions of nomenclature, but is always of value for the understanding of the thing itself.

II

The *terminus a quo* for the occurrence of the concept 'biblical theology' is in the first instance the time at which we first find the idea of 'theology' used to designate explanatory teaching of the Christian faith. Surprisingly enough, that first happens in the twelfth century.[1] But I defer for brief discussion later the importance of the history of the concept 'theology' for our problem. A further limitation of the *terminus a quo* for the occurrence of the concept 'biblical theology' is provided by the period at which it became possible and necessary to append as a criterion with polemical intent the epithet 'biblical' to the concept 'theology'. We might conjecture that that happened in the sixteenth century. The slogan 'biblical theology' would appear to be not inappropriate for certain biblicist tendencies in Humanism, above all in Erasmus. With much greater probability we might expect to find the concept 'biblical theology' in the Reformers as an expression of their biblical principles. Might not Luther's theology—to take him as a brief illustration—be best summed up under the formula 'biblical theology'? There is his radical attack on setting the authority of tradition and of the church

[1] Cf. the article 'Théologie' in the *Dictionnaire de Théologie catholique*, vol. XV, 1 (Paris, 1946).

alongside, which really means setting it above, that of scripture; his struggle against the scholastic method in theology and against the influence of Aristotle; the exclusive concentration of his own theological work on the exegesis of holy scripture; his incomparably profound instinct for the peculiarities of biblical usage and biblical ways of thinking. In fact one is bound to say that Reformation theology is the first attempt in the entire history of theology to take seriousiy the demand for a theology based on holy scripture alone. Only among the followers of the Reformation could the concept 'biblical theology' have been coined at all. Indeed, here the coining of the concept was obviously inevitable. And in everything else that we shall still have to say on the problem of 'biblical theology' this will have to be kept in view: that we have here to do with a path opened up by the Reformation, and indeed appointed and even enforced by it, however dangerous it threatened to become for the very theology that is committed to the Reformation.

Nevertheless, to the best of my knowledge, the phrase 'biblical theology' is not a creation of the sixteenth century. In Luther's case I venture to affirm that with fair certainty. There are also internal reasons that can be given for it. Luther was no biblicist. That is shown by his distinction between law and Gospel. '*Scriptura est non contra, sed pro Christo intelligenda, ideo vel ad eum referenda, vel pro vera Scriptura non habenda.*' '*Si adversarii scripturam urserint contra Christum, urgemus Christum contra scripturam.*' '*Si utrum sit amittendum, Christus vel Lex, Lex est amittenda, non Christus.*'[1] No biblicist speaks like that. What prevented Luther from adopting the only seemingly unequivocal formula 'biblical theology' was his insight into the hermeneutic problem.

Admittedly Luther's insight into the hermeneutic problem was limited, in so far as he had not thoroughly thought it through from the methodological point of view and therefore the methodology of theology in general remained obscure in decisive questions of fundamental importance. It was not made clear what the principle of *sola scriptura* means for the procedure of theology as a whole. This lack of clarity became apparent in the degree to which Reformation theology, like medieval scholasticism, also developed into a scholastic system. What was the relation of the systematic method here to the exegetical method? Ultimately it was the same as in medieval scholasticism. There, too, exegesis of holy scripture went on not only within systematic theology but also separately alongside of it, yet so that the possibility of a tension between exegesis and systematic theology was *a priori* excluded. Exe-

[1] *WA* 39/1, p. 47.3 f, 19 f, 23 f (Disputation theses *De fide*, 11th Sept. 1535).

gesis was enclosed within the frontiers fixed by systematic theology. Hence theology in the strict sense was the total explication of Christian doctrine, proceeding by systematic methods and normative for exegesis. In this, medieval and early Protestant scholasticism were completely alike. Hence also the agreement of both in using Aristotelian philosophy despite Luther's passionate struggle against the dominance of Aristotle in theology. Early Protestant Orthodoxy could understand that only as an individual eccentricity confined to Luther himself, as it did also his absolute rejection of the systematic method of scholasticism in favour of exegesis, although for Luther himself both belonged inseparably together and were of fundamental importance: '*Cum vocabula physica in theologia translata sunt, facta est inde scholastica quaedam theologia.*'[1] But just as this primacy of exegesis was not fully thought through by Luther himself from the methodological standpoint—it was of course really a case of incorporating the task of systematic theology in exegesis, and thus not of a simple antithesis of exegesis and systematic theology, in the modern sense—so also in early Protestant Orthodoxy the primacy of systematic theology was in no way connected with an awareness of departing from the basic approach of the Reformation. And from the historical point of view it is perfectly true that on the basis of the Reformation the intense concern of Orthodoxy with the problem of systematic theology must be judged to have been absolutely necessary, however strong the material objections may certainly be to the Orthodox solution of the problem.

The methodological problem which, as we have seen, was contained of necessity in Protestantism but at first only deferred—namely, the problem of the implications of the Reformation principle of *sola scriptura* for the procedure of theology as a whole—finally emerged at the point where the insufficiency and the dangers of the theological methods of early Protestant Orthodoxy were realized. The critical doubts which now arose and were voiced within Orthodoxy itself, and at the same time became the precursors of Pietism, based their claim to justification ultimately on the demand for a 'biblical theology', now for the first time advanced in those very words. To supply precise statistics on this point is naturally extraordinarily difficult. But subject to better information I would hold it a probable conjecture that the expression 'biblical theology' originated somewhere in the first half of the seventeenth century. A typical instance is supplied by Spener in his *Pia Desideria* (1675) from a funeral oration delivered at Tübingen in 1669 for the Württemberg

---

[1] *WA* 39/1, p. 299.22 f (Disputation of 1st June 1537).

court chaplain Christoph Zeller. On the occasion of a parliament at
Regensburg in 1652, so it says, Zeller and the chief court chaplain of
Saxony, Jacob Weller, conferred together '*de Theologia Scholastica*',
which had been expelled by Luther through the front door but obviously
let in again through the back door by contentious theologians, and also
'*de revocanda Theologia Biblica*'. Spener quoted this remark with approval,[1] and later also took over himself the antithesis of 'biblical theology' and 'scholastic theology'.[2] It would be of interest to go more
closely into the various trends and traditions which brought about the
origin of Pietism, in order to trace the historical roots of the concept
'biblical theology' and discover an earlier instance of it.[3]

For the understanding of the concept 'biblical theology' at the time
of its origin the following point is significant: it is the slogan of a programme of theological reform which directs its criticism neither at the
content of Orthodox dogmatics nor at its methodological form as systematic theology, but only at certain accretions, namely, at the fact that,
as Spener says, there has been 'much introduced into theology which is
alien, useless and savours more of the wisdom of the world',[4] 'presumptuous subtleties in matters where we ought not to be wise above the
scriptures',[5] so that the students become 'certainly *Studiosi* of what
might be called a philosophy *de rebus sacris*, but not *Studiosi Theologiae*'.[6]
The dominant theology may 'indeed have preserved the foundation of
the faith on scripture, but has built thereon so much wood, hay and
stubble of human presumption that one can scarcely see the gold any
more'.[7] 'The whole of *Theologia*' must therefore 'be brought back to the
apostolic simplicity',[8] to the true 'simplicity of Christ and his teaching'.[9]
Thus the slogan 'biblical theology' is used neither to propagate a new
theological discipline, nor even to advocate shifting the centre of gravity

---

[1] Philip Jacob Spener, *Pia Desideria*, ed. Kurt Aland, in *Kleine Texte für
Vorlesungen und Übungen*, No. 170, Berlin 1940, pp. 25 f.

[2] E.g. Phil. Jac. Spener, *Theologische Bedencken* IV, Halle 1715, p. 458.

[3] As against the original English version of the paper, in which I described
this instance as the earliest known to me at the time (and from which it was taken
over by *LTK*[2] II, p. 443), I can now refer to the title of a book to which I have
unfortunately not yet had access: Wolfg. Jac. Christmann, *Teutsche Biblische
Theologie*, Kempten 1629, quoted in Martin Lipenius, *Bibliotheca realis theologica omnium materiarum, rerum et titulorum in universo sacrosanctae theologiae
studio concurrentium*, Frankfurt 1685, tom. I, 170a. On the person of W. J.
Christmann cf. L. M. Fischlin, *Memoria theologorum Wirtembergensium*, pars II,
Ulm 1710, pp. 179 f, as also *ADB* IV, p. 224. See further below p. 86 note 2.

[4] *Pia Desideria*, p. 22.13 f.   [5] P. 22.34 f.
[6] P. 71.20 ff.   [7] P. 26.36 ff.
[8] P. 74.5 f.   [9] P. 27.2.

from systematic theology to exegesis (however great the importance Pietism attached also to that). It is rather a demand for the reform of systematic theology itself—and that too, it seems, in accordance with its own undisputed principles—to a certain extent only a reform of the style and ethos of theology. It is true that this demand derives its pathos from a comparison between the Bible, especially the New Testament, and the contemporary form of systematic theology. But the same result arises from the comparison of Orthodox with Reformation theology. In both cases the recognized ideal is that of simplicity.[1] Thus the difference in no sense affects the foundation of Orthodoxy. At this initial stage the demand for a 'biblical theology' remains completely on Orthodox ground in so far as it casts no doubt on the essential equation of holy scripture, Reformation doctrine and Orthodox dogmatics. Orthodox dogmatics is unscriptural only in respect of its scholastic form. But this apparently quite innocuous criticism has much more far-reaching consequences than were immediately perceived. It conceals within itself the seed of a theological revolution, in the varying history of which the slogan 'biblical theology' remained a prominent feature.

The momentous significance of this newly coined phrase 'biblical theology', which had a strong ring of the Reformation and against which the prevailing Orthodox dogmatics could raise no objection, stands in remarkable contrast to the theological naivety with which the slogan was introduced. For it never entered anyone's head that precisely by the apparent limitation to a purely formal critique of Orthodox scholasticism they were raising the fundamental problem of the methodology of Reformation theology. Under appeal to Luther's struggle against Aristotle, criticism was levelled at the influence of philosophy upon theology, but no attention at all was paid to the problem whether systematic theology is possible without contact with philosophy. For the first time since the Reformation, the Bible on the one hand and the dominant form of theology on the other were seen to be in tension with each other, even if only in a formal way. But no thought was given to the hermeneutic problem, whether such a tension does not, one way or another, always mark the relation of text and exposition. And it was not noticed that by thus setting up scripture as the formal pattern for theology the criterion of what is in conformity with scripture was tacitly transposed from the notion of correct theological views to the ideal of theological simplicity. Behind that there still stood untouched by any detailed material criticism the opinion, in itself Orthodox but now played

[1] Pp. 74.5 f; 27.2; 22.31.

off against Orthodoxy, that revelation is a sum of revealed doctrines and the Bible is a theological compendium dictated by the Holy Spirit himself.

How far the concept 'biblical theology' thus stood initially in the twilight between Orthodoxy and Pietism is shown by the fact that the sturdiest of Orthodox Lutherans, Abraham Calov, could likewise take over the concept at the very same time—and that, too, as a designation of what had hitherto been called *theologia exegetica*.[1] Here he fully shared in the increasing emphasis on the biblical tendency in theology—as, incidentally, he later also expressed warm approval of Spener's *Pia Desideria*. Thus the demand for a 'biblical theology' could apparently as a matter of course find favour within the Orthodox system, *viz*.—to the extent that, as the use of the analytic method in systematic theology increased, a need was felt for a separate account of the biblical foundation of dogmatics, and in the so-called *Collegia biblica* the biblical *dicta probantia* for the individual dogmatic *loci* were gathered together. This subsidiary discipline of dogmatics, originating about the middle of the seventeenth century, assumed the title 'biblical theology'.[2] In the well-known work of that title by Carl Haymann (1708, 4th ed. 1768) the growing influence of Pietism was undoubtedly already at work.[3] Yet even here there did not yet appear any antithesis to the Orthodox development of this discipline. Pietism showed itself to be incapable of drawing from the concept 'biblical theology' the decisive methodological

---

[1] Abraham Calov, *Systema theologicum*, 1655, I, 9. Cf. Ludwig Diestel, *Geschichte des Alten Testaments in der christlichen Kirche*, Jena 1869, p. 710.

[2] Following F. Chr. Baur (*Vorlesungen über neutestamentliche Theologie*, 1864, p. 3) it is usual to mention as an example of this kind Seb. Schmidt, *Collegium Biblicum, in quo dicta Vet. et Novi Testamenti iuxta seriem locorum communium theologicorum explicantur*, Strasbourg 1671. In this context, however, an older work deserves to be mentioned at the top of the list because of its key-word title: Henricus a Diest, *Theologia biblica*, Daventriae 1643. The sub-title indicates the programme: *Praeter succinctam locorum communium delineationem, exhibens testimonia Scripturae ad singulos locos, locorum singula capita, capitumque singula membra, pertinentia*. That we are here in the immediate vicinity of the time when this discipline made its appearance and was entitled 'biblical theology', seems to be implied in the following sentences from the introduction: ' . . . prima *Theologiae elementa, totius fidei Christianae fundamenta, nova ac facili methodo constructa, atque definitionibus (succinctis), rei tamen praecipuam materiam exhaurientibus, pertexta, sic ordinavi, ut omnes eorum sinus aura Spiritus Sancti, ex sacris literis spirans, perflaret; atque adeo singula definitionum membra ac propemodum verba, suis e sacra Scriptura testimoniis stipata prodirent: unde tandem orta est haec, quae et inde nomen suum accepit, Theologia Biblica*' (p. 3a).

[3] In the original English version of the paper I had wrongly described it as the first book to bear that title. R Bultmann, *Theology of the NT* II, 1955, p. 242 also requires similar correction.

consequences which, as we have seen, were nevertheless contained in germ within it from the beginning. The consequences first became evident when the theology of the Enlightenment quite logically took up the slogan 'biblical theology'. How easy the transition was here, too, is shown by Anton Friedrich Büsching, who took his stimulus from Pietism yet already belonged entirely to the so-called Neology, and was a contemporary and associate of the most important German theologian of the eighteenth century, Johann Salomo Semler. Büsching appeared only to be resuming the original demand of early Pietism when he produced a book with the title *Gedanken von der Beschaffenheit und dem Vorzug der biblisch-dogmatischen Theologie vor der alten und neuen scholastischen* (1758) ['Reflexions on the Nature of Biblical Dogmatic Theology and on its Superiority to Scholasticism old and new']. And in his *Dissertatio exhibens epitomen theologiae e solis literis sacris concinnatae* (1756) he seemed to be continuing the late Orthodox discipline that supplies a separate account of the scriptural basis of dogmatics. And yet at this point the decisive change occurred. From being merely a subsidiary discipline of dogmatics 'biblical theology' now became a rival of the prevailing dogmatics—itself, to be sure, nothing else but dogmatics, yet emphatically biblical dogmatics and not scholastic dogmatics, and thus a dogmatics which in accordance with the ideal of the simplicity of Bible teaching got rid of the ballast of dogmatic tradition, and in giving an account of Christian doctrine could disregard even the confessional documents of the Reformation and base its construction only on the purely biblical texts. The conflict in which Büsching thereupon became involved with the Göttingen theological faculty and with the government[1] proves that the slogan 'biblical theology' had now emerged from its original twilight and was taking a course which Pietism had certainly inaugurated, but without having had the faintest idea of its consequences.

For now it was impossible to call a halt. It was likewise only logical when, under the influence of the incipient critical historical exegesis, the biblical dogmatics that had thus asserted its independence of traditional dogmatics then became aware of its independence of dogmatics also from the methodological point of view and thereafter remained content neither with the role of a merely subsidiary dogmatic discipline

[1] Emanuel Hirsch, *Geschichte der neuern evangelischen Theologie* IV, 1951, pp. 102 f. Cf. further Gotthelf Traugott Zachariæ, *Biblische Theologie oder Untersuchung des biblischen Grundes der vornehmsten theologischen Lehren* I-IV, 1771-1775.

nor even with that of a rival species of dogmatics, but set itself up as a
completely independent study, namely, as a critical historical discipline
alongside of dogmatics. As is well known, that was first adopted as a
programme by Johann Philipp Gabler in his *Oratio de iusto discrimine
theologiae biblicae et dogmaticae regundisque recte utriusque finibus* (1787).[1]
But now, what is the meaning of 'biblical theology' as a historical discipline alongside of dogmatics? A juxtaposition without any sort of contact was obviously *a priori* impossible. For like 'biblical theology' as a
historical theological discipline, dogmatics as a systematic theological
discipline had of course also to remain tied to the Bible. Hence it could
only be a co-existence bristling with extraordinary difficulties: not only
was the relation between the two a matter of continuous controversy,
but also, because of this controversy, both the new discipline of 'biblical
theology' and the traditional discipline of dogmatics were involved in a
rapid movement of development and change. If the idea of 'biblical
theology' was originally conceived only as a reform of systematic theology, then its complete emancipation from dogmatics was bound to have
all the greater, and indeed downright revolutionary, repercussions on
the latter discipline. Although as a result of this change the theme of
'biblical theology' now seems to claim all our attention for the development of this historical discipline and its methodological problems, yet
since the Enlightenment the really acute difficulties for theology have
lain in the methodological problems of dogmatics.

The relation of 'biblical theology' as a historical discipline to dogmatics remains dominated from now on, through all its variations, by
the following apparently self-contradictory tendencies:—

First, as a historical discipline it rejects any directives for its own
work that derive from dogmatics. Its view of its task is, that the independence of its historical method which it has proclaimed in principle
should now also be asserted in detail by freeing itself from the traditional dogmatic viewpoint. It is indeed all out to justify its existence as
an independent theological discipline by discovering more and more
new and increasingly radical theories of an anti-traditional kind. That
does not exclude vacillation between an extreme critical and a cautious
conservative position. Yet the impulses which lead to real advance in
the development of this discipline are without question those which
sharpen the tension with traditional dogmatics. That has its ground in
the principle on which 'biblical theology' entered the field as a historical

---

[1] Excerpts can be found in W. G. Kümmel, *Das Neue Testament: Geschichte
der Erforschung seiner Probleme*, 1958, pp. 115 ff.

discipline. It necessarily adopts a critical attitude towards dogmatics. It must not let itself be hindered in any way by considering how the results of its researches are related to dogmatics.

Further, the more 'biblical theology' as a historical discipline derives its vitality from its detachment from dogmatics, the less it can be indifferent to the utterances of dogmatics. However much it may make a show of its lack of interest in systematic theology, yet it must at least make the claim to be respected by dogmatics—and that, too, not only in the negative sense that dogmatics should refrain from any interference in historical examination of the Bible, but also in the positive sense that dogmatics, so far as it appeals to the Bible, must bow to the results of historical study of the Bible. How dogmatics manages that is its own affair. 'Biblical theology' as a historical discipline has for its part no wish to interfere in the proper business of dogmatics. To that extent its attitude to dogmatics certainly remains that of a detached spectator, often not without a compassionate smile at the embarrassments in which dogmatic theology finds itself. It leaves entirely to dogmatics the doubtful advantage of providing normative theological statements for the present situation, considering that for its own part it can confine itself to the mere establishing of historical facts. Yet it cannot relinquish the claim that 'biblical theology' as a historical discipline exercises a normative function over against dogmatics in all matters concerning the relation to the Bible. Dogmatics must answer for its use of scripture at the bar of historical study of the Bible.

And lastly, there can be no mistaking the fact that although 'biblical theology' as a historical discipline adopts this detached, but at the same time critical and normative, attitude to traditional dogmatics, yet it is itself guided by a strong dogmatic interest, even (and more especially) where this fact is not conceded. From the beginning the appeal of the name of this discipline has of course been that it is a guide to the real, original, and pure source of theological knowledge. That imparted to it in the first instance a claim which, especially in the field of a theology that took its bearings from the Reformation, could hardly be challenged. But as a result of its necessarily critical attitude towards traditional dogmatics, 'biblical theology' as a historical discipline recognized first and foremost the untenability of the dogmatic presupposition from which it had taken its own start, namely, the Orthodox doctrine of verbal inspiration. 'Biblical theology' as a historical discipline, in its critical debate with dogmatics, had to begin at once at the very point where 'biblical theology' as a separate discipline had its own dogmatic basis.

The critical attitude towards dogmatics thus affected the foundation of
'biblical theology' itself. The result was necessarily a new examination
of its foundation, i.e. of the basis and nature of the authority of holy
scripture.

Owing to the nature of 'biblical theology' as a historical discipline
this fresh consideration of its foundation did not proceed in the traditional dogmatic manner, but partly by general reflexions of a scientific
and methodological kind regarding the nature of history and of historical knowledge, and partly by the process of interpreting the sources
themselves. But that certainly did not mean that definite dogmatic positions were not adopted precisely in so doing. For anyone who, even as
a historian, concerns himself with 'biblical theology' does so in full
awareness of the relevance of holy scripture for Christian faith, and
because of that relevance. It is therefore not merely a matter of fact, but
of principle, that general methodological reflexion upon the task and
nature of 'biblical theology' as a historical discipline already implies a
particular understanding of the Christian faith and of the meaning of
the Bible for it, and moreover that the concrete results of research are
partly determined by the question to which they are the answer—a question which in fact depends upon a specific view of the subject-matter of
the Bible. That is, 'biblical theology' as a historical discipline is, like
any historical work, not independent of the author's standpoint in history and therefore not of the conception either which the author has of
the Christian faith—a conception which in its general structure is of a
dogmatic kind even when in opposition to traditional dogmatics it considers itself undogmatic. The history of 'biblical theology' as a historical
discipline provides proof of that by reflecting the changes in the historical, and therefore also the theological, standpoint of its authors. As
to the detailed relations between historical research and theological
standpoint, the general framework here outlined leaves ample room for
possible variations. To indicate only two extremes: in the age of rationalism the findings of 'biblical theology' led, with the help of the distinction between the time-conditioned and the timelessly valid, directly to
the basic features of rationalist dogmatics. By this means the historical
distance from the Bible was eliminated. In the religious-historical school,
on the other hand, it was primarily the historical distance that was
brought into relief. The only thing left to assert an immediate claim
was a vague religious impulse. In both cases, however, there remains in
'biblical theology' itself a dogmatic element inseparably bound up with
the historical element—though admittedly, because of the conscious

exclusion of the dogmatic tradition, it is always a kind of dogmatic element which adopts a more or less critical attitude to that dogmatic tradition.

III

It is not possible here to trace out under these heads the history of 'biblical theology' as a historical discipline. I confine myself to the question: What has the history of this discipline contributed towards the explanation of its name, of the concept 'biblical theology'? The answer to that is, that the history of 'biblical theology' as a historical discipline brought to light for the first time the problematical nature of the concept 'biblical theology', and that in the following respects:—

The theological unity of the Bible has become problematical. It very soon proved necessary to divide the one discipline of 'biblical theology' into two—a theology of the Old Testament and a theology of the New Testament. Not merely as a sort of result of progressive specialization in historical methods of study, and the consequent necessary division of the field. For what theologian would today be capable of being equally expert in both Old Testament and New Testament studies? But the real reason for the division into two disciplines is rather that historical criticism of the Bible made the theological unity of the Old and New Testaments problematical. From a historical point of view it is impossible to see the statements of the Old and New Testaments without distinction on one level and to combine them together to produce a unified theology of the Bible. At first, it is true, the designation 'biblical theology' still formed the common title for accounts of Old and New Testament theology that followed each other in one and the same book. As this separation then also came to achieve outward recognition, the designation 'biblical theology' still remained for a time as a reminiscence of the lost unity in the titles assumed by the two disciplines, in that they did not speak simply of an Old Testament and New Testament theology, but of a 'Biblical Theology of the Old Testament' and a 'Biblical Theology of the New Testament'. But this usage did not become established. The title 'biblical theology' as the designation of a theological discipline has today practically ceased to exist.

But the theological unity of the Old and New Testaments respectively has also become problematical. The critical historical method, when consistently applied to the biblical writings, increasingly revealed the differences within both Testaments and concentrated attention primarily on these. Thus Old Testament and New Testament theology became an account of a variety of theologies in historical succession. The designation as Old Testament or New Testament theology was reduced to a formal collective idea for ordering under one head the 'doctrinal ideas' of the different biblical writers, without any narrower definition of the theological unity of the whole being possible. Even when historical criticism proved oversharp distinctions between the doctrinal ideas to be reading too much into the often very slender textual basis, and the exposition came to concentrate primarily on the main complexes, the unity of the whole was nevertheless asserted only from the evolutionary point of view. Old or New Testament theology became in practice a history of Old or New Testament theology. And even when alongside the genetic treatment, or indeed exclusively in place of it, there comes a purely systematic classification covering the whole (as e.g. in the Old Testament Theologies of W. Eichrodt and L. Köhler or in the New Testament Theology of E. Stauffer), yet there, too, the historical differences have to be brought out if such an account is not to be guilty of flattening out the historical form of the biblical testimony. Whatever the facts may be concerning the inner unity of the Old and New Testaments respectively, it is at all events highly questionable to understand that unity as a uniform theology, especially since theology (as distinct from doctrine or credal confession) has in each individual case its own particular character and thus e.g. the testimony of Paul and of John, regarded as theology, simply cannot be identical.

Another matter that has become problematical is the limitation to canonical scripture. For one thing because the study of the Old and New Testaments simply cannot avoid considering the religious-historical background, and in an Old Testament or New Testament theology the results at least of such a comparison must be allowed to have their effect. But further—and this is the decisive point—also because for an account of the historical development a limitation to the selection found in the canon is not justified. If a picture of the process as a whole is really to emerge, then an Old Testament theology can hardly refrain from extending its range beyond the canonical scriptures into pre-Christian Judaism. And still less can a New Testament theology overlook the extra-canonical literature of early Christianity belonging to the same period as the canonical scriptures. That of course punctures the normative idea contained in the concept 'canon'. But also quite apart from that it has in fact already been abandoned by the application of the critical historical method to the canonical scriptures themselves. For the historical approach excludes at all events any idea of a canon which implies the hermeneutic rule that without distinction and in all its parts the canon is of equal authority and discrepancies and contradictions within it are excluded in principle.

A further thing that has become problematical is the application of the concept 'theology' to the actual content of the Bible. This use of the concept 'theology' is the common heritage of medieval and Protestant scholasticism, according to which revelation consists in the communication of revealed truths, and the Word of God is therefore identical with theological propositions; theology and revelation or theology and the knowledge of God (or faith) are thus not distinguished from each other in principle and in structure. But this concept of theology has become problematical, not least as a result of the historical discipline of so-called 'biblical theology' itself. We may consider it unfortunate when in its place the general concept of religion came to the fore and the idea of a history of Israelite and Jewish religion, or of primitive Christian religion, threatened to displace the idea of Old or New Testament theology respectively. But at all events we must recognize the criticism it expresses—that what the Bible testifies to and strives after is not theology, but something that happens to man in God's dealings with the world. Even if we cling to the interpretation of this event as revelation and faith, we must not give up the distinction that revelation as such is not theology and faith as such is not belief in theological propositions. The highly questionable Orthodox concept of a *theologia revelata* does not do justice to the actual content of the Bible.

That of course is not to deny that the Bible, too, contains theology. But the question is: what exactly is to be claimed as theology in the Bible, and that means, what is our idea of theology as we approach the Bible? The fact that the Bible itself does not use the word 'theology' is obviously not in itself a reason for not applying it to the Bible. But it is also a doubtful proceeding to use the concept 'theology' in such a wide sense that any talk of God and any religious statement whatever may be designated as theology. This extension of the term theology to cover any conglomeration of religious ideas has come to be the usual thing in the modern study of religion, but its reverse side is, significantly enough that such study of religion in fact no longer regards itself as theology. I am of the opinion, which of course I cannot defend in detail here, that from the history of the concept 'theology' criteria can be derived for the proper use of the term. It could be shown that theology arises from the meeting of the biblical testimony to revelation with Greek thinking, and that these two elements are constitutive for the nature of theology. From this angle there would be real sense in speaking of theology even in the New Testament, above all in Paul and the author of the Fourth Gospel. On the other hand it would be questionable to describe, say, the preaching of the individual Old Testament prophets as theology. But it is certainly capable of theological explication. From this the conclusion follows, that although the Bible for the most part does not contain theology in the strict sense, yet it does press for theological explication. From this point of view there could therefore certainly be sense in speaking of a theology of the Old or New Testament, *viz.*—as long as in doing so the word 'theology' did not, or at least did not primarily, denote the content of the Old or New Testament, but rather the scientific explication of the content of the Old or New Testament. That would also be the only justification for the use of 'theology' in the singular. A New Testament theology would then be called 'theology' in the sense of a contemporary theological explication of the things which in the New Testament itself call for such theological explication, or of the things which in the New Testament itself have already entered on the beginnings of a theological explication yet nevertheless likewise require a contemporary theological explication if they are not merely to be repeated but are to be given scientific expression. That explains at the same time why the discipline which we call Old Testament and New Testament theology must be studied unceasingly and ever anew. It is in fact, like all historical study, not a photographic reproduction of the past, but expresses in terms of contemporary interpretation its understanding of the past. For that reason *the* Old Testament or *the* New Testament theology will never be written. It can never be written, because in principle the discipline of Old or New Testament theology is never a finally closed book but constitutes a task that continues with us all our days.

Looking back on our argument: our question was, what has the history of 'biblical theology' as a historical discipline contributed towards the explanation of its name, of the concept 'biblical theology'? Our answer was, that the history of 'biblical theology' as a historical discipline has brought to light for the first time the problematical nature of the concept 'biblical theology'. I illustrated that by referring to the problems connected with the theological unity of the Bible, the problems connected with the theological unity of the Old and New Testaments respectively, those connected with the limitation to the canonical scriptures, and those connected with the application of the concept 'theology' to the actual content of the Bible. It might appear that the result is no other than was already reached by William Wrede—namely, to show that the history of 'biblical theology' as a historical discipline is in every respect the *reductio ad absurdum* of the concept 'biblical theology'. There is certainly this much truth in that: that the understanding of the concept 'biblical theology' which was held at the time of its origin—that is, the understanding which has its home on the frontier between Orthodoxy and Pietism—suffered its refutation and dissolution in the course of its further history. There is an inexorable logic in that process. It cannot be remedied by attempting to turn it back to its starting-point. Yet the process contains (as was made clear in discussing the problematical nature of the concept 'theology' and of its application to the actual content of the Bible) a pointer which Wrede had not yet taken into consideration and which now certainly offers the possibility of seeing the problem in a new light. It would therefore be entirely wrong to interpret the development as a mistaken one, as a development whose result was purely destructive. On the contrary, it has uncommonly positive significance in that it sets aside all short cuts to a solution and leads right into the depths of the hermeneutic problem. Thus it has necessitated a consistent and precise definition of the problem of theological method posed by the Reformation. I venture to affirm that thanks to the developments that have taken place in the history of theology since the Enlightenment under the influence of the evolution of the critical historical method, we are now nearer than early Protestant Orthodoxy was to the correct understanding of the task of theology in the Reformers' sense. For we see more sharply the nature of the task that arises for theology from holy scripture. I do not say we have ready to hand solutions with which we can be satisfied. But we see ourselves confronted by problems in regard to which we can be glad that we do see them.

IV

The implications of that for the subject of this paper in the narrower sense can only be briefly outlined. For here there arises immediately a vast multitude of as yet unmastered tasks.

The task of a theology of the Old or New Testament must, in view of what was said above concerning the concept of theology, be defined as follows: In the theology of the Old or New Testament the theologian who devotes himself specially to Old or New Testament research has to give an inclusive account of his understanding of the Old or New Testament, i.e. above all of the theological problems that come of enquiring into the inner unity of the manifold testimony of the Old or New Testament.

On the basis of this definition the question would arise whether a discipline of 'biblical theology' is not in fact also a possibility, and indeed a necessity. Its task would accordingly be defined thus: In 'biblical theology' the theologian who devotes himself specially to studying the connexion between the Old and New Testaments has to give an account of his understanding of the Bible as a whole, i.e. above all of the theological problems that come of inquiring into the inner unity of the manifold testimony of the Bible.

In the contemporary theological situation a 'biblical theology' of that kind would demand the intensive co-operation of Old and New Testament scholars. For that reason alone it can certainly hardly be expected to develop into a separate discipline. It will rather have to remain dependent on the scientific conversation between the two disciplines and will sometimes be furthered more vigorously by the one, sometimes by the other. But now, just as the theology both of the Old and of the New Testament, as a result of its being involved in the hermeneutic problem, is dependent on close contact with systematic theology—for because of the hermeneutic problem the exegete must participate in the work of systematic theology—so also what I have defined as the task of a 'biblical theology' is even more dependent on the support of systematic theology; for in what I have defined as the task of a 'biblical theology' the hermeneutic problem arises in extraordinarily complicated form. The task of 'biblical theology' would then provide the compelling impulse towards close co-operation on the part of the various theological disciplines, from which the church historian also could not be omitted. But, be it noted, this 'biblical theology' would not then be a rival substitute for dogmatics and would hardly correspond either to the pietistic ideal of a 'simple' theology, but would be an uncommonly complex exercise in historical theology. Yet then it would be able also for its part to assist dogmatics towards a clearer grasp of the question of what constitutes scriptural dogmatics.

Thus the concept 'biblical theology', the false understanding of which caused theology—contrary to the original intention—to split up into different disciplines, when rightly understood points back again to the unity of theology—not of course a unity achieved by abolishing the different disciplines, but a unity consisting in the right theological use of the different disciplines, each of which has its own peculiar task and yet each is 'theology' in the sense of participating in the scientific expression of the Word of God. This understanding of the unity of theology, in which the conversation is kept open between the historian and the systematic theologian because the historian, if he is to be a historian, must also be a systematic theologian, and the systematic theologian, if he is to be a systematic theologian, must also be a historian, seems to me to be peculiarly in keeping with the Reformers' understanding of theology. For theology in this sense is never a completed task, never attains its goal. The goal is attained only by faith, or rather, by the Word of God as it awakens faith.

IV

THE
'NON-RELIGIOUS INTERPRETATION
OF BIBLICAL CONCEPTS'*1

I

THE formula 'non-religious interpretation of biblical concepts', which
Dietrich Bonhoeffer used in the last year of his life to mark the theo-

* ZTK 52 (1955), pp. 296-360. Also: Die mündige Welt II, Munich 1956,
pp. 12-73.
1 A paper read at the Theological Conference of Friends and Pupils of Bonhoeffer on 28th September 1955 in Berlin. The closing sections of the address
were revised and expanded for the press.
   Titles of the posthumously published writings of Dietrich Bonhoeffer here
quoted: Ethik, ed. Eberhard Bethge, Munich 1949, 4th ed. 1958 (ET, Ethics,
SCM Press, 1955). Widerstand und Ergebung: Briefe und Aufzeichnungen aus der
Haft, ed. Eberhard Bethge, Munich 1951, 8th ed. 1958 (ET, Letters and Papers
from Prison, SCM Press, 1953, revised ed. 1956). Cf. the Bonhoeffer biblio-
graphy in Die mündige Welt II, Munich 1956, pp. 204-13.
   Some of the essays so far published on Bonhoeffer are contained in the
collection, Die mündige Welt: Dem Andenken Dietrich Bonhoeffers, Vorträge und
Briefe, Munich 1955. It contains: E. Bethge, 'Dietrich Bonhoeffer: Person und
Werk' (=EvTh 15 [1955], pp. 155-63); H. Chr. von Hase, 'Begriff und Wirklichkeit der Kirche in der Theologie Dietrich Bonhoeffers' (=EvTh 15 [1955],
pp. 164-84); O. Hammelsbeck, 'Zu Bonhoeffers Gedanken über die mündig
gewordene Welt' (=EvTh 15 [1955], pp. 184-99); R. Grunow, 'Dietrich Bonhoeffers Schriftauslegung' (=EvTh 15 [1955], pp. 200-214); A. Schönherr,
'Bonhoeffers Gedanken über die Kirche und ihre Predigt in der "mündig"
gewordenen Welt' (=EvTh 15 [1955], pp. 214-27); W. Maechler, 'Vom Pazi-
fisten zum Widerstandskämpfer: Bonhoeffers Kampf für die Entrechteten'
(=EvTh 15 [1955], pp. 227-34); H. Schlingensiepen, 'Zum Vermächtnis Dietrich
Bonhoeffers' (=EvTh 13 [1953], pp. 97-106); 'D. Bonhoeffer und K. Barth:
Ein Briefwechsel' (expanded form of EvTh 15 [1955], pp. 234-45). In addition
I also had the following contributions before me: E. Müller-Gangloff, 'Theologie für die mündige Welt: Dietrich Bonhoeffer und die geistesgeschichtliche
Situation der Gegenwart' (in Die neue Furche 6 [1952], pp. 525-30); H. H.
Brunner, 'Am Ende des religiösen Zeitalters: Versuch einer Standortbestim-
mung, Zehn Jahre nach der Hinrichtung von Dietrich Bonhoeffer' (in Refor-
matio IV [1955], pp. 419-35); E. Bethge, 'Dietrich Bonhoeffer—der Mensch und
sein Zeugnis' (in Kirche in der Zeit X [1955], pp. 141-55). See further the independent treatment of Bonhoeffer's theme (which is of course only an indirect
contribution to the interpretation of Bonhoeffer) by Heinrich Vogel: Jesus

logical problem that exercised him,[1] causes shock and astonishment in three respects.

1. For those who stand outside the more recent developments in theology which began with Karl Barth, the antithesis between Christian faith and religion that is here taken into the theological agenda in such a downright provocative way appears a paradox in which clearly the effort to solve the old problem of the absoluteness of Christianity is violently stood on its head. But even those who share the approach of Barth—to whom Bonhoeffer repeatedly appeals in this context as the real path-breaker,[2] though only to reproach him at the same time with being illogical and with reverting to a 'revelational positivism'[3]—view with

[1] The formula is first heralded in the letter of 5th May 1944 (*WE* p. 183, Eng. p. 125) and then appears explicitly in the above form in *WE* pp. 233 and 239, Eng. pp. 158 and 162. Instead of 'non-religious interpretation' it can also be 'worldly interpretation' (*WE* pp. 185, 237, 242, Eng. pp. 126, 160, 164), instead of 'biblical concepts' also 'the theological concepts' (*WE* p. 219, Eng. p. 148). In order to forestall any foolish misunderstandings, let it be said that this is naturally only a formula for theological reflexion regarding our proclamation, not a slogan that is to be taken up into the vocabulary of the proclamation itself!

[2] 'Barth who is the only one to have started on this line of thought . . .' (*WE* p. 179, Eng. p. 123). 'Barth was the first theologian—and that remains his really great merit—to begin the critique of religion . . .' (*WE* p. 184, Eng. p. 126). 'He brought the God of Jesus Christ into the field against religion, "*pneuma* against *sarx*". That remains his greatest merit (2nd edition of Romans in spite of all the Neo-Kantian trappings!). By his later Dogmatics he has put the church in a position to effect this distinction in principle all along the line' (*WE* p. 219, Eng. p. 148).

[3] Cf. the continuation of the quotations in the last note, especially *WE* p. 219, Eng. p. 148: 'It was not that he subsequently failed in ethics, as is often claimed . . ., but he gave no concrete guidance either in dogmatics or in ethics on the non-religious interpretation of theological concepts. There lies his limitation, and because of it his theology of revelation becomes positivistic—"revelational positivism" as I would express it.' See also *WE* pp. 220, 260 f, Eng. pp. 149, 180. By 'revelational positivism' Bonhoeffer understands a defence and restoration of biblical and ecclesiastical tradition conditioned by the rejection of liberal theology, in which for want of interpretation the world is left to itself, the individual elements in the tradition are passed off without differentiation for equally significant and equally necessary parts of the whole, the question of faith is held to be answered by presenting the 'Faith of the church' and in that way a law of faith is erected. That that is characteristic of a tendency that is very much at work today in theology and in the church, is beyond question, as also that the theological work of Karl Barth has unfortunately contributed widely to a

---

Christus und der religionslose Mensch, Berlin 1955. While the present article was printing there appeared also the memorial volume, *Dietrich Bonhoeffer: Einführung in seine Botschaft*, published by the Presseverband der Evang. Kirche im Rheinland, with contributions by G. Leibholz, E. Bethge, A. Schönherr and a few texts of Dietrich Bonhoeffer.

some embarrassment the consequences Bonhoeffer for his part believes he must draw. Barth himself, apart from a somewhat puzzled shake of the head at being branded a revelational positivist, has only been able to say disparagingly of the problem called non-religious interpretation that he can summon up a certain understanding of it which he himself feels to be ultimately no understanding.[1] Bonhoeffer was aware that to pursue further the train of thought Barth had begun was by no means an easy and immediately obvious course.[2] He expected that even among his trusted friends his theological ideas and their consequences would cause surprise, perhaps even anxiety.[3] And he fully admitted the fragmentary and enigmatic character of his statements.[4] But he knew himself guided all the same by an instinctive idea of something completely new and revolutionary.[5]

2. From the standpoint of Bonhoeffer's own theological development, his statements on the non-religious interpretation of biblical concepts make it look as if a 'radicalism' that had somehow been peculiar to him

---

[1] *Die mündige Welt*, pp. 121 f (=*EvTh* 15 [1955], p. 244).

[2] 'Lutherans (so-called!) and pietists would get the creeps at such an idea . . .' (*WE* p. 113, Eng. p. 79). 'I am often shocked at the things I write . . .' (*WE* p. 268, Eng. p. 185).

[3] *WE* pp. 178, 185, Eng. pp. 121 f, 127.

[4] *WE* pp. 237, 239, 246, 262, 268, Eng. pp. 160, 162, 167, 181, 185. That is merely a crystallization of his insight into the fragmentary character of the life of this generation as compared with the preceding generation: *WE* pp. 80, 153 f, 202, Eng. pp. 61, 106, 137. For that reason the following remarks may be applied to his fragmentary allusions to the problem of non-religious interpretation:— 'But this very fragmentariness can of course point in its turn towards a higher fulfilment beyond the limits of human achievement. Even though our lives may be blown to bits by the pressure of events . . ., yet as far as possible there should still be clear indications of the way in which the whole was planned and intended, and at least it will still be recognizable what material was being built with here, or was to have been built with . . .' (*WE* p. 80, Eng. p. 61). 'The only thing that matters is surely that people should still be able to discern from the fragment of our life how the whole was in fact laid out and intended and of what material it consists. There are ultimately fragments which are only worth throwing into the dustbin . . . and others whose importance lasts for centuries, because their completion can only be a matter for God, and therefore they are fragments which must be fragments . . .' (*WE* pp. 153 f, Eng. p. 106).

[5] *WE* pp. 206, 215, Eng. pp. 140, 145.

---

strengthening of that tendency. How far that is contrary to Karl Barth's own intentions, so that Bonhoeffer's verdict possibly does not affect Karl Barth himself, cannot be discussed here. For the rest, such censures as 'revelational positivism' can naturally never count on the agreement of those so censured. They are merely a challenge to objective discussion in which the general (and therefore as good as meaningless) rejection of a revelational positivism stands *extra controversiam*. See also below, p. 103 note 3.

all along[1] had mysteriously turned in the opposite direction. What reader of his *Cost of Discipleship*[2] or his *Life Together*[3] ever thought of a positive verdict on irreligion, earthliness and this-worldliness? Astonishment at the change exhibited here can be seen more or less in all attempts to describe the final phase of Bonhoeffer's development. Bonhoeffer himself showed that it was no ill-founded astonishment when he looked back and spoke of the dangers of his book on Discipleship—though indeed without dissociating himself from that book, which he recognized as the end of a particular road.[4] His twofold verdict, expressing at once both continuity and change, may well serve only to intensify our astonishment at the non-religious interpretation which in spite of everything is supposed to be still linked up with his *Cost of Discipleship*—and then surely also our astonishment at the *Cost of Discipleship* which in spite of everything is supposed to be heading towards the non-religious interpretation. At any rate, it seems to me out of place to make the conjunction of these two slogans serve towards easing our minds and mitigating the startling effect—as if this business of non-religious interpretation ultimately cannot be so dangerous after all when we reflect that it is the author of *The Cost of Discipleship* who coined the slogan. If I am not mistaken, Bonhoeffer's name is widely held today in such great respect *in spite of* the strange things that are to be found in his last Tegel letters

[1] How little that is really characteristic of his nature, will be testified by all who knew him personally. Compare with this his remark—significant surely also for his own view of his theology—about the midland hills as 'the part of nature where I am at home'—'in the sense of what is natural, not exalted, modest and self-satisfied (?), non-speculative, content with concrete realities, and above all of "not given to self-advertisement" ' (*WE* p. 147, Eng. p. 102). If Barth ascribes to him what he likes to call the 'melancholy theology of the North-German Plain' (*Die mündige Welt*, p. 122=*EvTh* 15 [1955], p. 245), then perhaps this *bon mot* of theological geography must in Bonhoeffer's case be corrected after all to 'theology of the midland hills', among whose characteristics would surely also belong the very *hilaritas* in which Bonhoeffer saw a common link between Luther and Karl Barth (*WE* p. 156, Eng. p. 108) and which can hardly be denied to himself. Compare here what Bonhoeffer said about 'optimism' (*WE* pp. 29 f, Eng. pp. 25 f) and above all how he lived that optimism, of which surely the letters from prison in particular are a single undivided testimony.
On the question of radicalism cf. further *E* pp. 80 ff, Eng. pp. 85 ff: 'Christian life' is' neither a matter of radicalism nor of compromise'. 'In Jesus Christ . . . there is neither radicalism nor compromise, but there is the reality of God and man' (p. 81, Eng. p. 87). 'Radicalism always springs from a conscious or unconscious hatred of what is established' (p. 82, Eng. p. 87).
[2] *Nachfolge*, Munich 1937, Eng. Trans. *Cost of Discipleship*, SCM Press 1948, revised edition 1959.
[3] *Gemeinsames Leben* (*Theol. Existenz heute*, vol. 61, Munich 1939), Eng. Trans. *Life Together*, SCM Press 1954.
[4] *WE* p. 113 and above all p. 248, Eng. pp. 79 and 168 respectively.

and that were not able to destroy the credit he had earlier acquired in ecclesiastical and theological circles.[1] It is not easy to decide whether that credit would not now have been long overdrawn if his voice had remained longer among us and had not been silenced in a martyrdom whose gravity also silences any criticism that might come from those who have survived—whereby it must also be asked whether the message of his death is really understood unless it is heard in harmony with his startling words about non-religious interpretation.

3. It is astonishing, finally, that his thoughts take this direction during his time in prison—and in fact, as the dates of the letters show, of all times in the second year, from April 1944 on, which brought the final decisions.[2] Would one not have expected that the fruit of forced isolation from the active life of the world would above all be to concentrate more intensely upon meditation on the things that could not be taken from him, that the fruit of the apocalyptic happenings in which he shared from his cell would be reflexion on the end of the world, that the fruit of what from 20th July 1944 on was certain expectation of death would be to submerge himself in anticipation in the Beyond? Instead, his thoughts circle round the question of finding God not in inwardness and at the end of man's tether but in the midst of the fulness of life, round the fact that the world has reached adulthood and that Christianity is deeply of this earth.[3] Here Bonhoeffer certainly perceived connecting links. It is no accident that precisely in the letter of 21st July 1944 he takes account of the fact that he could only have perceived them on *the* way that he happens to have gone[4]—a way on which he banished from his mind as temptation the question whether it was really for the cause of Christ that he was now in prison,[5] and on which he then occupied himself, not for the sake of distraction but in pursuit of the course his own theological thought was taking, chiefly with the philosophy, the historical research and the belles-lettres of the nineteenth century.[6]

[1] The right to put it thus pointedly is by no means called in question by the increasingly strong echo struck by the *Letters and Papers from Prison*.

[2] The explicit treatment of the subject begins with the letter of 30th April 1944 (*WE* pp. 178 ff, Eng. pp. 122 ff).

[3] I cite here only the main passages, such as *WE* pp. 182, 236 and 247 f, Eng. pp. 124, 160 and 168 f.   [4] *WE* p. 249, Eng. p. 169.

[5] *WE* p. 92, Eng. p. 64, cf. E. pp. 162 f, Eng. pp. 181 f. Yet for the right understanding of this it must be added: 'that for me the conduct of my whole case is quite decisively a question of faith' (*WE* p. 128, Eng. p. 89).

[6] Cf. the many references to literature in his letters:—'In my reading I am now living entirely in the nineteenth century. In recent months I have read Gotthelf, Stifter, Immermann, Fontane, Keller with sheer admiration. An age in which men could write such a lucid, simple German must at bottom have

I have confined myself by way of introduction to a mere indication of aspects which in themselves press for much more detailed treatment. In dealing with the person and work of Dietrich Bonhoeffer it is very difficult to resist the tendency to dwell upon the close tie between the theological and the human aspects, as it speaks to us above all in the collection of *Letters and Papers from Prison* so touchingly and ever again so movingly. We can hardly keep from extensive quotation, in order to let him speak again and again for himself and to feel the influence which the unique atmospheric quality of his nature has on us. We might therefore be inclined to take everything that could be said on our present subject and group it round the points with which we began and work it out from there. We should then have to speak of Bonhoeffer's theological and spiritual ancestry and his place in the most recent history of theology, of the development he himself underwent, and of his personal life which presents in 'discipline', 'action', 'suffering' and 'death' as 'stations on the road to freedom'[1] the unforgettable commentary on his theological thinking. In spite of the variety of publications that have appeared about him, which all proceed more or less in that way, there would still be work to be done here.

As far as his place in theology is concerned, we must not abide by his own occasional remarks on the subject,[2] which in part, e.g. in regard to Bultmann, unquestionably contain mistaken judgments.[3] We should rather have to probe the links objectively, arriving thereby also at relationships of which he was completely unaware and even perhaps could not possibly be aware because they do not rest on direct contact but on unexpectedly parallel attempts to solve the same problems—such as the

[1] *WE* pp. 250 f, Eng. p. 170. This poem is an account of his own life under the immediate impact of the failure of the resistance movement.
[2] Above all *WE* pp. 218-221, Eng. pp. 147-149.
[3] See below, p. 139 note 2. To a certain extent that is true of all these incidental judgments, which are of purely illustrative significance for the pointing of particular problems in hand and could be expressed so unguardedly only in purely private letters. Cf. above, pp. 99 f note 3.

been substantially very sound' (*WE* p. 56, Eng. p. 45). 'There are so few nowadays who still have any real interest or sympathy with the nineteenth and eighteenth centuries. . . . Hardly anyone now has the slightest idea of what was produced and achieved last century—that is by our own grandfathers. And how much of what they knew has already been forgotten! I believe that one day men will not be able to get over their amazement at the fertility of that now so much despised and so little known age' (*WE* pp. 81 f, Eng. p. 62). 'My real ambition was to become as thoroughly acquainted as possible with the nineteenth century in Germany. The biggest gap up to now is a sound knowledge of Dilthey' (*WE* p. 144, Eng. p. 100).

relation to Gogarten or to Hirsch. Without thereby prejudicing his originality, we should not then see him in such isolation as is usually the case, but should notice that the questions which troubled him and the insights he was moving towards are really not after all solely his own. But then we should also get beyond the false question whether he is to be placed nearer Barth or nearer Bultmann, and should rather have to count him among the all too weakly represented younger generation whose discipleship of the great theological masters must prove itself in going on to their own proper tasks, one of which happens to be that of new work on the heritage of liberal theology.[1]

In regard to the development which Bonhoeffer himself underwent,[2] we should have to enquire into the basic impulse which remained constant amid all the changes, which also made these precise changes possible and demanded them. It would not only have to be noted how the seemingly so new and revolutionary developments of his very last period are already for the most part heralded in his *Ethics*, but in the same manner the whole range of the writings he has bequeathed to us would have to be examined in the light of his origin and his end. In so doing we should perhaps come to the conclusion that the phase characteristic above all of his *Cost of Discipleship* was only a detour, but a necessary detour, in order to enable him to digest theologically the very thing which here seems at first to be left out of account and which was then brought in by the question of non-religious interpretation, viz.— the secular heritage, with the full inclusion of which his theology first

[1] 'It was the weak point of liberal theology that it allowed the world the right to assign to Christ his place in that world; in the dispute between church and world it accepted the (comparatively clement) peace dictated by the world. It was its strong point that it did not seek to put the clock back, and genuinely accepted the battle (Troeltsch!), even though that ended with its overthrow' (*WE* p. 218, Eng. p. 147). 'I feel myself obliged to tackle these questions as one who, though a "modern" theologian, is still aware of the debt we owe to liberal theology. There will not be many of the younger men who combine both trends in themselves' (*WE* p. 257, Eng. p. 177). 'Not until that is achieved [viz.—the non-religious interpretation] will, in my opinion, liberal theology be overcome (and even Barth is still dominated by it, though negatively), and at the same time the question it raises be genuinely taken up and answered (which is *not* the case in the revelational positivism maintained by the Confessing Church!)' (*WE* p. 221, Eng. p. 149).

[2] 'I have certainly learnt a great deal, but I don't think I have changed very much. There are some who change a lot, but many hardly change at all. I don't believe I have ever changed very much. . . . Self-development is of course an entirely different matter. A break in our life is a thing neither of us has really experienced. . . . In the old days I often used to long for such a break, but I think differently about it today. Continuity with our past is surely also a wonderful gift' (*WE* p. 174, Eng. p. 119). Cf. also *WE* pp. 96, 173, Eng. pp. 66, 118 f.

came to maturity and, perhaps we may say in spite of all its fragmentary character, really attained its appointed goal.

And finally, as far as the man Dietrich Bonhoeffer himself is concerned, a comprehensive biography would unquestionably be an eminently important key to the understanding of what he was commissioned to say—a biography whose compass would have to be wide enough to embrace the whole realm of the traditions and decisions, the bonds and the freedom of this life, and deep enough to sound both the revealed and the hidden depths of his humanity, so as to allow what he has given us to go on working, and to leave room in what is hidden from us for the judgment of him to whom Bonhoeffer himself committed the answer to the question, 'Who am I?'[1]

Although there is thus a very great deal to be said for treating our subject in such a way and so concerning ourselves all the time directly, and essentially in narrative form, with the person and words of Bonhoeffer, yet another method nevertheless seems to me to be at least equally justified, if not indeed the first thing necessary—namely, to renounce all emotional effect and enter on a sober theological examination of the question what exactly the formula 'non-religious interpretation of biblical concepts' may mean. Certainly not without seeking to discover Bonhoeffer's own opinion from what statements of his we have, yet for all that making our own efforts to think his thoughts with him, think over them and think them further, until in the end we lose all interest in Bonhoeffer as compared with the subject itself—the problem he has indicated by the slogan 'non-religious interpretation of biblical concepts'.

II

We shall come within reach of this problem at all only if we are ready to adopt definite presuppositions which Bonhoeffer has expressed with all the clarity that could be desired. However much ground we may have for complaining of the enigmatic character of his remarks on the problem of non-religious interpretation of biblical concepts and the way they have not fully matured but remain at the stage of allusive *aperçus*, we have just as little cause to plead that any lack of clarity prevails in regard to these presuppositions. Here it is by no means a question of special presuppositions peculiar to Bonhoeffer, on which opinions could differ as to their justification. It is a case of the most universal presuppositions of theological thinking as such, of its simplest basic rules—though to

[1] *WE* pp. 242 f, in addition also p. 118, Eng. pp. 165 and 82 respectively.

recognize them in this their simplicity and hold fearlessly and inexorably
to them is certainly by no means a matter of course. If we turn first of
all to these presuppositions, then that will already provide us with the
first indications of what Bonhoeffer meant and did not mean by the
non-religious interpretation of biblical concepts.

    1. Theological thinking is concerned with Jesus Christ. How intensely
Bonhoeffer's theological outlook took its bearings from Jesus Christ
requires no substantiation. In face of large parts of his writings we
might sooner be troubled by the question whether he is not sometimes
too hasty, too uncritical, too massively dogmatic in speaking of Jesus
Christ, whether he does not indeed even cover up theological problems
by using this name as a formula, and largely fail to supply the explanation that is here of all places so badly needed. The reproach of Christomonism made by Althaus against Barth[1] would apply also to Bonhoeffer.
It would of course be a mistake to regard Barth and Bonhoeffer from
this viewpoint without more ado as on one and the same track. Just
because they are both theologians whose foundations are so radically
Christological, the differences between them necessarily stand out most
clearly in Christology. And apart from that the Christomonistic approach, to adopt Althaus' term for the moment, is not by any means a
thing peculiar only to Barth, however much Bonhoeffer may here have
been influenced by him. It is an approach characteristic also of Karl
Heim. And to trace the noteworthy connexions here only a little further
back in theological history, let me recall the Ritschlian school, in which
Wilhelm Herrmann made the problem of theological certainty depend
solely and entirely on the encounter with Jesus Christ and Johannes
Gottschick could declare: 'But for Jesus I should be an atheist.'[2] We are
reminded of utterances of that kind rather than of the Christological
foundation of Barth's *Church Dogmatics*, when in one of the last of
Bonhoeffer's letters we find it said, purposely in the simplest form: 'If
the earth was good enough to bear the Man Jesus Christ, if a man like
Jesus really lived in it, then, and only then, has life a meaning for us.
If Jesus had not lived, then our life, in spite of all the other people we
know and honour and love, would be without meaning.'[3] If, as E. Bethge
reports, the remark was once made at a pastors' conference that 'we can
only hope that at the very last Bonhoeffer recovered his faith again',[4]

[1] Paul Althaus, *Die christliche Wahrheit*, 1952, pp. 56 ff.
[2] Althaus, *op. cit.* p. 54. [Cf. J. Gottschick, 'Ohne Christus wäre ich Atheist',
Chr. Welt 2, 1888, pp. 461-463.]   [3] *WE* p. 266, Eng. p. 184.
[4] *Die mündige Welt* p. 19=*EvTh* 15 [1955], p. 157.

then that is certainly understandable from the standpoint of the common conception of faith, and also highly typical of it (one could say, shockingly typical!), yet on the other hand it is surely incomprehensible how anyone could overlook the fact that the letters show not even the slightest trace of any doubt of Jesus Christ, that on the contrary Bonhoeffer is chiefly concerned in ever more elementary ways with personal faith in Christ[1] and that to his mind speaking about God, which has certainly become problematical to a degree, can find its proper foundation solely in Jesus Christ.[2] In the Outline of the book he intended still to write it is said: 'What do we mean by God? Not in the first place an abstract belief in his omnipotence, etc. That is not a genuine experience of God but a piece of extended world. Encounter with Jesus Christ. Discovering here the reversal of all human existence in that Jesus only "exists for others". The "existence for others" of Jesus is the experience of transcendence! This freedom from self, this "existence for others" maintained to the point of death is the sole ground of his omnipotence, omniscience, omnipresence. Faith is participation in this existence of Jesus. (Incarnation, Cross, Resurrection.) Our relation to God is not a "religious" relation to some highest, mightiest, best Being imaginable— that is not genuine transcendence—but our relation to God is a new life of "existing for others", of participation in the existence of Jesus.'[3]

Let us in the first instance leave unspoken all the questions that could here be asked, and first of all merely take note of this: The problem of non-religious interpretation arises for Bonhoeffer not from any doubt of Jesus Christ, but precisely from faith in Jesus Christ. It is not Jesus Christ, but the word God, indeed all religious concepts as such, that he finds problematical.[4] The question of non-religious interpretation derives directly from the foundation and heart of his theology, from his Christology. Non-religious interpretation is for Bonhoeffer nothing other than Christological interpretation.[5] That is heralded already in

[1] 'The general thing in the Confessing Church: championing the "cause" of the Church etc., but little personal faith in Christ. "Jesus" disappears from sight' (WE p. 259, Eng. p. 178).

[2] 'All that we rightly expect from God and pray for is to be found in Jesus Christ. The God of Jesus Christ has nothing to do with all that we, in our human way, imagine a God can and ought to do. We must persevere in long, quiet periods of meditation on the life, sayings, deeds, sufferings and death of Jesus in order to learn what God promises and what he fulfils' (WE p. 265, Eng. p. 183).

[3] WE pp. 259 f, Eng. p. 179.   [4] WE p. 183, Eng. p. 125.

[5] This phraseology must not be misunderstood as if it were thereby assumed that what is called 'Christological interpretation' is obviously a matter of common knowledge and, say, identical with what Bonhoeffer in earlier years offered as examples of 'Christological' interpretation of the Old Testament: 'König

his *Ethics*: 'What matters in the church is not religion, but the form of
Christ and its taking form amidst a band of men.'[1] And in his letters he
once draws the astonishing hermeneutic conclusion that the Song of
Solomon has in fact to be read as an earthly lovesong, and that that is
probably the best way of expounding it 'Christologically'.[2] When we
have said that non-religious interpretation is Christological interpretation and consequently Christological interpretation is non-religious
interpretation, then of course what we said earlier of the danger of
speaking of Christ all too much as a matter of course and in an all too
massively dogmatic way, appears in a different light. Bonhoeffer was
obviously aware of precisely this danger. His first daring advance into
the realm of the problems of non-religious interpretation is entered in
the programme under the general heading: 'What exercises me incessantly is the question what *is* Christianity, or indeed what *is* Christ, for
us today?'[3] It is true that even the common ways of speaking of Jesus
Christ have become for him deeply problematical.[4] Not, be it noted,
Jesus Christ himself, not faith in him, not the assurance of Christ that
finds in Jesus Christ himself the ground of all assurance—on the contrary, that is according to Bonhoeffer 'the solid ground on which we
stand'.[5] One may well ask why that should be so; and if it is so, why he
must then still be exercised incessantly by the question what Christ

[1] *E* p. 26, Eng. p. 21.   [2] *WE* p. 213, cf. pp. 192 f, Eng. pp. 144, 131.
[3] *WE* p. 178, Eng. p. 122.
[4] 'It is only when one knows the ineffability of the Name of God that one can
utter the name of Jesus Christ' (*WE* p. 112, Eng. p. 79).
[5] 'Certain is, that we may always live close to the presence of God and that
that is newness of life; that then nothing is impossible for us, for all things are
possible with God; that no earthly power can touch us without God's will and
that danger and trouble can only drive us closer to God; certain is, that we have
no claim on anything, and yet we may pray for everything; certain is, that in
suffering is hidden our joy, in death our life; certain is, that in all this we are
sustained in a wondrous fellowship. To all this God in Jesus has given his Yea
and Amen. That Yea and Amen is the solid ground on which we stand' (*WE*
pp. 265 f, Eng. pp. 183 f).

David' in *Junge Kirche* 4 (1936), pp. 64-9, 157-61, 197-203; 'Der Wiederaufbau
Jerusalems nach Esra und Nehemia', *ibid.*, pp. 653-61; *Schöpfung und Fall,
Theologische Auslegung von Gen. 1-3*, Munich, 2nd ed. 1937 [ET, *Creation and
Fall*, 1959], 3rd ed. 1955; *Das Gebetbuch der Bibel, Eine Einführung in die Psalmen*,
Bad Salzuflen, 1940. On the contrary, it is a question of a new understanding of
the task of Christological interpretation. However little these attempts at exposition could in all respects be described as mistaken, it is nevertheless necessary
to submit their method to very far-reaching criticism from the standpoints provided by his reflexions on non-religious interpretation. That is unfortunately
not brought out in Richard Grunow's essay on Dietrich Bonhoeffer's exposition
of scripture (see above, p. 98 note 1).

really *is* for us today. Well, the answer to the first part of the question cannot escape concepts so taboo in theology today as 'experience' in both senses of the word (*Erfahrung oder gar Erlebnis*). The simple fact is: Jesus Christ has met him, he knows himself called and claimed by Jesus Christ, he too has allowed himself to be caught up into the way of Jesus Christ, he has become sure of Jesus Christ as the Lord. He has experienced him as the hope and driving-force of his life.[1] However we may describe it, for him it is beyond doubt that he belongs in the 'place at which God and the cosmic reality are reconciled . . . at which God and man have become one', at which we have therefore 'to set our eyes upon God and upon the world at the same time'.[2] But—and with this we come to the second part of the question—really to grasp that, to understand it thoroughly, to live it, to reckon with it in all its furthest implications, to make it expressible, communicable, to be able to express it liberatingly and redeemingly[3]—that is a task which demands our being incessantly exercised by the question, what Christ really *is* for us today. To answer that not merely in traditional, standardized and now in-effectual religious terms, but in full personal responsibility, is a thing to which the theologian has to dedicate all his thinking-power.

That is the decisive thing, and compared with it the problem raised by Althaus' criticism of the so-called Christomonistic thought of revelation takes a completely secondary place—indeed, it can and does acquire theological relevance only within the framework of the basic theological question what Christ really *is* for us today. The Christomonism which Althaus censures is at all events right in this: that Jesus Christ—as indeed Althaus, too, has ultimately no wish to deny—is not to be con-

---

[1] I am here taking up—and admittedly freely combining—phrases that occur here and there in Bonhoeffer's letters, e.g. pp. 231, 245, 252, 259, 264, Eng. pp. 157, 166, 172, 179, 183. It is true that in order to protect such remarks from misunderstandings that can easily arise, it must be very clearly recognized that he does not make them in the form of personal confessions. Nevertheless, this important proviso must not deter us from tracing out the significance of experience for Bonhoeffer's theological thinking. To that end we have also to take account of what appear to be entirely untheological remarks on 'experience', e.g. 'Time lost is time when we have not lived a full human life, time unenriched by experience, creative endeavour, enjoyment and suffering' (*WE* p. 9, Eng. p. 13); my life 'has been an uninterrupted enrichment of my experience' (*WE* p. 173, Eng. p. 119); further also observations such as that on 'moral memory' (*WE* p. 143, Eng. p. 99 omits the actual phrase) or on his own 'turning away from the phraseological to the real' (*WE* p. 174, Eng. p. 119 omits the whole sentence).   [2] *E* p. 15, Eng. p. 8.

[3] In *WE* p. 169 he speaks of the 'emancipating and liberating word' (Eng. p. 116, 'word of deliverance'), in *WE* p. 207 of the 'reconciling and redeeming word' (Eng. p. 140, 'word of reconciliation'). Cf. below, pp. 121 ff.

sidered in theology as *one* ground of faith among others, and therefore still less as an article of faith that has to be laboriously appropriated on the basis of some assurance grounded elsewhere, and must of course also be believed if we would be Christians.[1] Rather, Jesus Christ is considered in theology as *the* ground of faith.[2] If we are not capable of expressing that in a responsible way, then that does not indeed make us cease to be theologians—for when do we ever get the length of being really able to express it?—but we certainly do cease to be theologians, and should honestly and cheerfully admit it, if our theological thinking is no longer centrally dominated by the question what Christ really *is* for us today. In pursuing that question we may then come to the conclusion that Althaus' criticism of so-called Christomonism is justified up to a point, that precisely in order to express in a responsible manner what Christ really *is* for us today we must speak in ways that are after all other than strictly Christological in the accepted sense, and that Bonhoeffer's idea of non-religious interpretation gives Christological interpretation an accent which is noteworthy in that respect and which meets the danger Althaus sees in so-called Christomonism. But however that may be, this at all events is plain: that the question which drove Bonhoeffer to the problem of non-religious interpretation must be our question too, as long as we make any claim at all to be theologians, and that our prospects of understanding Bonhoeffer's approach to the problem—it may then be in taking a critical view of the solution he has indicated—depend on the extent to which in our whole theological thinking we truly allow ourselves to be incessantly exercised by the basic theological question, what Jesus Christ really *is* for us today.

2. The second basic presupposition we must be ready to adopt if we are to be open to the problem as Bonhoeffer sees it, is respect for the precept of intellectual honesty. 'Intellectual honesty in all things, including questions of belief, was the great achievement of the emancipated *ratio* and it has ever since been one of the indispensable moral requirements of Western man. Contempt for the age of Rationalism is a suspicious sign of failure to feel the need for truthfulness. If intellectual honesty is not the last word that is to be said about things, and if intellectual clarity is often achieved at the cost of insight into reality, this can still never again exempt us from the inner obligation to make clean

---

[1] That is surely what Bonhoeffer means in his criticism of revelational positivism, 'which says, "Take it or leave it"—whether it is the Virgin Birth, the Trinity or anything else, everything is an equally significant and equally necessary part of the whole, that must either be swallowed whole or not at all. That is not biblical' (*WE* p. 184, Eng. p. 126).   [2] See above, p. 108 note 5.

and honest use of the *ratio*. We cannot now go back on Lessing and Lichtenberg.'[1] Two fateful misunderstandings must here be countered, which are designed, allegedly for the sake of theology but in actual fact to the detriment of theology, to discredit the concept of intellectual honesty.

First, it would obviously be a grave error to consider intellectual honesty an achievement of the modern age in, say, the sense that it did not exist before and the preceding ages would therefore *ipso facto* fall under the verdict of lack of intellectual honesty. When for example Bonhoeffer says on one occasion that the *salto mortale* back into the Middle Ages could only be a step of desperation which must cost the sacrifice of intellectual honesty,[2] then that does not express a judgment on the men of the Middle Ages, but only on our relation to the Middle Ages at a time that in point of fact is not ours.[3] The trite maxim that

---

[1] *E* p. 37, Eng. p. 34.   [2] *WE* p. 241, Eng. p. 163.

[3] Bonhoeffer does indeed himself appear to express an absolute judgment on the Middle Ages when he describes 'heteronomy in the form of clericalism' as 'the fundamental principle of the Middle Ages' (*WE* p. 241, Eng. p. 163). Although that way of putting it is a most vulnerable historiographical abbreviation, yet by using the concept of heteronomy in contrast to the concept of autonomy that characterizes the modern age, it manifestly does express a characteristic mark of the Middle Ages. In the same way the remark that 'intellectual honesty in all things . . . was the great achievement of the emancipated *ratio*' (*E* p. 37, Eng. p. 34), in other words of the age of the Enlightenment, likewise seems to imply an absolute—and negative—judgment on the Middle Ages. That judgment may then be somewhat modified by the observation that 'the foundation of that freedom of thought that has made Europe great' lies already in the great controversies between emperor and pope (*WE* pp. 237 f, Eng. p. 161), and that out of the Middle Ages themselves there arose a ' "secularity" entirely different from the Renaissance variety', which was 'not an "emancipated" but a "Christian", though anti-clerical, secularity', which found its expression in thirteenth-century poetry and art and continued on into the nineteenth century in its peculiarity as a special branch developing in its own way' (*WE* pp. 156 f, cf. also pp. 215 and 167, Eng. pp. 108, 145 f and 115 respectively). But even when the relation between the Middle Ages and modern times is considered on all its many different levels, the aspect of the Middle Ages that could be roughly summed up under the concept 'clerical' can hardly be done justice to historically by such judgments as 'heteronomy' or even 'intellectual dishonesty'. We should then be setting out from presuppositions which for the Middle Ages simply did not exist. The problem of historical understanding and historical judgment which we are now touching on can of course only be glanced at here. But we must do that in order to be aware of (and not let ourselves be perplexed by!) the difficulty that attaches to all discussion of the so-called spirit of modern times, *viz.*—that on the one hand (despite all the detailed criticisms!) we must acknowledge it is right as against the Middle Ages, yet on the other hand that does not by any means entitle us to suppose that medieval man must actually have thought so too and that thus we must deny to the Middle Ages the right to be what they were. The problem is broached also by Bonhoeffer when he questions

history is a one-way street—and if I may picture it so, a one-way street
of such technical perfection that traffic in the opposite direction is
absolutely out of the question and a corresponding prohibition is really
superfluous—that trite maxim is far more difficult to keep fully in mind
than one would expect. For applied to our present problem it means
that the demands of intellectual honesty are subject to historical change.
To be clear in our own minds that the human *ratio* is itself historical, is
indeed the best way of showing that when we speak today of intellectual
honesty, we are not by any means connecting it with the ideals and
illusions of the Enlightenment and its unhistorically applied concept of
reason. The statement made by Bonhoeffer in the context of a totally
different problem that to tell the truth means to say how a thing really is,
and thus includes respect for mystery, for intimacy and for concealment,[1]
indicates that the concept truth, like the kindred concept freedom,[2] is
historical in kind,[3] and that both again must be seen in their relationship
to the concept reality.[4] That means: the demand for intellectual honesty

[1] *WE* pp. 114 ff, Eng. pp. 80 f. Cf. the essay written in prison (*WE* pp. 94,
119, Eng. pp. 65, 83) and never completed, 'What is meant by "Telling the
Truth"?' (*E* pp. 283-90, Eng. pp. 326-34); ' "Lying" is destruction of, and
hostility towards, reality as it is in God' (*WE* p. 119, Eng. p. 83).

[2] I can here only refer to the extraordinarily frequent occurrence in *WE* of the
concept freedom. Specially characteristic in that respect are the two poems
'Stations on the Road to Freedom' (pp. 250 f, Eng. pp. 170 f) and 'Der Freund'
(pp. 269 ff, omitted in English). Also the remarks on the concept freedom in *E
passim*, especially pp. 193 ff, Eng. pp. 216 ff.

[3] Particularly clear in *E* p. 289, Eng. p. 333: 'How can I speak the truth?
1. By perceiving who causes me to speak and what entitles me to speak. 2. By
perceiving the place at which I stand. 3. By relating to this context the object
about which I am making some assertion. It is tacitly assumed in these rules that
all speech is subject to certain conditions; speech does not accompany the
natural course of life in a continual stream, but it has its place, its time and its
task, and consequently also its limits.'

[4] *E passim*, esp. pp. 55-61, Eng. pp. 55-62. To analyse the connexion between
theology and ontology in Bonhoeffer on the basis of the concept reality is a task
we must the more firmly deny ourselves within the very limited possibilities of

Hegel's general conception of history as a developing continuum (*WE* pp. 157 f,
Eng. p. 109), and especially when he considers whether it may not perhaps be the
case that understanding of the sphere of freedom (art, culture, friendship,
recreation) can today be recovered only from the standpoint of the concept of
the church and that precisely thereby the connexion with the Middle Ages (!)
would also be regained (*WE* p. 136. Eng. p. 94). A genuine connexion of that
kind with the Middle Ages, which must not be confused with a return to the
Middle Ages, would then be comparable to 'becoming as little children'—which
indeed is also not possible through arbitrary renunciation of inward honesty but
only 'through repentance, i.e. through *ultimate* honesty', and that means by
including intellectual honesty after all (*WE* p. 241, Eng. p. 163).

is the obligation to keep my thinking in agreement with my reality. The concept 'my reality' here means, the indivisible complex of all that concerns me and the ways in which I can be expected to recognize it as concerning me.

With this definition it becomes possible and necessary to respect the historical, and consequently also the individual, differences in the meaning that intellectual honesty bears in various concrete circumstances. Anyone who in his thinking (from cowardice or laziness or whatever the reason) culpably by-passes a part of the reality that concerns him, or who does not exhaust the possibilities ascribable to him of recognizing what concerns him, transgresses the precept of intellectual honesty.[1] But now, to the reality that concerns modern man there belongs—and for this reason the duty of intellectual honesty does in fact acquire for him a significance that is entirely new, and compared with earlier ages entirely unique—the discovery of the autonomy of the

[1] A connexion therefore exists—though Bonhoeffer himself, as far as I can see, never considered it directly—between the precept of intellectual honesty and what he says about standing in the polyphony and multi-dimensionality of life in *WE* pp. 192 f, 195 and especially 209 f, Eng. pp. 131 f, 133 and 141 f: 'I have repeatedly observed here how few there are who can make room for many things at the same time. . . . They miss the fulness of life and the wholeness of an independent existence; everything subjective and objective is dissolved for them into fragments. By contrast, Christianity plunges us into many different dimensions of life simultaneously: we can make room in our hearts, to some extent at least, for God and the whole world. . . . We have to drag men out of one-track thinking—as a sort of "preparation" or "enablement" for faith, although it is only faith itself that can make possible a multi-dimensional life. . . .' I should not consider it too hazardous, at any rate not more hazardous than the last sentence as it stands already is, if it were to be altered to: We have to drag men out of intellectual dishonesty—as a sort of 'preparation' or 'enablement' for faith, although it is only faith itself that can make possible a life of intellectual honesty. But that is already jumping ahead of the above train of thought. See below, pp. 117 f.

this address, the more plainly we see just here a cardinal point not only in Bonhoeffer's thought—I recall his thesis, *Akt und Sein: Transzendentalphilosophie und Ontologie in der systematischen Theologie, Beitr. z. Förd. christl. Theol.* 34, 2, Gütersloh 1931, 2nd ed. 1956 [ET, *Act and Being*, 1962]—but also in modern theology as a whole. A quotation may suffice to indicate the bearing of the problem: 'In Christ we are offered the possibility of partaking in the reality of God and in the reality of the world at the same time, but not in the one without the other. The reality of God discloses itself only by setting me entirely in the reality of the world, and when I encounter the reality of the world it is always already sustained, accepted and reconciled in the reality of God. . . . Thus it is a case of participating in the reality of God and of the world in Jesus Christ today, and this participation must be such that I never experience the reality of God without the reality of the world or the reality of the world without the reality of God' (*E* pp. 60 f, Eng. pp. 61 f).

reason and accordingly the inescapable duty to make use of the autonomous reason[1]—not, be it noted, to make autonomous use of the reason;
for it is not man himself but reason which, rightly understood, is
autonomous,[2] whereas to confuse the automony of the reason with the
autonomy of man results precisely in a new heteronomy of the reason,
as can be abundantly illustrated from the history of modern times. This
rightly understood autonomy of the reason is so much a part of the
reality of modern man that he is not even asked whether he is willing
to make use of it, but only how in fact he does make use of it, namely,
whether he lets its use be subject to the precept of intellectual honesty,
and that means: neither considers the autonomous reason his entire
reality nor yet arbitrarily screens any areas of his reality from the autonomous reason.[3] It is obvious that within the framework of the problem
of intellectual honesty here generally outlined there would still be an
abundance of questions to be discussed. But one thing should be plain:
that modern man transgresses the duty of intellectual honesty if he does

---

[1] 'There is no longer any need for God as a working hypothesis, whether in
morals, politics or science; but just as little in philosophy or religion (Feuerbach!). Intellectual honesty involves dropping the working hypothesis, or dis-
pensing with it as far as is humanly possible. A scientist, physician, etc. who
seeks to provide edification is a hybrid. . . . The only way to be honest is to
recognize that we have to live in the world—"*etsi deus non daretur*" ' (*WE* pp.
240 f, Eng. p. 163).

[2] With that I am introducing a distinction which I cannot here establish and
develop in detail, as would have to be done. Verbally it seems to contradict Bonhoeffer's usage. He is accustomed to speak simply of the autonomy of man, or of
the world (*WE* pp. 215, 239, 240, Eng. pp. 145, 162, 162). Yet I consider such
a distinction necessary if we would pursue further Bonhoeffer's line of thought.

[3] This is where critical remarks about reasonableness necessarily belong. 'The
failure of "*reasonable*" people is evident. With the best of intentions, but with
a naive lack of realism, the reasonable man imagines that a small dose of reason
will be enough to put the world right. In his short-sightedness he wants to do
justice on all sides, but in the mêlée of conflicting forces he gets trampled upon
without having achieved the slightest effect. Disappointed by the unreasonableness of the world, he realizes at last his futility, retires from the fray, or weakly
surrenders to the winning side' (*WE* p. 11, Eng. p. 14). In the parallel passage
in *E* p. 12, Eng. p. 4, we find the noteworthy modification, that the failure of
reasonable people is connected with their inability to perceive the depths of the
holy. Further: 'We believed that reason and justice were the key to success, and
where both failed we felt we were at the end of our tether. We have constantly
exaggerated the importance of reason and justice in the historical process too.
You . . . are learning from childhood that the world is controlled by forces
against which reason is powerless. This knowledge will enable you to cope with
these powers more soberly and effectively' (*WE* p. 204, Eng. pp. 138 f). Cf. also
the observations on folly, *viz.*—'that it is essentially a moral rather than an
intellectual defect' and 'that the spiritual liberation of man to responsible life in
the sight of God is the only real cure for folly' (*WE* pp. 17-20, Eng. pp. 18-19).

not as far as can be expected of him in any given circumstances keep his thinking, whatever the subject, open to the facts that are posited with the autonomy of the reason. The difficulties that causes demand of modern man very special watchfulness where his intellectual honesty is concerned, *viz.*—that in most stringent self-criticism he should take care not to deceive himself but to keep his thinking in actual fact in agreement with his reality.

The second misunderstanding is the false notion that the demand for intellectual honesty ends up in a restriction of the development of faith. That of course is in actual fact the picture presented to us by the history of Christianity since the beginning of the modern age. Bonhoeffer repeatedly addressed himself anew to the task of analysing this movement of retreat that was forced on the Christian faith[1] and castigated in pungent terms both the 'attack by Christian apologetics upon the adulthood of the world'[2] and also the practice of resting content with a final, allegedly secure, place of retreat.[3] Even the Confessing Church is not spared from the judgment that it is not entirely fresh air that blows in it: 'A church on the defensive'.[4] The conflict here between Christianity

---

[1] *WE* pp. 181 f, 210 f, 215 f, 229 ff, Eng. pp. 124, 142 f, 145 f, 156 f. From these passages just one statement that frequently recurs in similar terms: ' . . . if . . . —as in the nature of things is inevitable—the frontiers of knowledge are always being pushed back further and further, then God, too, is being pushed back further and further along with them and accordingly finds himself in continuous retreat' (*WE* pp. 210 f, Eng. p. 142).

[2] *WE* pp. 216 ff, 221, 230, Eng. pp. 146 ff, 149, 156. Esp. pp. 217 f, Eng. p. 147: 'The attack by Christian apologetics upon the adulthood of the world I consider to be in the first place pointless, in the second ignoble, and in the third un-Christian'. 'The importunity of all these people is far too unaristocratic for the Word of God . . .' (*WE* p. 236, Eng. p. 160).

[3] 'Even though there has been a surrender on all secular problems, there still remain the so-called "ultimate questions"—death, guilt—on which only "God" can furnish an answer and which are the reason why God and the church and the parson are needed. Thus we live, to some extent, by these ultimate questions of humanity' (*WE* pp. 216, 230, Eng. pp. 146, 156). 'When God was driven out of the world, and from the public side of human life, an attempt was made to retain him at least in the sphere of the "personal", "inner", "private" life.' Then come the pungent remarks about 'the secrets known by a man's valet' as 'the hunting-ground of modern psychotherapists' and the characterization of this development from the sociological point of view as 'revolt of inferiority'. And then he sums up: 'From the theological point of view the error is twofold. First, it is thought that a man can be addressed as a sinner only after his weaknesses and meannesses have been spied out. Second, it is supposed that man's essential nature consists of his inmost and most intimate background, and that is defined as his "interior life"; and it is in these secret human places that God is now to have his domain!' (*WE* pp. 233-5, Eng. pp. 158-9).

[4] *WE* pp. 261, 259, also 220, 221, Eng. pp. 181, 179, 148, 149.

and intellectual honesty, which Bonhoeffer characterizes in drastic terms by saying that 'the only people with whom we can now make headway in "religious" things are a few "last survivals of the age of chivalry", or else one or two who are intellectually dishonest',[1] rests on a disastrous confusion regarding the relation of faith and reason.[2]

The right understanding of the relation between faith and reason has to prove itself by its ability to maintain two statements in all their fulness and to interpret them each in its own distinct reference as valid without limitation, *viz.*—Faith is the death of reason, and: Faith stands in agreement with reason.[3] But to do that, it is necessary to know what faith means. The confusion in regard to the relation between faith and reason is recognizable from the fact that we either feel able to accept only one of these two statements, but yet cannot then maintain a radical understanding of it—for an irrational faith is just as nonsensical as a rational faith—or that we reject both and put in their place a conciliatory formula of compromise. Either way, faith and reason are regarded as two factors on the same level, which contest each other's place or agree to an arbitrated peace in which the field is divided in favour of one or other of them.[4] In either case the cause of confusion here is a misunderstanding of what faith means. Faith is seen as an organ that competes with reason or supplements it, as a kind of reason projected into the suprarational. Faith thus understood, already secretly mastered by reason and therefore nothing else but pseudo-faith, strives to justify and safeguard itself by making itself as far as possible a law to reason and changing the latter's legitimate autonomy into heteronomy. This pseudo-

---

[1] *WE* p. 179, Eng. p. 122.

[2] What here follows also comes under the proviso that it can necessarily only indicate questions that would require fuller explication.

[3] Cf. *E* pp. 63 f, Eng. p. 65: 'Just as in Christ the reality of God entered into the reality of the world, so, too, what is Christian is to be found only in what is of the world, the "supernatural" only in the natural, the holy only in the profane, the revelational only in the rational. . . . And yet what is Christian is not identical with what is of the world. The natural is not identical with the supernatural or the revelational with the rational. But between the two there is in each case a unity which derives solely from the reality of Christ, that is to say solely from faith in this last reality. This unity is seen in the way in which the secular and the Christian elements, etc., prevent one another from assuming any kind of static independence in their mutual relations. They adopt a polemical attitude towards each other and bear witness precisely in this to their shared reality and to their unity in the reality which is in Christ.'

[4] Cf. Bonhoeffer's attack on 'thinking in terms of two spheres' in *E* pp. 61-9, Eng. pp. 62-72. Specially important in it is: 'to think in terms of spheres is to think statically and is therefore, theologically speaking, to think in terms of laws' (p. 64, Eng. p. 66).

faith is itself reason become heteronomous, and necessarily calls out the opposition of autonomous reason in the properly understood sense. The necessary and inevitable conflict between faith and reason, which finds expression in the theological statement that reason is blind as far as man's being before God is concerned, has now been shifted on to false ground and turned into a sham conflict (though certainly one of very great consequence) in which the statement about the blindness of reason is supported by all kinds of evidence of human irrationality—evidence of which there is certainly no lack, but the production of which ultimately (though that is not clearly realized) really speaks only in favour of reason. Only a theology that does not know the meaning of faith can promise itself any benefit for faith from a weakening of reason. Only a false faith, and that means only unbelief, can profit from a reason that has become heteronomous and therefore unbridled. The unbridled nature of a reason that turns against the Christian faith therefore cannot be complained of, as long as unbridled reason is promoted in the name of a wrongly understood Christian faith and allegedly for the benefit of the Christian faith. It is merely a sign of moral health when this twisted and depraved form of faith is opposed in the name of reason.[1]

The conclusion is: Christian faith rightly understood demands and promotes (*fordert und fördert*) the right use of the legitimately autonomous reason in the proper sense of that autonomy and within the limits of it. To that extent the Christian faith is interested, even if only indirectly, in the total range of human life; not only in the so-called things of faith but also in the things that are subject to the autonomous reason—and interested, too, in the sense that the reason should here be really reasonable and relevant, i.e. perceive and make perceptible the meaning of things. Faith can and must on occasion become in this respect the advocate of reason against human irrationality and inculcate in every sphere of human life the precept of intellectual honesty. At the

---

[1] Similarly, even if not at all parallel to the above: 'As . . . Luther protested with the help of the secular and in the name of a better Christianity against a Christianity which was striving for independence and detaching itself from the reality in Christ, so too today, when Christianity is employed as a polemical weapon against the secular, this must be done in the name of a better secularity and must on no account lead back to a static predominance of the spiritual sphere as an end in itself' (*E* p. 64, Eng. p. 65). In almost exact agreement with the above: 'The attack by Christian apologetics upon the adulthood of the world I consider . . . pointless . . . because it looks to me like an attempt to put a grown man back into adolescence, i.e. to make him dependent on a lot of things on which he is not in fact dependent any more, to thrust him back into the midst of problems which are in fact not problems for him any more' (*WE* pp. 217 f, Eng. p. 147).

same time, however, it must respect the demand for intellectual honesty
also in matters of faith itself, and will never be able to do the one without
the other. Faith does not here bow to an external law, but follows its own
law and that means, is free. For if, as we said, intellectual honesty means
keeping my thinking in agreement with my reality, then intellectual
honesty in matters of faith means that faith does not anxiously by-pass
a part of my reality but concerns itself with my whole reality,[1] and thus,
as Bonhoeffer rightly says, is not a partial act, but 'a whole, a life-act'.[2]
Intellectual honesty in matters of faith is not to be demanded as, say, a
concession to a reason that has turned tyrant, but faith itself demands it
for faith's own sake, because it seeks to be real faith.[3] The lack of
intellectual honesty in matters of faith is a symptom of secret unbelief,
of an unbelief that thinks it must isolate faith from reality. For that
reason it is a basic presupposition of theological thinking that the question of faith is neither put in the form: What *must* I believe?[4]—that
would be making faith a law to reason—nor yet in the form: What *can*
I believe?—that would be making reason a law to faith. The question
of faith must rather be, to turn again to Bonhoeffer's own words: 'What
do we really believe—i.e. in such a way as to stake our whole lives upon
it?'[5] That certainly does not mean that the language of faith is nourished

---

[1] 'Whoever professes to believe in the reality of Jesus Christ as the revelation
of God, must in the same breath profess his faith in both the reality of God and
the reality of the world; for in Christ he finds God and the world reconciled.
And for that very reason the Christian is no longer the man of eternal conflict,
but, just as the reality of Christ is *one*, so he, too, since he shares in this reality
in Christ, is himself also an undivided whole. His worldliness does not divide
him from Christ, and his Christianity does not divide him from the world.
Belonging wholly to Christ, he stands at the same time wholly in the world'
(*E* p. 65, Eng. p. 67).
   [2] 'The "religious act" is always something partial' (*WE* p. 246, Eng. p. 167).
When we think in terms of two spheres, 'the cause of Christ becomes a partial
and provincial matter within reality as a whole' (*E* p. 61, Eng. p. 63). Also the
frequent remarks about the 'whole man', the ἄνθρωπος τέλειος as opposed to the
ἀνὴρ δίψυχος (James 1.4, 8): *WE* pp. 141, 161 f, 193, 209, 236, Eng. pp. 98, 111 f,
131, 141 f, 160. For the question how that is related to the fragmentary character
of life (see above, p. 100 note 4) see below, pp. 153 and 161.
   [3] See above, p. 113 note 1.   [4] *WE* p. 260, Eng. p. 179.
   [5] *WE* p. 260, Eng. p. 179. Bonhoeffer indicates that that has far-reaching
consequences: 'Revision of the "creed" question (the Apostle's Creed); revision
of Christian apologetics; revision of the training for the ministry and the pattern
of clerical life' (*WE* p. 262, Eng. p. 181). In particular: 'The antitheses between
Lutheran and Reformed (and to some extent between Catholic and Protestant)
are no longer genuine. They can naturally be revived at any time with passion,
but they no longer carry real conviction. It is impossible to prove this. We must
simply take the bull by the horns. All we can prove is, that biblical Christian
faith does not stand or fall by these antitheses' (*WE* p. 260, Eng. p. 180). He was

by the believer's sole subjective view of himself. For here of course it must never be forgotten for a moment that faith is response to the Word of God which itself comes to fruition in faith, and therefore everything that professes to be faith has to prove itself by the standard of the original testimony of faith. But just as little must it be forgotten that faith has no other way of speaking, and thus there can be no other theological exposition of faith either, than in rendering account of itself—we could also say, in testimony, and that means in fact in ultimate 'honesty with ourselves',[1] *viz.*—not 'by repeatedly entrenching ourselves behind the "faith of the Church" ', but by 'quite honestly asking and answering the question what we ourselves really believe'.[2] For only so will faith be kept to being concrete faith, and only so will it be expounded in theology and in proclamation as concrete faith, not as the schema prescribed by some religious method that has been taken over and turned into a law,[3] but as a faith that stands in agreement with my reality (*im Einvernehmen*

---

[1] *WE* p. 261, Eng. p. 180. That the concept testimony, which theologians today are so fond of employing, implies 'being honest with ourselves', is naturally never disputed, but little account is taken of it either as far as its consequences are concerned.   [2] *WE* pp. 260 f, Eng. p. 180.

[3] E.g. in giving the reason why, in his 'Prayers for fellow-prisoners' (*WE* pp. 96-101, Eng. pp. 67-71), the prayer for forgiveness is not central: 'I thought it would be a mistake, both pastorally, and because of the hard facts, to be strictly "methodical" about it' (*WE* p. 149, Eng. p. 103). Or: to make the Cross, or suffering at any rate, an abstract principle would be 'an unhealthy devotion to method, that deprives suffering of its element of contingency upon a divine ordinance' (*WE* pp. 253 f, Eng. p. 173). Existential philosophy and psychotherapy as 'secularized methodism': *WE* pp. 217, 230, Eng. pp. 146, 156. Also *WE* pp. 218, 246, Eng. pp. 147, 167. 'To be a Christian does not mean to be religious in a particular way, to use some particular method of turning oneself into something (a sinner, a penitent or a saint), but it means to be a man—it is not a human type that Christ creates in us, but a man. It is not some religious act which makes a Christian what he is, but participation in the suffering of God in the life of the world' (*WE* p. 244, Eng. p. 166), and that in fact means, faith (*WE* p. 245, Eng. p. 167). That the process of 'being caught up into the Messianic suffering of God in Jesus Christ' takes place in very different ways, and thus not according to a definite methodical schema, is shown by New Testament examples: *WE* p. 245, Eng. pp. 166 f. 'When Jesus saved sinners, they were real sinners, but Jesus did not make every man a sinner first' (*WE* p. 231, Eng. p. 156) cf. also *E* pp. 77 f, Eng. p. 82. It seems to me certain that Bonhoeffer did not wish all this to contradict what Luther in his *Lectures on Romans* said on the subject of *magnificare peccatum* and *oportere peccatores fieri* (*WA* 56, pp. 3.6-11; 157.2-6; 229.7-230.8; 231.6-12; 232.34-233.33), but to safeguard the right understanding of it.

---

concerned to 'try to say simply and clearly certain things which we so often prefer to ignore' (*WE* p. 262, Eng. p. 181). 'We must also risk saying hazardous things if only vital questions are stirred up thereby' (*WE* p. 257, Eng. p. 177). What has happened in that respect in church and theology since then?

mit meiner Wirklichkeit stehend), or more correctly as a faith that embraces my whole reality (*meine ganze Wirklichkeit einvernehmend*). When
Bonhoeffer reflects on the question 'how the concepts of repentance,
faith, justification, rebirth, sanctification . . . are to be re-interpreted in
"secular" terms',[1] then by that he means nothing other than: What is
the actual concrete meaning of repentance, faith, justification, rebirth,
sanctification, in the strict context of the question, 'What do we really
believe?'[2] How are all these concepts to be understood in such a way
that they do not by-pass our reality, nor yet are somehow only a
separate part of our reality, but concern our reality as a whole? Thus we
can now register the further provisional result that non-religious interpretation means concrete interpretation.

3. Finally, the third basic presupposition which is at work in Bonhoeffer's reflexions on non-religious interpretation, and which must be
a basic element of all theological thinking, is the orientation towards the
task of proclamation.[3] In view of the dominant place assumed by the
church in the whole of Bonhoeffer's theological work,[4] it would be easy
to have recourse at this point to the concept of the church and to
characterize the basic presupposition whose definition now concerns us
by using, say, the formula that has become a commonplace of theology
today: that theology is a function of the church[5] and therefore all
theological thinking has to understand itself in that light. That, how-

[1] *WE* p. 185, Eng. p. 126.
[2] Cf. Otto Küster, 'Konkreter Glaube', *ZTK* 48 (1951), pp. 101-114.
[3] In what follows, 'proclamation' obviously must not only be understood as
the Sunday sermon, but certainly includes it more especially.
[4] At bottom all Bonhoeffer's publications, from his dissertation (*Sanctorum
Communio: Eine dogmatische Untersuchung der Soziologie der Kirche*, Berlin 1930,
New impression, *Theol. Bücherei Bd. 3*, Munich 1954) onwards, are oriented
towards the theme 'church'—Hans-Christoph von Hase, 'Begriff und Wirklichkeit der Kirche in der Theologie Dietrich Bonhoeffers' (see above, p. 98 note 1).
[5] E.g. Karl Barth, *KD* I/1 (1932), p. 1; Emil Brunner, *The Christian Doctrine
of God, Dogmatics I* (ET, 1949), p. 3; Paul Althaus, *Grundriss der Dogmatik* I
(1947), p. 7 (contrast the important reservations in *Die christliche Wahrheit* (1952),
pp. 4 ff); Heinrich Vogel, *Gott in Christo* (1951), pp. 74 f; Hermann Diem,
Theologie als kirchliche Wissenschaft (1951), pp. 21 ff; Otto Weber, *Grundlagen
der Dogmatik* I (1955), pp. 30 f. But also e.g. Michael Schmaus, *Katholische
Dogmatik* I (1953), pp. 22 f. In Bonhoeffer himself: *Akt und Sein* (1931),
p. 123 [ET, *Act and Being*, 1962, p. 143].
   It is time that the formulae 'theology as a function of the church' or 'theology
as a church science', which can have a really unequivocal meaning only in the
Roman Catholic sense, were critically examined and then at least somewhat
more cautiously applied; as it is also time to contest the idea that the motto of
the 'churchliness of theology' was a quite surprising new discovery of the
twenties of this century (thus Hermann Diem, *op. cit.*, pp. 22 ff), whereas in
fact it had its origin in the nineteenth century and was intensively debated then.

ever, would jeopardize the precise understanding of what requires to be noticed here. Not that it would not be a true indication of Bonhoeffer's incessant concern also in this last phase of his theological thinking. That indeed is proved precisely by the criticisms of the church for the church's sake which accompany his reflexions on the problem of non-religious interpretation. In the very years in which we seemed to have reached a new experience and understanding of the meaning of the church, the church in Bonhoeffer's judgment 'fought only for self-preservation . . . as though it were an end in itself',[1] and thus sinned against its own nature, which Bonhoeffer now defines by saying that 'The church is its true self only when it exists for others.'[2] The fact that Bonhoeffer's utterances on the church during the time of his imprisonment are almost exclusively pitched in this key of passionate criticism, can, however, neither be dismissed by saying that that is in fact only an expression of his love of the church, nor by saying that these utterances, taken in isolation, really contain only half the truth. That is all no doubt correct. But at the moment there is surely no call for a carefully balanced judgment of these years and one that avoids the sin of ingratitude. It is much rather a question of grasping the real theological element at work in Bonhoeffer's criticism. And that is surely that Bonhoeffer leaves the church utterly and completely to the mercy of what makes the church its true self, and that therefore his theological thinking, too, in order to be rightly oriented towards the church, is oriented towards what makes the church its true self. That, however, is the Word of God as proclaimed. This, the foundation of the church's existence, is the criterion of all that is said of the church. It is therefore on this foundation of the church's existence that Bonhoeffer lays his finger when he says our church is 'incapable of bringing the word of reconciliation and redemption to mankind and the world at large'.[3] It is with this foundation of the church's existence that he is concerned also in the cry that anticipates the whole pathos of the work he finally planned: 'The church must get out of its stagnation. We must move out again into the open air of intellectual discussion with the world.'[4]

It is thus a question of right proclamation. Certainly also a question of the form of the church.[5] Yet only in so far as the transformation and recasting which Bonhoeffer sees coming to it is connected with the

[1] WE p. 206, Eng. p. 140, see above, p. 115 note 4.
[2] WE p. 261, Eng. p. 180, see also E p. 66, Eng. p. 68.
[3] WE pp. 206 f, Eng. p. 140.
[4] WE p.25 7, Eng. p. 177.
[5] See below, p. 122 note 4.

question of proclamation and takes its start from there, so that any premature organization would only mean delaying the coming changes.[1] It requires to be noticed, however, that Bonhoeffer's view of the coming changes in this connexion is simply not concerned at all with the problem of form,[2] but with the problem of language: ' . . . the day will come when men will be called again to utter the Word of God with such power as will change and renew the world.' Thus he speaks of the world, where the immediately preceding sentences make us think of a change and renewal in the form of the church! And he then goes on: 'It will be a new language, perhaps completely unreligious, but liberating and redeeming like the language of Jesus, so that men are horrified by it and yet overwhelmed by its power. It will be the language of a new righteousness and truth, a language which proclaims the peace of God with men and the advent of his kingdom.'[3]

To be sure, we must ask ourselves whether justice is really done to Bonhoeffer's intention when this particular remark, according to which the whole problem of the church is concentrated in the problem of language, is focussed on as of decisive importance.[4] We should certainly

---

[1] *WE* p. 207, Eng. p. 140.

[2] The quotation that follows above is immediately preceded by the words: 'By the time you are grown up, the form of the church will have greatly changed. We are not yet out of the melting pot, and every attempt to hasten the organized deployment of the church's power will only delay its conversion and cleansing. It is not for us to prophesy the day—but . . .' (*WE* p. 207, Eng. p. 140).

[3] *WE* p. 207, Eng. pp. 140 f.

[4] For the inseparable association of the proclamation and form of the church in Bonhoeffer, two remarks made precisely in the context of the discussion of non-religious interpretation are characteristic. Thus he says in the same breath, *WE* p. 180, Eng. p. 123: 'How do we *speak* . . . of "God" in "secular" fashion, how *are* we Christians in a "non-religious" and "secular" way . . .?' Likewise, *WE* p. 182, Eng. p. 124, the question of speaking rightly about God is followed by the remark: 'What this non-religious Christianity looks like, what form it takes, is a thing to which I am giving much thought . . .' The same order is reflected also in the Outline when under 2 (c) the interpretation of biblical concepts is to be discussed, leading on to the discussion under (d) of the problem of the cultus (*WE* p. 260, Eng. p. 179). All this must not, in my opinion, be taken in the sense of a descending order in which the problem of non-religious interpretation finds its proper location not so much in 'word' as in practical existence, and thus the question of speaking rightly is relativized, if not indeed excluded from what is here really meant by 'interpretation'. The observations in Hammelsbeck's essay (see above, p. 98 note 1) seem ultimately to tend in that direction (*op. cit.*, pp. 60 f and 198 f respectively). It is true that various remarks of Bonhoeffer's could be appealed to in support of that:—'The time when men could be told everything by means of words—whether theological or pious words —is over' (*WE* p. 178, Eng. p. 122); ' . . . but perhaps we can simply no longer "speak" of such things as we used to' (*WE* p. 180, Eng. p. 123); 'So our traditional language must lose its force and fall silent, and our Christianity today will

still have to pay careful attention here to the special importance he attached in his *Ethics* to the concept of form[1] and to the theological principles he endeavoured to inculcate in regard to deeds and action.[2] That must now be left out of account. But I cannot refrain from saying that to my mind our critical sense needs to be very wide awake if we are to put in their proper theological place the things Bonhoeffer could say with a certain degree of telling exaggeration. As indeed it is true of all Bonhoeffer's individual sayings and thoughts that the gravest mischief can be caused if we do not appropriate them in theological work of our own but repeat them as canonical. That applies also e.g. to the celebrated demand that in order to make a beginning with the business of existing for others the church must give away all its property to the poor and the ministers should live solely on the voluntary offerings of their congregations or exercise a secular calling.[3] Understandable in that particular situation! Excellent as a test of the true state of the church, even without the experiment being carried out! Certainly worth taking seriously as a prick to the church's conscience! Yet how far would it really be a beginning of the church as a church existing for others? Existing for others with its *property* and providing a sensational demonstration of that could only obscure still more deeply the fact that in its *existence*, i.e. in the proclamation which is the foundation of its own existence, it was not existing for others. It could at any rate not have the effect of bringing the church to the recognition that as a church it is so far from being anything on its own account that its existence for others is strictly not at all *its* existence for others, but solely testimony to the

[1] Esp. *E* pp. 23 ff, Eng. pp. 17 ff.
[2] *E* pp. 149 ff, Eng. pp. 166 ff; *WE* pp. 203, 250, Eng. pp. 138, 170.
[3] *WE* p. 261, Eng. p. 180.

---

be confined to two things: praying, and doing the right among men. All Christian thinking, speaking and organizing must be reborn out of that praying and that action. . . . Until then the Christian cause will be a silent and hidden one; but there will be those who pray and do the right and await God's time' (*WE* p. 207, Eng. pp. 140 f); our church 'must not underestimate the importance of human "example". . . . It is not abstract argument but concrete "example" that gives its word force and power' (*WE* p. 262, Eng. pp. 180 f). Certainly these particular remarks are to be taken very seriously. But there is surely no overlooking the fact that in the last quotation the example presupposes the church's word, and that in the preceding quotations absolutely everything presses towards the question of proclamation, the coming to expression of the Word of God. And ultimately it must not be forgotten how very strongly in all this Bonhoeffer himself felt the urge towards writing and still more towards the conversation of which he was deprived. The problem of non-religious interpretation is therefore really decisively concerned with the task of proclamation.

fact that God in Christ exists for others, yet that testimony now truly as testimony for others. That is after all for Bonhoeffer really the breath-giving, or better the completely breath-taking thing—the tremendously troubling question, 'How can Christ become the Lord also of the non-religious?'[1] That is the problem of proclamation and therewith a problem of interpretation and therewith again a problem of language and in all that an eminently theological problem.

Let us try again here, too, to get to the bottom of the matter by discussing a misunderstanding that lies to hand. That is the misunderstanding according to which we have a more or less technical question of form, and are not involved in the real essence of theology, when we come to the problem of language. I purposely do not characterize this misunderstanding, as has here and there been done to the supposed theological vindication of Bonhoeffer's honour, by saying that here there is obviously no question of some sort of 'point of contact' or 'preconception'.[2] To my mind such a defence of Bonhoeffer rests for its own part also on a misunderstanding—to say the least, on the mistaken view that the adoption of particular rules of theological language can supplant thought and argument. It is of course possible that an old and doubtless bogged-down discussion of a by no means exhausted problem had to be set in motion again from a new angle. However, let us keep to the problem itself and not to this or that label.

Bonhoeffer obviously knew that our theology, and likewise also our proclamation, is constantly faced with the problem of translation. 'In ethics, as in dogmatics, we cannot simply reproduce the terminology of the Bible. The altered problems . . . demand an altered terminology'.[3] The reproach that has to be made against the Confessing Church (and truly not it alone!), *viz.*—'A church on the defensive. No risks for others'[4]—is explained to the effect that here the great concepts of Christian theology are indeed maintained, yet their real meaning remains unexplained and remote for lack of interpretation.[5] But now, the problem of speaking pertinently, of claimability, of making claims, of feeling the cap fit, of understandability, or however we may express[6] the thing

---

[1] *WE* p. 179, Eng. pp. 122 f.
[2] *Die mündige Welt* pp. 21, 122 (=*EvTh* 15 [1955], pp. 159, 244).
[3] *E* p. 173, Eng. p. 194.   [4] *WE* p. 259, Eng. p. 179.
[5] *WE* p. 220, Eng. p. 148.
[6] There is here no call to collect statistics on Bonhoeffer's use of terms. Cf. only such expressions as 'not claimable for God' (*WE* p. 230, Eng. p. 156), or 'There seems to me no way of getting hold of such a person and bringing him to his senses' (*WE* p. 143, Eng. p. 99).

that where modern man is concerned gives rise to the search for a non-religious interpretation, is so radically conceived by Bonhoeffer that not only speaking in undeveloped, traditional dogmatic terms[1] but likewise also all the modern efforts in Christian apologetics are presented as hopeless, and even downright un-Christian efforts[2] which with modern man as he really is—and normal, healthy man at that—simply get nowhere, but at best only with a few marginal cases, with people who are at the end of their tether or with those who have been made receptive by artificial preparation.[3] In face of our failure to affect the broad masses we must not let ourselves be pacified by the information that the elect are in fact only few.[4] Rather, it is a circumstance that must lead to serious criticism of the content of our proclamation.

One thing here, apart from any possible objections, is simply true: that the criterion of the understandability of our preaching is not the believer but the non-believer. For the proclaimed word seeks to effect faith, but does not presuppose faith as a necessary preliminary. The actual situation with the church's proclamation today is, however, that for the most part the believing congregation is made the criterion of whether the preaching is understandably, and thereby faith is made a prerequisite of the hearing of the Word. This reversal of the relation of Word and faith, which comes of not letting the non-believer be the criterion of whether our proclamation is understandable, results not only in making the proclamation a foreign language,[5] but also in silen-

[1] In conjunction with the remark about revelational positivism: 'For the non-religious workman, or the non-religious man in general, nothing that makes any difference is gained by that' (*WE* p. 180, Eng. p. 123).

[2] Cf. above, p. 115 note 2. 'Un-Christian—because Christ is confused with a particular stage in the religiousness of man, i.e. with a human law' (*WE* p. 218, Eng. p. 147).

[3] The immediate reference, it is true, is to 'secularized methodism' [cf. above, p. 119 note 3], but that makes no difference in this context: 'And whom does it reach? A small number of intellectuals, of degenerates, of people who regard themselves as the most important thing in the world and hence like occupying themselves with themselves. The ordinary man who spends his everyday life at work and with his family, and of course with all kinds of other interests too, is not affected. He has neither time nor inclination for thinking about his existential despair and regarding his perhaps modest share of happiness as a "trial", a "trouble" or a "disaster" ' (*WE* p. 217, Eng. pp. 146 f). Likewise pp. 230, 179, 181, Eng. pp. 156, 122, 123. 'Never did Jesus cast any doubt on a man's health, strength or happiness in themselves, or look upon them as evil fruits' (*WE* p. 231, Eng. p. 157).

[4] *WE* pp. 259, 179, cf. also p. 230, Eng. pp. 178, 122, 156.

[5] 'Atonement and redemption, regeneration, the Holy Ghost, the love of our enemies, the cross and resurrection, life in Christ and Christian discipleship—all these things have become so problematical and so remote that we hardly dare

cing the genuine faith which must repudiate any religious talk[1] that no longer speaks to real man because it does not speak of him. Thus the peculiarly sympathetic nearness of the believer to the non-religious man, as Bonhoeffer testifies to it in his own case,[2] becomes a genuine symptom of the present state of Christianity. There is simply no question here of attempting to find missionary avenues of approach, but it is a case of being driven back to first principles,[3] of finding new, stammering words for the Word of God, of a groping rediscovery of what Christian faith really means.[4] That is what is heralded in Bonhoeffer's struggle with the question of non-religious interpretation. Non-religious interpretation is interpretation of faith.[5]

III

If I have spoken of three basic presuppositions in the light of which Bonhoeffer's approach to the problem is to be understood and to which

[1] On the difficulty of 'speaking a Christian word to others', *WE* pp. 139 f, 142 f, Eng. pp. 97 [for 'a chance' read 'the ability'], 98 f; *E* pp. 79 f, Eng. pp. 84 f. But the following distinction is then important: 'While I often shrink with religious people from speaking of God by name—because that Name somehow seems to me here not to ring true, and I strike myself as rather dishonest (it is specially bad when others start talking in religious jargon: then I dry up almost completely and feel somehow oppressed and ill at ease)—yet with non-religious people I am able on occasion to speak of God quite openly and as if it were a matter of course' (*WE* p. 181, Eng. p. 124). Cf. *WE* p. 104, Eng. p. 73, on not uttering the name of God, also *WE* p. 200, Eng. p. 136. The general remarks, too, on 'talk' (*WE* pp. 114 f, 133, 148 f, 171, Eng. pp. 80 f, 92, 103, 117) are at least indirectly connected with that.

[2] 'I often ask myself why a "Christian instinct" frequently draws me more to the non-religious than to the religious—and that, too, not with any intention of evangelizing them, but rather, I might almost say, in "brotherhood" ' (*WE* p. 181, Eng. pp. 123 f). Here we must also recall the remarks in which Bonhoeffer himself confesses to being no '*homo religiosus*' (*WE* pp. 104, 96, 248, Eng. pp. 73, 66 [for 'going to pieces' read 'turning out a "man of the inner life" '], 168) and to knowing periods when it is remarkable how little he misses going to church (*WE* p. 119, Eng. p. 83) or to passing through weeks in which he reads little in the Bible (*WE* p. 163, Eng. p. 112, but contrast passages like pp. 93, 111, 139, 247, Eng. pp. 65, 78, 96, 168). For the whole question see also the remark that already anticipates all this in the letter from the period before his arrest (25th June 1942): *Die mündige Welt*, p. 20 (=*EvTh* 15 [1955], p. 158).

[3] *WE* p. 206, Eng. p. 140.

[4] *WE* pp. 206 f, Eng. p. 140. It is no accident that Bonhoeffer feels the urge to attempt poetry—a symptom of his being drawn into the event of word and language.

[5] Namely, in the sense that the proclaimed Word is aimed solely at faith, and that the profound difference thereby becomes apparent between faith and religion.

any more to speak of them' (*WE* p. 206, Eng. p. 140). Cf. also *WE* pp. 207, 220, Eng. pp. 140 f, 148.

we ourselves must also be unreservedly subject as theologians, viz.—
that theological thinking is concerned with Jesus Christ, that the precept of intellectual honesty must be respected, and that everything
depends on the orientation towards the task of proclamation—yet it has
surely become clear that here we are dealing not with a sum of hetero-
geneous elements, but only with the unfolding of an indivisible whole.
And if I have laid so much stress on the discussion of these presuppositions that the treatment of our proper subject seems on that
account to have receded into the background, yet I do think that the
startling slogan of the non-religious interpretation of biblical concepts
can be fruitfully studied only if we neither stare at the expression in
anxiety or fascination, nor yet ask impatiently for practical advice on
the carrying out of the programme, but let ourselves be guided on to its
path—a path that is no paved road but becomes a path as we take our
own steps upon it, a path on which we in fact already find ourselves as
theologians, yet possibly wandering without sense of direction or idly
marking time. If Bonhoeffer is to help us to get started on this our own
path, and therefore under our own steam, then what will further us
much more towards that end than the answer intended in the idea of
non-religious interpretation is the inculcation of the questions that lead
to it: What *is* Christ for us today? What do we really believe? How can
Christ become the Lord also of the non-religious? When we are exercised by these questions, when it is not so much we who pursue these
questions as rather they that pursue us, when they leave us no rest, keep
our theological thinking constantly on the move and under stringent
discipline, then the best result is attained that can come from occupying
ourselves with Bonhoeffer—namely, that he makes us independent of
himself, as free theologians who are themselves completely engrossed in
their own job. We know then what our task is: not to abide by definite
findings of past interpretation, but to abide by the never-ending work of
interpreting the Gospel. And then these basic presuppositions have
always supplied us with a few essential points to be going on with as
basic rules for that interpretation: it must be Christological interpretation, concrete interpretation, and interpretation of faith. Once more let
it be recalled that these are not three different things. The interpretation
with which we are charged is either all three together, or it is neither
Christological interpretation nor concrete interpretation nor interpretation of faith.

But now, if we nevertheless go on to ask further why Bonhoeffer
coined the expression non-religious interpretation manifestly for this

and for nothing else, then to my mind that can only serve to help us to a still sharper grasp of what was said regarding the basic presuppositions, and thus prevent any aberrations to one side or the other. Is it necessary to emphasize that the expression non-religious interpretation was not coined in order to loosen the reins of theological study but to tighten them, not in order that the traditional biblical and theological concepts could be cheerfully thrown overboard but in order to regain them, not in order to succumb to a snobbish freebooter jargon but to strive for new expression of the Word of God, not in order to play off life against doctrine, action against thought, but to incorporate life really in doctrine and action really in thought,[1] not purely and simply in order to enable the non-believer to understand but in order that we ourselves, we theologians, should come to the right understanding,[2] not in order that we should now proclaim non-religious interpretation as Gospel but in order that, if it should prove appropriate, we should really proclaim the Gospel in non-religious interpretation? Bonhoeffer was right in condemning so bitterly all the clericalistic subterfuges of theologians.[3] The concept of non-religious interpretation therefore must not be expected to provide a new and still cleverer subterfuge, the trick of doing things now. On the contrary, we must take the risk of entering still uncharted and dangerous territory. And we must try to think things through with greater theological sharpness than Bonhoeffer succeeded in doing.

The concept of non-religious interpretation derives from three sources: an analysis of our historical situation today, a definite conception of what religion is, and an insight into the nature of the Gospel. These viewpoints are all bound up with each other and condition each other. But they must nevertheless as far as possible be expounded separately.

1. Our situation today is determined by the fact that the fateful process of secularization that marks the modern age has reached a certain completeness in every sphere of human life, not only in science,

---

[1] 'For you, thought and action will have a new relationship. Your thinking will be confined to your responsibility in action. With us thinking was largely the luxury of the spectator; with you it will be entirely the servant of action' (*WE* p. 203, Eng. p. 138). It is true that, particularly in prison, Bonhoeffer learned the meaning of the 'stuffiness and spuriousness of a purely intellectual existence' (*WE* p. 228, Eng. p. 155). But he of all people must not be made into one of those who despise thinking. Cf. only *WE* pp. 209 f, 222, Eng. pp. 142, 150.

[2] 'We too are being driven back to the first steps in understanding' (*WE* p. 206, Eng. p. 140).

[3] *WE* pp. 234, 236, 261, Eng. pp. 159, 160, 180.

politics, art and morals but even in the things of religion,[1] and has become for modern man the naturally accepted key-signature of his views of existence and reality. The historical analysis of this process was for Bonhoeffer an important element in his theological thinking,[2] but need not concern us now. His sketchy remarks on that subject merely refer to thoroughly well known facts, and only theologians who are out of touch with history could find them anything of a new discovery. Even the fact that a theologian should evaluate the process on the whole so positively can appear surprising[3] only to those who have lost their continuity with the history of nineteenth-century theology and now see themselves confronted by what they imagine wholly new perspectives.[4] He stands on his own, however, in his way of concentrating the whole problem on the phenomenon of religion. The tremendous extension of the boundaries of human knowledge and ability has its correlate in the fact that God is edged more and more out of the realms of the knowledge and life of a world come of age.[5] God retains a place only on the utmost periphery. For normal life he is not required, neither as 'working hypothesis' nor as *'deux ex machina'*. That process and its result have in themselves nothing to do with an actively atheistic view of things. The operation takes place by inner necessity[6] in consequence of the principle now adopted as a matter of course for dealing with all world phenomena —the purely methodical and hypothetical principle of *'etsi deus non daretur'*,[7] which has nothing whatever to do with hostility towards religion. The drawback is only that, parallel to God's being pushed out of the world of experience, religion becomes more and more a special province on the outskirts of life, linked with the marginal experiences of human existence. Indeed, by combining observance of the facts with

---

[1] *WE* p. 215, Eng. p. 145.

[2] *WE* pp. 156 f, 215 f, 237 f, 239 f, Eng. pp. 108 f, 145 f, 161, 162 f. In greater detail, *E* pp. 35-46, Eng. pp. 31-45.

[3] Bonhoeffer himself encourages this mistaken judgment by the sweeping statement; 'Catholic and Protestant historians are agreed that it is in this development that the great defection from God, from Christ, is to be discovered' (*WE* p. 216, Eng. p. 146).

[4] Any reader in whom Bonhoeffer stimulates the desire to improve his knowledge of the historical developments and to find a broader basis for the discussion of the problems involved, may be referred, apart from Dilthey and Troeltsch, especially to Emanuel Hirsch, *Geschichte der neuern evangelischen Theologie*, vols. 1-5, Gütersloh 1949-54, and Friedrich Gogarten, *Verhängis und Hoffnung der Neuzeit: Die Säkularisierung als theologisches Problem*, Stuttgart 1953. These are at present the best expositions of what Bonhoeffer had in view when speaking of historical analysis.   [5] See above, p. 115 notes 1 and 3.

[6] Bonhoeffer says: 'as in the nature of the case is inevitable' (*WE* p. 210, Eng. p. 142).   [7] *WE* pp. 240 f, Eng. pp. 162 f.

prognosis Bonhoeffer comes to the conclusion that the day of religion is past altogether. 'We are moving towards a time of no religion at all; men as they are now simply cannot be religious any more.'[1]

To this seemingly decidedly summary verdict various objections can naturally be raised. That the concentration on the West leaves out of account the role played today by the great world religions, surely means very little, in so far as Western secularism has in fact become a competitor of all religions.[2] The objection that can perhaps be raised by appealing to statistics of church membership was anticipated by Bonhoeffer already in his *Ethics* by distinguishing between open godlessness and the kind that wears religious clothing.[3] To interpret, say, communist atheism as a pseudo-religion and therefore as evidence of man's indestructible disposition towards religion does indeed contain a grain of truth, but is hardly a convincing argument against Bonhoeffer's thesis.[4]

[1] *WE* p. 178, Eng. p. 122. '. . . when we really reach the stage of being radically without religion—and I think this is more or less the case already . . .' (*WE* p. 179, Eng. p. 122).

[2] The saying of Ibn Saud quoted in *E* p. 38, Eng. p. 35—'I have had machines brought from Europe, but I want no irreligion'—is surely, though Bonhoeffer at that point overlooks the fact, a sign of being on the defensive and as such a direct confirmation of the above statement. Cf. also H. Vogel, *op. cit.*, pp. 16 f.

[3] *E* p. 42, Eng. p. 39. See also the following note.

[4] In the observations on 'Western godlessness' (*E* pp. 41 f, Eng. pp. 38 ff) three viewpoints are interlocked which Bonhoeffer himself does not, I think, clearly enough distinguish:—1. Western godlessness is itself religious in character. 'It is totally different from the atheism of certain individual Greek, Indian, Chinese and Western thinkers. It is not the theoretical denial of the existence of God. It is itself a religion, a religion of hostility to God. That is precisely what is Western about it. It cannot break loose from its past. It cannot but be religious in essence. That is precisely why to the human eye it is so hopelessly godless.' That, he says, is why we must speak e.g. of the 'religion of Bolshevism'. 2. Western godlessness largely wears a Christian mask. It 'ranges from the religion of Bolshevism to the midst of the Christian churches. In Germany especially, but also in the Anglo-Saxon countries, it is a markedly Christian godlessness.' What the anti-Christian and the Christian forms of Western godlessness have in common is the 'deification' of man. That is why hostility to the church and membership of the church provide no unequivocal criterion by which to define the phenomenon of Western godlessness. Thus far Bonhoeffer's meaning is perfectly clear. What makes his observations difficult is the arrival of still another viewpoint. 3. A distinction has to be made between a hopeless and a promising kind of godlessness. Though Bonhoeffer had at first described Western godlessness as a whole in all its manifestations, including the Bolshevistic, as hopelessly godless because it is itself religious in character, yet now there comes a peculiar change of outlook:—'Alongside the godlessness in religious and Christian clothing, which we have called a hopeless godlessness, there is also a godlessness which is full of promise, a godlessness which speaks against religion and against the church. It is the protest against pious godlessness in so far as this has corrupted the churches, and thus in a certain sense, if only negatively, it defends

In one thing at any rate Bonhoeffer is decidedly right: where the phenomenon of religion is concerned, we are now in a totally new situation
compared with the whole of history. What is usually designated by the

the heritage of a genuine faith in God and of a genuine church. . . . This promising godlessness is, like the hopeless godlessness, a specifically Western phenomenon.' Thus some confusion now appears to arise as a result of the fact that
here only the godlessness in Christian clothing is described as hopeless, whereas
the godlessness that speaks in anti-religious and anti-Christian terms is supposed
to be promising. This turn to the train of thought has manifestly not been
sufficiently thought through. For what is the relation of the verdict on Western
godlessness as a whole as 'religious in essence', and in particular on Bolshevism
as a religion, to the assertion of a kind of Western godlessness which is now not
'religious in essence' after all and therefore in its anti-religious and anti-church
utterances (which surely includes Bolshevism!) is supposed to be promising?
   To straighten it out we should surely have to say:—1. It is plainly Bonhoeffer's
intention that what he says about promising godlessness should not cancel his
statement about Bolshevism as a religion and thus as a manifestation of hopeless
godlessness, but should certainly modify it. 2. For that reason a distinction must
be made where, say, Bolshevism is concerned, between the fact of the open
protest against religion and the church so far as it really *is* a protest against pious
godlessness, and the fact of the protest that is not radically maintained even here
because it has itself turned into religion again. 3. This differentiation, and therewith the co-existence of 'promising' and 'hopeless', can naturally only be grasped
from the standpoint of Christian faith properly understood, which can only be
served by the open protest against pious godlessness whereas the godlessness in
religious and Christian clothing can only endanger it. 4. But now, however, the
question arises whether, although to a certain extent it is right to characterize
Western godlessness as 'religious in essence' and therefore also Bolshevism as a
religion, we do not in so doing all too easily close our minds to the necessary
protest against pious godlessness by taking the religious character of, say, Bolshevism and exploiting it either apologetically to the advantage of religion in
general or polemically against the genuine protest which (even if not rightly
understood by Bolshevism itself) is voiced in it. Is there not a danger of obliter-
ating the contours, if we all too confidently and unequivocally interpret as
'religious' a phenomenon which explicitly wishes not to be so? 5. At this point
Bonhoeffer seems to me in the Tegel letters to go a step beyond the observations
in his *Ethics*, by confining the concept of religion to manifestations of it which
expressly describe themselves as such and distinguishing from these the phenomenon of modern non-religiousness—so that Western godlessness, so far as its
explicit intention is not to be religious, is not interpreted as 'religious' either.
That certainly does not deny us a certain right to such interpretation—as indeed
it is repeatedly forced on us on this very question of Bolshevism and its structural
kinship with religion—yet even then we should have to stick all the same to the
designation pseudo-religion in order to avoid an arbitrary confusion of terms.
6. In the Tegel letters, of course, when Bonhoeffer speaks of the non-religious
man he is not thinking at all of an explicitly anti-religious type like Bolshevism,
even if that is not *a priori* excluded from his mind. What he has in view is rather
modern man as such, as represented e.g. by the 'non-religious working man'
(*WE* p. 180, Eng. p. 123), but perhaps much more sharply by the type of well-
educated, aristocratic middle class, conscious of its public responsibilities and
well grounded in tradition—in other words, the class from which Bonhoeffer

caption 'secularism' is a novelty without parallel. Opinions on the present situation and the future may differ substantially in detail from Bonhoeffer's, but there can be no altering that exciting fact. But in addition to that we must surely grant that in principle Bonhoeffer's judgment is independent of statistics and prognosis. For ultimately, however surprising it sounds, the numerical relation between the religious and the non-religious is a matter of indifference for the point he is concerned to make. As a result of the change in the intellectual situation as a whole, the religious are now so to speak only partially religious—to be precise, in the religious province of their being, whereas for the rest over broad stretches of their life their existence is in fact as non-religious as any.[1] Even where religion is passionately clung to, it has nevertheless been revealed as a thing that in itself is highly problematical because it does not concern the whole of life. Hence in fact for Bonhoeffer, too, when we look closely, it is not the rise of a radical

---

[1] Cf. *WE* pp. 216, 230, 233 f, 236, Eng. pp. 146, 156, 158 f, 160, and see above p. 118 note 2. So-called 'purely religious' preaching is marked by the fact that it separates the Gospel from man's secular existence (*E* p. 247, Eng. p. 283). 'Pietism as the last attempt to maintain evangelical Christianity as a religion' (*WE* p. 258, Eng. p. 178) is surely a direct confirmation of the thinking in terms of two spheres which (in the modern age at any rate) is characteristic of religion. The remark on the subject of revelational positivism that 'the place of religion is now taken by the church' (*WE* p. 185, Eng. p. 126), in itself says something biblically correct, yet in the context in which it stands it is really meant as a criticism: by speaking, as revelational positivism does, of 'church' instead of 'religion', we gain nothing at all if the world is thereby made to depend on itself and left to its own devices. 'That is all wrong' (*WE* p. 185, Eng. p. 126). Cf. finally, 'Even those who honestly describe themselves as "religious", do not in the least act up to it, and so when they say "religious" they evidently mean something quite different' (*WE* p. 178, Eng. p. 122).

---

himself came. We must surely think of certain impressive figures from the resistance movement group—or let us say more generally, of the non-religious man in his noblest and most genuine representatives—if we are to understand what Bonhoeffer meant. 7. Only then shall we grasp why Bonhoeffer attacks both a 'moralizing' and traditional interpretation of 'idolatry' and also a moralizing condemnation of the phenomenon of godlessness. 'The usual exposition of idolatry as applied to "riches, wellbeing and honour" seems to me not at all biblical. That is a bit of moralizing. Idols are objects of worship, and idolatry implies that people still do worship something. We, however, worship nothing at all any more, not even idols. Therein we are truly nihilists' (*WE* p. 225, Eng. p. 153). 'The world that has come of age is more godless, and for that reason perhaps *nearer* to God, than the world as a minor was' (*WE* p. 246, Eng. p. 167). 'To that extent we may say that the process we have described by which the world came of age was the abandonment of a false conception of God and the clearing of the decks for the God of the Bible . . .' (*WE* p. 242, Eng. p. 164). This is a dimension of Bonhoeffer's thought into which H. Vogel's impressive work mentioned above (p. 98 note 1) unfortunately does not penetrate.

non-religiousness but—to be sure in the light of that—the phenomenon of religion today that is the real problem.

2. What does Bonhoeffer really mean by religion? Here we come upon a peculiar difficulty. On the one hand he sets the phenomenon of modern non-religiousness—rightly, as we have seen—over against the whole of preceding history. On the other hand he works with a concept of religion that in essence takes its bearings from the modern view of religion. Bonhoeffer repeatedly mentions two components as the marks of religion: metaphysical interest, and inwardness.[1] If it is already questionable whether the concept of the metaphysical can suitably be taken as a general mark of religion and not rather only of a particular form of religion, then it is certainly beyond doubt that it was not till modern times that inwardness or, as Bonhoeffer can also say, the note of individualism,[2] if it did not indeed appear as a mark of religion for the very first time, at least did for the first time acquire *the* significance Bonhoeffer attaches to it, whereas in particular religions it is entirely missing. Carefully thinking through this point as Bonhoeffer conceives it would naturally mean exposing ourselves to all the difficulties of defining the concept of religion.[3] It might at first sight appear hopeless to concern ourselves further with the concept of a non-religious interpretation so long as no complete clarity prevails regarding the underlying concept of religion. Does Bonhoeffer's concept of religion not in fact coincide only with the modern view of religion? But how can he then make it the basis of such general statements as that we are at the end of the age of religion altogether? However, I think that despite the unquestionable difficulties which here arise and which therefore also make the concept 'non-religious interpretation' an easily vulnerable formula, we are not really

[1] *WE* pp. 180, 183, Eng. pp. 123, 125. The remarks about a false understanding of transcendence as defined from the standpoint of theoretical epistemology serve to clarify what he means by 'metaphysical': *WE* pp. 182, 184, 210 f, 255, 259, Eng. pp. 124, 126, 142 f, 175, 179. It is on the concept 'inwardness' and the criticism of it that the stronger accent lies: *WE* pp. 178, 233 f, 236, Eng. pp. 122, 158 f, 160. Synonymous with it is 'heart', *WE* pp. 194, 218, Eng. pp. 132, 147 (contrast the statement on p. 236, Eng. p. 160 on the meaning of 'heart' in biblical language) or even 'conscience', *WE* p. 178, Eng. p. 122 (on this concept see also *WE* pp. 11 ff, Eng. pp. 14 f; *E* pp. 12 f, 134 ff, 188 ff, Eng. pp. 5, 148 ff, 211 ff. It is a sore defect that Bonhoeffer did not go further towards the attainment of a proper theological concept of conscience, as to my mind can and must be done on the basis of Luther's concept *conscientia*. On this point cf. now especially E. Hirsch, *Lutherstudien* vol. 1, Gütersloh 1954.)

[2] *WE* p. 183, Eng. p. 125.

[3] I can here only pose the problem, which would require to be discussed on a very broad basis. We urgently need a thorough examination of the concept of religion in the nineteenth and twentieth centuries.

in a cul-de-sac. Bonhoeffer was surely right in feeling that compared with the history of religion as a whole, the modern age is of peculiar significance in so far as its view of religion is steering towards the breakdown of religion altogether in the accepted sense and whatever may come after that at all events cannot be the refurbishing of an earlier view of religion. For that reason the modern concept of religion does in fact acquire genuine critical significance for the understanding of the phenomenon of religion in general so far as we are capable of saying anything about that from historical experience. The modern concept of religion brings to light so to speak *a posteriori* what was implied all along in religion in general, but hidden. The law of the irreversibility of the course of history will have to be taken seriously also in the case of the history of religion. If in the intellectual upheaval of modern times an absolutely unique change has taken place in men's view of themselves, as we must judge it has, then that most strongly affects the history of religion, too, and it more especially. As far as the phenomenon of religion is concerned we are on the way to something absolutely unknown. Being more cautious than Bonhoeffer, we shall not be able simply to forecast an entirely non-religious age. We shall nevertheless have to grant a certain justification to that forecast in so far as it brings out more sharply than would otherwise be possible the fact that not merely what we understand today by religion but also what in earlier times existed as religion is moving to its end—an end of which we can as yet form no more idea of what it will really be like than we can of what will follow it.

3. There can be no denying the fact that the discussion of Bonhoeffer's concept of religion on the historical and phenomenological level is certainly inescapable, and yet still leaves untouched the factor that really determines his use of the concept religion. The decisive thing is rather his theological view of the fundamental antithesis between Christian faith and all religion. What does that mean? This antithesis between the Christian faith and all religion has of course by and large always been asserted in the sense that Christianity as the *vera religio* has been opposed to all other religions as *religiones falsae*. We may set aside here the question as to how far any weight attaches to the fact that in so doing the concept of religion is nevertheless applied to both sides. At all events it was not till modern times that the concept of religion came to be of such systematic importance as a general concept that Christianity was first of all viewed in principle on one and the same level with the other religions, and the question was then only afterwards raised whether its superiority to all other religions is one of degree or is absolute. Compared

with that it was certainly a new departure when Barth in his *Romans* went beyond the traditional orthodox terminology and viewed the antithesis between Christian faith and religion as a fundamental one: Christian faith is not religion but the fundamental opposite of religion. To be sure, the new thing here was ultimately only on the terminological side. For Luther had already seen as essentially fundamental—and that means not merely based on a formal claim to revelation but displaying an essential difference of structure—the antithesis between Christian faith and all religions, in so far as the latter in spite of all the differences between them have without exception the structure of law, whereas faith in Christ is faith in the Gospel.[1] The antithesis here is in the nature of the case a radical one, for *lex est negatio Christi.*[2] Bonhoeffer, who took over from Barth the fundamental view of the antithesis, now went a bold step beyond Barth by taking the antithesis with its so far purely dogmatic foundation and applying it to the actual historical situation in which Christianity finds itself today in relation to religion and non-religiousness. This bold step was a simple necessity if Barth's starting-point was taken seriously. It was necessary to make practical proof of it, so to speak, in face of history. The result was as follows:

There is an unmistakable link between the Christian faith and modern non-religious man. A double one in fact. First, a genetic one: the Christian faith has a causative share in the modern process of secularization. And that, too, not merely in the sense of a fault on the church's part—though there is also something to be said of that[3]—but also in the sense that the radical secularization in question was possible only on Christian ground[4] and that, despite all the restrictions and reservations that would here have to be made, it is the working out in history of what the Christian faith itself implies for our relation to the world, *viz.*—the denial of the world's divinity. Secondly—and the above is in fact already

---

[1] E.g.: *Idolatria omnis religio, et quo preciosior, spiritualior, hoc pestilentior, quae avertit oculos a fide in Christum et in sua. . . . Extra Christum omnes religiones sunt idola* (*WA* 40/2, pp. 110.6-111.1). *Non est differentia inter Iudaeum, Papistam, Turcam. Diversi quidem ritus, sed idem cor et cogitationes . . . quia sic: si sic fecero, erit mihi deus clemens. Eadem passio omnium hominum in aminis, non media via inter cognitionem Christi et operationem humanam. Postea nihil refert, sive sit Papista, Turca, Iudeus, una fides ut altera. Ideo maxime stulti, quod invicem digladiantur propter religionem* (*WA* 40/1, pp. 603.8-604.3). *Amissa hac doctrina et articulo* (namely, the distinction of *iustitia activa* and *passiva*) *amisimus omnia. Sine eo qui est, est Turca, papista vel Iudeus et nihil aliud potest docere quam opera, quia aut iusticia legis aut gratiae est* (*WA* 40/1, p. 48.10-12).

[2] *WA* 40/2, p. 18.4.

[3] *E* pp. 49 ff, Eng. pp. 48 ff; *WE* p. 206, Eng. p. 140.

[4] *E* pp. 36, 38, Eng. pp. 32 f, 35.

an indication of this—there is also a material link. A paradoxical conformity exists between the Christian faith and radically secularized man. Bonhoeffer uses the relation to religion to make that clear: ' "Religious interpretation" . . . means . . . speaking metaphysically on the one hand and individualistically on the other. Neither of these is relevant to the Bible message or to the man of today.'[1] That obviously does not mean: Modern man is non-religious; the Christian faith is not religion; hence modern man is a Christian. That syllogism is of course a mockery even of the rules of logic. But what in fact certainly *is* meant is: the Bible message is not merely patient of non-religious interpretation, but for its own part ultimately demands it. Only such interpretation is really relevant to it. And therefore the vis-à-vis of Bible message and modern man is ultimately not hopeless but in certain respects most promising. For to be religious is not a prerequisite of understanding the Bible message.

But now, there also exists, as becomes more overwhelmingly plain than ever in the face of history, a link between Christian faith and religion—a link so close that for anyone familiar with history the fundamental distinction between the Christian faith and religion becomes wholly problematical. Bonhoeffer is naturally aware of that. Christianity, he says, has always been a form of religion or, as he can also put it the other way round, religion has always been a garment of Christianity, and a changing garment at that.[2] But can Christianity as a form of religion be severed from it, or religion as a garment be separated from Christianity? The terms employed certainly do leave the possibility logically open, so that the idea of a 'non-religious Christianity' is theoretically conceivable.[3] But are these terms 'form' and 'garment' appropriate? Even from a purely terminological viewpoint they are disastrous historiographical terms. But what of the material point of view? If Christianity and religion are to be distinguishable *realiter*—and in the last resort that means separable from each other—then, according at least to Bonhoeffer, only in the event of religion as such ceasing to exist. As long as religion were still a genuine potentiality of human nature, there would exist also the symbiosis of Christianity and religion which is the one and only thing historically known to us. If, however, that presupposition ceased to obtain, then and only then would the separation come to a head. Here two questions arise:—

[1] *WE* pp. 183 f, Eng. p. 125.
[2] *WE* pp. 178, 179, Eng. pp. 122 (for 'pattern' read 'garment'), 123.
[3] *WE* pp. 179, 182, Eng. pp. 123, 124.

First: what would religion be, if it could cease to be a genuine potentiality of human nature? Bonhoeffer thinks it would now be plain that religion 'was a historically conditioned and temporary form of human self-expression'. There would thus be no such thing as a religious disposition essentially belonging to human nature, a so-called 'religious *a priori*'.[1] If we accept that for the moment, then we must still perforce go on to ask: what, then, was the existentialist[2] condition that made religion possible as a passing and temporary historical form of human self-expression? What was it that sought 'expression' in the 'form' of religion, and in what 'form' does it find 'expression' when religion has disappeared? The purely negative term 'non-religiousness' is manifestly insufficient the moment we are faced, as is inevitable, by the problem of providing an existentialist interpretation of religion *and* non-religiousness, i.e. by the question of the relation both bear to man's human nature. For if, as Bonhoeffer holds, religion is a historically conditioned, passing form of human self-expression, then at its passing it surely does not leave simply nothing, but gives place to something else which, although negatively characterized as non-religiousness, must be understood in a positive sense as something which has this at least in common with religion: that it is a 'form of self-expression' on man's part which takes the place of religion and is therefore characteristic of man in the same way as religion hitherto was. It would thus be necessary to enquire into the common basis of religion and non-religiousness—to ask in what, for all their difference, they are identical. And it is with this element common to both, with the basis in which both are grounded—and not primarily with religion or non-religiousness—that Christianity has obviously really to do if it has hitherto worn the garment of religion[3] but now exchanges it for the garment of non-religiousness. That at least is surely how we should have to express it, unless we wish to foist on Bonhoeffer the opinion that non-religiousness as such is identical with Christianity, and permit ourselves to turn his statement that 'the Western brand of Christianity' is to be regarded 'merely as the prelude to a complete non-religiousness'[4] into the travesty that the Western brand of (hitherto religiously veiled) Christianity is merely the prelude to a complete non-religiousness (and therewith to a true, unveiled Christianity). To develop his train of thought in this way is to begin to

[1] *WE* pp. 178 f, Eng. p. 122.
[2] Cf. my note below, p. 331 note 1.—*Translator.*
[3] 'And even that garment has had very different aspects at different periods' (*WE* p. 179, Eng. p. 123).
[4] *WE* p. 179, Eng. p. 122.

realize how great are the terminological and material difficulties that encumber Bonhoeffer's exposition here. The problem of the 'religious *a priori*' will have to be very thoroughly thought through once again before we accept his assertion that it simply does not exist.[1] Yet we must not on any account allow such scruples to prevent our noticing two facts, *viz.*—that the rise of what Bonhoeffer calls 'non-religiousness' is after all something very different from a mere modification of religion (at least in its accepted sense), and second, that the task of taking stock of its own position which is imposed on Christianity by the change in question is, surprisingly enough, really nothing else but what a clear idea of the nature of the Gospel itself demands.

That brings us to the second question: How indeed was it possible for Christianity to exist so long 'in a religious form', if at bottom it has really no concern with religion? When Bonhoeffer says that religious interpretation ultimately by-passes the Bible message and is not in conformity with it—then had the Bible message been missing in the history of Christianity till now? And what of the Bible message itself? Does it, too, not wear the garment of religion? Of course, the fact of the matter could be that the actual symbiosis of Christian faith and religion had always the structure of a relationship of tension, but that the tension was mostly unnoticed and the Christian faith was almost swamped by religion and it was only at a few points—say for example in Paul, or in Luther—that the critical relation of the Christian faith to religion came sharply into theological focus. If we begin by assuming for the moment that this understanding of the Christian faith really fits the Bible message, then a proper interpretation of the New Testament would be concerned to bring to light this critical relation between Christian faith and religion, and also to maintain it for the sake of a sound understanding of the Gospel. If that is what Bonhoeffer means by non-religious interpretation—and to my mind there can be no doubt about it—then

---

[1] The readiness to agree with Bonhoeffer's criticism of the 'religious *a priori*' will in general be considerable today because of its connexion with the problem of natural theology. But apart from the terminological problems involved in the expression, originally coined by Troeltsch, it is surely one thing how a religious disposition on man's part that is accepted without question is assessed from the theological point of view, and quite another thing whether the very existence of such a religious disposition is contested. To suppose that in the latter case the problem of natural theology is then really radically eliminated, is to short-circuit the argument. Rather, it merely arises here in an entirely untraditional form. If we follow Bonhoeffer's theological train of thought, then I believe the very problem which in the accepted view is marked by the certainly most unfortunate designation 'natural theology' will still cross our path in a different way.

it does in fact bring him into close proximity to Bultmann. He himself also knew that perfectly well.[1] If in the few remarks we have on the subject the preponderant note is nevertheless one of criticism and contradistinction, then the following points must here be noted: first, Bonhoeffer's reproach that Bultmann succumbs to the typical liberal reduction process fails to recognize Bultmann's express intention[2]; secondly, Bonhoeffer himself in the course of his non-religious interpretation sees the mythological as conformate with the religious, so that non-religious interpretation in itself means the liberation of the Bible message from the so easily incurred mythological misunderstanding[3];

---

[1] 'Bultmann would seem to have somehow sensed Barth's limits' (*WE* p. 220, Eng. p. 149).

[2] *WE* pp. 183, 220 f, Eng. pp. 125, 149. Compare the following:—Bonhoeffer: 'Bultmann . . . succumbs . . . to the typical liberal reduction process (the "mythological" elements of Christianity are *subtracted* and Christianity is reduced to its "essence"). I am of the opinion, however, that the full content, including the "mythological" concepts, must be maintained . . . but that these concepts must now be *interpreted* in such a way as not to make religion a precondition of faith.' Bultmann: 'If we can say roughly that in the age of critical research the New Testament mythology was simply critically *eliminated*, then the task today— likewise roughly speaking—would be to provide a critical *interpretation* of the New Testament mythology.' Also the definition of his method as against that of liberal theology and of the religious-historical school (*Kerygma and Myth* I, pp. 13 ff). Whether, contrary to his intention, Bultmann's exegesis does in fact succumb to the danger of reduction, is another question, which must not be allowed to deter us from stating the simple fact that Bonhoeffer in the passage quoted has falsely described Bultmann's position. For the rest, it would then still have to be noted that alongside the 'liberal reduction' there exists also a reduction that is theologically legitimate (in the sense of the Reformers' concentration!). An example of reduction of this latter kind is of course the theology of Bonhoeffer himself.

[3] Cf. the section on the Bible message in relation to the redemption myths, *WE* pp. 225-7, Eng. pp. 153-4. Bonhoeffer considers the designation of Christianity as a religion of redemption 'a cardinal error, which divorces Christ from the Old Testament and interprets him in the light of the redemption myths'. 'The redemption myths deny history in the interests of an eternity after death.' 'The difference between the Christian hope of resurrection and a mythological hope is, that the Christian hope points a man to his life on this earth in a wholly new way which is even more sharply defined than it is in the Old Testament. The Christian, unlike the devotees of the redemption myths, does not still have a last refuge in the eternal from his earthly tasks and difficulties. . . . This world must not be prematurely written off. . . . Redemption myths arise from human experiences of the boundary situation. Christ, however, takes hold of a man in the centre of his life.' In all this Bonhoeffer is surely describing nothing else but the antithesis of Christian faith and religion. Compare with that e.g. Bultmann's description (and rejection!) of the concept of religion by which the religious-historical school is guided in its interpretation of the New Testament: 'Religion is man's yearning for something beyond the world, is the discovery of a sphere above the world in which only the soul can live, detaching itself from worldly

and finally, Bonhoeffer is convinced that he takes a decisive step beyond Bultmann, and only then acts really as a theologian, when he finds not only mythological ideas and concepts problematical, but religious concepts altogether, and therefore sees the decisive task precisely in the interpretation of concepts that are not indeed (or as little as makes no difference) in danger of being mythologically, but certainly of being religiously understood.[1] We do not require to discuss here what relation

[1] *WE* p. 183, Eng. p. 125. It is of course a question whether something of what Bonhoeffer has in mind does not take place in Bultmann's interpretation of concepts in his *Theology of the New Testament*. But even apart from that, R. Grunow's verdict (*Die mündige Welt*, p. 66 = *EvTh* 15 [1955], p. 204) that with Bonhoeffer's demand for non-religious interpretation 'Bultmann's demand for demythologizing is surpassed, in fact . . . even becomes out of date' seems to me to make somewhat overhasty use of Bonhoeffer's remark that Bultmann has 'not gone "too far" . . . but not far enough' (*WE* p. 183, Eng. p. 125).

---

things. In religion man is alone with God, fraught through by the powers of a higher world of truth. And religion shows itself not in the shaping of the life of the world but in the aimless action of the cultus' (*Kerygma and Myth* I, p. 14). But do we not have a striking contrast between Bonhoeffer and Bultmann when Bultmann designates as 'mythological' the way of thinking 'in which the unearthly and divine is viewed as earthly and human, the things of the Beyond as things of this world' (*op. cit.*, p. 10), whereas Bonhoeffer would say that the characteristically mythological outlook is precisely that of prematurely writing off the things of this world and escaping into the Beyond? And more so than ever, when Bultmann's concept of 'desecularizing' is set alongside Bonhoeffer's concept of 'secular interpretation' and the 'deep this-worldliness of Christianity'? We must not let ourselves be confused here by apparent antitheses, on the ground of the similar-sounding terms employed. In the one case it is a question of the mythological way of thinking (hence in Bultmann, the things of the Beyond as things of this world), in the other case of the mythological understanding of ourselves (hence in Bonhoeffer, escape from the things of this world into the Beyond). In the one case it is a question of marking the eschatological dimension (hence in Bultmann, desecularizing—which, however, must be clearly distinguished from desecularizing in the sense of a mystic idea of religion!), in the other case of safeguarding the eschatological as eschatological (hence in Bonhoeffer, the things of this world—and that means the 'penultimate things'—must for the very sake of the 'last things' not be prematurely written off, cf. *E* pp. 79 ff, Eng. pp. 84 ff). Thus we must not be surprised when e.g. on the very question of the concept of the 'Beyond' the agreement between them becomes clear, in that Bultmann calls it mythological to think of God's beyond-ness as spatial distance (*op. cit.*, p. 10) and Bonhoeffer says: 'The Beyond is not infinitely remote, but close at hand' (*WE* p. 255, Eng. p. 175), and, 'The "Beyond" of God is not the beyond of our perceptive faculties! The transcendence of epistemological theory has nothing to do with the transcendence of God. God is the "beyond" in the midst of our life' (*WE* p. 182, Eng. p. 124). Even a remark that seems so radically contrary to Bultmann as, 'This mythology (resurrection, etc.) is the thing itself!' (*WE* p. 221, Eng. p. 149), appears in a different light when taken along with all we have said—that Bonhoeffer (like Bultmann!) refuses to eliminate, but certainly does demand interpretation, and that, too, an this last point in actual fact bears to Bultmann's theological approach. But it is necessary to ask in conclusion in what way the expression non-religious interpretation, encumbered as it is by all the above problems attaching to the concept religion, can be given more precise theological definition.

IV

Is there a theological category which makes it possible for the problem of religion in its theological relevance, i.e. in its relation to the Christian faith, to be grasped and thought through in such a way as to bring to full clarity the insight into the nature of the Gospel which is at work in Bonhoeffer's conception? What theological category—and that surely means, what category based on and determined by the Gospel itself—is suited to define the place of religion and non-religiousness in theology? Bonhoeffer sensed with a sure instinct the category that was necessary, but then unfortunately did not make thoroughgoing use of it after all. He says: 'The Pauline question whether circumcision is a condition of justification is today, to my mind, the question whether religion is the condition of salvation. Freedom from circumcision is at the same time freedom from religion.'[1] Accordingly, the non-religious interpretation of biblical concepts means, 'that these concepts must now be interpreted in such a way as not to make religion a precondition of faith (cf. circumcision in Paul!)'.[2] Here, I think, lies the decisive starting-point from which to reach a comprehensive theological solution of the problem of non-religious interpretation. The analogy with circumcision points to the law. The problem of religion (and with it of course also the phenomenon of non-religiousness!) falls under the theological category of the law. The relation of religion and Christian faith has to be thought through in the light of the relation of law and Gospel. That note is occasionally struck also elsewhere in Bonhoeffer—e.g. when he says that to confuse Christ with a particular stage in the religiousness of man would be to confuse him with a human law,[3] or that the thinking in terms of two spheres which is typical of religion is—theologically speaking—

[1] *WE* pp. 180 f, Eng. p. 123.
[2] *WE* p. 221, Eng. p. 149.
[3] *WE* p. 218, Eng. p. 147.

interpretation that is non-mythological (in the sense of the redemption myths!).
It is not by any means my intention that these marginal comments should simply equate Bonhoeffer with Bultmann. There would be a great deal to be said of the real differences. But we ought to take the trouble to determine them at the correct place.

legalistic thinking.[1] Let it be carefully noted that the introduction of the concept law naturally does not imply the identification of religion and law. The parallel with circumcision is already a warning against that; for circumcision is of course not identical with the law as such. An identification of religion and law would rest, moreover, on the mistaken idea that non-religiousness is lawlessness, which of course is not at all what Bonhoeffer means. The introduction of the concept law implies rather that the phenomenon of religion (and likewise that of non-religiousness!) has its place in theology within the problem of the law—so much so, indeed, that on the basis of the concept religion the correct distinction of law and Gospel is quite out of the question, and thus the domination of the concept religion in theology can only lead to falsely turning the Gospel into law.

The path which that indicates for theological thought and the judgment it implies could be anticipated in summary form by saying:— Religious interpretation is legalistic interpretation. Non-religious interpretation means interpretation that distinguishes law and Gospel. And looking back to what we worked out in section II, we should now have to say: legalistic interpretation can neither be Christological interpretation nor concrete interpretation nor interpretation of faith, but destroys all these things together, however much it allegedly speaks Christologically, or concretely or in faith. On the contrary: only the interpretation that distinguishes law and Gospel is at one and the same time and without possibility of separation Christological interpretation, concrete interpretation and interpretation of faith.

To show the basis of this approach and to develop it in detail is a task we cannot come anywhere near to mastering within the scope of this paper. For of course it is not as if the doctrine of law and Gospel provided a ready-made framework which can be taken for granted and into which the problem raised by Bonhoeffer has only to be fitted in order thereby to find an immediate solution (and therewith certainly also to lose its revolutionary power!). The task is rather to think through the doctrine of law and Gospel anew in the light of this way of formulating the problem, to bring it back again from the sphere of the history of theology into the sphere of systematic theological thinking and thereby at the same time to make it no longer a separate theological *locus* but the essence of our doctrine of the fundamental principles of theology. To

---

[1] *E* p. 64, Eng. p. 66. Cf. also *E* p. 247, Eng. p. 283: 'The false antithesis of moralizing and religious themes must be replaced by the true distinction and connexion between the law and the Gospel.'

put a point on it: the doctrine of law and Gospel is not a sort of master key to the problem of non-religious interpretation, but the problem of non-religious interpretation could well lead to a new opening up of the doctrine of law and Gospel. That, however, is a very vast task, in which the whole doctrine of the Word of God would have to be discussed in strict relation to reality, whereby it would then not be possible to evade the intermingling of the theological and ontological problems, i.e. the question of the connexion between being, word and language.

Instead of that, I must confine myself to a few remarks that may serve, at least by way of indication, to make clear that Bonhoeffer's approach does in fact tend in this direction, and the way in which it does so:—

1. The analogy between the problem of religion and the problem of circumcision would be misunderstood at once if we overlooked the fact that Paul only uses the question of circumcision to illustrate what is true of the relation of law and Gospel in general. If the Pauline χωρὶς νόμου were understood solely of the ceremonial law and not of the whole law, then his doctrine of justification would merely amount to an alteration of the law, and the Gospel would then be nothing else but a *nova lex*. That circumcision is not a condition of justification, is merely the concrete application to the Jews of the fact that the law as such is not a condition of justification. The mere absence of circumcision, or abrogation of the ceremonial law, is not yet by any means freedom from circumcision in the strict sense. For freedom from circumcision is not radically understood until it is taken as freedom from the law altogether: 'that a man is justified by faith without the deeds of the law' (Rom. 3.28). Correspondingly, to be non-religious would still be far from meaning in the strict sense freedom from religion. For freedom from religion would likewise not be understood radically until it is taken as freedom from the law altogether. The truth therefore is: 'circumcision is nothing and uncircumcision is nothing' (I Cor. 7.19), religion is nothing and non-religiousness is nothing! But now, the freedom from the law which in Christ is bestowed on faith requires an interpretation which involves two main considerations in regard to the law.

Firstly, the preaching of the Gospel necessarily and abidingly includes preaching of the law—and that, too, for the sake of a right understanding of the Gospel. Without the preaching of the law, the Gospel cannot be preached as Gospel at all. That Christ is the fulfilment, and therefore the end, of the law, can only be testified by giving expression to the law. If we seek to preach the Gospel without preaching the law, then by this very fact we make the Gospel into a law, and therewith at the same time falsify the law by making the Gospel into a special religious law which has nothing to do with the reality that concerns man as man, but alienates man from reality in order to make him a Christian. It depends therefore on the preaching of the law whether the Gospel is preached in ways that are concrete, understandable and binding, and in all that truly as Gospel, i.e. redeeming and liberating. We can also say: the reason why the preaching of the law belongs to the preaching of the Gospel for the sake of the preaching of the Gospel is, that the preaching of the Gospel is concerned with man as he really is. Thus we must not say: although we have really only to preach the Gospel, nevertheless the law must unfortunately also be preached alongside of it. That would amount to saying: although we have to preach the Gospel, we must nevertheless unfortunately also speak of the concrete reality of the man with whom the Gospel is concerned. If that were so, then the Gospel would be a kind of fairy-tale whose validity is more purely expressed the more it causes us to forget our real existence. Rather we must say: because we have to preach the Gospel, we must for that very reason speak of man in his concrete reality. And correspondingly: because we have to preach the Gospel, we must preach the law. The preaching of the law does not curtail the preaching of the Gospel, but serves, rightly understood, towards making the preaching of the Gospel really preaching of the Gospel. Without the preaching of the law, the preaching of the Gospel would cease to be preaching of the Gospel.

Secondly, Christian proclamation differs, however, from other 'proclamation' in religions, world views, etc., not only in its being preaching of the Gospel, but also in the way in which it preaches the law, *viz.*—in preaching it for the sake of the Gospel. The preaching of the Gospel is not added on to a preaching of the law that preceded it and was untouched by it, but the preaching of the law is itself altered from the standpoint of the preaching of the Gospel. In order to guard that statement against misunderstanding, let me add at once by way of explanation: the Christian message does not preach a different law, but it preaches the law differently. 'Differently', that is, in testifying to what only the Gospel allows us to testify, *viz.*—to what the law can do and what it cannot do, and that means to the fact that the *lex* is *non necessaria*, indeed *impossibilis ad iustificationem*.[1]

But now, would it not likewise have to be said that the Christian message preaches also a different law? Must we not notice alongside the freedom from law altogether which the Gospel promises to faith, that is

---

[1] This familiar expression of Luther's requires no special documentation.

alongside the abrogation of the law that has taken place in Christ as the fulfilment and end of the law, also the fact of a partial abrogation of the law, and one that is by no means valid only for faith, i.e. an abrogation that applies only to definite parts of the law (e.g. to the Old Testament ceremonial law) and thus in fact amounts in the end to an alteration of the law? If this manifest fact is to be rightly understood, however, then we have to bear in mind a distinction which I can here only lay down without expounding it further. A distinction has to be made between the law as always already existent and the preaching of the law—in other words, between the law in the light of the fact that it belongs inseparably to my existence, and is in fact my very reality,[1] and the law in the light of the fact that a specific exposition of it is taught. The only reason why the law can be preached to man at all is, that the law is always present to man in the first place, that man would not be man at all were he not subject to the existence of the law. In view of that, the concept of a *nova lex* is, strictly speaking, self-contradictory. We could speak at best of a *renovatio legis*.[2] Thus even in regard to the preaching of the law which is perforce included in the Christian message for the sake of the preaching of the Gospel, we cannot speak of a *doctrina novae legis*, but only of a *nova doctrina legis*. From that standpoint the above-mentioned partial abrogation of the law would have to be interpreted as a coming into force of the *lex ipsa*. The Gospel here becomes the criterion of the abrogation, in so far as the qualification which the Gospel imparts to the preaching of the law (*viz.*—that the law is *impossibilis ad iustificationem*) enforces one part of the accepted *doctrina legis* even more strongly than ever, whereas it means the complete abolition of another part. And indeed, inasmuch as the law is preached for the sake of the Gospel, the part of the accepted *doctrina legis* that is completely abolished is the part

---

[1] Cf. Luther's concept of the law. For example: '*Prior pars doctrinae* (namely, the preaching of the law) *ostendit illas res, quae iam existunt in natura humana*' (*WA* 39/1, p. 361.29 f). Against the phrase '*lex requiritur*': '*Hi sunt improprii et incommodi sermones, nec veri sunt. Nam lex iam adest, is already there. Lex prius adest in facto*' (*op. cit.*, p. 477.6 f, cf. also pp. 446 f). '*Lex ... nulla nostra necessitate, sed de facto iam invitis nobis adest ...*' (*op. cit.*, p. 353.37 f). '*Haec tria, lex, peccatum, mors sunt inseperabilia. Quatenus igitur mors adhuc est in homine, eatenus peccatum et lex est in homine*' (*op. cit.*, p. 354.24 ff). Cf. my essay, 'On the Doctrine of the *triplex usus legis* in the Theology of the Reformation' (pp. 62 ff above).

[2] '... *coactus est Deus a novo nobis, ne prorsus suam legem obliviseremur, metam proponere, ut sic recordaremur saltem, qui iam antea fuerimus et qui iam simus. Itaque renovata lex est, et quidem scripta et tradita certo populo, in quantum scripta, sed non in quantum dicta, quia hae notitiae communes erant omnibus gentibus, sicuti experientia ipsa testatur*' (*WA* 39/1, pp. 539.13-540.3).

which is rendered pointless by the realization that the law is not a means
to the attainment of salvation.[1] The fact that in making this critical distinction regarding the accepted *doctrina legis* the Gospel and the rationalism of the Enlightenment not only appear to be in very questionable
proximity but can in fact even undeniably join hands, need here only be
mentioned in passing—although it would of course bring us explicitly
into touch again with Bonhoeffer's angle on the problem.

The above is only a scant outline, and therefore one left open to attack
from various quarters, of the train of thought that is occasioned by the
parallel Bonhoeffer draws between the problem of religion and the
problem of circumcision. Let me go on to illustrate it, and thereby at the
same time to bring out its real point, by referring to an argument of
Luther's. The effect which the Christian's freedom from the law has
upon the preaching of the law is to reduce it to the law written in all
men's hearts. That comes to light in the question how far the preaching
of the law is binding. If someone says to me, 'You are not circumcised',
then that does not come home to me as the accusing voice of the law, it
does not have anything at all to do with me. If, on the other hand, the
charge is: 'You do not believe in God, you do not fear him', etc., then
that is an accusation because it has to do with me.[2] But what of today?
Does that also get home to the modern non-religious man? We must
surely grant that it does not. What is the change that has come about
here? That modern non-religious man is no longer *de facto* under the
law? Not at all—if indeed, as we have said, the law belongs inseparably
to man's existence and is in fact his very reality! That the law under

---

[1] There would certainly be further differentiations to make here, as Luther
does e.g. in regard to circumcision: '*Circumcisio et lex fiat tandem definita: quod
non necessaria ad iustificandum . . . gentibus non debet imponi, quia esset eis novitas,
ergo nemo cogatur ad Circumcisionem neque aliquis cogatur vi a Circumcisione. . . .
Paulus non cogit nec facto, verbo Iudeos a Circumcisione sed addit: per quam non
potestis iustificari. . . . Neminem coge a Circumcisione; maneat, si vult, modo hoc
sciat: non esse necessariam ad iustificationem*' (*WA* 40/1, pp. 158.1 f, 6 f; 159.6 f,
8 f). But the latter clause did in fact after all lead to the abrogation of the
ceremonial law also among Jewish Christians.

[2] Continuing the passage cited above p. 145 note 2: '*Nam si hoc non esset, iam
nihili fecerimus, si lex diceret: Tu non fidis Deo, non times Deum, abuteris nomine
eius, quam iam nihili facimus, si quando diceretur: Tu non es circumcisus, tu non
affers bovem, vitulum, pecudes. Nam haec cum audio, nihil moveor neque perhorresco
et tamquam ludum iocumque puto. At quando dicit: Tu es incredulus Deo, non credis
Deo, non times Deum, es adulter, moechus, inobediens et quicquid tale est, hic statim
perhorresco et pavesco et sentio in corde, me certe hoc debere Deo, non quia traditus
et scriptus decalogus sit nobis, sed quod scimus vel leges has nobiscum in mundum
attulimus et hac quidem praedicatione statim velamen tollitur et ostenditur mihi,
quod facio peccatum*' (*WA* 39/1, p. 540.3-13).

which he *de facto* stands is not truly God's law? It would be the end of the Christian message if that were so! But the change we find here is surely that the traditional 'religious' exposition of the law under which even the non-religious man *de facto* stands is manifestly no longer able to speak of the law in ways he finds understandable and binding—because it no longer speaks of this modern non-religious man and his reality, but considers it necessary to add on and hold over against him a law which is not verifiable as the law under which the modern non-religious man *de facto* stands. And the reason for that is plainly that the traditional 'religious' interpretation of the law has completely failed to make the law as a whole, and therewith reality as a whole and therewith also the whole man the object of its statements and its claims. Precisely because it speaks of God the way it does—namely, so to speak as an additional reality bordering on the world and the existence of man—therefore it is the one thing that no longer testifies to the law as God's law. Thus there cannot be the slightest question of doing modern non-religious man a favour by giving up testifying to the law as God's law. Rather, the task is precisely to ask ourselves anew in view of modern non-religious man what it means to take the law that belongs inseparably to the existence of man, and is in fact his very reality, and testify to it as God's law. The accepted religious interpretation of the law has become a special religious law which—like the law of circumcision—lacks universal validity and which, if its acceptance is nevertheless made a prerequisite of faith, must, precisely from the standpoint of the Gospel, be declared abrogated.

The decisive question therefore is: how do we preach the Gospel to the non-religious man as freedom from the law—and that means, Jesus Christ as the fulfilment and end of the law—without first laying on him beforehand a law that is strange to him and does not concern him? How does the law really get home to the non-religious man? What is it that unconditionally concerns him? How do we bring to expression the law under which he stands *de facto*? That, I say, is the decisive question; for whether our preaching of the Gospel is understandable and binding all depends on whether our preaching of the law is understandable and binding.[1]

---

[1] 'It is only when one knows the ineffability of the Name of God that one can utter the name of Jesus Christ. It is only when one loves life and the earth so much that without them everything would be gone, that one can believe in the resurrection of the dead and a new world. It is only when one submits to God's law that one can speak of grace, and only when one sees the anger and wrath of God hanging like grim realities over the head of one's enemies that one can know

2. What do Bonhoeffer's observations on religion and non-religious-ness contribute towards the problem of the preaching of the law, or as we can now also say, of the coming to expression of the reality that concerns us? If we here disregard for the moment the question marks set against Bonhoeffer's use of the concept religion (see above, part III), then the following picture emerges:—

The basic structure of 'religion' is the supplementing of reality by God. That could, I think, be taken as the common denominator of all the many different things Bonhoeffer says about religion: the thinking in terms of two spheres that is characteristic of religion,[1] striving to make room for God,[2] understanding transcendence in the epistemo-logical and metaphysical sense[3] or in the sense of what surpasses the possibilities of man,[4] localizing the experience of transcendence on the

---

[1] See above, p. 116 note 4 and p. 118 note 2. 'So long as Christ and the world are conceived as two opposing and mutually repellant spheres, man will be left in the following dilemma: he abandons reality as a whole, and places himself in one or other of the two spheres. He seeks Christ without the world, or he seeks the world without Christ. In either case he is deceiving himself. Or else he tries to stand in both spheres at once and thereby becomes the man of eternal conflict. . . . It may be difficult to break the spell of this thinking in terms of two spheres, but it is nevertheless quite certain that it is in profound contradiction to the thought of the Bible and to the thought of the Reformation, and that consequently it aims wide of reality. There are not two realities, but *only one reality*, and that is the reality of God, which has become manifest in Christ in the reality of the world' (*E* p. 62, Eng. pp. 63 f).

[2] See above, p. 115 notes 1 and 3. '. . . it always seems to me that in talking thus we are only seeking frantically to make room for God' (*WE* p. 182, Eng. p. 124). '. . . that they all had as their objective the clearing of a space for religion in the world or against the world' (*WE* p. 219, Eng. p. 148). 'At this point nervous souls start asking what room there is left for God now . . .' (*WE* p. 241, Eng. p. 163). 'That is why I am so anxious that God should not be smuggled into some last secret place . . .' (*WE* p. 236, Eng. p. 160).

[3] See above, pp. 139 f note 3. 'The "Beyond" of God is not the beyond of our perceptive faculties! The transcendence of epistemological theory has nothing to do with the transcendence of God' (*WE* p. 182, Eng. p. 124). 'The Beyond is not infinitely remote, but close at hand (*WE* p. 255, Eng. p. 175). 'God . . . not in the abstract form of the Absolute, Metaphysical, Infinite, etc.' (*WE* p. 260, Eng. p. 179).

[4] 'Man's religiosity makes him look in his distress to the power of God in the world' (*WE* p. 242, Eng. p. 164). '. . . all men do so, Christian and unbelieving' (*WE* p. 246, Eng. p. 167). 'What do we mean by "God"? Not in the first place an abstract belief in his omnipotence, etc. That is not a genuine experience of

---

something of what it means to love them and forgive them. I don't think it is Christian to want to get to New Testament ways of living and thinking too soon and too directly. . . . You cannot and must not speak the last word before the second last one. We live with the second last and believe in the last . . .' (*WE* pp. 112 f, Eng. p. 79).

boundaries of existence,[1] treating it schematically as the solution of unsolved problems,[2] God's role as a 'stop-gap',[3] spying out and exploiting man's weaknesses as proof of his need of God,[4] the view that being a Christian is a special kind of human existence,[5] shifting the emphasis

[1] 'Religious people speak of God when human perception is (often just from mental laziness) at an end, or human resources fail: it is in fact always the *deus ex machina* who is marched on to the stage either for the so-called solving of insoluble problems or as support in human failure—always, that is to say, in exploitation of human weakness or on the borders of human existence. Of necessity, that can only go on until men can, by their own strength, push those borders a little further, so that God becomes superfluous as *deus ex machina*. I have come to be altogether doubtful about talking of "borders of human existence" (is even death today, since men are scarcely afraid of it any more, or sin, which they scarcely understand any more, still a genuine borderline?). . . . On the borders it seems to me better to hold our peace and leave the insoluble unsolved. . . . The church stands not where human powers give out, on the borders, but in the centre of the village' (*WE* pp. 181 f, Eng. p. 124). '. . . we must not wait until we are at the end of our tether: God must be found at the centre of life' (*WE* p. 211, Eng. p. 143). 'Redemption myths arise from human experiences of the boundary situation' (*WE* p. 227, Eng. p. 154). 'Of course Jesus took to himself the creatures on the outskirts of human society, harlots and publicans, but never them alone, for he sought to take to himself man as such' (*WE* p. 231, Eng. p. 157). See also above, p. 115 note 3.

[2] '. . . God becomes the answer to life's problems, the solution of its distresses and conflicts' (*WE* p. 230, Eng. p. 156). 'We should find God in what we know, not in what we don't; it is not in the unsolved questions but in the solved ones that God would have us comprehend him. This is true not only for the relation between God and scientific knowledge, but also for the wider human problems such as guilt, suffering and death. . . . (Jesus Christ) is the centre of life and in no sense did he "come to order to" answer our unsolved problems. From the centre of life certain questions are seen to be wholly irrelevant, and so are the answers commonly given to them. . . . In Christ there are no "Christian problems"' (*WE* p. 211, Eng. pp. 142 f.).

[3] Regarding the experience of separation: 'It is nonsense to say that God fills the gap; he does not fill it at all, but rather what he does is precisely to keep it empty . . .' (*WE* p. 131, Eng. p. 91). '. . . how wrong it is to use God as a stopgap for the incompleteness of our knowledge' (*WE* p. 210, Eng. p. 142). ' "God" as a working hypothesis, as stop-gap for our embarrassments . . .' (*WE* p. 258, Eng. p. 178).

[4] See above, p. 115 notes 2 and 3, p. 125 note 3, p. 149 note 1. 'That is why I am so anxious . . . that we should not "pick holes in" man in his worldliness . . .' (*WE* p. 236, Eng. p. 160). Cf. here also the criticism of 'religious blackmail', *WE* pp. 140, 179, 181, 218, 234 f, Eng. pp. 97, 122, 124 (for 'helping out' read 'exploiting'), 147, 158 f.

[5] *WE* p. 244, Eng. p. 166, quoted above, p. 119 note 3. Cf. also p. 118 note 2.

God but a piece of extended world. . . . Our relation to God is not a "religious" relationship with some highest, mightiest, best Being imaginable—which is a spurious conception of transcendence . . .' (*WE* p. 259, Eng. p. 179). 'The transcendent consists not in tasks beyond our scope and power but in the nearest thing to hand' (*WE* p. 260, Eng. p. 179).

on to an individualistic view of salvation,[1] on to inwardness[2] or into the Beyond,[3] whereby the world is left to its own devices,[4] its godlessness is religiously covered up[5] and God's gifts and his 'hours' misjudged.[6] These are notes that would have to be comprehensively developed beyond the rudimentary treatment supplied by Bonhoeffer, and if need be also in critical review of it, if we are to work out the 'religious' view of the law envisaged in them. The theological problem would then be whether and why a basic outlook that ultimately means the supplementing of reality by God misses both the right understanding of the law and also the right understanding of the Gospel.

The basic structure of 'non-religiousness', on the other hand, is coping with reality without God. In that phrase we have the culmination of

[1] 'Is it not true to say that the individualistic concern for personal salvation has almost completely left us all? Are we not really under the impression that there are more important things than bothering about such a matter? (Perhaps not more important than the *matter* itself, but certainly more important than *bothering* about it!?) I know it sounds pretty monstrous to say that. But is it not, at bottom, even biblical?' (*WE* p. 184, Eng. pp. 125 f).

[2] See above, p. 115 note 3 and p. 133 note 1. 'The Bible does not recognize our distinction of outer and inner. . . . The "heart" in the biblical sense is not the inner nature, but the whole man as he is before God' (*WE* p. 236, Eng. p. 160). Cf. also the polemic against the tendency to spiritualize, *WE* pp. 126, 160, 253, Eng. pp. 88, 111, 173.

[3] See above, pp. 139 f note 3. 'The emphasis now falls beyond the boundary of death. And it is just here that I see the mistake and the danger. Redemption now means redemption from cares and needs, from fears and longings, from sin and death into a better Beyond. But is that really the distinctive feature of Christianity as proclaimed in the Gospels and in Paul? I am sure it is not' (*WE* p. 226, cf. also p. 184, Eng. pp. 154 and 126 respectively).

[4] *WE* p. 185, Eng. p. 126.

[5] Man 'must therefore really live in the godless world, without attempting to gloss over its godlessness with a veneer of religion or trying to transfigure it' (*WE* p. 244, Eng. p. 166). 'When we speak of God in a "non-religious" way, we must speak of him in a way that does not gloss over the godlessness of the world, but rather exposes it . . .' (*WE* p. 246, Eng. p. 167).

[6] 'We ought to find God and love him in the things he gives at the moment; if he pleases to grant us some overwhelming earthly bliss, we ought not to go one better than God and spoil that bliss by our presumption and arrogance, by letting our religious fancies run riot and refusing to be satisfied with what God gives. God will surely see to it that the man who finds him in his earthly bliss and thanks him for it has plenty of opportunities to remind himself that earthly things are only transitory, and that it is good for him to accustom himself to the idea of eternity, and there will not fail to be times, too, when he can say with all sincerity: "I would that I were home. . . ." But everything in its season, and the important thing is to keep step with God and not get a step or two in front of him (nor for that matter, a step or two behind him either). It is arrogant to want to have everything at once, matrimonial bliss, and the cross, and the heavenly Jerusalem . . .' (*WE* pp. 123 f, Eng. p. 86).

Bonhoeffer's analysis of modern non-religious man.[1] Yet how does he mean it? In the sense of approval? There is surely no need to start pointing out that of course it is superfluous to bother any more about the Christian message and Bonhoeffer's question how God can be spoken of in non-religious, secular ways is a simple breach of the law of contradiction and a sheer absurdity, if it is a plain, unqualified matter of fact that non-religious man copes with reality without God. It would be sufficient merely to say that the statement is obviously totally unrealistic. For what reasonable, sober-thinking man would wish to maintain that in the strict sense we can speak of coping with reality at all, entirely irrespective of whether it is under the heading 'without God' or 'with God'? Yet are theology and Christian proclamation not then compelled after all to take the way so passionately rejected by Bonhoeffer—the way of demonstrating the fact and the extent of man's *failure* to cope with reality, and of basing on that demonstration its own right to exist? That indeed is ruled out by the fact that according to Bonhoeffer the Christian message's claim to validity is not derived from solutions it offers to any problems.[2] Nevertheless the task of entering into critical debate also— and more especially—with modern non-religious man still remains inescapable. It does indeed look as if Bonhoeffer directs the full sharpness of his criticism against the religious man, whereas he is peculiarly sparing of the non-religious. That impression, however, is completely false in such general form. If he assents to the adulthood of the world, then what he means by that is naturally 'not the shallow, commonplace this-worldliness of the enlightened, of the busy, the comfortable or the lascivious'.[3] There is surely no need to start listing all the expressions of incisive criticism, sometimes even of horror, where certain manifesta-

---

[1] By the 'movement towards the autonomy of man' he understands 'the discovery of the laws by which the world lives and copes in science, social and political affairs, art, ethics and religion'. 'Man has learned to cope with all questions of importance without recourse to God as a "working hypothesis"... It is becoming evident that everything gets along without "God", and just as well as before' (*WE* pp. 215 f, Eng. pp. 145 f). 'In practice—and in every age it has been so—men do cope with these questions even without God' *viz.*—'the wider human problems such as guilt, suffering and death' (*WE* p. 211, Eng. p. 142. Note here the parenthesis [omitted in English], 'in every age'!).

[2] 'It is possible nowadays to find human answers to these problems too [see the previous note!] which leave God right out of the picture.... It just isn't true to say that Christianity alone has the answers. As far as the idea of an "answer" goes, the fact is rather that the Christian answers are no more—and no less— compelling than other possible answers' (*WE* p. 211, Eng. pp. 142 f). Cf. above, p. 149 note 2.

[3] *WE* p. 248, Eng. p. 168.

tions of modern man are concerned,[1] but it should be sufficient merely to recall the opponents he resisted to the death. That alone should rule out any mistaken ideas as to his seeking to gloss over a frivolous or dubious 'coping without God'.

But the problem lies deeper. The debate with modern non-religious man must not be made too easy by confining ourselves only to his degenerate aspects. What of his best possibilities for coping without God? Is it not really necessary after all to talk here of 'boundaries', to address this kind of man with an eye to his boundaries and at these boundaries to speak of God? Can it be seriously maintained that to talk of the boundaries of human life has become altogether questionable and even death and sin are today not genuine boundaries any longer?[2] Did Bonhoeffer himself not testify to the significance for his own personal life of such boundary-line experiences,[3] and moreover, does his ultimate theological development not come under the head of consciously maintaining his stand in a 'boundary situation'?[4] That is why even in his fundamental statements we repeatedly come across remarks that put a question mark against the idea of 'coping', point to the problem of the 'boundary', and as correctives of his other statements must not be simply left out of account. For example, when he distinguishes between coping with dying and coping with death,[5] when he observes that 'most men do not know what they really live by' and thinks to see in that 'an

---

[1] As examples let me mention only the observations on the 'sense of quality' and the 'levelling down in all ranks of society' (*WE* pp. 24 ff, Eng. pp. 22 f), on 'cynical, ungodly frankness' (*WE* pp. 108, 114 ff, Eng. pp. 75, 80 f), on the loss of 'moral memory' (*WE* p. 143, Eng. p. 99), on the miserable behaviour of fellow-prisoners (*WE* pp. 145 f, Eng. pp. 100 f), on vestiges of a belief in some 'supra-sensual' reality (*WE* pp. 159 f, Eng. p. 110), on 'a dreadful desolation and impoverishment' as a result of de-personalization (*WE* pp. 171 f, omitted in Eng. p. 118), on one-track thinking ('when the bombers come, they are all fear; when there is something good to eat, they are all greed; when they are disappointed, they are all despair; when they are successful, they can think of nothing else', *WE* pp. 209 f, Eng. p. 141), etc. Cf. also above, p. 114 note 3.

[2] See above, p. 149 note 1.

[3] '... these heavy air raids ... lead me back to prayer and to the Bible just like a child. ... In more than one respect my confinement is acting like a wholesome though drastic cure' (*WE* pp. 110 f, Eng. p. 78). '... it is true that it needs trouble to shake us up and drive us to prayer ...' (*WE* p. 139, Eng. p. 96).   [4] *WE* p. 92, Eng. p. 64 translates 'facing the worst'.

[5] 'Easter? We think more of the act of dying than of death itself. We are much more concerned about how to cope with dying than about how to conquer death. Socrates mastered the art of dying, Christ overcame death as the ἔσχατος ἐχθρός, the last enemy. ... To cope with dying is still not to cope with death. To master the art of dying is within human capacity, to overcome death means resurrection. We need not the *ars moriendi* but the resurrection of Christ to

unconscious waiting for the emancipating and liberating word',[1] when he shows how modern man's coping with the dangers that threaten him from the side of nature confronts him all the more sharply with the problem of coping with himself,[2] and when he emphasizes that it is never on his own, but only in encountering his neighbour and therefore only in experiencing his own limitedness—thus, paradoxically enough, ultimately only as a fragment!—than man can be a whole.[3]

But all these facts, which of course ultimately crystallize into the experience of guilt and the encounter with death, do not cancel out, but rather render the more poignant, the fact that modern non-religious

---

[1] *WE* p. 169, Eng. p. 116.

[2] 'The goal is to be independent of nature. Nature formerly conquered by spiritual means, with us by technical organization of various kinds. Our immediate environment not nature as formerly, but organization. But this bulwark against the threats of nature produces a new danger, viz.—the very organization. The spiritual power is now lacking! The question is: what protection is there against the danger of organization? Man is once more faced with the problem of himself. He has coped with everything, excepting only himself! He can safeguard himself from everything, excepting only from man. In the last resort it all turns upon man' (*WE* p. 258, Eng. p. 178). Cf. also *WE* pp. 200 ff, Eng. pp. 136 f. 'The task laid on our generation will not be once more "to desire great things", but to save ourselves alive from the debris, as a brand plucked from the burning' (*WE* pp. 202 f, Eng. pp. 137 f).

[3] 'We want to do everything ourselves, but that is a mark of false pride. Even what we owe to others belongs to ourselves and is a part of our own lives. . . . It is with what we are in ourselves and what we owe to others that we are a complete whole' (*WE* p. 111, Eng. p. 78). 'Witiko "does everything there is to be done" by adapting himself to the realities of life, by always listening to the advice of others more experienced than himself, thus showing himself a member of the "whole". We never achieve this wholeness on our own; it can only be acquired with the help of others' (*WE* p. 141, Eng. p. 98). In regard to the phenomenon of growing insensitive to hardships, he thinks 'that it can surely also be a case of coming to a clearer and more sober estimate of our own limitations and possibilities and thereby being enabled genuinely to love our neighbour' (*WE* p. 175, Eng. p. 120). 'After all, human relationships count for more than anything else. The "successful man" of the modern world cannot alter this —neither can the demi-gods and lunatics who know nothing about human relationships. God himself lets us serve him in the human sphere. All else is closely akin to *hybris*.' There is of course also the danger of perversion into a 'cult of the human', 'which does not fit in with reality. What I mean here, however, is the simple fact that people are more important in life than anything else. Of course that does not mean we should belittle the world of things, or success in that sphere. . . . For many today man too is just a part of the world of things. That is because the experience of the human simply eludes them' (*WE* pp. 263 f, Eng. pp. 182 f).

---

invigorate and cleanse the world of today. *Here* is the answer to the δός μοί ποῦ στῶ καὶ κινήσω τὴν γῆν, give me where to stand and I will move the earth' (*WE* p. 168, Eng. p. 116).

man must cope with reality without God. He does not have God as compensation for his weaknesses, as the Beyond over his boundaries, as prolongation of the world, as extension of reality. He is wholly dependent on this world, utterly exposed to the pressure of reality and therewith to its claims. As man come of age he is man given his freedom and thereby summoned in person to the free exercise of his responsibility. He is prohibited from acknowledging as God a God whose place would be only in the gaps and at the boundaries of his, man's, existence but who at the centre of his existence, 'in the free responsibility of free man',[1] would be no concern of his—a God, that is, who lives so to speak from man's being a minor and does not make his presence felt precisely in the godlessness of the world. Naturally modern non-religious man, too, has many possibilities of escape from reality,[2] yet really only in transgressing the precept of intellectual honesty—for 'the only way to be honest is to recognize that we have to live in the world—"*etsi deus non daretur*"'.[3]

But now, the passage just quoted goes on to define, in terms as surprising as they are fundamental, what this recognition of reality involves: 'And this is just what we do recognize—before God! God himself compels us to recognize it. So our coming of age leads us to a true recognition of our situation *vis-à-vis* God. God gives us to know that we must live as those who cope with life without God. The God who is with us is the God who forsakes us (Mark 15.34!). The God who makes us live in the world without the working hypothesis God is the God before whom we are ever standing. Before God and with him, we live without God.'[4] Two things in this are extraordinarily significant: first, the way God is here spoken of not in abrogation but in confirmation of the 'without God', and secondly, the fact that in the recognition in question the intellectual honesty of modern man and the testimony of Christian faith meet in a peculiar way. Yet how is that to be understood? There can of course be no doubt that it is only as a theologian that Bonhoeffer can speak as he does here, and that the assertion that our coming of age leads to a true recognition of our position before God is the theological interpretation of a fact whose existence is certainly independent of this interpretation but whose truth is disclosed, recog-

---

[1] *WE* p. 14, Eng. p. 17. On the concept of responsibility cf. the observations 'After Ten Years' in their context (*WE* pp. 9 ff, Eng. pp. 13 ff).

[2] To these must be reckoned also the possibilities discussed in the section 'Who stands his ground?' (*WE* pp. 10 ff, Eng. pp. 14 ff).

[3] *WE* p. 241, Eng. p. 163.

[4] *WE* p. 241, Eng. pp. 163 f.

nized and brought into force only on the basis of the Christian message. Thus it is not a case of bowing to a cut and dried item of extra-theological knowledge to which merely a theological finishing touch would then be added, but 'the world's adulthood' 'is now really better understood than it understands itself, namely, on the basis of the Gospel, and in the light of Christ'.[1] The assertion that an intellectually honest view of reality and the testimony of the Christian message thus intersect is of course a thing we come across in Bonhoeffer again and again,[2] but always in such a way that the assertion of this intersection is a theological assertion, and the peculiar occurrence ultimately presupposes the Christian faith because maintaining one's 'adulthood' and standing one's ground in face of the intellectually honest view of reality is possible only 'before God'.[3]

With that we have sketched the methodological problem of theology as it underlies the whole of Bonhoeffer's statements. Hence the real approach to what he says of 'non-religiousness' can be found only from the angle of his understanding of the Christian faith. And it here becomes plain that the basic idea characterized by a pure 'coping with reality without God' does in one particular respect (namely, as against all 'religious' concealment) uncover the law under which we stand *de facto* and which is our reality; but that it is not capable of expressing it in truth, i.e. to the exclusion of all escape attempts, because it does not perceive and express the law as God's law.

[1] *WE* p. 221, Eng. p. 149, cf. also p. 219, Eng. p. 148: 'Of course the world does *need* to be understood better than it understands itself!—but on no account "religiously" . . .', that is, not in the sense of a supplementing of reality by God, as I have expressed it, but as we could now say: 'theologically', in the sense of recognizing reality before God.

[2] Specially instructive, apart from the above-quoted passage *WE* p. 241, Eng. pp. 163 f, are: *WE* pp. 183 f, Eng. p. 125 (see above, p. 136 note 1), pp. 209 f, Eng. pp. 141 f (see above, p. 114 note 1), pp. 217 f, Eng. p. 147 (see above, p. 115 note 3), pp. 242 and 246, Eng. pp. 164 and 167 (see below, p. 159 note 2). Cf. also the conjunction of the Christian and the 'man of liberal education' (*WE* p. 141, Eng. p. 97), the reference to ' "Christian" worldliness' (*WE* p. 157, Eng. p. 108) and to 'profound this-worldliness' (*WE* p. 248, Eng. p. 168), the relation between being a Christian and being a man (see below, pp. 160 f), the nearness to the non-religious man (see above, p. 126 note 2), the remarks on 'The Gods of Greece' (*WE* p. 222, Eng. p. 150), on 'the question of "unconscious Christianity" ' (*WE* p. 252, Eng. p. 172) and many other passages.

[3] 'Who stands his ground? Only the man whose ultimate criterion is not his reason, his principles, his conscience, his freedom, his virtue, but who is ready to sacrifice all these things when he is called to obedient and responsible action in faith and exclusive allegiance to God—the responsible man seeks to make his whole life a response to the question and call of God. Where are these responsible men?' (*WE* p. 13, Eng. pp. 15 f).

3. The direction our thought now necessarily takes is, in traditional theological terminology, the question of the spiritual exposition of the law. That, however, would necessitate entering into Christology, whereby we should have to adhere strictly to the fact that Christ is not *legislator*, but is certainly *impletor legis* and consequently *interpretator legis*. I am outlining the task in scholastic terms, not in order to subject it to the automatism of a dogmatic schema but to indicate the wide theological implications that would here have to be taken into account. For when given proper theological treatment law and Gospel cannot in any way be isolated from each other. The law interprets the Gospel and the Gospel interprets the law. The principle of their relationship is as much a '*coniunctissime*' as a '*distinctissime*'. The correct doctrine of law and Gospel has to show in what respect the law precedes the Gospel, but also in what respect the Gospel precedes the law—in such a way, of course, that the order 'Gospel and law' serves to confirm the order 'law and Gospel', and on no account *vice versa*. In the context here formally outlined there belong statements of Bonhoeffer's to which I would make at least a brief reference in conclusion because (or, in view of the necessary brevity, although) here all the previous threads now come together.

'Jesus does not call men to a new religion, but to life.'[1] 'Christ is . . . not an object of religion, but something quite different, indeed and in truth the Lord of the world.'[2] 'Jesus claims for himself and the kingdom of God the whole of human life in all its manifestations.' The subject that concerns Bonhoeffer is therefore: 'the claim made by Jesus Christ on a world which has come of age'.[3] Therein God issues 'the Gospel summons into his kingdom'.[4] For God's Word 'reigns'.[5] Hence for Bonhoeffer's Christological approach the statement is fundamental that in Christ the reality of God and the reality of the world are *one* reality.[6] 'Jesus Christ . . . is the centre of life.'[7] And accordingly Christ 'takes

[1] *WE* p. 246, Eng. p. 167.
[2] *WE* p. 180, cf. p. 218, Eng. pp. 123, 147.
[3] *WE* p. 231, Eng. p. 157, cf. p. 179, Eng. pp. 122 f (see above, p. 124).
[4] *WE* p. 194, Eng. p. 132: 'A kingdom stronger than war and danger, a kingdom of power and might, a kingdom signifying to some eternal terror and judgment, to others eternal joy and righteousness, not a kingdom of the heart but one as wide as the earth and the whole world, not transitory but eternal, a kingdom which makes a way for itself and summons men to itself to prepare its way, a kingdom worthy of our life's devotion.'
[5] *WE* p. 236, Eng. p. 160.
[6] See above, p. 109 note 2, p. 112 note 4, p. 116 note 3, p. 117 note 1, p. 118 note 1, p. 148 note 1.
[7] *WE* p. 211, Eng. p. 143. Likewise: 'Is not righteousness and the kingdom of God on earth the focus of everything?' (*WE* p. 184, Eng. p. 126).

hold of a man in the centre of his life'.[1] Likewise 'the church . . . stands not where human powers give out, on the borders, but in the centre of the village.'[2] Therefore God must be testified to at the centre of life.[3] Man must be 'confronted by God at his strongest point'.[4] God wishes to be found and loved in this life and in the things he gives at the moment.[5] For 'in the events themselves is God.'[6] Although such remarks when viewed superficially could, surprisingly enough, be misunderstood partly in a theocratic sense but partly also in the sense of Cultural Protestantism, yet when read in their context there can certainly be no doubt of the common Christological root of all these statements.[7] Nor is there any sort of one-sided creationist or incarnationist theology behind them, but we are bound to notice how it is precisely in the light of the resurrection that Bonhoeffer most strongly underlines the aspect of this-worldliness,[8] seeing in it the sharpening of a line that

---

[1] *WE* p. 227, Eng. p. 154. Precisely because it is a question of the kingdom of God, the following holds: 'It is not with the next world that we are concerned, but with this world as created and preserved and ordered and atoned for and made new. What is above the world is, in the Gospel, intended to exist *for* this world—I mean that not in the anthropocentric sense of liberal, mystic, pietistic, ethical theology, but in the Bible sense of the creation and of the incarnation, crucifixion and resurrection of Jesus Christ' (*WE* p. 184, Eng. p. 126).

[2] *WE* p. 182, Eng. p. 124.

[3] ' . . . I should like to speak of God not on the borders of life but at its centre, not in weaknesses but in strength, not therefore in man's death and guilt, but in his life and prosperity' (*WE* p. 182, Eng. p. 124). 'We should find God in what we know, not in what we don't; it is not in the unsolved questions but in the solved ones that God would have us comprehend him . . . not at the end of our tether, but he must be found at the centre of life; it is in life and not only in death, in health and strength and not only in suffering, in action and not only in sin that God wishes to be known (*WE* p. 211, Eng. pp. 142 f). Cf. also *WE* p. 231, Eng. p. 157 (see above, p. 125 note 3).

[4] *WE* p. 236, Eng. p. 160. For that reason Bonhoeffer demands 'that we should frankly recognize that man and the world have come of age, that we should not "pick holes in" man in his worldliness'.

[5] See above, p. 150 note 6. 'I am sure we ought to love and trust God in our *lives* and in all the blessings he sends us, so that when our time comes and the hour strikes—but not before!—we may go to him in love and trust and joy' (*WE* p. 123, Eng. p. 86).

[6] *WE* p. 134, Eng. p. 93. ' . . . through every event, however untoward, there is always a way through to God' (*WE* p. 120, Eng. p. 84). 'God encounters us not only as a Thou, but also "disguised" as an "It"; so in the last resort my question is how we find the "Thou" in this "It" (i.e. "fate") . . .' (*WE* p. 151, Eng. p. 104).

[7] Continuing the second quotation in note 3 above: 'The ground for this idea lies in the revelation of God in Jesus Christ' (*WE* p. 211, Eng. p. 143).

[8] 'The difference between the Christian hope of resurrection and a mythological hope is, that the Christian hope points a man to his life on this earth in a wholly new way which is even more sharply defined than it is in the Old Testa-

derives from the Old Testament.[1] This unusual, Christologically grounded antithesis between the this-worldly and the Beyond, the 'centre' and the 'boundary', has surely the ultimate aim not of abrogating transcendence in favour of immanence, the 'boundary' in favour of the 'centre', nor of turning it into a matter of indifference, but of countering a false understanding of transcendence and 'boundary'[2] by working out the proper view of them: 'God is "beyond" in the midst of our life.'[3]

Yet what does that mean? Both the Christological understanding of 'this-worldliness' and 'secularity' (when the lines from creation and from the Old Testament are held together in the light of the incarnation and the resurrection) and also its relation to 'religion' and 'non-religiousness' become fully clear only when the *theologia crucis* is seen to be the keynote of Bonhoeffer's thinking. Not that that means any retraction or limitation of what he says of 'the claim made by Jesus Christ on a world which has come of age',[4] of the kingdom of God as 'a kingdom of power and might . . . as wide as the earth and the whole world',[5] and of his wish to speak of God 'not in weaknesses but in strength, not . . . in man's death and guilt, but in his life and prosperity'[6]; on the contrary, all that must now appear for the first time in its proper perspective and be clearly seen as universally understandable and universally binding. For what warrant is there for speaking of God in such a way? The process of 'forcing God out of the world'[7] which results from the movement towards autonomy finds its correlate precisely in the event of Christ: 'God allows himself to be forced out of the world and on to the Cross, God is weak and powerless in the world, and that is exactly the way, the only way, in which he is with us and helps

---

[1] Cf. especially *WE* pp. 112 f, 182, 184, 185, 193, 225-7, 253 f, Eng. pp. 79, 124, 126, 126, 131, 153-4, 173. This view of the significance of the Old Testament for the Christian faith calls for special examination.

[2] See above, p. 148 notes 3 and 4.

[3] *WE* p. 182, Eng. p. 124. Cf. also: 'The boundary arises from the centre and fulness of life with the commandment of God; it is not the other way round' (*E* p. 221, Eng. p. 252).   [4] See above, p. 156 at note 3.

[5] See above, p. 156 note 4.   [6] See above, p. 157 note 3.

[7] *WE* p. 233, Eng. p. 158; ' . . . that God is being increasingly edged out of the world now that it has come of age, out of the realms of our knowledge and our life and since Kant has been relegated to the world beyond experience' (*WE* pp. 229 f, Eng. p. 156). Cf. also above, p. 115 note 1.

---

ment' (*WE* p. 226, Eng. p. 154). ' . . . I mean the profound this-worldliness which is completely disciplined and in which the knowledge of death and resurrection is ever present' (*WE* p. 248, Eng. p. 168).

us.'[1] The very thing 'religion' stands to prevent is revealed 'before God', and that means in Christ, to be our reality but therewith at the same time—and this remains hidden even in the process by which the world came of age—also the reality of God.[2] Is it not true that God's impotence in the world is our reality? It is in virtue of that impotence that Christ helps.[3] That is the revelation of God's omnipotence.[4] The life to which Christ calls is participation in God's impotence in the world.[5] And precisely that, and that alone, is the meaning of 'faith'.[6]

Yet are these not paradoxes which there is no means of verifying? It is quite true that here we have to do with *metanoia*,[7] with 'a complete re-orientation of human being'.[8] The encounter with Jesus means the reversal of all human values.[9] That cannot be demonstrated to anyone. Faith is verified only by faith. But what makes faith's testimony, as a

[1] *WE* p. 242, Eng. p. 164.

[2] 'This is the decisive difference between Christianity and all religions. Man's religiosity makes him look in his distress to the power of God in the world: he uses God as the *deus ex machina*. The Bible, however, directs him to the powerlessness and suffering of God; only a suffering God can help. To this extent we may say that the process we have described by which the world came of age was the abandonment of a false conception of God and the clearing of the decks for the God of the Bible who gains power and place in the world by his weakness. This must surely be the starting-point for our "secular interpretation" ' (*WE* p. 242, Eng. p. 164). ' "Christians range themselves with God in his sufferings", that is what distinguishes Christians from the heathen. . . . That is the exact opposite of everything the religious man expects from God. Man is challenged to participate in the sufferings of God at the hands of a godless world' (*WE* p. 244, Eng. p. 166). 'When we speak of God in a "non-religious" way, we must speak of him in a way that does not gloss over the godlessness of the world, but rather exposes it and thus sheds a surprising light upon the world. The world that has come of age is more godless, and for that reason perhaps *nearer* to God, than the world as a minor was' (*WE* p. 246, Eng. p. 167). Cf. also above, p. 107 note 2.

[3] 'Matt. 8.17 makes it crystal clear that it is not by his omnipotence that Christ helps us, but by his impotence and suffering!' (*WE* p. 242, Eng. p. 164). Cf. the previous note.

[4] 'This freedom from self, this "existence for others" maintained to the point of death, is the sole ground of his omnipotence, omniscience, omnipresence' (*WE* p. 259, Eng. p. 179).   [5] *WE* p. 246, Eng. p. 167.

[6] 'It is not some religious act which makes a Christian what he is, but participation in the suffering of God in the life of the world' (*WE* p. 244, Eng. p. 166). 'This is "*metanoia*": it is not in the first instance bothering about one's own needs, problems, sins and fears, but allowing oneself to be caught up into the way of Christ, into the Messianic event, and thus fulfilling Isaiah 53!' (*WE* pp. 244 f, Eng. p. 166). 'Participation in the suffering of God in Christ . . . that is . . . "faith" ' (*WE* p. 245, Eng. p. 167). 'Faith is participation in this existence of Jesus' (*WE* p. 259, Eng. p. 179).

[7] Cf. previous note and *WE* p. 249, Eng. p. 169.

[8] *WE* p. 259, Eng. p. 179.   [9] *WE* p. 231, Eng. p. 157.

word that rouses faith, understandable and binding is the fact that it does verify reality and to that extent of course certainly does have a bearing on experience. For it addresses man with an eye to his humanity and has no other aim than that he should be really man. Being a Christian does not add anything to being a man, but puts our humanity into force. 'The Christian is not a *homo religiosus* but a man pure and simple, just as Jesus . . . was man.'[1] Here we have once again to take into account all that Bonhoeffer says about the 'wholeness' of man[2] and about existence in the multi-dimensionality and polyphony of life.[3] If we established earlier the fact that the basic structure of 'religion' is supplementing reality by God, and the basic structure of 'non-religious-ness' is coping with reality without God, then we can now express the basic structure of faith as enduring reality before God.[4] Thus defined, faith is concrete faith and finds 'worldliness' at once both a necessity and a gift.[5] Bonhoeffer learned this by experience, whereas he had earlier thought we can acquire faith by trying to lead some sort of holy life.[6] 'Later I discovered, and am still discovering to this day, that it is only by living completely in this world that one learns to believe. One must abandon every attempt to make something of oneself—whether it be a saint, or a converted sinner, a churchman (a so-called priestly type!), a righteous man or an unrighteous one, a sick man or a healthy one. This is what I mean by worldliness—taking life in one's stride with all its duties and problems, its successes and failures, its experiences and perplexities. Then we throw ourselves right into the arms of God, then we no longer take seriously our own suffering but the suffering of God

[1] *WE* p. 248, Eng. p. 168. Noteworthy is the parenthesis omitted above: 'as distinct, I suppose, from John the Baptist'. On this identification of being a Christian and being a man—it could be said that the Christian is man properly identified!—cf. further *WE* pp. 136, 244, 249, Eng. pp. 94, 166, 169.

[2] See above, p. 118 note 2, p. 153 note 3.

[3] See above, p. 113 note 1. To this there belongs also the frequently recurring thought that being a Christian has nothing to do with indifference towards wishes and with restraining the feelings, but rather shows itself in the enduring of fierce tensions: *WE* pp. 68, 95 f, 121 f, 131, 134 f, 141, 142, 146, 161 f, 171 f, 175, 192 f, 209 f, 212, 256, Eng. pp. 53, 66, 85, 91, 93 f, 97 f, 99, 101, 111 f, 117 f, 120, 131 f, 141 f, 143, 175.

[4] The Christian 'must drink the earthly cup to the lees like Christ himself ("My God, why hast thou forsaken me?"), and only in his doing that is the crucified and risen Lord with him, and he crucified and risen with Christ' (*WE* p. 227, Eng. p. 154).

[5] 'He must live a "worldly" life and so participate in the suffering of God; he *may* live a "worldly" life as one emancipated from all false religious obligations' (*WE* p. 244, Eng. p. 166).

[6] *WE* p. 248, Eng. p. 168.

in the world, then we watch with Christ in Gethsemane, and I think that is faith, that is "*metanoia*"; and that is what makes a man, and a Christian. . . .'[1] Thus the 'enduring of reality' amounts to 'being finished off'—a process which in the very renunciation of the attempt to make something of oneself, and that means in remaining a fragment, makes man a 'whole man'—not 'man on his own', but 'man existing for others'.[2]

That man becomes man in this way only 'before God', and that means in the 'encounter with Jesus Christ', that 'the "existence for others" of Jesus is the experience of transcendence' and 'faith is participation in this existence of Jesus',[3] that therefore only the proclamation of the Word of God as law and Gospel creates this man by killing and making alive—that proves itself true only *ubi et quando visum est deo* and not even 'non-religious interpretation' can compel it to happen. But that our task is to 'endure reality before God' and in doing so to let ourselves be driven back to first principles, to spell out and work around the concrete interpretation of law and Gospel, and to let ourselves be drawn into the service of a new coming to expression of the Word of God—of that Dietrich Bonhoeffer is a solemn reminder to us, and one we are obliged to heed.

[1] *WE* pp. 248 f, Eng. p. 169. And continuing the quotation on p. 160 note 1: 'To be a Christian does not mean . . . to use some particular method of turning oneself into something (a sinner, a penitent or a saint) but it means to be a man.'

[2] *WE* p. 260, Eng. p. 179.

[3] *WE* p. 259, Eng. p. 179.

V

THE SIGNIFICANCE OF DOCTRINAL DIFFERENCES FOR THE DIVISION OF THE CHURCH[1]

1. *On the Definition of the Problem*

THE question of the significance of doctrinal differences for the division of the church is formulated in very general terms and must first of all be defined in such a way as to make clear what can be regarded as standing *extra controversiam* and what primarily requires to be discussed. This preliminary task may be served by three theses:—

1. Only doctrinal differences have divisive significance for the church.
2. Doctrinal differences that have divisive significance for the church are a necessary element in the church's existence.
3. Not all doctrinal differences have divisive significance for the church.

However formal these propositions may be, and however free (as I think) from the influence of any particular confessional and theological standpoint, they nevertheless require closer examination if they are to meet with general agreement.

1. The following objections may be chiefly expected to the thesis that only doctrinal differences have divisive significance for the church:—

(*a*) The old distinction between heresy and schism appears to tell against it. That distinction, however, cannot possibly be maintained in the strict sense that doctrinal differences are concerned only in the one case, whereas in the other case questions of doctrine are not touched on at all. When for example Victor of Rome broke off communion with the churches of Asia Minor on the question of the date of Easter, and thus on a question which according to all concerned did not as such

[1] A paper read to the theological commission of the E.K.U. [*Evangelische Kirche der Union*] at Berlin on 7th January 1956, and at the conversations between the theological commissions of the E.K.U. and the V.E.L.K.D. [*Vereinigte Evangelische Lutherische Kirche Deutschlands*] at Loccum on 17th October 1957.

affect doctrine, yet in fact the real difference here was a different conception of what is necessary for the unity of the church, and thus ultimately a doctrinal difference after all. The same is true, say, of the Novatians, whose orthodoxy was never in doubt, yet the importance they attached to a different administration of discipline as a reason for dividing the church in fact pointed back after all to differences in regard to the doctrine of the church. Even with schisms that appear to have come about purely on grounds of ecclesiastical politics there is generally a doctrinal difference involved, even if an indirect and hidden one. If, however, neither of the parties concerned in the schism should even attempt to indicate it, then that would be an admission that the schism was devoid of any legitimate ground and thus existed *per nefas* on both sides.

These considerations are not meant *a priori* to nullify the distinction between heresy and schism and to set it aside as meaningless. Rightly understood, however, it does not affect the question whether only doctrinal differences have divisive significance for the church, but only the question of the modifications which the divisive significance of doctrinal differences for the church can assume. That, again, depends on the state of the recognized standard of church doctrine at the time in question. Further reflexion on that point will of course bring us to the problem whether any agreement is possible e.g. between Roman Catholic and Evangelical thought even on the purely formal definition of the concepts heresy and schism, and whether these concepts as they are traditionally understood do not defy being taken up into the usage of evangelical theology. But let us not pursue that question further here.

(*b*) Another objection could appeal to the fact, true enough in itself, that it is by no means only the individual objective differences in doctrine that play a role in the antithesis between the confessions, but also a different basic idea of the function to be assigned to doctrine in the existence of the church. The thesis that only doctrinal differences have divisive significance for the church is liable to be suspected of already having its source in a definite confessional position—namely, one which, as distinct from others, puts all the emphasis on doctrine. A suspicion of this kind is of course obviously nothing to be afraid of in a theological debate. Where would we get to, if we sought to avoid even the appearance of a definite confessional position! But it is quite true that we are here concerned in the first instance to determine a general, supraconfessional proposition which is to stand *extra controversiam* and so prepare for the precise definition of the controversial point. We therefore ask: does the thesis that only doctrinal differences have divisive significance for the church already contain an *a priori* confessional decision?

We are not concerned here with the point that belongs to the third thesis, *viz.*—that there can be distinctions when it comes to estimating whether specific doctrinal differences are divisive or not divisive for the church. Rather, we are here concerned with the more elementary question whether anything else besides doctrinal differences can have divisive significance for the church. This question, however, cannot well be answered in the affirmative for the very simple reason that all further description of anything that could be alleged to cause division in the church besides and apart from doctrinal differences is, in the way it is expressed in words, already of the nature of doctrine. Even a church division whose ground was the protest against over-estimating the importance of doctrine would by that very fact be rooted in a doctrinal difference. That holds in the extreme case even of the Darbyites. It does however certainly become plain that in our thesis, 'Only doctrinal differences have divisive significance for the church', the very concept doctrine itself at once becomes controversial and that thus the doctrinal differences that divide the church can at least also amount, and perhaps indeed ultimately always do amount, to differences concerning the real meaning of the concept 'doctrine' as such. That is a thing which will have to be our primary concern in the later part of our discussion.

(c) Finally, one could bring against the first thesis the nowadays much-discussed role of the so-called non-theological factors in causing and maintaining confessional splits. Church history is full of instances. No church division, and still less any church division that has become a tradition, has any lack of non-theological factors. We need only mention catchwords like 'Prussia', 'Bavaria' or 'Guelphs' in order to put a name to contributing factors of that kind from our own immediate neighbourhood. Sober historical analysis of the story of the confessions seems to lead to very different results than that only doctrinal differences have divisive significance for the church. Certainly doctrinal differences are always involved. But are they not often completely overlaid by other motives? Are they not often enough pressed into the service of very different interests? And—not to give the critical questions only a negative tone—is church history not something incomparably more alive, more full of real things and real people and therefore also richer, than is brought out by the suggestion that what really keeps it going can be reduced to questions of doctrine and is thus a matter of theological calculation? There is undoubtedly much truth in all that. Even when over-hasty judgments are toned down and corrected on more careful examination—when we do not e.g. employ *a priori* a concept of doctrine so narrow as to become doctrinaire, or in combination with the extra-theological factors referred to even see a sort of magnetic power in the working of doctrinal differences—nevertheless in view of the history of the confessions we shall hardly be able to advance as a purely descriptive statement the proposition that only doctrinal differences have divisive significance for the church.

Rather, it is a normative proposition for purposes of criticism, though it certainly does express a mere statement in so far as anyone who is personally involved in dealing with the fact of church division must require both of himself and of the other party valid reasons for the division, and can regard as really valid only such reasons as are susceptible of a theological exposition because they relate to the Christian faith's understanding of itself and therefore to the church as a factor in faith. It is therefore unnecessary to give the proposition a normative form, *viz.* that only doctrinal differences may rightly have divisive significance for the church. For it would be inherently contradictory if, when personally involved in a concrete instance of the problem of church division, one could cite only so-called extra-theological factors as the cause of the division and simply left it at that, instead of going on at once to draw the conclusion that there is no difference here of a kind to divide the church and that anyone who does not admit that is indulging in an error of Christian doctrine. We can see of course how any further attempt to reach agreement on the proposition that only doctrinal differences have divisive significance for the church must immediately also kindle the theological discussion of the concept of the church. For the very proper reference to the so-called non-theological factors compels us in speaking of the church to remain constantly aware of the real historic church situation, and therefore also in asserting the divisive significance only of doctrinal differences to beware of an unhistorical conception of doctrine, i.e. of the illusion that the doctrinal differences which divide the church can, just because they are doctrinal differences, be understood without regard to their envelopment in the age in which they arose and were expressed. That implies, however, that traditional doctrinal differences which divide the church have still divisive significance only when they can be expounded as such today.

2. The proposition that doctrinal differences of divisive significance

for the church are a necessary element in the church's existence appears at first sight even more vulnerable than the previous thesis. The discussion of it, however, need not detain us so long. The objection that the church is by nature *one* could have real force as an objection only if this essential unity that belongs to the church could be understood as one that is demonstrable in history from the start and can be exhibited unequivocally also today, while the fact of church division could be viewed on the other hand as an accident that took place later and can in principle be made good—one that strictly does not touch the unity of the church at all, in so far as that continues to exist all along as the *unitas* of a single ecclesiastical body, whereas the fact of church division is properly speaking only the separation between what is church and what is not church. On this interpretation, of course, which typifies the Roman Catholic position, even the Romans could accept the proposition that doctrinal differences of divisive significance for the church are a necessary element in the church's existence. For then the concept of *church* division has the real edge taken off it and the idea of necessity is understood in the sense of the actual fate of the church, which it so happens must constantly defend itself against heresy. The Reformers' concept of the church did indeed affirm the essential invisibility of the *unitas* (!) of the *ecclesia universalis,* but took no steps, or only few and certainly insufficiently thoroughgoing ones, to bring about a corresponding correction of the traditional Catholic view of church history. For that reason the statement that the church never existed in unequivocally demonstrable unity sounds startling and offensive even in Protestant ears. Protestantism therefore submits in the same manner as Catholicism to the fact stated in our second thesis, without allowing that fact its full weight in accordance with the Reformed concept of the church. Or else we let the threat here of relativization lead us into becoming indifferent towards doctrinal differences, and as far as the church's past is concerned are strangely biased towards letting our sympathies always go out to the heretics.

To face up squarely to the proposition that doctrinal differences of divisive significance for the church are a necessary element in the church's existence, would mean to allow the validity of two things at the same time:—First, the unity of the church can paradoxically enough never be exhibited without church division—and thus never only in distinguishing the church from the so-called world, but always at the same time in distinguishing church from church—unity in the Spirit only through separation of spirits, *consensus* only in contrast to a *dissensus.*

The unity of the church can always be manifested only on the plane of an *ecclesia particularis* and therefore only as a proof of the dividedness of the church. Alongside of that, however, the second thing must also always remain valid: the church cannot exist otherwise than in wrestling for its unity, which is yet never visible except as party unity. It must therefore take the doctrinal differences seriously, although the boundaries of the church as they are thereby defined are never identical with the boundaries of the Church of Christ, but rather cut it up into bounded parts. Whoever refuses to have anything to do with doctrinal differences that divide the church, is attacking the very existence of the church.

3. Finally, the thesis that not all doctrinal differences have divisive significance for the church cannot be opposed at all. For who would wish to assert the contrary, namely, that all doctrinal differences have divisive significance for the church? Although we are thus here dealing with what is apparently the most self-evident and commonplace of our statements on the subject, yet it is precisely the one that conceals within it the whole explosiveness of the problem of the divisive significance for the church of doctrinal differences. For if we accept the two previous propositions—*viz.* that only doctrinal differences have divisive significance for the church, and that doctrinal differences of divisive significance for the church are a necessary element in the church's existence—then the fact that not all doctrinal differences are of divisive significance for the church must surely touch off the whole battle on the divisive significance for the church of doctrinal differences. *Which* doctrinal differences are divisive for the church and which are not? It might be thought that any further general discussion of the divisive significance for the church of doctrinal differences is now fruitless and hopeless, and that in order to make any progress we should have to turn to individual concrete doctrinal differences, so as to make plain from one case to another which doctrinal differences have divisive significance and which have not. But that would be a mistake. The mere statement of a concrete doctrinal difference has in itself no bearing whatever on the question whether it is to be considered divisive for the church. A criterion is here required which the individual concrete doctrinal difference as such cannot possibly supply but itself seeks to be measured by. Unless we wish to incur the suspicion of ultimately regarding all doctrinal differences as divisive for the church after all, or else of making arbitrary judgments, then we must be able to supply a criterion for the divisive significance of doctrinal differences. Nor must we seek to supplant this

criterion by judging according to a kind of moral feeling, whether in the
sense of taking as strict as possible, and therefore as comprehensive as
possible, a view of doctrinal differences as divisive for the church or in
the sense of applying that verdict as magnanimously as possible and
therefore as rarely as possible. It might well be that a very cautious
classification of the divisive nature of doctrinal differences could result
from genuine theological stringency, and that an extremely rigorous
judgment could come of theological carelessness and laxity. At all events,
the man who considers a doctrinal difference to be divisive must not *a
priori* accuse the other who does not consider it to be so of an indifferent
attitude to questions of doctrine—as of course on the other hand the
latter likewise must not accuse the former *a priori* of a doctrinarian
attitude.

Therefore the discussion must really be kept to the fundamental
problem of the divisive significance for the church of doctrinal differences and must be fought out there. Only so, I believe, can we also reach
the real roots of the difference between the E.K.U. [*Evangelische Kirche
der Union*] and the V.E.L.K.D. [*Vereinigte Evangelische Lutherische
Kirche Deutschlands*], which is simply not the case when the discussion
is limited, say, to the doctrine of the Lord's Supper. For even when we
fully recognize the doctrinal difference which does in fact exist here, it
would surely still not necessarily be proved that this doctrinal difference
is of a kind to divide the church. Or on the other hand, it might well be
—to consider an extreme possibility for the moment—that an agreement
could in fact be reached on the question of the Lord's Supper, and
therewith the obstacle that causes division of the churches removed in
the eyes of the V.E.L.K.D., but that then on the other hand the E.K.U
on its side, at some point that was hitherto concealed but became
manifest in the course of the fundamental discussion on the divisive
significance for the church of doctrinal differences, would have to bring
out a doctrinal difference of divisive significance and declare: 'Your
spirit is different from ours; your underlying doctrine of what is called
"church doctrine" and of the relation of church and doctrine is one we
cannot regard as in accordance with scripture.' I do not mean that to be
the writing on the wall. But it does seem to me really necessary to
indicate the decisive point of difference, which is perhaps not to be
found within the circle of the traditional doctrinal differences between
Lutheran and Reformed, but has to do with a different understanding
both of the Reformation and also of so-called Modernism, and for that
very reason with a different understanding of scripture.

2. *On the Relation between the Word of God and the Church*

The connexion between church and doctrine is to be determined by the relation in which both church and doctrine stand to the Word of God. Church and doctrine belong together in virtue of the Word of God and for the sake of the Word of God. The relationship of church and doctrine can therefore be properly viewed only in the light of its basis in the Word of God. How church and doctrine are related to each other is thus a secondary question which depends on how church and doctrine are comprised in the Word of God.

As a basis for considering the relation of the Word of God and the church, I quote an observation of Luther's in *De captivitate babylonica:* '*Ecclesia ... nascitur verbo promissionis per fidem, eodemque alitur et servatur, hoc est, ipsa per promissiones dei constituitur, non promissio dei per ipsam. Verbum dei enim supra Ecclesiam est incomparabiliter, in quo nihil statuere, ordinare, facere, sed tantum statui, ordinari, fieri habet tanquam creatura. Quis enim suum parentem gignit? quis suum autorem prior constituit? Hoc sane habet Ecclesia, quod potest discernere verbum dei a verbis hominum. ...*'[1] I would expound that as follows:—

1. The Word of God has absolute priority and superiority over the church as the thing that calls it to life and maintains it in life, as the constitutive ground of its existence. The church does not exist on its own alongside the Word of God, but its existence has in the strict sense its source in the Word of God, so that in virtue of this fact that its existence has its source in the Word of God its *actio* is nothing but *passio*: *in quo nihil statuere, ordinare, facere, sed tantum statui ordinari, fieri habet.* The *verbum dei* is *creator ecclesiae*, the *ecclesia* is *creatura verbi dei.* This passivity of the church on the ground of the *actio* of the Word of God does not by any means merely belong to the past as a once-for-all event by which the church is founded, but it is and remains constitutive of the being of the church in the sense of a *creatio continua.* This Luther underlines by using the present tense. He does not say: *ecclesia nata est verbo promissionis, ipsa per promissiones dei consituta est,* but: *nascitur* and *constituitur.* Its *esse* is a continual *fieri.* That certainly does not exclude the perfect forms *factam esse, natam esse, constitutam esse.* Rather, it includes them. We shall have to come back to that later. At any rate it is also true the other way round: that the *factam esse* of the church is rightly understood only when the present tense of the *fieri* is not excluded but included. For the church lives from the proclamation

[1] *WA* 6, p. 560.33 ff=Clem. 1, p. 497.37 ff.

as the present coming to expression of the Word of God. It is, to quote here also Article VII of the Augsburg Confession, *perpetuo mansura* only in virtue of this continual action of the Word of God. In this sense the relative clause, *in qua evangelium pure docetur et recte administrantur sacramenta*, certainly emphasizes the fact that the proclamation of the Word of God which takes place here and now derives from the proclamation that has always already taken place before, and for that reason already presupposes the existence of the church. Yet it surely calls for special attention that the linking pronoun is not a '*quae*' but an '*in qua*'. True, we are often given the impression today that the Augsburg Confession defines the church as the entity *quae evangelium pure docet et recte administrat sacramenta*; as if the constitutive relation of church and proclamation consisted in the church's being subject. The expression 'word of the church' is gradually entering into strange competition with the concept of the Word of God, while interest in a word of the church competes with the desire for the Word of God. Although the Word of God is uttered only by human lips, since it is in being testified to by men that it awakens testimony, although the church as the place where the Word is spoken is thus at the same time also the bearer of the Word that is spoken, and the proclamation as the ground of the church's existence is at the same time also the expression of the church's existence, yet that must never lead us to forget that the Word of God must always remain above the church and the church under the Word of God, that the Word which is uttered in it and through it is also addressed to it, and that it is one and the same Word of God which summons us to the church and keeps us in the church and without whose coming the church would cease to be church. Much would be gained if all that is said of the church were to set out from the fact of its thus being unceasingly constituted by the working of the Word of God.

2. But now we must once more give special consideration to what was already mentioned in connexion with the time factor: the tension in the being of the church between its *factam esse* and its *fieri*. Is not the church, as a result of its temporal origin, a historical entity which maintains itself continually within history without in the strict sense depending upon its being unceasingly constituted by the working of the Word of God? Is it not the church itself that accomplishes the movement from its *factam esse* to its *fieri*? Now, we shall also have to speak as well of a continuity of the church within history independent of the Word of God. But when we said the church is *perpetuo mansura* in virtue of the act of the Word of God, which as proclamation in the present, always

comes from past proclamation and is on the move towards new proclamation, then this continuity of the act of the Word must not be
identified as a matter of course with the observable continuity of the
church within history. Rather, it is a question of the continuity of the
Word of God itself which, as *verbum caro factum* in the strict once-for-
all-ness of the perfect tense, seeks to be ever proclaimed anew and thus
engages in continual *verbum fieri*, so that in this *fieri* it may give proof
of its *factum esse* in the unity and identity of the *verbum caro factum* with
the *Christus praesens* as *Christus praedicatus*. Instead of saying that the
church is the place of the action of the Word of God, it would b emore
correct to say that the action of the Word of God is the place of the
church, *viz.*—that the church with the *factam esse* and *fieri* of its being
has its place in the Word of God and its *factum esse* and *fieri*. For the
fact that the *fieri* of the church must be spoken of in view of its *factam
esse*, and that its *factam esse* can be intelligibly spoken of only in view of
its *fieri*, has its ground solely in the fact that the present *fieri* cf the Word
of God can be spoken of only in view of its *factum esse*, but that its
factum esse must also be spoken of in view of its present *fieri*.

Luther indicates this in the observation quoted by using *promissio dei*
as an alternative term for *verbum dei*. For the *verbum dei* as *caro factum*
is the Word that pledges, that promises, that points into the future
because it opens the future, the *verbum pro-mittens* which, translated
literally, sends forwards what it itself is, lets it spring forth, holds it in
prospect and makes it come; a Word that gives hope and therefore in
its *factum esse* contains the *futurum* within itself and emits it from itself.
For that reason it will, and it can, and it must ever be proclaimed anew
as *promissio*, as the coming of God himself coming towards us. The
church lives from this *promissio*, in taking it to itself *per fidem*. The *fides*
in which the *promissio dei* on each several occasion achieves its end is the
act of what Luther at the end of the quotation designated as *discernere
verbum dei a verbis hominum*. For the *fides* recognizes the Word of God
as what it truly is, in distinction from the word of men: as *promissio* and
not as law. That however means: the Word of God which is constitutive
of the church is Gospel, not law. For only the Gospel, not the law, has
the power to effect faith. However necessary it is that a detailed doctrine
of the Word of God should deal with the fact that the Gospel cannot be
proclaimed without the law, and should explain how far it is true that
the law, too, is God's Word, yet the supremely important thing is, that
we should not let ourselves be seduced into starting with a formal conception of the Word of God, but should take the expression 'Word of

God' in the proper sense, namely, in its radical contrast to man's word, as Gospel. For: *quoties verbum dei praedicatur, reddit laetas, latas, securas conscientias in deum, quia est verbum gratiae, remissionis, bonum et suave, quoties verbum hominis, reddit tristem, angustam, trepidam conscientiam in seipsa, quia est verbum legis, irae et peccati, ostendens, quid non fecerit et quanta debeat.*[1]

Here I appear to have advanced far beyond our proper subject. Throughout the discussion of the problem of church doctrine it is of supreme importance to keep two things in mind:—First, that all that is said of the Word of God must take its bearings strictly from the distinction of law and Gospel and therefore any purely formally applied concept of the Word of God leads to hopeless confusion. Secondly—and materially connected with it—everything that is said of the Word of God must be said in strictest relation to its correlate, *fides*—and that means to *fides* as *fides iustificans*, for we must strictly forbid ourselves to use the concept of faith in any other way than as *fides iustificans*.

3. On the question of a continuity of the church within history, independent of the continuity of the Word of God itself, let us consider the expression *tanquam creatura* in the Luther quotation. The *tanquam* is not intended to mark as a mere simile the designation of the church as *creatura verbi*, but means that the word *creatura* really expresses what the church is: creature, creation. For that reason analogous statements are valid of the creation and of the church. Both have the ground of their existence in the Word of God, and in both cases the problem arises whether the entity in question is not in fact capable of existing in independence of this, the ground of its existence. The fact is, that man exists even when he does not consider himself a creature of the Word of God. And yet, even if he will not allow the truth of it, he exists only because God nevertheless does not let go of him and does not abandon him as his creature. Hence even in his fallen state he exists in virtue of the fact that the Word of God accompanies and upholds him. Thus faith can regard fallen man, too, as God's creature and recognize in him the will and ordinance of God. In the same way the church, too, does not simply cease to exist when it does not attend to the Word of God which is the ground of its existence. But as far as it does exist thus independently of God's Word, it is a creature of the Word of God in the same paradoxical way as the fallen creation, i.e. it is world and not *ecclesia proprie dicta*. When the church seems to be independent of the concrete act of the Word of God and yet continually distinguishes itself

[1] *WA* 2, p. 453.2 ff.

as church from the so-called world, then the very fact of its historically self-contained existence shows precisely that church and world are inseparably bound up with each other and that the proclamation of the Word of God even as proclamation to the church always remains *eo ipso* proclamation to the world. It comes to the same in the end whether it has then to be addressed rather as churchly world or as worldly church.

3. *On the Relation between the Word of God and Doctrine*

It is substantially more difficult to reach agreement on the relation of the Word of God and doctrine than on the relation of the Word of God and the church, because we must now take up questions which could be left out at first in a discussion of the relation of the Word of God and the church confined to essentials. The difficulty is, that we have now to deal with an ambiguity attaching both to the concept of the Word of God and also to the concept of doctrine—an ambiguity which raises problems no one today can evade. Here it is not the least help complaining of the destructive influence modernistic thinking has on theology and trying to cut it out and refurbish the old ways. For the fact is, it has made men aware of problems which were always contained in substance, if also latently, in the concepts 'Word of God' and 'doctrine'. Hence the influence of modernism, so far as it is in fact destructive, can only be countered by really facing up to these problems. Lest at this point we should completely lose our bearings, I shall now approach the problems from the standpoint that the concept doctrine tends partly to be almost equated with the concept Word of God and partly to be sharply distinguished from it.

1. A use of the term doctrine which tends to be almost equated with the concept Word of God is found for example both in early Protestant Orthodoxy and also in the theology of the Reformers. And yet, without prejudice to the fluidity of the boundary between the two, there is an unmistakable shift of accent. The orthodox usage may be illustrated by the following expressions (from Hollaz):—*Articulus fidei est pars doctrinae verbo Dei scripto revelatae.* Or, *materia specialis et primaria, circa quam sacra scriptura versatur, sunt dogmata fidei et praecepta morum.* Or the thoroughly typical concept of a *theologia revelata.* It is doing no injustice to Orthodoxy if we define its standpoint by saying that the Word of God is doctrine and that revelation is a sum of revealed doctrines. The best illustration of that is the carefully worked out doctrine of the *articuli fidei fundamentales* and *non fundamentales.* Nevertheless it must not be overlooked that even here the concept doctrine and the

concept Word of God are only *almost* equated. We must recall among
other things the distinction between *fundamentum fidei reale sive sub-
stantiale* and *fundamentum fidei dogmaticum sive doctrinale*. Thus even
Orthodoxy cannot make the two concepts coincide completely and, say,
replace *verbum dei* by *doctrina dei* or *doctrina de deo*. But all the same the
concept of the *verbum dei* is here very largely interpreted in the light of
the concept of *doctrina*, and the concept of *doctrina* in turn has its real
prototype in theology.

If it is said on the other hand that the Reformers' concept of *doctrina*
means simply preaching, and thus finds its real prototype not in theology
but in proclamation, in the *viva vox evangelii*, then that is right enough
in a way, yet here too matters are more complicated. The concept
doctrina in Art. VII of the Augsburg Confession, at any rate, must not
be interpreted without more ado according to the German version. It
gives the Latin text, in contrast to the German, possibly a stronger
Melanchthonian accent which already points in the direction of Orthodoxy. But even for Luther it cannot by any means be affirmed that
doctrina means simply preaching. When he says, for example, 'Distingu-
amus vitam et doctrinam, quae ad deum pertinet, vitam ad nos',[1] or when
he tells us, 'Our life may well be impure, sinful and sickly, but our
doctrine must be pure, holy, sound and steadfast. . . . For doctrine is
God's Word and God's very truth',[2] then although that is a downright
equation of doctrine and Word of God, so that he can even on occasion
say God's doctrine instead of God's Word[3]; and although in thus equat-
ing them he is undoubtedly thinking in the first instance of the proclamation, yet here as everywhere a sharp distinction between proclamation
and theology is naturally very far from his mind. Any form of Christian
doctrine or teaching, including the theological form proper, is comprised
without reflexion in the concept *doctrina*, and doctrine for him is thus
also certainly doctrine expressed in articles of faith. *Doctrina debet esse
rotundus et aureus circulus sine rima . . . si unum articulum amittimus, omnes
amittimus*.[4] Nevertheless these observations cannot by any means be
taken simply as synonymous with Orthodoxy. To bring out the contrast
it could be said that in Luther the concept of *doctrina* is very largely
interpreted in the light of the *verbum dei*.

But now, what separates us today both from the age of the Reformation and from the age of Orthodoxy, is that we must go much further
than they did in distinguishing between Word of God, holy scripture,

[1] *WA* 40/2, p. 46.5 f.   [2] *WA* 30/3, p. 343.3 ff.
[3] *WA* 30/3, p. 344.13.   [4] *WA* 40/2, p. 47.3 ff, 11.

proclamation, doctrine and theology. That is not merely a question of terminology, but deeply affects the very essence of the matter. Yet it does not prevent us, in the task imposed on us, from having a very great deal to learn from the theology of the Reformation and of Orthodoxy, or from finding ourselves, even if in ways that are not immediately obvious on the surface, ultimately in agreement with it. In the context of our present problem that would have to be proved by showing that a really penetrating examination of the distinction between Word of God, holy scripture, proclamation, doctrine and theology, far from leading to a separation, is the very first way of re-establishing their essential inner connexion. That necessitates a new exposition of the doctrine of the Word of God in which we decisively turn our backs on a metaphysical interpretation of the concept 'Word of God' (the Reformation can be appealed to there!) and instead interpret the act of the Word of God in a context whose nature I can here only very briefly indicate by referring to such phenomena as word, language, history and exposition. If for example I define proclamation as expressing in words the Word of God, church doctrine as expressing in confessional language the Word of God, theology as expressing in scientific language the Word of God, then I intend such ways of putting it, which I cannot here ground and expound, merely to indicate how a more sharply formulated distinction could now be the very means of establishing the fact and the manner in which it is really the Word of God itself we have to do with in proclamation, church doctrine and theology.

2. If we now ask why a distinction has to be made between Word of God and doctrine, and how, then something like the following possibilities present themselves:—It can be said that in contrast to the Word of God, the subject and author in the case of doctrine is always man. That sounds quite obvious. But we must then be clear that in the very same way preaching and even holy scripture would have to be contrasted with God's Word, and that for the rest God's Word is never uttered at all except by men in human words. On the other hand, it is plain that the proposition is really not by any means intended to imply that Christian doctrine as such is in this qualitative sense human doctrine as opposed to God's Word. If we seek help by saying that doctrine is only response to God's Word, only testimony to God's Word, then that will likewise have to be countered by the fact that the same applies also to preaching and even to holy scripture itself. But if the formula seems suspect in that context, then why not also in regard to doctrine? Or it can be said by way of variation that God's Word is an event, it has

always the character of address, it posits a personal relation between God and men; whereas doctrine objectifies, is teaching about God and about men. True enough! But does that give us a really unequivocal grasp of the difference, say, from the uttering of the Word of God in the sermon? Is e.g. the character of address a stylistically ascertainable criterion of the Word of God and the character of objective statement a criterion of the same kind on the negative side? Or it can be said that God's Word creates faith and thereby makes us free to a right obedience; whereas doctrine has always at least a tendency to legalism, presents the *credenda* and is easily set in the notorious key of the Athanasian Creed, '*Quicunque vult salvus esse . . .*'. But can the ground of faith and the content of faith be so simply apportioned to the Word of God and to doctrine respectively?

Perhaps, though, we have left unnecessary free play to these definitions of the relation between God's Word and doctrine by speaking of doctrine in a completely general way. That prevents from the start a clear distinction from holy scripture, preaching and theology. For the latter is surely nothing else but doctrine; and both scripture and preaching at least contain doctrine. Yet our question was really at bottom one about doctrine in the specific sense of church doctrine and about its relation to the Word of God. For this more precisely formulated question too, of course, the answers we have considered and the problems they involve are not without significance. Can we now find a more convincing answer?

It may be said: God's Word is to be found solely in holy scripture, whereas church doctrine comes under the category of the *traditio ecclesiastica*. Only scripture is therefore binding in the strict sense, whereas church doctrine is only relatively binding to the extent that it must always be left open to testing by scripture. How should any evangelical theologian fail to assent to the intention of this answer?—irrespective of the questions that now surely also arise as to the meaning and limits of the scripture principle, as to the rightness of excluding scripture from the concept of tradition and as to the understanding of what is meant by 'relatively binding' or by the (even logically so unsatisfactory) distinction between *norma normans* and *norma normata*. But let us here leave all that aside and now take up a doubtful point that is perhaps not immediately obvious at first sight! According to the view both of the Reformers and of Orthodoxy we have indulged in a fatal *quid pro quo*. For never do they rank church doctrine as such under the category of *traditio ecclesiastica*. It is always a question of the *doctrina christiana*, the doctrine that accords with the Word of God, in which nothing else but the Word of God itself comes to expression. What does in fact, however, come under the concept of tradition is everything that supplies Christian doctrine in the form of testimonies and writings alongside holy scripture, and hence also the early Christian creeds and the confessions of the Reformation. But, be it noted, only in regard to the question of their being formally binding. As far as their content is concerned, the fact of confessing to them settles the question and declares that they contain the doctrine which accords with God's Word and that this doctrine is now in fact absolutely binding. Moreover, it is not binding as the doctrine of a particular confessing church, but it is binding as the pure doctrine of the Word of God itself—and to that extent certainly as the doctrine of the Church of Christ, but not church doctrine in the sense that it could compete with other types of church doctrine. There is only *one* pure doctrine, and beside it only heresies. Who would wish to dispute the inner logic of this argument, or even the theological correctness of the proposition that when we speak of church doctrine we must claim its validity as doctrine which accords with scripture and therefore testimony to *the* church doctrine proper, or rather, not doctrine of the church, but doctrine of the Word of God itself?

But now, this argument rests on a presupposition which we cannot possibly make our own any more. In order to fix clearly this decisive point, let us deliberately leave aside for the moment all the questions that since the collapse of Orthodoxy have arisen in exegesis and dogmatics with regard to concrete individual points of church doctrine, and which no theologian who is to be taken seriously today could dismiss as pointless. I grant it is understandable when people say: 'Please do not come to us with the general reservation about the church's doctrinal statements being liable to error, in order by that means to undermine *a priori* their bindingness. We, too, recognize that general reservation. Show us in concrete instances where the recognized creeds and confessions are not in accord with scripture. Until that is demonstrated, they are binding in the strict sense.' Yet I think that really glosses over the decisive problem. We saw that according also to the view of the Reformers and of Orthodoxy the church's creeds and confessions are naturally not binding *per se*, that is, that they have no formal authority. What is binding is exclusively the scriptural doctrine they contain, whereby the old debate about *quia* or *quatenus* is at bottom irrelevant. But now, the question is: What is really meant by the binding nature of the content of the confessions? Does it mean also the binding nature of their linguistic and reflective form? Let us not immediately become impatient because that raises anew a question we have already had more than enough of—the question of a distinction between the wording and the real meaning, between the formulation and the intention, between the letter and the spirit, between the theological form and the doctrinal content of the confessions. That these distinctions solve nothing must surely be clear to all of us; for how can the content of a proposition be taken seriously without taking its wording seriously? But there should be just as little disputing the fact that the distinctions in question do pinpoint a problem which we cannot evade.

The nature of this problem can best be realized by asking: How are we to test and determine whether someone is in agreement with the teaching of the confessions or not? Surely not by his signing the confessions! Nor by the fact that he does not explicitly contradict them. Nor yet by the fact that in case of doubt he takes up and repeats certain phrases from the confessions. All these things provide no criterion, but at bottom only render more difficult the task of testing and determining whether he is in agreement with the teaching of the confessions. The task of testing and determining this is not only necessitated by the fact that in his preaching, teaching and theology he does not simply repeat the wording of the confessions but expresses himself in his own way: rather, the task of testing and determining the point in question is also made *possible* only by the fact that in his preaching, teaching and theology he does not simply repeat the wording of the confessions but expresses himself in his own way. Whoever evades independent expression when it comes to the bit, thereby evades our testing and determining whether he is in agreement with the teaching of the confessions. Agreement with the teaching of the confessions can be proved at all only as a result of independent theological statements. To be bound to the teaching of the confessions therefore means to be bound by that very fact to theological work on one's own. And that, too, not merely, say, in the sense of subjecting the teaching of the confessions to a critical examination in the light of holy scripture, nor yet merely in the sense of taking advantage of the margin which the teaching of the confessions still leaves open, but also and above all in the sense of being bound to an independent study of the confessions which identifies the church's doctrine in them. Yet how can this be tested? Solely by participating in the theological task of identifying church doctrine.

We are confronted here, precisely as with holy scripture, by the hermeneutic problem. The agreement between text and exposition can be determined only by means of the exposition itself. Demonstrating and testing agreement with the teaching of the confessions is possible only by means of theological study. Identity with the doctrine of the church can be established only in the process of identifying the church's doctrine. That is where the problem lies, and in the first instance it exists entirely irrespective of the question whether the teaching of the confessions in turn also agrees with scripture—however acute that question may also become in the task of identifying church doctrine. But apart from that, the immediate implications of the problem as such will surely be plain to anyone who puts himself in the position of a judicial commission of the church which had to decide the question of agreement with the teaching of the confessions in a concrete case—for example, that of the theology of Bultmann. The best thing in such an undertaking would be the theological endurance tests to which the judicial commission would be exposed and the resulting realization of how difficult the question of agreement with the teaching of the confessions in actual fact is. For surely one thing which was not sufficiently realized and thought through in the days of the Reformation and was entirely lost sight of in the days of Orthodoxy, but which we cannot possibly overlook today, is, that every formulation of church doctrine, precisely as an exposition of scripture, is a piece of theology. The doctrine of the church, however, can never be identified with a particular theology, since it would then after all come under the category of the *traditio ecclesiastica*—a possibility which both the Reformation and Orthodoxy most passionately and rightly rejected. But now, it is beyond question that every church creed and every confession is not only testimony to the Word of God but also testimony to a particular ecclesiastical and theological tradition —both things, in fact, inseparably bound up together. Hence for us— and here indeed we are, rightly understood, in agreement with the Reformation and even with Orthodoxy—it is totally inadequate to say that the creeds and confessions are admittedly not binding *per se*, thus not formally, which means not without the authority of holy scripture behind them, but that their content is scriptural until the contrary is proved, and is consequently absolutely binding. That statement says nothing of the fact that the wording—and taken strictly, that really means also the content—of the creeds and confessions is in certain respects *traditio ecclesiastica* and as such cannot be absolutely binding.

If the concept of church doctrine is related to the particular documents and formulae which are held to define church doctrine, then the following alternatives arise:—Either a difference must be allowed in principle between the teaching of these documents and church doctrine as the teaching of the Word of God itself—a difference which is necessarily given with the theological form of these documents and which therefore compels to further theological study. Or else the concept of church doctrine has to be limited to an unqualified identity with the teaching of these documents, and therewith to the doctrinal tradition of a particular church. But even then it is necessary to reckon with a difference, *viz.*—the difference between church doctrine in this sense as a historical phenomenon and the actual contemporary teaching of the church in question. In both cases we are forced to the realization that to speak of church doctrine can be meaningful only in view of the fact that the doctrinal tradition which constitutes a particular church is currently vindicated as constitutive of the existence of the church, i.e. that it is asserted not as ecclesiastical tradition but in concrete testimony to the Word of God, and accordingly is not simply repeated but serves by way of interpretation to identify the doctrine of the church. Anyone who holds that to point to the confessions is *the* answer to the question of the church's doctrine, turns church doctrine into a historical phenomenon, and thereby furthers the much-lamented doctrinal chaos in preaching and theology.

3. A final remark on terminology may also shed light on the problem. In speaking of church doctrine there is a widespread tendency to use the terms dogma and confession indiscriminately. Is that appropriate? I think not! Involuntarily we usually make a distinction by speaking of the trinitarian or Christological 'dogma', yet not, say, of the Lutheran 'dogma of the Lord's Supper' but of the Lutheran 'doctrine of the Lord's Supper'. That points to the fact that the concept of dogma really belongs to the doctrinal definitions of the ancient church, whereas the Reformation statements of church doctrine bear the designation *confessio*. That is no accident. The concept dogma with its two root meanings 'tenet' and 'decree' provides the possibility of bracketing together the claim to truth and the claim to formal absolute authority. The concept dogma covers completely the Catholic understanding of church doctrine. But to bring the concept dogma into harmony with the Reformers' understanding of church doctrine must involve violently wresting its literal meaning, without thereby being really able to prevent the Reformers' understanding of church doctrine from suffering in the process. The meaning of church doctrine in the Reformers' sense can be appropriately designated only by the concept confession and can be really expounded only in the light of that concept. Its difference

from the concept dogma relates both to the question how statements of church doctrine come about and also to the question how far they are valid.

4. *On the Relation of Church and Doctrine*

The question of the relation of church and doctrine may at once be put in a more precise form: What has the church's doctrine to do with the unity of the church? I begin from the relevant passage in Article VII of the Augsburg Confession.

1. What is the meaning of '*vera unitas ecclesiae*'? At all events not the organizational unity of an ecclesiastical body. That falls under the '*nec necesse est*', including e.g. the apostolic succession. Since the church is in its essence one, what constitutes the unity of the church is nothing other than what makes the church its true self. What makes the church its true self, by definition makes the church *una ecclesia*. The Augsburg Confession does not treat the question of the unity of the church as an additional problem alongside the question of its essence, but considers the question of the church's unity answered with the question of its essence, as the conjunction 'for' in the German version shows. Thus it is with good reason that in the positive statement on the true unity we find '*satis est*' and not '*necesse est*'. For the question is not put in the form: What must happen, that the church may be one? But it is: What is the criterion of a right or wrong understanding of the essential unity of the church? Art. VII of the Augsburg Confession is clearly and exclusively aimed against the Roman Catholic understanding of the church and its unity. And in the concrete confessional situation the point is: You must not make the unity of the church depend on anything else but what makes the church its true self.

After all that, it is beyond doubt that the *vera unitas ecclesiae* which is spoken of in Art. VII of the Augsburg Confession is the unity of the body of Christ, as is underlined by the quotation from Ephesians 4. When it is said that Art. VII of the Augsburg Confession can be applied today only to 'a church with a clear confession' ('*eine konfessionell klare Kirche*'), then that is dubious on various counts:—First, the question of the unity of a particular church is not at issue here at all, or at least not primarily. Further, even 'a church with a clear confession' provides no guarantee of any kind that within it the Gospel is everywhere and always purely preached. Again, to set up the formal ideal of a 'church with a clear confession' without regard to the nature of that confession, is to pay remarkably little attention to the *pure* and *recte* of Art. VII of the Augsburg Confession, or rather to supplant it by a confessional purism that is bound to history. And finally, it would mean that if the *pure* and *recte* is taken into account, then locigally Art. VII of the Augsburg Confession would obviously be applicable only to a single confession, this confession would be identical with the church as such, and its unity as a confessionally determined ecclesiastical body would be the visible presentation of the *vera unitas ecclesiae* itself.

2. If it is now asked all the same what is the indirect bearing of Art. VII of the Augsburg Confession upon the question of inter-church communion and inter-church division among individual ordered churches, then first of all we must point again to the '*nec necesse est*'. We naturally cannot here go into the whole question of the founding of church law. There is no doubt that with the event which makes the church its true self certain basic ordinances are laid down for the existence of the church. It is obvious that in that respect special significance accrues to baptism and the Lord's Supper. It is only natural that out of these basic ordinances given with the act of the Word of God there arises the need to safeguard them by forming an abundance of further church ordinances, both within the local ἐκκλησία and also with regard to the mutual relations between the individual ἐκκλησίαι. But we must be quite clear that this whole process is at best only a consequence that follows from the *vera unitas ecclesiae*, but does not create the *vera unitas ecclesiae*. Indeed, it cannot even be said that it serves to make increasingly manifest the *vera unitas ecclesiae*. It can at best serve to testify to the nature of the *vera unitas ecclesiae*, but even then only when this process of the judicial shaping and safeguarding of church unity is understood as a thing that is not essential *ad veram unitatem ecclesiae*. The *unitas* of an organized ecclesiastical body above congregational level is a different thing in principle from the *vera unitas ecclesiae*. For the unity of such an ecclesiastical body does in fact require very many things that are not essential *ad veram unitatem ecclesiae*. And to confuse the *vera unitas ecclesiae* with the organizational unity of an ecclesiastical body inevitably leads to a false view of the true unity of the church, because precisely then non-essential marks of unity are elevated into essential marks of unity and consequently to essential marks of the church. The '*nec necesse est*' must be interpreted strictly in the sense that none of the things which do not make the church its true self may be declared essential for the true unity of the church, because precisely that would be in contradiction to the true unity of the church. For that reason we must go so far as to say that even the existence of a unified

confessional statement does not belong essentially *ad veram unitatem ecclesiae*, nor indeed even the explicit recognition of an existing *consensus de doctrina evangelii et de administratione sacramentorum*. On the contrary sufficient for the true unity of the church is the actual fact of a *consentire*, even without going on to expound the *consentire*.

That may appear an over-subtle interpretation of Art. VII of the Augsburg Confession. But when for example the 'in unanimity' ('*einträchtiglich*') in the German version is left out, so that it reads, 'For it is sufficient for the true unity of the Christian church that there the Gospel is preached in its pure sense and the sacraments are administered in accordance with the divine Word', or when the Latin version is put in the form, '*Et ad veram unitatem ecclesiae satis est evangelium pure doceri et recte administrari sacramenta*', then that does not alter the real point in the very slightest. For where the Gospel is purely preached and the holy sacraments are administered according to the Gospel, then of course that is done at all simply because it is done *pure et recte*, in the unanimity of a factual *consentire*. Yet there is no trace of the statement: *ad veram unitatem ecclesiae necesse est consensum statutum esse de doctrina evangelii et de administratione sacramentorum*. Now of course it is indisputable that in the confessional situation in which it arose, the Augsburg Confession had also an eye to the concrete fact of a division in the church and to the question of overcoming it and hence of course also to the recognition, or the re-establishing, of a *consensus*. Yet what has that to do with the *vera unitas ecclesiae*?

With almost every question concerning the concept of the church the discussion is hopelessly encumbered by the one-sided identification of 'church' with an ecclesiastical body organized above congregational level —a thing which has implanted itself ineradicably in German usage but which, in spite of the difference in Greek and Latin usage, is really a result of the early Catholic concept of the church and its understanding of the unity of the church. That understanding has left its mark on the phrase ἐκκλησία καθολική ever since its first appearance in Ignatius. I can therefore only consider it harmful and hopeless to seek to possess ourselves of the concept 'Catholic', 'Catholicism' in an evangelical sense. In saying that, I am well aware that it occurs in the Apostles' Creed and the Nicene Creed, but also that Luther constantly interpreted it by 'Christian'. For the simple fact is, that the concept 'Catholic' involves the confusion of the *vera unitas ecclesiae* with the *unitas* of an ecclesiastical body—which means it involves the tendency to bind the holy, Christian Church 'to place and time, to person and gesture, by means of laws and outward pomp' (Schwabach Articles, 12). For myself, it serves only to strengthen me in this view when W. Maurer interprets the claim to Catholicity in a positive sense as the claim 'to possess and administer the undivided heritage of early Catholicism in its authentic meaning'.[1] Do we not here have a fundamental *dissensus* in regard to the understanding of the Reformation?

But so far as it is a question of inter-church communion and inter-church division at the level of individual ordered churches, the basic proviso of *'nec necesse est'* will certainly not make everything here a matter of indifference. Although the formation of organized individual churches falls under the *'nec necesse est ad veram unitatem ecclesiae'*, yet it surely cannot be affirmed that it is superfluous. We shall have to say on the contrary: it is in certain respects even a very necessary thing. Only, necessary not *ad veram unitatem ecclesiae*, but on the ground of the *vera unitas ecclesiae* for charity's sake, which is intent on the creating and maintaining of good order with a view to mutual service. To what service? Naturally to the service of and with that which makes the church its true self, and to that extent of course indirectly also to the service of the *vera unitas ecclesiae*. Yet certainly not with the claim to be essentially constitutive of the *vera unitas ecclesiae*. We can visualize that more clearly by taking the concrete question of why in the sixteenth century the formation of state churches took place and why in our day the formation of the E.K.U. or the V.E.L.K.D. Anyone who sought to assert that it is strictly necessary for churches of the same confession to form a single ecclesiastical body with a common church constitution, would be falsifying the *vera unitas ecclesiae*. We should then have to protest against such an undertaking precisely for the sake of the *vera unitas ecclesiae*.

3. But now, the decisive point at issue is the question of the manner in which what is done for charity's sake in the direction of individual church unity must take its bearings from the *vera unitas ecclesiae*. There is no question as to *whether* it must do so. Everything that constitutes the unity of an individual church—even, say, to the unified regulation of church taxes—must ultimately justify itself by proving that it serves what makes the church its true self. The unity of an individual church therefore presupposes that unanimity prevails as to what makes the church its true self, and consequently also as to what belongs to the true unity of the church. In regard to the question of individual church unity we must certainly instead of *'satis est'* say: *necesse est consentire de doctrina*

---

[1] *TLZ* 77 (1952), pp. 4 f.

evangelii et de administratione sacramentorum. But now, what does that mean?

(*a*) Although the *consentire de doctrina evangelii et de administratione sacramentorum* is a necessary condition of the unity of an individual church, yet the unity of an individual church is never to be identified with the *vera unitas ecclesiae.* But of course the thing is now to provide the correct basis for this assertion. It is obvious that not any and every *consentire de doctrina evangelii et de administratione sacramentorum* could be identified with the *vera unitas ecclesiae.* If the *consentire* were thus formally understood, then the Roman Church would be the ideal of a confessional church. The critical definitions *pure* and *recte* must also be added in the sense of the Augsburg Confession. Now of course every confessional church understands its *consensus* in that sense. Yet that must not confuse us or lead us to see it all as a relative question and conclude that since everyone asserts the *pure et recte* it presumably does not apply anywhere and therefore the *vera unitas ecclesiae* is only a pious dream. Rather, we must set out from our own confessional standpoint and from the assertion of the *pure et recte* necessarily bound up with it. But even then identity with the *vera unitas ecclesiae* must not be asserted. Why not? Because not all members of this individual church are *vere credentes,* and there can be such also in other individual churches? However correct that is, yet the decisive thing for the definition of the nature of the *vera unitas ecclesiae* is certainly not that, but rather what makes the church its true self, that is, the preaching and the administration of the sacraments. Must we therefore argue that the *consensus* which constitutes the individual church does not in any way guarantee the *pure et recte* in the concrete act of the church's proclamation? To a certain extent every confessional church must and will grant that, but will assert on the other hand: the fact that everyone recognizes the confession is the decisive thing. That provides the basis for the confession repeatedly to assert itself and bring its influence to bear. It is then at all events established in principle what doctrine the church in question regards as binding.

Although the point just discussed has really made clear that the unity of a confessional church can never be identified with the *vera unitas ecclesiae,* yet to put the assertion on a completely solid basis we must still take a further step. For we must take seriously the objection that the *consentire* and the *pure et recte* in the Augsburg Confession surely obviously mean the *consensus* presented in the Augsburg Confession itself, i.e. at least the Articles I-XXI. Then, however, what belongs to the true unity of the church would really have been voiced here, and consequently the confessional unity of Lutheranism, and only of Lutheranism, would give evidence of, and visible form to, the true unity of the church. We should then have to go on to the further conclusion that at least since 1530 recognition of the Augsburg Confession has belonged to the true unity of the church. Now the view that the *consentire* which Article VII of the Augsburg Confession means is the one articulated and documented in the Augsburg Confession can obviously appeal to the 12th Schwabach Article, which says explicitly: 'This church [*viz.*, the one holy Christian Church] is nothing else but the believers in Christ who hold, believe and teach the above-named articles and items.' But what nonsense would result from saying in place of that: the one holy Christian Church is nothing else but the believers in Christ who hold, believe and teach the Schwabach Articles—or from saying: *ad veram unitatem ecclesiae satis est consentire de Confessione Augustana.* If, however, we seek to avoid this absurdity by having recourse to such expressions as 'the sense of . . .', 'the doctrinal content of . . .' and so on, then in fact we are back at the very point which I marked as decisive in my observations on the relation between doctrine and the Word of God. The authors of the Augsburg Confession naturally did not reflect on the distinctions which we have to make here. The concrete confessional situation gave them the right to that. For a confession is no dogmatic treatise. Moreover, the idea of a confessional church based on the Augsburg Confession never occurred to them at all. And lastly and above all, being bound as they were to the general thought-forms of their day, they did not see the problems that necessarily arise from historic thinking. We, however, do see these problems and must therefore affirm that no confessional statement can rank as *the* symbol of the *vera unitas ecclesiae.*

(*b*) That makes a further remark necessary on the question of the forming of confessional statements. Can the confession in the sense of a particular confessional statement be described as a formative ground of the church? In the case of the church in the strict theological sense as *ecclesia universalis* that is impossible. But in the case of the *ecclesia particularis*, which always bears some sort of confessional stamp, it is up to a point correct. The proviso holds in two respects. First in view of the fact that every individual church as a part of the Church of Jesus Christ naturally cannot see itself, whether in its origin or in its continued existence, as founded by its confession, but confesses itself to be founded on and by the event which makes the church its true self. And secondly, by the confessional statement as such it will constantly have to let itself be reminded also of the concrete event in church history which gave rise to its appearance as an individual church, which is its source and determinant as an individual church, and whose power to determine the future is present in the stated confession. With these two provisos, however, it will have to be granted as a fact that for the concrete individual church as an *individual* church the stated confession is of constitutive significance. For every confession has a separatist function. It draws the line between true and false doctrine. A Uniting Confession in the sense of one that refrained from drawing any distinctions from false doctrine would be a contradiction in terms. For a confession always presupposes a *casus confessionis*. It is the pronouncement of a decision. But, rightly understood, not the pronouncement of a decision of the church on doctrine and consequently on the understanding of the Word of God. For then indeed the church would stand *supra verbum dei incomparabiliter*. But the pronouncement of a decision which is the result of the Word of God coming to new expression and thus affects the church itself and concerns it as a whole. Confession in the strict sense is only what calls for a decision on what makes the church its true self, and consequently compels the church itself to make a decision (*Entscheidung*) but therefore also a distinction (*Scheidung*).

When we survey the history of the forming of confessions, then we must realize that there have been only few periods in the history of the church that were really formative of confessions and therefore exceptional periods of decision. Ultimately only two: the period of the early church and the period of the Reformation. The power of these exceptional periods of decision and of their confession-making is shown by the fact that in either case it was now laid down for long years to come in fundamental terms of a clear-cut alternative what makes the church its true self. What, then, of the question whether it is possible and necessary to form new confessions? Basically it must be said that the forming of confessions cannot be a thing that is finished once and for all. Yet the question of the possibility and necessity of forming new confessions calls for extremely careful thought. Why is it that Catholic promulgation of dogma, despite the character of finality that attaches to dogma, goes ahead with a swing, whereas on the evangelical side the forming of confessions seems to have come to a standstill with the sixteenth century and the attempts to continue it today are to say the least very much in dispute? How is it that the churches grounded on the Reformation seem to be much greater traditionalists than Rome? Is the lack of further confession-making to be charged upon Protestantism as a sin of omission? And then also the fact that the conflict with Pietism, the Enlightenment, and so on, did not lead to decisions that divided the church? There is not only a danger of too little confession-making, but also a danger of too much of it. That is linked with the question of whether we can really distinguish between forming confessions and promulgating dogmas. I believe that we must, and that there is therefore good reason why it is still only the confessions of the Reformation that are really constitutive for the Reformed churches today. Barmen is not in the strict sense a confession, for the reason that it has not become a confession dividing the church. Its significance, as I see it, lies in the fact that it inculcates anew the fundamental alternative which was at stake in the Reformation and is at stake in the churches of the Reformation still. We do not know, of course, whether Barmen is not the precursor of a really new confession of divisive significance for the church. We must neither wish for that, nor be afraid of it.

(c) If for the churches of the Reformation today the Reformers' confessions still have constitutive significance, then is the course of uniting churches of different Reformed confessions by definition to be described as illegitimate? The discussion of this question will always encounter the following major problems:—What does 'church doctrine' mean? What is to be said of the manner in which church confessions are valid? What is the fundamental alternative that arises in the Reformation with regard to what makes the church its true self? And what is it that separates us irrevocably from the sixteenth century and its ways of thinking? I have been able to make only fragmentary remarks on these questions. Yet I think the most important points that have to be considered in order to reach a conclusion on the concrete question of union have at least been touched upon. The exposition of this conclusion is a task I have not been able to include in my paper, since it would now be necessary to speak in concrete terms of the doctrinal differences between Lutheran and Reformed and the question of their continued divisive significance for the church. I have given an indirect indication of the conclusion by trying to show that the real point of difference in the discussion between the E.K.U. and the V.E.L.K.D. is not by any means to be sought among the traditional doctrinal differences between Lutheran and Reformed.

4. In conclusion I would merely sum up in thesis form the sort of general criteria our exposition provides for deciding the question of how far the *consensus* which is necessary for the unity of an individual church

must extend, or in other words, what makes doctrinal differences divisive for the church.

(a) The *consensus* must not seek to attain the ideal of a numerically complete definition of all articles of faith. It must not be a sort of dogmatic compendium.

(b) The *consensus* therefore must not be misunderstood and misused in the sense of imposing the widest possible uniformity on theology. A view of church doctrine and of the binding nature of the confessions shows itself to be erroneous when it results in a standard church theology; it proves itself to be correct when it both frees us and obliges us to pursue unceasingly the theological task of identifying church doctrine.

(c) The *consensus* must cover, but also be limited to, what makes the church its true self. This point rules out the mistaken idea that church doctrine depends on a continual forming of confessions in the sense of a summarizing of church decisions on doctrine that draws ever tighter the net of the church's doctrinal declarations. We have to require of a confession, as a testimony to the doctrine of the church, that it should seek nothing else but to express the one, fundamental thing, *viz.*—to lay down what makes the church its true self.

(d) The account which such a *consensus* gives of what makes the church its true self must therefore be a necessarily self-contained whole. The exposition in different articles must submit to the test of whether the removal of an article really destroys the whole.

(e) The scope of the account is conditioned by the *dissensus* at issue regarding what makes the church its true self, and that means by the question of the warrant for dividing the church. Only a doctrinal difference as to what makes the church its true self can have divisive significance for the church, and only in face of doctrinal differences which are in fact dividing the church can there be a definition of what has to rank in the strict sense as church doctrine.

(f) The verdict on the divisive significance for the church of traditional doctrinal differences is in principle open to revision. The concrete occasion for such a revision can be of very different kinds. The possibility and necessity of such a revision depends (apart from the case where the doctrinal differences are directly overcome) on whether the divisive significance for the church of traditional doctrinal differences can still be responsibly clung to also in the present, and that means, whether they are necessary in order to bear clear testimony to what makes the church its true self or whether they are a direct hindrance to such clear testimony. That has to show itself as much in preaching as in the study of theology.

From these standpoints we shall, to say the least, not be able to dismiss as light-hearted indifference to church and theology the remarks made on our subject by Dietrich Bonhoeffer: 'The antitheses between Lutheran and Reformed . . . are no longer genuine. They can naturally be revived at any time with passion, but they no longer carry real conviction. It is impossible to prove this. We must simply take the bull by the horns. All we can prove is, that biblical Christian faith does not stand or fall by these antitheses.'[1]

[1] *WE* p. 260, Eng. p. 180.

VI

THEOLOGY AND REALITY*[1]

I

I t is right for theology to be critical of itself. It is bound to be so not only because of its character as a science, but also because of its object, Christian faith. Just as science ceases to be science when it no longer subjects itself to testing, so faith ceases to be faith when it is no longer on its guard against perversion into unbelief, false belief or superstition (*Unglaube, Irrglaube oder Aberglaube*). Just as science is threatened by the possibility of being unscientific while appearing to be science, so faith is threatened by the possibility of being unbelief while appearing to be faith.

Theology stands or falls with the question whether this twofold definition of its function of self-criticism makes sense, or whether it is an irreconcilable dualism which renders theology self-contradictory and therefore self-destructive. Theology at any rate, so far as it takes its own claims seriously, will insist on a correlation in which faith, for the sake of the critical watchfulness so necessary to it, demands the scientific mind of theology and the scientific mind of theology serves towards faith's being real and true faith, while on the other hand faith in turn holds science to the course of respecting reality and so abiding by the truth.

That of course sounds like imposing a superficial harmony on an exceedingly profound conflict which in the course of its varied, yet peculiarly logical, history became the cause of the Western world's greatness, but seems also to have become its ill-starred fate. There are signs which promise the return in our day of a more peaceful co-existence and co-operation between Christian faith and scientific knowledge, yet a sober view of them surely cannot obscure the fact that we sense a note of discord the moment we ask about the relation between theology and reality. And it is quite true that we should be indulging in a disastrous piece of false comfort if we took the introductory sentences on the

* ZTK 53 (1956), pp. 372-83.
[1] Inaugural lecture at the University of Zurich, 10th November 1956.

relation of faith and the scientific mind to mean that theology is un-
molested in its own camp and exposed to attacks only from without.
The question of the relation of theology and reality would then only be
one of an apologetic kind for theology itself, would not affect theology
in its essence, would thus strictly not be a genuinely theological question
at all but only one introduced into theology. If that were so, then of
course we should have lost our own starting-point. We spoke of theology's obligation to self-criticism. It was in relation to that that we spoke
of the conjunction and co-operation of faith and the scientific mind.
Seen in that light, theology is not by any means a system of fortifications
built for defence purposes: it is nothing else but the very battle which
faith constantly engenders in the world of thought. Were theology
rightly studied, it could never come under the fire of any criticism that
was not already anticipated and outdone by the fire of self-criticism.
And the problem 'Theology and Reality' is then a question which arises
within theology itself, affects it in its essence, and is the expression of
its self-critical function. It is therefore *the* basic theological question.

We started with the relation of faith and the scientific mind in theology and introduced the problem 'Theology and Reality' only incidentally as a test case, so as not to fall into the trap of over-hasty harmonizing.
Even without now going into details of the links between the two
questions, we can surely see how the second not only takes up the first
but, so to speak, rounds it off. Faith too, like science, claims to be concerned with reality in the emphatic sense of discovering and expressing
it as true reality in distinction from all deceptive appearances. If we ask
about the relation of theology and reality, then in doing so we obviously
raise the question of the relation of faith and science in a particularly
sharp and problematical form, by appealing to reality itself as criterion.
At the same time, however, the problem reaches far beyond the narrow
field of scientific methodology. For reality is, in a word, surely infinitely
more than science, viz.—the utter pre-existent which transcends it in
every respect, can never be mastered by it, and always asserts absolute
primacy over it. And faith? Well, one might say that on the one hand
faith is itself only a tiny sector of reality, a vanishing speck in the
surrounding sea of reality, while on the other hand it is a relation to
reality which divides it fundamentally into two—into a reality which is
known only to faith and is its foundation and support, and a reality
which opposes faith and forces itself on every man with the evidence
of fact. Thus when we address ourselves to the problem of 'Theology
and Reality', then we are indeed swept up into an endless process of

questioning and being questioned, yet at the same time are also thrown back upon the most rudimentary of all first principles—upon the *punctum mathematicum*, so to speak, where the rule and compass of theology have to be applied if they are to be right in the midst of reality.

We shall now follow this road to first principles by abandoning for once the statutory path of theology and making clear to ourselves how the topic of 'Theology and Reality' becomes a part of everyone's experience.

II

First of all: Theology—it seems—speaks of something which is not verifiable as reality.

Theology, according to its name, has to do with God. But what about the reality of God? We cannot evade this question, if we are in earnest about the self-criticism of theology. For if theology runs away from the question of the reality of God, then it has already surrendered. Yet neither can we counter the question by asserting that at bottom it surely settles itself automatically for any intelligent man—that if a man only thinks deeply enough he cannot get on without accepting the existence of God. Theology had in earlier days almost always, explicitly or tacitly, built upon the assumption that the reality of God may be pre-supposed as self-evident. Yet what confronted theology with a new situation was not only the realization of the lack of strict conclusiveness in the so-called proofs of God, nor only (though much more than that) the mass production of views of self and of reality in which God had no role to play: it was also theology's own realization that a God who is self-evident, or who is proved and established by argument, would not be God. The reality of God makes itself known only by revelation to faith. Is that, however, an answer to the rudimentary question of the reality of God? Does there not remain a host of questions, even—especially—when all so-called natural theology is radically rejected? How can the *claim* to be revelation convince me of the reality of revelation? *What is the criterion for distinguishing real and merely alleged revelation?* What is the relation between speaking of God on the basis of revelation and the plain, undeniable fact of other ways of speaking of God? The distinction, say, between a mere knowledge of God's existence and the knowledge of his nature attainable only through revelation is surely hardly satisfactory. For knowledge of the mere existence of God would all the same be knowledge of God as a reality. But how, we must go on to ask, can speaking of God on the basis of revelation be intelligible, if the word

'God' outside of revelation is to be void of any relation to reality, or has even become in fact an empty and unintelligible term void of any relation to reality? It can hardly be said that theology on the whole has faced up to the full measure of the problem which arises from the fact that the word 'God' has today lost not only its self-evident character (*Selbstverständlichkeit*) but largely also its intelligibility (*Verständlichkeit*). And further, how can reality be ascribed to something which only faith can know? Incidentally, how would faith then be safeguarded against being confused with superstition? It is better, too, not to seek help here in analogies—e.g. that only a musical person perceives the reality of a Bach fugue, whereas to the non-musical man it is simply a noise. Quite apart from the fact that such an analogy contains a distorted view of the problem of reality in any case—what would be left of the binding nature of revelation if it were only something for people of a religious temperament?

But supposing the fact of God's reality is undisputed—what then is the nature of this reality? Is God a Being alongside all other beings? Even as *ens perfectissimum* crowning a reality conceived in pyramid form, he would of course still be a mere part of reality as a whole. Even in the infinite qualitative distinction of non-created from created being, of the Creator from the creature, he would still, conceived as a Being, be at once relegated all over again to a place in the order of being as such. Does the affirmation of the reality of God not demand at least the idea of an *analogia entis*? Yet does that not lie fundamentally on the same plane as the problematical necessity of speaking of God in anthropomorphic ways? We know about their figurative character, but we know also how easily the dissolving of naive ideas of God shatters the conviction of his reality. Is it not a fatal dilemma: the more concretely we try to express the reality of God, the more figurative our way of speaking of him becomes; yet the more we try by the *via eminentiae* or *via negationis* to approach a proper way of speaking of God, the more his reality vanishes before us into abstract ideas? If, however, we follow the ancient view of classical theology that God himself cannot be defined and his reality can be appropriately spoken of only on the basis of his action and his relations to the world; if we thus take our stand quite exclusively on the ground of revelation, so as not to seek in revelation merely a means of knowing God in himself again after all, but to confine ourselves to God in his revelation, to his Word, to his actions, to the 'saving acts' wrought by him—are we not precisely then confronted by the problem of reality in still sharper form? For a reality of God that utterly transcends the reality of the world is easier to accept than a reality of God that interferes at individual points in the complex of the world's reality and interrupts it—a reality which then displays on the one hand all the sensual marks of worldly reality while on the other hand, likewise in sensual ways, it is supposed to be demonstrably a divine reality.

The scientific and historical thinking of the modern age has destroyed the naive attitude of accepting without question that everything the *Bible* says is fact. That does not apply merely say to the miracles, but widely affects the whole question of the historicity of what bears, or appears to bear, the form of historical narrative. There is no need for us to enter here into details of critical historical research. Everyone who reads the Bible with his eyes open knows these questions: whether the world was really created in six days, whether the serpent really spoke, whether the speeches of the Johannine Christ really report the words of the historical Jesus, whether the Virgin Birth is to be taken as real, whether Jesus really rose bodily from the grave, and so on. Obviously these questions are of widely varying importance and require very different answers. But this much is surely clear: merely to abide inflexibly by the claim to reality may certainly have the appearance of strong faith, but causes confusion as to the true nature of faith. Yet merely to surrender the claim to reality, in the sense of rejecting the biblical testimony wholesale or of being indifferent to the question of reality in matters of faith, has certainly the appearance of consistency, yet likewise mistakes the true nature of faith. But above all, to suppose that the sort of questions just raised are the only form in which the problem 'Theology and Reality' is directly and primarily forced upon us is to overlook the question of the reality of faith itself.

III

Without abating anything of the disturbing nature of what we have said so far, we now approach the question again from a totally different angle. If we began before by asking whether the subject of which theology speaks can be verified as reality, we now ask whether the subject of which theology speaks verifies reality.

To verify a thing means, to show it to be true, prove its truth. That verification is necessary at all has its ground in the fact that deceptive appearances are a part of reality itself. When we say here that deceptive appearances are a part of reality itself, then we are already speaking of reality inclusive of man and his relation to reality, and thus of reality as something that encounters man. And that of course undeniably accords with reality; for how could we speak to a thing's being reality unless in some way or other it encountered us—spoke to us in the encounter, as it were, and by thus speaking to us challenged us to speak of it? And this, too, is surely beyond all doubt: that the encounter with reality always contains already the possibility of illusion, of a mistaken understanding that does not agree with reality but is contrary to it. That again, however, points not only to the *necessity* of testing but also to the *possibility* of it, i.e. to criteria which are nevertheless to be found nowhere but in the very reality that encounters us and therefore have no other effect but to urge a better understanding of that reality. We normally use the word 'observation' for the understanding of reality that encounters us. Yet whether an act of observation [*Wahrnehmen*= lit. 'receiving, or registering the truth of' something] is really what its designation claims, requires to be tested by verifying that the thing observed is in fact reality. Verification is making sure of the truth of observation. Now I grant that we usually employ the word observation only in the sense of a quite definite way of encountering and understanding reality—*viz.* of observation through the senses—and that we consider such observation to be not so much a thing that requires verification as rather the proper means of verifying mere opinions and ideas. However, let us not allow the possible objections to seduce us into remaining within the field of questions we are just on the point of leaving behind us. For as long as we continue to ask whether the subject of which theology speaks is verifiable as reality, then we are in the realm of epistemological theory and formulating the question in a way which presupposes that objective observation is the proper sphere of the problem of verification. When, however, we ask how the subject of which theology speaks verifies reality, then the problem of verification arises at a totally different point.

We can clarify our minds here by first of all considering a use of the terms 'observe' (*wahrnehmen*) and 'prove true' (*wahrmachen*) which we have here so far left out of account. If for example I say: 'I observe an opportunity', or 'I observe my office', then there is certainly also an element of knowledge included in that; yet the whole point surely does not lie at all in my merely knowing something, but in the fact that I make use of something—that is, that I take advantage of the opportunity or exercise the office, and that means that I am personally implicated, that I identify myself with something. Or if I say: 'I prove my promise true', or 'I prove true what another expects of me', then of course here, too, there is an element of knowledge also involved; but the proving and verifying in question is not testing the truth of an item of knowledge but giving proof of myself in the fulfilment of my existence. The act of observing and proving understood in this way belongs to a dimension of the encounter with reality in which it is not only the truth of our knowledge that is at stake, but the truth of our own reality itself.

How can the problem 'Theology and Reality' in *this* dimension become a disturbing part of everyone's experience? Well, first of all, by way of a corrective to what was said above, it must be emphasized that theology certainly does not speak only of God—as if theology somehow meant, in the same way as the names of other sciences like geology, zoology or psychology, the study of a clearly defined realm of reality requiring separate treatment, i.e. in this case not the formation of the earth, nor the animal world, nor the reality of the soul, but the reality of God. Nor indeed does theology speak only of a special reality of divine revelation, a history of salvation with its saving acts. Theology surely speaks, to say the least, *also* of the world, of history, of man, and thus of all the things which everyone encounters as reality and whose reality no one calls in question. And theology surely speaks of the two not in unrelated juxtaposition, but in such a way that in speaking of God and of his revelation it has no other aim whatsoever than to speak correctly of the world, of history, of man, and thus of our reality—i.e. to speak of our reality in a way that is to the point. How to the point? Surely in such a way that this reality of ours is observed in the sense of being properly used and administered, and that this reality of ours is proved true in the sense that its appointed purpose is fulfilled.

But now we must make an admission: Theology does indeed claim to be to the point in speaking of this reality of ours. But does it justify the claim? *Does* it speak to the point? Does it not rather talk past it? Does theology bring this reality of ours to expression in such a way that it is observed and proved true in the above sense? Or does theology somehow compel us to disregard our reality, to forget it and leave it to its own devices, to raise ourselves into an alien reality that borders on this reality of ours like a dream-world, and since that can never quite succeed, to be content with a split reality and a split existence?

Let us give these questions a more concrete base by not dwelling upon theology but going on for a moment to look at the event theology exists to serve: the *proclamation*. Let us consider frankly our experience where preaching is concerned! I am not by any means thinking here only of people who merely chance to be at a church service one day and merely find it proved again that they can make nothing of it. I am certainly thinking also of them, but primarily of the so-called believing Christians for whom churchgoing is not just a habit or a duty but also a necessity—and not least of the ministers of the Word, who are often just as much burdened by the sermon they have behind them as by the one ahead. Thus I am not thinking either, in the first instance, of the sort of people who are troubled by intellectual doubts and disappointed that in that respect the sermon leaves them in the lurch, nor of the sort who think it does them credit that their faith has so far always managed to evade thinking, and are annoyed if the sermon does not justify them in that. Those who know what is really to be expected of preaching have surely of all people cause to be most deeply disturbed that so little happens, so little gets going, that so little is really understood here, that the sermon mostly remains so remote, so unimportant, so non-committing. Despite all the theological arguments that lie to hand, the common complaint is simply true: it has so little to do with life, it remains an optional extra, it does not get to the root of reality. And all that surely in contradiction to what the Christian message stands for. It would therefore be poor advice to say our preaching should talk less of faith and appeal instead more strongly to action. For the message does not seek to be realized by man, but man is to be realized by the message— i.e. exposed to the whole truth of his reality. For that reason there is also little help in homiletic advice about enlivening the sermon by means of practical illustrations or making it topical by digressions into contemporary history. For the message has no wish to be illumined by our reality, but our reality is to be illumined by the message. But what does that mean? And how does it happen?

IV

It seems absurd to turn in face of this question once more to theology, as if it would here be in a position to help. Compared with preaching is the danger of being out of touch with reality not many times greater in theology which, as a science, floats with its abstract jargon in regions whose connexion with concrete reality is unintelligible at all events to the non-theologian and—as we may suspect—is often not clear even to the theologian himself? Is not the concept 'reality'—ironically enough! —one of the most abstract things one can imagine? However, a physicist's formula is likewise an extremely abstract thing, yet can be the key, say, to the splitting of the atom. If theology is to serve the Christian message, and therewith reality, then it will certainly not be able to evade the labour of abstract thinking. It is called to clarify its mind on the problems we have outlined. Let me now add at least a brief indication of the nature of the tasks that arise from that.

1. Theology has to clarify its mind as to how far it has to do with reality. If it is incapable of doing that, then it is empty talk. If it addresses itself to this question, then that includes the readiness to check itself by that reality in constant, rudimentary self-criticism, as well as the readiness to bear responsibility for that reality in participating in that reality.

2. Theology has to do with reality as a totality—not with the sum of all the realms of reality and all the ways in which reality encounters us (which would be nonsense), yet just as little with a mere single sector of reality, such as the phenomenon of the Christian religion, but rather with reality in view of the way it encounters man in its totality. And that means in view of the way man, who in all kinds of partial encounter with reality is himself always only partially involved, is concerned in the totality of his existence between God and the world. However much theology is based upon the testimony of Christian faith, it has yet to make good faith's claim by bringing to expression what unconditionally concerns every man in his totality. That demands openness towards every kind of experience of reality.

3. Theology must take equally seriously in both dimensions we have discussed the problem of reality which arises in the theological field. In doing so it must not isolate the one dimension from the other and will at all events have to approach the first in the light of the second. But it must not suppress the first altogether in favour of the second. For it might well be that a false understanding of God and his revelation could have the effect of preventing what theology says of this reality of ours from being to the point.

4. Theology must clarify the concept of reality and consequently take upon itself the ontological task. In place of merely contrasting personal and ontological thinking, the aims of personalism must be turned to good account for fundamental ontology. The result will then be a concept of reality which takes its bearings not on objectification but on historic encounter, not on the availability of reality but on its linguisticality, not on the existing present but on the future that is still to come. An ontology of this kind will certainly be nourished by theological insights and intended for theological use, yet it will be no theological ontology but a fundamental ontology open to general discussion, and one in which the derivative modes of reality, such as natural science's concept of reality, will also have their place. Yet that will make it no

longer possible to go to work in theology with, for example, a naively positivistic concept of reality—except where it should happen to be a case of purely positivist statements of fact.

5. Theology must bear in mind that a theological statement is a believing statement. Consequently God, man and the world cannot be spoken of in theology separately and on their own, but only as a single coherent reality. Thus revelation of God, for example, is *ipso facto* also a revealing of the world and of man. Or man in his worldly existence is by definition the man who is called by God. There is here no completion of one reality by the other. The decisive differentiation is no longer covered by a metaphysical and epistemological distinction between transcendence and immanence, supernatural and natural, etc., but solely by the alternative of a believing or unbelieving relation to reality.

6. The theologian must be clearly aware that the possibility of his believing statement thus viewing God, man and the world together depends on his confession to Jesus: true God and true Man. Thus understood, Jesus is the witness to faith, and faith in turn is the witness to Jesus. And therefore to the question of what is real, concrete faith that embraces at once the relation both to God and to the world—the faith, that is, which arises when the proclamation gets home, the faith in which the observing and proving of our reality in the sense described takes place—to that question, too, our best answer will be to point to Jesus, of whom we confess that in him God became Man in order that we through him may become real.

VII

JESUS AND FAITH[*][1]

THE subject 'Jesus and Faith' is intentionally stated in such a way as to hold the balance between a historical and a dogmatic approach. This accords with the present situation in theological study as a whole, and it is not my purpose here to embark on a theoretical discussion of the methodological problems it involves, although the proposed subject is certainly more than just a casual example of the conjunction of the historical and dogmatic aspects. We are enquiring into the relation between Jesus and faith. It is true that what we have to say will centre mainly on the question of the historical relation, and will even be still further limited to that aspect of the matter which has to do with the history of concepts. But nevertheless the wider context in which this examination belongs ought at least to be indicated.

I

The question of the relation between Jesus and faith affects the heart of Christology, and indeed the prime datum of Christian dogmatics as such. It is the cardinal point of the whole account of what Christianity really means. For there is no doubt that what makes a Christian is faith in Jesus Christ. And the one basic problem of Christology is precisely the meaning of the statement, 'I believe in Jesus.' The name 'Christology' is thus not to be understood here in the sense of a clearly-defined part of Christian dogmatics, but as a pointer to what is absolutely constitutive for everything discussed in Christian dogmatics. It is plainly a fundamentally mistaken understanding of the Christian faith when Jesus Christ is seen as a *credendum* among other *credenda*, and then no doubt also, in view of the traditional statements of faith, as a *credendum* to be attained only with the utmost difficulty. Rather, in the testimony the Christian faith bears to him Jesus is rightly understood only when

* *ZTK* 55 (1958), pp. 64-110.
[1] The essay goes back to lectures I first gave in the summer semester of 1957 in Zurich during a course on Christology and then in January 1958 as guest lectures at the Kirchliche Hochschule Berlin. Cf. further my paper, *Was heisst Glauben?*, SGV 216, Tübingen 1958.

he is not an object of faith, but its source and ground. The widely felt weakness, perplexity, inhibitedness and unintelligibility of our Christian proclamation today comes, I think, ultimately from the fact that it is apparently so difficult to grasp and express in the proper way what faith in Jesus means, namely, that Jesus is the source and ground of faith. In general today there is certainly no lack, either in our preaching or in our theology, of so-called Christological orientation. Yet the self-evidence and superabundance of Christological references does not remove the real difficulty, but rather threatens only to conceal it and so make it the more hopeless. For that reason where Christology is concerned (in the above broad and basic sense) the question of understanding confronts us with peculiar urgency.

The task of Christology, then, is to give an account of the statement, 'I believe in Jesus.' That seems perfectly obvious, but already contains a far-reaching decision on the nature of Christological thinking, *viz.*—that the question of who Jesus is and the question of what faith means cannot be answered apart from each other, but only in conjunction with each other. That of course involves a difference from the traditional way of treating the Christological problem.[1] The traditional 'orthodox'

---

[1] I am naturally likewise aware of the difference from Karl Barth, although his treatment of Christology attempts at vital points to correct the faults of the traditional schema ('Person and Work of Christ', 'Christology—Soteriology'). In his extraordinarily far-reaching doctrine of the atonement Barth deliberately moves the explicit discussion of the concept of faith to the periphery and gives this § 63 (*KD* IV/1, pp. 826-72) what by the standards of the *Church Dogmatics* is an unusually modest length: it is by far the shortest of the twelve paragraphs to appear so far on the doctrine of the atonement. It is his antimodernist outlook that makes Barth do so: 'Our objection to the more deep-seated, but therefore all the more influential, presupposition underlying these modern "Doctrines of the Faith" is directed, to use a moral category, simply against their *immodesty*. They rest on the fact that the Christian of the last centuries (on the long road from early Pietism to the contemporary Existentialism inspired by Kierkegaard) has begun to take himself seriously in a way that is not at all in accord with the seriousness of Christianity. They have presented the Christian truth as if its highest honour was to be permitted to revolve around the Christian individual with his little bit of faith, and one had even to be glad if they did not present him outright as its producer and master. Such pomposity cannot be allowed to the Christian individual. The procedure of the modern "Doctrines of the Faith" is one which the very fact of its being thus rooted made us unable to commend and to follow. The attention that is due to the Christian individual and his faith must now be duly paid to him, but only here, not at the beginning but—and briefly—at the *end* of our road' (*KD* IV/1, p. 828). This quotation may serve not only to mark Barth's position but also to typify his way of arguing—one that would compel us to a sharp rejoinder did we not prefer in non-polemical objectivity to devote all our attention (not just at the end but from the start) to the concept of faith, and not let ourselves be impressed

Christology suffers from a faulty concept of faith. It is infected, from the time of the Christian dogma's rise in the ancient church and the time of its broader dogmatic development in scholasticism, by the conception of faith which determined the theological thinking of that time, *viz.* the Catholic view. The church dogmatics of both main types of Protestantism astonishingly enough took over with only slight modifications the existing Christology in its traditional form. The Reformers' understanding of faith had no effect on the formation of Christology—not, at least, in normal church dogmatics.[1] It is not given dogmatic treatment until the doctrine of the appropriation of salvation which is separated from Christology, in the *locus* on *iustificatio sola fide.* But in the section on Christology in the narrower sense faith is taken into account only in the form of the general heading that applies to church teaching as a whole, *viz.* that it is teaching which cannot be grasped by reason but ultimately only accepted in faith.

A distinction is drawn between a *fides generalis* in this noetic sense and a *fides specialis* in the soteriological sense of the *fides iustificans.* But the connexion between the two and the point of making such a distinction is normally given too little attention. It is said that faith as such is a completely empty and formal thing (a mere 'organ', only a means to an end) which receives its content and its closer definition from the particular object of the moment. But how then can we make for faith the stupendous claim that it alone justifies? According to the usual conception of faith the answer is: on the presupposition that faith has as its object the thing that provides the basis and possibility of justification. But what is that? The *doctrine* of justification by any chance? But if we point to Jesus Christ as the object of faith, then in what way is he that? How can any object of faith, even when the salvation that has been 'objectively' effected confronts me in it, communicate that salvation to me by means of faith? And why is it faith of all things that is required for that? On what ground do Jesus and faith belong thus closely together? The answer that Jesus Christ is the centre of the Christian

[1] Hence the difficulty—Melanchthon is the supreme instance of it in the theology of the Reformers, but it can be traced more or less through the whole history of Protestant theology—of maintaining the strict inner connexion between Christology and the doctrine of justification. The Christology mostly does not lead by any compelling necessity to the doctrine of justification, and the latter in turn usually leaves it an open question how far Christology is really needed as its ground.

by the labels that are then to be expected, like 'anthropological approach' and so on, because they do no sort of justice to the situation.

religion and therefore religious faith has here its primary object in him, leads completely astray. For purely from the point of view of the history and phenomenology of religion it is an unusual thing for faith to be understood as *the* religious relationship and the communication of salvation to be ascribed to that faith alone, as happens not only in Paul but throughout the whole of the New Testament. It is a simple fact that the concept of faith assumed its absolutely dominating position only in conjunction with the person of Jesus Christ. Despite our being so accustomed to the language of the New Testament, we must learn anew to marvel at the nature of this correspondence between Jesus and faith, and to ask why faith alone should be the proper relation to Jesus and why Jesus alone should have a claim on faith. It requires no great stretch of imagination to suppose that the fact that Jesus and faith belong together already implies the statement which is the basic content of Christology, *viz.*—that the *sola fide* corresponds to the *solus Christus* because Jesus is the essence of faith and faith is the essence of the work of Jesus and consequently no 'organ', no 'means to an end', but—the gift of Jesus himself. According to Gal. 3.23, 25 the coming of Christ is the coming of faith, and according to Heb. 12.2 Jesus is τῆς πίστεως ἀρχηγὸς καὶ τελειωτής.

By concentrating Christological thinking on the most rudimentary of all rudiments—*viz.* on the understanding of the statement, 'I believe in Jesus'—we bind it at one and the same time to both the points from which it must not on any account be loosed if it is not to abandon the theme of Christology: to the historical Jesus and to our own reality. For faith is manifestly not Christian faith if it does not have a basis in the historical Jesus himself. And it is likewise not Christian faith if it is not we ourselves who in faith are concerned with Jesus. Here, too, there is a correspondence: it is only along with each other that the real humanity of Jesus and our real humanity can come to expression in Christology. The secretly docetic tendency which, despite all protestations to the contrary, is at work in 'orthodox' Christology was made manifest by the conflict between the quest of the historical Jesus and Christology. The quest of the historical Jesus unquestionably dealt critical blows at traditional Christology which dogmatics cannot ignore. Christology cannot, for example, remain untouched by critical historical analysis of the Easter stories, or of the so-called Messianic consciousness, or of the legend of the Virgin Birth. On the other hand it has become equally clear that the quest of the historical Jesus cannot somehow take the place of Christology. Rather, the quest of the historical Jesus and Christology are tasks that have to be distinguished. Yet the triumph over the embarrassments of so-called life-of-Jesus research and the practice of conveniently utilizing them for the purpose of carefree dogmatism are totally out of place. The strange dogma has spread abroad that we must not seek for the historical Jesus beyond the New Testament witness. Who, then, is going to forbid it? It is another question how far the search is still possible at all. The fact that we cannot, as the eighteenth and nineteenth centuries imagined, reconstruct from the sources a biography of Jesus surely must not be confused with the idea that the historical Jesus is completely hidden from us behind the New Testament witness and totally unknown to us.[1] Were that really so, then all we should be left with would in very truth be only a Christological myth. In contradition, of course, to Christian faith's understanding of itself, for it is certainly interested in the historicity of Jesus—and indeed not just interested, say, in the mere fact of a man named Jesus, but thoroughly concerned that faith in Jesus should have a basis in Jesus himself. In view of this question we cannot by any means consider ourselves emancipated from historical research. If the quest of the historical Jesus were in fact to prove that faith in Jesus has no basis in Jesus himself, then that would be the end of Christology. On the other hand it is not meaningless for Christology, but can be of great critical and positive importance to it, if we can ascertain anything by historical means regarding the question how far faith in Jesus has a basis in Jesus himself. Would it not be significant if it could be historically shown that Jesus and faith are inseparably joined together, so that whoever has to do with the historical Jesus has to do with him from whom and in view of whom faith comes?

[1] On the now resuscitated question of the historical Jesus cf. above all: E. Käsemann, 'Das Problem des historischen Jesus', *ZTK* 51 (1954), pp. 125-53; N. A. Dahl, 'Der historische Jesus als geschichtswissenschaftliches und theologisches Problem', *KuD* 1 (1955), pp. 104-32; E. Heitsch, 'Die Aporie des historischen Jesus als Problem theologischer Hermeneutik', *ZTK* 53 (1956), pp. 192-210; E. Fuchs, 'Die Frage nach dem historischen Jesus', *ZTK* 53 (1956), pp. 210-29; G. Bornkamm, *Jesus von Nazareth*, 1956 [ET, 1960]; P. Biehl, 'Zur Frage nach dem historischen Jesus', *TR* 24 (1956/57), pp. 54-76; E. Heitsch, 'Über die Aneignung neutestamentlicher Überlieferung in der Gegenwart', *ZTK* 54 (1957), pp. 69-80; E. Stauffer, *Jesus: Gestalt und Geschichte*, 1957 [ET, *Jesus and His Story*, 1960]; E. Fuchs, 'Glaube und Geschichte im Blick auf die Frage nach dem historischen Jesus. Eine Auseinandersetzung mit G. Bornkamms Buch über "Jesus von Nazareth" ', *ZTK* 54 (1957), pp. 117-56; H. Diem, *Der irdische Jesus und der Christus des Glaubens*, 1957; H. Braun, *Spätjüdischhäretischer und frühchristlicher Radikalismus: Jesus von Nazareth und die essenische Qumransekte* I/II, 1957.

That is a question that calls for comprehensive examination through-out the whole range of the tradition about Jesus. I confine myself here to a very narrow, though not accidental, section of it—*viz*. the question whether anything can be discovered as to the use of the concept faith by Jesus himself.

II

The question whether any significance is to be ascribed to the histori-cal Jesus in the history of the concept faith necessitates going further afield in the history of the concept. The point of this section cannot be to provide new results of research; I must rely substantially on existing inquiries.[1] Nor would I endeavour to supply a more or less complete report. Rather, I restrict myself to a few major points and combine them with a few marginal comments by way of interpretation.

When the study of religions frequently borrows concepts from Chris-tian usage and employs them as general concepts relating to the structure of religion (e.g. 'church', 'theology', 'sacrament', etc.), then that not only betrays the spiritual origin of the discipline in question, and often a somewhat naive failure to notice its own historical conditionedness, but perhaps also the deeper fact that it is precisely Christianity which provides the kind of questions, the possibilities of understanding and the means of interpretation which are the prerequisite of the scientific study of religion. At any rate it would be foolish to seek to forbid in principle the interpretation of historic phenomena in a different language from that in which they have expressed themselves. For that would be the end of all historical study. But special caution is called for here, e.g. when a uniform terminology employs, say, the concept of faith to express the basic relationship of religion. We must at all events from the hermeneutic point of view be clear as to the extent of the linguistic difference. Hence we badly need not only a thorough investigation of the question of forming concepts appropriate to the study of religion but as well as that also a comprehensive examination of religious con-ceptuality from the point of view of linguistic comparison. The diffi-culties that stand in the way of that lie not only in the enormous demands with regard to the necessary linguistic knowledge, but also in the material problems involved in making comparisons where there is often little historic contact or none at all. Despite the lack of preliminary studies

[1] A. Schlatter, *Der Glaube im Neuen Testament*, 4th ed. 1927; Art. πιστεύειν κτλ. *TWNT* VI, pp. 174-230 (R. Bultmann, A. Weiser), 1955—which also gives further bibliographical references [ET in BKW, 1961].

in this field, the essential point for our present problem nevertheless stands out fairly clearly: the view that the fundamental religious relationship is 'faith' is by no means a general element in the language of religion, but rather belongs to a limited area in history.[1] Naturally we find in many places individual elements of the conception of faith familiar to us. Yet the latter as such is so peculiarly rooted in the linguistic tradition of the Bible that by comparison the religious employment of the concept of faith independently of the usage of the Bible is at all events decidedly poverty-stricken and not at all characteristic. That is shown specially clearly by the difficulty of finding an equivalent for the biblical concept of faith when translating the Bible into foreign languages, as well as by the process of creating new terms which that always to a great extent involves.[2]

In the history of the concept faith, the New Testament is the place where it is suddenly employed with unusual intensity and is given the stamp that determines its future. For that reason the fixed point on which the examination of the concept has to take its bearings is the word πιστεύειν and its derivatives, although it is not the Greek but the Hebrew which is the real root of the concept of faith. But just because of this link with the past, the words coming from the root πιστ- perform the service of determining among the abundance of possibilities provided by the Old Testament for expressing man's relation to God the root word that may be taken as the real nerve-centre of the concept of faith. For in the LXX the Greek root corresponds with uncommon regularity to the Hebrew root אמן. It is true that in the numerical sense the Hiph. form הֶאֱמִין does not by any means take first place among the related terms, yet in substance it proves to be the dominating concept in the group.[3] The kinship with concepts like אֱמֶת and אֱמוּנָה sets the Old

---

[1] Edvard Lehmann (Chantepie de la Saussaye, *Lehrbuch der Religionsgeschichte*, ed. by A. Bertholet and E. Lehmann, 4th ed. 1925) for example affirms: 'It was only for the Semitic peoples that faith ranked as the highest relation to God' (I, p. 128).

[2] For the Latin language: E. Fraenkel, 'Zur Geschichte des Wortes Fides', in *Rhein. Museum für Philologie, Neue Folge*, vol. 71 (1916), pp. 187-99; R. Heinze, 'Fides', in *Hermes, Zeitschrift für klass. Philologie* vol. 64 (1929), pp. 140-66. For the German language: Art. 'Glaube', in *Deutsches Wörterbuch* by J. and W. Grimm, IV/1, 4, pp. 7779 ff (1949). Instructive examples of the problems of translating the word 'faith' in the modern mission fields are given by F. Melzer, *Unsere Sprache im Lichte der Christus-Offenbarung* (1946), pp. 287 f, 297 f.

[3] A. Weiser says: 'The view of the LXX and the New Testament was surely substantially correct when they linked their concept of faith (πιστεύειν) to the Old Testament root אמן; for that is the one which brings out the peculiar, and also the deepest aspect of what the Old Testament has to say of faith. Though

Testament concept of faith from the start in the context of the problems that concern the understanding of truth and of reality.[1] The elusive abundance of possible meanings which the verb can assume above all in the Niph. form could (to touch on the peculiar structure of Hebrew thinking) be defined by saying that the meaning of נֶאֱמַן is: that a thing corresponds to what it promises to be—whereby the terms 'correspond' (*entsprechen*) and 'promise' (*versprechen*) are meant to indicate the character of word, event and relation which belongs to reality in the Old Testament view.[2] We could also say: that a thing does not disappoint the expectations it raises. There is always more than one relation concerned here: that between the essence of a thing and its reality, then also that between a thing's present and its future, and finally that between the thing and the person it concerns. In connexion with religion the root אמן is therefore employed to express God's faithfulness, and in regard to his work (whether promise, threat or command) to express its becoming reality, coming into force, being valid, taking place. In fact the reason why 'Amen' signifies as much as 'It holds', 'It is valid' and therefore 'It is true' is, that it means: 'It happens', 'It becomes reality'.[3]

[1] Cf. the contrast of the Old Testament and Greek views of truth in H. von Soden's rectorial address at Marburg (1927), 'Was ist Wahrheit?', now published in H. von Soden, *Urchristentum und Geschichte. Ges. Aufsätze und Vorträge*, ed. H. von Campenhausen, vol. I (1951), pp. 1-24, esp. pp. 7 ff. Also Quell, Kittel and Bultmann in *TWNT* I, pp. 233-51.

[2] A. Weiser: 'אמן proves to be a formal concept whose content is differently determined in each case by the particular subject. It expresses the fact that on each several occasion the attributes to be ascribed to the subject concerned are correspondingly present in reality. Thus אמן here contains something of what we could describe by "specific", and means the relation of reality to that which is characteristic of the particular subject concerned' (*TWNT* VI, p. 184.19-24: BWK, p. 5).

[3] For that reason, if also with a certain change of nuance (cf. Schlier in *TWNT* I, p. 340.7 ff), the LXX mostly rendered אמן by γένοιτο. On that basis one could offer the definition: Real is what has a future. Cf. von Soden's brilliant way of putting it: 'The peculiarity of the Hebrew concept of truth is . . . on the one hand its temporal determination, its specifically historic character. It is always a case of something that has happened or will happen, not of something that by nature is, is the way it is and must be so. To that extent truth and from the purely quantitative point of view the use of the word הַאֲמִין may lag behind other root words, its qualitative superiority is undoubtedly to be seen from the fact that assimilation to the sense of אמן, combined with a more or less violent change of meaning, must be designated one of the essential marks of the linguistic development of the other root words' (*TWNT* VI, p. 197.1-10: BKW, pp. 32 f).

The Hiph. form הֶאֱמִין has, in the causative or declarative sense, the meaning: to let something be נֶאֱמָן or declare it to be נֶאֱמָן, that is, to let it be valid or adjudge that it corresponds to what it promises.[1] It is, strikingly enough, always employed in a personal relation—in fact, applying either directly to a person or to his word. But that of course is strictly one and the same thing. The הֶאֱמִין ultimately cannot apply to a person otherwise than in applying to his word; and *vice versa*, by the very fact of applying to the word of a person, it applies to the person himself. When it is said in Gen. 15.6 that 'Abraham believed the Lord', then that obviously refers to what God had said to him. Or when Ps. 106.12 says, 'Then they believed his words', that means that they believed *him*, as is shown by the following clause: 'and sang his praise'. Because of its personal application הֶאֱמִין belongs within the sphere of the word-event. For that reason faith is a mode of encounter. For the essence of personal encounter lies in the sphere of the word—whereby the word is not only the thing that demands faith but also the thing that evokes it. Faith can be directed only to the person who awakes faith. Not everyone of course can be believed, but only the person who corresponds to what he promises, who stands by his word, who identifies himself with his word, whose word does not disappoint, on whose word one can depend, whose word, or rather who himself through his word can be the ground of faith. For that reason God alone can claim faith unconditionally.[2] It is true that הֶאֱמִין can perfectly well denote also

[1] A. Weiser: 'To say Amen to a thing, with all the consequences that has for object and subject' (*TWNT* VI, p. 186.26 f: BKW, p. 10).

[2] For that reason man is warned against putting his faith in what in actual fact promises nothing and therefore abandons him to nothingness: 'Let him not trust in vanity—he is deceived; for vanity shall be his recompense' (Job. 15.31).

---

reality would here not be distinguishable at all, but truth is reality seen as history. Truth is not something that lies somehow at the bottom of things or behind them and would be discovered by penetrating their depths or their inner meaning; but truth is what will transpire in the future. The opposite of truth would so to speak not really be illusion, but essentially disillusion (in the commonly accepted sense of disappointment). What is lasting and durable and has a future is true, and that holds supremely of the eternal as being imperishable, everlasting, final, ultimate. The law of history would be truth for the Hebrew not in the sense of a regularity or natural law that is always confirmed in all that happens, but in the sense of the fulfilled determination of its unique course, of its divinely appointed rightness. . . . The second thing to be emphasized is, that questions of truth for the Hebrew are not really questions about whether something is so or not, but questions about the existence or non-existence of the man himself who is interested in it . . .' (*op. cit.*, pp. 10 f).

the relation to men. But the word always has the tendency to remain reserved for the relation to God.[1]

The personal relation of the הֶאֱמִין must be further underlined by stating explicitly that there is not a single passage in the Old Testament where believing is directly related to a fact.[2] It is true that in the secular application the word or person communicating the information can recede so far into the background as compared with the information communicated that in practice it amounts after all to believing or not believing a fact.[3] With the religious application, however, it is a different matter. Apart altogether from the occasional absolute use of הֶאֱמִין it is striking how sparing is the addition of further definitions. Frequently mention is made only of the person believed, i.e. God or the prophet, even when a concrete word is presupposed to which the faith relates. But there is e.g. in Gen. 15.6 good reason why it does not say, 'Abraham believed *this* of the Lord', but quite indefinitely, 'Abraham believed the Lord.'[4] It is in essence exactly the same when without reference to any definite single word faith is expressed in the Word of God, his promises and commands.[5] Besides, such promises and commands are of course essentially not simply statements of fact, but claims for the future.[6] The Old Testament—seemingly in striking contrast to the New Testament —never speaks of faith with its eye on a state of affairs or a fact as the objects of faith.[7]

The reason why הֶאֱמִין in its religious as distinct from its secular use cannot relate to a fact instead of a person, is as follows :—What is said by men can be concerned with things that have nothing to do with the person of the speaker. Hence the content of the statement can here be completely detached from the person. Likewise the content of the

---

[1] Cf. Num. 23.19 and Micah 7.5. That does not exclude the claiming of faith for the words of the prophets, but includes it (cf. the *parallelismus membrorum* in II Chron. 20.20). The prophets are to be believed because of God's speaking with them (Ex. 19.9), and God is to be believed because of the testimony of the prophets or of Israel (Isa. 43.10).

[2] The twice found negative saying that one cannot trust one's life (Deut. 28.66; Job 24.22) merely confirms this.

[3] E.g. Gen. 45.26; I Kings 10.7; II Chron. 9.6.

[4] Likewise Ex. 14.31; Num. 14.11; Deut. 1.32; II Kings 17.14.

[5] Ps. 106.12, 24; 119.66.   [6] That holds also e.g. of Isa. 53.1.

[7] The sole exception seems to be Ex. 4.5: 'that they may believe that the Lord hath appeared unto thee'. But even here the purpose is obviously not faith in a fact (and a past one at that!), but that they should believe Moses as one whose authority comes from God. Likewise with the conjunction elsewhere of faith and miraculous signs (Ex. 4.8; Num. 14.11; Ps. 78.32), the sign is not *qua* miracle an object of faith, but seeks to be a sign language (לְקֹל הָאֹת Ex. 4.8) that causes the person to be believed.

statement can be without any relation to the person of the hearer, who can accept ('believe') the statement or not without his personal existence being affected. When God speaks, however, the content of the statement is identical with the will of God and therefore cannot be detached in any way from the person of the speaker. What God says, he also personally sees to, so that to believe the statements of God's Word—even if they should be statements of fact!—is not to believe 'something', but by definition to believe God. That hangs together with the fact that the content of what God says always unconditionally concerns the person of the hearer, that is, that God's Word rightly understood is never statement but always address. A word is received as God's Word only when it is not in itself an isolated object of faith, but opens the way for faith to find its ground in God. In the light of the Old Testament concept of faith, the concept of an object of faith becomes questionable, so far as it is supposed to mean a fact as distinct from the person (or word of the person) who claims faith. Nevertheless I should not like to express this peculiarity of the Old Testament concept of faith by reducing it to the concept of trust, in contrast to 'merely accepting as true'. The concept of trust would not necessarily ensure for the act of faith the characteristic of having to do with a person and his word. And on the other hand the concept of accepting as true, if properly interpreted, could be a most excellent rendering of the character of הֶאֱמִין: inasmuch as faith is concerned to accept God as true, and that means, to insist that God asserts himself and proves himself true—and, correspondingly, to accept God's Word as true and to insist on this Word as something that God makes true and brings to pass.

The structure of the Old Testament concept of faith would oppose its being understood as a human virtue. Faith arises on the ground of a divine initiative, an act of God, in which—instead of in himself—man is challenged to find the ground of his being, as is incomparably portrayed in the story of Abraham. Now, one would think that this relation *ad extra se* which belongs intrinsically to faith really prohibits the absolute use of הֶאֱמִין.[1] Yet we come across it, even if not very often, employed with particular emphasis above all in Isaiah,[2] and may well

[1] See below, p. 218 note 1.
[2] Isa. 7.9; 28.16, and also Ps. 116.10. Isaiah has been regarded by many as in fact the creator of the religious application of faith. According to B. Duhm (*Das Buch Jesaia*, Göttinger Handkommentar z. AT III, 1, 4th ed. 1922, p. 73) we find in Isa. 7.1-9 'for the first time in the history of Israelite religion . . . the expression which one day, to be sure only centuries later, was to be of such prodigious importance—the expression faith'. We have here, he says, 'a passage in which the

see this absolute use as a specially radical expression of the Old Testament view of faith.[1] The absolute use of הֶאֱמִין certainly leaves no doubt that the faith in question has to do with God and only with God. But it is precisely the absolute use that makes plain how far faith is necessary, how far man is dependent on believing; what this faith has really to do with our existence and why the relation to God must have the character of faith. 'If ye do not believe, ye shall not be established' [*habt keinen Bestand*, lit. 'have no subsistence'] surely means that faith has to do with what establishes existence [gives it subsistence], and that it is thus a question of to be or not to be. Faith is not something that takes place on the basis of an existence whose subsistence is already assured, and thus something that would only be a single act grounded on the fact of our existence. Rather, faith is that in which our existence receives its ground.

The bond re-established here between believing and having subsistence, believing and being, would be misunderstood if it were interpreted as a relation of cause and effect, i.e. as if faith were the condition that must be fulfilled and subsistence were the result and reward of faith. That would be to misinterpret faith as a human achievement and understand it in a way that would leave it completely unintelligible why faith of all things should be the act that has to be achieved—the more so as in fact the very concept of achievement contradicts the concept of הֶאֱמִין. Faith is the renunciation of everything man can achieve to-

[1] M. Buber, *Zwei Glaubensweisen* (1950), pp. 21 f: 'The omission to add in whom this believer believes has . . . its good reason and ground. It is not by any means a shortened expression arising from the omission of what is felt to be an obvious "in God". . . . Rather, to add that would rob the concept of its proper character, or at least weaken it. The absolute construction conveys to us . . . the absoluteness of what is intended. Which naturally must not and cannot mean that "a general faith" is intended (on the contrary, neither the Old nor the New Testament knows anything of that), but merely that any addition, because usually associated with a state of the soul, would be liable to miss the fulness and power of what is intended, of the reality of a relationship that essentially transcends the world of the person' [ET, *Two Types of Faith*, 1951, p. 23].

birth of faith, that wondrous bond between this earth and the world above, is superbly portrayed. . . .' W. Eichrodt (*Theologie des AT* I [1933], p. 189): 'When Isaiah in the decisive struggle with the false religion of his day denotes the right attitude of the religious man by the term "faith", then he thereby expresses the sum of concentrated spiritual activity in a word of enormous significance which, as the grasping of the unseen hand of God, has become the name for the central religious act' [cf. ET (1961) of 6th ed. 1959, pp. 245 f]. I cannot here enter into the problem of the temporal relationship with Gen. 15.6, nor into the question whether such a creation of a new word is probable in conjunction with the sort of word-play contained in Isa. 7.9 or whether the very word-play presupposes the concept.

wards assuring his own existence; the recognition of the fact that his existence in itself has no ground and no subsistence and that therefore the question as to the ground of existence, when asked in the radical sense, can be answered only by not relying on himself but on what is absolutely outside himself and really reliable. We could also say it is literally a case of abandoning oneself (*Sich-selbst-Verlassen*), of not being at home with oneself, not being grounded in oneself, being pointed *extra se*, but for that very reason of relying (*Sich-Verlassen*) on the ground of existence that lies *extra se*, of letting oneself be grounded in what grounds existence and gives it subsistence. To seek to rely on oneself is a contradiction in itself, a perversion of human existence. To rely on the true ground of existence, however, must necessarily have the character of faith, because it is the relation to One who addresses us and whose addressing us supplies the ground to allow the validity of which —to recognize it as that which subsists in itself and thus is reliable and bestows subsistence—is the only appropriate way for existence to be sure of its subsistence. For that reason God and faith certainly belong so closely together that faith is the only way of responding to him who addresses me and of letting myself be grounded in him who is my ground. And for that reason faith and existence likewise belong so closely together that faith alone is the existence which is sure of its ground and therefore has ground and subsistence.[1]

[1] Such an interpretation may appear to do violence to the text, owing to the fact that what Isaiah says in concrete relation to the people of Israel in a particular historic situation has been related to the understanding of existence in general. But is it not a fact that the employment of the concept הֶאֱמִין by Isaiah sheds a light on the state of human existence in general? For the rest cf. A. Weiser (*TWNT* VI, pp. 189 f: BKW, pp. 16 f)—'Faith and being (are) for Isaiah identical; for in . . . Isa. 7.9 . . . "having subsistence" in the sense of man's total existence is not thought of as a sort of reward for faith, so that faith would be the prerequisite of existence, but . . . it expresses the identity of faith and subsistence (= existence); interpreted positively, the sense of the statement would be: in faith itself lies the special mode of being and the subsistence of the people of God. This and the rejection of all fear of, and all confidence in, human power transient as it is, as well as the incorporation of the fear of Yahweh alone into faith's relationship, shows further that for Isaiah faith means the only possible form of existence, which radically excludes every other attitude of independence on man's part or any bond with anyone other than God.' M. Buber (*op. cit.*, p. 27): 'The two different meanings of the verb in the saying [Isa. 7.9] can be traced back to one—the original one: standing one's ground. The prophet is saying, in terms of our way of speaking: Only when in the essential relation of life you hold your ground (*standhaltet*), do you essentially subsist (*Bestand haben*). The true stability (*Beständigkeit*) of the foundations of a man's existence derives from true stability in the basic relation of that man to the power that founds his being' [ET, p. 28].

A further conclusion from what we have said is, that faith is a total
concern. That would not be the case if in faith man were alone with
himself. For man alone with himself is essentially not complete. Nor
does he become complete through completion by fellowship with others.
He is 'complete' and therefore 'whole' only in relation to the ground of
his existence. Because faith is concerned with this relation, it is concerned
with the true wholeness of man. That does not contradict the fact that
faith is wholly and solely concerned with God. Precisely because faith
is concerned absolutely exclusively with God alone, who suffers no
other gods beside himself, and because it is concerned wholly with God
and not merely with partial manifestations of God and partial statements
of his will, which would only have to affect us under certain conditions
and at certain times—just for that reason faith is concerned also wholly
with man, with his self. For God wishes to be loved with the whole
heart, the whole soul, the whole mind and with all our powers. Only in
the light of the divinity of God can man be addressed as a whole. And
only with an eye to the whole man can God be addressed as God. And
precisely this is the event of faith: that God and man are wholly involved. This characteristic of totality and exclusiveness is incidentally
reflected also in the fact that האמין is never made a formal and neutral
expression to describe the relationship with other gods. Not just because
of course faith must be given only to Yahweh, but also because faith
can be given only to him. Only the relation to the true, living God can
be faith. The relationship with other gods by its very nature cannot be
called faith at all.

If it is true that the wholeness of existence is disclosed in the light of
faith, it is also true that the historicalness of existence is disclosed only
in the light of faith. The connexion of faith with historicalness is seen
most clearly in the fact that faith has to do with the future. Not as if
faith were directed primarily to future things. It is related to God and
his Word. But precisely that provides it with a future, because the
reality and truth of God is, that the future belongs to him. Faith therefore has to do not with an unhistorical, timeless generality, but with the
God who keeps his Word and makes it true. Faith in the Old Testament
sense does not mean thinking something about God, but expecting
something from God. It does not believe in the presence of God, but in
the coming of God. The Word of God is believed as Word of God only
when it is understood as a Word that points to the future. God is believed as God only when he is believed as the Future One. Man is
involved in faith only when his future is abandoned to God and ex-

pected as his future from God. Yet this is not to be separated from what comes to faith from the past. As it is expectation, so also it is remembrance, calling to mind what God has done and what he has said; preserving what seeks to give ever further proof of itself. For faith the past is therefore no mere past, but a past that approaches the believer full of promise. As indeed the future is never mere future, but a pledged and promised future. In the same way the present, too, is not an instantaneous present without remembrance and without expectation, but the *transitus* from yesterday to tomorrow, the journeying, the nomadic existence for which the seasons do not revolve in a circle as for the settler, but time like one's own movements is directed towards a goal.[1] In this historicalness, faith is of course blind faith that must let itself be led without seeing the way, a faith that continually steps into the darkness. But being faith, it is patience. If M. Buber is right, Isa. 28.16 should be translated, 'The believer will not hasten.' And he adds by way of interpretation: 'To believe in the Old Testament sense means to walk in all things according to God's will, also in regard to the temporal realization of his will: the believer works in God's tempo.'[2]

The understanding of the concept of faith in the Old Testament is manifestly very closely connected with the fact that the God of Israel is the God of history. The concept of faith appears in the Old Testament, significantly enough, by far the most often in contexts which are connected with the historic guidance of Israel. That is why הֶאֱמִין is normally used of Israel as a whole. Even the fact that Abraham believed is of course recounted in view of his significance as founder of the race. Though his case also makes clear that in faith it is precisely the individual, too, who is concerned. And if the above conjecture is correct, then it is surely no accident that the concept of faith is bound precisely to the figure of the nomad Abraham. In that case the results of scientific analysis of religion and the tradition of the Bible would then coincide in regard to the origin of the concept of faith.

If this Old Testament concept of faith is compared directly with that of the New Testament, then we are forced at once to two conclusions

---

[1] My colleague V. Maag was kind enough to point out to me this connexion which the origin of the concept faith and the discovery of historicalness have with the nomadic existence.

[2] *Op. cit.*, p. 21: ET, p. 22. [That this is in fact the translation of the English AV might well escape the notice of a German scholar accustomed to the different rendering of the Luther Bible and the much-argued interpretations and emendations of the critics.—*Translator.*]

which admittedly characterize the situation only very roughly, yet remain valid also on detailed examination. On the one hand there is
undoubtedly a strong and close link between the concept of faith in the
Old Testament and its employment in the New Testament, so that at
least the tap-root of the New Testament concept of faith reaches back
into the Old Testament. On the other hand certain differences are so
obvious—the extraordinary quantitative intensification of its use,[1] which
we already mentioned, new syntactical forms[2] and altered shades of
meaning[3]—that the mere derivation from the Old Testament is not
enough to explain it. Here the attempt at further explanation must concentrate primarily on three questions. First, what contribution was the
history of the meaning of the Greek stem πιστ- able to make where it
was uninfluenced by the Old Testament? Second, how far does the
continuing effect of the Old Testament concept of faith in pre-Christian
times (whether in Palestinian or Hellenistic Judaism or in the form of a
wider and perhaps only indirect influence on Hellenistic usage) provide
a link to explain the situation in the New Testament? And finally, to
what extent and at what more exactly definable historical point in

[1] In the New Testament, derivatives of the stem πιστ- occur (according to
C. H. Bruder) 610 times in all; of these, 492 are instances of πιστεύειν and πίστις
—and that, too, in roughly the same proportion: πιστεύειν occurs 247 times,
πίστις 245 times. In every New Testament book (except II and III John) one at
least of these two terms is found several times, in almost all both of them. A
striking exception is John's Gospel in which, of all the New Testament books,
πιστεύειν occurs by far the oftenest (100 times—thus about 40% of the total
instances), whereas πίστις is totally absent. In consequence of this predominance
of the πιστεύειν passages in John, πίστις is found in the other New Testament
books more often than πιστεύειν. Only in Matt., Mark, Acts, I Cor. and I John
is it the other way round. Apart from this difference, instances of the concept of
faith are distributed very evenly (from the purely stylistical point of view)
throughout the whole linguistic field of the New Testament. If one were to
collect from the total vocabulary of the New Testament the words which in spite
of the variations in the linguistic situation from book to book belong to all levels
of the New Testament scriptures as fundamental concepts, then πιστεύειν etc.
would stand among the first.

[2] Totally new is the prepositional construction πιστεύειν εἰς and πίστις εἰς
(*TWNT* VI, p. 203.30-32 [BKW, p. 58]; II, p. 430.19-35), as is also the joining
of πίστις with an objective genitive (on which point of course the discussion on
the meaning of the genitive πίστις Ἰησοῦ Χριστοῦ has to be taken into account,
see *TWNT* VI, p. 218 note 325: BKW, p. 87, note 2). It is noticeable that
precisely these two new syntactical possibilities are found primarily in describing
the relation to Christ.

[3] Cf. R. Bultmann's exposition of the relation of Christian faith to the faith
of the Old Testament, *TWNT* VI, pp. 216-18: BKW, pp. 82-6. The structural
difference between the Old Testament and Christian concepts of faith is the
basic thought of M. Buber's book, *Zwei Glaubensweisen*, 1950 [ET, *Two Types
of Faith*, 1951].

Christianity could some kind of creative event have taken place in the linguistic realm where the concept of faith is concerned?

The examination of the classical usage of the words from the stem πιστ- contributes nothing directly to our question.[1] This negative result completely accords with the non-Greek character of the biblical concept of faith.[2] It is true that in Hellenistic times the employment of the stem πιστ- in religious contexts increases. But if—as is indispensable on grounds of method—we first of all confine ourselves only to the development of the Greek language apart from external influences, then although the religious reference does come more strongly to the fore in the usage of πιστ-, yet it does so in complete continuity with the usage of classical Greek and without abandoning the specifically Greek attitude. It is a continuation of the understanding of πίστις in the sense of firm conviction[3] when in face of increasing religious scepticism philosophic discussion takes up the question of a πιστεύειν θεοὺς εἶναι.[4] And it likewise remains both linguistically and materially within the framework

[1] R. Bultmann: 'Words formed from πιστ- did not become religious terms in classical Greek.' There are indeed a few faint beginnings. 'But in no sense did πιστός become a designation of the proper religious relationship to God or a designation of the basic religious attitude of man' (*TWNT* VI, pp. 178.29 f, 179.2-4: BKW, pp. 38 f). To the literature Bultmann cites on classical Greek usage there should be added: Harry Austryn Wolfson, 'The Double Faith Theory in Clement, Saadia, Averroes and St. Thomas, and its origin in Aristotle and the Stoics', in the *Jewish Quarterly Review* 33 (1942/43) pp. 212-264—especially § 1: 'The Aristotelian "Faith" and the Stoic "Assent" ' (pp. 215-223).

[2] M. Pohlenz (*Der hellenische Mensch*, 1947, p. 39): 'That there are gods is for the Greeks a matter of course. They would not need any "supernatural" revelation in order to believe in them. They do not speak of "believing" in the gods at all. The word νομίζειν has a totally different meaning: it means that a people conforms in outlook and worship to definite ideas about the gods and that an individual joins in these. The πίστις, however, by which the Christians designate their faith based on revelation, means for the Greeks always acceptance as true, and rests on "persuasion", not on instruction and clear intellectual knowledge; and though Plato does occasionally use this word also of religious conviction, yet he is then thinking of the unprovable myths of retribution in the Beyond which he believes in, or of philosophical arguments which he recognizes. The Greek does not "believe" in the existence of the gods, but he knows that there are gods, because he "sees" them in his mind's eye and experiences them. He feels in fact all the time that he is surrounded by beings of superhuman power.'

[3] Plato understands πίστις as a mode of δόξα, Aristotle as ὑπόλημψις σφοδρά, the older Stoa as ὑπόλημψις ἰσχυρά. References in R. Bultmann, *TWNT* VI, pp. 176 f, 181 [BKW, pp. 35 f] and H. Wolfson, *op. cit.*, pp. 215, 219.

[4] In the place of the earlier νομίζειν, see above note 2. Cf. R. Bultmann, *TWNT* VI, pp. 179 f [BKW, pp. 39 f], who emphasizes that πίστις is here understood not only as theoretical conviction but at the same time also as piety. The question whether the Neo-platonist use of πιστ- can still be considered entirely uninfluenced by the biblical usage, is one I would leave open.

---

of Greek thought when πίστις is understood in the later Stoa as the virtue of reliability and being true to oneself.[1] On the other hand it seems to me that the employment of πίστις as a slogan of religious propaganda in late Hellenism is to say the least already influenced by Jewish, if not indeed already partly by Christian usage.[2] As indeed I also consider it inadequate to explain the intensified employment of the concept faith solely by the entry of the religions into a missionary situation.[3]

[1] R. Bultmann, *TWNT* VI, p. 181.34 ff: 'πίστις is accordingly firmness of character, and it is a sign of that that πίστις and πιστός are used absolutely and no longer require to be completed by an object. πιστός is merely the reverse side of ἐλεύθερος with which it is not seldom combined. As God is πιστός and ἐλεύθερος, so man also is meant to be. . . . πίστις is thus primarily an attitude of man towards himself, not to others. . . . πίστις in the Stoa has thus no religious meaning in the sense of denoting the relationship of man to the deity, or of the deity and its ways being the object of πίστις. But the attitude of πίστις certainly is a religious attitude in so far as in it man, as πιστός, ἐλεύθερος and αἰδήμων realizes his kinship with God' [not all translated in BKW, pp. 39 f]. See further the passage in Epictetus, Diss. II, 4, 1, which is very informative for the distance between tne Stoic and the biblical concepts of πίστις (but also for the formal nearness which gives food for thought): ὁ ἄνθρωπος πρὸς πίστιν γέγονεν καὶ τοῦτο ὁ ἀνατρέπων ἀνατρέπει τὸ ἴδιον τοῦ ἀνθρώπου (quoted in *TWNT* VI, p. 181.27 f).

[2] R. Bultmann (*TWNT* VI, p. 180.11 ff: BKW, 41)—'The use of πίστις as a religious term was . . . further expedited by the fact that πίστις became the slogan of the propaganda-making religions, not only of Christianity. Every missionary sermon demands "faith" in the deity it proclaims.' This fact should not be rejected outright, even if the evidence, when examined more closely, is perhaps not so extensive as would appear from the general verdict based on it. The decisive thing, however, is the question of the origin of this usage. E. Wissmann (*Das Verhältnis von ΠΙΣΤΙΣ und Christusfrömmigkeit bei Paulus*, FRLANT, Neue Folge 23 [1926], pp. 43 ff) makes it look as if we had here a general aspect of Hellenism which is totally independent of Judaism and Christianity, and in which the Jewish and Christian concept of faith also participates. The Mandaean and Manichaean texts adduced as evidence can hardly be regarded as uninfluenced by Jewish and presumably even Christian usage (cf. also R. Bultmann, *TWNT* VI, p. 181 note 76: BKW, p. 41 note 4). Even in the case of the *Corp. Herm.* there would be room for certain reservations in this respect. The usage of the *Odes of Solomon* (cf. *TWNT* VI, p. 181.13 ff: BKW, p. 41) undoubtedly stands under Christian influence. And the Celsus quotation adduced by Bultmann (Origen, *Contra Cels.* VI.11: *GCS* 3, p. 80.33 ff) surely likewise indicates Christian usage—irrespective of whether its its being general propaganda jargon used by all religions was an idea invented by Celsus for the occasion or met him as an already existing fact. To be cautious in our judgment we should have to say that the spread of the concept faith in the late Hellenistic religious world is a linguistic result of syncretism, not without a certain preparation in Greek usage, but certainly not without Jewish and then also Christian influence. For the rest, no significance of any importance attaches in my opinion to this phenomenon as a link towards New Testament usage.

[3] W. Bousset simply makes the concept faith arise according to a definite evolutionary law of the phenomenology of religion: 'The religious concept of faith . . . first arises within the history of religion at the point where the religions

Judaism, by its use of the Old Testament concept of faith, both continued the history of its meaning and also took the decisive step in the history of its translation by supplying it to the Greek language. The two aspects can hardly be separated, since an isolated examination of the history of the meaning of the Hebrew and Aramaic concept of faith in Palestinian Judaism lights upon the well-known problems of textual tradition, while the process of translation into Greek naturally touches also on the history of the meaning, yet in such a way that on this point —in spite of certain nuances—the developments in Palestinian and Diaspora Judaism are closely interlocked. The astonishing regularity with which the words formed from the stem πιστ- stand in the LXX

---

separate themselves from national soil, strive towards universalism and begin to lead their own life outside and above national culture. As long as religion is predominantly nationally defined, it is in essence completely bound up with the national life, with custom, use and wont; only with the separation of nation and religion does the factor come to its own which we call faith, the personal conviction of the individual' (*Kyrios Christos*, 3rd ed. 1926, p. 145). In the weaker sense of an explanation of the more intensive employment of the concept faith: 'The development of religion towards church, confession and dogma . . . involves the concept of faith acquiring a central importance for piety. Faith of course is actually present in every living religion—indeed it is everywhere central. For in germ all living religion is the lifting up of the heart to the deity in love, fear and trust. But the consciousness of faith's significance always comes only at the point where the emancipation of religion from the national element begins, and therewith the development towards a church. As long as that has not yet happened, faith is too much a matter of course, a given part of life as a whole, for the consciousness of its central significance to arise. But as soon as the development towards a church begins, as soon as within the nation itself the deep gulf appears between the believing (confessing) and the unbelieving, the godless and the pious, as soon as religion begins to make the claim that its basic views are valid for everyone and not only for its own nationals, and as soon as it regards the nations as "heathen" (unbelieving)—then the note of faith becomes important in it. The demand for believing acceptance of the church's confessional statement, which at first can be very superficial, gradually brings about an understanding of the decisive place of faith in religion' (*Die Religion des Judentums im späthellenistischem Zeitalter*, 3rd ed. 1926, p. 193). R. Reitzenstein (*Die Formel Glaube-Liebe-Hoffnung bei Paulus: Ein Nachwort, Nachr. d. kgl. Ges. d. Wiss. zu Göttingen, phil. hist. Kl.* 1917, p. 132): 'Where a religion develops missionary activity, there arises by inner necessity the deepened and intensified evaluation of faith.' Not only Wissmann (*op. cit.*, p. 46), but also Bultmann (*Theology of the NT* I, p. 89; *TWNT* VI, p. 205.30: BKW, p. 62) takes a positive view of this point. It really does indicate a factor which above all in late Judaism affected the employment of the concept faith and accordingly also played a part in the Christian concept of faith. But just as it does not enable us to explain the origin of the concept of faith, but only a modification of it in a very definite historical context, and therefore does not affect the essence of the religious employment of the concept of faith, so also it seems to me impossible from this point of view to explain the striking situation in the New Testament.

for the words formed from the stem אמן[1] has its ground in the way both actually agree in combining the meanings of reliability, faithfulness and trust; save that in the light of the Hebrew concept of faith the way is now opened, beyond the existing scant beginnings, for the words from the stem πιστ- to be applied for the first time to any great extent in the religious realm, and consequently the concept is deepened and enriched by taking up new elements into its structure. It must certainly also be asked how far in this process of translation the Greek heritage did not *vice versa* also have the effect of helping to formalize and intellectualize the Jewish concept of faith. Yet we must beware of stark alternatives, since certain evolutionary tendencies in later Judaism were manifestly also moving that way in any case. From the very varied material[2] a few features stand out as characteristic of the concept of faith in late Judaism in general: first, the purely quantitative increase in the use of the concept faith,[3] second, its firmer conceptual moulding into a

---

[1] Cf. the list in *TWNT* VI, p. 197 note 149: BKW, Additional Note, pp. 55 f.

[2] Apart from R. Bultmann (*TWNT* VI, pp. 197-202: BKW, pp. 43-52) cf. above all: A. Schlatter, *op. cit.*, pp. 9-60; Strack-Billerbeck III, pp. 187-201; A. Wissmann, *op. cit.*, pp. 40-43, 50-54; A. Meyer, *Das Rästel des Jakobusbriefes*, Beih. zur ZNW 10 (1930), pp. 123-141. On Philo see below, p. 222 note 1.

[3] Specially impressive is the list and comment in A. Meyer, *op. cit.* Cf. his summing up: '. . . we have recently learned to grasp better what great importance faith acquired also in Judaism. Certainly Judaism speaks more of the Thora and the keeping of its commands than of faith; but the relation to God and his law is increasingly characterized also as faith' (p. 123). 'There is a specially lively emphasis on faith in the century before and the century after Christ, and Christianity is itself a consequence of this trend in Israel towards faith' (p. 137). On the retrogressive movement which then after all set in, see Strack-Billerbeck in the following note.

It should be noticed that Bultmann attempts to combine this general point from the phenomenology of religion directly with his emphasis on the unique element in the New Testament concept of faith: 'The acceptance of the message is called faith. . . . The significance of this act of believing acceptance of the proclamation, by which the believer is incorporated in the congregation, led to the concept of faith acquiring a significance which it had neither in the Old Testament nor in other ancient religions. It was in Christianity that the concept of faith first became the prevailing designation of man's relation to the deity, and faith was understood as the religious attitude that dominates the whole of life. The preparation for this was given in the missions of Judaism, as also of pagan religions that carried on propaganda in the Hellenistic world. For it is only in mission that this concept of faith arises as the embracing of the message of a new religion, whereas in the Old Testament as in all ancient national religions the worship of the national deity (or deities) is a matter of course' (*Theol. of the NT*, p. 89). Who knows but what, if a missionary situation and an intensive use of the concept faith belong together, the unique significance of the concept of faith in Christianity was cause rather than effect of its missionary ardour?

designation of the basic religious relationship,[1] but thirdly, the consequent formalizing and blunting of the concept of faith,[2] and lastly, likewise connected with the second point, a one-sided emphasis on, and an objectification of, individual elements in the structure of a radically understood Old Testament concept of faith.[3] A peculiar position is

[1] E. Wissmann (*op. cit.*, p. 41), oversimplifying the relation to the New Testament concept of faith: 'Thus in fact the very same is true of the term "faith" in late Judaism as for the early Christian churches: "faith" is the technical term for piety, and "believers" are the adherents of one's own religion.' Strack-Billerbeck (III, p. 187): 'The ancient synagogue in its early days, as especially the pseudepigrapha show, was by no means unaware of faith's central importance for moral and religious life. A clear proof of that is the very fact that the righteous and pious were roundly called the "believers".' But the literature of late Judaism reflects a break—manifestly caused by the debate with Christianity, which thereby reveals itself as a debate on the nature of faith. The main evidence for the strong emphasis on faith is provided according to Strack-Billerbeck by passages from the non-rabbinic writings. 'The rabbinic literature proper, although it too can commend faith, nowhere rose to such exalted views on faith and the life of faith as we find in the pseudepigrapha and in Philo. The legalism of rabbinic Judaism laid faith, too, completely in chains. . . . Legalism no longer ranked faith as a unified attitude to life, but on the contrary resolved the life of faith into many individual acts of faith. Each several act of faith was thereby reduced to the level of a single achievement to which a man in that particular situation in his life was bound in exactly the same way as he would have been bound in another situation to fulfil this law or that. Faith then no longer stood in contrast to works, but had now itself become a work, which in certain circumstances God could credit to men as a merit like any other fulfilment of the law' (p. 188). Hence it is not surprising to find the statement: 'The rabbinic world only seldom uses the designation "believers" for the righteous or pious' (p. 189).

[2] E. Wissmann (whose interpretation of the Pauline concept of faith must here be disregarded), *op. cit.*, p. 43: 'Faith means primarily taking as true and denotes the acceptance of one's own religion.' Cf. e.g. the way it is regarded even in the sense of 'conversion' in Judith 14.10, or the neutralization—impossible with the Old Testament concept of faith—in *Enoch* 46.7: 'whose faith turns to idols that they have made with their own hands'.

[3] Cf. Strack-Billerbeck, note 1 above; also phrases like 'to believe the law' (Strack-Billerbeck III, p. 191) or 'merit of faith' (*ibid.*, pp. 195 f; A. Meyer, *op. cit.*, pp. 132 f). Bultmann excellently diagnoses as the real weakness of the concept of faith in late Judaism its loss of genuine historicalness: 'History is brought as it were to a standstill, and a real bond with history is lacking. The significance of past history is limited to giving the Jew the awareness of belonging to the called and chosen people. The present can no longer carry on history and its tradition in living ways, but merely mediates the canonized tradition. The codex of scripture, given as a timeless present, is appropriated and interpreted in theological and legal study. Faith loses the character of being decision in the particular historical situation of the moment and "thereby appears as something static and constant, as the frame of mind that results from the mind's being penetrated by the teaching of scripture". The idea of the inspiration of scripture limits the working of the Spirit to the past, and it limits the divine acts to the historical events of the past. The result is, that there arises "also a contempt for the natural conditions of life" and that faith, in so far as it does hope for acts of

occupied by Philo,[1] in whom the concept of faith does come relatively strongly to the fore,[2] but now certainly also takes on a shade which is much more strongly determined by specifically Greek traditions than in the rest of Judaism.[3]

The development of the concept of faith in late Judaism really does prove to be an essential link between its Old Testament and its Christian use, so that one might be inclined to see the Christian concept of faith simply as an immediate result of that of late Judaism.[4] Of the things which we provisionally singled out as striking peculiarities of the New Testament situation,[5] we could in this way certainly explain to some extent the purely quantitative intensification in the use of the concept

[1] R. Bultmann, *TWNT* VI, pp. 202 f (BKW, pp. 52 ff); A. Schlatter, *op. cit.*, pp. 60-80 and 575-81 (summary of Philo's usage); W. Bousset, *Die Religion des Judentums*, pp. 446 ff; M. Preisker, *Der Glaubensbegriff bei Philo,* 1936; W. Völker, *Fortschritt und Vollendung bei Philo von Alexandrien* (1938), pp. 239-59; H. A. Wolfson, *Philo, Foundations of religious Philosophy in Judaism, Christianity and Islam* I/II, 1947.

[2] W. Bousset: 'For the first time in the history of religion, apart from Isaiah, we find the thought of faith at the centre of religion in Philo' (*Die Religion des Judentums*, p. 447); 'The Jewish philosopher is the first theologian of faith' (*Kyrios Christos*, p. 145). A. Schlatter on the other hand says (*op. cit.*, pp. 74 f) 'that faith does not form for Philo the chief concept in which he sums up his relation to God. That was no longer possible after he had placed it at the end of piety as its goal.' For according to Schlatter 'the concepts which tell how contact with God is acquired are the centre of every theological system. This position, however, is occupied in Philo not by faith, but on the one hand by knowledge ... and on the other by aversion of the desire from natural good. ...' The interpretation of the concept of faith in Philo is much disputed. W. Völker gives strongly divergent views (*op. cit.*, pp. 239 and 248).

[3] R. Bultmann (*TWNT* VI, p. 202.46 ff: BKW, p. 54): 'πίστις is ... at bottom the firmness and steadfastness of the man who is grounded in dependence on the only thing that is firm and that truly is. In so far as it means turning away from the transient and towards the eternal, Philo follows the Platonic tradition; but in so far as he terms such an attitude πίστις, he follows the late Stoa.' This statement of course does not bring out clearly enough that Philo's use of the concept πίστις cannot simply be explained from the Greek tradition, but only from the meeting of Old Testament and Jewish with Greek ways of thought.

[4] So e.g. Windisch (*RGG*² II, p. 1201): 'That faith in the New Testament has central importance is a heritage of Judaism. For Judaism had already become a religion of faith.' More cautious is Dom. Jacques Dupont, *Gnosis: La connaissance religieuse dans les épitres de Saint Paul* (1949), p. 403: 'Si la foi chrétienne ne se réduit à aucune autre notion antérieure, il n'en est pas moins vrai que c'est à partir de la foi juive qu'il faut l'expliquer; l'influence de la terminologie hellénistique sur le vocabulaire de "foi" du Nouveau Testament est, en tout cas, très secondaire et n'atteint pas la signification proprement religieuse du terme.'

[5] See above, p. 216.

God, is one-sidedly directed towards miracles ...' (*TWNT* VI, p. 201.14 ff: BKW, pp. 50 f—with quotations from Schlatter).

faith, though it is nevertheless also true that in that respect a not immaterial step is taken here beyond anything that can be shown elsewhere in Judaism at the time of the beginnings of Christianity. It is, however, a striking symptom that there still remain unexplained the new syntactical forms which the New Testament contains in the context of the concept of faith. In conjunction with that we must carefully examine the question whether the difference from late Judaism cannot be perceived also in the concept of faith itself more clearly than appears at first sight, and indeed, whether it is not precisely here that we have to grasp the decisive difference between Judaism and Christianity. But that can be answered only in the light of an analysis of the New Testament concept of faith.

III

The methodological difficulties involved in making decisions on Jesus' use of terms are well known. They may be so great that in concrete instances the question whether Jesus used this term or that and how he understood it can only be answered by a '*non liquet*'. Nevertheless it is a sensible question, and there is no reason to capitulate before it right at the start. In the course of the history of the concept of faith, in which the transition from Jewish to Christian usage certainly claims special interest and raises several problems, it is therefore not out of place at least to examine the possibility of whether anything can be discovered about the use of the concept of faith by Jesus. I therefore find it a defect of Bultmann's otherwise excellent article in the *Theologisches Wörterbuch zum Neuen Testament* that he does not even ask this question.[1]

[1] That is the more surprising since Bultmann in his book on Jesus (1959 edition, pp. 135-59) supplied a detailed treatment of faith ('faith and providence', 'faith and miracle', 'faith and prayer') and finally added a paragraph, albeit a short one, on the concept of faith itself (pp. 159 f). He there answers the above question in the affirmative: 'For faith in miracles and in prayer Jesus uses also the word "faith".' As evidence he adduces Matt. 17.20; Mark 9.23; 9.19; Matt. 6.30. And he comes to a not uninteresting conclusion: 'Little as . . . he ascribes any special role to the term "faith", it is yet characteristic of his thought of God. Namely, in so far as Jesus does not speak of faith in God in a general way, but only in regard to definite, current possibilities.' And in opposition to a faith that is understood as 'a piece of *Weltanschauung*' he says: ' . . . faith for him is the power to take seriously in particular moments in life the conviction of God's omnipotence, is the certainty that in such particular moments one will really experience an act of God, is the conviction that the distant God is really near, if man will only relinquish his usual attitude and is really ready to see God near.' That Bultmann then does not enter into this question in the πιστεύω article in *TWNT* (nor in the *Theology of the New Testament* either), can be due either to

When we analyse instances in the Synoptics of words from the root πιστ-, then it is a striking thing that by far the greatest majority occur in sayings attributed to Jesus.[1] That is naturally not yet proof that this usage derives from Jesus himself. But all the same the fact does catch our attention—the more so as it becomes still more impressive when the material outside the sayings of Jesus is arranged according to subjects and so compared with the instances in sayings of Jesus. It then emerges that 11 of the 17 passages in question occur in contexts in which the concept of faith also appears in sayings of Jesus, so that its occurring in the narrative framework could give the impression of being merely a

---

[1] On the basis of Nestle's text I count 87 passages in all, 66 of them in direct speech by Jesus. If we omit the spurious ending of Mark, the result—giving in brackets in each case the figures for sayings of Jesus—is 80 (63) passages. In a detailed table:

	Matthew	Mark	Luke
πιστεύω	11 (9)	10 (7)	9 (6)
πίστις	8 (7)	5 (4)	11 (9)
πιστός	5 (5)	—	6 (6)
ἄπιστος	1 (1)	1 (1)	2 (2)
ἀπιστέω	—	—	2 (–)
ἀπιστία	1 (–)	2 (–)	—
ὀλιγόπιστος	4 (4)	—	1 (1)
ὀλιγοπιστία	1 (1)	—	—
	31 (27)	18 (12)	31 (24)

πιστικός (Mark 14.3) is ignored because of its disputed etymological origin (see Arndt and Gingrich, *Greek-English Lexicon of the NT*, 1957: = Baur⁴ 1952; E. Lohmeyer, *Das Evangelium des Markus*, 1954, on the passage concerned).

---

the fact that he has more critical views on historical ascertainability than in the book on Jesus, or to the fact that in the course of the historic development of the concept he does not ascribe any importance to the usage of Jesus because he considers it no different from that of late Judaism. At all events, Bultmann in the *TWNT* discusses the Synoptic material essentially from the point of view of the continued working of the Old Testament Jewish tradition (pp. 204-208: BKW, pp. 62-8). I should think the second possibility the more probable—with which, to be sure, the question would then arise whether the characteristics stated in the book on Jesus do not after all stand in remarkable contrast to late Judaism's concept of faith.

The question of Jesus' concept of faith is raised by among others A. Schlatter, *Der Glaube im NT* (4th ed. 1927), pp. 94-176 (uncritical in the analysis of sources yet deeply penetrating in interpretation); H. Windisch, Art. 'Glaube (im NT)', *RGG²* (1928), pp. 1202 f; A. Meyer, *Das Rätsel des Jakobusbriefes* (1930), p. 138; W. G. Kümmel, 'Der Glaube im NT, seine katholische und reformatorische Deutung', *Theol. Bl.* 16 (1937), pp. 209-21, esp. 210 f; M. Buber, *Two Types of Faith*, *passim*; G. Bornkamm, *Jesus of Nazareth*, pp. 129-32; E. Fuchs, 'Glaube und Geschichte im Blick auf die Frage nach dem historischen Jesus', *ZTK* 54 (1957), pp. 117-56 *passim*; U. Neuenschwander, *Glaube: eine Besinnung über Wesen und Begriff des Glaubens* (1957), pp. 22-34.

usage derived from the instances in sayings of Jesus—namely, above all
in the context of miracle stories,[1] as also in the context of logia on the
power of faith[2] and in the context of the question of authority.[3] There
are then only very few passages left in which the concept of faith is
found without any corresponding employment of it in sayings of Jesus,
viz.—twice each in Luke's introductory narrative,[4] Luke's Easter story,[5]
and the Passion story.[6] If the 11 passages we mentioned first above are
taken along with the analysis of the situation in the sayings of Jesus,
then it can be said of the remaining 6 that in regard both to syntax and
to meaning they remain entirely within the framework of the pre-
Christian possibilities. In Luke 1.20, 45 the concept of faith has an Old
Testament colour. In the other passages faith or unbelief as the case
may be does indeed have to do indirectly with Jesus[7]—one passage
alone expresses the direct relation to him[8]—but in a usage bordering on
the profane. With this group of passages at least, there is—in striking
contrast to John's Gospel—as good as no influence of the Christian
concept of faith to be found. The concept of faith is employed only
negatively in order to express the unbelief of the spectators at the
crucifixion and of the disciples in regard to the appearances of the Risen
Lord. There is no question of faith in Jesus Christ in the Christian
sense.

Of the material found in sayings of Jesus we can now dismiss from
further examination the passages which provide instances of πιστός (it

[1] In the Pericope on the Healing of the Paralytic (Matt. 9.2; Mark 2.5; Luke
5.20) and on the Healing of the Epileptic Boy (Mark 9.24 [*bis*]), as also in
accounting for the scanty performance of miracles at Nazareth (Matt. 13.58;
Mark 6.6). Cf. below, pp. 230 f.
[2] The disciples' request for faith (Luke 17.5) is an editorial introduction
added by the evangelist to the logion handed down in various forms about the
power of faith. Cf. below, pp. 227 f.
[3] Matt. 21.25; Mark 11.31; Luke 20.5, where the question about John the
Baptist, διὰ τί οὖν οὐκ ἐπιστεύσατε αὐτῷ is laid indirectly on Jesus' lips, whereas
Matt. 21.32 brings the same thought again in direct speech by Jesus. For a
critique cf. below, p. 227.
[4] Luke 1.20, 45.
[5] Luke 24.11, 41. That Luke once also makes the Risen Lord speak of the
unbelief of the disciples (24.25)—incidentally the only time in the Synoptics,
apart from the spurious ending of Mark, that a word from the root πιστ- is found
on the lips of the Risen Lord—is naturally of no significance in the present
context.
[6] Matt. 27.42; Mark 15.32.
[7] Once constructed with the dative, of the women who are not believed (Luke
24.11), otherwise used absolutely (Mark 15.32; Luke 24.41).
[8] Matt. 27.42 supplements Mark 15.32 by ἐπ' αὐτόν. Yet the readings fluctuate
significantly (also αὐτῷ, ἐπ' αὐτῷ and εἰς αὐτόν).

is only used in the sense of 'faithful', 'dependable'),[1] of πιστεύειν in the sense of 'entrust',[2] and of πίστις in the sense of 'faithfulness'.[3] The material which really concerns us clearly falls into two groups according to how it occurs, *viz.* the instances occurring in logia, and those in the spoken parts of narratives, primarily indeed of miracle stories. It can be seen at once that the concept of faith in the second group presents a unified profile, whereas the situation in the first group varies.

Within this first group of passages we find first of all a few in which, as can be seen from the language, we have doubtless to do with constructions of the church: the πιστεύετε ἐν τῷ εὐαγγελίῳ in the summary of Jesus' preaching (Mark 1.15),[4] the designation of the disciples as πιστεύοντες in the saying about offence (Mark 9.42; Matt. 18.6),[5] the use of πιστεύειν as a formula actually meaning to be a Christian in Luke's interpretation of the Parable of the Sower (Luke 8.12, 13),[6] the use of πίστις meaning 'true Christianity' probably likewise as a technical term (Luke 18.8),[7] and finally the use of the concept of faith in the context of the question of authority, which admittedly bears a less

---

[1] In the Parable of the Unjust Steward (Luke 16.10 [*bis*], 11, 12), in the Parable of the Talents (Matt. 25.21 [*bis*], 23 [*bis*]; Luke 19.17) and in the Parable of the Faithful and Wise Servant (Matt. 24.45; Luke 12.42). Curiously enough, primarily in an eschatological context and exclusively with reference to the faithfulness and dependability of men. Parallels in rabbinic usage are abundantly cited in Strack-Billerbeck I, pp. 968, 972; II, pp. 221 f.

[2] Luke 16.11.

[3] In Matt. 23.23 πίστις is to be understood of the relation to our fellowmen: R. Klostermann, *Das Matthäusevangelium*, HNT, on the passage. Cf. also H. Braun, *Spätjüdisch-häretischer und frühchristlicher Radikalismus: Jesus von Nazareth und die essenische Qumransekte*, II. *Die Synoptiker* (1957), pp. 39, 84, 90 f. The parallel passage Luke 11.42, on the other hand, points to the relation to God, but in place of Matthew's ἔλεος and πίστις has ἀγάπη τοῦ θεοῦ. Whether πίστις means 'faithfulness' also in Luke 22.32 is questionable. R. Bultmann affirms it does (*SynT*, p. 267), though only as the original meaning of the piece of tradition here used, while he considers that the evangelist understands 'faith' (*TWNT* VI, p. 204 note 227: BKW, p. 60 note 1).

[4] The construction πιστεύειν ἐν, which goes back to the Hebrew and is occasionally used in the LXX, is found in the New Testament only here. Cf. E. Lohmeyer, *Das Evangelium des Markus*, on the passage in question. In John 3.15 ἐν αὐτῷ of course belongs not to πιστεύων but to ἔχῃ ζωὴν αἰώνιον.

[5] The more so when Matthew expands Mark's ἕνα τῶν μικρῶν τούτων τῶν πιστευόντων by adding εἰς ἐμέ. From there the addition also got into some MSS of the Marcan text. Matt. 18.6 is the only passage in which the combination πιστεύειν εἰς, which first occurred in Christian usage, is found in the Synoptics —here indeed, as everywhere else, relating to Jesus Christ.

[6] E. Klostermann (*Das Lukas-Evangelium*, HNT, on the passage in question) says: 'Christianized'. The concept of the ἄπιστοι in Luke 12.46 is presumably to be taken the same way.

[7] E. Klostermann, *op. cit.*, on the passage in question.

specifically Christian stamp, yet—most probably at any rate—does not belong to the genuine context of the tradition of Jesus (Matt. 21.25, 32; Mark 11.31; Luke 20.5),[1] as also in the warning against eschatological credulity (Mark 13.21; Matt. 24.23, 26).

We come nearer to the sphere of what is possibly to be seen as Jesus' own usage when we turn to the concept ὀλιγόπιστος[2] or ὀλιγοπιστία.[3] This concept is non-Greek,[4] is a literal translation of late Judaism's concept of 'those of little faith' (קְטַנֵּי אֱמוּנָה),[5] and is found in the New Testament only in Matthew and Luke (who took it over from Q) —and indeed exclusively on the lips of Jesus and applied to his disciples. If Jesus did use this word, then it is a case of merely taking over a current concept from the religious language of the world about him.

More noteworthy, however, is the case of the logion handed down in various forms about the power of faith.[6] In its primary form, though with various modifications, it appears four times,[7] and twice in a secondary form which is perhaps to be seen as a separate, independent logion.[8] In the composition of the Synoptic Gospels this logion has been inserted at three different places: in the conversation about the Withered Fig Tree (Mark 11.22-24; Matt. 21.21-22), in the Healing of the Epileptic (Matt. 17.20), and also as an independent unit (Luke 17.6). In the first case both Gospels give the two forms of the logion following each other—viz. first as the saying that ascribes to faith the power to give a mountain the effective command to cast itself into the sea, and then as the saying which promises unconditional fulfilment to the prayer made in faith.[9] Both sayings serve here to explain the power of

---

[1] Matt. 21.25, 32; Mark 11.31; Luke 20.5. See above, p. 235 note 3. Similarly also Luke 22.67.

[2] In Q: Matt. 6.30 (=Luke 12.28); in the section peculiar to Matthew: 8.26, 14.31; taken over by Matthew from Mark: 16.8.

[3] Matt. 17.20, unless the reading ἀπιστίαν is to be preferred.

[4] The LXX does not have it either.

[5] Strack-Billerbeck I, pp. 438 f. For example: 'He who lets his voice be heard in his prayer (i.e. prays aloud) belongs to those of little faith.' Or particularly appropriate for comparison with Matt. 6.30: 'He who has bread in his basket and says, "What shall I eat tomorrow?", belongs to those of little faith.'

[6] Cf. above all E. Lohmeyer, *Das Evangelium des Matthäus* (1956), pp. 271-74; *Das Evangelium des Markus* (1954), pp. 238 f.

[7] Mark 11.23; Matt. 21.21; 17.20; Luke 17.6.

[8] Mark 11.24; Matt. 21.22.

[9] The preliminary introduction in Mark (11.22), ἔχετε πίστιν θεοῦ, is the editorial work of Mark. The phrase πίστιν ἔχειν is there taken from the saying about the faith that moves mountains which in Matt. (17.20 and 21.21), as also in the altered form in Luke 17.6, has preserved the original version ἐὰν ἔχητε πίστιν or εἰ ἔχετε πίστιν, which Mark has abandoned in favour of the formula in

Jesus' word, which caused the fig tree to wither. In the second case the saying about the faith that moves mountains provides a positive comment on the censure of the little faith, or unbelief, of the disciples who were unable to heal the epileptic. That the concept of faith is already firmly established in this miracle story in any case, is shown by the expression that stands in all three Synoptic Gospels: ὦ γενεὰ ἄπιστος.[1] The καὶ διεστραμμένη added by Matthew and Luke has a link with the Old Testament (Deut. 32.5) and also rabbinic parallels,[2] whereas the expression γενεὰ ἄπιστος is clearly unusual. It is equally offensive whether we choose to relate it to the people round about or to the disciples, and derives from an idea of faith that is more radically conceived than usual. In the third and last case (Luke 17.6) the logion about the power of faith is altered, in that it speaks about the uprooting of a fig tree instead of about moving mountains.[3]

The complicated situation in the tradition is, I think, to be interpreted as follows. Matt. 17.20 is to be taken as the original form of the logion about the power of faith: ἀμὴν γὰρ λέγω ὑμῖν, ἐὰν ἔχητε πίστιν ὡς κόκκον σινάπεως ἐρεῖτε τῷ ὄρει τούτῳ μετάβα ἔνθεν ἐκεῖ καὶ μεταβήσεται. The continuation in Matthew, καὶ οὐδὲν ἀδυνατήσει ὑμῖν, will already no longer belong to the original saying.[4] In favour of the originality of this form is the fact that with the powerful pictorial paradox of the tiny mustard seed and the vast mountain, much as in the paradoxical conjunction of the camel and the needle's eye, it brings out the point most sharply—*viz.* the improbable power of faith.[5] The comparison with the mustard seed falls out in Mark's version and its

---

[1] Matt. 17.17; Mark 9.19; Luke 9.41.

[2] Strack-Billerbeck I, pp. 758 f.

[3] On the editorial character of Luke 17.5 see above, p. 225 note 2. Cf. the rabbinic parallel in Paul Fiebig, *Jüdische Wundergeschichten des neutestamentlichen Zeitalters* (1911), pp. 31 f: 'On that day Rabbi 'Eli'ezer raised all the objections in the world (in order to carry his point), but they (i.e. the other scholars) did not accept (them). He said to them: if the Halakah (is fixed) as I (i.e. according to my view), then may this acacia tree prove (it is right). Thereupon the acacia tree lifted its roots (and moved) from its place 100 ells. . . . Then they (i.e. his opponents) said to them: One does not prove things by an acacia tree.'

[4] R. Bultmann, *SynT*, pp. 75, 89.

[5] Cf. R. Bultmann, *SynT*, pp. 93 f.

---

his editorial introduction. The addition of θεοῦ, which is lacking in some MSS, is unusual from the linguistic point of view—θεοῦ as objective genitive with πίστις is found only here, though on the other hand the phrase πίστις Ἰησοῦ Χριστοῦ often occurs—and is best explained from the missionary situation for which Mark's Gospel was written.

parallels in Matthew and is supplanted by the demand not to doubt, apparently because the comparison of faith with a mustard seed was already felt unsuitable, or was misunderstood in the sense of 'a little faith' whereas its point is the insignificant appearance of faith as such. Luke did indeed retain the comparison with the mustard seed, yet apparently considered the contrast with a grown tree more suitable than with a mountain.[1] As regards the placing, it seems to me that neither the conjunction with the story of the withered fig tree nor with the account of the healing of the epileptic is original. Rather, we have here to do with an independent logion that gives strong grounds to suppose it derives from Jesus himself:[2] the fact of its being firmly anchored in the Synoptic tradition despite all the variations, the unusual expressive power of the picture, the absence of parallels in late Judaism to this form of the concept of faith,[3] and also the quotation of this logion by Paul in I Cor. 13.2.[4] The saying about the faith that moves mountains

---

[1] Whether there is any connexion between Luke's version and the rabbinic parallel quoted above p. 228 note 3 must remain an open question.

[2] Bultmann in the section on the concept of faith in his book on Jesus sets out from Matt. 17.20, and thus presumably considers the saying authentic. So also G. Bornkamm, *Jesus of Nazareth*, p. 129.

[3] In Strack-Billerbeck the net result of the material in late Judaism that can be compared with the synoptic passages in question is (apart from the idea of those of little faith, see above, p. 227 note 5) completely unimportant. We do of course sometimes find also in the thought of late Judaism a reference to the power of faith. But in A. Meyer, who in view of James 1.6 and 5.15 f had every reason to pay particular attention to this material, I find only one instance reported which points in this direction: 'Of special importance for the rabbinic view of the power and significance of faith is the affirmation that it is not the men of God nor their doings but only faith in God that produces the miracle. When Moses painted the doorposts at the *pesach* (Ex. 12.7), when he raised his arms at the battle with Amalek (Ex. 17.11), when he lifted up the brazen serpent (Num. 21.9), then it was not these signs that helped, but the looking up in faith to the Father in heaven' (*Das Rätsel des Jakobusbriefes*, p. 135). When he goes on, 'Just as Jesus also said, "Thy faith hath saved thee!" (Matt. 9.22; Mark 5.34, and frequently elsewhere)', then he overlooks not only the considerable difference of aim, but also above all the essential difference between making such a statement (in a historical and dogmatic sense) about Moses, and employing the concept of faith in an actual concrete situation, as Jesus does, and speaking there of the improbable power of faith.

[4] In view of the complete absence of parallels—to show the existence of the expression 'uprooting mountains' in the sense of 'making possible the impossible' (Strack-Billerbeck III, p. 451) of course does not explain its application to faith —I hold it hardly feasible to imagine anything else but that I Cor. 13.2 contains an allusion to the saying of Jesus, which R. Bultmann also considers at least possible (*Glauben und Verstehen* I [1933], p. 191; *RGG*[2] IV, p. 1028; cf. *SynT*, p. 75). Naturally this allusion as such would not exclude the possibility of its being a product of the church. But the rest of the findings are against that.

is of such elemental force, penetrates so deeply to the basic relations of being, and stands so completely alone in the world of late Judaism that it would be hard to find a ground for denying it to Jesus and considering it an anonymous product of the church. Possibly the logion about faith and prayer is also to be seen as an independent and likewise genuine saying of Jesus,[1] in which case Mark 11.24 is presumably the original form: πάντα ὅσα προσεύχεσθε καὶ αἰτεῖσθε, πιστεύετε ὅτι ἐλάβετε, καὶ ἔσται ὑμῖν.

But now, the concept of faith testified to above all in the saying about the faith that moves mountains is strikingly similar to the extremely marked use of the concept of faith in the healing miracles.[2] Once again

[1] Here of course the further question intrudes itself, how we are to view its relation to what is said in James about faith and prayer (1.6; 5.15 f). When M. Dibelius quotes Ecclus 7.10; 32.21 in support of the view that we have here a current element in the proverbial wisdom of Judaism, then that of course will not by any means pass muster. It is true that Ecclus 7.10 is a parallel in point of subject-matter, yet it is no accident that the concept of faith is not used, but it says: μὴ ὀλιγοψυχήσῃς ἐν τῇ προσευχῇ σου. In Ecclus 32.21 πιστεύειν does occur, but in a context whose meaning is so totally different that it certainly cannot be taken as a parallel. To see in the passages quoted from James the result, admittedly faded, of the Jesus logion would not be utterly misguided, but I should not like to commit myself to it by any means.

[2] It is a case of nine healing stories (the parallels of course not counted separately), which means about half this group of the synoptic narrative material. Only in the *Story of the Paralytic* (Matt. 9.1-8; Mark 2.1-12; Luke 5.17-26) does the concept of faith stand in the narrative part: ἰδὼν (ὁ Ἰησοῦς) τὴν πίστιν αὐτῶν (Matt. 9.2; Mark 2.5; Luke 5.20). Otherwise it is always found on the lips of Jesus. In the *Story of the Woman with the Issue* (Matt. 9.20-22; Mark 5.25-34; Luke 8.43-48) all three Gospels have in common ἡ πίστις σου σέσωκέν σε (Matt. 9.22; Mark 5.34; Luke 8.48). In the *Healing of Bartimaeus* (Mark 10.46-52; Luke 18.35-43; Matt. 20.29-34) the same phrase is repeated in Mark (10.52) and Luke (18.42), whereas it is missing in Matthew's version, which also varies somewhat in other ways. But in another story of the *Healing of Two Blind Men* (Matt. 9.27-31) Matthew sets the concept of faith in the centre with Jesus' question, πιστεύετε ὅτι δύναμαι τοῦτο ποιῆσαι; (v. 28) and the promise, κατὰ τὴν πίστιν ὑμῶν γενηθήτω ὑμῖν (v. 29). In the *Story of Jairus' Daughter* (Matt. 9.18 f, 23-36; Mark 5.21-24, 35-43; Luke 8.40-42, 49-56) Mark and Luke have the exhortation to faith in common: μὴ φοβοῦ, μόνον πίστευε (πίστευσον) (Mark 5.36, Luke 8.50). In Matthew, who here more severely abbreviates the whole story, it is missing. In the *Pericope on the Healing of the Epileptic* (Matt. 17.14-21; Mark 9.14-29; Luke 9.37-43) all three Synoptics have in common the censure, ὦ γενεὰ ἄπιστος (see above, p. 228), while Mark alone gives the conversation between Jesus and the father of the epileptic: τὸ εἰ δύνῃ, πάντα δυνατὰ τῷ πιστεύοντι (v. 23), πιστεύω· βοήθει μου τῇ ἀπιστίᾳ (v.24). Matthew and Luke here together follow a shorter source. Matthew, however, adds on the saying about the faith that moves mountains (Matt. 17.20, see above, p. 228). In the *Pericope on the Nobleman of Capernaum* (Matt. 8.5-13; Luke 7.1-10) Matthew and Luke have substantially the same: παρ' οὐδενὶ τοσαύτην πίστιν ἐν τῷ Ἰσραὴλ εὗρον (Matt. 8.10, with slight variation in Luke 7.9), while Matthew alone has Jesus say at the end: ὡς ἐπίστευσας,

the absence of parallels in late Judaism is noticeable, so that it is not possible to explain the use of the concept of faith in the healing stories as a general element of form.[1] In other narratives the Synoptic Gospels hardly ever use the concept of faith. Luke 7.50 is clearly constructed on the model of the synoptic healing stories.[2] And in other miracle stories the concept of faith is found only on the circumference.[3] I am naturally aware of the difficulty of drawing conclusions about Jesus' own usage from what is found as direct speech by Jesus in the synoptic narrative tradition. I am far from claiming specific passages as authentic renderings of words of Jesus. But the way in which reference is made in the healing stories to faith, taken along with the logion about the faith that moves mountains, makes it seem to me very probable that Jesus affirmed a connexion between faith and the event of healing—and that, too, in a thoroughly unusual way—and that this became an element in the form of the healing stories in the synoptic tradition. It has thus nothing to do with a particular wording, but only with the peculiar structure of this concept of faith. The expression which is repeated like a formula seven times in the Synoptic Gospels, ἡ πίστις σου σέσωκέν σε,[4] points in my opinion as much to Jesus' concept of faith as does the manifold coupling of faith and event[5] or faith and power.[6] Thus I consider we are justified in adducing also this material from the healing

---

[1] I refer again to the fact that Strack-Billerbeck is not able to cite any material for comparison, and the Paul Fiebig's collection *Jüdische Wundergeschichten des neutestamentlichen Zeitalters* likewise produces no results in this respect. The rabbinic parallel to Luke 17.6 cited above (p. 228 note 3) really shows in essence only the profound difference.

[2] For the parallel passages in the healing stories see note 4 below.

[3] In the pericope on the Storm on the Lake (Matt. 8.23-27; Mark 4.35-41; Luke 8.22-25) and on the Walking on the Water (Matt. 14.22-33; Mark 6.45-52). But here the accent lies somewhat differently. The concept of faith is only introduced negatively, in that the disciples' unbelief is censured (Matt. 8.26; Mark 4.40; Luke 8.25; Matt. 14.31). Moreover, the tradition here is not very unified.

[4] Matt. 9.22; Mark 5.34; 10.52; Luke 7.50; 8.48; 17.19; 18.42.

[5] Matt. 8.13: ὡς ἐπίστευσας γενηθήτω σοι. Matt. 9.29: κατὰ τὴν πίστιν ὑμῶν γενηθήτω ὑμῖν. Matt. 15.28: μεγάλη σου ἡ πίστις· γενηθήτω σοι ὡς θέλεις.

[6] Mark 9.23: πάντα δυνατὰ τῷ πιστεύοντι. Matt. 9.28: πιστεύετε ὅτι δύναμαι τοῦτο ποιῆσαι; Matt. 17.20: καὶ οὐδὲν ἀδυνατήσει ὑμῖν.

γενηθήτω σοι (Matt. 8.13). In the *Story of the Syro-phoenician Woman* (Matt. 15.21-28; Mark 7.24-30), which is perhaps a parallel form to the story of the Nobleman of Capernaum (R. Bultmann, *SynT*, p. 39), Matthew alone has: ὦ γύναι, μεγάλη σου ἡ πίστις· γενηθήτω σοι ὡς θέλεις (Matt. 15.28). And finally, in the *Healing of the Ten Lepers* (Luke 17.11-19) it is said to the thankful Samaritan: ἡ πίστις σου σέσωκέν σε (v. 19). To that there falls to be added the conjunction between faith and healing in the report of the rejection at Nazareth (Matt. 13.58; Mark 6.6).

stories as well as the saying about the faith that moves mountains, in order now to expound the peculiar structure of the view of faith thereby expressed.

IV

1. It is very necessary to ask ourselves whether we have here a religious use of πίστις and πιστεύειν at all. Apart from the undoubtedly secondary instance in Mark 11.22, ἔχετε πίστιν θεοῦ,[1] it is nowhere explicitly said to be a question of faith towards God. In all the passages concerned πιστεύειν or πίστις is used absolutely. Even the occasional combination with a ὅτι-clause serves not so much to define the concrete content and object of faith, as rather to explain a structural peculiarity of faith. When it is said in Mark 11.23, 'Whosoever shall say unto this mountain, etc. . . . and shall believe that those things which he saith shall come to pass', or in Mark 11.24, 'What things soever ye ask and pray for, believe that ye receive them', then the that-clauses merely express that the essence of faith is certainty, without indicating *materialiter* the individual grounds of this certainty. The concrete content of the concept of faith comes on each occasion only from the concrete situation to which it refers, thus e.g. from being affected by an illness. But even this concrete reference to the situation does not, at least for the most part, provide any kind of indication that this faith has to do with God. It is not a case of a faith which expresses itself in some kind of dogmatic confession. Certainly, to the extent that explicit reference is made to prayer, the religious context is clearly given. But in most cases that is not so. It could indeed even look as if it were a question of an immanent psychic power possessed by the man who concentrates with unshakable certainty on a definite goal. Yet that would be a manifest misunderstanding.

Although the relation of this faith to God is not directly expressed in any way, it results indirectly from what is ascribed to faith. Just as it belongs to the essence of prayer that it can only be fulfilled by God and seeks only to be fulfilled by God—so that the introduction of faith as a condition of the fulfilment does not mean a limitation of what is expected from God, but rather the radical affirmation of the fact that everything is expected exclusively from God—so also it belongs to the essence of faith, even when it is not spoken of in relation to prayer, that it has to do with something that is God's concern. The phrase about moving mountains opens up eschatological perspectives, and thus alludes to

[1] See above, p. 227 note 9.

what is solely a matter for God. In faith, word and fulfilment are bound as firmly together as in the word of creation that speaks and it is done. The power of faith is marked outright as the power of God. For just as it says, πάντα δυνατὰ τῷ πιστεύοντι (Mark 9.23), it says also, and primarily, πάντα δυνατὰ παρὰ θεῷ (Mark 10.27 and parallels)—and that, too, while explicitly underlining that it is a case of things which are ἀδύνατα παρὰ ἀνθρώποις. That is obviously not meant in the sense of faith's competing with God—which of course would be self-contradictory. Nor would it be doing justice to the situation to weaken it into a mere hyperbolic manner of speaking. Rather, the whole point is to declare that faith is letting God work, letting God go into action, and that therefore it is legitimate to ascribe to faith what is a matter for God.

That is underlined by the contrasting fact that the man who is addressed as a believer is the helpless man, who cannot help himself, who is dependent on the help of another and who is really finished with still expecting help from any other. The only reason why there is any talk of faith here at all is, that the man in question has no confidence whatsoever in himself, but is so to speak thrown entirely off himself on to ground over which he has no command yet which is itself endowed with infinite power to command. Where faith is spoken of in these stories, it is always a case of men who have ground for despair—which is the same as to say that the ground of their existence is shattered—and who now (it remains to be seen how), without their situation in itself changing in any way, find ground for faith. It is because, and only because, it is here *eo ipso* implicitly a question of being thrown upon God, that it can be a question of faith in that absolute sense—not of an uncertain idea or an impotent wish, but a faith whose certainty and power are the certainty and power of God himself. For that reason these statements about faith would be completely meaningless, if they were not understood as referring to God, i.e. in such a way that faith can exist only as a relation to God.

But it is nevertheless astonishing—and on no account must we tone down the shock of it—that faith is here still spoken of in such a completely non-religious way. Jesus does not speak in this context of God. He does not exhort to faith in God, nor does he ask what sort of views of faith and what sort of ideas of God the people have with whom he has to do in these encounters. He imputes faith to the Samaritan, the Syro-phoenician woman, the Gentile nobleman irrespective of any confession of faith—and such a faith, too, as he has not found in Israel. If the faith in question here is really faith towards God, then it is

manifestly directed concretely towards God in concrete encounter with
him.

2. What has this faith of which Jesus speaks to do with Jesus himself?
Is it primarily a matter of Jesus' own faith? The evangelists themselves
say nothing of the faith of Jesus. And there is at all events no explicit
saying of Jesus about his own faith. Admittedly, the saying πάντα δυνατὰ
τῷ πιστεύοντι (Mark 9.23) in the light of the context in which it stands
can hardly be understood otherwise than primarily of Jesus, and likewise
also Mark 11.23 and parallels, in the context of the conversation about
the withered fig tree. It would be necessary to examine Jesus' usage on a
broader basis, *viz.* to enquire whether Jesus includes himself along with
the others in a 'we' and accordingly in the same kind of statements, and
also how far the evangelists show Jesus in a practical attitude which coincides with that indicated in his sayings about faith. Yet however that may
be, it is surely impossible, in view of the manner in which Jesus speaks of
faith, to except him from faith himself. We must not let scruples that
arose later on the ground of Christological considerations and took their
bearings from a particular concept of faith[1] deter us from granting that
Jesus himself is not to be dissociated from the faith of which he testifies,
but rather identified himself so closely with it that he very properly did
not speak of his own faith at all but devoted himself to awakening faith.
For whoever is concerned to awaken faith will have to bring his faith
into play without speaking of his faith.

But now, what of the other possible way of bringing the faith of
which Jesus speaks into relation with Jesus? Is it a case of faith *in* Jesus?
Apart from the undoubtedly secondary passage Matt. 18.6 where the
πιστεύοντες εἰς ἐμέ are spoken of,[2] the concept of faith in sayings of
Jesus is never related to Jesus as the object of faith. In marked contrast
to what happens later in John's Gospel, the Synoptic Jesus never links
the concept of faith with his own person. That is undoubtedly not a

---

[1] The question, *Utrum in Christo fuerit fides?* is a stock part of scholastic
dogmatics. E.g. Peter Lombard, *Sent.* lib. III, dist. 26, cap 4: '... *Christus,
in quo fuerunt bona patriae, credidit quidem et speravit resurrectionem tertia die
futuram, pro qua et Patrem oravit; nec tamen fidem-virtutem vel spem habuit, quia
non aenigmaticam et specularem, sed clarissimam de ea habuit cognitionem, quia
non perfectius cognovit praeteritam, quam intellexit futuram. Speravit tamen
Christus, sicut in Psalmo ait: "In te, Domine, speravi"; nec tamen fidem vel spem-
virtutem habuit, quia per speciem videbat ea quae credebat.'* Thomas Aquinas,
Summa theol. III, qu. 7, art. 3: '... *excluso quod res divina sit non visa excluditur
ratio fidei. Christus autem a primo instanti suae conceptionis plane vidit Deum per
essentiam. . . . Unde in eo fides esse non potuit.'*

[2] See above, p. 226 note 5.

subsequent correction of the tradition. If ever anything bore the stamp of authenticity, this does. It is amazing how faithfully the synoptic tradition has preserved the original facts in this respect and not imported into the logia and narratives the Christian concept of faith that is explicitly related to Jesus Christ. Yet for all that, a peculiarly close connexion has to be affirmed between the faith which is spoken of in sayings of Jesus and Jesus himself. Wherever faith is spoken of here, Jesus has part in that faith, and faith cannot be separated from him. In all the healing stories faith, even without its being explicitly said so (as it is in the exceptional case of Matt. 9.28), is faith in the power of Jesus. At the same time, however, it is faith that relates to Jesus only because it is faith awakened by Jesus himself! The whole point of all these healing stories is surely that Jesus in a peculiar way awakened confidence, hope, courage in the people concerned, that something went out from him which drew them to him. Add to that that he did not merely awaken faith, but also ascribed this faith to those who had no idea what was really happening to them, told them as it were to their face: You just do not know what has really happened—$\dot{\eta}$ $\pi\iota\sigma\tau\iota\varsigma$ $\sigma\sigma\upsilon$ $\sigma\epsilon\sigma\omega\kappa\epsilon\nu$ $\sigma\epsilon$! Such a concrete imputation of faith is without parallel. Even if for a moment we completely disregard the testimony of the healing stories and concentrate solely on the saying about the faith that moves mountains, then here, too, we shall have to say that this saying includes also him who has the authority to say it. All this is not intended for a moment to cancel the fact that Jesus does not speak of a faith in himself. But he who is able to speak so concretely of faith is obviously able to do more than merely speak of faith, *viz.* to awaken faith, to summon to faith. We confine ourselves here solely to the question of the *concept* of faith. A comprehensive examination of the subject 'Jesus and Faith' would also have to enquire, quite apart from the occurrence of the concept of faith, into the question how far the words, deeds and attitude of Jesus make it plain that he summoned to faith. Then, for example, the call to $\dot{\alpha}\kappa o\lambda o\upsilon\theta\epsilon\hat{\iota}\nu$[1] would come into close connexion with the concept of faith. If however the faith to which Jesus awakened men was faith as such and

---

[1] E. Schweizer, 'Der Glaube an Jesus den "Herrn" in seiner Entwicklung von den ersten Nachfolgern bis zur hellenistischen Gemeinde', *Ev Th* 17 (1957), pp. 7-21: 'That Jesus called disciples to follow him, is beyond doubt. The word $\dot{\alpha}\kappa o\lambda o\upsilon\theta\epsilon\hat{\iota}\nu$ is firmly embedded in the tradition, and from the very beginning denotes something new and unique, to which there is no parallel either in Greek or in Jewish writings' (p. 7). Cf. G. Kittel, Art. $\dot{\alpha}\kappa o\lambda o\upsilon\theta\epsilon\omega$ $\kappa\tau\lambda$. *TWNT* I, pp. 210 ff; E. Schweizer, *Erniedrigung und Erhöhung bei Jesus und seinen Nachfolgern* (1955), pp. 8 ff [ET , *Lordshipand Discipleship*, 1960, pp. 11 ff].

by definition faith in God, then it was manifestly a case of concrete faith, i.e. of encountering God concretely. This observation can perhaps be further underlined by the way in which Jesus used the word אמן which belongs to the same root as האמין.

The use of the word ἀμήν[1] as a formula to introduce one's own sayings is found only in the New Testament, and here in turn exclusively on the lips of Jesus.[2] It was not imitated in later Christianity either. It is undoubtedly a case of a peculiarity of Jesus' manner of speaking. Three things apply to the Old Testament and Judaistic use of ἀμήν: 1. There is always a religious meaning implied in its use, hence not only when it is employed in prayer, but also when it is used in a benediction, a curse or any other binding statement. 2. It always stands in corroboration at the end of the statement to which it refers. 3. It is always spoken by someone else in response to the statement, never by the speaker himself. The usual custom among us of ending our own prayer with amen accords neither with the usage of late Judaism nor with that of primitive Christianity.[3] For primitive Christianity, too, as for late Judaism, what a man says can have amen added to it only by another. The use of the word ἀμήν thus means that someone assents to the words of another as valid and true—and that, too, in such a way that they are affirmed to be valid in God's eyes and have their guarantee in God, and also in such a way that they bind the man who says amen, that he identifies himself with them, that he accepts these words from the speaker as valid for himself.

What does it mean, then, that Jesus deviated so strangely from the prevailing usage, yet without thereby founding a new usage that became generally established, but instead the deviation remained confined to

[1] H. Schlier, Art. ἀμήν *TWNT* I, pp. 339-342; P. Glaue, Art. 'Amen', *RAC* I, pp. 378-80; G. Dalman, *Die Worte Jesu* I (1898), pp. 185-7 [ET, 1902, pp. 226-9], 2nd ed. 1930, p. 383; G. Dalman, *Jesus-Jeshua* (ET, 1929), pp. 30 f; A. Schlatter, *Der Evangelist Matthäus* (2nd ed. 1933), p. 155; Strack-Billerbeck I, pp. 242 ff, III, pp. 456 ff; J. Jeremias, 'Kennzeichen der ipsissima vox Jesu', in *Synoptische Studien, Alfred Wikenhauser zum 70. Geburtstag dargebracht* (1953), pp. 86-93, esp. 89-93.

[2] In Matt. 30 times, Mark 13 times, Luke 6 times (plus 4 times rendered by ἀληθῶς or ἐπ' ἀληθείας), John (only in him—and always in him—double: ἀμὴν ἀμὴν λέγω ὑμῖν) 25 times. (According to H. Schlier, *TWNT* I, p. 341.29-31.) Naturally that does not mean that each individual instance is to be considered authentic. Here too, I think, the usage of Jesus has provided an element that continues to influence the form of the tradition.

[3] In numerous passages where ἀμήν appears in the New Testament outside the Gospels at the end of prayers and doxologies, the state of the text is uncertain. In part it will have been introduced into the text from the practice of reading aloud at divine service.

Jesus himself?[1] Possibly a knowledge of Jesus' unique usage still lingers in two New Testament passages in which ἀμήν becomes outright a designation of Jesus himself, *viz.* II Cor. 1.19 f[2] and Rev. 3.14. Yet quite apart from that, Jesus' use of ἀμήν will have to be understood as follows:—It gives expression to the fact that Jesus understood his statements, and wished to have them understood, as statements made before God, in which God himself is the Guarantor of what is said and watches over the authentication of this word, i.e. sees to it that it comes about. Just as by saying amen to the prayer or word of another we do not merely signify our assent to it, but in and with this word put ourselves at the mercy of God and consequently of the reality of the word concerned—a reality which cannot again be cancelled but must now of necessity be fulfilled—so Jesus uses the amen to bring out the fact that the truth and reality of his words is the truth and reality of God. For that reason Jesus' use of amen gives expression, secondly, to the fact that Jesus identifies himself entirely with his words, that in the identification with these words he surrenders himself to the reality of God, and that he lets his existence be grounded on God's making these words true and real. That means, he is so certain of these words that he stakes his whole self on that certainty. And this absolute certainty that puts his whole existence at stake is so much the decisive thing in Jesus' proclamation that he sometimes begins with ἀμήν as a sort of slogan to mark the tenor of the whole. This ἀμήν is primarily not at all a question of corroborating the individual saying that follows. Rather, the latter arises

---

[1] A. Schlatter: 'Perhaps we are not only to suppose that Jesus turns to the disciples with his amen in order to give them the certainty that they have to depend on his word; the amen can also arise from considerations which preceded the formulation of the saying in question. Jesus was not only the speaker, but first the hearer who listens to God speaking. In embracing the certainty of what is shown him he answers it with amen and now passes it on to his disciples, that it may be for them too the rule which controls their conduct' (*Matthäus*, p. 155). H. Schlier: ' . . . the amen which precedes Jesus' own word marks it as one that is certain and dependable. And indeed certain and valid because and in that in the amen he, Jesus, acknowledges his own word and makes it valid for himself. This word has very different things to say in detail, even if it always concerns the history of the kingdom of God which is bound up with his person. That means, however, that the ἀμήν in front of Jesus' λέγω ὑμῖν contains *in nuce* the whole of Christology. He who sets up his word as true (=established) is at the same time he who acknowledges it and establishes it in his own life and so makes it in turn in its fulfilment a summons to others' (*TWNT* I, pp. 341.34-342.3).

[2] The ναί is a Greek rendering of אמן. Paul means: Christ is the Amen to the promises of God, and therefore our saying amen is also related to Christ as the absolute Amen.

from a fundamental certainty which already precedes it—we could also say, from a decision that has already been made, an assent given once for all to the reality of God, an absolute readiness to obey, an irrevocable act of being cast upon God and grounded in him. And lastly, Jesus' use of ἀμήν gives expression to the fact that Jesus here performs a vicarious act. He does not wait till those he is addressing can decide to say amen for their own part. He is not dependent on such corroboration on the hearer's side. He is even able to impart along with his words also the assuring power which flows from the assurance in which he himself is one with these words. The obedience in which that certainty consists has vicarious power in this: that it becomes the source from which certainty flows, that it is the origin of a testimony which awakens faith, i.e. a testimony which gives certainty not only in this respect or that, but *in toto*—and that means, which gives certainty to existence itself, makes it a believing existence, provides it with the ground on which it can depend. Jesus' use of אמן is the most concentrated way of saying that all he says and does—that indeed he himself has no other aim than to awaken האמין.

This has opened up for us perspectives which really could be termed a 'Christology *in nuce*'[1]—the fact that the decisive gift of Jesus is the faith which makes existence sure, i.e. which points it to its ground and so grounds it, and that the communication of faith takes place solely out of the certainty of Jesus, which in turn consists in his obedience, so that this obedience has a vicarious function, *viz.* as vicarious obedience it becomes the source of faith, and it can be vicarious obedience at all only as it becomes the source of faith. Then, however, Jesus is the source of faith.

3. We now ask once more in particular what the faith of which Jesus speaks has to do with the believer's existence. It seems to me another strikingly peculiar thing that in the passages we are concerned with here the concept of faith is frequently joined with the personal pronoun: ἡ πίστις σου σέσωκέν σε, μεγάλη σου ἡ πίστις, κατὰ τὴν πίστιν ὑμῶν γενηθήτω ὑμῖν.[2] I know of no parallels to that in late Judaism. In later Christian usage the combination ἡ πίστις ὑμῶν does occur;[3] but even here there is no evidence of such a pointed personal use of the concept of faith as in the healing stories. The concentration upon the individual

[1] H. Schlier, *TWNT* I, p. 341.40 f.
[2] Matt. 9.22; Mark 5.34; 10.52; Luke 7.50; 8.48; 17.19; 18.42; Matt. 15.28; 8.13; 9.29.
[3] E.g. Rom. 1.8, 12; I Cor. 2.5; 15.14; II Cor. 1.24; 10.15.

of what is said about faith is particularly striking as compared with the usage of late Judaism. Nothing is said, as it is there, of the faith of the fathers or the faith of the people. Not that there could be any question of denying it. But the way men took for granted both their participation in the faith of the fathers or of Israel as a whole and also the possibility of falling back on it, has now a question mark set against it. It is not without reason that the figure of the hypocrite is set in such a sharp light by Jesus. For the hypocrite is not merely the seeming saint but also, and primarily, the seeming believer. Of the hypocrite it is true, by definition, that he does not believe. Jesus on the other hand speaks of faith in such a way as to make unambiguously clear that it is a question of real faith, and that means of a man's own faith. A seeming faith, a faith that is merely believed in and imagined, a faith that is merely appropriated in thought, that is practised only in half-hearted participation in the life of the community, is manifestly not the faith which moves mountains and of which it could be said, ὡς ἐπίστευσας γενηθήτω σοι, or, πάντα δυνατὰ τῷ πιστεύοντι, or, ἡ πίστις σου σέσωκέν σε. The faith that moves mountains involves the believer's being unmistakably and entirely himself. That indeed is why this faith also becomes so acute in the healing stories: because man cannot be concerned more strongly in his personal being than when his existence is prejudiced or threatened. The blind man, for example, knows that he himself, inalienably he himself, is blind.

In this relation to existence as a whole it also becomes clear that faith is not a partial act—whether partial in the sense of merely grasping one particular object of faith among, and in preference to, others and thus requiring to be supplemented by other acts of faith directed towards other objects of faith, or partial in the sense of faith's being confined to one particular function of man, say his thinking, while other functions remained untouched by faith and had to be set to work separately and then placed on the same level as faith. Rather, faith seeks to be understood as something that concerns the whole of existence, as a movement in which the whole of existence is given aim, definition and ground. Faith is thus not a pale, empty category; rather it has to do with the concentratedness of existence, with the fact that man, prior to all the separate partial aspects in which he manifests himself and into which he divides himself and dissipates his energies, is one and the same and a whole. Precisely through the movement of being thrown upon God the wholeness of existence comes into view. Once more that is clearly illustrated by the healing stories: the blind man who cries out to Jesus, the Syro-phoenician who does not give up praying for her daughter—all these figures are outstanding in this: that they are totally involved, totally concerned, not merely half-heartedly interested in what now happens or fails to happen, but rather, just like the dog watching tensely for the morsel that falls from the table, they are concentrated on one single point with every nerve of their being tense with attention and expectation. This faith which sums up our existence in one concentrated whole can be regarded in various structural aspects on the basis of what we may learn from Jesus' concept of faith:—

a. Faith gives certainty to existence, indeed it is really nothing else but existence in certainty. Faith therefore sets itself against fear (μὴ φοβοῦ, μόνον πίστευε)[1] and against doubt (ἐὰν ἔχητε πίστιν καὶ μὴ διακριθῆτε).[2] It even appears as will. Instead of ὡς ἐπίστευσας γενηθήτω σοι,[3] it can also be said with entirely the same meaning, γενηθήτω σοι ὡς θέλεις.[4] What is not willed is not believed either—and willed, too, not in the colourless sense of wishing, but in the utmost intensity of concentrated will-power. The figures in these healing stories could not be believers without their whole will being set on help. This conjunction of faith and will is really what constitutes its certainty. It is not a case of the certainty of views, insights, etc. Whether and how far anything of that kind may also be legitimately connected with faith is at all events not the point at issue in Jesus' concept of faith. Here it is a matter only of the decisive point: the certainty of faith is a certainty that concerns our very existence, it is taking sure steps although no road is visible, hoping although there is nothing to look for, refusing to despair although things are desperate, having ground under us although we step into the bottomless abyss.

b. Faith is therefore directed towards the future, indeed it is really bringing about the future. The healing stories are eminently reminders of that: faith has to do with an event. It has its place in the movement of time and in all that that may bring and present. Where faith is, there something happens. It may then be a completely open question, what happens. But at all events everything does not remain simply what it was. If nothing at all had happened in the healing stories, if at the end the condition of the sick had been exactly the same as before, then Jesus could not have spoken of their faith, then there obviously would not have been real faith at work here. This direction of faith towards an

[1] Mark 5.36; Luke 8.50. Cf. Matt. 8.26; Mark 4.40; Luke 8.25.
[2] Matt. 21.21. Cf. Matt. 14.31.   [3] Matt. 8.13. Cf. Mark 11.23.
[4] Matt. 15.28.

event, however, is necessarily direction towards the future. A faith that did not point to the future would be a pseudo-faith. Even a faith directed towards so-called facts is really only faith in so far as a future opens up in the light of these facts. Thus it is by no means the case that among many other objects of faith there happen more or less accidentally to be also objects of faith that lie in the future. Rather faith, as that which makes existence a concentrated whole, is essentially a faith that relates to the future. For existence stands essentially in a movement towards the future—in hopeful, anxious or resigned expectation of the future, but at all events so that what is still to come, the 'not yet' of the future, belongs to the wholeness of existence, and the man without a future is, as is rightly said, only half a man. But now, faith's concern with what is to come, with the future part of existence, is not only that of hope; rather, faith has really an active function in regard to what is to come. It is bringing about the future.

c. For that reason faith is power, indeed it is really participation in the omnipotence of God. We must not seek to evade the alarmingness of that way of putting it. As a matter of fact it corresponds exactly to the saying about the faith that moves mountains, to the πάντα δυνατὰ τῷ πιστεύοντι, to the οὐδὲν ἀδυνατήσει ὑμῖν. This must at once be seen against the background of the pictures of powerlessness which are inseparable from Jesus' words about faith: as a mustard seed is obviously absolutely powerless against a massive mountain, so these people in the healing stories are likewise powerless against the massive realities of sickness, of permanent infirmity, of death. We are presented here with a whole range of different aspects of powerlessness: not merely the powerlessness of the sick people themselves, but also the powerlessness of their nearest and dearest who in love tend them and suffer with them; and then also the powerlessness of those who are expected to help, the doctors and finally the disciples of Jesus, who have to disappoint these expectations because they go beyond their power. And now it is said, startlingly enough, that this powerlessness is unbelief. Faith on the other hand is not powerless in such a situation, but rather achieves the unbelievable.

Do not let this be dismissed with the tag 'miracle faith'! 'Miracle faith' is either uncritical acceptance of the truth of miracles recounted by others, which however means of someone else's reality—but faith here has to do with a man's own reality. Or 'miracle faith' is subsequent pious interpretation of what has happened to us—but faith here has to do not with what has happened, but with what has not yet happened.

Or 'miracle faith' is a general theoretical conviction of the possibility of miracles—but faith here is concretely realized in defiant faith that defies the superiority of the massive realities. For the rest, we do well to exclude the concept of miracle in this context altogether. It is encumbered for us by confusing associations with the idea of breaking through the laws of nature. Here however it is (more properly) a case of the category of the unusual and exceptional—in contrast to the normal things of everyday. It belongs to the nature of faith as it understands itself, that it can do unusual, exceptional things. It is not surrendering oneself resignedly to reality, but acquiring power over reality. Even in the form of genuine self-surrender, faith is not powerlessness, but power. It is not contradiction of the nature of God, but rather accords with it, to say that where God is believed in, faith participates in the omnipotence of God. Nor indeed may that be watered down, as if it were only a case of faith being rewarded with some sort of outward demonstration of God's power. Rather, this faith seeks to be understood as being itself power, and as such then certainly also a demonstration of God's power. For faith is power only to the extent that God suffers it to be powerful. But at the same time it is also true that faith is faith only as powerful faith. Its nature is to be powerful. The power of faith is not a second thing alongside of faith, but faith itself. Hence participation in the omnipotence of God is not something that follows upon faith as effect follows upon cause. Rather, it is a description of the essence of faith to say: faith is participation in the omnipotence of God.

Then however one could also say: the essence of faith is participation in the essence of God. We fail to see what faith is all about if we do not perceive the dimension to which this daring way of putting it points. Faith cannot possibly be comprehended within the framework of a method of study which understands man as a self-contained and rounded whole that can be isolated from everything else. But man can exist only in participation in another. The reason why faith is so eminently concerned with the existence of man is, that in the question of faith the question of man's participation is posed in radical form. If however faith is understood as participation, then it cannot possibly be regarded in isolation as a human act, but the thing in which faith participates belongs inseparably to faith itself. For that reason not only the nowadays much discussed subject-object pattern is highly problematical as applied to faith, but also other alternatives which lie to hand. Is faith highest activity or pure passivity, utmost exertion of the will or complete surrender of the will, is it power or the extreme of powerlessness?

But the truth is, it is the coalescence of both: its activity is its passivity, its strength of will is its surrender to the will of God, its power is its absolute powerlessness before God.

d. Faith takes place in the encounter with other men. I am not thinking here of the point involved in the concreteness of faith, *viz.* that man as a believer cannot and must not abstract from his relation to his fellows, say on the supposition that faith affects only his relation to God. As if it did not for that very reason affect man in the whole of his existence and consequently also in his existing with others! But the point here is, that the healing stories all take place through the encounter with the man Jesus. On the face of it, that means that the encounter with Jesus was necessary for the simple reason that he alone was able to heal. But then Jesus would be no more than a wonder doctor, endowed with particular powers of healing peculiar to himself alone, who had brought about the cure. To be sure, we know little about the course of the cures as such. The tradition was unquestionably very active here in elaborating and intensifying the facts of the case. Yet it does seem to reflect the historical facts in this: that there is little to tell of any particular healing techniques, that the emphasis did not lie in the act of healing at all, and that in that act itself the way of employing the concept of faith is meant actually to distract attention both from the effecting of a cure and also from Jesus' healing action. The formula ἡ πίστις σου σέσωκέν σε forbids regarding the cure as the result of a particular healing technique on Jesus' part. It would not fully meet the case if instead it were said: ἐγὼ σέσωκά σε. Certainly, it would not be untrue, just as little as it would be to say: ὁ θεὸς σέσωκέν σε. But the fact of God's having helped would surely be rightly understood only if there were no obscuring the fact that his help took place in the encounter with Jesus. And the fact of Jesus' having helped would surely be rightly understood only if it were noticed that he helped by awakening the faith of which it can be said: ἡ πίστις σου σέσωκέν σε. That is certainly not to declare Jesus superfluous. For faith does not arise in a man automatically. No man can awaken faith in himself by his own power, decide for faith by his own power. But whatever may have to be said about the rise of faith in the light of the New Testament testimony as a whole, the testimony of the tradition about Jesus, which is the only thing we are considering now, is that the rise of faith always depended on the encounter with Jesus. That means: to evoke and to claim faith is possible only for a person empowered to do so. That is the element of truth in the view that faith has its origin in authority. Authority exists, however, only as personal authority. That is not to deny that faith comes of preaching, and thus by word. For personal authority is in itself authority which makes its claims by word. But the only word that is genuinely authoritative and therefore becomes *auctor fidei* is the word spoken in such a way that the person who speaks it identifies himself with it. Only the word of a witness can be a word that has power and authority and awakens faith. Whatever peculiarity about the person of Jesus may also have to be taken into account, at all events one structural characteristic of faith is, that the rise of faith depends on encounter with witnesses to faith.

  e. Faith is concrete faith in its being related to a concrete situation. The unique force of the healing stories as examples lies in the fact that they make clear that we have to believe concretely. Here of course there is also a danger that the healing stories, through the concreteness of their faith, threaten to make the nature of faith unrecognizable by pinning the attention on the unrepeatable way it became concrete, which cannot dispense from the decision to make it concrete anew. For that reason the point at issue in faith certainly cannot be discussed exclusively by pointing to a concrete event of faith. But we must let such concrete instances remind us of the fact that faith seeks concrete belief—and of what that means. Our usual use of the concept of faith to denote the sum of religious convictions and ideas is an abstraction from the real nature of faith. Faith receives its concreteness not by expressing the believer's ideas in the most specific possible form. In that case faith, as Jesus spoke of it, would have been as far from concreteness as one could imagine. For here there is not the slightest reference to definite believing ideas. Jesus does not demand the recitation of a Creed, he does not hold an examination in the faith. Certainly we must not be over-hasty in deducing from that the right to reject statements of faith as such. Yet in terms of Jesus' concept of faith it is surely entirely appropriate that in the only passage in the Synoptic Gospels where believing appears in the 1st person singular, this 'Creed' is confined to the words: πιστεύω· βοήθει μου τῇ ἀπιστίᾳ.[1] And if we care to adopt the idea of an examination in faith, then it could be said that the healing stories most certainly are examples of genuine examinations in faith, *viz.* of obtaining faith and displaying faith in a concrete situation, not as a particular act alongside other acts, but as the fundamental act of existence, in the sense of a faith that masters and overcomes the concrete situation on the basis of the ground of existence. Only a faith which thus concretely authenticates itself and proves its truth can be claimed as faith. For that reason faith can also

---

[1] Mark 9.24.

only be learned in relation to a concrete situation. And for that reason faith is ultimately always something exceptional, something which does not become concrete in just any situation.

f. Finally, faith is always saving faith, indeed it is salvation itself. The conjunction of πίστις and σωτηρία which is so characteristic of the New Testament is prefigured in the healing stories. The form and manner of the conjunction, it is true, here remains strangely fluid. On one occasion it is to the faith of the sick man himself that the healing comes;[1] on another it is the faith of someone else, who takes the sick man's part and so to speak mediates the healing to him;[2] on another it is manifestly on the faith of Jesus himself that everything in the healing story depends.[3] It would not be doing justice to the understanding of faith that prevails here if we sought to harmonize it and make it calculable. The decisive thing amid the manifold variations is this: with the arrival of faith on the scene, something has changed, a saving power has arrived on the scene, the power that counters the power of the massive facts is already at work, the cause of the future so to speak has been espoused and consequently the old—all that comes from the past to discourage the present—has been declared to be past. Faith itself is the really salutary turning-point, because it is the power that saves. The healing stories would be misunderstood if they were taken as a pattern of how the power of faith primarily and properly works. Perhaps they should not be called healing stories at all, because that shifts the real point. It is a case of stories of faith, of *exempla fidei* with all the problematical character that always attaches to an *exemplum fidei*. We should therefore be better to say: a case of testimonies to faith, in which the thing that repeats itself is not what faith once effected, but the effective power of faith itself. For that reason it is no accident that in these encounters Jesus explicitly names faith as the point of the encounter. Not that the healing should then become irrelevant. For where there is faith, there, by definition, one way or another, existence becomes whole, is healed. The fact that πιστεύειν and σώζεσθαι thus belong essentially together gives the power of faith its direction and supplies the πάντα δυνατά with its proper interpretation. For faith can do nothing insalutary. But faith alone—and that, too, in the strict sense of this *particula exclusiva*—can heal, can save: μόνον πίστευε![4]

---

[1] Matt. 9.28 f; 9.22; Mark 5.34; Luke 8.48; Mark 10.52; Luke 18.42; 17.19.
[2] Matt. 8.10, 13; Luke 7.9; Mark 5.36; Luke 8.50; Matt. 15.28; 9.2; Mark 2.5; Luke 5.20.
[3] Mark 9.23.   [4] Mark 5.36.

The above exposition requires further development in various respects. What we have tried to say of the historical Jesus on a very narrow basis would have to be related to the whole of the tradition about Jesus and so tested and elucidated. Then the history of the concept of faith would have to be traced further into primitive Christian usage, in order to discover what relation Jesus' concept of faith (which, certainly not entirely without contact with the usage of the contemporary world of late Judaism yet in astonishing independence of it, takes up the deepest intentions of the Old Testament concept of faith, and yet develops it further in ways that are peculiar also in comparison with the Old Testament) bears to the Christian concept of faith, and what the death and resurrection of Jesus mean for the understanding of the nature of faith. And finally the insights resulting from that would have to be thought through in their bearing upon Christology.

VIII

REFLEXIONS ON
THE DOCTRINE OF THE LAW*[1]

W HEN we survey all the debates on the doctrine of the law, then we can hardly resist the tiresome impression of an utterly hopeless discussion. There is little point in taking some well-known position and defending it anew against its opponents, or even in introducing some sort of modulated view, without taking account of the methodological problem involved in a doctrine of the law. That includes in the first instance the effort to reach an agreement on the concept of law. If we think for example of the criticism of the Reformers' doctrine of law and Gospel advanced by Karl Barth under the title 'Gospel and Law',[2] or of the discussion on the *tertius usus legis*, then it is easy to see that the antitheses which here arise hang together with a difference already in the definition of the concept law. That could mean that the contradiction between the views is resolved, or at least looks somewhat different from at first sight, as soon as we take into account that the two parties are using the concept of law in different ways. It could of course also mean that when careful attention is paid to the difference in terminology, the real antithesis merely shifts elsewhere and the fact of different definitions of the concept law confirms that the roots of the difference already lie very much deeper. And one could perhaps even be driven to affirm that not only is the actual difference in the understanding of the concept law significant, but there is already a divergence of views on the formation

---

* *ZTK* 55 (1958), pp. 270-306.
[1] A paper read to the theological study circle of 'old Marburgers' at Jugenheim on 21st October, 1958. For the press I have left the text of the paper unaltered and in the added footnotes have confined myself essentially to supplying references for the quotations in the paper itself. To go on to mention and discuss the abundance of literature on the subject in the realms of exegesis, church history and systematic theology, would have been beyond the scope of an essay which is so to speak only an experiment in 'short-distance border traffic' between the theological disciplines.
[2] Karl Barth, 'Evangelium und Gesetz', *Theol. Existenz heute* 32 (1935). Reprinted in *Theol. Ex. heute* Neue Folge 50 (1956). [ET in *God, Grace and Gospel*, SJT Occasional Papers No. 8, 1959.]

and criteria of theological concepts. For if, as we have said, in view of the methodological problem of a doctrine of the law our efforts must be directed in the first instance towards reaching an agreement on the concept of the law, then that involves the necessity of considering also the question of the forming of theological concepts in general. It would certainly be an illusion to see in that a way of simplifying theological disputes. But if the conversation between theologians is not to be pointless altogether, then it must be possible to discuss also the forming of theological concepts.

However, we certainly do not mean to let ourselves be edged away from the problem of the law into general preliminary reflexions on methodology. Rather, we shall use the concept of law as a perhaps specially instructive example in the light of which to discuss the question of the forming of theological concepts in general. Merely in order to indicate the vast and difficult background against which the problem of the concept of law arises for discussion, I begin with a few preliminary remarks of a general kind.

I

The *forming of theological concepts* is obviously a part of the problem of forming concepts in general. As an attempt to characterize this extremely delicate subject in as elementary a way as possible, we could perhaps say that to deal with concepts in a responsible manner is to know oneself bound to two cardinal points: attentiveness to the history of language and openness towards the reality that confronts us. Here we are touching on the basic structure of the hermeneutic task, for which the twofold relation, to linguistic expression and to the object therein expressed, is fundamental. And of course seeking agreement about concepts is in fact a fundamental matter of hermeneutics. Now, the two cardinal points I have just distinguished belong for hermeneutics inseparably together in a relation of reciprocal interaction. The fact of reality's confronting me and the manner in which it does so are conditioned by the language spoken to me. And again, the understanding of language spoken to me, together with my own ways of using language, are conditioned by the way in which reality confronts me and the manner in which I let myself be confronted by it. Within the framework of this basic structure, the bearing of the two cardinal points on each other varies according to the particular thing to be conceived. But—at all events with concepts which touch on man's humanity and consequently on his understanding of himself—it may well be adopted as an elementary rule for dealing conscientiously with such concepts that we have to take our bearings on the history of the concept and also on the phenomenon itself. We cannot with impunity ignore the history of language —to be made the uncritical prey of a particular linguistic tradition is of course one of the penalties of disregarding the history of language. But neither can we with impunity lose contact with reality; otherwise our concepts unexpectedly turn into empty shells.

Now it is beyond question that every science, and in the wider sense every approach to reality from a particular standpoint, forms its own particular concepts. These can even on occasion be its own particular words, but for the most part they are words also used elsewhere which separate into different concepts according to the particular context in which they are employed. The concept of law in natural science differs from that of jurisprudence.[1] It is a matter for the methodology of the individual scientific disciplines to clarify their specific concepts. Theology has naturally to watch over the forming of specifically theological concepts. Here it can only in exceptional cases, as we have said, be a question of using special theological terms. It is chiefly a case of giving precise definition as theological concepts to words which are also used elsewhere, in everyday life as in other sciences. Luther here laid down the basic principle: '*Omnia vocabula fiunt nova, quando e suo foro in alienum transferuntur.*'[2] The concept *opus*, for example, undergoes a change when we turn from the *forum politicum* of the lawyer to the *forum theologicum*.[3] There remains of course the problem of what it is that despite all the differences forms the common element which makes it meaningful to employ the same word. And the question arises whether it is not surely an over-simplification when a parallel text of the remark from the dissertation just quoted says: '*Omnia vocabula fiunt nova, quando transferuntur ex philosophia in theologiam.*'[4] But at all events the warning against careless use of philosophical concepts in theology is fully justified: '*Si tamen vultis uti vocabulis istis, prius quaeso illa bene purgate,* give them a good bath.'[5] And it is also right to warn against

---

[1] Cf. e.g. the collection of essays, *Das Problem der Gesetzlichkeit*, published by the Joachim-Jungius-Gesellschaft der Wissenschaften e.V., Hamburg, vol. 1 *Geisteswissenschaften*, vol. 2 *Naturwissenschaften*, 1949.

[2] *WA* 39/1, p. 231.1-3 (*Disp.* 1537).

[3] *Physicus, iurista dicit: Opera sunt bona, iusta, necessaria, et recte quidem illi iudicant, et secundum suum finem. Sed theologus contra dicit: Opera nostra quantumvis bona sunt coram Deo mala et damnata, non necessaria* (op. cit., p. 231.4-9).

[4] *Op. cit.*, p. 231.1-3.

[5] *Op. cit.*, p. 229.16-19.

adopting certain kinds of concepts—Luther speaks of the *vocabula physica*—in theology at all; for introducing too many foreign elements into theological language through the use of inappropriate concepts can have unforeseeable results: '*Cum vocabula physica in theologiam translata sunt, facta est inde scholastica quaedam theologia.*'[1]

When we regard the problem of the forming of theological concepts in the light of the two points mentioned above, namely, paying attention to the history of language and taking our bearings on reality itself, then the one to a certain extent meets with unquestioning acceptance while the other encounters severe misgivings. For how should taking our bearings on reality possibly be relevant where the content of theological statements is concerned? Is this not a case of being enticed on to the false paths of empirical theology and natural theology? The precept that theological concepts must be determined by the Bible apparently tells unequivocally and indisputably against it, at all events for a theology that is true to the Reformers. Luther's theology took its rise, long before the theoretical statement of the so-called scripture principle, from paying attention to the peculiarity of biblical usage as distinct from that of philosophy or scholasticism.[2] One could even go so far as to say of Luther that for the forming of theological concepts the study of languages takes the place that had been occupied in scholasticism by the study of philosophy: '*primo grammatica videamus, verum ea Theologica.*'[3] Who would wish to dispute the binding character of this instruction? But as a result of changes in the intellectual climate we can see as Luther did not the problems involved in making the Bible the norm of theological concepts. Luther and his age could, generally speaking, hold that the task of forming theological concepts is identical with conscientiously collecting the data of biblical usage. The Reformers' theology, it is true, was generally free of any formal biblicist tendencies. Luther was perfectly able to agree with e.g. the adoption of the traditional concept 'sacrament', although it is not of biblical origin.[4] And he was magnanimous enough to distinguish between substance and expression: 'We must retain the *res*, whatever term we like to call it by.'[5] Yet on the other hand the dominant thing with him is nevertheless the exhortation to adopt the biblical usage: 'For it is dangerous indeed

---

[1] *Op. cit.*, p. 229.22-24.

[2] Cf. my essay, 'Die Anfänge von Luthers Hermeneutik', *ZTK* 48 (1951), pp. 191 f.　　　　　　　　　[3] *WA* 5, p. 27.8 (*Op. in ps.* 1519).

[4] *Non enim habet universa scriptura sancta hoc nomen sacramentum in ea significatione, qua noster usus, sed in contrario* (*WA* 6, p. 551.9-11 [*De capt. Bab.* 1520]=Clem. 1, p. 487.20 f).　　　　　　　　　[5] *WA* 39/2, p. 305.22 f (*Disp.* 1544).

to speak of the things of God in other ways or other words than God himself uses.'[1] '*Manendum est in formulis praescriptis Spiritus sancti.*'[2] The Formula of Concord expresses it in a similar way, yet with a somewhat different aim, namely, that of avoiding theological disputes by recourse to the terminology of the Bible (and significantly enough also of the church tradition): 'But as concerns the words and manner of speaking, the best and surest course is to use and keep to the pattern of sound words provided in holy scripture and in the books noted above in this article.'[3] And as a horrible warning of the fact that recourse to the biblical line serves on occasion towards the suppression of clarity of concept, let us recall the ὅμοιος κατὰ τὰς γραφάς of the Arian controversy.

We know very well today that there are two reasons why the task of forming theological concepts cannot be dispensed with simply by taking over the usage of the Bible—first, because the Bible itself contains wide linguistic differences, so that e.g. *the* biblical concept of law simply does not exist, and second, because linguisticality is the same as historicality, and therefore the hermeneutic distinction between text and exposition arises at once, even when we think we are only repeating what we were taught. The task of forming theological concepts is consequently perceived to be an uncommonly difficult matter. More difficult in a way than, say, the task of forming philosophical concepts. The latter is, of course, also bound to concern itself with the history of language and cannot behave towards it in a completely arbitrary fashion. But it is not bound to a definite linguistic tradition, as is the case in theology. Even when we are perfectly clear that restriction to the vocabulary of the Bible would be a completely senseless thing to ask, because it breaks down already on the problem of translation, and that moreover the specifically scientific character of theology necessitates the forming of concepts beyond the usage of the Bible, yet on the other hand it cannot be denied that from the purely lexicographical standpoint a large number of basic biblical concepts supply and must supply the major part of the theologian's vocabulary. The transmission of the Christian message,

[1] *WA* 15, p. 43.12 f (*An die Ratsherren*, 1524); '. . . that we should be content to speak of his works simply in his words, as he has bidden us speak of them and teaches us, and should not propose to speak of them in our own words as being different and better, for we shall certainly go astray where we do not simply repeat after him what he teaches us . . .' (*WA* 26, pp. 439.37-440.2 [*Vom Abendmahl Christi*, 1528]).

[2] *WA* 39/2, p. 105.2 f (*Disp.* 1540).

[3] *Form. Conc. Sol. Decl.* Art. I: *Die Bekenntnis-Schriften der Ev. Luth. Kirche*, 2nd ed. 1952, p. 860.11-16.

and therefore also the scientific reflexion directed towards that end, cannot emancipate itself at its own discretion from the use of the words in which the Christian message originally came to expression. It is unthinkable that Christian preaching and theology could ever dispense with such concepts as sin, faith, Holy Ghost, God, etc. But these now constantly require interpretation. And a central part of that is doubtless the effort to reach a genuine understanding of biblical usage in all its differentiations. But that is not a task that can be isolated and confined within these limits. On the one hand it is absolutely necessary to pay attention also to extra-biblical usage, so as to illuminate the special linguistic conditions and peculiarities of biblical usage; while on the other hand it is likewise essential in the task of forming theological concepts today to enquire also into the further history of theological, but in addition also of secular usage.

A comprehensive philological orientation of this kind cannot, of course, supply the concepts themselves, but can only provide the necessary material and sharpen the awareness of our own responsibility for the forming of theological concepts. Nevertheless taking our bearings on the history of language does not leave us without any sense of direction. Not in virtue of a formal authority but because of its varying degrees of nearness to the root of the matter, the history of language exhibits cardinal points that command supreme respect. Apart from the Bible the cardinal point for us happens to be the theology of the Reformers. That does not alter in any way the verdict that neither is the usage of the Bible uniform in itself, nor is that of the Reformers identical with it, nor indeed can our own theological language be simply that of the Bible or the Reformation. Nevertheless the forming of theological concepts has to face the question of its conformity to scripture and also (though the relation between the two need not here be more closely defined) the question of—let us say in general terms—its evangelical character. That means that in the forming of theological concepts the historical disciplines play an essential role, yet without being able as such to solve the problem of forming theological concepts. It is the task of systematic theology, with an open ear to the diversity in the history of language, to work out concepts which take the reality itself that confronts us—this aspect now comes to the fore—and give expression to it in the way it has to be given expression by the Christian message. It goes without saying that we are here setting out the difference between the disciplines only in principle. In actual practice they are perforce bound up with each other, so that in the work of exegesis and of systematic theology we have only differences of accent in the work of carrying out the hermeneutic task.

I turn now—not to the doctrine of the law as a whole, but only to the problem of the concept of law, and must confine myself even here to a few limited aspects of it, as they emerge above all from comparing the concept of the law in the Bible and in the Reformers. That will bring us only to the threshold of the tasks that would have to be dealt with in forming systematic theology's concepts today.

II

When we enquire into the theological concept of the law—and that, too, with a view to a theological doctrine of the law—then we do so as followers of the Reformers (whereby I permit myself, for the sake of brevity, to leave aside the question of internal differences between the Reformers and to keep to Luther). The significance which the theology of the Reformers has for our question does not arise purely and simply from our own chance confessional position. Naturally Catholic theology, too, is interested in the concept of the law and develops a doctrine of the law.[1] The difference, however, does not consist merely in the form given to it in detail, but in the function which the doctrine of the law has in theology as a whole. The concept of the law fits into Catholic

[1] On this point we must now refer above all to the very notable book by Gottlieb Söhngen, *Gesetz und Evangelium: Ihre analoge Einheit. Theologisch, philosophisch, staatsbürgerlich*, 1957: 'To examine the relation between law and Gospel is to go to the heart of Christianity and enquire into the essence of Christianity' (p. 1). But Söhngen is very well aware of the important terminological difference, *viz.* 'that the Catholic way of stating our subject is "law and grace", not "law and Gospel", which is the Reformers' form' (pp. 6 f). He admits and regrets the neglect of this subject on the Catholic side, and explains it as resulting from the fact that it had become the battleground of the Reformation. 'Not as if the Catholic theologians of recent times and of today had written off our subject, and dismissed it; and yet most of them do "write off" here in a different sense—they merely copy out the great scholastic tradition on the subject, and do not even do that without touching it up and smoothing it out in legalistic style, they do not go on to add anything new to the subject. The subject, one of the most exciting since the Epistles to Galatians and Romans, largely ceases to be particularly stirring to Catholic theologians. I cannot resist the impression that the exciting and thorny topic sometimes seems actually to be evaded; thus there is something occasional about its treatment—it is treated on occasion, but no longer with ultimate thoroughness' (pp. 7 f).—Certain elements in this picture of the situation could be applied *mutatis mutandis* also to evangelical theology.—Cf. further the important work (which Söhngen also values as an exception) by Bernhard Häring, *Das Gesetz Christi: Moraltheologie*, 4th ed. 1957.

theology so to speak without a break, and is for that reason itself relatively free of problems, whereas in the theology of the Reformers the problems all concentrate themselves so much on the concept of law that the whole of theology (in the sense of the essential structure of theology) stands or falls with it. Not that in a purely quantitative sense the concept of law dominates more strongly in the Reformers than in Catholic theology. Rather the contrary. But just because in the theology of the Reformers it is primarily the questionable aspect of the law that is discussed, the doctrine of the law here acquires an importance that affects the whole of theology, while in the other case, where the concept of law is a theological category of undisputed positive significance, reflexion upon it can take a back seat. It is only in the law-to-Gospel relationship that the concept of law becomes a problem for theology and the doctrine of the law therefore also acquires that total theological relevance which we have in view in our approach to the question.

Just as the outstanding theological significance of the *distinction of law and Gospel* is familiar to us from the Reformed tradition, so also it appears to us a matter of course that the distinction is in conformity with scripture. Yet what are the facts? If we here keep strictly to the angle of terminology, then naturally the Old Testament can be completely left out of account for a start. We shall come back later to the question of the contribution made by the Old Testament concept of law (or its variations) to the question of the theological concept of law.[1] At all events the Old Testament concept of law as such is entirely void of any antithetical determination in the sense of the distinction of law and Gospel. And also in the New Testament the theme of law and Gospel is found, as is well known, essentially only in Paul, and even in him almost exclusively in Galatians and Romans.[2] Yet even here we must note that Paul never sets νόμος and εὐαγγέλιον directly over against each other or applies them as a dialectical formula in the manner of the Reformed usage familiar to us. Harnack has called attention to this (so far as I am aware he was the first to do so): '... Paul himself, although the antithesis agrees in general with his convictions, nevertheless never formulated it in that way. Where he speaks of νόμος he never speaks of εὐαγγέλιον, and *vice versa*.' 'The two words seem even to shun each other in Paul, i.e. they appear wholly disparate. In contexts in which

[1] See below, pp. 264 ff.
[2] For that reason I confine myself in what follows to Paul. That is no arbitrary narrowing of the field when it is borne in mind that here we are not considering the attitude to the law in general, but the application of the concept of law, and that the antithesis for the first time casts new light on that.

Paul uses "law", the Gospel is never found and *vice versa*.'[1] Molland has added to that only the minor correction that in I Cor. 9.20 f Paul explicitly touches on the question of law in a context whose centre is in fact the Gospel: 9.12-23. 'But here Paul is saying,' (so Molland interprets it) 'that for the sake of the Gospel he adapts himself both to the people of the law and those who are free of the law. With that he is in fact saying that the proclamation of the Gospels [*sic*!] transcends the dispute about the law—that is, that Gospel and law lie on different planes. The hermeneutic conclusion *e silentio*, that "law" and "Gospel" are disparate concepts, is directly supported by that.' And Molland for his part goes on to draw the further conclusion: 'Hence the content of the Gospel is not the doctrine of the law. And consequently not the doctrine of justification either.' 'The doctrine of justification is not the content of the Gospel message, but its theological consequence.'[2]

We shall not discuss that view further here, but merely note that it is undoubtedly correct that the Reformers' contrast of *lex* and *evangelium* is at all events not found stated explicitly in Paul, however tremendous the significance which the concept νόμος has for him and however much he, too, uses εὐαγγέλιον with a definite stamp that seems essentially in complete agreement with the Reformers' concept of Gospel. (The Johannine writings, in which above all John 1.17 comes very close to the Reformers' distinction, may be left out of account, because εὐαγγέλιον and its derivatives are totally absent.)

The first to join the concepts *lex* and *evangelium* as a pair of contrasting concepts was, so far as we know, Marcion. '*Separatio legis et evangelii proprium et principale opus est Marcionis*', Tertullian reports,[3] and with that he is doubtless repeating here as in other passages Marcion's own terminology. When Harnack then designates Augustine as the first 'who after Marcion . . . perceives and works out the full sharpness of the contrast of *lex* and *evangelium*, and brings it to light especially in the work "*de spiritu et littera*" ',[4] then with qualifications that does tally from the point of view of content, but not where terminology is concerned. The direct contrast of the concepts *lex* and *evangelium*, to the best of my knowledge, probably does not occur in Augustine at all; rather, alongside *littera* and *spiritus* he has *lex* and *gratia*, or *lex operum* and *lex fidei*. That is then also what determines scholastic usage, in which the antithesis of

---

[1] A. von Harnack, *Entstehung und Entwicklung der Kirchenverfassung und des Kirchenrechts in den zwei ersten Jahrhunderten*, 1910, p. 218 note 1.

[2] E. Molland, *Das paulinische Euangelion: Das Wort und die Sache*, 1924, pp. 62 f.

[3] *Adv. Marc.* I, 19: *CSEL* 47, p. 314.22 f.   [4] *Op. cit.*, p. 239.

lex and *evangelium* plays no part, though we do have the distinction of *lex* and *gratia*, combined with the other distinction of *lex vetus* and *lex nova* or *lex evangelica*. Thomas Aquinas in a carefully weighed and most illuminating definition characterizes as *lex nova* what we might expect to be designated *evangelium*: '*Principaliter lex nova est ipsa gratia Spiritus sancti, quae datur Christi fidelibus. Habet tamen lex nova quaedam sicut dispositiva ad gratiam Spiritus sancti et ad usum huius gratiae pertinentia, quae sunt quasi secundaria in lege nova; de quibus oportuit instrui fideles Christi et verbis et scriptis, tam circa credenda quam circa agenda. Et ideo dicendum est, quod principaliter lex nova est lex indita, secundario autem est lex scripta.*[1] Thus according to him the distinction of *lex vetus* and *lex nova* coincides with that of the revelation of the Old Covenant and the revelation of the New Covenant. And in regard to the latter there is the further distinction that *lex nova* in the strict sense is the *lex indita*, that is, the grace of the Holy Spirit himself shed abroad in the heart, while the *lex nova* in the derivative, secondary sense is doctrine, but then also doctrine fixed in writing, which is related to the *gratia spiritus sancti* as preparation and instruction—and that, too, in such a way that it communicates what men must believe and do.

The Reformers' distinction of law and Gospel is a new departure in the history of concepts, in so far as the terminological association with Marcion must not create any delusions as to the fundamental material difference and the material association with Augustine (and surely also with the scholastics) must not obscure the terminological difference, whose material relevance is by no means so trifling. What now of the relation of the Reformers' formula to Paul? For the time being we still refrain as far as possible from a special comparison of the concept of the law itself in the Reformers and in Paul, and attend first of all merely to the relation that obtains between law and Gospel.

The Reformers' way of opposing law and Gospel did at all events—as everyone must admit—bring out the sharp contrast which Paul has in view when he speaks of νόμος. Except that then, as we have said, Paul does not employ as the opposite member the concept εὐαγγέλιον, which he otherwise finds so important, but names as the antithesis to νόμος either 'Ιησοῦς Χριστός himself, or πίστις or χάρις or πνεῦμα. It is a simple step to replace these varied forms of expression by taking as a term that comprehends them all the concept εὐαγγέλιον, which of course was Paul's unmistakable and stereotype description of the κήρυγμα, the saving message of Jesus Christ. But then it would surely

[1] *Summa theol.* I, II, q. 106, a. 1.

be missing the point of Paul's choice of expression if we were to say that the Gospel is just the particular message and doctrine whose content and object is Jesus Christ, $\pi i \sigma \tau \iota s$, $\chi \acute{a} \rho \iota s$, $\pi \nu \epsilon \hat{v} \mu a$. If the distinction of law and Gospel were understood in this way as the difference of two kinds of doctrinal content, then the law-and-gospel terminology would in very truth involve a false interpretation of Paul. Compared with that, Augustine's interpretation which contrasts *lex* and *gratia* (and moreover, be it noted, not a *doctrina de gratia* but grace itself, not a communication about grace but the communication of grace itself, the *ipsa praesentia spiritus sancti*) would have the advantage of fitting Paul's intention better. Paul certainly does not simply take two forms of doctrine which in themselves have qualitatively the same essential structure, and contrast them in the light of their difference of content. The only head under which he can comprehend together the two things he means, is $\delta \iota a \theta \acute{\eta} \kappa \eta$[1] (with the *differentiae specificae* $\pi a \lambda a \iota \acute{a}$ and $\kappa a \iota \nu \acute{\eta}$), which is to be understood as 'disposition', 'declaration of will'—indeed, one could even go so far as to render it freely 'constitution', in order to bring out the fact that it is a case of a power which determines absolutely the reality it affects. That is also why Paul compares the two $\delta \iota a \theta \hat{\eta} \kappa a \iota$ not really in regard to their content, but in regard to their power, their effect. Whereas the law cannot give life, cannot bestow the Spirit,[2] but on the contrary in fact kills,[3] the $\kappa a \iota \nu \grave{\eta}$ $\delta \iota a \theta \acute{\eta} \kappa \eta$ is the act of the life-giving Spirit himself;[4] and $\pi i \sigma \tau \iota s$ has no other meaning. And precisely that is the reality of the Risen One.

Did the Reformation now prejudice this state of affairs by using the concept '*evangelium*' instead? Its use could be appropriate at all events only if it were clearly grasped—as in fact it undeniably was in the original Reformation theology—that the Gospel is that proclamation which creates faith and imparts the Holy Spirit—as it is very well expressed in the 7th Schwabach Article: 'For the attainment of such faith or the bestowing of it on us men, God has ordained the preaching office or spoken word, namely the Evangel, through which he causes such faith and its power, profit and fruit to be proclaimed, and also uses the same as a means to bestow faith and the Holy Spirit, as and where he will. Apart from that there is no other means nor method, way nor path to acquire faith.'[5] The Reformers' employment of *evangelium* as an

[1] In the wider sense, still other concepts of course bring out the common point of reference of both $\delta \iota a \theta \hat{\eta} \kappa a \iota$, such as e.g. $\delta \iota \kappa a \iota o \sigma \acute{v} \nu \eta$.
[2] Gal. 3.21; cf. 3.2, 5.   [3] Rom. 7.10; II Cor. 3.6.
[4] II Cor. 3. Cf. my article 'Geist und Buchstabe', *RGG*[2] II, pp. 1290 ff.
[5] *Bekenntnis-Schriften* (see above, p. 251 note 3), p. 59.2-12.

antithesis to *lex* would then of course not serve as a mere collective term for the varied terminology of Paul, but would perform an interpretative function, namely, that of describing the reality of the καινὴ διαθήκη so to speak in the light of its historic effective principle. And the latter happens to be—here the Reformation grasped a decisive Pauline standpoint— the event of proclamation. Let us recall only Rom. 10.17, ἡ πίστις ἐξ ἀκοῆς, and the phrase ἀκοὴ πίστεως Gal. 3.2, 5. The καινὴ διαθήκη has its existence determined by the act of a proclamation whose absolute peculiarity and therefore also its distinctive mark over against the law, is the power to awaken faith, to confer the Holy Spirit.

The significance of such interpretation by means of the concept Gospel becomes clearer from a comparison with the interpretation of Augustine and the scholastics. Here the question of the historic effective principle of the καινὴ διαθήκη is given a different answer. On the positive side we should have to speak at this point of the view of the sacrament. But the negative marks may suffice. The proclamation is not in the proper sense what constitutes the reality of the καινὴ διαθήκη. It has significance only as preparation and accompaniment, while the real coming of grace and the Spirit takes place in another way. That is why for the Catholic mind the καινὴ διαθήκη can without hesitation be subsumed under the concept of the law, partly in the sense of a law that fulfils itself in practice, partly in the sense of a law that makes demands. And as far as any account is thereby taken of the event of proclamation, it is no accident that the movement, as was shown by Thomas' definition,[1] is in the direction of a New Testament *lex scripta*, whereas Luther put quite decisive emphasis for the New Covenant on the spoken word.[2]

[1] See above, p. 256.

[2] 'For in the New Testament the sermons are to be spoken aloud in public and to bring forth in terms of speech and hearing what was formerly hidden in the letter and secret vision. Forasmuch as the New Testament is nothing else but the unlocking and revealing of the Old Testament. . . . That, too, is why Christ himself did not write his teaching, as Moses did his, but delivered it orally, also commanded to deliver it orally and gave no command to write it. . . . For that reason it is not at all the manner of the New Testament to write books of Christian doctrine but there should everywhere, without books, be good, learned, spiritually-minded, diligent preachers to draw the living word from the ancient scriptures and constantly bring it to life before the people, as the apostles did. For before ever they wrote, they had first preached to and converted the people by word of mouth, which also was their real apostolic and New Testament work. . . . That books had to be written, however, is at once a great failure and a weakness of spirit that was enforced by necessity and not by the manner of the New Testament. . . .'—*WA* 10/1, 1, pp. 625.19-627.3 (*Weihnachtspostille*, 1522). Cf. also my book, *Evangelische Evangelienauslegung: Eine Untersuchung zu Luthers Hermeneutik*, 1942, pp. 366 ff.

The interpretation of Paul by Catholics and Reformers indicates their different views of word and reality, which then came to a head in the most significant antithesis on the point whether *iustificatio* takes place *fide charitate formata* or *fide sola*. Difficult as a critical comparison of both views with Paul may be, it must surely be designated a weakness of the Catholic interpretation of Paul that it is unable to maintain the Pauline understanding of πίστις and therefore supplants the relation to the word-event by an immediacy of spirit,[1] a reality of grace as an anthropological state. The Reformers' use of the concept Gospel therefore serves, rightly understood, towards an anti-enthusiastic interpretation of Paul. The rightness of that can of course only be tested by considering which interpretation is demanded by the eschatological factor in Paul. In the Catholic view the eschatological character of the καινὴ διαθήκη is interpreted as a new period in history (the age of the church), in the Reformers' view as the realization of true historicalness through being determined by the end of history. It seems to me characteristic of these two interpretations of the eschatological factor that the Gospel is interpreted on the Catholic side as *lex*, on the Reformers' side as *promissio*. The latter, it is true, contradicts the traditional schema promise/fulfilment, and seemingly also the Pauline distinction of ἐπαγγελία and εὐαγγέλιον, but should surely serve the very purpose of keeping open the eschatological character of εὐαγγέλιον and πίστις.

These pointers, to be sure, bring us to new difficulties in making conceptual comparisons between the Reformers and Paul. It would have to be asked in the first instance whether the Catholic use of the concept of law in the sense of a category embracing both the Old and the New Covenant cannot very well appeal to Paul. Augustine's terminology of *lex operum* and *lex fidei* is of course taken direct from Rom. 3.27. And Paul again puts it similarly in Rom. 8.2: ὁ νόμος τοῦ πνεύματος τῆς ζωῆς ἐν Χριστῷ Ἰησοῦ, and can also construct in Gal. 6.2 the expression ὁ νόμος τοῦ Χριστοῦ. As of course James 1.25; 2.12 also speak of the νόμος ἐλευθερίας. The terminology which then became usual, *lex nova* or *lex evangelica*, appears to be entirely justified on that basis. Now of course the Pauline expressions in Rom. 3.27 and 8.2 are obviously formed *ad hoc* to contrast with νόμος τῶν ἔργων and νόμος τῆς ἁμαρτίας καὶ τοῦ θανάτου. They show no sign of a desire to coin a permanent terminology. But that is hardly sufficient to condemn a corresponding terminological expansion of the concept of law. For to do so would be

---

[1] Cf. Luther's remark that 'popery is also mere enthusiasm' in the *Schmalkald Articles*, II, 8: *Bek.-Schr* (see p. 251 note 3), pp. 453.16-456.18.

to remain at the level of the type of argument used by biblicists. Why should an expression Paul uses only in passing not be developed from the terminological point of view into a concept of law which would then be directly synonymous with the concept διαθήκη? But that kind of formal treatment of the concept of law, although Paul does in fact provide a certain possible starting-point for it, would, if it got out of hand, make it at least very difficult if not impossible to bring out the point on which the real accent in Paul's discussion of the law lies. There is therefore good reason not to follow out the occasional pointers in Paul towards an expanded application of the concept of law to the New Covenant, but to make the concept of law by means of stricter theological definition into as precise as possible an instrument by which to acquire a theological grasp of the *decisive* point in Paul's doctrine of the law.

If the question just discussed could create the impression that the Reformers' terminology has sharpened the Pauline antithesis, yet we find another, and far greater, difficulty which could give rise to the opposite opinion: that the Reformers' doctrine of law and Gospel has peculiarly weakened the radical sharpness of the Pauline antithesis. For surely, when we turn from the Reformers' doctrine of law and Gospel to Paul, the most striking difference is, that the successive elements in a unique transition which can never again be reversed are turned by the Reformers' schema into a peculiarly simultaneous conjunction, so to speak a permanently occurring transition which is suspect of not being a transition at all; we could also say, that the Pauline alternative has apparently become in the Reformers' schema a 'Both—And', even if a very dialectical 'Both—And'. Those who in the formula 'law and Gospel' (which is after all not merely Lutheran but common to all the Reformers) censure the idea of a rigid order, a strangely 'methodistic' succession, would to my mind have much more cause in the light of Paul to criticize the fact that the definite temporal succession of *tempus legis* and *tempus evangelii* is the very thing that is eliminated in the Reformers' schema, or at all events interpreted in an altered way, so that fundamental Pauline statements can apparently no longer be accepted without reservation—such as Gal. 2.25: ἐλθούσης δὲ τῆς πίστεως οὐκέτι ὑπὸ παιδαγωγόν ἐσμεν, or Rom. 6.14: οὐ γάρ ἐστε ὑπὸ νόμον ἀλλὰ ὑπὸ χάριν, or Rom. 7.4: ὑμεῖς ἐθανατώθητε τῷ νόμῳ διὰ τοῦ σώματος τοῦ Χριστοῦ εἰς τὸ γενέσθαι ὑμᾶς ἑτέρῳ τῷ ἐκ νεκρῶν ἐγερθέντι etc. In Paul we have to do with a total change in the situation, with a mutually exclusive 'then' and 'now', 'old' and 'new'—indeed, essentially old and essentially new, and therefore conclusively old and conclusively new—with a change qualified by resurrection from the dead. The Reformers' formula on the other hand gives this transition *to* the New Covenant so to speak the structure of existence *under* the New Covenant. For Paul it seems an impossible form of expression to say that law and Gospel have constantly to be preached and that the *praecipuus usus legis* also among Christians is the *usus paedagogicus* or *elenchticus*—as indeed, significantly enough, the terminology *usus legis* is connected with an expression that is not Pauline but deutero-Pauline.[1] Here we meet all the differences between Luther and Paul that have already been so often discussed:[2] the different view of the statements in Romans 7, the fact that in Paul the concept of μετάνοια retires completely into the background, whereas Luther characterizes the whole Christian life as *poenitentia*; further, the different background of experience from which Paul and Luther came to the understanding of the Gospel, and so on. I can here only indicate these things as the wider context of the problems which present themselves when we examine the law-and-Gospel terminology. If we abide by this narrower circle of problems, then the difference could also be defined by saying that the concepts law and Gospel are largely stripped of the concrete historical references they bear in Paul and made into hard and fast general basic concepts of theology, so that they find a more universal application than in Paul. To that extent one might suppose that the Catholic terminology of *lex vetus* and *lex nova* with its pronounced historical orientation recalls more strongly the Pauline schema of the turn of the ages. But nevertheless, or perhaps for that very reason, it can hardly be affirmed that the Catholic version maintains the radicalness of the Pauline antithesis. What is to be said however of the Reformers' view in this respect is a question which, considering the abundance of problems connected with it, could now be taken up from a great many different angles. We approach it here from that of a closer examination of the concept of law.

---

[1] I Tim. 1.8 Vulgate: '. . . *bona est lex, si quis ea legitime utatur.*' Cf. my essay, 'On the Doctrine of the *triplex usus legis* in the Theology of the Reformers', pp. 62 ff above.

[2] Above all: A. Schlatter, *Luthers Deutung des Römerbriefs*, B.f.Chr.Th. 1917; W. G. Kümmel, *Römer 7 und die Bekehrung des Paulus*, 1929; R. Bultmann, 'Römer 7 und die Anthropologie des Paulus', in *Imago Dei (Festschrift für Gustav Krüger)*, 1932, pp. 53-62; P. Althaus, *Paulus und Luther über den Menschen*, 1938; R. Bultmann, 'Christus, des Gesetzes Ende', in *Beitr. z. Ev. Theol.* I, pp. 3-27; W. Joest, *Gesetz und Freiheit: Das Problem des Tertius usus legis bei Luther und die neutestamentliche Parainese*, 2nd ed. 1956; W. Joest, 'Paulus und das Lutherische *Simul Iustus et Peccator*', *KuD* I, 1955, pp. 269-320.

III

The difference most likely to strike us between the Pauline *concept of
law* and that of the Reformers is, that by νόμος Paul normally understands the Torah, whereas the Reformers' doctrine of the law strictly
means the law which concerns every man as man. This difficulty, it is
true, can seemingly be very easily removed by reducing the difference
to mere nuances: Paul (it would then be said) certainly touches likewise
on the problem of how far the νόμος can be spoken of also with regard
to the Gentiles, while the Reformers' doctrine of the law surely takes
its bearings very largely also on the problem of the validity of the Old
Testament law. It might therefore appear as if all the problems could
be resolved simply by keeping in mind that Paul takes his bearings
primarily on the situation of the Jews, and the Reformation on the
situation of the non-Jews. But that would be only a superficial explanation of the symptom from which we set out. If we go into it more closely,
then we find ourselves faced with a problem of a very complicated kind.

Even in Paul himself the situation is decidedly complex. To be sure,
the basis of his νόμος concept is quite plainly, that νόμος is a positive
factor in history—'the law of the Old Testament, or the whole Old
Testament considered as law'.[1] In this basic and dominant use νόμος is
indeed a proper name. With or without the article, and independently
of qualifying additions, νόμος clearly denotes the Mosaic Law, or the
Old Testament record of revelation as a whole. It is thus not one law
among others, though it may perhaps be the only true, or at any rate
the only binding one. Νόμος as a generic term is surely a thing that must
have occurred easily to the mind of a Greek speaker. But Paul has so
little feeling for νόμος as a generic term, that even when he turns aside
from his normal view of νόμος as a positive factor in history or, as we
have said, a proper name and employs νόμος in the 'general sense of
norm or constraint, obligation',[2] to my mind he does not then take up
an already existing general concept, but starts with νόμος as a proper
name and goes on from there to a usage that generalizes in one respect
or another. This tendency to take the basic meaning in the sense of
Torah and so to speak transcend it by way of figurative application in
various directions (the νόμος of the Gentiles, the νόμος of faith, etc.)
has the effect of sparks given off on various sides from a highly charged
core.

[1] R. Bultmann, *Theology of the NT* I, p. 259. On the following cf. also the
article νόμος κτλ. *TWNT* IV, pp. 1016 ff [BKW, *Law*].

[2] R. Bultmann, *op. cit.*, p. 259.

For us the interesting thing must in the first instance be the inner tension that belongs to the word νόμος in Paul even in the apparently quite straightforward use as the proper name of a positive historic phenomenon. On the one hand Paul simply takes over here the existing usage of late Judaism, which has primarily three characteristic marks: the absolute use (תּוֹרָה/νόμος is the proper name of the Mosaic Law); second, the strictly singular use (the Torah itself is an indivisible whole); and lastly, the unlimited preponderance of the law in the Old Testament revelation as a whole (hence νόμος can denote the whole Old Testament, and the relation to the law is absolutely constitutive of the relation to God). On the other hand the Pauline view displays quite astonishing critical differences from the view of the law in late Judaism. To be sure it is for Paul, too, a case of the νόμος θεοῦ; but although he can even allude to the Old Testament idea of Tables of the Law written by God himself,[1] yet he then takes up after all the gnostic thought of the derivation of the law from angelic powers,[2] that is, of its limited dignity; and that is surely also one of the underlying notes in the pointed ascription of the law to Moses.[3] There is an immediate connexion between that and the fact that Paul—in sharpest antithesis to rabbinic ideas of the pre-existence and eternity of the law—stresses even to the point of defiance its episodic character.[4] Further, he does indeed link up with the idea of the soteriological function of the law, but then gives it a totally new interpretation. He is already almost on the very edge of self-contradiction when on the one hand he assents to the statement that theologically speaking the aim of the law is life, yet then not only affirms that because of sin its actual effect is to kill, but even argues on that basis that the law was not given to make alive.[5] To be sure, it is πνευματικός. But that does not mean that it confers the Spirit. Rather, it is precisely in its impotence, its killing effect, that it fulfils its soteriological function. Is it not the case that Paul's version of the concept of law, including his critical statements on it, is so strongly determined—partly in a positive, partly in a negative way—by the late Judaistic and rabbinic view of the law that he misses the genuine Old Testament outlook altogether, and that his whole doctrine of the law therefore makes sense at all only in the conditions of its time, in relation to its immediate opponents? In its sharpest form: is Paul really engaged in a debate with the Old Testament law, or only with a deformed view of the Old Testament law?

From this standpoint I really must touch fleetingly for a moment on

---

[1] II Cor. 3.3, 6. [2] Gal. 3.19. [3] R. Bultmann, *op. cit.*, p. 268.
[4] Gal. 3.17. [5] Cf. Rom. 7.10 ff; Gal. 3.12.

the topic Mr Würthwein will deal with tomorrow.[1] There can be no suggestion of a unified view of the law in the Old Testament. Apart from the diversity in terminology and in form we have to notice above all how it is only in the course of Israel's history that the concept of the law comes to acquire the sense of the comprehensive whole of the revelation of the divine will. That can be traced in the history of the term תורה, which was at first used only of an individual priestly instruction and therefore with a plural form in view, and was only in Deuteronomy given the stamp of a comprehensive term and one now singular in principle. More recent Old Testament research, however, is rightly very cautious in its approach to the question whether even here תורה can really already be rendered 'law'.[2] Von Rad, for example, considers the question of when תורה has first to be understood as 'law in the theological sense of the word'.[3] Where, however, does von Rad find the norm which he here applies with the phrase 'law in the theological sense of the word'? It is of course the legalistic understanding of the law, that is, the late Judaistic concept of law in the light shed on it by the New Testament. Judged by that norm von Rad denies that תורה in Deuteronomy is already 'law in the theological sense of the word' and may be rendered by 'law'. He joins Noth in holding that the word תורה did not assume the meaning of 'law in the theological sense of the word' until the period after the exile, because here (apart from other symptoms) the law becomes an absolute factor with a timeless validity, detached from the thought of the covenant.[4] In this von Rad sees a disastrous error. That means, then, that 'law in the theological sense of the word' is in itself a concept which is theologically illegitimate. It is the symptom of a theological misunderstanding and can be applied in theology only to the extent that it is used to designate that legalistic misunderstanding in its own terms. That of course is a very problematical view. Von Rad begins with the perfectly correct point that in using the concept of law in theology today we simply cannot, and surely also must not, disregard the Pauline doctrine of the law and the critical light it casts upon the law. Then, however, he short-circuits the argument by making the

---

[1] The paper by E. Würthwein [*ZTK* 55, 1958, pp. 255-70], which was originally to have been delivered first at the Jugenheim conference, had to be postponed to the second day in view of his being prevented by official duties. The contents of his paper were not known to me in advance.

[2] E.g. G. von Rad, *Theol. d. AT* I, 1957, pp. 197, 271 [cf. ET with revisions, *Old Testament Theology*, 1962, p. 195].

[3] *OT Theology*, pp. 92, 230.

[4] Von Rad, *op. cit.*, p. 91—M. Noth, 'Die Gesetze im Pentateuch', in M. Noth, *Ges. Studien zum A.T.*, 1957, pp. 112 ff.

concept of law into the self-designation of a theological misunderstanding. That of course would lead perforce to the further conclusion that the way to overcome the late Judaistic view of the law is to return to the deuteronomic concept of the Torah, which from the theological standpoint still so rightly holds together what later got separated and went wrong. For Torah in Deuteronomy still means in the comprehensive sense the revelation of God's will, in which the obedience demanded is not the prerequisite of election but 'rather the order is the other way round.'[1] One might interpret von Rad by saying, 'So the order is "Gospel and law"!', were it not that his view of 'law in the theological sense of the word' would really forbid the use of the concept law at this point. But von Rad after all points out with satisfaction that Deuteronomy exhibits the same structure as the apostolic exhortation.[2]

H.-J. Kraus[3] differs from this position only in that he sees the covenant idea as still the foundation even in the post-exilic concept of the Torah, and then goes on without hesitation to claim the concept of law for this unity of covenant and law. He is concerned with the right to 'rejoice in the law' and, as he says explicitly, with the rightness of Barth's order 'Gospel and law', the proof of which from the Old Testament scriptures he now considers assured.[4] It would even appear here to be a great pity that Paul carried on his struggle against the legalism of late Judaism so much under the spell of the late Judaistic concept of law, and therefore in the light of a sharp antithesis between νόμος and χάρις instead of in the light of the unity of χάρις and νόμος found in the

---

[1] Von Rad, *op. cit.*, p. 230.

[2] Von Rad, *op. cit.*, p. 232. The problem rightly raised by von Rad as to the proper translation of תּוֹרָה naturally remains. To discuss it completely would involve going into the hermeneutic problem in detail. My purpose here was merely to warn against being overhasty in utilizing the difficulty for theological purposes. The fact that law and grace are indistinguishably bound up together in the deuteronomic concept of the Torah is a sign not of its nearness to the New Testament, but of its distance from it!

[3] H.-J. Kraus, 'Freude an Gottes Gesetz: Ein Beitrag zur Auslegung der Psalmen 1, 19b und 119', *EvTh* 10 (1950/51), pp. 337-51; 'Gesetz und Geschichte: Zum Geschichtsbild des Deuteronomisten', *EvTh* 11 (1951/52), pp. 415-28.

[4] 'The theological significance of Noth's work in particular should be recognized at last by the systematic theologian. It is time that the discussion of the problem "Gospel and law" took its bearings on the results of exegetical research. When that happens, then in view of Noth's work it will be difficult still to maintain with a good conscience the priority of the "law" over the "Gospel" as a basic principle of dogmatics' (*EvTh* 10 [1950/51], p. 340 note 14). A correct principle is here made the basis for jumping to highly disputable conclusions. (Incidentally, what does 'priority' mean in this case?)

Old Testament. According to Kraus, Deut. 30.11-14 for example is a sheer 'Gospel of the law'.[1] Paul himself quoted this passage in Rom. 10.6 ff, yet not as a 'Gospel of the law', but in contrast to the δικαιοσύνη ἐκ νόμου as a testimony to the δικαιοσύνη ἐκ πίστεως, by boldly taking the ῥῆμα that is here inculcated and interpreting it as ῥῆμα τῆς πίστεως, whereas he had adduced immediately before as testimony to the δικαιοσύνη ἐκ νόμου a quotation from Leviticus (18.5) whose sense is completely identical with what the Deuteronomy passage intends to be the content of the ῥῆμα. It is not at the moment a question of the correctness of Paul's exegesis here, but of observing a point which rests on a much broader basis. The intention of the Pauline exegesis of the Old Testament is precisely to distinguish clearly and hold apart what in the Old Testament is confusingly mixed up together: the line deriving from Abraham and the line deriving from Moses, the ἐπαγγελία and the νόμος, the πίστις and the ἔργα. In the Old Testament, it is true, both are so closely intermingled that we first have to have our eyes opened before we have the necessary sharpsightedness to perceive clearly the specific nature of either element. The Old Testament, taken on its own, is in fact ultimately not clear—and Paul happens to be concerned with a question of ultimate clarity. Hence to my mind it is completely wide of the mark to say that the Pauline view of the law takes its bearings only from the view of late Judaism, but altogether misses the genuine Old Testament view, and that Paul is thus engaged in a debate only with a particular understanding, or misunderstanding, of the Mosaic Law, but not with the Mosaic Law itself. A detailed analysis would show moreover that Paul—in noticeable contrast to the Synoptic tradition of Jesus—in his observations on the law takes nothing at all to do with the typical late Judaistic phenomenon of legalistic, casuistic interpretation of the law. Rather, going much deeper, he has in view the Mosaic Law as a whole, and precisely as it is embedded in the totality of the Old Testament revelation of the divine will, yet regards it in such a way as now to show the fundamental differences of theological structure which in the Old Testament view are interlocked and never became conscious differences. Admittedly, his own concept of law is then not identical with that of the Old Testament, and cannot be identical with it—as little as the Pauline and late Judaistic concepts are identical.

We cannot here follow out in detail all the subsidiary problems connected with the relation between Paul and the Old Testament. Yet we must still say something more of a far-reaching problem in systematic

[1] *EvTh* 10 (1950/51), p. 342.

theology which presents itself in connexion with what has just been said. Is the only proper course from the theological point of view not surely to set out from a comprehensive concept which transcends the antithesis of law and Gospel and gives unbroken expression to the divine will, in other words, strictly from the unity of Gospel and law, in the way Barth impressively advocates that as the basic principle of his whole theology —however misshapen his formula about the law as the form of the Gospel and the Gospel as the content of the law?[1] It could then be a

[1] The formula is, quite apart from its theological intention, unclear from the standpoint of logic. For one thing, as concepts 'form' and 'content' are related to a third factor. That happens only occasionally in Barth, in that as form of the Gospel he mentions the law and as content of the Gospel grace (or Christ). Thus the Gospel is then itself the third factor, the comprehensive concept, and there is no longer any real question of defining the relation of Gospel and law as form and content. But sometimes also the Gospel is called the form of the law, so that Gospel and law would be content and form of some factor X.

Secondly, the concept of 'form', so overloaded in view of the history of philosophy, remains unclarified. The antithesis to 'content' suggests the modern (depreciative and externalizing) view of 'form'. But in part we might also think again of the Aristotelian concept of εἶδος. G. Söhngen (see above, p. 253 note 1), who naturally sets out from the scholastic concept of *forma*, arrives at the opposite definition of the relationship: 'The law . . . cannot be understood as the form of the Gospel, as if the Gospel without the law would be formless. If the concept of form is here understood not in the external sense, but at the same time and primarily in the internal sense as essential form, then it can be said the other way round that the Gospel is the new form, the grace-form of the law. And since form thus conceived of the inward essence cannot be separated from the essential inner content, the law can further be spoken of as the content of the Gospel. As was said a moment ago, the Gospel contains its antithesis, the law, and impresses its form upon it, reshaping it into the new, unprecedentedly new form of the law of grace. The Gospel is formative for the law, not the law for the Gospel. From the standpoint of the history of redemption the law exists in twofold form—the law in its own form of law and legalism, and the law in the "extra-legal" form of the Gospel and its grace' (pp. 27 f). What now? Is this deviation of Söhngen from Barth merely the result of a different concept of form, so that in substance they would be in agreement? Or is the difference in concept already the symptom of a difference in substance? At all events it is certainly no help towards conceptual clarity when Barth (see above, p. 247 note 1) explains: 'The differentiation of content and form denotes an infinite difference. . . . That the content of the Gospel has also a form, is not merely *also* a work of God, but is precisely the work of God which makes room for the Gospel among us men and room for us men in the Gospel' (p. 12). In what common aspect can content and form be designated as an infinite difference? Do they not themselves represent different aspects, so that their difference is incapable of intensification? And what, if need be, are we to imagine by a content without a form?

Finally, let me further observe that this formula of Barth's is linked up in a way I cannot understand with the picture likewise employed by him: 'So the law thus lies in the Gospel like the Tables of Sinai in the ark of the covenant' (p. 11, cf. also p. 3). After all, then, the law is the content of the Gospel, and the Gospel the form of the law?!

matter of relative indifference what concept we choose for it: whether
law or covenant or testament or revelation or Word of God or even—
why not a foreign word?—Torah. Each of these concepts would first
have to be related to the point of unity and consequently submit to a
certain degree of neutralizing and formalizing, in order to bring out only
the one fact that here we have something that derives from God and not
somehow something that derives from men. Instead of allowing the
antithesis between law and Gospel to dominate, the basic antithesis
would be made that between man and God. Then law and Gospel alike
would both be God's Word, or as it would have to be put according to
Barth, would only be different, inseparable elements in the structure of
the one Word of God. One would first of all have to grasp the nature of
God's Word as distinct from man's word, before approaching the
distinction of secondary character between law and Gospel within the
one Word of God.[1] This indeed is the path recommended also by the
Old Testament scholars quoted, who in view of the scripture principle
must surely also be given a hearing when it comes to forming the
theological concept of the law.

In order to pursue this problem, whether the distinction of law and
Gospel has to be made in the light of the nature of the Word of God or
whether the nature of the Word of God has to be defined in the light of
the distinction of law and Gospel, I now take up a Luther passage which
admittedly appears somewhat venturesome and isolated even within
Luther's theology, but can help to put the problem in its very sharpest
form. On Gal. 1.1 in his 1519 Commentary[2] Luther explains the nature
of the apostle's office on the basis of his being sent by God: '*Quis enim
potest praedicare, nisi sit Apostolus? Quis autem est Apostolus, nisi qui
verbum dei apportat? Quis autem potest verbum Dei apportare, nisi qui
deum audierit?*' The Word of God, however, stands in contrast to the
word of man: '*At qui vel sua vel humanarum legum, decretorum aut
philosophorum dogmata affert, numquid is dicendus est Apostolus?*' No—

[1] I am well aware that it is definitely not in the light of a formal concept of
the Word of God that Barth seeks to define the unity of Gospel and law, but in
the light of the Gospel—on which point I fully agree with him. I see the difference in the manner in which the statement of the unity of law and Gospel is
reached in the light of the Gospel, and in the sense in which they are one. Cf. my
observations at the end of Section III, p. 270 below.
But it remains to my mind unclear in Barth what is the relation in his formula
between Gospel *qua* 'content' and Gospel *qua* that of which 'content' and 'form'
have to be predicated—and whether his approach does not ultimately conceal
within it after all a formal concept of the Word of God.
[2] *WA* 2, pp. 452.28-453.6.

whoever comes in his own name is a thief and a robber, a destroyer and murderer of souls. In this antithesis between the Word of God and the word of man the decisive thing is thus primarily the question of origin. The one word is the Word which God speaks himself and out of his own resources, the other word is that in which man speaks—and speaks in virtue of the highest of all the possibilities he has of using words, *viz.* in a legislative and philosophic way. Whereas the nature of God's Word is first of all left in its essence without further elucidation and no more is said of it than that in God's Word God himself speaks, the human word contrasted with it is at once more closely defined in its essence as a thing which in its highest possible forms is '*humanarum legum et decretorum aut philosophorum dogmata*'. That heralds the conjunction of *lex* and *ratio* which was so important for Luther later. Man's word as springing from human reason has the character of a legalistic word. That is intended in the sense of a definition of function, yet at the same time results in a surprising definition of effect. Man's word is in itself a soul-destroying word. Luther now proceeds to speak also of God's Word on corresponding lines. By allegorizing the etymological associations he comes from the concept of apostle via the Hebrew word שלח to the name Siloah and says in allusion to John 9.7: '*In Siloa lavatur caecus et visum recipit, et Siloe aquae salutares sunt.*' And what that means is then directly expressed in the words of Ps. 107.20: '*Misit verbum suum, nempe deus, et sic sanavit eos.*' God's Word has in itself saving effect, is a saving Word, whereas man's word is a destructive word, comparable with the doctors who instead of improving the condition of the woman with the issue only make it worse: '*Venit homo et verbum suum, et haemorrhoissam peius habere facit.*' That brings Luther to the point of setting God's Word and man's word in clear and sharp antithesis: '*Hoc est, ut clare dicam: quoties verbum dei praedicatur, reddit laetas, latas, securas conscientias in deum, quia est verbum gratiae, remissionis, bonum et suave, quoties verbum hominis, reddit tristem, angustam, trepidam conscientiam in seipsa, quia est verbum legis, irae et peccati, ostendens, quid non foecerit, et quanta debeat.*' And he later underlines this antithesis still further by designating the '*verbum dei*' as '*verbum fidei*', the '*verba hominum*' on the other hand as '*verba moralia sine fide*'.[1]

Thus Luther here equates God's Word with Gospel, man's word with law. That looks like a grotesque foreshortening of the problem. And the cause of the confusion seems easy to see. On the one hand Luther speaks of the *humanae leges*, the *decreta* and *statuta*, but on the

---

[1] *Op. cit.*, p. 462.23 f.

other hand he then sums up all these things together in the concept
verbum legis as such, as if there were no such thing as a law of God. On
the one hand he emphasizes that the church has to hold solely to the
Word of God and not to the words and precepts of man: '*Sicut enim
primum et maximum ecclesiae beneficium est verbum dei, ita contra nullo
maiore detrimento ecclesia perditur quam verbo hominis et traditionibus
huius mundi.*'[1] That, it would seem, surely means asserting the formal
principle of scripture while rejecting the principle of tradition. On the
other hand, however, he suddenly interpolates in place of this antithesis
that of Gospel and law.

But is that really so completely misguided? When Luther sees in the
'*verbum hominis*' and the '*traditiones huius mundi*' the bane of the church,
and in the '*verbum dei*' on the other hand the '*primum et maximum
ecclesiae beneficium*', then he obviously means in fact that the '*verbum
dei*' is the remedy against the said bane of the church only in view of its
being Gospel, but not by any means that a revealed divine law has to
take the place of these human laws and traditions. The abrogation of
these human precepts takes place not through the obedient fulfilment
of divine precepts, but through the faith-creating Gospel. For it is not
a matter of replacing a false law by the true, revealed one, but of men's
consciences being freed from the law by the Gospel: '*pereat maledictaque
sit omnis doctrina de coelo, de terra, undelibet allata, quae docet in opera,
in iusticiam, in merita alia confidere, quam ea quae sunt Iesu Christi.*'[2]

No doubt the treatment of the problem of law and Gospel is at this
point very incomplete. For the law cannot be given adequate theological
treatment until it has been made clear how far it is in fact a case of the
law of God. That however is a thing whose full depth can be recognized
only in the light of the Gospel, i.e. of Christ as the τέλος τοῦ νόμου.
Hence the correct theological way of looking at the law came only when
the fact that it is a case of God's law had lost its self-evident character
and the law had presented itself in a way that made it seem impossible
to reconcile God and law. It is a fundamentally different way of studying
theology whether our thinking is carried on from the standpoint where
God and the law obviously form a unity, or from one where that unity
can be asserted only in the face of a contradiction. Then of course the
concept of law is also very differently defined in the one case and in
the other.

---

[1] *Op. cit.*, p. 453.33-5.
[2] *Op. cit.*, p. 462.29-32.

IV

I shall not now pursue the problem into the doctrine of the Word of God, but attempt instead to take a step further in the precise definition of the theological concept of law. I would do so by means of the *question of the abrogatio legis*. This question was already touched upon a moment ago in the Luther passage—and in the double sense at that: first in the sense that specific individual precepts are annulled, and second and above all in the sense that the law is abolished as a way of salvation, that is, as teaching '*quae docet in opera, in iusticiam, in merita alia confidere, quam ea quae sunt Iesu Christi*'.[1] The problem of the *abrogatio legis*, which is extraordinarily significant for the understanding of the concept of law, naturally turns our attention first of all back again to Paul.

It would be not only superficial but false if the Pauline doctrine of the law, and that really means of freedom from the law, were understood as a piece of theologizing to justify the Gentile mission. The undertaking of a mission to the Gentiles was never, or hardly ever, in dispute, but only of a mission that was free of the law. If Paul was not the first champion of that, he was certainly the most effective and thoroughgoing one. Yet it was not a supplementary point tacked on to his κήρυγμα, but a direct consequence of it. As far as we can see, his conversion to Christ and his call to be missionary to the Gentiles coincided with each other. That means, however, that the Gentile mission which is free of the law was only the immediate consequence of the fact that Christ means for sinners the end of the law. So the Pauline doctrine of the law thus had the closest connexion from the start with the question of the Gentile mission, but was valid in principle independently of it. In the doctrine of the law the saving significance of Christ for the Jews was expounded. It was not a case of a change in the law, whether in the sense of a partial abrogation or of a re-interpretation. The law remained, as far as its individual commandments were concerned, unchangedly valid. There was no cause to regard it, in its individual demands, as too difficult and as such to ease it or make it fulfillable. Rather, it was a case of making the law nothing for the Jew to glory in and, at one and the same time, conferring in place of the curse that proceeded from the law a share in the promised blessing. With the coming of the πίστις τοῦ Χριστοῦ this had become reality, and that was the end of the law as a way of salvation. Admittedly, one could say: in that case merely a particular view of the law is abolished, but the law in itself remains after all—indeed, in a way

---

[1] *Op. cit.*, p. 462.30-32.

it is now set up for the first time, as far as the proper understanding of it is concerned. Yet for Paul the law is not a mere codex, but a force. Looked at from the proper angle the interesting thing is not the mere ideas the law contains but the execution of it—not the content it has but so to speak the content it does not have: the fulfilment which is still outstanding. For that reason the law, when it is really fulfilled, is no longer law in the proper sense. To be sure it continues to exist, but it has ceased to be an unfulfilled law and as such a power of destruction. If it is fulfilled, then that in fact means its proper function is also fulfilled and done with. Because, indeed, in the man who is a believer it no longer has an object on which to work as law. Be it noted: it is not the law itself that is dead, but man is dead to the law; and for that very reason the law has nothing more to do, because the task for which it exists is done. Thus Paul cannot speak of the law at all as a thing in itself, but only in respect to the man to whom it is given and to whose reality it belongs one way or another: if a change occurs in man's relation to the law, then precisely therewith a change occurs also in the nature of the law.

So far, then, it has been a case of the *abrogatio legis* in the proper, soteriological sense, as it takes place for the Jew who comes to faith. The Gentile, who of course does not stand under the Mosaic Law, is affected by that, it would seem, only in so far as the eschatological salvation is thereby opened likewise also to him, without the imposition of the Mosaic Law. But strictly, one might think, this negative statement need not interest him at all, if only the Gospel is in actual fact preached to him without the imposition of the Mosaic Law. That the Gentiles are to have part in salvation and belong to the eschatological people of God without adopting the law, that the promised incorporation of the Gentiles thus takes place by the going out from Jerusalem not of the law but of the Gospel—that need be a problem to disturb only the Jew. But now, all this has certain further implications.

1. For the Jewish Christian it must sooner or later become a question whether any real meaning and obligation still attach to the things laid down in the Mosaic Law which are *materialiter* most closely connected with the view of the law as a way of salvation—that is, in a word, the ceremonial and judicial law. If the law is no longer a way of salvation, then that really takes away the ground of the existence of these parts of the Mosaic Law. Not of course that the Pauline doctrine of the law may be reduced to an abrogation of the ceremonial and judicial law. The freedom from the law which he means naturally applies to the whole law. But it is a question here of cause and effect. It is indeed theoreti-

cally conceivable that the ceremonial regulations might continue to be observed, yet without thinking to attain righteousness thereby. Do they not then, however, in actual fact have their validity undermined and become ripe for abolition? For Paul this problem, so far as we know, did not yet present itself. The early expectation of the end made it superfluous to make any alteration in the station in which one was called. Moreover, the separation of ἐκκλησία and Jewish people was not yet final. And lastly, the factual authority of the Old Testament as holy scripture made it difficult to introduce alterations in detail. (The historical process of a partial material *abrogatio legis* for the Christian converts from among the Jews cannot be traced here.)

2. What did on the other hand become supremely acute for Paul was the problem of what the understanding of the Gospel as freedom from the law implies for the co-existence of Jewish and Gentile Christians. The cause of the conflict was in the first instance the question of the observance of the regulations on ceremonial cleanness in view of the common meals in mixed congregations. Either the Jewish Christians had to be required to disregard the law; or the Gentile Christians had to be required to remove the stumblingblock by adopting the Mosaic Law; or Jewish and Gentile Christians had to form separate congregations—or at least refrain from common meals and thus also from common celebration of the Eucharist. Paul did not decide this problem in principle. But a general separation into Jewish and Gentile Christian congregations would for him have been self-contradictory, and to require the Gentile Christians to adopt the Mosaic Law out of consideration for the Jewish Christians would inevitably have been misunderstood as a condition of salvation. So the thing was for the Jewish Christian from one concrete instance to another to exercise also *materialiter* his freedom from the law. In the course of further developments this problem then solved itself relatively quickly.

3. Had the Pauline doctrine of the law any further significance for the Gentile Christians themselves beyond the mere fact that they did not need to become Jews in order to become Christians? Through the use of the Old Testament as holy scripture also in the Gentile churches the question arose, how far the Old Testament was still valid for a Gentile Christian or, if valid without distinction as an inspired book, how it was to be understood, since it was surely obvious that not everything could be binding in the literal sense. In the ancient church this problem was not dealt with strictly in the light of the Pauline doctrine of the law, but did find various solutions which owed something to it.

The possibilities open can be tabulated as follows:[1] Either help was sought after all in a merely selective validity—partly founded on the theory of the intrusion of counterfeit passages (so that the 'original' divine law was now restored), partly founded on the limited validity which the plan of salvation conferred on individual passages. Or re-interpretation was employed—partly founded on the transposition to a different stage in the history of redemption, partly founded on what was alleged to be the original intention of the text. In the former case the Pauline derivation of the law from angels was specially suited to serve as justification, in the latter case the Pauline distinction between γράμμα and πνεῦμα, now turned into a hermeneutic rule. It is quite true that the Pauline doctrine of the law must be adduced as being in actual fact the only fundamental theological indication in the New Testament as to how the question of the use of the Old Testament in the church would have to be thought out. But as a result of operating only with half-understood fragments of the Pauline doctrine, the process ended up in a mere alteration of the law. The soteriological sense of the Pauline doctrine of the law was lost. And the acceptance of the Old Testament as inspired holy scripture became the gateway to a legalistic under-standing of scripture.

If, however, the significance for Gentile Christians of the Pauline doctrine of the law is not to be exhausted by the sketch just given, if indeed it is to play a proper part even only in regard to the use of the Old Testament, then it must be applicable in a soteriological sense also to the non-Jews. Paul, to be sure, did not show that directly. He con-fined himself virtually exclusively in his doctrine of the law to the prob-lem of the Mosaic Law. However, there are sufficient indications to show that he ascribed to this doctrine immediate significance for the Gentile Christians. Not only where the churches, as in Galatia, were threatened by false teachers—whether these were Jewish Christians in the ordinary sense or, as Schmithals[2] is presumably right in supposing, judaizing gnostics. Rather, the contrast with the law was, as is shown by Romans and also II Corinthians, one of Paul's main themes in the doctrinal explication of the kerygma also for the non-Jews. Paul ob-viously did not merely expect the Gentiles to be interested in the problem of the Jewish law, but apparently also believed that they would

[1] Cf. the important chapter 'Das Problem der Aufhebung des Gesetzes' in M. Werner, *Die Entstehung des christlichen Dogmas, problemgeschichtlich dar-gestellt*, 2nd ed. 1953, pp. 197-237.

[2] W. Schmithals, *Die Gnosis in Korinth: Eine Untersuchung zu den Korinther-briefen*, FRLANT Neue Folge 48, 1956.

discover in these discussions of it something which directly concerned themselves. There is no need here to quote individual passages to show that Paul, despite his strong consciousness of the difference between Jews and Gentiles, saw them where the kerygma was concerned as ultimately in the same situation: God is the God not only of the Jews, but also of the Gentiles; they are all sinners; Christ died for them all; all are justified not by works of their own, but solely through faith.

But now, if the Pauline doctrine of the law interprets the kerygma from an angle that concerns Jews and Gentiles alike, yet we must nevertheless proceed only with the greatest care to the exposition of the doctrine of the law in its universal character. It is not sufficient merely to eliminate as it were the Jewish colouring from the Pauline doctrine of the law. It might well be that to do so would be to eliminate also what are essentially the central problems involved in the whole argument. Two main difficulties have to be considered: the extension of the concept of law, and the question of the actuality of freedom from the law.

Certain essential elements in the Pauline concept of νόμος appear to oppose the extension of the concept of law which takes place in the theology of the Reformers. It is a question here of a definite, positive law—*viz.* the Mosaic Law—so that as we said already, νόμος is here indeed a proper name. Is there any other possibility than either to interpret it in the direction of a supra-historic law (and thereby surrender the relation so essential for Paul to the concrete, historic law), or to transfer the application to corresponding positive laws (but thereby sacrifice the strictly singular form of the Pauline concept of law)? That is connected with another point: the Mosaic Law considers itself to be revealed, and Paul takes over this view. The law has its place in what for him, too, is the invisible holy scripture of the Old Testament. Would there be any other possibility left than either to sever altogether the connexion between law and revelation, or else along with the concept of law to expand at will also the concept of revelation and remove it from its base in holy scripture? And finally, the event of Christ not only had its actual historical place within the sphere of the Mosaic Law, but had also been expounded by Paul in this relationship to the Mosaic Law. Does an extension of the concept of law not leave open only two possibilities: either to drop the exposition of the event of Christ where the law is concerned as confined to the Mosaic Law, or else to generalize the paradoxical teleological connexion of the law with Christ in such a way that the Old Testament is robbed of its unique place in the history of redemption not only as law but also as promise? What becomes of statements like Gal. 3.24 (ὁ νόμος παιδαγωγὸς . . . εἰς Χριστόν) or Rom. 10.4 (τέλος νόμου Χριστός), and consequently of the whole Pauline doctrine of the law, if law is no longer equated, as he equated it, with the Mosaic Law?

On the other hand there is no lack of signs in Paul which cast doubts on this equation and point beyond it. Indeed even the Mosaic Law itself, as also the whole Old Testament, already has a universalistic tendency, even if a hidden one. It concerns—at all events at a definite stage in the development of its own understanding of itself—by no means only the people of Israel. Above all, however, Paul sought, as we said already, to express with his doctrine of the law something that concerns both Jews and Gentiles, and the reason why he could do so is obviously that the Mosaic Law makes clear symptomatically something which *mutatis mutandis* holds of every man. It is true that Paul speaks of the non-Jews as the ἄνομοι or νόμον μὴ ἔχοντες.[1] But just as the occasional references to a stage previous to the law in the history of the people of Israel (or the individual Jew)[2] must not be understood in the sense of a total absence of law, so likewise the non-possession of the Mosaic Law by the Gentiles cannot be taken in the sense that here there is no analogy whatsoever to the law. Paul indicates in Rom. 2.14 ff that even outside the sphere of the Mosaic Law we can and must speak of the reality of the law.

The theology of the Reformers derived from this its justification for the extension of the Pauline concept of law, which it took to mean, transposed into universal terms, the law written in every man's heart. This was supported firstly by the traditional doctrine of the *lex naturalis*, secondly by the reduction of the Mosaic Law (as a result of the *abrogatio legis* that took place in Christ) to the moral precepts of the Decalogue, and finally by the identification of the *lex naturalis* and the Decalogue. In the tangle of problems which confront us here, the following necessarily brief points may perhaps bring some clarification.

It is an undeniably correct criterion when Luther allows validity as 'law' in the theological sense only to what touches and binds the conscience. It is precisely in that that it proves its binding character. What does not touch man's conscience, what does not concern him unconditionally as charge and commitment, is not law as it must be understood in interpreting the Pauline doctrine of the law. Luther illustrates that by the fact that the precept of circumcision, for example, is not able to

---

[1] I Cor. 9.21; Rom. 2.14.
[2] Cf. Rom. 5.20; Gal. 3.17, 19; Rom. 7.9.

touch our conscience: '*Nam haec cum audio nihil moveor neque per-horresco et tamquam ludum iocumque puto. At quando dicit: Tu es incredulus Deo, non credis Deo, non times Deum, es adulter, moechus, inobediens et quicquid tale est, hic statim perhorresco, et pavesco et sentio in corde, me certe hoc debere Deo, non quia traditus et scriptus decalogus sit nobis, sed quod scimus vel leges has nobiscum in mundum attulimus. . . .*'[1] According to that, then, I can be legitimately confronted by a thing as law and claimed by it as such only when it is that in which I myself am involved and which has therefore been with me all along, has always claimed me, because it belongs inseparably to my existence. That is why *in foro theologico* the concept of a *nova lex* is strictly speaking self-contradictory, because then some external factor, some supplement added on to man's being, would be making a claim that was at once neither understandable nor binding and that could gain recognition only by deceiving and doing violence to the conscience. There could be point only in speaking of a *renovata lex* which expresses anew what has already been said from the start.[2]

For the elucidation of this view of the law written in the heart Luther made use of the traditional view of the *lex naturalis*, which in the form of definite *notitiae communes* is supposed to belong to man inalienably from birth. That facilitated the departure from an understanding of the law in terms of revelational positivism, and at the same time served as a protection against the charge that the introduction of conscience as a criterion was surrendering to subjectivism. We have become aware today of the flaws in this method of arguing from natural law. But that does not by any means do away with the Reformers' doctrine of the law written in the heart. It merely requires a different grounding and eluci-dation. And a basis for that is provided precisely by Luther's doctrine of conscience,[3] in which it is not a case of registering what we know but of pointing to a claim made on us. Luther knows very well that the conscience is no infallible source of information about the ideal contents of the law. Even—and precisely—when it is led astray, the conscience still functions as conscience. The decisive question put to the conscience is concerned not with its knowing but with its hearing. For conscience

---

[1] *WA* 39/1, p. 540.6-12 (*Antinom. Disp.* 1538).

[2] '*Itaque renovata lex est, et quidem scripta et tradita certo populo, in quantum scripta, sed non in quantum dicta, quia hae notitiae communes erant omnibus gentibus, sicuti experientia ipsa testatur*' (*WA* 39/1, p. 540.1-3).

[3] Cf. especially G. Jacob, *Der Gewissensbegriff in der Theologie Luthers*, 1929, and E. Hirsch, *Drei Kapitel zu Luthers Lehre vom Gewissen*, Lutherstudien vol. 1, 1954.

is the question 'Where?' knocking at man's door, and by conscience that question is decided to the effect: in prison or in freedom. The problem of conscience is thereby regarded at a level where it is not a case of better information on the content of the law, but of instruction on the right use of the law. For it is not false knowledge of the law's contents that accuses the conscience, but the law itself. It is not a change in the contents of the law, but so to speak a change in the position of the law, that frees the conscience, i.e. the fact that the law is assigned the place that belongs to it, which is in point of fact not to dominate the conscience—a change of position which is merely the complement of a change in man's own position: from the ἐν νόμῳ to the ἐν Χριστῷ εἶναι.

This view can be brought into harmony with the concept of the law written in the heart only when we free ourselves from the abstract understanding of the law as a codex and from the usual domination by the question as to the ideal content of the law.[1] The law is primarily an event and only secondarily teaching. Whereas the Gospel is in essence spoken word, sermon, and never exists in any other way, the law is primarily and properly factual reality and only so to speak in a subsidiary sense, as a makeshift, also teaching. The preaching of the law, says Luther, brings to light the things *'quae iam existunt in natura humana'*.[2] It is therefore absurd to speak of a necessity of the law in the sense of its being necessary for the law to be added on to man's reality as a supplement. *'Nam lex iam adest*, is already there. *Lex prius adest in facto.'*[3] *'Lex nulla nostra necessitate, sed de facto iam invitis nobis adest.'*[4] Hence even the so-called 'man without the law' is not outside the real event of the law. *'Omnium quidem est lex, sed non est omnium sensus legis.'*[5] From that point of view the law written in the heart cannot be interpreted as a detailed legal codex, but only as the state of being utterly open to question. The law written in the heart is so to speak the question mark that is branded upon man: Where art thou? It would then be the task of a detailed doctrine of the law to show how this question mark

---

[1] Cf. also R. Hermann, *Zum Streit um die Überwindung des Gesetzes: Erörterungen zu Luthers Antinomerthesen,* 1958. Hermann emphasizes 'that Luther understands the concept of law as it were in a functional sense, and does not bind it to its origin (Old Testament, New Testament, Moses, Christ, Decalogue, Sermon on the Mount, codes of laws, admonitions, etc.) . . . the law is not so much statute as rather principle. For the law it is not really court and signature that are constitutive, but its function' (p. 20).

[2] *WA* 39/1, p. 361.30 (*Antinom. Disp.* 1537).

[3] *Op. cit.,* p. 437.7 (*Antinom. Disp.* 1538), cf. pp. 446 f.

[4] *Op. cit.,* p. 353.37 f (*Antinom. Disp.* 1538).

[5] *Op. cit.,* p. 406.1 (*Antinom. Disp.* 1537).

that is branded upon man sets in motion the whole reality that concerns man and brings it to expression, thereby summons to the interpretation of reality, and then crystallizes also in positive laws. In this way, of course, the *lex ipsa* becomes concrete only in varying historic forms. But each positive *lex* has therefore also perforce to be ordered under the critical head of the *lex ipsa*, i.e. of the event of the law, compared with which each positive law is a mere consequence or interpretation.

That provides us with a further point for the forming of the concept of law in the theological sense. The question primarily appropriate to the law is the question of what it can do. Luther went so far as even to define the law on that basis—*viz.* that it is *impossibilis ad iustificationem*. That is not an accidental, appearing only under definite conditions, but points exactly to the *essentia legis*, seen *theologice*: in its essence it is *lex non impleta*, for as *lex impleta* it would no longer be *lex*. It is essentially *lex accusans*. '*Lex non damnans est lex ficta et picta sicut chimaera.*'[1] And in so far as it can be said that the law provides knowledge, it is not a case of knowledge of the good, but of knowledge of sin; not knowledge of what ought to happen, but knowledge of what has already happened; not knowledge of possibilities that are open, but knowledge of possibilities that are excluded and lost. But now, that implies that the law, taken on its own, is always law that is misused and therefore also law whose true nature is not perceived. What makes its impotence into power is the fact that it determines the structure of human existence. Whether Jew, or sinner, or Gentile, whether pious or godless, every mode of existence despite all the differences is the same as the others in that all are existence under the law. Every religion or world-view, including an atheistic one, but also the Christianity that has been perverted from faith into a religious ideology—all have the common structure of the law.[2] They are all one as against faith. For *lex est negatio Christi*.[3] The special thing about the Mosaic Law is only that in the light of the Gospel it has illustrated with fundamental and universal clarity the nature of the law in its antithesis to faith: ὁ νόμος οὐκ ἔστιν ἐκ πίστεως (Gal. 3.12). Because of the soteriological sense of the doctrine of the law, the Pauline concept of law requires existentialist[4] interpretation.

But now, that already implies that this extension (or, as we now say

---

[1] *Op. cit.*, p. 358.26 (*Antinom. Disp.* 1540).

[2] 'It is *religio falsa, quae concipi potest a ratione*. It is *religio Papae, Iudaeorum, Turcarum* . . .'—*WA* 40/1, p. 603.5 ff (*Gal.* 1531).

[3] *WA* 40/2, p. 18.4 f (*Gal.* 1531).

[4] See my note below, p. 331 note 1.—*Translator.*

more accurately, this systematic interpretation) of the concept of law cannot take place in isolation but, as we already indicated, is most closely connected with the question of the actuality of freedom from the law. Freedom from the law is neither a general truth nor a historically given fact. It could be the one or the other only if the law were understood as a definite legal codex which could be abrogated, or whose claim to validity could be evaded. Within the pattern of existence under the law, however, it is possible only to repeal a law by means of another one, but not to annul the domination of the law as such. But now, freedom from the law does not mean freedom from a legal codex, but freedom from the power of the *lex ipsa*. This freedom, which is opened up in Christ, is faith. Paul understands the change it brings as an eschatological one. The pattern of redemptive history, however, in which he describes this change presents the difficulty of how it can be understood at present. In this identification with the pattern of redemptive history the eschatological change is not transmissible. It thereby inevitably becomes a thing of the past—even when it is understood as the dawn of a new period in history. Its eschatological character can be preserved only when the πίστις that came in Christ continues coming, that is, when the change that took place in Christ is actualized in faith. The aorists are then certainly valid: the law is fulfilled and done with, as sin and death are also over and done with. But testifying to that and recognizing its truth in faith is not by any means over and done with. Hence the difference of mere temporal succession is turned into the difference of existence in two ages. '*Vides utrumque tempus in Christiano in affectu.*'[1] '*Christianus est divisus in duo tempora: quatenus est caro, est sub lege; quatenus spiritus, est sub Euangelio.*'[2] But, be it noted, with the distinction: '*Tempus legis non perpetuum . . . tempus gratiae* is to be *aeternum.*'[3] 'There are *distinctissima tempora, et tamen oportet coniunctissima peccatum et gratia, lex et Euangelium.*'[4] Here lies the ground of the necessity to interpret the Pauline doctrine of the law as a doctrine of the *usus legis*, and moreover not only of the *praecipuus usus*, the *usus theologicus*, but also and more especially of the so-called *primus usus legis*, whose real nature is disclosed and given free course at all only on the basis of the *usus theologicus*, and upon which—in seeming divergence from Paul, but in logical execution of the task of translation—the main task of a detailed doctrine of the law is then concentrated. Not that the preaching has chiefly to employ the *primus usus legis*. Rightly understood, it has only

---

[1] *WA* 40/1, p. 524.11 (*Gal.* 1531).   [2] *Op. cit.*, p. 526.2 f.
[3] *Op. cit.*, p. 526.8 f.   [4] *Op. cit.*, p. 527.7-9.

to disclose it and give it free course—precisely by means of the law in its proper *usus theologicus* which, however little it can be confined as an actual event to the preaching, can be brought to expression as such only in the light of the Gospel and for the sake of the Gospel in the preaching. For for the sake of the Gospel the law must come to expression, if the Gospel itself is not to be misunderstood as law. The Gospel would lose its meaning if it did not have an eye to the law. For the sake of the intelligibility of the preaching of the Gospel—and that means at the same time, for the sake of the concreteness of the Gospel—the law belongs in the preaching of the Gospel. For the *homo peccator* belongs in the preaching of the Gospel. The *peccator*, however, according to Luther is the *materia legis*. Hence it can be stated as a valid basic rule for our subject: '*Si vis disputare de lege, materiam legis accipe, quae est peccator.*'[1]

The question as to what this '*materia legis*' is today in concrete terms, and thus as to how the law really affects contemporary man, would now be the most burning question of the theological doctrine of the law.

[1] *Op. cit.*, p. 535.1.

IX

DIETRICH BONHOEFFER*

THE life of Dietrich Bonhoeffer was extraordinarily full and despite its brevity—he was not yet forty when hanged by Hitler's minions—it was of unusual radiative power. And this life was entirely dedicated to the church. Passionate devotion to the church is not to be taken for granted even in a theologian.

Bonhoeffer began his career as a scholar with a dogmatic examination of the sociology of the church.[1] This dissertation, written at the age of twenty-one, is reckoned today among the most important works on the concept of the church. With it he struck the theme of all his further theological work. One cannot speak of Bonhoeffer's theology, however, without recalling how it merges with his life. He was heir to the best social and academic tradition. To his many gifts there were glittering possibilities open. But he resolved to be a servant of the church. And striking decisions mark also the rest of his way. He sacrificed his academic career to enter into the church struggle. And when a refuge was made available to him abroad, he was hardly there when—just because of the threat of war, and now doubly in danger—he returned again from a sense of solidarity with his brethren. He was not exercised by mere thoughts about the church. The existence of the church determined his existence. In all his many activities that came impressively to light: as university teacher, as pastor in congregations abroad, as associate in the ecumenical movement, as catechist to the unruly youth of Berlin, as university chaplain and above all as director of a Preacher's Seminary of the Confessing Church.

The determination with which he concerned himself with the church nevertheless did not make him a church functionary. He did not by any means neglect secular things for the Christian faith, the life of this world for the Beyond, the humanities for the things of the soul, the work

* In *Kritik an der Kirche*, ed. H. J. Schultz, Kreuz-Verlag Stuttgart/Walter-Verlag Olten, 1958, pp. 313-18.
[1] *Sanctorum Communio: Eine dogmatische Untersuchung zur Soziologie der Kirche*, 1930, second ed. 1954.

of critical theological reflexion in favour of practical action. On the contrary, the one thing experience taught him was, 'that it is only by living completely in this world that one learns to believe'.[1] He therefore laboured to overcome the fateful habit of thinking in two spheres which separates the world of religion from the rest of reality. On a superficial view he does indeed himself seem for a time to have taken an almost sectarian view of the true path of Christianity as one of separation: when he saw everything concentrated in the idea of discipleship, when he sounded notes of Kierkegaardian criticism of Luther, when his exposition of scripture took on a biblicist character, when he maintained the thesis that 'whoever purposely cuts himself off from the Confessing Church in Germany cuts himself off from salvation',[2] and when in turning his back on the university he relegated 'the whole education of the next theological generation' to 'church and cloister schools in which pure doctrine, the Sermon on the Mount and the cultus are taken seriously'.[3] But then he was stirred during his imprisonment by ideas at which, so he felt, 'Lutherans (so-called!) and pietists . . . would get the creeps.'[4] 'The church,' he says in one of his last letters, 'must get out of her stagnation. We must move out again into the open air of intellectual discussion with the world.'[5] The radical protagonist of the Confessing Church now reproaches it with having 'lapsed into conservative restoration'[6] and says it is 'not entirely fresh air' that blows in it.[7] 'Our Church,' he declares unsparingly, 'which in these years has fought only for self-preservation as though it were an end in itself, is incapable of bringing the word of reconciliation and redemption to mankind and the world at large'.[8]

It would be misconstruing these statements if we sought to explain them as dark thoughts of a lonely and perhaps even despairing prisoner. Indeed, the thing we particularly sense in them is just the unbroken sharpness of a mind that sees deep. For the rest, Bonhoeffer was not only now for the first time turning a sharply critical eye on the church. Everything clericalistic and stuffy had always been repugnant to him. As a young assistant minister in Spain he was already expressing thoughts that read like an anticipation of his last writings. Thus he wrote as early as 1928: 'Here one meets men as they are, far from the masquerade of

[1] *WE* p. 248 (Eng. p. 169).
[2] 'Zur Frage nach der Kirchengemeinschaft', *EvTh* 3 (1936), p. 231.
[3] *Ges. Schriften* I, *Ökumene. Briefe, Aufsätze, Dokumente 1928-1942*, ed. E. Bethge, 1958, p. 42.   [4] *WE* p. 113 (Eng. p. 79).
[5] *WE* p. 257 (Eng. p. 177).   [6] *WE* p. 220 (Eng. p. 148).
[7] *WE* p. 260 (Eng. p. 180).   [8] *WE* p. 206 (Eng. p. 140).

the "Christian world"; people with passions, criminal types, small people with small aims, small urges and small misdeeds—all in all, people who feel themselves homeless in both senses of the word, who thaw out when you speak to them in a friendly way—real men; I can only say I have the impression that these of all people stand much more under grace than under wrath, but the Christian world in particular stands much more under wrath than under grace.'[1] And three years later, as a bursary student in America, he comes with deep disquiet to the conclusion: 'The gigantic work of American missions is hollow within, the mother church itself is really dying.'[2] Only in the negro churches in the United States did he see seeds of promise. But his eye takes in—almost resignedly—the world-situation as a whole: 'A great land', he says in 1931, 'I should like to see if perhaps the great solution comes from there—India; for otherwise it seems to be all over, the great death throes of Christianity seem to be upon us.'[3] That was already very early an accompanying undertone in Bonhoeffer: 'It could be that everything we . . . are undertaking in the way of church action is too late, pointless, simply playing.'[4] It would be suspicious if we were not at all exercised by the dubious character of the church. 'If . . . any should wish to protest emphatically . . . that he has never despaired of the church, then let him ask himself if he has ever really believed in the church. Faith in the living church of Christ breaks through only where we see most clearly the dying of the church in the world, the process of ever new collapse . . . —and where despite it all we then . . . hear how the New Testament proclaims life to the dying and how in the Cross of Christ living and dying clash together and life swallows death—only where we see that do we believe in the church under the Cross.'[5]

It is not to be disputed that Bonhoeffer's theology went through changes and that—when we review it as a whole—we find unresolved tensions. But the expressions of extreme joy in the church and those of extreme criticism of the church spring, as it seems to me, from a single basic impulse which is maintained amid every change: faith has to do with reality. The concept of reality runs through the whole of Bonhoeffer's theological work alongside the concept of the church. It is this very fact of being engaged with the question of reality that raises, for the Christian faith, the question of the concrete reality of the church. And from the fact of being engaged with reality there arise at the same time also criteria by reference to which theological thinking has to be tested

[1] *Ges. Schr.* I, pp. 51 f.   [2] *Op. cit.*, p. 61.   [3] *Op. cit.*, p. 61.
[4] *Op. cit.*, pp. 162 f.   [5] *Op. cit.*, p. 163.

in intellectual honesty. It is not a case, rightly understood, of opposing tendencies that have to be brought to agreement in terms of compromise: concentration on the Word of God and consideration for the reality of the world. Rather, the Word of God embraces the reality of the world. The Christian is therefore not 'the man of eternal conflict'. 'His reality does not separate him from Christ; and his Christianity does not separate him from the world. Belonging wholly to Christ he stands at the same time wholly in the world.'[1]

One thing that follows from that is the readiness to make a sober diagnosis of the situation in which the church finds itself. 'It is only when we look at reality with open eyes and without any illusions about our morality or our culture that we can believe. Otherwise our faith becomes an illusion.'[2] We have already seen samples of such diagnosis from his early days. In the end, reflexion on the great modern process of secularization acquired decisive significance in his eyes. 'We are on the way', he says, 'to a time of no religion at all; men as they now are simply cannot be religious any longer'.[3] But instead of now lamenting the fact and searching for ways and means of bringing the process to a halt, he is concerned with the proper understanding of it. It is a mistake to think the coming of age of the world is in itself an antichristian thing. And the idea that with the extension of the boundaries of our knowledge God finds himself in constant retreat merely betrays the great misunderstanding of God as the stop-gap for our imperfections. In place of the senseless 'attack of Christian apologetics on the adulthood of the world',[4] which aims to spy out man's weaknesses and there keep a corner still open for religion, the church must reflect that Christ is 'not ... an object of religion but ... the Lord of the world'[5] and ask itself how he therefore becomes Lord also of the non-religious. With that Bonhoeffer set the church a task of barely conceivable dimensions: not to barricade itself inside a wall of traditional habits of thinking, not to fight for the possession of property, not to consider itself an end in itself, but really to exist for others and to submit itself to the great transformation without which it is not capable of testifying 'what Christ actually *is* for us today'.[6]

Along with that goes a second thing which likewise runs like a red thread through the whole of Bonhoeffer's theological existence: 'The problem of making our proclamation concrete.'[7] 'When will the time

[1] *E* p. 65 (Eng. p. 67).   [2] *Ges. Schr.* I, p. 163.   [3] *WE* p. 178 (Eng. p. 122).
[4] *WE* p. 217 (Eng. p. 147).   [5] *WE* p. 180 (Eng. p. 123).
[6] *WE* p. 178 (Eng. p. 122).   [7] *Ges. Schr.* I, p. 34.

come when Christians speak the right word at the right moment?'[1] For
the church the question of authority depends on that. 'I can be addressed
with authority only when a word spoken out of deepest knowledge of
my humanity affects me in my whole reality here and now. Every other
word is impotence. The church's word to the world must therefore come
of deepest knowledge of the world and affect it in its whole present
reality, if it seeks to be authoritative.'[2] This problem, which we are
mostly so blind to because we have resigned ourselves to the church's
proclamation being of no consequence, drove Bonhoeffer like a goad:
'How can the Gospel and how can the commandments be proclaimed
by the church with authority—and that means utterly concretely?'[3] At
first the problem concentrates itself for Bonhoeffer above all on the
question of the concrete demand, that is, of bringing to expression what
is commanded here and now, and not just general ethical principles. In
the peace question, in the confessional question, and finally in the
resistance question he personally practised attending to the concrete
demand of each individual case: 'To venture and do not what is agreeable but what is right, not to hover in the realm of possibilities but
boldly to grasp what is real, not in escaping into thought but alone in
action is freedom.'[4]

But now, along with the problem of the concreteness of the Christian
message goes also the general problem of its understandability. Bonhoeffer saw himself towards the end of his life 'driven back again
entirely upon the first steps in understanding. Atonement and redemption, regeneration, the Holy Ghost, the love of our enemies, the cross
and resurrection, life in Christ and Christian discipleship—all these
things have become so problematic and so remote that we hardly dare
any more to speak of them. In the traditional words and ceremonies we
are groping after something completely new and revolutionary, without
being able to understand and utter it yet.'[5] Bonhoeffer sees that as the
church's fault. Instead of handing on the great words of the Christian
message without interpretation, that is without understanding their
real meaning, the church could better keep silent and being a Christian
could 'consist today in only two things: in praying and in doing the
right among men. All Christian thinking, speaking and organization
must be reborn out of that praying and that action.'[6] In such a transformation of the church Bonhoeffer sees something promising: 'It is

[1] *Op. cit.*, p. 117.   [2] *Op. cit.*, pp. 144 f.
[3] *Op. cit.*, p. 145.   [4] *WE* p. 250 (Eng. p. 170).
[5] *WE* p. 206 (Eng. p. 140).   [6] *WE* p. 207 (Eng. p. 140).

not for us to prophesy the day—but the day will come when men will be called again to utter the Word of God with such power as will change and renew the world.'[1] That, however, is a legacy that obliges us not to despair of such a promise, but for that reason not to grow weary either of 'protesting against any kind of church that does not honour above all things the quest of the truth'.[2]

[1] *WE* p. 207 (Eng. p. 140).   [2] *Ges. Schr.* I, p. 143.

X

THE QUESTION OF THE HISTORICAL JESUS AND THE PROBLEM OF CHRISTOLOGY*[1]

To Rudolf Bultmann on his 75th birthday

A theological sketch on the subject of the problem of the 'historical Jesus' must, I think, take up three questions:

1. What is the meaning of the phrase 'historical Jesus'?
2. What came to expression in Jesus?
3. Has faith in Jesus Christ a basis in Jesus himself?

The question of the historical Jesus is manifestly grasped as a theological question only when we perceive that it is aimed at the problem of Christology. Now of course, in some form or other we constantly come across this connecting link by which the question of the historical Jesus and the problem of Christology are bound up together.

If we set out from the latter, the problem of Christology, then this at all events is true: that the relation to Jesus is constitutive for Christology.[2] It must, if it understands itself aright, make the claim to be doing

---

* *ZTK* 56 (1959), Beiheft 1, pp. 14-30.

[1] The wording of the paper read at Tutzing [at a study group on the problems of Life-of-Jesus research, 25-26th May 1959, at the invitation of the Evangelical Academy in Tutzing] has been subjected only to stylistic revision at a few points. The footnotes supply a few references and elucidations, yet they cannot provide the scientific apparatus that would really be required, nor enter into a discussion of the literature, but must keep within the framework of an outline sketch.

[2] The word 'Christology' along with many other scientific terms of the same structure (in the theological realm e.g. soteriology, ecclesiology, eschatology, etc.) to the best of my knowledge first appeared in the eighteenth century. The form of the word as such allows of two interpretations: as teaching about faith's views concerning the Christ idea (corresponding to the usual use of 'Messianology'), or as teaching about a definite historical Person (whereby Christ would then be understood as a proper name, so that we could also say 'Jesuology'). Scientific terminology can quite well use words formed with '-ology' also (though only exceptionally) as applied to historical phenomena (e.g. Egyptology), though admittedly not as applied to individual persons (say, Constaninology). The term 'Christology' as it is in actual fact employed no doubt means the combination of both points of view: that it is a case of something general (and thus to that extent of teaching) as also of something historical and individual. A

nothing else but saying who Jesus is. Hence Jesus is the criterion of Christology.[1] If it were to be shown that Christology had no basis in the historical Jesus but was a misinterpretation of Jesus, then that would put paid to Christology.[2]

But the connexion arises also for the opposite approach: the historical question about Jesus cannot be posed at all without thereby having an eye also to the Christological problem, even if it should perhaps be in an attitude of deliberate dissociation and with the intention of criticism.[3] Not merely the influence of the Christian tradition upon the mind of the investigator, but also the nature of what has been handed down about Jesus makes it quite impossible to pursue the question of the historical Jesus without any knowledge of the connexion between Jesus and Christology.

The merging of the two questions must not, of course, be prematurely taken as a soothing confirmation of the tradition. Rather, the result of the merging could be precisely that the question of the historical Jesus when pursued to its logical conclusion brings about the destruction of Christology. So long as this radical point is not reached, it is of course usually supposed that the two, as different tasks, can be kept apart in principle: the question of the historical Jesus and the problem of Christology. For in fact (so it is supposed) the one is a historical question, the other a dogmatic one.

[1] That of course is not all that is to be said on the subject of criteria of Christology. For inasmuch as Christology is concerned precisely with the relation of Jesus and faith and therefore with the encounter between the real man Jesus and the real man that we severally are, it is plain that human nature itself belongs to the criteria of Christology. But that merely indicates an aspect of the problem which I am not explicitly examining here.

[2] Modern Jesus-research has largely been carried on precisely with the purpose of putting paid to Christology in this way. (To cite from the contemporary discussion an example of the opinion that the primitive church misunderstood Jesus, let me mention the observations of Ernst Heitsch in *ZTK* 53 [1956], pp. 208 f.) The intention is to put paid to Christology as a misinterpretation of Jesus not as regards his authority, but as regards its claim to interpret his Person.

[3] The history of Life-of-Jesus research is an impressive example of this.

bridge between the two could be provided by the point that Jesus is to be regarded not as *persona privata* but as *persona publica*.

That is meant merely to indicate that even reflexion on the concept 'Christology' already gives rise to competition between the dogmatic and the historical outlook. For if Christology is *a priori* meant only as teaching about Jesus Christ, then it is plainly impossible that a doctrine of the Christ idea should provide the framework into which Jesus as a historical phenomenon would then only have to be fitted. Rather, Jesus himself must rank as constitutive for Christology (and consequently also for the 'Christ idea'). Anything that has no reference to Jesus has therefore no place in Christology.

The real problem however, as it seems to me, is whether we can be content with this juxtaposition. Was it not saying too little when we began by stating that the question of the historical Jesus is obviously grasped in its theological relevance only when we perceive that it is aimed at the problem of Christology? Must it not be expressed—more radically—by saying: either the question of the historical Jesus destroys Christology, or else the question of the historical Jesus must show itself to be identical with the Christological problem—*tertium non datur*? If that were so, then it would have far-reaching consequences.

1. *What is the meaning of the phrase 'historical Jesus'?*

1. The adjective 'historical' has first of all a critical and polemical character. It expresses the modern view of truth—a view which compels us where history is concerned to make a critical distinction between the tradition of history and the facts of history, between the picture that has been handed down of an event and the reality of the event itself. This attitude arose from the general revolution in the Western world's understanding of itself when it broke free of the authority of tradition and began to subject the tradition to examination in responsible historical research of its own.

The vast background of problems—what it was that once gained for the tradition such respect that it could itself rank as a criterion of truth; secondly, what made it necessary and possible for men to dissociate themselves from tradition-bound views of truth; and finally, how much of this basic modern attitude is problematical and how much of it can never be surrendered—these things we must here omit from our discussion. It is sufficient to underline the meaning of the adjective 'historical' from the standpoint of method.

'Historical', then, means the appropriate method of perceiving historic reality. 'Historical Jesus' is therefore really an abbreviation for: Jesus, as he comes to be known by strictly historical methods, in contrast to any alteration and touching up to which he has been subjected in the traditional Jesus picture. Hence the 'historical Jesus' as good as means the true, the real Jesus.

The student of history likewise seeks to discover the 'historical' Francis of Assisi as distinct from the Francis of the legends.[1] If the historical method allows the phenomena of history to be seen for what

---

[1] On this illustration and the analogy between it and the problem of the historical Jesus, cf. Ernst Benz, *Ecclesia spiritualis: Kirchenidee und Geschichtstheologie der franzikanischen Reformation*, 1934, esp. pp. 57, 61 f.

they are, then the adjective 'historical' is not required at all. For what is meant is—in this instance—nothing else but Francis himself. For that reason, too, the historian normally hardly ever uses the adjective 'historical' added in such an emphatic way to the name of a historical figure, unless for polemical reasons. For that Francis of Assisi is in fact the historical Francis of Assisi is for the historical mind a matter of course.

With Jesus, too, the adjective 'historical' should therefore at bottom be considered superfluous. That here of all places it is used so much and appears indispensable, is obviously due to the fact that here the historical task is specially difficult and therefore a permanent insistence on the historical method is necessary. It cannot by any means be considered a matter of course that when we speak of Jesus we really mean the Jesus the historian means.

2. The difficulty does not merely lie in the peculiar number of transforming influences in the tradition (of which no further details are required here). It derives above all from the fundamental motive for the transformation: the interest which faith and preaching have in Jesus. That determines completely the nature of the tradition. Indeed, it likewise determines the present relation to Jesus, at least for the Christian. But the non-Christian, too, is touched by it in actual fact in the manner of his approach, even if negatively.

In this situation the phrase 'historical Jesus' is directed not so much, as is fundamental in all historical study, against additions and errors of some kind in the tradition; nor even only against the legendary Jesus. We could much sooner say, against the mythologized Jesus. But even that does not exactly touch the heart of the difficulty. Rather, the slogan 'historical Jesus' is really directed against the kerygmatic or dogmatic Jesus or, as is also said with a significant change of name, against the 'dogmatic Christ' or the 'biblical Christ' or the 'Christ of faith'.

The fact that it is primarily a case of making a critical distinction from the 'dogmatic Christ' (to put it briefly) gives the concept 'historical Jesus' a peculiar note. It now excludes in particular, as not belonging to Jesus, three elements which are essential to the dogmatic and kerygmatic tradition:—

(a) everything that belongs to the subsequent interpretation of the life of Jesus in the light of the post-resurrection faith in him;[1]

---

[1] The critical exclusion of this is a self-evident principle for 'historical Jesus' research.

(*b*) those statements in the tradition which seem indeed to have the character of historical reports, yet cannot by any means be considered as historical statements about Jesus, such as above all those on the resurrection, the risen appearances and the ascension;[1]

(*c*) confessional statements on the person and work of Christ, which as statements *sub ratione Dei* do not have the character of historical statements.[2]

How what is then left as the 'historical Jesus' can be reconciled with the kerygmatic and dogmatic tradition, is usually separated from the historical question as a dogmatic one. But the idea of a peaceful co-existence of the two points of view is an illusion. For from the historical standpoint—in apparent contradiction of the Christological dogma—Jesus can be considered only as man, without any room being left over for statements of another kind. And from the dogmatic standpoint we cannot somehow subsequently alter the historical statements. The only option left is, either to reduce the dogmatic statements to what can be stated historically of Jesus, or else to interpret the dogmatic statements in such a way that they do not come into competition with the historical ones. In the latter case the historical Jesus is simply certain to exercise an eminently critical function over against the traditional form of Christology.[3] For the '*vere homo*' must now be understood in such a way that it keeps within the bounds of the historical (and that means at the same time of the historically possible). And the '*vere Deus*' must be understood in such a way that it does not cancel out the view of the '*vere homo*' as just defined. The question would then still remain, what right there is for going on to add to the historical statements about Jesus also dogmatic ones.

[1] Death is the boundary of historical statements. For the rest, the modern view of history cannot make an exception even in the case of the historical Jesus.

[2] This at once sums up and includes (*a*) and (*b*).—Notice the linguistic difference heralded here: ἱστορεῖν is a different matter from ὁμολογεῖν.

[3] Thus it is not merely a case of criticizing the Christological dogma on the basis of the history of dogma (as in the thesis of D.Fr. Strauss, *Die christliche Glaubenslehre in ihrer geschichtlichen Entwicklung und im Kampfe mit der modernen Wissenschaft* I, 1840, p. 71: 'The true criticism of the dogma is its history'), but of the possibility which was likewise discovered only in modern times and which, in spite of the many false paths to which it has led, is of the greatest significance for theology—the possibility of criticizing the traditional Christology in the light of Jesus. That there are links here with the Reformation, is a thing I would merely indicate by recalling Luther's radical ways of taking seriously the '*vere homo*'.

3. But now, it is not by any means only the dogmatic statements that become problematical, but in fact also the historical ones, in so far as they share in the problem of the understanding of history in general. From that standpoint the concept of the 'historical Jesus' takes on the note of relativity. Doubly so, in fact:—

(a) The expression 'historical Jesus' now contains the underlying note: the Jesus subject to the march of time, who in many ways is so far from us and can become all the stranger to us—or more accurately, whose strangeness we must become all the more conscious of—the more strictly we seek him by historical means. The tension with the so-called dogmatic Christ now becomes still sharper. We are bereft in principle of the possibility of making the historically reconstructed Jesus himself the basis of faith.[1] The historical in itself now seems to exclude the dogmatic. The historical Jesus becomes *purely* historical.

(b) But now, it is not only the Jesus thus apprehended with what is imagined to be 'historical objectivity' who appears relative. The note of relativity extends perforce also to the historical apprehension itself. What was imagined to be objective apprehension turns out to be an objectification and hence actually a question of standpoint. That is illustrated by the failure of the quest of the historical Jesus to attain its end. Instead of the real Jesus himself, we are again provided with historically changing pictures of the historical Jesus. The 'historical' Jesus, *thus* understood, is in fact by its very nature not the real Jesus. Just as the person regarding him from a distance is only partially involved, viz. in respect of his historical interest, so, correspondingly, the Jesus regarded from a distance likewise comes only partially into view.[2]

The historical aporia to which the concept of the 'historical Jesus' reduces us is a thing it is of course wrong to regard as a free permit for the return of Christology to the old ways. For to the extent that historism jeopardizes the historical understanding, it also—and all the more—

---

[1] For the clarification of the concept 'basis of faith' (and such like), which is mostly used in a very confused way and is employed also here primarily in the common sense, see below, pp. 303 f.

[2] This correspondence between the coming into view of the one partner in the encounter and the involvement of the other is important for the structure of encounter and understanding. When a man is involved only in a particular respect, then it is also only in that particular respect that anything can concern him (whereby it remains for the moment an open question where the critical points lie). The question arises whether the relation to the historical necessarily has the character of a merely partial way of encounter. It is with this that contemporary study of the hermeneutic problem is concerned.

jeopardizes the dogmatic understanding. To that extent history and
dogmatics are in like danger. Since however Jesus, as we said, is the
criterion of Christology, we cannot simply pass over the historical
approach to him. Hence in overcoming historism Christology is possible
only by means of new reflexion on the historical Jesus.

4. The concept 'historical Jesus' has undergone in the course of these
reflexions a kaleidoscopic change. But it would be a mistake to imagine
that that is the end of it. Indeed, it must not even be considered the
complete end of any of the different individual aspects we have discussed,
although they partly appear to be in flat contradiction to each other. All
the nuances of the concept 'historical Jesus' which we have touched on
—the real Jesus, the purely human Jesus, the purely historical Jesus
subject to the march of time, and the Jesus objectified into a historical
picture and so made unreal—are in certain respects right enough in
their own way. It would be oversimplifying the problem of the historical
Jesus if any one of these aspects were ignored.

That, however, means that in spite of all the difficulties—not by any
means merely of the state of the sources in this particular case, but
primarily also of the fundamental historical problem—the task posed by
the slogan 'historical Jesus' still remains. It is the task of giving expression to what came to expression in Jesus.[1] The defeatist attitude to this
problem, which is partly an accommodation to indolence and partly
arises from dogmatic perplexity, is unjustified both in regard to the

[1] The somewhat peculiar sense in which Professor Ebeling uses this phrase is
not easy to render exactly in English, and the links with other related terms are
also more obvious in German than English can make them. The phrase itself—
zur Sprache kommen (bringen)—means literally 'to come (bring) to speech', and
is normal German for 'to come (bring) up for discussion'. Here, however,
'speech' is used not in the sense of the thing in question being spoken about,
but in the active sense of the thing itself speaking. One might perhaps say in
English 'to come (bring) on the scene'—especially when it is remembered that
an actor comes on the scene in order to say something. The rendering 'come
(bring) to expression', which has been adopted throughout this book, is an
attempt to indicate more directly the important association with words and
language.
    The event in which something thus comes or is brought to expression may
be referred to in a general way as a *Sprachgeschehen,* which I render 'linguistic
event'. More particularly, and more often, it is called a *Wortgeschehen,* which I
translate by 'word-event'.
    Other related terms may also be noted:—A *Sprachgeschehen* or 'linguistic
event' is part of *Sprachgeschichte*='the history of language' and is bound up
with the *Sprachlichkeit,* or 'linguisticality', of existence. And a *Wortgeschehen* or
'word-event' can be described in verbal form as an event in which a word
geschieht='happens', 'takes place' and thus becomes *geschehenes Wort*='a word
that has taken place'.—*Translator.*

state of the particular sources here concerned and also in view of the problem of historical understanding in general.

The historical aporia is certainly inevitable if we abide by a view of history that takes its bearings on the concept of fact. That does not mean that the concept of fact could be done without altogether. But we must be clear as to the limits within which it is justified. The only thing that can lead us out of the historical difficulty is the view of history which takes its bearings on the word-event and consequently on the linguisticality of reality.[1] Hence the proper question regarding the past is not: What happened? What were the facts? How are they to be explained? or something of that kind, but: What came to expression?

That holds in principle of our whole relation to history as such, and is not merely trimming the question to suit the historical Jesus. The fact is, that concern with the problem of the historical Jesus can help us to acquire the proper historical approach to history as such—as against the suspicion (in view of the prevailing circumstances unfortunately not unjustified) that a theological interest destroys the purity of historical methods. When, however, theology approaches history in a proper way, i.e. with the question what it was that came to expression, and when it understands this coming to expression as something that happens in the word-event, then it is pursuing the hermeneutic task in a way that begins to bridge the modern gulf between the historical and the dogmatic.

Christology would then be nothing else but interpretative handing on of what came to expression in Jesus. The historical Jesus would then, rightly understood, be nothing else but Jesus himself. And the right to believe in Jesus—and that is what Christology is concerned with—must then consist in the fact that faith is the particular relation to Jesus which is appropriate to the historical Jesus, because it corresponds to what came to expression in Jesus. But whether that is really the case must be decided on the basis of the text itself.

2. *What came to expression in Jesus?*

I can treat this part very briefly—on the one hand because I can refer to earlier publications,[2] and on the other hand because it is here merely a question of stating the main point.

---

[1] The root of historism is, as it seems to me, a depraved view of 'word': abstraction from the live word-event and reduction to a matter of statement. To that there corresponds the inability to take a transmitted word and interpret it in the light of its character as word-event instead of as a mere statement. Cf. my essay, 'Word of God and Hermeneutics', below pp. 305 ff.

[2] *Was heisst Glauben?* SGV 216, Tübingen 1958; 'Jesus and Faith' (see above,

1. When I put it in the form, 'Faith came to expression in Jesus', then my right to do so is not by any means based exclusively, or even only primarily, on considerations of the history of the concept such as those on which my essay 'Jesus and Faith' was primarily centred. I was conscious there of operating on a very narrow basis.[1] Even if that argument, which centred on the instances of the word 'faith' should prove untenable, it would still be proper to say it was faith that came to expression in Jesus. For that way of putting it is meant to sum up in a word what is the one absolutely decisive and all-determining characteristic in the life and message of the historical Jesus. However imperfect in many ways our knowledge of Jesus is, we can yet see perfectly plainly the point on which all lines converge with astonishing unanimity. It is, however, to my mind absolutely necessary that in thus stating the main point the word 'faith' should substantially be understood in the sense I have tried to work out in that essay.[2] It is here a question of the basic structure of what came to expression in Jesus.

2. The possibility of characterizing the whole of a historical phenomenon as concentrated on one single point, instead of confronting us with a complex variety of aspects, is a peculiar exception. We must ask ourselves whether that is merely the result of a particular shaping of the tradition which excluded everything that did not fit this one point of view. Certainly a strong tendency to omission was at work here. The suspicion that misrepresentation consequently arose in the form of idealization and simplification is not to be rejected *a limine*.

That brings us to a specially critical point in the quest of the historical Jesus. Should the matters on which nothing can be learned—even indirectly—from the tradition call in question our knowledge of Jesus? Ought we thus to reckon with the possibility that it may be a completely false, or at least inadequate, view of Jesus to say that faith came to expression in him? Certainly where the historical is concerned nothing whatsoever can be exempted from questioning. But—apart from more immediate arguments—in this case it is simply convincing that the convergence of all lines of the tradition on the coming to expression of faith came about in real life and not in imagination. And it can rank

---

[1] *ZTK* 55 (1958), pp. 69, 110, see above, pp. 206, 246.

[2] Cf. especially *ZTK* 55 (1958), pp. 95 ff (see above, pp. 232 ff); also *Was heisst Glauben?* pp. 15 ff.

---

pp. 201 ff); *Das Wesen des christlichen Glaubens*, Tübingen 1959, 2nd ed. 1960, esp. ch. IV 'Der Zeuge des Glaubens' (pp. 48 ff) and V 'Der Grund des Glaubens' (pp. 66 ff) [ET, *The Nature of Faith*, Collins 1961, ch. IV 'The Witness of Faith' (pp. 44 ff) and V 'The Basis of Faith' (pp. 58 ff)].

indeed as a result of this concentration of Jesus upon the coming to expression of faith that he himself has rendered superfluous all interest in exact biographical detail and in psychological presentation. For if it was a matter of the coming to expression of faith, then it was impossible to bring to expression alongside of this anything contradictory or even supplementary, but things of that kind were superfluous and confusing accessories.

It is surely due to the view of faith here involved that to say it was faith that came to expression in Jesus does not by any means end up by interpreting Jesus on psychological lines, however much it has the aim of interpreting not only the teaching of Jesus but certainly also the man Jesus as such. This unity of Jesus with faith comes properly to expression not really in what Jesus says of his own faith, but as a witness to faith in existing for others—in a word, in the communication of faith.[1]

If this concentration of a man upon one single point (which of course in itself is of inexhaustible fulness) appears from the historical point of view to be strange and incomprehensible, then we certainly cannot well adduce analogous cases to make it completely clear. For it is only where faith is concerned that this concentration of a man on one single point can take place. But as for the fact that it is true only of Jesus that all that can be said of him may be summed up by saying that faith came to expression in him—that belongs under the head of historical contingency.

It is also part of the historical uniqueness of the person of Jesus, as a result of the concentration on faith, that the encounter with Jesus himself coincides entirely with the encounter with the witness to faith. That is why what happened here could come to expression entirely as a word-event. It explains why the death of Jesus made a decisive contribution towards the coming to full expression of what came to expression in Jesus. And it also explains, finally, why the death of Jesus does not prevent, but on the contrary actually makes truly possible, the encounter with Jesus himself as the witness to faith although, or in fact even because, he is not encountered directly but as one who belongs historically to the past.

It is not only here that the encounter with a historical figure can be claimed as an encounter with the actual person concerned. To deal historically with Plato, Francis or Luther—or whoever it may be—is of course in certain respects also to encounter the man himself. Admittedly, that is true 'in certain respects', and therefore within limits. For there

[1] *ZTK* 55 (1958), pp. 97 f (see above, pp. 234 f).

is always an abiding discrepancy between 'person' and 'work'. The encounter with Jesus as the witness to faith, however, is without limitation an encounter with himself. For the concentration on the coming to expression of faith—and that alone!—is the ground of the unity of 'person' and 'work', but for that reason also the ground of the totality of the encounter.

3. In answering the question, 'What came to expression in Jesus?', I have as good as entirely dispensed with the exposition here required of the content, and instead have placed relatively strong emphasis on what it means for Jesus as a historical phenomenon that faith came to expression in him. It goes without saying that these observations are unthinkable without a knowledge of the subsequent proclamation of Jesus Christ. But I am very much concerned to make this one thing clear: that we can find entirely in Jesus himself, and not first in some sort of additional new happenings of a historical or supranatural kind, the ground both of the fact that what came to expression in Jesus continues to come to expression and of the way in which it does so. Indeed, it must even be laid down as fundamental that also where Christology is concerned nothing may be said of Jesus which does not have its ground in the historical Jesus himself and does not confine itself to saying who the historical Jesus is.

That is exactly what the church's dogma meant by emphasizing that Jesus did not become the Son of God only after his death, but was and is Son of God already as the historical Jesus. In the same way we could now say: the historical Jesus is the Jesus of faith. Faith's view of Jesus must therefore assert itself as a furtherance to the historical view of Jesus. For faith itself is the coming to its goal of what came to expression in Jesus. The man who believes is with the historical Jesus.

Yet that, if it is not to appear a mere construction, now requires to be tested against the way in which faith in Jesus Christ and the proclamation of Jesus Christ arose after the death of Jesus.

3. *Has faith in Jesus Christ a basis in Jesus himself?*

1. The quest of the historical Jesus, as it arose from the modern historical consciousness, has run into difficulties. A striking thing about these is, that step by step difficulties of a dogmatic and a historical kind go hand in hand. There are two groups of problems, which in turn are interconnected.

(*a*) The quest of the historical Jesus, taken in itself, largely called in question the traditional church picture of Jesus, but finally discovered that it was itself involved in the problem of whether and how any historical picture at all of Jesus can be acquired in its place.

(*b*) The result of that was, that it became questionable how the transition from the historical Jesus to faith in Jesus Christ is to be understood. The traditional dogmatic view of the connexion between them proved untenable for historical thinking. But at the same time the way in which the transition takes place remained an enigma for historical research itself.

We shall here concentrate on this second problem regarding the continuity between Jesus and faith in Christ, although in doing so we shall inevitably be thrown back on the questions discussed in section II concerning the historical Jesus himself.

2. The New Testament tradition and, following its lines, the traditional view of the church answer the problem of the connexion here by pointing both to the element of 'continuity' and also to the element of 'discontinuity'.[1] Continuity is said to be vouched for by Jesus' own message and his understanding of himself, i.e. above all by the fact that he himself already thought of himself in the same way as later Christology taught. That is considered to include above all his Messianic self-consciousness, his foreknowledge and prophecy of his death and resurrection, and his action of deliberately founding the church. Thus in Jesus himself, it is said, the continuity with what follows is already prepared. That, however, is combined with an aspect of abrupt discontinuity is so far as the way from Jesus to faith in Christ led through death and resurrection, and thus through a sheer miracle which is the opposite of continuity. For between death and resurrection there is no natural continuum. It is true, though, that this traditional definition of continuity and discontinuity is then somewhat modified on both sides by the fact that to the continuity itself there is added an element of discontinuity (the Messianic secret and the disciples' failure to understand in Jesus' lifetime) and that likewise the discontinuity itself has an element of continuity (the assertion of the identity of the Risen Lord with the Crucified, which became palpable in the continuum of his corporeality).

Historical research appeared at first to direct its criticism above all against the statement of the resurrection of Jesus. But while that was

---

[1] The terms that are usual in this context are employed here only to provide a provisional characterization of the difficulties. On closer inspection these concepts (as belonging dialectically together) are inadequate for a proper grasp of the problem involved.

the case, the element of discontinuity that was emphasized primarily in the testimony to the resurrection was not by any means abolished by historical research. On the contrary, even historical research itself was also impressed by a discontinuity, although it now took a totally different view of it and extended it so radically that the element of continuity threatened to be forgotten altogether. It was not only that everything in the traditional view of the resurrection that was connected with the idea of continuity (including the teaching instructions of the Risen Lord) now lost that character of continuity. But everything, too, in the traditional picture of Jesus itself which seemed to guarantee the continuity was now almost entirely demolished at the hands of the critics. To that extent the critical examination of the statements about the historical Jesus himself (i.e. Messianic consciousness, prophecies of the passion, etc.) became much more disturbing as far as our problem is concerned than the critical analysis of the Easter tradition. For now the end of the matter seemed to be, that the church's proclamation of Christ stands in contradiction to Jesus himself.

If, however, help was sought in taking what nevertheless remained of the genuine heritage of Jesus and making that the foundation of preaching and faith, then there arose a threefold difficulty:

(a) It was contrary to the whole tradition of the church including the New Testament itself. For never did the Christian message confine itself simply to passing on the message of Jesus.

(b) The view of the genuine heritage of Jesus as the foundation of preaching and faith was based—at least very largely—on a presupposed authority of Jesus which was a relic of the traditional faith in Christ.[1]

(c) And finally, careful exegesis made it necessary to realize that the so-called genuine tradition of Jesus in itself alone is simply not transmissible as the foundation of preaching and faith, in so far as it largely implies a connexion with his person which either makes the isolated transmission of his teaching meaningless or else raises the problem of how it should now be possible after all to transmit and communicate not merely the teaching of Jesus but the person of Jesus himself.

3. Although historical research almost exclusively left the impression of discontinuity, yet it was compelled, precisely as historical research, not to rest content with establishing the discontinuity, but to strive to

---

[1] The attempts to bring about a theological elimination of the problem of Christology by going back to the genuine heritage of Jesus suffer from the contradiction of presupposing that the authority of the genuine heritage of Jesus is self-evident (in view of the person of Jesus!), but thereby still resting tacitly on a Christological presupposition.

understand that discontinuity—which, however, means to search after all for the continuity that was nevertheless at work in it. For it is undeniable that a historic connexion exists between Jesus and the primitive church.

In order to enter into this problem it is necessary to turn to the Easter story. For the tradition is undoubtedly right in this: that here, from the purely historical point of view, lies the cardinal point in the transition from the historical Jesus to the church's proclamation of Christ. I must naturally abstain here from the analysis of the Easter tradition[1] and content myself with emphasizing two main aspects.

(a) The point of the Easter story is, that Jesus as the witness to faith became the ground of faith and that those who thus believe are witnesses to faith as witnesses to Jesus. It can hardly be denied that the point of the appearances of the Risen Lord, which form the heart of the Easter tradition, is the rise of faith in Jesus. Nobody was granted an appearance who did not thereby become a believer, and likewise nobody who did not already know Jesus before and thus in some measure recognize him.

This interpretation of the appearance events as events of faith requires to be further elucidated by adding: To be sure Jesus did not now meet with faith for the very first time. But now for the first time it is a case of the faith awakened by Jesus and founded on him becoming proclaimable. For that reason the occurrence of appearances is an exceptional occurrence in a limited period of time; it has the character of a call and has to do with the constituting of the Christian kerygma, but is not typical of the general way of coming to faith.

On the other hand the occurrence of appearances does not in any sense mean somehow making faith easier on the basis of an evident miracle. Such 'making faith easier' would in any case be self-contradictory and in actual fact a hindrance to faith. Rather, the appearance of Jesus and the coming to faith of the man who is granted the appearance, or his becoming a witness to faith, are one and the same thing. Indeed, it must even be said that for those who received them the appearances made faith more difficult in so far as they could become the very means of obscuring the nature of faith. The first witnesses to faith were not in any way exempted by the appearances from believing. Rather the appearances, so far as they were matters of seeing and hearing, were only concomitant phenomena of the faith-awakening encounter with Jesus.

For it was not a case of disclosing a new object of faith over and above

---

[1] Cf. the attempt at a brief review in *Das Wesen des christlichen Glaubens*, pp. 73 ff (ET, *The Nature of Faith*, pp. 63 ff).

others already existing. It was not a case of a single additional *credendum* (the fact of the resurrection), but of faith itself—and that, too, in relation to Jesus as the source of faith. Hence what is so confusingly called the 'Easter faith' is really a case of nothing else but faith in Jesus. The faith of the days after Easter knows itself to be nothing else but the right understanding of the Jesus of the days before Easter. For now Jesus appeared as what he really was, as the witness to faith. But we recognize the witness to faith only when, believing ourselves, we accept his witness and now ourselves as witnesses to Jesus become witnesses to faith.[1]

(*b*) That faith confesses Jesus as the Risen Lord, that faith in Jesus thus expresses itself as faith in him as risen, becomes understandable in the light of what is the whole point of faith. Faith as such is directed towards God as the act of entering into relations with (*Sicheinlassen auf*) God. To believe in Jesus therefore means: to enter into relations with God in view of him, to let him give us the freedom to believe, to let him as the witness to faith be the ground of faith and therefore to enter into relations with him and his ways, to participate in him and his ways and consequently to participate in what faith is promised participation in, namely, the omnipotence of God. To believe in face of the Crucified, of *this* man crucified, and indeed of this his dying consummation of his witness to faith, means in effect to confess to the omnipotence of God in him and that means to the power of the God who raises the dead. To believe in Jesus and to believe in him as the Risen Lord are one and the same thing. Yet we cannot rejoice in the resurrection of Jesus unless we perceive that the Cross of Jesus now had to become the central content of the message of faith.

4. What we have said of how the proper understanding of the Easter tradition makes clear the connexion between Jesus himself and the faith in Christ after Easter, finds its confirmation when we consider the Christian concept of faith itself. To a considerable extent the confusion regarding the relation between the historical Jesus and faith in Christ arises from failing to notice essential elements in the primitive Christian concept of faith. I recall here only a few outward symptoms, without being able to enter into an exposition of the concept of faith.

With primitive Christianity—and that, too, in all its forms—the employment of πιστεύειν and πίστις suddenly assumes an intensity not found before.[2] It is no mere chance that this coincides with the confes-

[1] I am here in part repeating expressions from *Das Wesen des christlichen Glaubens*, pp. 81-84 (ET, pp. 69-71).
[2] Cf. *ZTK* 55 (1958), p. 79 note 1 (see above, p. 216 note 1).

sion of Christ. Rather, faith is almost without exception related explicitly to Jesus Christ or (where the words πιστεύειν and πίστις are used absolutely) certainly meant in the sense of this relation to Christ.[1] It is manifestly because of this orientation towards Jesus that faith appears as the appropriate attitude towards him.[2] To belong to Jesus means to believe, and to believe means to belong to Jesus. Faith is not a form that can be given any content at will, but is the very essence of the matter, the thing that came with Jesus Christ, the content of revelation, the gift of salvation itself.

That the new thing that came with Jesus has to do with faith shows itself also in the new syntactical construction πιστεύειν εἰς, or πίστις εἰς, which is primarily employed only in relation to Christ, as also in the unusual genitive construction πίστις 'Ιησοῦ Χριστοῦ which, at all events if taken as objective genitive, is entirely new;[3] it can of course hardly be a pure objective genitive, as is shown by the parallel in Paul with πίστις 'Αβραάμ,[4] but on the other hand it cannot be a pure subjective genitive either. This genitive construction to my mind expresses in a very characteristic way the fact that faith in Christ is a faith which derives from Jesus, has its source and ground in him and therefore clings to him, receives from him its life, its very being as faith. 'Εκ πίστεως εἰς πίστιν[5] could surely be interpreted as this movement in the event of faith ἐκ (διά) πίστεως 'Ιησοῦ (Χριστοῦ) τοῖς πιστεύουσιν (εἰς πάντας τοὺς πιστεύοντας).[6]

5. The fact that Jesus and faith belong together forms the ground of the continuity between the historical Jesus and the so-called Christ of faith. Jesus is therefore not an object of faith in the sense in which we are accustomed to speak of objects of faith. Rather, he is the ground of faith. This relation is what is meant by the εἰς with πιστεύειν.

What does 'ground of faith' mean? Not on any account a support that would partially exempt us from faith. In the discussion about the historical Jesus the concept ground of faith or foundation of faith is again and again falsely employed in that way, whether in order to produce as

---

[1] I am thinking here only of primitive Christian usage. Cf. on the other hand *ZTK* 55 (1958), pp. 98 f (see above, pp. 234 f).

[2] The exclusive relation of faith to a man in the sense of faith's being—precisely so—exclusively related to God, and consequently in the sense of a radical understanding of faith, is a thing which stands out also in the history of language as a peculiarity of the Christian concept of faith.

[3] On both cf. *ZTK* 55 (1958), p. 79 note 2 (see above, p. 216 note 2).

[4] Cf. especially the parallel between ὁ ἐκ πίστεως 'Ιησοῦ Rom. 3.26 and ὁ ἐκ πίστεως 'Αβραάμ Rom. 4.16.

[5] Rom. 1.17.   [6] Gal. 3.22; Rom. 3.22.

an assured result of historical study a foundation of this kind which exempts from faith,[1] or in order to maintain polemically that historical study has nothing whatever to do with the ground of faith, since then faith would of course become dependent on historical study.[2] Rather, the ground of faith is that which makes faith what it is and so maintains it that it really remains faith—in other words, that on which faith in the last resort depends. The ground of faith in the biblical view is not isolated and objectified matters of fact, not facts like what was falsely presented and passed off as the objective fact of the resurrection of Jesus. Thus neither can any 'picture' (not even a picture of Jesus),[3] any 'idea', nor any proposition or group of propositions either, serve as a ground of faith. Rather, the sole ground of faith is Jesus as the witness to faith in the pregnant sense of the 'author and finisher of faith'.[4]

As such, however, the ground of faith is certainly to be brought to expression also by historical study, because it came to expression in history. The quest of the historical Jesus is the quest of this linguistic event which is the ground of the event of faith: ἄρα ἡ πίστις ἐξ ἀκοῆς ἡ δὲ ἀκοὴ διὰ ῥήματος Χριστοῦ.[5]

The further conclusions for Christology cannot be drawn here. But the decisive starting point should surely be clear: the task of Christology is in fact no other than to bring to expression what came to expression in Jesus himself.[6]

---

[1] Hans Conzelmann uses the expression 'foundation of faith' in this common sense in the concluding section of his article 'Jesus Christus' in *RGG*³ III, p. 651.

[2] Cf. the pertinent remark by Ernst Fuchs, *ZTK* 54 (1957), pp. 117 f.

[3] Thus I am here in complete agreement with Hans Conzelmann: 'Only when we include the process of proclamation as part of the problem, do we escape the danger which threatens today as always—the danger of making a picture of Jesus the foundation of faith again after all, and thus providing again a psychological ground for faith', *RGG*³ III, p. 651.

[4] Heb. 12.2.   [5] Rom. 10.17.

[6] The interpretation of the traditional Christological titles is also a part of that. The vast problem of their significance for Christology would require special examination and could not also be included in the present sketch.

XI

WORD OF GOD AND HERMENEUTICS*[1]

I

THE subject 'Word of God and Hermeneutics' combines two concepts which are perhaps more representative than any others of the approach that has determined theological thinking in the last four decades, and that still determines it today and also must determine it in the train of the Reformation. For by concentrating on the Word of God the Reformation conferred on the problem of hermeneutics a significance which, in spite of Origen and Augustine, it had never attained before. One might also say: a significance which had never before been perceived in these dimensions. For the *Catholic view of tradition* was in point of fact an answer to the hermeneutic problem—holding as it does that the revelation testified in scripture cannot be correctly understood without the tradition presented in the church. For in the strict sense this tradition is interpretative in character, even where in less strict terminology it is accorded a supplementary function.[2] Now if the exclusive

* ZTK 56 (1959), pp. 224-51.

[1] The paper was first read at the editorial conference of the ZTK on 18th April 1959 at Sindlingen, and then repeated on 10th May at the Interfac 1959 (Swiss Conference of Reformed Students of Theology) at Vaumarcus (Neuchâtel) and on 3rd June at the University of Heidelberg on the invitation of the Faculty of Theology.

For what follows cf. my article 'Hermeneutik' in RGG[3] III, pp. 242-62.

How profoundly I agree with Ernst Fuchs and how much I owe to him from many years' exchange of views can be seen from the many connexions between this paper and the recently published first volume of the collected essays of Ernst Fuchs: *Zum hermeneutischen Problem in der Theologie: Die existentiale Interpretation*, Tübingen 1959.

[2] *Tridentinum Sess. IV*, Denzinger 783, 786; *Vaticanum Const. dogm. de fide cath.* cap. 2, Denzinger 1787, 1788. On the discussion on the interpretation of these texts see R. J. Geiselmann, 'Das Konzil von Trient über das Verhältnis der Heiligen Schrift und der nicht geschriebenen Traditionen. Sein Missverständnis in der nachtridentinischen Theologie und die Überwindung dieses Missverständnisses', in *Die mündliche Überlieferung: Beiträge zum Begriff der Tradition*, ed. Michael Schmaus, Munich 1957.

The different verdicts on the question whether the tradition has to be assigned interpretative or supplementary character hang together with the divergence of views on the nature of interpretation. But according to the view of the Roman

particle 'sola scriptura' was directed against this Catholic view of tradition, yet the so-called *scripture principle of the Reformers* did not really
consist in a reduction of the sources of revelation, a quantitatively
narrower definition of the norm. Rather the '*sola scriptura*', as opposed
to the hermeneutic sense of the Catholic principle of tradition, was itself
already a hermeneutic thesis. Holy scripture, as Luther puts it, is *sui
ipsius interpres*.[1] Incidentally, that is strictly speaking also the point of
the Orthodox doctrine of verbal inspiration and of the *affectiones scripturae*, its *auctoritas, perfectio* and *perspicuitas*.[2] That holy scripture is *sui
ipsius interpres* was not a second point added to the '*sola scriptura*', but
only made explicit its hermeneutic sense. It is not as if the scripture
principle of the Reformers were joined by a hermeneutic principle, but
rather *the scripture principle of the Reformers* is, rightly understood,
nothing else but a hermeneutic principle. It says: scripture is not obscure,
so that the tradition is required in order to understand it. Rather,

[1] Luther's first explicit discussion of the sole authority of scripture (in
Assertio omnium articulorum, 1520: *WA* 7, pp. 96 ff) is exclusively concerned
with the problem of scripture exposition. It is a question of the correct understanding of the rule (introduced as an objection to Luther himself, but claimed
by him against the Roman view): *Non esse scripturas sanctas proprio spiritu inter-
pretandas* (96.10 f). *Error itaque manifestus est, hoc verbo, 'non licet scripturas
proprio spiritu intelligere' nobis mandari, ut sepositis sacris literis intendamus et
credamus hominum commentariis* (96.35-37). Rather, the truth is: ... *scripturas
non nisi eo spiritu intelligendas esse, quo scriptae sunt, qui spiritus nusquam prae-
sentius et vivacius quam in ipsis sacris suis, quas scripsit, literis inveniri potest* (97.1-3).
The exclusive sense of the '*sola scriptura*' is thus aimed against the alleged
insufficiency of scripture on the hermeneutic side: ... *ut sit ipsa* (sc. *scriptura*)
*per sese certissima, facillima, apertissima, sui ipsius interpres, omnium omnia probans,
iudicans et illuminans*. ... (he appeals to Ps. 119.130:) *Hic clare spiritus tribuit
illuminationem et intellectum dari docet per sola verba dei, tanquam per ostium et
apertum seu principium* (*quod dicunt*) *primum, a quo incipi oporteat, ingressurum ad
lucem et intellectum* (97.23-29).
[2] The consistent development of the early Protestant doctrine of verbal inspiration took place under pressure of the Catholic argument that the very
concept 'canon' already presents the authority of tradition, and the '*sola scriptura*' is thus a contradiction in terms inasmuch as this 'principle' is in fact a
confessional statement of the church. In face of that, the sufficiency of scripture
also in regard to the very point of the authorization of scripture had to be
expressed with the utmost sharpness. The hermeneutic sense of the doctrine of
verbal inspiration (which then caused so much confusion precisely in the
hermeneutic field) becomes very clear from the conclusion that the pointing of
the Hebrew text must also be inspired since the unequivocal meaning of the text
seemed to depend on it.

church the tradition naturally contains nothing that contradicts scripture and is
not provided for at least in germ in it. The concept of development, on which
the discussion of the Catholic concept of tradition concentrates itself, therefore
involves the hermeneutic problem.

scripture possesses *claritas*, i.e. it has illuminating power, so that a clarifying light shines from it, among other things also on the tradition.[1]

Now it is true that the consequences of this hermeneutic sense of the '*sola scriptura*' were not sufficiently clearly recognized at the Reformation itself, and still less in *Orthodoxy*. Both in the understanding of 'Word of God' and also in the conception of hermeneutics this showed itself in a certain lack of clarity and later even in grave errors. Luther, it is true, was aware that the proposition of the *claritas scripturae* demands a distinction between the unrestricted clarity of the *res* of scripture and a partial obscurity of its *verba*[2]—a distinction which, when pursued further, makes a problem of the relation of Word of God and scripture. But the later efforts to safeguard the Reformers' position led to the Orthodox identification of scripture with the Word of God. That jeopardized alike both the Reformers' concept of the Word of God and the Reformers' understanding of the *claritas scripturae*.[3] And the

[1] On Luther's doctrine of the *claritas scripturae* cf. esp. *De servo arbitrio* (1525), *WA* 18, pp. 606.1-609.14; 652.23-653.35 (=Clem. 3, pp. 100.34-103.22; 141.1-142.19). *Nam id oportet apud Christianos esse imprimis ratum atque firmissimum, Scripturas sanctas esse lucem spiritualem, ipso sole longe clariorem, praesertim in iis quae pertinent ad salutem vel necessitatem. Verum quia in contrarium persuasi sumus iamdudum pestilenti illo Sophistarum verbo, Scripturas esse obscuras et ambiguas, cogimur primum probare illud ipsum primum principium nostrum, quo omnia alia probanda sunt, quod apud philosophos absurdum et impossibile factu videretur* (*WA* 18, p. 653.28-35=Clem. 3, p. 142.11-19; cf. J. I. Packer and O. R. Johnston, trans., *Martin Luther on the Bondage of the Will*, New Jersey 1957, p. 125). Cf. R. Hermann, *Von der Klarheit der Heiligen Schrift: Untersuchungen und Erörterungen über Luthers Lehre von der Schrift in De servo arbitrio*, Berlin 1958.

[2] *Hoc sane fateor, esse multa loca in scripturis obscura et abstrusa, non ob maiestatem rerum, sed ob ignorantiam vocabulorum et grammaticae, sed quae nihil impediant scientiam omnium rerum in scripturis. . . . Res igitur in scripturis contentae omnes sunt proditae, licet quaedam loca adhuc verbis incognitis obscura sint. Stultum est vero et impium, scire, res scripturae esse omnes in luce positas clarissima, et propter pauca verba obscura res obscuras dictare. Si uno loco obscura sunt verba, at alio sunt clara. Eadem vero res, manifestissime toti mundo declarata, dicitur in scripturis tum verbis claris, tum adhuc latet verbis obscuris. Iam nihil refert, si res sit in luce, an aliquod eius signum sit in tenebris, cum interim multa alia eiusdem signa sint in luce* (*WA* 18, p. 606.22-37=Clem. 3, p. 101.20-38; Packer and Johnston, *op. cit.*, pp. 71 f).

[3] In order to emphasize that the *res* of scripture can remain *mysteria*, but that the grammatical sense of scripture can nevertheless be clear to anyone, Luther's observations on the *claritas scripturae* are in Orthodoxy seemingly turned upside down: *Clara dicitur scriptura sacra non ratione rerum sed verborum: quia res inevidentes etiam claris et perspicuis verbis proponi possunt* (Hollaz). *Disting. inter evidentiam rerum, quae in scripturis revelantur, et claritatem verborum, quibus res revelatae significantur; non de illa sed de hac nobis sermo est: agnoscimus enim, tradi in scripturis multa mysteria . . . abstrusa et humano intellectui in hac praesertim vita imperverstigabilia; sed negamus, illa obscuro sermone et verbis ambiguis in scriptura*

lack of clarity in regard to hermeneutics took its toll in exegesis and dogmatics. Exegesis found itself again, as before, under the domination of the dogmatic tradition which was always decisive in case of doubt. And dogmatics fell back into its traditional form, without sufficient attention being paid to the significance of the scripture principle for the method of dogmatics.

Thus it is not only the close connexion of the subjects Word of God and hermeneutics that has its origin in the Reformers. The heritage of the Reformation also includes where the concept Word of God is concerned the latent tension with holy scripture, and in regard to hermeneutics the at first likewise latent tension between exegesis and dogmatics. And because of that the close conjunction of Word of God and hermeneutics was in jeopardy of being transformed by criticism into its opposite. This became clear in the *theology of the modern age*. Using the lever of hermeneutics, it first brought out the tension between exegesis and dogmatics, as also between scripture and the Word of God, and finally called in question the concept of the Word of God itself. It was the concentration on the Word of God at the Reformation that had conferred such importance on hermeneutics. And now in the modern age hermeneutics threatened to lead to the dissolution of the Word of God. If we still bear in mind the internal links indicated with the Reformation, then such a condensed formula may perhaps be applied to the problem of modern theology, without implying an irresponsible condemnation of the development in theological history that has here taken place.[1]

The more recent decided *transition to a theology of the Word of God* was in danger of regaining this Reformation theme at the cost of thoughtlessly overlooking the hermeneutic problem. In point of fact, too, some theological oddities did get out of hand, and what is much worse, a late by-product was the intensification of the stuffy atmosphere of a narrow churchiness. Yet we must not judge by such incidental

[1] Cf. *RGG*[3] III, pp. 253 f.

---

proponi (Quenstedt). Quoted according to H. Schmidt, *Die Dogmatik der evang.-luth. Kirche*, 7th ed. 1893, p. 46: trans. *The Doctrinal Theology of the Lutheran Church*, C. A. Hay and H. E. Jacobs, Philadelphia 1889, pp. 85 f. To be sure, it is not a case of direct contradiction, when we consider Luther's distinction between *externa* and *interna claritas* and notice that the statements quoted from the early Protestant dogmatic theologians concentrate in essence on the problem which Luther puts under the head of *interna claritas*. Nevertheless there are highly significant changes of emphasis, which of course could only be brought out in a detailed analysis of the early Protestant doctrine of scripture and of Luther's (not completely thought out) doctrine of the *duplex claritas* (and *obscuritas*) *scripturae*.

accompaniments. The return to the theology of the Word of God resulted from a passionate wrestling with the hermeneutic problem. The various prefaces to Barth's *Romans* are impressive testimonies to that.[1] We are assured that it is not to be a case of breaking with modern, critical historical hermeneutics, but only of necessary corrections to it. 'The critical historical people are not critical enough for me', said Barth.[2]

This critical advance seemed indeed to have purely theological motives, but fitted completely into the general contemporary movement of the hermeneutic problem. In contrast to the traditions of the earlier part of the modern age, the hermeneutic interest had slackened since about the middle of the nineteenth century. But in the debate with positivism and historism the problem of hermeneutics was more deeply and more and more widely involved and so acquired new acuteness. Thus it was not unconnected with general, comprehensive historic changes when in the theology of the last decades the subject of hermeneutics came so much into the foreground once more—and that, too, in critical reflexion on the inadequacy of modern hermeneutics hitherto.

But now, it is no accident that at this point the prevailing *dissensus* within theology arose. It is usually marked for simplicity by the names of Barth and Bultmann. In the framework of the present sketch of the problem it seems to present itself as follows: on the one side the passion for the Word of God tends towards disparagement of the hermeneutic problem; on the other side the interest in the hermeneutic problem

[1] Above all the prefaces to the first (1918) and second (1921) editions. I quote from the 5th impression of the revised version, Munich 1929.

[2] *Op. cit.*, p. xii. 1918: 'The critical historical method of research into the Bible is right enough: it aims at a preparation for understanding, and that is never superfluous. But if I had to choose between it and the old doctrine of inspiration, I would definitely take the latter: it has the greater, profounder, *more important* right, because its aim is the work of understanding itself, without which all preparation is worthless. I am glad not to have to choose between the two. But my whole attention has been directed to seeing *through* the historical to the Spirit of the Bible, who is the eternal Spirit' (*op. cit.*, p. v). 1921: 'I have been called a "declared enemy of *historical criticism*". . . . But what I reproach them with is not the historical criticism, the right and necessity of which on the contrary I once more explicitly recognize, but the way they stop at an explanation of the text which I cannot call any explanation, but only the first primitive step towards one, namely, at establishing "what is said". . .' (*op. cit.*, p. x). The basic hermeneutic impulse of so-called dialectical theology, as it comes to expression in these prefaces of Barth's, has not lost anything of its drive even after four decades. Cf. also R. Bultmann's remark from the year 1924: 'It is no accident that the latest movement in theology was not born from the matrix of Orthodoxy but in point of fact from liberal theology' (*Glauben und Verstehen* I, p. 1).

appears to jeopardize what is said of the Word of God. But we must be very much on our guard against drawing the differences too crudely. It is correct at all events to say that Barth and Bultmann form a very different estimate of the theological revelance of the hermeneutic problem and that this is connected with a difference also in their view of the Word of God. Yet Barth has not by any means surrendered his initial hermeneutic impulse, but has let it lead him on to the path of his *Church Dogmatics*. For if his direct treatment of the hermeneutic problem is relatively meagre, the *Church Dogmatics* presents over and above it an implicit answer to the hermeneutic problem.[1] On the other hand Bultmann's continuous concern with the theme of hermeneutics has no other aim than to be the methodological vindication of a theology of the Word of God.[2]

The differences are thus bound up with what they have in common. Common to both is, that in opposition to historism and psychologism they address themselves to the specific 'matter' of theology. But in distinction from the objective approach of the *Church Dogmatics* Bultmann considers the understanding to belong to the matter itself. That is why for him the problem of the preliminary understanding acquires such importance. Common to both is, further, the tendency to surmount the dualism of historical and systematic theology. But while in Barth the methodological tension is set aside altogether and the separation of the disciplines is reduced to a certain practical division of labour, Bultmann finds that precisely where methodology is concerned the element of tension remains, yet so that each theological discipline contains it within itself. Common to both is, lastly, that on no account will they return to the Orthodox distinction of *hermeneutica sacra* and *hermeneutica profana*. Barth, however, brings out the unity of hermeneutics by claiming general validity for the hermeneutics dictated by the Bible,[3] while

[1] The hermeneutic problem in Barth (as far as his intentions are concerned) has been taken up without remainder into the discussion of the subject-matter of theology.

[2] Perhaps—in addition to the concept of the kerygma which is central for Bultmann's theology—I may recall as an illustration of this the fact that the essay on de-mythologizing ends: 'The Word became flesh.'

[3] 'Where does the theory of hermeneutic principles just sketched come from? Well, the very fact that although in itself it is surely as clear as day, yet it does not after all enjoy general recognition, shows that it can hardly have been derived from general reflexions, i.e. from reflexions that are possible in a general way, upon the nature of man's word, etc., and thus from a general anthropology. Why do the reflexions that are possible in a general way upon the nature of man's word not usually lead to the propositions just stated? I would answer: because special care is taken not to let the theory of hermeneutic principles be dictated,

Bultmann on the contrary approaches the hermeneutic problem in theology from definite standpoints provided by general hermeneutics.[1]

The discussion of the Word of God and hermeneutics appears today to have become bogged down. But it is not by any means over and done with and, as it seems to me, has not even advanced to final alternative answers. One could attempt to take the conversation further by a detailed analysis of the controversy we have just fleetingly touched on between Barth and Bultmann. Yet it seems to me more helpful to approach the phenomena themselves by way of a few remarks on the structure of the problem our subject involves.

II

Whatever precise theological definition may be given to the *concept of the Word of God*, at all events it points us to something that happens, *viz.* to the movement which leads from the text of holy scripture to the sermon ('sermon' of course taken in the pregnant sense of proclamation in general). As a first definition of the concept of the Word of God the reference to this movement from text to proclamation may suffice. For this is in fact according to Christian tradition the primary place of the concept of the Word of God. We here set aside questions that probe behind that—why the holy scripture that presses for proclamation or the proclamation that takes its stand on holy scripture should be marked out in particular above other things as Word of God; or what form of the Word of God to some extent precedes scripture; and whether the Word of God is not found also outside the relation of text and sermon. For according to Christian conviction the answers to all these questions can be truly known only in connexion with that movement from the text to the sermon. But it is of decisive importance to choose this movement as the starting-point for the definition of the concept of the Word of God.

---

[1] 'The interpretation of the biblical scriptures is not subject to any different conditions of understanding from any other literature' (*Glaube und Verstehen* II, p. 231).

as has of course happened here, by holy scripture. . . . It was with the only possible exposition of holy scripture in mind that we laid down the principles of exposition just given. Certainly not in the belief that they are valid *only* for the exposition of the Bible, but fully believing that *because* they are valid for the exposition of the Bible they are valid for man's word *in general*, and that they thus have a claim to *general* recognition. . . . There is no such thing as special biblical hermeneutics. But precisely the general, and only valid hermeneutics must be learned by means of the Bible as the testimony to revelation' (*KD* I/2, p. 515; cf. *Church Dogmatics* I/2, pp. 465 f.).

The criticism usually made of the Orthodox doctrine is, that it identifies scripture and the Word of God without distinction. And the correction then made is to say instead of 'Scripture *is* the Word of God' something like, 'Scripture *contains* or *witnesses to* the Word of God.' In other words, to refer to a factor distinct from scripture which has to be sought within or behind it. There is no doubt some truth in that. Yet the decisive shortcoming of the Orthodox position lies in the fact that holy scripture is spoken of as the Word of God without any eye to the proclamation,[1] and thus without expression being given also to the

[1] The Orthodox understanding of the Word of God is completely dominated by the aspect of the becoming scripture of God's Word. *Scriptum Dei verbum est μόνον καὶ οἰκεῖον theologiae principium* (Joh. Gerhard, *Loc. theol. Prooem. De natura Theologiae*, ed. Cott. II, 8). *Nullum igitur aliud Theologiae principium quam Verbum Dei scriptum agnoscimus* (Joh. Wolleb, *Christ. Theol. Compend., Praecognita* Can. V). Orthodoxy too, of course, knew of the *verbum Dei* as *viva vox*, and indeed knew both of the necessity of preaching by word of mouth and also of the historic priority of the *verbum Dei non scriptum*. For the rest, the strong emphasis on the *verbum Dei scriptum* can surely be understood and approved of in so far as it was a case of deciding the question of the normative authority unequivocally in favour of scripture and disputing the normative significance of an oral tradition that vaguely develops and uncontrollably claims a hearing alongside of scripture. For that reason not only the necessity but also the dependability of scriptural fixation had to be emphasized. Yet in doing so, all too little attention was paid to the tension that exists between the character of the *verbum Dei* as spoken word and the character of writtenness. Here we see a startling divergence from the Reformation. Luther, as is well known, insisted that the Gospel is really oral preaching: ' . . . in the New Testament the sermons are to be spoken aloud in public and to bring forth in terms of speech and hearing what was formerly hidden in the letter and in secret vision. Forasmuch as the New Testament is nothing else but the unlocking and revealing of the Old Testament. . . . That, too, is why Christ himself did not write his teaching, as Moses did his, but delivered it orally, also commanded to deliver it orally and gave no command to write it. . . . For that reason it is not at all the manner of the New Testament to write books of Christian doctrine, but there should everywhere, without books, be good, learned, spiritually-minded, diligent preachers to draw the living word from the ancient scriptures and constantly bring it to life before the people, as the apostles did. For before ever they wrote, they had preached to and converted the people by word of mouth, which also was their real apostolic and New Testament work. . . . That books had to be written, however, is at once a great failure and a weakness of spirit that was enforced by necessity and not by the manner of the New Testament' (*Kirchenpostille* 1522, *WA* 10/1, 1, pp. 625.12-628.8. Further, *WA* 10/1, 1, pp. 17.4-18.1 and 10/1, 2, pp. 34.12-35.3. Cf. G. Ebeling, *Evang. Evangelienauslegung*, 1942, pp. 365 ff; H. Østergaard-Nielsen, *Scriptura sacra et viva vox*, 1957). On the distinction between scripture and spoken word depends not only the right understanding of the difference between the Old Testament and the New Testament, but also—as a presupposition of that, though not identical with it— the right understanding of the relation of law and Gospel. For the distinction of law and Gospel concerns their *efficacia*, and that in turn goes with a difference in their word-character. The difference between written and spoken word,

future to which holy scripture points forward as its own future. On closer inspection the concept of the Word of God certainly seeks to be interpreted in a still more comprehensive sense in terms of event. Yet that results from the basic starting-point in the process of the text becoming proclamation. The question as to the real nature of this event must therefore be at least one essential element in the doctrine of the Word of God.

And now, whatever the precise definition that may be given to 'hermeneutics', at all events as the theory of understanding it has to do with the word-event. And indeed, like every science, ultimately with a practical aim, as an aid to the word-event, *viz.* as guidance on how a word that has taken place comes to be understood. That is not intended by any means to simplify hermeneutics by reducing it to a collection of rules. But even when the hermeneutic problem is entered into radically, teaching about understanding must give proof of itself by serving the understanding, be it only in providing a critical indication of its limits.

Now if in the Word of God we have a case of the word-event that leads

---

however, is no purely formal one. Reading aloud what is written does not yet produce spoken word in the sense Luther means here. He is concerned with the insight into the different possibilities in the language event which contain within them the difference of law and Gospel and can be rightly interpreted only in the light of the distinction of law and Gospel. *Nam longe alia debet esse praedicatio Euangelii quam legis. Lex in tabulis scribebatur et erat scriptura mortua, limitibus tabula clausa, ideo parum efficax. At Euangelium vivae et liberrimae voci in auras effusae committitur, ideo plus energiae habet ad convertendum* (*Enarr.* 1521: *WA* 7, p. 526.12-16). It is symptomatic of the impoverishment of the understanding of the Word in Orthodoxy that those insights were completely lost from sight. It was no longer borne in mind that to the essence of the Word belongs its oral character, i.e. its character of an event in personal relationship, that the Word is thus no isolated bearer of meanings, but an event that effects something and aims at something. In Joh. Gerhard I find the point of view we have just discussed mentioned only once, but significantly enough in the form of a Catholic objection which is rebutted. Gerhard (*Loci theol. loc. I De script. s.*, cap. 2, q. 3, ed. Cott. II, 30) quotes among other things remarks of the Catholic apologetic theologians Lindanus (*Natura verbi evangelici a scripto et literis plane abhorret*) and Pistorius (*Apostoli non scripserunt ex proposito, sed propter incidentem necessitatem*). The Orthodox understanding of the *verbum Dei* as *verbum scriptum* stood on its own in isolation from the proclamation that has taken place and from the proclamation that is to take place, and so shrunk to an unhistoric understanding of the Word. From the standpoint of Luther it is obvious that that endangered both the right distinction between the Old and New Testaments and also the right distinction of law and Gospel. These critical considerations are not mentioned in the otherwise so praiseworthy book by Bengt Hägglund, *Die Heilige Schrift und ihre Deutung in der Theologie Joh. Gerhards: Eine Untersuchung über das altlutherische Schriftverständnis*, Lund 1951.

from the text of holy scripture to the proclamation, then the question is, whether hermeneutics can be expected to help towards that happening rightly. Here doubts arise at once. Can the event of the Word of God be served at all by scientific methods? Must the hermeneutic approach as such not at once have a destructive effect on the concept of the Word of God, as also on the corresponding concept of the Holy Spirit? But doubts, too, of a less radical kind also call in question the service of hermeneutics here. Can hermeneutics not deal only with an exposition which is subject to scientific criteria? Even then there are, as is well known, already great methodological difficulties. Now in so far as the sermon is preceded by a scientific exposition of the text, hermeneutics may also have significance for it. But then the question remains what the scientific exposition contributes to the sermon and what distinguishes it from the exposition that takes place in the sermon itself; whether it is appropriate to contrast the latter as 'practical' exposition with the scientific kind and so withdraw it from the strict standpoint of hermeneutics, or to distinguish it as *applicatio* from the *explicatio* and thereby deny that the sermon in its essential nature is exposition at all, however much it may contain textual exposition. Yet is it not bringing the event of the Word of God into dangerous isolation from word-events in general, if we withdraw it from the reach of hermeneutics? Indeed, is it not the case that the concept of the Word of God can be used at all only when hermeneutic justification can be given for it? But what does 'hermeneutics' then mean? Let us therefore attempt first of all a more precise clarification of the concept hermeneutics.

III

According to the common view there is a sharp distinction between exegesis as the process of exposition itself and hermeneutics as the theory of exposition. And here indeed it is assumed that verbal statements are the object of exposition, i.e. the thing requiring exposition. According to the several kinds of verbal statement, general hermeneutics may be differentiated into various special hermeneutics, though of course without departing from the comprehensive framework of general hermeneutics.

This customary view of hermeneutics requires correction in various respects.

1. On the threshold of the Enlightenment the *distinction of general and special hermeneutics* had taken the place of the very differently articulated Orthodox distinction of *hermeneutica sacra* and *hermeneutica*

profana.[1] The basic proposition that holy scripture is not to be differently interpreted from other books[2] seemed, it is true, now to allow of only one single science of hermeneutics and to relieve theology of any special discussion of the hermeneutic problem, indeed even to forbid it. But owing to the colourlessness and abstractness of the proposition of a general hermeneutics, it did not exclude the introduction of various special hermeneutics applied and related to concrete subjects, as long as these various special hermeneutics remained subject to and derived from general hermeneutic criteria. Indeed, modern hermeneutics developed at first almost entirely in the form of special hermeneutics of such kinds,[3] in the construction of which theology played an outstanding part along with classical philology and jurisprudence. It can even be said that the principle of a single science of hermeneutics worked itself out in practice as the principle of an increasing hermeneutic specialization.

For theology this meant in the first instance that, although specifically theological hermeneutics disappeared, there arose within theology various hermeneutics in different degrees of specialization, such as biblical, Old Testament or New Testament hermeneutics, or (the demand for this at all events has already been made) in such a way that each biblical book requires a special hermeneutics.[4] We must not let

[1] It was still retained in Pietism, where also for the first time the concept hermeneutics coined in the middle of the seventeenth century (cf. *RGG*[3] III, p. 255) had made possible the formula *hermeneutica sacra.* Joh. Jak. Rambach defines this (with characteristic emphasis on the requisite subjective presuppositions): *Priori modo accepta, est facultas practica, qua homo Christianus, bona mente et obviis bonae mentis adminiculis instructus ac spiritus sancti lumine adiutus, scripturae sensum, ex ipsa sacra scriptura, ad suam utilitatem ac salutem scrutatur. Posteriore modo accepta hermeneutica sacra est habitus practicus, quo doctor theologicus, necessariis adminiculis sufficienter instructus, praelucente spiritus sancti lumine, idoneus redditur ad sensum scripturae legitime investigandum, investigatumque aliis exponendum et sapienter adplicandum, ut hoc modo Dei gloria et hominum salus promoveatur* (*Institutiones hermeneuticae sacrae,* 1723). J. A. Ernesti on the other hand gives a general definition of hermeneutics: *Hermeneutice est scientia, adducens ad subtilitatem tum intelligendi, tum explicandi auctoris cuiusque sententias, sive tradens rationem sententiae quorumque verborum subtiliter et inveniendae et explicandae* (*Institutio interpretis N.T.,* 1761).

[2] For the first time in J. A. Turrentini (*De sacrae scripturae interpretandae methodo tractatus bipartitus,* 1728): *non aliam esse Scripturae interpretandae rationem quam reliquorum librorum.*

[3] An early exception is: J. M. Chladenius, *Einleitung zur richtigen Auslegung vernünftiger Reden und Schriften,* 1742.

[4] 'Today we know that it is only the kind of material and the special interest we take in it that puts a peculiar stamp on hermeneutics. Now we must make, and fulfil, the demand to set alongside the special hermeneutics for the New Testament as a whole also an individual hermeneutics for each New Testament book' (E. von Dobschütz, *Vom Auslegen des NT,* 1927, p. 16).

ourselves be deceived about the real nature of this state of affairs by, say, the fact that such extreme specialization was never realized, and that biblical or Old or New Testament hermeneutics owing to the theological dignity of these books at once gives the impression of theological hermeneutics. Strictly, however, the basic conception is, that there is no such thing as theological hermeneutics. For the differentiation in hermeneutics is held to be justified indeed from the standpoint of different literary complexes, but not on the basis of particular, non-universal epistemological principles such as those of theology. Thus hermeneutics in theology became the methodology of definite individual disciplines—*viz.* the biblical ones—and therewith at once the boundary separating them from dogmatics, which as such had nothing to do with hermeneutics.

The fact that in contrast to this, historical and systematic theology today join hands in the hermeneutic problem and hermeneutics has expanded to become the methodology no longer merely of individual theological disciplines but of theology as a whole, is to a great extent a distant result of *Schleiermacher.* For his pioneer view of hermeneutics as the theory of the conditions on which understanding is possible modified the relation of general and special hermeneutics in a twofold way.

First: a special hermeneutics must now take strict account of what can here be *differentia specifica.* The view which Schleiermacher himself here put forward in detail[1] is doubtless obsolete. His basic demand,

---

[1] 'The answer, then, to the question whether and how far New Testament hermeneutics is of a special kind is as follows. On the linguistic side it does not appear to be special, for here it is to be related in the first instance to the Greek language. On the psychological side, however, the New Testament does not appear as a unity, but a distinction has to be made between didactic and historical writings. These are different types (*Gattungen*), which certainly demand different hermeneutic rules. Yet that does not yet give rise to a special hermeneutics. All the same, New Testament hermeneutics is a special kind, but only in relation to its compound linguistic ground or the Hebraizing character of its language.... For when a spiritual development takes place in a people, then there also arises a new linguistic development. Now as every new spiritual principle has a formative effect on language, so also has the Christian spirit. But that does not in other cases give rise to any special hermeneutics. If a people begins to philosophize, then it displays a vast linguistic development, but it does not require any special hermeneutics. The new Christian spirit, however, appears in the New Testament in a hybrid language, in which Hebrew is the stem in which the new thing was first thought, but Greek was grafted on to it. For that reason New Testament hermeneutics is to be treated as a special kind. As the mixture of languages is an exception, and not a natural condition, so too New Testament hermeneutics as special hermeneutics does not derive from general hermeneutics in the regular way' (D. F. Schleiermacher, *Hermeneutik und Kritik mit besonderer Beziehung auf das NT,* ed. F. Lücke, *Sämtliche Werke* I, 7, 1858, pp. 27 f).

however, is still valid. The view emphatically advanced today by Bultmann that the difference as to what one is after in the interrogation
(*Woraufhin der Befragung*) has differentiating character in the hermeneutic sphere[1] is a first step towards further clarification of this side of
the hermeneutic problem—a step that is capable of being developed
and certainly also stands in need of further development. This provides,
without relapsing into an alleged *hermeneutica sacra*, the possibility of
speaking of a hermeneutics related to theology as a whole, which on the
basis of the specifically theological approach works out structures and
criteria of theological understanding that apply in theology not only to
the exegetical but also to the dogmatic understanding. It is absolutely
necessary that this should then be done in demonstrable connexion
with a general theory of understanding. The nature of the connexion,
however, raises difficult problems.

The other impulse which Schleiermacher gave to the further history
of hermeneutics is today discernible above all in a surprisingly *extended
use of the word hermeneutics*. It is not only that hermeneutics can now
be spoken of in sciences in which it was not possible before and which
do not have to do with texts at all but with phenomena—for example
psychology. Rather, the development from Schleiermacher via Dilthey
to Heidegger shows that the idea of a theory of understanding is on the
move towards laying the foundation of the humanities, indeed even becomes the essence of philosophy,[2] that hermeneutics now takes the
place of the classical epistemological theory,[3] and indeed that fundamental ontology appears as hermeneutics.[4]

Thus outside of theology, too, hermeneutics today is breaking through
the old, narrow bounds of philological or historiographical hermeneutics,
or is plumbing their depths. For theology the hermeneutic problem is
therefore today becoming the place of meeting with philosophy. And
that always involves at the same time both community and contrast.
This confirms once again that in an approach so radical as this there is

[1] R. Bultmann, 'Das Problem der Hermeneutik' in *Glauben und Verstehen* II,
esp. pp. 217 f, 227 ff [ET, *Essays Philosophical and Theological*, pp. 240 ff,
252 ff]; *Geschichte und Eschatologie*, 1958, pp. 131 ff [ET, *The Presence of Eternity*, pp. 113 ff]. It would be well to raise the problem of a systematic statement
of the possibilities as to what one is after in the interrogation, as also of the
criteria of its application.
[2] O. F. Bollnow, *Dilthey: Eine Einführung in seine Philosophie* (1936), 2nd ed.
1955, pp. 24 f, 212 f.
[3] Cf. W. Wieland, Article 'Erkenntnistheorie', *RGG*[3] II, pp. 559 ff.
[4] M. Heidegger, *Sein und Zeit*, pp. 37 f [ET, *Being and Time*, London and
New York 1962].

point in speaking of theological hermeneutics without in any way refurbishing the division into *hermeneutica sacra* and *profana*.

2. The customary view that *hermeneutics is the theory of the exposition
of texts* already seemed a moment ago to have undergone correction in
that phenemona can also be objects of exposition. If we followed that
further, then we should doubtless have to limit it to phenomena in so
far as they have to do with the linguisticality of existence, and are thus
'texts' in the wider sense. Hermeneutics would then also remain related
to the word-event. But what is now to be held against the usual view is
something other than that.

It is usually taken for granted that the reason why hermeneutics has
to do with the word-event is, that verbal statements pose the problem
of understanding. Now however much the need for hermeneutics does
in fact arise primarily from difficulties of understanding in the word-
event, it is nevertheless completely false to take this situation as the
point of orientation for one's basic grasp of the relation between word
and understanding and of what is ultimately constitutive for hermeneutics. The superficial view of understanding turns matters upside down
and must therefore be completely reversed. *The primary phenomenon
in the realm of understanding is not understanding* OF *language, but understanding* THROUGH *language*. The word is not really the object of understanding, and thus the thing that poses the problem of understanding,
the solution of which requires exposition and therefore also hermeneutics as the theory of understanding. Rather, the word is what opens
up and mediates understanding, i.e. brings something to understanding.
The word itself has a hermeneutic function. If the word-event takes place
normally, i.e. according to its appointed purpose, then there is no need
of any aid to understanding, but it is itself an aid to understanding. It
is to my mind not unimportant for the proper grasp of the hermeneutic
problem whether we set out from the idea that a verbal statement in
itself is something obscure into which the light of the understanding
must be introduced from elsewhere, or whether, on the contrary, we
set out from the fact that the situation in terms of which and into which
the verbal statement is made is something obscure which is then illumined by the verbal statement. This starting-point opens up three
important perspectives for the question of hermeneutics.

First: interpretation, and therefore also *hermeneutics*, is *requisite* only
in the case *where the word-event is hindered* for some reason or other. But
for that reason also the hermeneutic aid can only consist in removing
hindrances in order to let the word perform its own hermeneutic

function. And the removing of hindrances to understanding can usually likewise take place only by word. For hermeneutics is of course not a departure from the linguistic realm in order to understand language, but a deeper penetration into the linguistic realm in order to understand by means of language.

From the point of view that it is a question of removing hindrances, we can now also grasp that the scope of the hermeneutic task can vary in extent. There is relative justification for restricting ourselves to what immediately concerns the grammatical and philological understanding of a text. We can include in the realm of the hermeneutic task also the very much wider problem of historical understanding. We can extend hermeneutics also to the understanding of what confronts us with the task of understanding by encountering us in the present. And we can thus, moving ever further afield, relate hermeneutics to the problem of understanding as such, i.e. to the problem of the ultimate conditions under which it is possible for understanding to take place at all. We are not, of course, left to choose at will. How radically we have to consider the hermeneutic problem depends on the extent to which lack of understanding arises.

Secondly, because hermeneutics can only make room for the word's own hermeneutic function, and thus because, as we could also say, hermeneutics only serves the word's own intelligibility, the content and *object of hermeneutics is the word-event as such.* For where a word happens, understanding is made possible. If hermeneutics, in order to be an aid to understanding, has to reflect on the conditions under which understanding is possible, then it has to reflect on the nature of words. *Hermeneutics as the theory of understanding must therefore be the theory of words.*

If that is formulated with the help of Greek by saying that hermeneutics is the theory of the Logos, then within the limits of Greek thinking that would doubtless seem very reasonable.[1] For the Logos which holds equal sway alike in things and in the knowing subject himself is the condition of the possibility of understanding. The Logos is for the Greek a hermeneutic principle. It is a question, of course, what relation responsible hermeneutics today could adopt towards this Greek conception of hermeneutics. However little explication we have as yet given to our references so far to word-event and linguistic event, there is nevertheless obviously a considerable difference from the Greek Logos

---

[1] Cf. Kleinknecht on the Logos in Greek thought and Hellenism, *TWNT* IV, pp. 76 ff.

concept. Yet for all that, wherever the subject of hermeneutics is taken up, contact with the problems of Greek thinking is surely *conditio sine qua non*. For the taking up of the hermeneutic problem has its origin in Greek thinking. And however far we may diverge in our view of the word-event, hermeneutics will never be able to enter into complete opposition to the Greek Logos. Otherwise it would have to be denied altogether that hermeneutics is an undertaking which makes sense.

An lastly, if what is constitutive for hermeneutics is the word that does not require to be made understandable but itself opens up understanding, then hermeneutics, just because it has to do with the word-event, has always to do at once with the thing that is to be brought to understanding by means of the word-event. For that reason it is false to hold that hermeneutics is restricted to pure matters of form. For *in that hermeneutics addresses itself directly to the word, it addresses itself directly to the reality* that comes to understanding through the word. True, to speak of the formal character of hermeneutics is right enough in a way, if it is borne in mind that 'formal' is the designation of a relation, so that the selfsame thing which in one regard is a definition of content can in another respect be a formal definition.

That hermeneutics must always in some way or other have a bearing on actualities, is a thing I now merely indicate by mentioning a few symptoms in a disconnected list:—We can get to the root of understanding only when we encounter what is not understood and what cannot be understood. We can know about the nature of words only when we come upon what is underivably given and is beyond the reach of words. Words produce understanding only by appealing to experience and leading to experience. Only where word has already taken place can word take place. Only where there is already previous understanding can understanding take place. Only a man who is already concerned with the matter in question can be claimed for it.

The significance of this for the grasp of the hermeneutic relationships is, that the hearer's relation to the verbal statement must always be coupled with a corresponding relation to reality (to which incidentally there is added a third, at least potential relation to his fellow men, in order to verify his understanding by joint understanding). It follows for the hermeneutic removal of hindrances to understanding that apart from difficulties of understanding that can be removed by the manifold means of philological and historical interpretation, there are also difficulties of a kind that have their ground in the relation to the matter in question and to overcome which we must therefore also begin with that relation.[1]

3. A third correction of the common view relates to the seemingly so straightforward and sensible *distinction between exegesis* or interpretation *and hermeneutics*. It is true that this distinction brings us into certain difficulties with the wide use in Greek of ἑρμηνεύειν, which of course is really a synonym of ἐξηγεῖσθαι and *interpretari*.[2] But why should a terminology of somewhat arbitrary coining, such as appeared in the seventeenth century with the concept hermeneutics, not be left as valid?

Now I think all the same that the basic meaning of ἑρμηνεύειν, 'to bring to understanding', which combines the various meanings 'state', 'expound' and 'translate', accords very well with the real sense of hermeneutics. Indeed, I hold it moreover to be in the nature of the case that the words 'interpretation' and 'hermeneutics' at bottom mean the same. True, it is at first sight one thing to interpret and another to reflect on the method of interpretation. We do not expect the same of New Testament exegesis as of New Testament hermeneutics. Yet how is hermeneutic insight actually acquired? Where does hermeneutics itself find the basis of its knowledge? If hermeneutics is the theory of understanding, then how, we must surely ask, does understanding itself come to understanding? If hermeneutics as the theory of understanding is the theory of words, how then does 'word' itself come to expression[3] so that there can be a theory of words? If hermeneutics is to be an aid to understanding, an auxiliary in the word-event, then where is understanding opened up in such a way that aid to understanding is to be expected from that quarter? Where do words so encounter us, where do words so take place, that therein the word-event itself comes into view? If, as we have made clear, 'word' itself is a hermeneutic principle, i.e. is that from which understanding proceeds and in which it has its origin, then hermeneutics as the theory of words must thus arise from the word-event itself. *Hermeneutics therefore, in order to be an aid to interpretation, must itself be interpretation.* Here we have the famous

---

[1] Luther knew about that: *Res sunt praeceptores. Qui non intelligit res, non potest ex verbis sensum elicere. Quare Munsterus saepe errat, quia res non intelligit. Ego plures locos explicavi per cognitionem rerum quam reliqua cognitione grammatices. Si iureconsulti ȵon intelligerent res, verba nemo intelligeret. Quare studium rerum,* that's the thing (*WA Table Talk* 5, p. 26.11-16, No. 5246). *Sola ergo superest grammatica, quam decet Theologiae cedere, cum non res verbis, sed verba rebus subiecta sint et cedant, et vox merito sensum sequatur et litera spiritum*—*WA* 5, p. 634.14-16 (*Op. in ps.*).

[2] *RGG*[3] III, p. 243.

[3] Cf. my note on terms, p. 294 above, note 1.—*Translator.*

hermeneutic circle in its methodological significance for hermeneutics itself.

The question which is now constitutive for hermeneutics—the question where we are encountered by *the* word-event which becomes the source of the understanding of word-events, which is thus of relevance for fundamental ontology, and which we have to hold to in order to achieve hermeneutic insight—is a question which obviously calls for ultimate decisions and therefore also, as we must suppose, gives rise to ultimate differences. For although hermeneutics is meant to serve understanding, and therefore assuredly also agreement, yet it is part of the phenomenon of understanding that the ground of the understanding, being a point beyond which no further questioning is possible, confronts us with a decision. Comprehensive differences of understanding, such as those for example between the confessions, are therefore of a hermeneutic kind and by their antithetical character point the ultimate limits of the possibility of agreement, just because they touch upon ultimate mysteries of the ground of understanding. This much, however, can be said in general terms on the question of what has to be the guiding light of hermeneutics: it must be a word-event in the comprehensive sense that it embraces both linguistic tradition and encounter with reality. Only by facing up to both of these together can hermeneutic knowledge be acquired.

IV

Our observations on the nature of hermeneutics, which were meant to take us beyond the common view, have remained still in abstract generalities and have also still left aside entirely the question of theological hermeneutics. In the short space at my disposal I can neither develop the first step I have indicated towards a hermeneutic theory of 'words' and thereby make it concrete, nor can I enter into all the many important theological problems which now present themselves again the more forcibly for having been left out of account meantime. Any reasonable man will pardon that, provided I add a few pointers at least to bring us to the *basic problem of theological hermeneutics.* I do so in three steps, by remarking on the relation between general and theological hermeneutics, on the relation between word and Word of God, and finally on the point with which we started—the relation between text and sermon.

1. In our introductory deliberations the question arose whether the Word of God and hermeneutics do not stand to each other in a relation-

ship of outright hostility, so that faith in the Word of God would forbid
the hermeneutic approach and the hermeneutic approach would destroy
the concept of the Word of God. The central point in our deliberations
on hermeneutics—*viz*. that 'word' itself has a hermeneutic character
and hermeneutics is the theory of 'word'—now suggests as a corresponding proposition: *theological hermeneutics is the theory or doctrine of
the Word of God.* The seeming simplicity of this step, however, must
not allow us to overlook the problems it involves. For in fact the very
point in dispute is, whether and how far there is room for the two propositions alongside of each other.

This much, however, must be clear: if the concept of the Word of
God is to be taken strictly, then of course the Word of God must be
ascribed hermeneutic relevance for theology, i.e. the Word of God must
then in itself be a source of theological understanding; and the structure
of the understanding peculiar to theology must result from the essential
structure of the Word of God. The fact that hermeneutics of such a kind,
as a theological doctrine of understanding, is then a doctrine of the
Word of God and consequently already *materialiter* interpretation of
theological statements, is surely just as little objection as the fact that
then hermeneutics is ascribed the role of a basic theological methodology
and its restriction to the methodology of individual theological disciplines *viz.*—the exegetical ones—is set aside.

On the other hand, we must explicitly consider the rightness of the
proviso we have just made in regard to these statements. Is *the concept
of the Word of God to be taken strictly*, i.e. does it mean *word in the proper
sense*, or is Word of God a mythical concept and therefore only symbolical in character, and is the speaking structure that belongs to the so-
called Word of God consequently also that of mythical speaking and the
structure of understanding that belongs to it that of mythical understanding? This is the decisive point for determining whether the Word
of God allows of conjunction with the idea of hermeneutics with its roots
in the Greek concept of the Logos. For the mythical as such does not
tolerate that conjunction. *In face of the mythical, hermeneutics must become de-mythologizing.* For we have departed from mythical thinking
the moment we adopt the hermeneutic approach. That Christian faith
has adopted the hermeneutic approach is indeed identical with its having
assented to the possibility and necessity of theology. And that again was
expressed in its asserting an association between the biblical concept of
the Word of God and the Logos concept of Greek philosophy. It is true
that in doing so, the considerable difference between the two was largely

obliterated. But an interpretation in terms of pure antithesis would not do justice to the significant fact that what the Bible means by 'word' does not, for all its differences, put out of commission what the Greek understands by 'word', while on the other hand the Greek conception of hermeneutics, with its root in the Logos idea, allows of being corrected in the light of the biblical understanding of 'word'.

This is true in the first instance quite apart from the concept of the Word of God. For in what the Bible understands by 'word' and (not unconnected with that) in the characteristic way the biblical thinker's understanding works and in what he understands by 'reality', experiences are comprised and dimensions of understanding opened up which permitted of an exceedingly fruitful encounter with Greek thought. But now, the concept of the Word of God forms no exception to that, in so far as 'Word' here does not mean any special, supernatural Word (and incidentally, God does not mean any separate, special Reality), but true, proper, finally valid Word.[1] For that reason theological hermeneutics can find itself over wide areas in agreement with non-theological hermeneutics, but where the hermeneutic problem reaches the ultimate ground of understanding, must enter into conflict with all non-theological hermeneutics—not in order to defend its own special right to independent existence, but in order to maintain responsibly to all comers in the field of hermeneutics the fact that God's Word is the ultimate ground of understanding because it is here in the last analysis that word is encountered as word and understanding as understanding. For the claim to truth which is made here means truth absolutely. And for that reason it always combines both things: agreement with all truth and opposition to what everyone is expected to reject as untruth.

2. The point we have just mentioned, the *relation between Word of God and word in general*, requires some further elucidation. It is a cardinal error in theology when God is spoken of as a part of reality and when for that reason God is thought of as something additional to the rest of reality, so that we should first of all have to speak of God and the world in themselves as two separate entities side by side and only then of their relationship as one of mutual supplementation or of mutual competition; whereas the fact is, that God cannot be spoken of in theology without the world thereby coming to expression as event, and the

---

[1] On what follows cf. the chapters 'The Communication of Faith' and 'The Word of God and Language' in G. Ebeling, *The Nature of Faith*, 1961, pp. 84 ff, 182 ff.

world cannot be spoken of in theology without God thereby likewise coming to expression as event.

This cardinal error by which theology is constantly threatened is also the ground of the fundamental misunderstanding according to which God's Word is so to speak a separate class of word alongside the word spoken between men, which is otherwise the only thing we usually call word. God's Word is here said to be not really word at all in the sense of the normal, natural, historic word that takes place between men. It is said that, if it would reach man, then it must first be transformed into a human word, translated as it were from God's language into man's language—a process in which, as in every process of translation, we have naturally to reckon with certain foreshortenings and distortions. These short-comings are then exculpated by means of the idea of accommodation, or the process is interpreted as analogous to the incarnation: As God finally took the highest, or lowest, step of becoming man, so (it is said) God's Word earlier, and in another form of course also later, becomes at least a human word. But this is a conglomeration of dreadful misinterpretations which cannot here be submitted to detailed critical analysis. Let me make only this one brief remark: when John 1.14 says that the Word became flesh, that surely means (interpreted of course in very abbreviated terms) that here word became event in a sense so complete that being word and being man became one. But that does not allow of any analogical transference to the relation of two kinds of word—let us say for the moment, in order to lay bare the metaphysical misunderstanding it contains, of heavenly word and earthly word. When the Bible speaks of God's Word,[1] then it means here unreservedly word as word—word that as far as its word-character is concerned is completely normal, let us not hesitate to say: natural, oral word taking place between man and man.

The Bible can, of course, radically contrast God's Word and man's word, but not in regard to the question of the verbal, or to put it still more sharply, spoken character of the word concerned, but in view of the question who is the real speaker of it: God, who is *verax*, or man, who is *mendax*.[2] Thus the point of the contrast is whether the word-event is one that is misused and corrupted by man, or whether it is one that is sound, pure, and fully realized—which is what is meant to be the

---

[1] Cf. G. Bornkamm, 'Gotteswort und Menschenwort in NT', in *Studien zu Antike und Urchristentum* (*Ges. Aufs. II*), Beitr. zur evang. Theol. 28 (1959), pp. 223-36; R. Hermann, *Gotteswort und Menschenwort in der Bibel: Eine Untersuchung zu theol. Grundfragen der Hermeneutik*, Berlin 1956.

[2] Rom. 3.4.

destiny, and indeed the natural destiny, of words in human society. And that implies at the same time a contrast in what the word produces: whether it is a destructive and deadly word or one that brings wholeness and gives life. The full theological bearing of this difference, however, can come to light only when word is really taken as word, and when it is clear that God and word are no more contradictory than man and word, but on the contrary it is 'word' that unites God and man.

To make that clear would require a comprehensive analysis which must certainly take its bearings on the Word of God, yet in such a way that in so doing the whole range of experience with words is kept in view and called upon. Here of course it would then be necessary for the profound *difference between the Greek and Hebrew understanding of word, truth and reality*[1] to be examined—*viz.* that (in accordance with the different etymology) Logos on the one hand means 'coherence',[2] and on the other hand דבר means that in which a thing shows itself:[3] on the one hand a timeless, on the other a historic understanding of word. And no doubt it is only the latter that really lays hold of what words mean for man's existence between God and the world. Word is, taken strictly, happening word. It is not enough to enquire into its intrinsic meaning, but that must be joined up with the question of its future, of what it effects. For ultimately the questions as to the content and the power of words are identical. Word is therefore rightly understood only when it is viewed as an event which—like love—involves at least two. The basic structure of word is therefore not statement—that is an abstract variety of the word-event—but apprisal, certainly not in the colourless sense of information, but in the pregnant sense of participation and communication.

That helps to clarify the question of why words are required at all. It is a long way off the mark when 'word' is understood as a technical means of rational intercourse. Certainly it must serve as that, too; and if we traced that idea to its roots, then we should doubtless also come

---

[1] H. von Soden, 'Was ist Wahrheit? Vom geschichtlichen Begriff der Wahrheit', in *Urchristentum und Geschichte I* (1951), pp. 1-24; L. Köhler, *Der hebräische Mensch*, 1953, pp. 117 ff; Thorleif Boman, *Das hebräische Denken im Vergleich mit dem griechischen*, (1952), 2nd ed. 1954, esp. pp. 45 ff. [*Hebrew Thought compared with Greek*, trans. J. L. Moreau, 1960, pp. 58 ff.]

[2] *TWNT* IV, p. 78.34.

[3] Whether this attempt to formulate the specific character of the Hebrew understanding of word can be justified also from the etymological standpoint is admittedly questionable. On the disputed etymology of דבר cf. O. Grether, *Name und Wort Gottes im AT*, Beih. zur ZAW 64 (1934), pp. 59 ff; O. Procksch in *TWNT* IV, pp. 89 f; T. Boman, *op. cit.*, p. 52 [p. 65].

upon the decisive point. More appropriate is the more comprehensive answer for which our discussion has already paved the way: word serves understanding. Where word happens rightly, existence is illumined (and that naturally always means: existence in association with others). We could, however, still go a step further and in seeming tautology say: word serves speaking. And the mocking counter-question whether it is really such a serviceable thing would have to be met and mastered by a 'Yes indeed!' If the word is the thing which shows what the speaker is, then we should have to say: the precise *purpose which the word is meant to serve is, that man shows himself as man.* For that is his destiny. And for that reason word is absolutely necessary to man as man. For his destiny is to exist as response. He is asked what he has to say. He is not destined to have nothing to say and to have to remain dumb. His existence is, rightly understood, a word-event which has its origin in the Word of God and, in response to that Word, makes openings by a right and salutary use of words. Therein man is the image of God.

The fact that man fails towards man, and so for that very reason also towards God, in the right use of words lends urgency to the search for that word which is a true, necessary, salutary, remedial and therefore unequivocal and crystal clear word, for the word which, because it accords with man's destiny, corresponds to God, that is, for the word by means of which one man can speak God to another so that God comes to man and man to God. That salvation is to be expected solely from God and that salvation is to be expected solely from words and is therefore at one and the same time a wholly divine and a wholly human thing —these are no paradoxes and whimseys.

This opens up a deeper insight into the nature of the word-event. As communication word is promise. It is most purely promise when it refers to something that is not present but absent—and that, too, in such a way that in the promise the absent thing so to speak presents itself; that is, when in word the speaker pledges and imparts himself to the other and opens a future to him by awakening faith within him. The conjunction of God, word, faith, future as the prime necessity for the good of man's human nature requires to be understood as a single vast coherent complex and not as some sort of chance conglomeration to be accepted on positivist terms.

This word-event takes place, Christians confess, in the Gospel. It is savingly related to the word-event which always proceeds from God and strikes the foolish man as the law which kills. But for that reason, too, it is only in the light of the Gospel that we can grasp what God's Word

really means and how far the law is God's Word. For God's Word must
not on any account be reduced to a formal concept which would be
indifferent towards any intrinsic definition of the Word of God.[1] For
God's Word is not various things, but one single thing—the Word that
makes man human by making him a believer, i.e. a man who confesses
to God as his future and therefore does not fail his fellowmen in the one
absolutely necessary and salutary thing, *viz.* true word.

3. There is no need to state here the reasons *why* the proclamation of
the Word of God appeals to scripture, and scripture thus becomes the
text of the sermon. I would merely go on to add in conclusion an
explanation of *how* that happens, in what sense scripture is the text of
the sermon, and thus how *text and sermon* are related to each other.

We begin with the question: What is the aim of the text? It aims at
all events to be preserved, read and handed on—and that, too, in the
service of the proclamation. Here of course we should at once have to
make differentiations, not only between Old and New Testament texts,
but also in both cases between different degrees of explicitness with
which the aim is proclamation. The question of the aim of the text
could indeed be shifted from the individual text to the biblical canon as
such. It would of course be a question whether the original intention of
the canon would be done justice to by asserting that it aims at being a
collection of sermon texts. But above all in face of the individual text it
would be a doubtful proceeding to ignore that text itself where this basic
question is concerned. It should not be supposed that any and every
text in holy scripture is in itself a sermon text. What is claimed to be a
sermon text must at all events seek to serve the proclamation of the Word
of God. Yet it would not be right to say: *the text* seeks to be proclaimed.
Apart from the fact that such a direct, authoritative aim is present in
relatively few texts, that way of putting it would also be fundamentally
wrong. For it is not *texts* that are to be proclaimed. Rather, it is God's
Word that is to be proclaimed, and that is one single Word, but not
Words of God,[2] not a variety of different texts.

---

[1] Cf. above, pp. 247 ff, esp. 267 ff.

[2] L. Köhler in his *Theologie des AT*, 1936, p. 90 [*Old Testament Theology*,
trans. A. S. Todd, London 1958, pp. 106 f] draws attention to a 'linguistic point
that is usually neglected. What the prophets are given to deliver is always called
the Word of Yahweh. It is never called *a* Word of Yahweh, in fact that expression
probably never occurs at all. Each individual revelation is called not a Word, but
the Word of Yahweh, so that when a string of individual messages follow each
other, each of them can be introduced by the formula: "then the Word of
Yahweh came." Thus in each individual revelation the whole Word of God is
always expressed.'

Indeed, we must put a still sharper point on it: if the word-character of God's Word is taken strictly, then it is absurd to designate a transmitted text as God's Word. Not out of contempt for its content or for its being written, but rather precisely out of respect for both. It is of course entirely true of sermon texts by and large that they are concerned with proclamation that has taken place, and to that extent—if it was right proclamation—with past occurrence of the Word of God. Naturally the form of direct speech on God's part cannot here rank as criterion. It is significant that with Jesus (apart from Christian imitations of the prophets) the stylistic form 'Thus saith the Lord' ceases—a fact well worth bearing in mind for the doctrine of the Word of God. But if it is a case of proclamation that has taken place, then we shall have to say of the sermon text: its aim is, that there should be further proclamation —and that, too, with an ear open towards the text, in agreement with it and under appeal to it.

The process from text to sermon can therefore be characterized by saying: proclamation that has taken place is to become proclamation that takes place. This transition from text to sermon is a transition from scripture to the spoken word. Thus the task prescribed here consists in making what is written into spoken word or, as we can now also say, in letting the text become God's Word again. That that does not normally happen through recitation, should surely be clear. If the concept of exposition can now be applied to this process, then we should have to say it is a question of interpreting the text *as word.*

But is the application of the concept 'exposition' here not questionable? This misgiving is in fact justified. Yet we must be very careful in giving place to it. For it is manifestly true all the same that the movement from the text to the sermon is a hermeneutic process in which, indeed to an eminent degree, it is a case of understanding and bringing to understanding. It would undoubtedly be wrong to assert that this movement from the text to the sermon does not come within the scope of the hermeneutic problem as posed by that text. For if its aim is, that what it has proclaimed should be further proclaimed, then the hermeneutic task prescribed by the text in question is not only not left behind when we turn to the sermon, but is precisely then for the first time brought to its fullest explication. The problem of theological hermeneutics would not be grasped without the inclusion of the task of proclamation; it is not until then that it is brought decisively to a head at all. And that, too, because the biblical texts would not be rightly heard unless they were seen to present us with the task of proclamation.

As it happens, the coming to a head of the hermeneutic problem in this way is not by any means peculiar to theology alone. We have an analogous case in legal hermeneutics. The *problem of legal hermeneutics* would be inadequately characterized if we left out of account the question of how to master the task of understanding that arises from the relation between the legal sources and the task of giving legal decisions in the present—in such a way, namely, that the traditional legal sources point the way to legal decisions in the present and thus become an illuminating source of understanding for the complications of the present legal case. It is true that one can also stop at a purely historical interpretation by examining the traditional legal sources with regard to the situation in which they arose and the sense in which they were then meant. Yet it cannot be called a falsification of the hermeneutic task when the legal sources, so far as they are presently still in force, are examined with regard to their bearing on this or that legal case. Certainly the text makes an unconditional demand for historical interpretation. But the so-called application to the present case is nevertheless not something entirely independent of that. For the judge must be expected to give a legal decision according to the laws that are presently valid. It is expected that in encountering the present concrete case the received text as an illuminating, clarifying, guiding word will become the source of legal understanding and therefore too the source of legal decision. Thus not merely the source of past legal decision, but as the source of past legal decision it becomes the source of legal decision in the present. Certainly the accents shift where hermeneutics is concerned. But they allow of only relative separation from each other. The man who has no interest in giving legal decisions will be a poor legal historian. And the man who does not trouble himself with historical interpretation jeopardizes the purity of his legal decisions in the present.

The reference to this analogy would require to be further developed in order to bring to expression the difference between it and the problem of theological hermeneutics. But neither is a special case. Rather, both make clear the structure of the hermeneutic problem in general, since in every case historical understanding joins with some form or other of expectation of further present understanding, interest in the past unites with interest in the future (as also conversely interest in the future with interest in the past). The relative distinction between the two hermeneutic aspects can perhaps also be given terminological expression as follows:—The sermon as such is in point of fact not *exposition* of the text—whereby exposition here means the concentration on the historical task of understanding. For to understand this text as a text means to understand it in its historical givenness as proclamation that has taken place. Now of course the sermon certainly does presuppose intensive efforts towards such understanding of the text. How could it otherwise appeal to it? And it contains also according to the particular circumstances a greater or less degree of explicit interpretation of the text. But the sermon as a sermon is not exposition of the text as past proclamation, but is itself proclamation in the present—and that means, then, that *the sermon is* EXECUTION *of the text*. It carries into execution the aim of the text. It is proclamation of what the text has proclaimed. And with that the hermeneutic sense of direction is so to speak reversed. The text which has attained understanding in the exposition now helps to bring to understanding what is to attain understanding by means of the sermon —which is (we can here state it briefly) the present reality *coram Deo*, and that means, in its radical futurity. *Thus the text by means of the sermon becomes a hermeneutic aid in the understanding of present experience.* Where that happens radically, there true word is uttered, and that in fact means God's Word.

The real rub in the hermeneutic problem, as it presents itself for theology, consists in the connexion between exposition of the text as proclamation that has taken place and execution of the text in proclamation in the present. The *concept of existentialist*[1] *interpretation* has been employed to characterize this fundamental hermeneutic problem. The efforts towards a closer definition of it are still going on.[2] I think the concept can be meaningful and helpful if it brings out the fact that existence is existence through word and in word. Then existentialist interpretation would mean *interpretation of the text with regard to the word-event*. There, in my opinion, lies the decisive startingpoint from which to direct historical exposition towards the utmost fulfilment of its task, and precisely in so doing to gain

---

[1] The German word is *existential*, and in seeking to understand Bultmann and his associates it is of paramount importance to distinguish between this word and *existentiell*. The latter is used in the now familiar sense of complete personal involvement, whereas *existential* is what relates to the nature of existence or to the (proper) understanding of it. Thus e.g. an 'existential statement' (*existentiell*) is one that in some way vitally involves the speaker's personal existence and gives expression to it. An 'existentialist interpretation' (*existential*) of such a statement is one that interprets it in terms of the real truth of existence as such. In the interests of uniform translation policy I follow here the practice adopted by the editors of the American series 'New Frontiers in Theology', *viz.* of using 'existentialist' to render *existential*, and 'existential' for *existentiell*.—*Translator*.

[2] See above all E. Fuchs, *Ges. Aufsätze* I, pp. 65 ff.

criteria for the inner hermeneutic connexion between text and sermon. *The hermeneutic principle* would then, in accord with what we said earlier, be the word-event itself. For hermeneutics, we said, is the theory of words. And we can now designate as identical with that, because merely the radicalization of it, the fact that theological hermeneutics is the doctrine of the Word of God, but that for that very reason there can also be doctrine of the Word of God only as theological hermeneutics. In view of that the hermeneutic principle could be given various precise definitions. With an eye to the real sphere of the word-event I suggest for consideration the formula: the hermeneutic principle is *man as conscience*. I refrain here from further attempts to ground and elucidate that. For a principle should surely be something that is obvious of itself, or at all events gives clear guidance and proves its fitness in use.[1]

[1] This does not rule out the need to form an exactly defined *concept* of conscience. Let me merely recall, as against the superficial objections that are to be expected on the ground of the dominant rules of theological language, that for Luther *'theologice'* was synonymous with *'in conscientia'*: (on Gal. 5.1) *Est libertas a lege, peccatis, morte, a potentia diaboli, ira dei, extremo iudicio. Ubi? in conscientia, Ut sic iustus sim, quod Christus sit liberator et reddat liberos, non carnaliter non politice, diabolice, sed theologice i.e. tantum in conscientia* (*WA* 40/2, p. 3.5-8).

XII

RUDIMENTARY REFLEXIONS ON SPEAKING RESPONSIBLY OF GOD*

To Emil Brunner on his 70th birthday

I F in the doctrine of God we are not content to treat the subjects in the order in which they usually appear in dogmatics, but begin where the question of understanding is at its most urgent, then it seems to me we are not pointed to this or that question of detail in the doctrine of God. Rather, we are faced in embarrassing ways by the whole problem of how a 'doctrine of God' is possible and necessary at all. For what 'God' may mean must not be left as a presupposition to be taken for granted, but must be faced as a real question. The best sort of instruction we can expect at all from a doctrine of God is surely precisely that it should tell us what 'God' means, if indeed that can really be learned by instruction. If, however, the doctrine of God thus forces itself upon us as one comprehensive subject, then within the scope of an essay we must surely be content to marshall a few points which serve to fix the bearings of the position in which we find ourselves with regard to the task of producing a doctrine of God.[1]

I

The doctrine of God is *the most comprehensive and most difficult task of theology*, because it concerns the ground of theology itself. In view of the etymology of the name of this science, it does indeed seem tautological to say that the doctrine of God is concerned with the essence, and therefore the whole, of theo-logy. But if we keep in view the terminological difference between 'theology' in the narrow sense as doctrine of God and 'theology' in the normal, comprehensive sense as

---

* In *Der Auftrag der Kirche in der Welt. Festgabe zum 70. Geburtstag von Emil Brunner*, Zwingli Verlag Zurich and Stuttgart, 1959, pp. 19-40.
[1] In what follows I take up in somewhat greater detail questions that were touched on in my book *Das Wesen des christlichen Glaubens* (Tübingen 1959) in chapter VI under the heading 'Die Wahrheit des Glaubens' (pp. 86-101) [*The Nature of Faith*, ch. VI, 'The Truth of Faith' (pp. 72-83)]. Occasionally I have taken over a phrase from there.

the doctrinal statement of the whole content of the Christian message, then it is surprising to be told that the special statement of the doctrine of God is the most difficult task of theology, because it is the one that concerns the ground of theology itself.

It could possibly be taken to mean that the doctrine of God performs a kind of propaedeutic function. After all, the people to whom Jesus Christ is to be preached as the Son of God obviously must already have some sort of knowledge of God and faith in God if they are to understand such preaching. Accordingly, traditional dogmatics built itself a general metaphysical foundation in the doctrine of God. But just because of that propaedeutic function one would be inclined to rank the doctrine of God among the humble first steps in theology.

The average Christian, indeed, is more or less of the opinion that the 'higher regions' of Christian doctrine, like the doctrine of the Trinity, Christology, the theory of satisfaction and so on, are hard for him to approach and can only with difficulty be incorporated into his faith, whereas the simple belief in God the Father is what he lives by as a Christian. The theological rigorist usually makes the same gradations, but then exalts himself above the poverty of a minimum faith of that kind. I confess that I find the theological rigorists suspect and my heart beats more and more for those for whom the great traditional formulae of Christian doctrine are stones instead of bread.

The discrepancy between what theology, and also preaching, recognizes and puts forward as central and decisive and what Christians in practice live by where the spirit is concerned, is uncomfortably large today. We theologians, too—and we in particular—have to ask ourselves how far our theological insights and also our theological interests are really things from which and in which our faith lives, or to put it simply: things that can also shape our prayers. That is not by any means intended to break a lance for a primitive outlook in theology. Differences must certainly be maintained here. Prayer must not become theological, and theology must not become liturgy or be reduced to our own personal piety. But it is not in order either when the accents are totally different in theology and in prayer, and when we have thus only a contemptuous smile for, say, the theology of the Enlightenment, while on the other hand we find ourselves in our own prayers at the level of a completely undogmatic piety. It is not good when theology resembles a perfect arrangement of glass beads instead of a sorely suffering hospital service —that is, when it is not related to real man as so to speak a theology of blood and tears.

But now, the very mention of contemporary man destroys the illusion that the doctrine of God is the most easily approached gateway to theology, the point at which we can still most likely reckon on general understanding and even on a certain amount of agreement. The word God widely encounters today such a fundamental lack of understanding that from this angle, if indeed God is what makes theology to be really theology, the whole of theology is also called in question. And rightly so, as surely as the truth and reality of every theological statement depends on the truth and reality of God, and as surely as theology must be expected to convince itself radically of the truth and reality of its statements. To that there corresponds also the fact that the particular doctrinal statements in Christian proclamation are not additions of some kind to a general faith in God, but nothing other than the explication of faith in God. Then, however, as we could now also say, with the doctrine of God our subject becomes not a single theological proposition, but the essence of all theological propositions and consequently the logic and ontology of theological statements.

II

If we enquire into the possibility of a doctrine of God, then we find ourselves *pointed to tradition and dependent on tradition*. I might have been expected to emphasize instead of that the dependence on revelation. Here, however, we are concerned with a phenomenological observation that does not exclude that aspect, but merely puts a bracket round it.

That in the doctrine of God we are pointed to tradition and dependent on tradition means not only that we are then committed to an imposing tradition of an intellectual, theological kind from which we have to learn and with which we have to enter into debate. That is of course correspondingly true of all scientific work. We come nearer to what is meant when in, beside and behind that kind of intellectual, dogmatic tradition concerning the doctrine of God we become aware of a tradition of speaking about God which springs from entirely different depths and sweeps through the ages with overwhelming breadth and power—a tradition by which our speaking of God is supported and on which it is entirely dependent, even if we should struggle against it and the way it determines like some primeval river the whole mental landscape. It leaves us no room for real independence, no possibility of an independent and creative grasp of the subject 'God'. We are dependent on what this stream of tradition brings us and says to us. It is the source from which, if at all, we must derive our doctrine of God. That, too, has its parallel in everything that has any connexion at all with the historical roots of our existence: in the tie that binds us to traditional mental associations stretching back far out of sight. Save that where religion is concerned the predetermining, moulding power of the historical has doubtless its greatest effect—so much so, indeed, that religious and historical ties largely merge altogether into one.

As far as our own situation is concerned, it is evident that the task of stating the doctrine of God points us to the biblical Christian tradition. To go on to ask why that should actually be so, leads to problems of a far-reaching and complex kind. For the formal reference to revelation of course merely describes the authority of this tradition, but does not explain it. We content ourselves here with stating the fact of our being bound to this tradition which leaves us as Christians—apart from the inexhaustible task of understanding—basically nothing new to discover or invent in the doctrine of God. Indeed, even the man who finds himself only under the more distant influence of this stream of biblical tradition cannot possibly develop a doctrine of God which would not be most deeply determined by it, even if only by way of antithesis. For here, over and above the actual power of the biblical tradition, there is also an element at work which in essence is highly significant and to which we shall return later, *viz.* the fact that contact with the biblical tradition of the understanding of God has consequences which can never again be undone.

But now, it would be an illusion to suppose that in regard to the doctrine of God we can confine ourselves exclusively to the biblical stream of tradition. For already at the very beginning of church history the traditions of biblical Christianity and of Greek philosophy entered, precisely in the concept of God, into an alliance which determined the whole future history of the doctrine of God. On the one hand the doctrine of God in dogmatics was, and largely still is, erected on the basis of this union. And indeed, from the historical point of view, to affirm this union is the very shibboleth of Orthodoxy. While on the other hand it has been regarded as the source of every false development in the history of the Christian doctrine of God.

The emphasis on the antithesis is an outstanding mark of the more recent evangelical theology. 'The ":God" of Plato and Aristotle', as Emil Brunner, for example, puts it, 'stands to the God of the biblical revelation in the relation of Either-Or. The same is true of every other idea of God acquired in purely philosophical speculative ways.'[1] Or Friedrich Karl Schumann: 'Augustine's proposition, apparently so harmless and to our ear—even an ear tuned to the Bible!—so self-evident, that "God" is the *aeterna veritas*, is the proposition that has the most far-reaching and disastrous consequences in all European thought.'[2] The affirmation of such an antithesis between—to use the customary slogans —the God of the Bible and the God of metaphysics can certainly only be rightly worked into theology when we realize that it is impossible to undo the problematical alliance that now happens to have been made and that therefore the doctrine of God can only be discussed in constant mutual contact and debate between the two streams of tradition. To try to achieve final separations here would betray not only a lack of historical training but also a lack of proper insight into the problem of the doctrine of God, which has obviously not by accident become the place of encounter between the two traditions—be it now in friendship or in mortal enmity.

But now we must take a step further. The whole complex of the other religious traditions of humanity is also a thing that must not be left out of account in striving to form the doctrine of God. For the simple reason, apart from all else, that the search for God demands the greatest possible openness towards reality. It is true, though, that in two respects we must at once lay down a sharply-defined boundary against any false intrusion of this point of view.

First, it must be recalled that early Christianity adopted not without reason a different attitude towards pagan religion and towards what in its historical origin was equally pagan philosophy. That heralds the very significant point that Christianity and philosophy join each other in their critique of pre-Christian religion. And that, as it seems, is connected with the point we have already indicated and shall later have to consider explicitly, *viz.* the element of irreversibility in the history of religion.

Secondly, however, it has to be noticed that the path of a neutral scientific study of religion can lead only to a phenomenology of the consciousness of God, but never to a doctrine of God. A phenomenology of the consciousness of God is unquestionably of significance for the doctrine of God. But theology would cease to be theology if it did not understand itself—in sharp contrast to the way the general scientific

[1] E. Brunner, *The Christian Doctrine of God, Dogmatics* I (ET, 1949), p. 136.
[2] F. K. Schumann, *Der Gottesgedanke und der Zerfall der Moderne*, 1929, pp. 7 f.

study of religion understands itself—as doctrine of God; which then certainly results in difficult problems of scientific methodology. For it presupposes being bound as a confessing Christian to the Christian understanding of God, since a doctrine of God is only possible when we are bound to a concrete religious tradition. That holds also of philosophy's speaking of God, in so far as it likewise springs from a definite religious soil and remains dependent on the existence of religious tradition.

That brings us down to a final substratum of the problem of the relation between God and tradition. What is the cause of this strange and, as it seems, contradictory association? Is God a historical phenomenon then, that he comes to us by way of tradition? Is he even himself only a piece of tradition? Now it would be a simple matter to correct that by saying: Naturally God is not a historical phenomenon; rather, the historical thing is only particular ideas of him, doctrines about him —in Christian terms, his revelations, his Word addressed to men. He himself, however, is eternal, unchangeable, beyond all history. Yet if that is supposed to mean that God can be given directly alongside of the tradition, so to speak for checking purposes, then it merely destroys our insight into the peculiar relationship of God and tradition. For God is no phenomenon immediately confronting us, no ascertainable object of direct investigation. Had we not heard of God, had we not been taught about him, were he not proclaimed to us, were he not announced to us, were he thus not handed down by tradition to us, what resources would we then really have for contesting a doctrine of God—indeed, how would the idea of a doctrine of God ever occur to us at all? The givenness of God means his existence in history.

This is indicated by the fact that at all events the original sphere in which God is spoken of is that comprehensive historical complex which we are accustomed to call 'religion' and which by its very nature is constituted by a tradition that has power to mould society and determine the whole context of life. Philosophical talk of God, on the other hand, whose nature is to dissociate itself from concrete religion with its community-building and its cultus, is from the purely phenomenological point of view not an equally original way of speaking of God, but one that is derived from that and dependent on it. But even philosophy in view of the actual history of our talk of God should grant that speaking of God has its proper sphere where God is accorded a place in history, and that on the other hand God can be spoken of only in borrowed ways where it appears contradictory in principle to think of

God and history together and to become involved in a definite tradition in order to encounter God.

It is true that there seem to be primarily two things which tell against this strong emphasis on the fact that God and tradition belong together. First, the problem of the origin of religious tradition in the first place. Even if it is a question here of an extremely rare event, and dependence on tradition is thus the normal thing, yet it does seem here that precisely the essential, because creative, relation to God is of a different kind. It belongs, however, to the very structure of that exceptional event, in which (as we might say) God has come to new expression, that men have experienced it purely passively as something that happened to them, something that they received, that was—albeit so to speak vertically—handed down.

A second objection, and one that concerns us directly, relates to the problem of the criterion of religious tradition. It would be senseless if in speaking of God we were completely at the mercy of the tradition with no mind of our own. That would mean surrendering our responsibility. But it would be self-contradictory to seek to relieve man of all responsibility at the very point where his responsibility is most sharply seen, in his relation to God. And surely the tradition itself constantly sets the task of using criticism to preserve and keep pure the tradition. A purely traditional relation to God is only a special kind of godlessness.

The question therefore arises: If we are rightly to understand what tradition says of God, and responsibly to assent to it, does that in itself not require that there should be a direct knowledge, a personal experience, an objective contact with God himself, unless what we say of God is to be speaking of something unreal and unverifiable? There is no doubt that the aspect of being dependent on tradition needs to be supplemented, or at least elucidated, in the direction of present experience of reality. For what does not stand in any demonstrable and intelligible connexion with the experience of reality that can be expected of me, cannot be responsibly appropriated by me at all. Presumably any attempt here to strike a balance between tradition and experience is *a priori* the sign of a false start—and the real point of being dependent on tradition is precisely that by means of the tradition God comes to be experienced in the real present. Here we find a profound link with the whole problem of language and reality. If we probe into the problem of language and consider the ontological problem in that context, then tradition and encounter with reality prove to belong very closely together as it is. But let us leave that merely as a pointer, and turn to a new aspect.

III

Our place in the history of religion is marked by the fact that *poly-theism is for us a thing of the past, while atheism is the possibility attaching to our own situation and as such determines our reality*. Now of course concepts like polytheism or monotheism and atheism are very indefinite. Their relativity may be illustrated by the fact that the apologist Athenagoras was able to say that Christians are really also polytheists, because they believe in divine hypostases such as light, power, etc., as also in a Son of God, in the Spirit and in angels,[1] while the apologist Justin sometimes (admittedly only in relation to the pagan gods) allowed the description of Christians as ἄθεοι (godless),[2] although the sole instance of the word in the New Testament applies on the contrary precisely to existence in pagan polytheism.[3]

Moreover, it is obvious that the antithesis between polytheism and monotheism must not by any means be identified with that between pagan and Christian faith in God, as if the question of God could ultimately be reduced to an abstract problem of arithmetic. At all events we should then have at some point to face questions such as:—Why should a plurality in the divine really be such an abhorrent thing? Might it not perhaps actually correspond to reality? And does the unquestioning acceptance of a monotheistic view not come under suspicion of obeying the dictates of a logical necessity, *viz.* of tracing everything back to one single principle and letting it all culminate in one single point? Even the very true observation that biblical monotheism sets God over against our reality as a whole, whereas pagan polytheistic thought lets the divine merge in our reality and our reality in the divine, has to be treated with caution, so far as the conclusion might possibly be drawn from it that it is peculiar to paganism to think of and experience the divine when it looks at this reality of ours, whereas it is the mark of Christianity to think in terms of two separate spheres of reality.

Yet polytheism is certainly an understanding of the divine which within the province of the biblical understanding of God has to be regarded as definitely over and done with, so that we can say in somewhat abbreviated form that there is no possibility of a return from Christianity to polytheism. The history of religion, too, like history in general, is subject to the law of irreversibility. And perhaps we may even see in the history of religion and its irreversibility the ultimate cause of the irreversibility of history in general. At all events, apart from

---

[1] *Plea for the Christians* 10.   [2] *I Apol.*, 6.   [3] Eph. 2.12.

fluctuations of a secondary kind, we know of a movement only in one direction, from polytheism to monotheism. This is obviously connected with certain laws of mental development.

So now, as it happens, the Christian faith agrees in certain respects with philosophical, rational enlightenment. It was so in the ancient world, and it is likewise observable today where Christian missions penetrate what is still originally pagan territory. It is certainly not the same thing whether the conscience is freed by faith from pagan religious or superstitious bonds, or whether the mind is enlightened on the emptiness of such ideas. But cross-links do legitimately exist. One must of course beware of thinking only the religious opponent vulnerable to criticism of myths and miracles. Thus the procedure of Boniface in demonstrating the nonentity of the pagan gods by felling the sacred oak was decidedly two-edged as if it were not the case that (if I may say so) just as little would have happened on overthrowing Christian altars, and thus the same line of argument could likewise have proved the nonentity of the Christian God. Or think how theologians today like to explain non-Christian religious phenomena in immanentist terms (psychologically, sociologically, etc.), but when it comes to their own statements of faith suddenly operate with a different concept of reality. Even such questionable inconsistency is still a reminder that with the coming of the Christian faith the understanding of reality underwent a change which cannot again be reversed. I need only recall slogans like de-idolizing the world, de-mythologizing, secularizing and giving historical form to reality, in order to indicate problem complexes which would here require examination but cannot be further pursued.

It is true that there is no lack of attempts to revitalize the mythical way of thinking and the pagan polytheistic reminiscences bound up with it. We might think, say, of Heidegger's remarks on the 'quaternity' of 'earth and heaven, divine beings and mortals'.[1] We should of course likewise have to note in it the clear symptoms of post-Christian thinking, such as the peculiar hovering between the divine beings as the 'beckoning heralds of the deity' and the God who appears in person as a result of their sacred offices—or the striking note of waiting and hoping, to which Heidegger atunes the attitude of the mortals towards the divine beings—or finally the sharp distinction drawn over against the manifestly pagan: 'They do not make for themselves their own gods and do not indulge in the service of idols.'[2] Much more rigorous is Walter Bröcker

---

[1] M. Heidegger, 'Bauen—Wohnen—Denken', in *Vorträge und Aufsätze*, 1954, pp. 149 f.   [2] *Op. cit.*, p. 151.

who, appealing to Hölderlin and going far beyond Heidegger, has recently championed a re-mythologizing in which Christianity of all things, interpreted as 'pagan Christianity', is now to be the means of regaining the mythical understanding of the world as it was originally given in the Greeks.[1] But Bröcker, too, lets it be seen that a simple return is impossible. For that reason, he says, even Hölderlin 'in his later years preferred to speak of spirits rather than of gods . . . in order to eliminate that element in the early Greek idea of god which is all too human and for us impossible'.[2]

If we would do justice to such attempts to regain the mythical, then we must see them against the background of an atheism which governs our spiritual situation to an extent that church and theology as a rule do not even come anywhere near to adequately realizing. A doctrine of God today, moreover, is abstract speculation if it does not have the phenomenon of modern atheism before it from the start. When I said earlier that atheism is the possibility attaching to our own situation and as such determines our reality, then I meant more by that than just the statistical fact that today a large section of humanity is subjected to the propaganda of a militant atheism and the part of humanity that lives in different circumstances is no less exposed to the problem of atheism. It is cold comfort to say that alarming forecasts were already made long ago but have not been fulfilled and that one would no longer venture to repeat them in such a form today. Thus already twenty years before the French Revolution, so Winckelmann reports, the idea was put forward in Rome that in half a century there would no longer be either pope or priest in the holy city.[3] Or in the second decade of the nineteenth century it is said to have been discussed at the dinner table on the Prussian minister of culture Altenstein (that is, within the sphere of the intellectual influence of Hegel) whether Christianity would only last another twenty or fifty years.[4] Despite one or two notable changes since then, we must not indulge in any illusions as to the fact that the full measure of the results of modern atheism is doubtless still ahead of us. But I am not concerned with statistics, or with forecasts either. I am concerned with the inner grasp of something which is far more complex than short-winded apologists suspect, and which does not by any means

---

[1] W. Bröcker, *Dialektik, Positivismus, Mythologie*, 1958.
[2] *Op. cit.*, p. 80.
[3] Quoted from E. Frank, *Philosophical Understanding and Religious Truth*, 1945, pp. 5 and 20.
[4] Quoted from K. Löwith, *Von Hegel zu Nietzsche* (1941), 2nd ed. 1950, p. 464.

threaten Christianity only from without, but has already also penetrated as it were through the walls of the heart into our inmost being as a sort of atmosphere whose influence no one can evade. If we enquire into the causes of atheism, then it is impossible to disregard the role which Christianity itself has played here. We might feel ourselves stung to remark that Christianity has proved itself to be the transition from polytheism to atheism. That with the same thoroughness with which it destroyed polytheism it has meanwhile also undermined its own foundation and prepared the way for atheism. And that as in the first case it rejoiced in the alliance with philosophy, so now in the second case it has been outplayed by philosophy, in that now the very thought of God, or at all events the biblical view of the personality of God, is being cleared aside as a remnant of mythological, anthropological belief in gods that has inadvertantly been left over. It is a fact that atheism in the form that troubles us is only to be understood from the history of Christianity. If for a moment we equate atheism with non-religiousness (which in view of phenomena such as Buddhism can only be done with reservations), then it is not to be found among the original historical potentialities of mankind. Modern ethnology has nowhere discovered peoples without religion. That is certainly not to be turned to apologetic account. To modern man it is of course hardly a convincing argument to prove to him that primitive peoples, mentally still under-developed, without exception were or are religious. The attempt has rightly been made to explain why it was only on Christian ground that atheism became a powerful possibility by pointing to the radical nature of the Christian understanding of God: only where God is so radically proclaimed and believed can he then also be so radically denied.[1]

If we would begin to sense the depth of the problem, then we must not stop at the phenomenon of common atheism, which is a changing mixture of rightly rejecting false ideas, and of simple-mindedness, presumption and volitional impulses of various kinds. Rather we must think of that basic experience which bursts upon a man with primeval force and in which nihilism is learned to be the dire truth of atheism. The sort of experience Jean Paul has presented in the form of a terrible dream in his so-called 'Rede des toten Christus, vom Weltgebäude herab, dass kein Gott sei' (Address by the dead Christ, from the heights of the cosmic system, to the effect that there is no God),[2] or the kind that

---

[1] H. Kössler, Art. 'Neuzeitlicher Atheismus, philosophisch', *RGG*³ I, p. 672.
[2] In *'Der Siebenkäs'*. Now also printed in G. Bornkamm, *Studien zu Antike und Urchristentum (Ges. Aufs. II)*, Beitr. z. ev. Theol. 28 (1959), pp. 245 ff.

Friedrich Nietzsche in the section entitled 'Der tolle Mensch' in *Fröhliche Wissenschaft* has described much more portentously as premature awakening from a dream.[1] We must surely go on to consider Heidegger's deeply penetrating interpretation of Nietzsche's saying, 'God is dead',[2] according to which nihilism heralds the end of Western metaphysics, yet not as an accident that befalls it from without, not as a mere phenomenon of decay, but in such a way that nihilism as the basic process in Western history is at the same time and above all the law to which that history conforms.

But we shall also have to consider alongside of that, or more correctly in conjunction with it, the phenomenon which may be called the limited, methodical atheism of modern science, the deliberate bracketing out of God, the way of encountering reality which *a priori* does not admit God. For to adopt the objective approach is in itself to look away from God. But how could theology venture simply to bring a charge of unbelief here? For indeed the very constraint of the confessional divisions contributed powerfully towards the development of modern science, since the co-existence of divided Christians made it necessary to leave the question of God strictly out of account in considering binding truth. And moreover, it was precisely a theology ruled by a false anxiety for the continuance of the Christian faith that to a great extent first drove modern science, contrary to its natural tendency, into hostility towards Christianity, and by foolish opposition gave rise to a distorted and compromising idea of the nature of the Christian faith itself. And furthermore, there is still behind all this confusion an unquestionable, if also indirect, connexion between the freedom towards the world which is disclosed in the Christian faith and the freedom which modern man uses in science. And indeed theology itself was unable to help opening its doors to the methodological demands of the modern view of science, so that, as can be seen from the effects on the principles of theology, rumblings of the problem of atheism made themselves heard in modern theology itself. If we thus take into account the full depth and breadth of the problems that go to make up the phenomenon of modern atheism, then it cannot surprise us that theology, as it seems to me, is only gradually beginning to grasp the breadth of the tasks confronting the doctrine of God today.

[1] *Fröhl. Wiss.* p. 125. Printed in M. Heidegger, *Holzwege* (1950), 2nd ed. 1952, pp. 198 f, as also in my book, *The Nature of Faith*, pp. 77 ff.
[2] 'Nietzsches Wort "Gott is tot" ', in *Holzwege*, pp. 193-247.

IV

Our thoughts must therefore turn to the *relation of God and reality*. We set them under the following head: real knowledge of God is knowledge of the reality of God. The reality of God, however, is on no account to be thought of like the reality of the world and consequently as a piece of the world's reality; nevertheless the reality of God can be expressed solely in view of the reality of the world. Knowledge of reality where God is concerned is assent to the claim which God in reality means. We emphasize three points in this.

1. We can be convinced of the reality of God only in absolute assent to God. There is no such thing as a preliminary and neutral discovery of the reality of God which would then only afterwards be followed by adopting a position of acceptance or possibly rejection. We cannot accept the existence of God in earnest—and knowing what 'God' means —and nevertheless refuse God. The man who denies God has not known him either. The knowledge of the reality of God, strictly understood, leaves no room to dissociate ourselves from God. The man who truly knows him, must also recognize and confess and worship him. Assent to the existence of God in the sense of a mere *praeambulum fidei* is therefore ultimately pointless and cannot be expected at all. Assent to the existence of God can be expected only in the form that faith in God is expected as such, with all that that means.

2. The man who accepts God accepts in his whole confession to God the reality of God. Thus the acceptance of God also cannot leave the question of the reality of God disinterestedly in the balance, but must face the full weight of that question. Consequently we can accept God responsibly only when in doing so we take responsibility for the statement of his reality.

3. Asserting our acceptance, and thus standing personally to what is said, is an essential element in speaking of God. A neutral, purely objective statement about God that left our own person entirely out of account would be a contradiction in terms or merely proof that we have not understood what we are talking about. By the very fact of my making a statement about God I am myself also involved in that statement. That does not mean that this fact of the speaker's also being involved must be brought out in so many words in the statement about God. But even a seemingly wholly objective statement about God, such as 'God is omnipotent', would be fundamentally misunderstood if it were not interpreted in view of the fact that the man who makes that statement

is also himself included in it. And indeed not merely in the sense that what is said has an application also to him, but also and above all in the sense that the man who makes the statement must stand surety for it, is responsible for the truth of the statement. And indeed so very much responsible that he cannot free himself by citing proofs or authorities of any kind, but must also take over the responsibility for it. The man who makes a statement about God, thereby—in spite of his dependence on tradition, in spite of the support he has in the fellowship of the faithful—stands entirely on his own feet as one who ventures to defend the cause of God, to stand surety with his own reality for the reality of God, with his own existence for the existence of God.

That sounds paradoxical, indeed downright impious, since the relation would surely really have to be expressed the other way round by saying that God's reality stands surety and provides for our reality, God's existence for our existence. How could we ever go further in the direction of the other statement? Should we say that speaking of God means we must stand surety with our love for God's love, with our wisdom for God's wisdom, with our power for God's power? Would it not then rather have to be said that we must stand surety with our lovelessness for God's love, with our foolishness for God's wisdom, with our impotence for God's omnipotence? But to what extent would that still be 'standing surety for'?

Is our speaking of God, if it really has this *assertio* character[1] that moves the whole responsibility on to our shoulders, not just a string of unfounded and unfoundable assertions? Is Feuerbach's anthropological interpretation of our talk of God not justified, if the whole responsibility, so to speak the whole burden of proof, for what is said of God falls in this way to the speaker, who yet fails to supply the proof? Our talk of God does in fact have so much *assertio* character, is in fact so little objectifiable and so closely bound up with the person of the speaker, that there is no certain safeguard against misunderstanding it as subjective caprice and pure illusion. For if it is true that the reality of God can be upheld only by the man who believes in God, then it is easy to infer that the reality of God is not the ground, but the result, of faith. It belongs to the affirmatory, assertive character of our talk of God that even this interpretation, fatal as it is to faith and consequently to speaking of God at all, cannot be resisted and refuted in any other way than by the practical proof of the confession that expresses the real truth, of

---

[1] Cf. Luther's use of the concept *assertio* in *De servo arbitrio*.

the *assertio* in which faith ascribes everything to God and nothing to itself.

There seems, however, to be a weighty objection that tells against this blunt emphasis on the *assertio* character of our talk of God: Is it not necessary to presuppose at all events an understanding of the word 'God', but therewith obviously also a knowledge which, whatever is to be said of it, is a knowledge of God? For the sake of the question of understanding, something else must surely still be added if acceptance of God is not to assume the character of a magic circle.

V

The thing would now be to enter into the problem of the so-called proofs of God on the one hand and the biblical idea of knowing God on the other. But being free to confine myself to one or two remarks, I will only point to the following problems.

1. *The understanding of what the word 'God' means has its place within the sphere of radical questionableness.* The question how God is actually experienced, how it can actually become clear what God means in the context of the reality that encounters me, can be answered in the first instance only by the pointer: God is experienced as a question. In the context of the reality that encounters me God encounters me as the questionableness of that encountering reality. What the word 'God' means can in the first instance according to its structure be described only as a question. The man who does not venture to ask questions is closed to the meaning of the word 'God'. To him the word 'God' says absolutely nothing. The questionableness which encounters us along with the encountering reality provides, however vaguely, the reason why it can be claimed that what is said of God concerns every man and therefore can also in principle be intelligible to every man—*viz.* because it relates to something that has to do with the reality which encounters him.

This is not a matter of some kind of natural knowledge of God in the sense of a positive consciousness of God. We could perhaps say it is a question of the condition on which it is possible for the problem of a natural knowledge of God to arise—unless indeed we prefer to leave aside the tainted concept 'natural'. Even what claims to be revealed knowledge of God must of course, since it includes the claim to be intelligible and binding, make its claim in view of something which has to do with the person addressed. It would be premature to designate that an inborn, original knowledge of God. It would likewise be premature to characterize it as the quest *for God* that is native to man as man, if indeed the quest for God already presupposes some kind of knowledge of what it seeks. Rather, the thing to which our talk of God relates as the common ground of every man's experience is: the questionableness that encounters us in the reality that encounters us. That, however, must now be more precisely defined.

It is not a case of just any questions that are answered sooner or later by the reality that encounters me. Rather, it is a case of radical questionableness, and that means: a questionableness to which reality itself does not contain the answer. It cannot be answered by some element which is admittedly not yet known, but is to be discovered after all in the end, in the reality itself that concerns me. Rather, this questionableness— and that is part of its radicality—seeks to be answered by me myself, in fact through me myself. For it is a case of my own questionableness. The fact that the reality which encounters me gives me cause to ask questions does not yet mean, of course, in the first instance that it is a questionableness which has to do with myself, or at any rate not a questionableness which calls me myself in question. Of course every question which I feel to be a question at all, even the question I myself raise, has to do with me myself to the extent that I myself am then the questioner and the person questioned in one. As indeed it ultimately comes to the same whether I say that I am questioning reality or that reality is putting questions to me. Yet the radicality of the questionableness comes only when I become questionable in my own eyes, when the questionableness of the reality that concerns me and my own questionableness are thus identical.

We could also say: the condition on which it is possible to understand what the word 'God' means is a lack of understanding. Of course we must not stop at merely penultimate and provisional lack of understanding and consequently assign God some sort of place among the gaps in our knowledge,[1] so that as these gaps in our knowledge close, there is so to speak less room for God and his reality is pushed ever further afield with the bounds of our knowledge, and God thus finds himself on the retreat—as has been thought in modern times owing to a fundamental misunderstanding. Rather, it is a case of experiencing a radical and comprehensive lack of under........ng, which is precisely that questionableness that embraces myself and the world.

---

[1] C. F. von Weizsäcker, *Die Geschichte der Natur* (1948), 2nd ed. 1954, p. 87; D. Bonhoeffer, *WE* pp. 131, 210 f, 215 f, 241, 258 (Eng. pp. 91, 142 f, 145 f, 163, 178).

The task of a comprehensive analysis of reality, which cannot be completed once for all, but the study of which is the constant, historically conditioned and historically motivated act of reflective questioning, would now be: to observe the radical questionableness of reality. This task has certain things in common with the undertaking of the so-called proofs of God, which demonstrate only the questionableness that belongs to reality. In their traditional form they could certainly speak to us of radical questionableness only if we understand their disclosure of the questionableness of the world's reality as explication of the world in which we understand ourselves. Radical questionableness—or as we could now also say with the help of a traditional concept, the problem of true transcendence—seems to us to arise at a totally different point from where the usual so-called proofs of God placed it: not with the question of the *primum movens* or such like, but with the problems relating to personal being, like the question of meaning, the question of guilt, the question of communication, etc. It is of course not ruled out that the transcendence problems in the traditional proofs of God also harbour within them the experience of radical questionableness and thus, rightly understood, likewise refer in the end to the radical questionableness which concerns personal being as a whole.

If this questionableness which strikes to the roots of personal being and thereby proves its radicality is described as concerned with the conscience, then we could now also say that the place where we experience what 'God' means is the conscience. For that we should of course require an interpretation of the concept of conscience which takes a critical view of its customary use, in order to guard against the misunderstanding that the conscience delivers definite material teachings and instructions, whereas in fact it is man himself under the aspect of his involvement in radical questionableness.

For the rest, it would be a falsification of the relation between knowing God and what we have described as radical questionableness, if knowing God were to mean the abrogation of radical questionableness. According to biblical usage the quest of God and search for God certainly does not mean that he is then found in a way that puts an end to the searching and questioning. Rather it is a searching and questioning which is stimulated more than ever by the true knowledge of God, so that the true quest for God is possible only for the man who has found him. To have found here means, to abide by the quest of God and the search for God. Thus not only some sort of first, provisional understanding of what the word 'God' means, but the knowledge of God itself has and retains its place within the sphere of radical question-ableness.

2. The nature of the radical questionableness which affects man can be further defined as *experience of passivity*. The decisive events of our existence, birth and death, point to the passivity that underlies all human activity. We may settle the question of God whatever way we please, yet we shall have to say that man at all events is not his own creator, but is brought into existence without any possibility of choosing time and place and circumstances. We may look at death whatever way we can, at all events it remains a fact that man must die, and thus even when he goes to death of his own free will he merely anticipates the fate that hangs over him. In his existence between birth and death man is also exposed to passivity in various ways as one who is involved, called, challenged, questioned. There is a close connexion between finitude and passivity. Finite existence is an existence exposed to the possibility of suffering. Even man's freedom has its ground in passivity, in that he has freedom conferred on him, or from another point of view, that he is condemned to freedom, or at all events that he is called to freedom. So, too, the phenomenon of radical questionableness points to the passivity of being called in question. Indeed, the experience of passivity becomes the cause of being called in question, and the fact of being called in question becomes the explication of passivity. The concept of conscience in the sense of man's being affected in his personal being also represents the factor of passivity.

In the end, passivity is not only of importance where the *quest* of God is concerned, but is an essential element in the relation to God precisely from the standpoint of revelation. For here activity belongs to God alone, and to man nothing but receiving. Knowledge of God is essentially determined by the fact that God *gives* himself to be known, and so gives man to know himself as the creature already known by God. The knowledge of God has therefore nothing of the character of spontaneous investigation and discovery on man's part. Rather, the fact that God is man's Creator is a basic principle of revelation. Man's knowledge of God rests on his being known by God, his love of God on his being loved by God, his addressing God as God on his being addressed by God, his acceptance of God as God on his being accepted by God. Revelation certainly does not mean that some kind of additional, new objects appear on my horizon and now become objects of my activity. Rather, revelation means the brightening, the illumination of the whole of my existence with everything it embraces. Revelation does not mean that something is handed to me which I must then take the trouble to clarify and understand and relate to my reality. Rather, revelation is itself light and therefore a source of light, not a single object offered for consideration, not anything at all that seeks to be considered in itself, as little as the source of light is there to be looked into (which everyone knows blinds instead of illumining). Rather the source of light serves the illumination, and therefore the knowledge, of the reality which concerns me in any case, so that strictly I myself together with the reality which concerns me am the object of revelation, the object on which revelation is bestowed and which is therefore brought to light. Thus as passive receiver I myself together with the reality which concerns me belong of necessity to the event of revelation. Luther would say, as the '*materia*' of God.[1]

3. *Knowledge of God is a linguistic event*, in accordance with the wordliness of reality. The structure of radical questionableness in fact already implies the structure of wordliness. For where questions are asked the word-event is already taking place in the conjunction of word and answer (*Wort und Antwort*). It might arouse misgivings that here the connexion is made so directly between the wordliness of reality and the wordliness of revelation. It seems to me wrong to explain this by introducing the idea of adaptation—that God adapts himself to our human ways by using speech as the vehicle of his revelation—as if God in himself were so to speak wordless. Despite all the doubts that have to be raised against the early church's Logos doctrine, it is definitely right in its grasp of this: that 'word' is what links and binds God and our reality, that God and our reality are thus one in their wordliness and that this, too, is one of the things that give sense to calling man the *Imago Dei*.

It now depends, of course, on the right understanding of what 'word-event' means. It cannot be that the word-event which is to be designated as revelation is directed towards communicating individual truths, towards answering individual questions. It is altogether problematical to see the connexion between what we have called radical questionableness and revelation simply as the relation of question and answer. As if it were not revelation that lets us see rightly for the first time what actually stands in question, and thus for the first time reveals the radicality of the questionableness. And as if conversely in the very questionableness of reality the word-event that comes from God were not already taking

---

[1] E.g. *WA* 39/1, p. 177.3 f (*Disp. de homine*, 1536): *Quare homo huius vitae est pura materia Dei ad futurae formae suae vitam.*

place. In the doctrine of the Word of God this would have to be thought through on the basis of the distinction of law and Gospel. In the word-event that has to be understood as revelation it is not primarily a case at all of that function of the word which consists in communication of meaning, but, however little it can be abstracted from, primarily of that function of the word in which it presses for fulfilment. As indeed the distinction of law and Gospel can be central only when 'word' is understood in ways that are not governed by the question of meaning but by the question of fulfilment. We could therefore also say briefly: in the understanding of revelation as word-event it is primarily a case not of the logical, but of the historical function of words, just because it is a case of a word that affects existence itself in its existing, of a word that does not simply supply answers, but waits for an answer, gives power to answer; whereby no less is at stake than that man himself in his existence is empowered to exist as one who answers—we could even say, as an answer.

For that reason the linguistic event which is constitutive of the knowledge of God is, rightly understood, not a word about God, but Word of God. For it is only as one who himself speaks that God can reveal himself as God. It is true that we should have to go on to ask how far God's Word makes words about God necessary and also possible, and thus how in answer to God's Word there can be, and as a highly necessary thing also must be, in actual fact talk about God, doctrine of God. But the doctrine of God that founds on God's Word will in the first instance have to make it its purpose to understand this its ground.

It will therefore in the first instance have to be explication of the confession of God as Person. Knowledge of God as word-event implies knowledge of God as a Person. For that reason what is called knowledge of God stands or falls with the possibility of prayer. Prayer is the most direct expression of the knowledge of God, in so far as it is answer to God's Word. Thus everything now comes to this, that knowledge of God is knowing God as a Person. This, however, cannot be presented on its own, but only in the context of the doctrine of the Word of God. The doctrine of the Word of God is at heart nothing else but the doctrine of God as a Person. The question whether the way of speaking of God as a Person is not really a highly problematical anthropomorphism, is certainly not to be lightly dismissed—as indeed, to press it further, even the application of the concept of existence to God already leads to perplexities in our speaking of God that have to be taken very seriously. If we were to pursue this point further, then it would certainly transpire that we can speak *properly* of God only when in doing so we have an eye to man as a person. The personal being of God and the personal being of man, however, are not so to speak two separate things, but are to be grasped only in relation to each other. And only with an eye on this relation can there be talk of God which is not improper but proper talk of God.

XIII

WORLDLY TALK OF GOD*

'WORLDLY talk of God' is an ambiguous phrase. It could be taken—this is the most obvious interpretation—as the designation of something absurd, wicked and blasphemous, as if it meant 'godless talk of God'. But it can also be given a positive meaning as the slogan for something appropriate, necessary and desirable, in the sense of 'real talk of God'. To accept the one is to reject the other. The man who has the face to approve of godless talk of God thereby denies that there can be real talk of God at all. And on the other hand, the man who longs for real talk of God separates himself as a matter of course from godless talk of God, indeed he feels even pious talk of God which does not prove itself real talk of God to be insupportable, godless.

We are familiar with the fact that contrasting values are put on the word 'worldly'. Piety—so it has been drilled into us—despises 'worldly' things. Correspondingly, emancipation from religion takes its effect in devotion to what is worldly. That indeed is putting it somewhat crudely. But the essential characteristic does in fact seem to be: the fear of God leads to unworldliness, contempt for God drives to worldliness.

Here, however, we are not to be concerned with these contrasting evaluations of the worldly, which depend on whether God is affirmed or denied. Rather, the question arises whether affirmative talk of God, confession to him, can be combined with such a divided view of worldly things that in the one case worldly talk of God is an absurd expression and in the other case a meaningful one: in the one case the epitome of false talk of God, in the other case the epitome of true talk of God.

It could be a mere dispute about words. Then it must be possible to settle it by reflecting calmly on the motley concept world and introducing clarifying distinctions. But a dispute about words seldom arises by accident. At the least there is a material lack of clarity behind it, and very likely it also indicates a material difference. That the phrase 'worldly talk of God' points in contradictory directions—godless or real

* In *Frömmigkeit in einer weltlichen Welt*, ed. H. J. Schultz, Kreuz-Verlag, Stuttgart/Walter-Verlag, Olten, 1959, pp. 63-73.

talk of God—presumably does not depend on a mere chance difference in the use of the word 'worldly'. It is connected at all events with the fact that talk of God as such harbours contradictory possibilities, and is thus a matter of dispute. And that is surely what the adjective 'worldly' talk of God, whatever way it is to be understood, seeks to bring out: Talk of God requires reflexion, for it can miss the mark and we can be left with a mere semblance of speaking of God. But if the dispute is on the question of reality or deceptive appearance, then it does not affect our speaking alone, but also our understanding, and indeed God himself. For in speaking of God a decision is made about God. Either God is spoken of in such a way that he loses his divinity, or God is spoken of in such a way that he really comes to expression as God.

Our subject thus points us to something questionable in the proper sense of the word question-able (*frag-würdig*, lit. question-worthy), *viz.* that it is something which is worthy of questioning, deserves thinking about. In that sense, talk of God is indeed the most questionable thing of all. For if incisiveness, exactness, conscientiousness and responsibility matter anywhere in our talk, then most of all in our talk of God. Here it is well to be silent before we open our mouth, to enquire before we make assertions, to test each word before we let it pass our lips.

We live in an age in which talk of God has become specially questionable. 'Questionable' of course in the first instance, as most people suppose, in the hackneyed sense of an openness to question that has really already been decided in the negative and leaves no more room for promise; as if it were simply no longer worth while to think about speaking of God. For how can we speak of God today without facing the fact that a considerable section of our contemporaries must honestly confess that they have really no idea what we are talking about when we talk of God? Could the reason for that possibly be, that God is spoken of thoughtlessly?—with a supposed self-evidence that can only hinder understanding the evidence, with such lack of awareness of our own questionableness that no genuine questions arise and we therefore also lose the power to arouse genuine questions? The man who ventures to speak of God today and does not wish to be without conscience and love, must venture to face with a wakeful heart the questionableness of speaking of God. Our subject seeks to guide us to that, by being formulated in a way that already compels us to ask questions.

That speaking of God has become so questionable today could now of course lead to the view that the decisive question is *whether* God is spoken of at all or not; that we should therefore be glad of every attempt still to bring up the subject of God, and not be so frightfully choosey about how it is done. Yet that is wrong. For *how* God is spoken of decides *whether* God is really spoken of at all. The problematical slogan 'worldly talk of God' raises this decisive question how. Thus the meaning is not that our talk of God so far as its content is concerned is obviously plain and free of problems, and only the supplementary question of the form and method of our speaking is open to discussion. Rather, our talk of God as such is called to account.

But now, why can the little word 'worldly', whichever way it is understood, become as it were the tongue of the balance where our talk of God is concerned? We can give the following provisional answer to that, and one which perhaps already hits the nail right on the head, even if we may not yet fully grasp it:—Our talk of God as such, we said, must be called to account. Before whom? Certainly our talk of God has to be answered for before God. But how could this answering for it take concrete form otherwise than before the world? Man has in fact to answer for himself before God and before the world at the same time. Strictly, however, it is not a second thing added on to our speaking of God when we now also answer for it before the world. For that in fact is precisely what it means to speak of God: to answer for God before the world. In that case, then, the world necessarily belongs to our talk of God.

To answer for (*verantworten*) God before the world means: to let God and the world come together by means of 'word' (*das Wort*). Only so will man be affected by our talk of God. And the only responsible talk of God is that which aims at the place where God and the world meet as it were in a mathematical point. That place is the conscience. Because responsible talk of God aims at the conscience, the world necessarily also becomes a question when talk of God stands in question. For conscience sake we cannot speak of God without speaking of the world. For as conscience man stands between God and the world. What is real in our talk of God comes to light in how that talk of God is related to the world. For that reason the slogan 'worldly talk of God' points the way for the questions that should be asked about our talk of God. It leads us to the central problem, *viz.* how God can be spoken of in such a way that precisely in so doing the world is rightly spoken of. And that means: how God can be spoken of in such a way that God and the world are rightly distinguished, but also rightly come together?

Now for the sake of the right distinction between God and the world it does in fact seem absurd, and indeed the very epitome of all false talk of God, to speak of God in worldly terms. There is no grosser way to rob God of his divinity than to consider him a piece of the world, to give him a place in the world and subject him to its laws. The confusion of God with a part of the reality of the world is the essence of idol-worship. Idols are God thought of in worldly terms.

This method of robbing God of his divinity is not by any means confined to what we are accustomed to call idol-worship in the grosser or subtler sense. Even enlightened atheism is in fact still nourished by this way of imagining God as a piece of the world. Only so can it think of 'God', yet for that very reason it must consider him an absurd thought. For atheism—at all events the modern atheism that has now for the first time made its public appearance as one of the great powers and has widely become a tacit self-evident assumption—presupposes at once the Christian, radical distinction between God and the world, yet can see this likewise only as a contradiction. A God distinguished from the world is, if he is a God really conceived and objectified, in fact a piece of the world after all—even if it is called the reality above and beyond the world. If, however, he is radically separated from all conceivable reality, then he himself has consequently to be denied reality.

This atheistic logic is not at all so easy to escape. For by no means only pagan, but also Christian talk of God is full of worldly notions. Naturally, it is said, these so-called anthropomorphic features which speak of God in finite, human ways are not to be taken literally. But in the positive sense this apologetic statement is by no means so convincing as to prevent the effort to understand what 'God' really means from being caught in this tangle of worldly thoughts of God whose logical consequence is atheism. Even emphasizing the fact of God's being above and beyond the world does not necessarily by any means really break through the circle of worldly notions. How many Christians there are for whom the talk of God therefore remains confused and powerless and gives no steadfast heart! And how many non-Christians there are whom such talk of God only drives the deeper into this confusion and hinders them from understanding the message of faith!

Yet it is not only a question of the fusion of God and the world that arises from the attempt to picture God to ourselves. The false talk of God that robs God of his divinity is to be found wherever what is expected of God is subjected to worldly standards—and that applies both to what has to be considered his will and also to what we may promise ourselves from him. It is pagan talk of God to understand God as guaranteeing, confirming, supplementing or overtowering worldly existence. The most pious work is then—as a means of ensuring oneself God's favour—a sign of this kind of worldly, and therefore strictly godless, thought of God, *viz.* the idea of conciliating God by sacrifice. Even Christianity is constantly in danger of becoming pagan precisely where it seeks to be most pious, of thinking and speaking of God not in godly, but in worldly and therefore ultimately godless ways. Even where the spiritual is determinedly opposed to all things worldly, the danger likewise threatens. The spiritual realm is then made into a world on its own, a separate reality which passes by the world as it really is, instead of engaging with it (*auf sie eingehen*).

With that, however, our train of thought has taken a strange turn. The conclusion that worldly talk of God is the epitome of all false talk of God forces itself upon us for the sake of the distinction between God and the world. We recalled various ways of confusing God and the world, but then ended unexpectedly with the possibility of separating God and the world. That appeared to us, however, to be merely a variation of the danger we had previously discussed. Is that correct? Could it be that the separatist, unworldly talk of God which builds a world apart is likewise worldly talk of God in that negative, basically godless sense?

It is indeed! Not only the fusion, but also the separation of God and the world is worldly talk of God in that contradictory sense. In fact, to separate God and the world is merely a deceptive way of fusing them. The extreme possibilities of separation join hands: atheistic and, as it is called, purely religious, purely spiritual talk of God. Both leave the world without God and God without the world. Both, however, take their cue from a way of thinking which allows what is said of God to be dictated by a definite understanding of the world. Atheism, it is true, seems from its name to be merely a statement about God. In fact, however, it is, at all events *also*, saying something about the world. The real purpose is in fact to speak atheistically of the world. Likewise, purely religious, purely spiritual talk of God seems indeed to have to do only with God. But in fact this way of speaking, which separates God from the world, very much includes speaking of the world—whether it speaks in ways that make the world a thing of indifference and leave it to its own devices, or in ways that do violence to the world by seeking to force an alien law upon it and do not trouble in the least about the world as it really is. In both kinds of talk, the atheistic and the purely religious, God is antithetically determined by the world. But for that reason, he is also stamped by the understanding of the world. And thus the very separation is explained as the result of a fusion.

It is therefore by no means sufficient, in face of the fusion of God and the world to proclaim their separation, and then *vice versa* no doubt in face of the separation to proclaim their fusion. That would merely be moving in a circle of speculative and religious possibilities which are all of the same structure. It would likewise be beside the point simply to set the 'purely religious', 'purely spiritual' talk of God over against the worldly talk of God in the possible negative forms we have just sketched. For that too, surprisingly enough, would fit into our picture along with the rest as a masked form of 'worldly' talk, and therefore with the unpleasant flavour of insincerity, hypocrisy and untruthfulness.

We conclude from that: all talk of God is worldly talk of God. We cannot speak of God without the world being also included one way or another—not indeed in the sense of an unfortunate necessity, but because our talk of God is addressed to the world; indeed, if we speak rightly of God, because God himself addresses himself to the world in such a way that he is its absolute concern and to that extent belongs absolutely to the world. If we thus cannot speak of God without the world being also included, then everything now depends entirely on *how* the world is included, on the sense in which our talk of God is worldly, on what is false and what is true worldly talk of God.

Rightly understood, 'spiritual' talk of God stands in contrast only to false worldly talk of God; but it is identical with true worldly talk of God, which is identical with true spiritual talk of God. And the quest of true worldly talk of God, which is identical with true spiritual talk of God, is not a special concern of those who for apologetic or missionary purposes wish to adapt themselves to the world in order to secure better success for their talk of God. Then everything would be lost. For true worldliness is not a supplement tacked on to our talk of God, but is what is brought about by our talk of God if it is correct, real talk of God.

For there are not two different problems: how God and the world are to be rightly distinguished and how they rightly come together. Only where God and the world truly come together are they truly distinct. Speaking of God and speaking of the world are inseparably one. Where God is falsely spoken of, the world is falsely spoken of also. Where God comes to expression in truth, the world also comes to expression in truth. And only where the world attains its truth is God known in truth. If, however, in order to speak of God, we speak of the world in a distorted way and will not observe and allow the truth of what presents itself

as real, then that betrays that we are not in truth speaking of God.
I will try to bring out a few easily instilled marks of true worldly talk
of God.

Worldly talk of God is *concrete talk of God*. We know from numerous
disappointments and our own manifold failures that talk of God mostly
persists in non-committal and ineffective generalities. For that reason it
provokes no opposition, yet neither is it heeded in revolutionizing ways,
but spreads abroad that possibly tranquillizing, but actually killing,
atmosphere of unimportance and boredom which is the death of faith.
Already most people expect nothing else from talk of God. Indeed, they
even justify this by withdrawing explicitly to the inner life—which, they
say, is the only thing talk of God is concerned with. If they only knew
what they were saying! It is true that our talk of God aims solely at the
inmost being, the conscience. But precisely what happens in the inmost
part has the outmost effects. The nature of man's inmost being, his
conscience, is grasped only when it is clearly realized that here it is not
a case of man in the abstract, separated from the world, and of his then
necessarily likewise abstract relation to God; rather, the conscience is,
as we said already, the place where God and the world meet. If our talk
of God is aimed at faith, then faith, because it has to do with God, has
to do with the world. And the conscience is only really affected when
our talk of God concretely pins man down, but also frees him, at the
point where he thinks himself free but is actually bound, or also where
he considers himself bound but is actually free. Speaking of God does
not suffer the concrete point at which we exist in the world to be forgotten; but when it is done in truth, then its authority lies in the fact
that it lays a finger on that concrete point and therefore calls things by
their true names, summons them forth from concealment, brings them
out of darkness into light, and thereby sets them in motion and puts
them to work. Then, for example, 'sin' is no longer a pious term—sin
leaps at us. And then 'forgiveness' is no longer an edifying phrase, but
the coming of that freedom which changes the face of the world.

Worldly talk of God is therefore *clear talk of God*. It confers the
freedom to let God be God and the world be world; not to fuse them
together, but never to separate the one from the other. For that reason
we could also say: worldly talk of God is godly talk of the world. There
is no place here for unclear, pious jargon, evasion of problems, obscuring
of facts. One might say that the tone itself betrays the man who shies at
clarity in his talk of God. For where there is in the true sense a spiritual
approach, there is freedom to be natural and to face the world un-

inhibited. There we are able to engage with the world in such a way that the world knows itself recognized, understood, concerned, affected. And to that there belongs the freedom to allow also worldly talk of the world free scope within its limits. There is in point of fact a purely worldly way of speaking of the world which is well justified as long as it confines itself to businesslike, rational concern with partial aspects of reality, and does not seek to be an answer to the question of the whole, and that means, to bind the conscience. It is faith that has to do with the conscience. But for that reason even faith should not tie reason to its apron strings, but rather set it free to cultivate what is reasonable. It is unbearable, indeed godless, when our talk of God takes refuge in lies because something which is undoubtedly true in the world's eyes is foolishly thought to be dangerous to the truth of God.

Worldly talk of God is, lastly, *active (wirkendes) talk of God.* Here we come to the real heart of the matter. For what we have said is valid only in view of the fact that it is 'word' that brings God and the world together, and that this word is no abstract statement, but a concrete word-event, address, call, by which God is proclaimed in the world. Because God and the world come together in the word-event, their coming together is itself an event: event of God and event of the world. God is only really spoken of when God comes to expression[1] as an event and for that very reason the world comes to expression as an event, and in this linguistic event God becomes wholly divine because he loves the world, and the world becomes wholly worldly because it becomes what it is: the world that belongs to God, God's creation.

I called these marks of true worldly talk of God—that it is concrete, clear and active talk of God—easy to instill. But to put them into practice is a never-ending task. In all unguardedness three pointers of that by way of example:—

First: the man who is responsible for speaking of God—and that certainly does not mean only ministers, but primarily them—must allow himself time for it, a great deal of time. Naturally that alone will not stem the usual ineffectiveness of the sermon. But when ministers and congregations begin to take seriously the fact that true worldly talk of God results only from most intensive theological reflexion, then that is at least one necessary step.

Second: the church must see to it that all the activities by which its talk of God is accompanied, explained and put into practice are given, if I may put it so, a natural style. It has certainly no cause for hectic

---

[1] Cf. my note on terms, p. 294 above, note 1—*Translator.*

modernization, in which it always comes too late in any case. But it has every ground to be uninhibited and to the point. There are many visible symptoms today of an inhibitedness which by the standard of the Gospel is not to the point, and pseudo-spiritual. That could be illustrated from painful experiences with bishops (I am thinking of Evangelical bishops!), with theologians and with congregations.

And lastly: Christians, as those who belong to the crucified Jesus, must know that their life in the world is the proper exercise-ground of worldly talk of God. For talk of God drives men to experience and ripens in experience in the place where we believe, that is, in the world.

XIV

THE WORLD AS HISTORY*

To Fritz Blanke on his 60th birthday

I

F OR King Midas, legend says, everything he touched turned to gold. For modern man everything, the whole of reality, turns to history. Does this parallel extend also to the results? The gift that opened undreamed-of possibilities led perforce to destruction. Only a miracle, it is said, saved Midas: by bathing he was freed of his fatal power. The total transformation of the world into history likewise opens up fascinating perspectives. Yet we are becoming increasingly aware of the doom that lurks in it. Is this doom inevitable? Or is there still a hope for the modern age? And on what would the hope rest? On changing man back again, freeing him from his headlong historicalness? Or—contrary to the indication of the legend—precisely on rightly embracing his historicalness, and thus not only on understanding (*verstehen*), but also on enduring (*durchstehen*) and bearing (*bestehen*), the world as history?

Opinions differ even among profound thinkers, and indeed often in unexpected ways. A philosopher, Gerhard Krüger, says: 'Pure historicalness . . . would be the disappearance of all constant, self-continuous human nature in the whirlpools of the stream of time. Man, however, cannot be man without some kind of eternity, wherever he may seek it.'[1] On the other hand it is a theologian, Friedrich Gogarten, who writing on the subject 'The Bane and Hope of the Modern Age' declares: 'What is not historical is for modern man not real. In face of that, however, we have not the slightest right to say that this modern man must just decide between his modern views and the Christian faith; here modern man in his historical thinking has the Christian faith on his side.'[2] Despite all the contrasts of opinion, there is widespread agreement today that history has to a peculiar degree become the destiny of

---

* In *Mensch und Kosmos: Eine Ringvorlesung der Theologischen Fakultät Zürich*, Zwingli-Verlag, Zurich/Stuttgart 1960, pp. 103-114.
[1] G. Krüger, *Grundfragen der Philosophie*, 1958, p. 10.
[2] F. Gogarten, *Verhängnis und Hoffnung der Neuzeit*, 1953, p. 109.

modern man. If we consider the subject 'Man and the Cosmos' in the form which troubles us today—and the threat it contains is surely what drives us to this subject—then the world must come to expression as history. For indeed it is not the cosmos with its natural forces that threatens man today. But man in his historical power threatens the cosmos and so drags all reality into his history.

II

The course taken by these joint lectures on the subject 'Man and the Cosmos' may serve as an immediate illustration of the nature of the historification that marks modern man. As a matter of course, without giving any explicit justification for doing so, the hearer has so far in more than two-thirds of the semester been served up with a review of history. To be sure, that was a result of the plan to have the composition and working method of the theological faculty present itself as a whole. But that is precisely what makes the thing all the more typical. A theological faculty today consists primarily of historians. And even the so-called systematic theologians must constantly be able to justify themselves in the historical field. In this respect theology shares in the contemporary situation of the humanities in general. Whatever the problem that is taken up, it transforms itself, at all events in the first instance, into a historical problem.

By way of contrast, let us try to imagine how a theological faculty in the seventeenth century would have approached the subject 'Man and the Cosmos'. A theological anthropology and cosmology would have been put forward with the claim to be the true and therefore perennially valid doctrine. If historical authorities were appealed to in so doing, then it would only be in order to demonstrate unchanged agreement with them, in contrast to other teachings which, likewise unchangeably, have always the character of false teachings. For truth, it was held, can surely only be an unchanging truth, remaining eternally the same. Never in the whole history of theology up to modern times was there such a thing as taking a historical view of a theological problem. Indeed, the constraint towards this kind of historical thinking is something new in the history of mankind altogether. Naturally there was also in earlier times an interest in the past. But the completely new thing in historical thinking consists in the fact that it relativizes all historical things as 'merely historical'. What earlier ages thought of man and the world has to be historically understood, but for that reason also its validity is historically limited. The Bible is no exception to that. Its statements, too, as statements that have to be historically understood, are not simply timeless truths.

What has so far been said on the subject 'Man and the Cosmos' by way of historical review therefore certainly could not be, and certainly did not seek to be, definitive teaching on man and the cosmos—however much it requires to be taken into account when we come to the question what we have to think of man and the cosmos today. In putting it that way, however, we already make clear that historification has not only relativized the past, but relativizes also the present. It would be naive if we now wished to state the finally correct view of man and the cosmos in contrast to all that has gone before. It is true that the present calls for decision. We cannot stop at historical reviews. A theological faculty of all bodies cannot evade present responsibility by excursions into history. Those who have been listening properly were in fact even in the historical orientation already being challenged to present responsibility. Moreover the whole course is to close with the explicit 'Summons to Responsibility', following a reminder of the concrete sphere of present responsibility in the phrase 'industrial world'. But all the same, it is not a definitive picture of man and the cosmos, not a timeless doctrine, that is the aim. The question about man and the cosmos is meant to point us to our own historical situation. It is not meant to encourage us to cosmological speculations. And if the task of today's lecture is to give, at this point of transition from the history from which we have come to the history we are about to enter, a basic account of the relation between man and the world, then our reflexions must in fact be directed towards this historicalness which for us determines the co-existence of man and the world.

III

But now, have we not ascribed to the modern age as a new discovery something that in one way or another is an element of every understanding of the world? It is true that on the one hand the world is conceived as order in space in such words as κόσμος or *mundus*, but at the same time it is also viewed on the other hand as happening in time in such words as αἰών or *saeculum* or even our own word 'world', which by etymology means 'age of man'. Biblical thinking in particular emphasizes the temporal extension of the world between the event of creation and eschatology—which in itself could already suggest the understanding of the world as history. But mythical thinking, too, displays in various forms the character of event that attaches to the world.

It was only in modern times that a sharp distinction began to be made between nature and history by dissociating the cosmos from man and therefore also conversely isolating man from the cosmos. The extreme attempts to force both together again must certainly be regarded as failures: the idealistic incorporation of nature, too, into the history of absolute spirit, and the materialistic interpretation of spiritual history, too, as a product of natural events. Nevertheless the merging of the interconnexions and blending of different aspects has come ever more strongly to the fore. The natural science of today provides a double proof of that. It has shown that the world of nature is not something that remains eternally the same, but is history in so far as it is a case of an irreversible, finite operation, a total process whose very substratum, matter, likewise proves to be a pure process. And secondly, it has made clear the subjective conditionedness even of objective examination of nature. A favourite example adduced today is the fact that in what happens in the atomic sphere, physics has reached the limits of what can be unequivocally objectified; for the decision on the appearance of corpuscle or wave is made with the choice of the method of experiment. But more important than this limiting case in physics is the general recognition that natural science's knowledge of the world is historically conditioned as such. It was only in a definite phase of mental history that it became possible. Its accomplishment depends constantly on the adoption of a definite attitude. For indeed objectifying, as the greatest possible exclusion of human references, means the strongest conceivable activation and inclusion of the man who deliberately takes up the detached position of the purely knowing subject. The realism of natural science is a supreme degree of abstraction from reality as a whole. It presents the world, not as it is 'in itself', but as it appears to the man who is capable of this abstraction. To that extent the natural science of today does not explode, but confirms the historical relativity of all understanding of the world.

Yet how far does this aspect of historicalness really point to a peculiar feature of the modern age in particular? Was it not always the case that with man's historical changes his understanding of the world has also changed, and that the latter has always corresponded with man's understanding of himself? And has 'world' not likewise always been an ambiguous term, which expresses on the one hand the tendency to seek the whole of reality, and on the other hand betrays the fact that the whole as such is never an object of experience? For that reason the concept of the world either becomes ultimately a matter of conviction, of a '*Weltanschauung*' as it has been called since the beginning of the nineteenth century; or else its application splits up into limited wholes, such as outer world, inner world, world of nature, world of history, industrial world, child's world, or some other particular form.

It is quite true that to a certain extent that has always been so. For in a general sense man in his existence in the world has always been historical. But he has not always recognized himself as such. The enigma which this knowledge involves is a thing he did not see himself subject to until modern times. In earlier times he was always able to keep his understanding of himself absolute, and to banish the tendency to split into many worlds thanks to his convincing idea of one all-embracing whole. The new thing about modern man is, that his reality has become radically historical as a result of an all-determining awareness of his historicalness. And the aspect of historicalness, destroying all solidity as it does and making all things relative, becomes paradoxically enough the one thing that still holds the whole together.

IV

The peculiarity of the modern age forces itself upon us in the indisputable experience that the world has become different—and that, too, in such a way that peculiar structural transformations have come to light in the historical itself. Gerhard Krüger has pointed to the fundamental significance of the following well-known features of the history of modern times, especially of this century.[1] For the first time there has come to be a unified history of mankind. And to this global totality there corresponds also the total participation of all social classes and the total interdependence of all realms of life. These are marks of contemporary history which were unknown to earlier times. Still more characteristic, however, is the constant acceleration of the pace of historical events that accompanies this comprehensive totalification of the historical. We must acknowledge Krüger to be right in this: 'All the facts mentioned—the spatial and social universality of events, the historical interaction of the various provinces of things, and the increasing tempo —manifestly belong together: they entitle us to feel that we are living in an age of intensified and outstanding historicalness and that precisely this is the peculiar feature of our age.'[2]

It would be presumptuous to try here to draw a complete sketch of the shape of our times. But it is surely plain that this outstanding

[1] G. Krüger, 'Geschichte und Tradition', in *Lebendige Wissenschaft*, Heft 12 (1958), pp. 8 ff.　　　　　　　　　　　　　　　　[2] *Op. cit.*, p. 11.

historicalness is the key to a great many phenomena which we meet for the first time in the modern age. A few notes may serve at least to indicate the interconnexion of a number of aspects.

First we might point to the highly characteristic revaluation of 'old' and 'new'. If in earlier times the old, the traditional, the established—as such—ranked as venerable and as true, whereas the new was first of all suspect, now the standard is reversed: the old is viewed in principle as out of date, while the new is considered as such to be superior. 'Modern times' is therefore not the changing self-designation of each present moment in the march of time, but the typical expression of a world-view whose basic feature is the constant wish for what is modern. The radical determination to look to the future is the cause of the intense changeability and of the disappearance of tradition. For man knows himself responsible for his world. It is the object he has to explore to master and to shape.

The interest in history which now flourishes so rampant and unbounded is only in seeming contradiction to this orientation towards the future. For a basic impulse of the modern interest in history is in fact precisely the emancipation from the past—retrospective mastery, so to speak, of the world. Therein it is the twin of the forward-looking mastery of the world which shows itself most startlingly in the technical interest that is revolutionizing every realm of life. Its appearance in modern times is not simply the result of an increase in man's intelligence, but results in the first instance from a new way of approaching the world, a new understanding of reality. The specifically modern intelligence is only a phenomenon resulting in turn from that. Man's attitude is now consistently searching. For his understanding of reality is determined by its calculability. For that reason he is concerned not simply with perception but with achievement, not with being but with becoming, not with states but with facts and existence. The interest in the future transforms given facts into tasks. The strictly real thing about reality is its potentialities.

The whole world, but therefore also man himself, both as an individual and as a social being, is sucked up into this stream. Human life, too, is now mastered according to plan. Man becomes his own material. Growth is supplanted by manufacture, the natural by the artificial, the organic by organization. The dialectic of this process once more recalls King Midas. That things become so much subject to man leads to turning man himself into a thing. Unbridled freedom pushed to extremes becomes meaningless and changes into constraint. Man who has become the measure of all things finds himself without measure. In making himself absolute he finds all things, including himself, relative. In his very power he experiences his powerlessness. In mastering the world and consistently making it his own, he estranges himself not only from it, but also from himself. In encountering the whole universe as never before, he encounters nothingness. This historicalness has turned malignant, and nihilism seems to be the only—and self-abrogating—sense in it.

V

If we trace out the roots of the modern age, and therewith the grounds of this exciting development in which the world has not merely become the stage of potential history but has so to speak itself been given the potential to become history, then we find ourselves faced by an extremely complicated tangle of problems. A major element in responsible education today is to take account of the differentiations involved in the rise and nature of the modern age. Here we can only warn against oversimplifications of the catchword type. Nevertheless everything ultimately concentrates on the one point that the evolution of the modern age is connected with the process of secularization. Yet the connexion has not been radically understood when it is taken as one of cause and effect; as if the historification and everything that has arisen from it were the result of secularization. Rather, the historification of the world requires to be understood as itself secularization of the world, and therefore also the secularization as historification.

The fact that we are compelled to include the problem of secularization as a decisive point in our reflexions has two results. Firstly, it brings us to a still deeper level of our subject 'The World as History'. For the fact that modern man sees everything as history is now only the reverse side of the fact that he sees absolutely everything as world. Reality is in his eyes exclusively worldly reality and therefore history is exclusively worldly history. Hence the historification of the world, as secularization of the world, is for him the world's coming to its own, the discovery of the world as world. And secondly, penetrating to this level suddenly brings to light the theological relevance of our subject. And indeed, here theology seems to be challenged to a life and death struggle. Does it not amount in the end to a choice between the modern understanding of reality and the Christian faith? For does secularizing not mean de-Christianizing?

The problem is too serious for us to be able to engage in the usual

apologetic ways of short-circuiting the argument. It is short-circuiting
the argument simply to dismiss wholesale as false the process whose
description we ended with the caption 'nihilism'. The modern age has
also won advantages that can never again be surrendered. What is to
become of it has not yet by any means been decided. And even its
sinister features have perhaps a different meaning from what appears
on the surface. At all events it does not at all become the Christian faith
to join in a mood of panic and a black-and-white analysis of our times,
still less to be the pacemaker for such things. For it is short-circuiting
the argument to suppose that one can withdraw from the modern age
as a spectator who knows better. For in the total historicalness of the
modern world, quiet islands and retired corners can be had only at the
price of self-deception. Indeed even the Christian—though he may still
be ever so fast asleep and retarded and ignorant of the world—has yet
so much of the modern man about him that to be a Christian and disregard the problems of the modern age (which would then mean being
a Christian only in appearance!) is a thing he can do only at the cost of
splitting reality. It is another short-circuit to charge the modern age
with apostasy from Christianity and to see in that the source of all the
trouble. At all events, so far as there is any question of apostasy, the
Christians themselves have surely failed. To say nothing at all of the
terrible guilt incurred by the church where the rise of modern unbelief
is concerned, above all by speaking of faith in such a way that by comparison one can only admit unbelief was right. And it is a short-circuit,
lastly, to suppose the change that has taken place can be reversed. The
secularizing movement cannot be dealt with by de-secularization. The
associations, as we have seen, go far deeper. For indeed secularization
is one with historification. But can radical historification also be termed
antichristian?

   That question certainly cannot be answered in the affirmative without
reservations. For the Christian faith stands essentially in a close relation
to history. It is well known that the significance of history in Western
thought goes back to the Old Testament. For God is here understood
as the God who acts and reveals himself in history. In accordance with
that, the manner of his revelation is the concrete event of the Word and
the aim of that event is faith. God and man stand in a personal relation
to each other. For that reason man as a historical being is responsible
to God in all he does. And the individual is taken up into God's plan for
his chosen people, which is a plan of salvation affecting the whole
world. To speak of God therefore means to speak of God's history with

the world. From there the relation to history becomes an essential part also of Christian faith, and indeed to a certain extent in a sharpened form—*viz.* in its being related exclusively to Jesus of Nazareth as the ground of faith, in the universality of its mission to the whole world, and in its freedom from the world in existing for others.

But now, these references do not only make it clear that it was only on Christian ground that history could acquire this tremendous significance in the modern age, but also point to the fact that despite all outward appearances the secularization process also derives to a certain extent from Christian faith. For to the faith which confesses God as the Creator and Lord of the world, the world is stripped of its divinity. Indeed, the faith which in view of Jesus Christ is certain of final, eschatological salvation is given no other law for its dealings with the world than the law of love. All ceremonial and ritual division of reality into the realms of clean and unclean, sacred and profane, is over and done with. For in faith all earthly things are profane in the sense of our being free to use them in natural, matter-of-fact ways. And in faith everything is sanctified at the same time in the sense of being employed before God in Christ through the Holy Spirit.

Now of course by relating it back in this way to what has been mediated and disclosed by the Christian faith, the phenomenon of modern historification and secularization cannot simply be explained, and certainly not uncritically justified. But to be aware of these double-sided, but for that very reason *also* positive, relations between the basic characteristic of the modern age and the Christian faith produces enormous tasks.

VI

I can only add a few sentences to indicate what in this situation seems to me to be our most urgent task in regard to Christianity and in regard to the contemporary world.

In regard to Christianity we are given the job of striving for a real understanding of the nature of Christian faith, i.e. for an understanding in which we take part as what we are, as men of the modern age, as men of this world that has become entirely worldly and entirely historical, and thus for an understanding that does not allow of a split mind. Certainly, that is in the first instance the theologian's business; yet surely only in order to help every man to his own responsible understanding of the nature of Christian faith. It is plain that generally speaking we are in a bad way with this task of understanding. We are being dangerously deceived about it (at all events in the West) by the seeming recovery and apparent flourishing of Christianity. I am convinced that Christians are heading sooner or later for a terrible awakening because of their carelessness regarding the relation of faith and understanding. There appeared recently from the pen of a decided non-Christian, Gerhard Szczesny, a book entitled 'The Future of Unbelief',[1] which ends by saying, 'As long as public opinion in the West insists that only accepting the truth of the postulates of Christian faith can save the world, it will forcibly prolong the age of unbelief and drive ever new generations into the arms of cynicism, superficiality and stupidity.'[2] Two things about this book are equally disturbing: that this is how Christian faith is represented in the minds of our contemporaries, and that Christianity today in actual fact to a great extent only justifies these ideas and therefore also the corresponding unsparing criticism.

For Christians as a whole have still shirked the inevitable transformation of what has traditionally been given out to be Christian faith. The shyness to face this task is understandable. For it is not only a case of making room for historical thinking along with all that that involves in the way of destructive criticism of what till now belonged to the content and ideas of faith. But it is also and above all a case of speaking of the reality of faith in such a way that in doing so we do not simply suppress or deny what we are compelled to understand by reality. That most certainly does not mean making deletions in the Christian faith in accommodation to the spirit of the times. But it means coming of age as a Christian; not confusing yesterday's metaphysics with the Christian faith, but precisely in the light of faith helping modern thought to discover the truth in its understanding of reality. For indeed it is not by any means the case that this modern understanding of reality is an established fact. Anyone who is at all familiar with the philosophical and scientific discussions on the concept of reality[3] knows of the perplexity that exists here. Yet if in spite of everything there is some irrenouncible truth about the fact that modern man's understanding of reality takes its bearings so decidedly on the historical and worldly nature of the world, then we should be doing that understanding of reality a decided service by learning to speak in truly historical and truly worldly ways of God.

---

[1] *Die Zukunft des Unglaubens*, Munich (1958), 7th-10th Thousand 1959.
[2] *Op. cit.*, p. 220.
[3] Cf. *Wirklichkeit heute: Referate und Arbeitsberichte vom Kirchentagskongress Hamburg*, ed. H. H. Walz, 1958.

With that we have already passed to the task which is set us in regard to the contemporary world. It would of course be basically wrong if what we have said about the relation of faith and understanding were intended to help Christianity to assert itself in the contemporary world. On the contrary: much of Christianity in its present form may be ripe for death. It depends on faith. Faith, however, is faith exercised *in* the world. It ceases to be faith when it flees the world. That is the other task I have in mind: that something of faith's freedom has to be made plain in this world of ours. It may well be that this freedom must then express itself in words and acts of protest against all the various kinds of madness and crime that go on for want of being aware of the true historicalness and true worldliness of the world. In the first instance, however, it is the business of the freedom of faith to pass on this freedom of faith. For it is in the freedom of faith that the world becomes truly worldly and the responsibility which is the essence of historicalness is observed.

That of course only points to the place in which we belong. Our place —and moreover, because it is the place of existence, it is therefore also the place of faith—is this: the world as history. What has to happen in this place, is no longer my task to speak of here. Today it was only a case of pointing out the place.

XV

FAITH AND UNBELIEF
IN CONFLICT ABOUT REALITY

I

L ET us think together about faith. That of course means presupposing faith, in so far as one can only think about something that is already given. To the question how faith is given, we offer the provisional answer: it is handed down—from Jesus, and inseparable from Jesus. For the tradition of Jesus Christ is the tradition of faith. Reflexion on faith will therefore not be slow to ask whether by any chance it is only tradition. A merely traditional faith is either a faith appropriated without thinking or a now merely mental repetition of past faith. Neither of these, however, is real faith. Yet in reflecting on faith what we are after is real faith. If faith is presented to us by tradition, then we must keep in view above all the question whether it is a tradition that concerns us, that makes convincing claims on us, that stands up to our reality and engages with it—in a word, whether faith is something that is necessary to us.

This, then, is how faith is to be presupposed: as a tradition which we would examine conscientiously with an eye to ourselves, stirred by the question of faith; for it is in fact handed down to us with the claim to be absolutely necessary, and that means to be necessary for salvation, indeed the only thing necessary for salvation. Paul, who knew a thing or two about faith, has made the well-known statement that man is justified by faith (Rom. 3.28). And Luther likewise showed his competence here when he deftly added the exclusive 'alone' to elucidate Paul's statement: 'by faith alone'.

Be it well noted: I am not presupposing faith in the hearer, but rather only that he is stirred by the question of faith and for that very reason is ready to think. Certainly to think about faith. But that is no sort of reason for not being scrupulous about his thinking. The man who in thinking about faith is not as scrupulous as his thinking capacity will allow, incurs at least the suspicion of not being scrupulous about faith itself. And such a man ought not to appeal to faith. The fact that I do not presuppose faith in the hearer should not cause surprise. For faith is not an acquired capacity which could be pre-supposed, like the capacity to think, and made the prerequisite of joining the audience. Those who confess to faith should of all people know that. Yet quite apart from that, it would be senseless to speak of faith on the assumption that no unbeliever is present. Christian talk of faith does indeed mostly take place on this tacit assumption. Faith is spoken of in more or less dark hints which are meant only for the initiated; we can only speak in such a way because we are among ourselves and do not reckon with anyone who thinks differently. But that only betrays the fact that we do not reckon with the power of words, which can become the communication of faith, and that moreover we do not take seriously the necessity (*Not-wendigkeit*) of faith, which must ever prove itself anew as the transition (*Wende*) from unbelief to faith. When faith is spoken of, the non-believer is the most appropriate listener. He is at all events a salutary criterion, which compels us not to speak too glibly of faith.

I may assume that both faith and unbelief are represented among us. These words designate a blunt alternative: either the one or the other. There can be no third element, no half-way, no 'both—and', no 'neither—nor'. So it is in truth. But for us that truth is hidden amid the confusion of appearances, so that we observe only a multitude of outward symptoms which cause the alternative of faith or unbelief to melt into an endless range of possibilities. Yet that need not worry us here. To think together about faith is a thing that can be asked of believers and unbelievers of all shades. Many a man, it is true, has his own special problem where faith is concerned. But the decisive and essential thing is the same for all, *viz.* to attain to the point where faith and unbelief are plainly seen and unambiguously part company. Believer and non-believer alike need to do that. In that purpose they ought to be one.

The non-believer will not, by thinking about faith, simply automati-cally become a believer. But neither should the believer, on the other hand, imagine that thinking about faith robs him *a priori* of his faith. The faith that is afraid to think is unbelief in the mask of piety. And the unbelief that is afraid to think is a pseudo-faith with Enlightenment trimmings. Believers and non-believers largely merit the same reproach: that they do not think, and therefore prevent their being in truth what they consider themselves to be. Not as if thinking could relieve us of deciding between faith and unbelief. On the contrary! It should help

us to make the decision between faith and unbelief and to prove the
truth of the conflict between faith and unbelief.

For faith and unbelief must be in conflict with each other. They must
therefore know each other, and lie hard upon each other. Not only in
thought, but also in reality. But for that very reason also in thinking,
because in reality faith and unbelief are so hard by each other that it
must be said: 'I believe, help thou mine unbelief!' (Mark 9.24). In
practice, however, those who champion the cause of faith have often
very little idea of those who deny faith, and only a completely distorted
picture of them. The idea that a non-believer, a decided non-Christian
or (to put it with rather blunt vagueness) a convinced atheist must be a
morally disreputable man, ought really to have been refuted long ago
not only in principle but also in practice. That it is nevertheless so deeply
rooted, betrays not only lack of knowledge of the opponent, but also
misunderstanding of our own position. The same is true *vice versa* of
the picture which the so-called non-believer has of faith. To a great
extent we can only admit that he is right in his rejection of faith. For if
faith were really what he considers it to be, we should have to be
ashamed to be believers. But even if it is a miserable caricature of faith,
the believer has cause to be ashamed of it. For it is somehow a charge on
the believers after all, if the non-believers have no idea of faith. And
indeed this dreadful ignorance about faith on the part of non-believers
corresponds only too closely with the dreadful ignorance about faith on
the part of believers. What sort of knowledge and understanding of faith
does the normal Christian today really have? No wonder the non-
believer feels himself thereby confirmed in his attitude, though of course
without guessing that he is a dupe who has let a muddled faith drive
him into muddled unbelief and keep him there—save that the muddled
unbelief very probably like the muddled faith is in fact unbelief.

But now, what is the conflict about, if faith and unbelief are truly in
conflict with each other? It would not be right to say simply: the conflict is about faith. Then it would seem as if there were here some special
cause which the one party upholds while the other rejects it, yet only
in the way of not accepting something that is supplementary. Faith
would then be something accidental to human nature, one of the infinitely many human possibilities. Strictly, it would be something superfluous, a sort of luxury which some indeed consider they cannot miss,
yet to which others, without missing anything, attach no value. Faith
would then only have to do with a particular sector of reality, interest
in which is simply not everyone's cup of tea. Or it might even relate to

some secret reality which is accessible only to the believer, a super-reality which the non-believer cannot possibly recognize as reality. That, however, would be a complete misunderstanding of the conflict between faith and unbelief, as if faith, being the object of the conflict, were also the cause of the conflict, and as if the whole conflict would have no object for the man to whom faith means nothing.

We could much sooner say: the conflict between faith and unbelief is about the 'either-or'—either faith or unbelief. That would bring out the fact that it is not a case of an accidental and supplementary interest but of a question which concerns every man and decides upon his human nature. Unbelief is only seemingly a mere negation, but in fact it is, just like faith itself, a position of a decisive kind; it is no mere absence of something ultimately superfluous, but an affirmation and assertion that runs counter to faith with regard to the absolutely necessary.

Then, however, we could also say: the conflict between faith and unbelief is about the very thing with which both faith and unbelief are concerned. It seems indeed a questionable undertaking to bring what faith is concerned with and what unbelief is concerned with to a common denominator, and thus to assert that both are concerned with the same thing. For there readily occur to us ways of putting it which make that appear absurd. Faith, it could be said for example, is concerned with God, with the Beyond, with eternal salvation, etc. In the case of unbelief, on the other hand, we could only note the constant absence of all that and say instead: it is concerned only with man, with this world, with temporal life. Yet this characterization is a wholly inadmissible caricature, as if unbelief were nothing else but naked materialism; and we must make a corresponding protest also in the name of faith against the suggestion of its being rightly characterized by saying it is concerned only with God, with the Beyond, with eternal salvation and consequently, so one must suppose, is indifferent to everything else. In that case the conflict between faith and unbelief could of course be settled by a peace of partition: the Beyond for faith, this world for unbelief. But this suggestion has so far been made only by cynical politicians, not by conscientious men.

It would not by any means, however, be correcting the mistake to say: naturally faith is not concerned only with God, the Beyond and eternal life, but also with man, this world and temporal life. For that still abides by the idea of two spheres bordering on each other. Rightly understood, however, faith is concerned with the world, with human nature; and

what it says of God, of the Beyond and of eternal life has no other point
at all than to bring man and the world to expression as what they truly
are. That does not amount in the end, as is so often feared, to shifting
the centre—to putting man in the centre instead of God, to thinking
anthropocentrically instead of theocentrically. It would certainly be a
foolish way of speaking to say that faith is concerned with God only for
the sake of man. But the very fact of its certainly having to do with God
alone is the way in which it has to do with real man. We cannot here
make separations and play off one against the other. Otherwise we turn
God into a supernatural ghost that has still to be added on to reality, yet
stands in competition with it and is therefore after all only a part of
reality as a whole. What the conflict between faith and unbelief is about
comes to light in greatest clearness only when the antithesis is sharpened
to the point of saying: reality itself is what the conflict is about between
faith and unbelief.

II

Now of course that does not yet make it all sufficiently clear. For
what is to be understood by that hard-worn word 'reality'? Or, to start
a little deeper down, without thereby losing sight of this question as to
the understanding of reality: what is actually at the bottom of the
expression 'conflict about'? Now, conflict is a thing with which we men
are all too familiar. So perhaps this expression 'conflict about' can help
to give some guidance in the maze of apparently increasingly difficult
questions in which our subject is involving us.

When two have a conflict, that can have an infinite number of causes.
But we can try to bring all imaginable causes of conflict under one single
head: the point is always that in one respect or another the right is in
dispute in point of reality. Both things, then, have to be taken into
account: conflict is in principle conflict about right. And conflict is
equally fundamentally conflict about something real. Both these statements admittedly appear problematical. Above all the first one seems
to fly in the face of experience. For how many conflicts on earth come
solely of not asking about right, but trusting to might and bringing
about a decision by force instead of in the way of justice! Yet that is no
objection to the observation that conflict by its very structure is conflict
about right—even if it is often enough not the right that is a man's due,
but the right that he takes to himself as the much-disputed right of the
stronger. Incidentally, in a very remote sense right and might do belong
together—and that, too, because the question of right is always a

question that concerns reality. And however endless the efforts to define the concept of reality may be, there is surely no option but to take the aspect of might as a guide.

The German word for 'reality' (*Wirklichkeit*) brings out the fact that the real is one way or another something which is effective (*wirksam*), active, mighty, which has the capacity to impress as real, to assert itself and gain recognition as real, to concern man as real, and which, in that it contains possibilities and hence has capabilities, has a reference to the future. So it is thus no accident that the one observation, that conflict is in principle conflict about right, combines with the other that conflict is fundamentally conflict about something real. The objection that there is surely often enough a conflict about phantoms or a conflict about mere words, does not tell against that. Phantoms, too, in fact can in certain cases come on the scene as enormously real things. This warns us to beware of a one-sided adherence, say, to the physical concept of reality, if we are not to do violence to reality. Strictly and indisputably valid as the physical view of reality is within its limits, it is yet precisely because of the method of objectification a most violent abstraction from reality as a whole. And it is all the more necessary to be cautious about coming out too quickly with the phrase 'conflict about mere words'. For reality as a whole is a thing one can only have a conflict about in words. A conflict about words can thus be a conflict about what reality as a whole mediates to us. Perhaps the very point at which the conflict about reality has broken out at its deepest is the one where words are the sole means used in the conflict—or better: where the only remaining means of identifying oneself is a defenceless word. Ultimately of course a conflict dies out as one that has no object, the moment it is perceived to be in actual fact a conflict about phantoms or about mere words. So that confirms what we have said: conflict is fundamentally conflict about something real. But for that reason too, it is only from the real that an end of the conflict can be expected to come. The man who refuses to let a conflict be decided in the light of what proves to be real and has the character of indubitability, is fighting to no purpose.

Now in the short space at my disposal these sketchy suggestions cannot be shaded in and protected against misunderstandings as they ought to be. But perhaps we can venture one further step. If 'conflict about something' means that in one respect or another the right is in dispute in point of reality, then the possible causes of conflict can be grouped under three heads. For the right can be in dispute in point of reality in three ways. The most immediate one is the conflict about the claiming and possessing of reality, about the right way of dealing with it, and thus about the command over reality and the moulding of it. Another kind is the conflict about the correct perception of reality, about the establishing of facts and of links between events. A third kind is the conflict about the true understanding of reality, about the grasping and conferring of meaning. These three forms of the conflict about who is in the right where reality is concerned, are interconnected in manifold ways and condition each other; but they are different spheres that are subject to different laws. Thus for example in the first sphere, in which action dominates, the conflict can be decided on occasion by force. In the second sphere, where it is a question of knowledge, it would be senseless to decide a question at issue by force. And in the third sphere, where understanding is in question, it would again be senseless to seek to decide the conflict as a question of knowledge. But in every case it is true that reality itself is not only the object of the conflict, but at the same time so to speak the forum of the conflict, the authority by which the conflict about right is decided. That is plainest where questions of knowledge are concerned. On these a judgment can be made only in strict, methodical reference to the object itself. But also in questions of active dealings with reality the conflict is not left to the mercy of chance and brute force, but is subject to the criterion of appropriateness: it is necessary to do justice to reality. And lastly, the conflict too about questions of understanding is not by any means a hopeless matter of personal taste, but here, in the proper home of language, it is a case of giving intelligible linguistic expression to the reality that concerns man and so shedding a convincing light on man's existence.

III

Let us now leave this somewhat laborious excursus and turn back again to our subject: faith and unbelief in the conflict about reality. This way of putting it does not add one element to the other, but merely sets side by side things that form an inseparable unity. That alongside of faith there appears also unbelief, is not something additional to faith. Faith is only faith in the neighbourhood of unbelief. That faith and unbelief are in conflict with each other, is therefore likewise not adding a further new aspect, as if there were many possible relations between the two and among others occasionally also conflict. Rather, the association of faith and unbelief is essentially one of conflict. And lastly, that this conflict is a conflict about reality is not a special case, so that apart from that many other things could also be in dispute between faith and unbelief. Rather, the addition 'about reality' merely elucidates the nature of the conflict between faith and unbelief and consequently the nature of faith and unbelief as such. Every conflict is, as we have made clear, a conflict about something real. The conflict between faith and unbelief, however, is not about this or that part of reality, but about reality as a whole—and from the standpoint of the whole certainly also about the concrete, individual aspect.

For that reason absolutely everything that is to be said on the question of faith must be considered from this standpoint. We can derive from it a general rule to guide us in all possible problems affecting faith, *viz.* that we ask ourselves: what has this to do with reality? Faith does not incite us to turn our backs on reality, but precisely to observe it in the deepest sense of the word 'observe', as one observes an opportunity, a commission, an office.[1] Faith does not flee reality, but stands up to it. And rightly understood, faith is never in conflict with reality, as is usually supposed—faith, it is said, largely stands in contradiction to reality and reality to faith. But that is true only in a superficial sense of reality that has been misused and violated. In truth, faith never stands in conflict with reality, but only in conflict with unbelief *about* reality. And the issue is in fact, who is right in point of reality, that is, who has reality on his side. The man who assents to faith can truly do so only in the certainty of thereby agreeing with reality, doing justice to it. For what other possibility could there be than that he, who is justified before God, should do justice to reality? Unbelief declares that faith is ignorant of reality and hostile to it. It is not a sign of faith to meet this with a bad conscience and a fifty-fifty mixture of admission and excuse. But faith's reaction is a decided: 'No! Unbelief is ignorant of reality and hostile to it.' Only so does the conflict between faith and unbelief acquire clarity and sharpness. In its conflict with unbelief about reality faith has reality itself on its side. It has no need to fear the bar of reality. Rather, faith can appeal to reality against unbelief. That is what Jesus did. That is the secret of the authority of his words.

What I have just propounded were certainly very risky propositions which oblige us to further reflexions of a kind at once bold and circumspect. I can only indicate with a few strokes the broad outlines of what would now have to be considered. And in fact I shall elucidate a little further the conflict between faith and unbelief about reality by maintaining the distinction made above between three groups of questions. I shall change the order, however, and begin with the conflict about

[1] Cf. the fuller explanation of this point above, p. 196.—*Translator.*

knowledge. Then follow some remarks on the conflict about understanding and finally on the conflict about action.

I begin with the conflict about knowing, because here the chief
conflict seems to lie. At all events for us men of the modern age. By the
modern age we understand the period of the total revolutionizing of the
world which, to date it roughly, broke upon all realms of life after the
Enlightenment. The historical roots of this revolutionary event, it is
true, reach very much further back, and the transformations have come
about in a highly complicated and many-sided historical process. But
we cannot and need not go into that in detail here. The phenomenon as
a whole stands plainly enough before us all. The shape of the world has
changed in such a way and to such a degree that the process is without
parallel in history. And surely the most exciting thing about it is, that
it is not simply a historical change of scene that has brought a few
upheavals and then returned to the same old static condition of things.
Rather, the revolutionary element has actually become an abiding principle. History has become an ever more comprehensive, all-embracing
movement that leaves nothing untouched, and one that above all has
assumed an ever more furious pace, bringing changes with a speed that
constantly surpasses itself. We have no idea where this is taking us.
One thing only is plain: here there is no going back. We can see that
most palpably in the technical mastery of the world and, linked in frightful ways with that, in political events.

As the seed from which this revolutionizing of the world sprang, we
can point to something entirely unpretentious—to the work of quiet
men of learning who ventured to elicit nature's secrets from her by
experiment, in order to master her; as also to subject historical tradition
to critical examination, in order to free themselves thereby from the
domination of traditional prejudices. Naturally, that is an extremely
stylized picture for the moment. There were many other factors also
involved. Yet this is surely the essential root of the process: that man
began to adopt a new attitude towards reality. To a hitherto unknown
degree he took advantage of the possibility to increase his knowledge, in
order thereby to increase his ability. For knowledge is power. And a
power, too, that counters the power of nature and the power of the past.
From the freedom of a new attitude towards reality there arose the
means to make ever greater use of human freedom through the mastering of nature and history.

Today we are ready all too quickly to condemn this process. For we
are confronted by unexpected results: man seems to be more threatened

and enslaved by powers of evil than ever. And what began so harmlessly in the name of science seems to be proving itself the revolt of unbelief against faith. The modern age has started off a landslide of secularization in every realm of life, of extensive de-Christianizing of public life, of widespread apostasy from the faith. Certainly with fluctuations and periodically with counter-currents. We are now living in the West once again in a phase of restoration. But it would be short-sighted to see in that a basic change in the situation. The Christian faith finds itself, despite the churches' occasional gains in prestige, on the defensive—a hopeless defensive, many think. The number of those to whom God has become an unintelligible word is not merely in the East, but also in the West, far greater than explicitly Christian circles usually imagine. That is not simply ill-will. People find it simply no longer possible to reconcile the traditional Christian faith with what they know of reality. Christianity is made to feel this within its own camp in a disturbing way. The methods of critical historical research when applied to the Bible have given many a shake to the traditional views. And the modern understanding of reality, which of course the Christian, too, as a modern man is unable to evade, causes at least uncertainty and anxiety, a bad conscience and an unhappily split mind, when the attempt is made to maintain nevertheless the traditional statements and ideas of faith. A faith of that kind has then understandably enough no power to carry conviction either.

The confusion that has taken place is too great for me to be able here to enter into the problem in detail. I must abide by fundamentals. The solution can only come from rightly grasping the proper meaning of faith. If faith comes into conflict with what is knowable and what stands conscientious testing as an indisputable item of knowledge, then that so-called faith proves itself to be pseudo-faith. For faith is not a matter of knowledge (in the sense of what is scientifically ascertainable) and can therefore never enter into competition with such knowledge either (unless the latter can be shown scientifically to be pseudo-knowledge). In individual cases this distinction may raise difficult problems. But the fundamental thing about it is plain. Faith is so little threatened by knowledge that on the contrary, if it is true faith, it sets us free to conscientious examination of what is knowable and takes up the cudgels against unbelief's behaving as if it were knowledge. For that reason faith is never by any means indifferent towards scientific examination of reality. For faith actually demands and promotes the right and proper use of the reason. That is what distinguishes it from superstition.

Faith has its proper place where it is a case of understanding reality. And indeed, understanding reality as a whole. This wholeness is not a sum of individual parts, but the experience that at one particular point everything stands or falls together. That sounds very strange. But perhaps it can be guessed what I am after when I say: this one point at which everything stands or falls together is the conscience of man. Not the conscience in the common, moralized sense as a moral law written in the heart. But the conscience in the radical sense as the place where it is decided what man truly is. If he is there under the pressure and anxiety of despair, then that does not merely affect the whole of his own being, but he also finds the whole world dragged into his despair. If on the other hand his conscience is cheerful and confident, then not only the man himself is cheerful and confident, but the whole of reality also takes on a different shape for him. Whatever binds him in conscience, decides how reality as a whole concerns him. If his conscience is set free, then he is absolutely free and no power on earth can alter that. It is therefore better not to call conscience a place *in* man but—however surprising it may sound—the place *of* man. For in the conscience it is decided where man belongs, where he is and where he has his abode.

And that is now, in its most rudimentary form, the decision between unbelief and faith: where does man belong, where is his place, where has he his abode? In himself and under the constraining law of the reality which concerns him—or outside himself and outside the constraint of the law in that freedom from himself and that freedom from the law of sin and death which Paul calls the glorious freedom of the children of God (Rom. 8.21)? This freedom we can only have imparted to us by the Word that frees the conscience and awakens faith, the Word that is proclaimed in the name, and that means with the authority, of Jesus, because, as Paul says, the coming of Jesus is the coming of faith (Gal. 3.23). That is no more than a pointer to what calls for a decision between faith and unbelief. It is a question of man's place. For with that the decision is made on the whole of reality—the decision between assurance and despair, between freedom and servitude, between life and death. And for that reason faith knows itself one with the purpose of reality, with the purpose of the creation.

But what, now, of the conflict between faith and unbelief about reality, in so far as reality is the field of our action? Faith at all events conducts no crusade of force against unbelief for the possession of the earth, for the lordship over reality. But that is not at all to say that faith withdraws into some realm of thought. Faith urges towards work. However little it is itself a human work or appeals to a human work or glories in it, it is yet the source of works. For it is God's work and therefore the origin of such works as we otherwise seek in vain and can hardly consider possible—*viz.* really good works, and that means at once: such works as have a future and are therefore not foolish and vain works but meaningful and rewarding ones, not inhuman works but truly human ones, works performed in following Jesus and in representing him. As the Johannine Christ says: 'He that believeth in me, the works that I do shall he do also; and greater works than these shall he do' (John 14.12).

Faith is thus so certain of being right in true reality that it is free to love and free to suffer, free, like Jesus, not to exercise lordship but to serve, to do justice to its neighbour, to the world, to reality as such. For where faith does justice to reality through love (and indeed even to the point of death), there the world is observed as creation, and that means: there the kingdom of God is at hand. Before this reality unbelief must pass away. For unbelief is at bottom hatred of reality. Unbelief, it is true, can combine with a love of many things. But it cannot love reality as a whole. For it cannot from the heart praise him who created the world. Faith, however, is at bottom nothing else but praise of the Creator.

XVI

THE NECESSITY OF THE
DOCTRINE OF THE TWO KINGDOMS

I

F o r more than two decades the doctrine of the two kingdoms has been the subject of particularly violent debate, and of various detailed examinations.[1] The sense in which I venture to make it the subject of a paper is indicated by my asking about its theological core, i.e. its necessity. The man who considers something to be necessary which appears to others to be of little help, or even to be pernicious, does not hesitate to repeat the necessary teaching and is ready to make clear its necessity by summing up its essential elements. At the same time, precisely from the standpoint of necessity we cannot stop at summary repetition.

Nor, of course, is it a case of giving a neutral presentation of the facts and then having to add recommendations of an apologetic kind. If the doctrine of the two kingdoms is not of itself evidently necessary, then no additional arguments are of any avail. The question of necessity points us strictly to the subject itself. The subject itself in this case is not a historical matter, however much it comes to us by way of history. The doctrine of the two kingdoms has widespread links with history and is primarily indebted to the theology of Luther. What now follows comes from the study of that theology.[2] Nevertheless, I shall not confine myself to a historical presentation of Luther's two kingdom doctrine. If it is a case of necessity (*Notwendigkeit*) in the sense of what answers a need (*das Notwendende*), then the doctrine of the two kingdoms must be accounted for in the present as something that opens a way to the future. It is true that the historical approach, too, brings with it the problem of present understanding. But in taking this problem explicitly as our subject, our purpose is dogmatic clarification, and consequently

---

[1] Cf. *EKL*[2] III, pp. 1927 ff and *RGG*[3] IV, pp. 495 ff, esp. pp. 509 f, 519.

[2] The following discussion of the problem is based above all on the rich material supplied by the 1531 *Lectures on Galatians*: *WA* 40/1 and 2.

doctrine whose necessity is its salutariness. We could thus speak of the two kingdom doctrine's necessity for salvation. Only, two misunderstandings must be ruled out—one, that it could be a necessary prerequisite of salvation, whereas salvation itself is surely the thing whose necessity is to come to expression in the doctrine of the two kingdoms; and the other, that salvation could be bound in a doctrinaire way to a theory instead of to that world-event towards which the doctrine of the two kingdoms is directed. The standpoint of necessity for salvation, in the sense of the one thing that is absolutely and finally needed, is, rightly understood, really always the specifically theological standpoint. For when we are concerned with God, we are concerned with salvation and the *eschaton* in inseparable unity. To enquire into the necessity of the two kingdom doctrine is to enquire into the theological justification of its at once soteriological and eschatological claim.

This approach allows the abundance of detail and variety of opinion to recede into the background and concentrates the attention on the aim. In that way the question as to the necessity of the two kingdom doctrine becomes the question as to its clarity. For that reason, too, accounting for the necessity of the two kingdom doctrine does not mean bringing clarity *into* a difficult and obscure doctrine, but *by means of* the two kingdom doctrine bringing clarity into the maze of reality that concerns us. As a theological doctrine it seeks in fact to serve the Word that is 'a lamp unto my feet, and a light unto my path'.[1] That, however, forces us away from secondary problems involved in this or that part of the two kingdom doctrine to the question of its ground, the fundamental point where the sense of the duality is determined. Usually the two kingdom doctrine centres on examining the consequences of that duality, while the duality itself is presupposed as a known fact and therefore given no further consideration. The question of the necessity of the two kingdom doctrine, however, fixes the attention precisely on these presuppositions. Not in order to distract it from the practical consequences, but in order to consider these in the light of their ground. This requires much patience, and a single paper can only point the first steps. But it is a safeguard against interpreting the necessity of the two kingdom doctrine as a mere makeshift, as an unfortunate or welcome compromise between faith and reality.

II

We shall trace out first of all the breadth and depth of the Reformers'

[1] Ps. 119.105.

distinction of the two kingdoms, as a way of approaching the problem of this duality.

The prevailing impression is, that the two kingdom doctrine has to do with a problem of ethics, or even *the* problem of ethics—to be more precise, the problem of theological ethics, the behaviour of the Christian in the world. For that reason the doctrine of the two kingdoms is usually dealt with not in dogmatics but in ethics. And indeed it takes concrete form primarily in two groups of questions. On the one hand it is concerned with the understanding of the Sermon on the Mount, with its validity for the life of the Christian amid the ordinances of this world (and thus with such questions as military service, oaths, etc.). On the other hand it is concerned with the relation of church and state, of ecclesiastical and secular government, and especially with the problem of the basis of church law. It is certainly granted that the two kingdom doctrine as an ethical problem rests upon dogmatic presuppositions, as indeed the separation of ethics and dogmatics is supposed altogether to be merely of a technical, not a fundamental kind. But the tension which comes up for examination in the doctrine of the two kingdoms is nevertheless understood in this common view to be an ethical conflict between the principles of political order and the radical demands of the Sermon on the Mount, or a tension, at least latent, between two judicial orders, the *ius civile* and the *ius ecclesiasticum*, the secular and ecclesiastical government.

However much the two kingdom doctrine has always found, and always will find, its primary application in these groups of questions, it is nevertheless inadmissibly narrowed down if we let our consideration of it be determined *a priori* by these two major spheres of its application. Primarily, at any rate, it is not a question of the relation of two different kinds of statute or code, or even of two different laws, but of law and Gospel. That at all events is Luther's terminology, which Johannes Heckel does not at all do justice to in his book *Lex charitatis*.[1] However permissible it may be to speak at times—paradoxically, according to Luther—of a '*lex Christi*', and however much we may see also in the Gospel the foundation of a *ius divinum*, yet strictly speaking, and in the terminology which is absolutely dominant in Luther, the Gospel is not law. But the Gospel is constitutive for the *regnum Christi*, while the *lex*

---

[1] Johannes Heckel, *Lex charitatis: Eine juristische Untersuchung über das Recht in der Theologie Martin Luthers*, Abh. d. Bayer. Akad. d. Wiss. Phil.-hist. Kl. Neue Folge, Heft 36 (1953). Cf. *WA* 40/1, p. 141.6: *Faciunt ex Euangelio legem charitatis*.

is constitutive for the *regnum mundi*. It is true that on thorough examination much more careful differentiations will have to be made in relating the distinction between the two kingdoms to the distinction between law and Gospel. Nevertheless, the co-ordination of the one *regnum* with the *lex* and the other *regnum* with the Gospel is fundamental.

III

If the doctrine of the two kingdoms has thus to be understood in co-ordination with the doctrine of law and Gospel, then the point at issue is not some partial aspect of theology, but the fundamental problem of theology. This fundamental problem is, to state it simply, how the Gospel comes to be heard as Gospel. It is with the ἀκοὴ πίστεως that theology is properly and ultimately concerned. For the sake of the purity of the ἀκοὴ πίστεως, and that means for the sake of its clarity and its power, the doctrine of *law* and *Gospel* is required. Correspondingly, because theology is concerned with the *regnum Christi*, theology unfolds itself as the doctrine of the *two* kingdoms. The nature of this logic, according to which we must speak of law and Gospel for the sake of the Gospel and therefore of the two kingdoms for the sake of the kingdom of Christ, is the *one* theme of all the reflexions that follow. For that is precisely what the question of the necessity of the two kingdom doctrine amounts to in the end. But now already we can make a few explanatory statements on the point.

Although it is only on the basis of Christian faith and to that extent for the sake of the *regnum Christi* that the two kingdoms can be spoken of (but also must be spoken of), yet it would be fundamentally wrong to say that the two kingdom doctrine concerns Christians alone. As truly as the Gospel concerns every man, so the two kingdom doctrine has to do with what concerns every man as man. The two kingdom doctrine undoubtedly deals with an antithesis, a conflict, a struggle, whatever way this basic dualism may be more precisely defined. What is the cause of that conflict? It would be a superficial judgment to say that the cause is the coming of Christ, of the Gospel, of the ἀκοὴ πίστεως, and thus that the *regnum Christi* has appeared beside, and in antithesis to, the *regnum mundi* which primarily existed alone; or to put it in terms of the individual, that man has become a Christian. That of course is to make it look as if the *regnum mundi* as such and in itself is in order and without contradiction, as is naturally true also of the *regnum Christi*. The discord—one would have to go on to say—comes of having the two mutually incompatible kingdoms side by side and face to face. It is only when we become Christians that we find ourselves in the conflict, only then do the problems arise that were indicated above in regard to the Sermon on the Mount or to the relation of church and state. The man who is not a Christian is spared these problems and can exist free of problems in the *regnum mundi*. Then of course, what need is there of the *regnum Christi*, if that is what first brings the contradiction? What is really the sense of becoming a Christian, when that brings a split existence in the place of an existence free of contradiction?

But now, the fact is, that it was through the preaching of the Gospel and through faith that the conflict was first perceived and was kindled as such. This is amply confirmed by scripture and by experience. But that is not by any means to say that the cause of the conflict was thereby superimposed on the world and on human nature for the first time. The ἀκοὴ πίστεως surely seeks, on the contrary, to be a message of *salvation* to the world. And that means that the Gospel engages with (*eingehen auf*) the *lex* and does not appear as some sort of supplementary factor accidentally competing with the *lex*. The *regnum Christi* does not appear beside the *regnum mundi* without a motive. For the necessity of the *regnum Christi* is its engaging with the godlessness of the *regnum mundi*. The cause of the conflict which comes up for discussion in the two kingdom doctrine thus lies in the *regnum mundi* itself. And that, too, not simply in the sense that the *regnum mundi* is in fact the negative, and therefore guilty, factor in the conflict. Rather, in the sense that the *regnum mundi* itself already bears this contradiction *within* it. Self-contradiction indeed is its very nature. '*Regnum mundi*' is, rightly understood, a contradiction in terms.

We said above that both kingdoms must be spoken of *for the sake of the kingdom of Christ*. It amounts to the same in the end if we now put it apparently in the opposite form: the doctrine of the two kingdoms is necessary *for the sake of the regnum mundi*—which, however, now means, for the sake of resolving this self-contradictoriness of a *regnum mundi*, and hence, for the liberation, for the deliverance of the world from its self-contradiction. For that reason the two kingdom doctrine claims to be true teaching about the world and for it, but not to deal with the sort of special problems that arise only for the Christian because although he exists in this world he has also bound himself to the *regnum Christi*.

It is understandable if the two kingdom doctrine appears primarily or exclusively as a means of coming to the Christian's help in the situation of conflict in which he finds himself in regard to the problems of the Sermon on the Mount or of ecclesiastical government. But we do not do full justice to the two kingdom doctrine until we bring it to the help of the world in its self-contradiction. Then, however, the impetus towards asserting the two kingdom doctrine is not provided by ethical deliberations on this or that particular decision about concrete action, whereby the actual meaning of the *regnum Christi* is carelessly taken for granted as known—which, however, means in practice that nothing is said of it. Rather, the cardinal point for a helpful application of the two kingdom doctrine is, that it should be made convincingly clear what the real nature of the *regnum Christi* is and in what sense it is opposed to the *regnum mundi*. It is abysmal when a particular ethical or political decision is declared in the name of the Gospel to be required of us, but the Gospel itself cannot be intelligibly and convincingly proclaimed. The perplexity in which Christian preaching finds itself in face of the burning political questions of today is certainly disturbing. But the perplexity on the point of how to proclaim the Gospel intelligibly and convincingly is much greater still, and it is more disturbing; for it is the cause of the other perplexity, or of the way we flee from that other subject—or even into it. The helpful light that should come from Christian preaching in the sense of the two kingdom doctrine can shine only when the ἀκοὴ πίστεως brings the *regnum Christi*. Then we shall be sure to engage with the world in the right way.

IV

Let us now press on with the attempt to grasp the breadth and depth of the distinction between the two kingdoms. If we start from the basic relation between *regnum mundi* and *lex* on the one side and *regnum Christi* and Gospel on the other—let us call them briefly the left and the right side—then we notice the following: There is little scope for alternative expressions to characterize the right side. Alongside of Christ and Gospel there appear as *differentiae specificae* of this kingdom *gratia, fides* or *spiritus*. We could add further characteristics from Luther's rich vocabulary, such as *pax, certitudo*, etc. But it is superfluous to name them all, since they form so to speak a list of identical terms. It is a different matter on the left side. Here we encounter a confusing welter of terms which characterize this kingdom. Instead of *mundus* or *lex*, it can be: *diabolus, mors, peccatum, caro, ira, ratio, opus, mores, politia, oeconomia, philosophia, creatura*—indeed, even *charitas* can appear in certain circumstances on this side opposed to *fides*. Even that is only a selection from the wealth of terms. But it marks clearly enough the problematical width of the scope here.

This difference between the two poles in the tension makes it easy to understand that in the two kingdom doctrine no further attention is normally given to the *regnum Christi*, because everything here is thought to be plain, and that therefore hardly anything is said about the nature of the duality before proceeding at once to its ethical consequences. One thing is certainly right in this: that the whole problem with which the two kingdom doctrine is concerned is essentially the problem of the *regnum mundi*. As indeed also in the doctrine of law and Gospel the *lex* is the factor in connexion with which all the problems appear. Yet just as for the theological doctrine of the law everything depends on the clarity of the Gospel, so everything that relates to the *regnum mundi* can only be clear when the nature of the *regnum Christi* is not merely supposedly clear, but really so. Of course, there is so much interlocking in the whole that it is not possible, say, to take first of all the *regnum Christi* alone and bring it clearly to expression in and for itself. For it is only in relation to the *regnum mundi* that the *regnum Christi* shows its clarity and power. As the doctrine of law and Gospel is no supplement to the Gospel, so the doctrine of the two kingdoms is no appendix added on later to the doctrine of the *regnum Christi*. Rather, the doctrine of the two kingdoms is itself the doctrine of the *regnum Christi*. This is not by any means intended in the sense of a Christocratic dissolution of the two kingdom doctrine. Rather, it means that the *regnum Christi* can be spoken of only when the *regnum mundi* is spoken of at the same time. To that extent the clarity of the *regnum Christi* is dependent on the presence of the *regnum mundi*. But that does not contradict what we said before. For from the clarity of the *regnum Christi* there comes clarity *about* the *regnum mundi*. Yet the *regnum Christi* becomes clear only *in relation to* the *regnum mundi*.

V

That is confirmed when we turn to the confusing variety of ways in which Luther can characterize the *regnum mundi*. It looks as if he here mixed up together things which require to be carefully distinguished, as if he forced under a single head things which cannot reasonably be brought to a common denominator and which therefore also compel him to speak of the *regnum mundi* in very contradictory ways. Sometimes one has the impression that the phrase *regnum diaboli* is used to brand absolutely everything, including reason and ethos, as devilry. Sometimes on the other hand the pendulum seems to swing hard to the other extreme of deifying the creation. Luther's contrasting statements on the civil magistrate are as well known as his judgments on the *ratio*, which seem to swing back and forward between coarsest vilification and unsurpassable praise. But instead of now pointing excusingly to Luther's supposedly unsystematic nature with its tendency towards exaggeration, we should stop to reflect that the remarkable state of affairs we have mentioned is highly noteworthy. Three things are notable here.

First, it shows once again that the usual practice of taking the two kingdom doctrine only as a basic formula of political ethics is unjustifiably one-sided (and disastrously straitening as a result). The concept *regnum* of course—this makes it understandable, but not excusable— leads to *regnum mundi* being associated in the first instance, if not indeed altogether, only with the state. Quite apart from the dubiousness of employing the concept 'state' in the interpretation of Luther's statements, it is misleading to tie his two kingdom doctrine down to the subject of the Christian and the state. Certainly this is where the main emphasis in Luther's own application of it lies. For that reason his *Von weltlicher Obrigkeit* together with the political writings that are substantially akin to it, and the exposition of the Sermon on the Mount, are the favourite sources for the presentation of his two kingdom doctrine. Yet when we have acquired some familiarity with Luther's theological thinking, and take the trouble to view his statements not just statistically but reflectively, then it should be reasonably clear that under *regnum mundi* there falls the whole of reality *extra Christum*, and that means *extra fidem*—not merely its political aspect, but in the widest sense everything that concerns man, and thus everything that has to do with his *ratio*, but also everything that has to do with his will and his passions, and hence absolutely everything from the most trifling human activity to science, morals and religion. Only in this broad sweep can the two kingdom doctrine be rightly interpreted.

A second thing goes closely along with that: if it is strictly a case of the direct counterpart of the *regnum Christi*, then it is the whole of life (including death!), the whole of reality in all its diversity, and even contradictoriness, that must so to speak come on to the stage as this *regnum mundi*. Here nothing in the vast range of its possibilities can be excepted in principle: all the filth and all the beauty of the world, all its foolishness and all its wisdom, all evil and all good, is the counterpart with which the *regnum Christi* has to do. The kingdom of Christ comes upon all these things, does not pass them by but rather engages with them. It would be falsely setting limits to the *regnum Christi* if we did not allow the *regnum mundi* to be as wide and as great as it is.

But now, from that there follows a third thing, which helps us to the precise formulation of the decisive question. The difficulty is surely this: how far do all these things which now appear on the side of the *regnum mundi* represent a meaningful unity in contrast to the kingdom of Christ—and that, too, not under an empty general head, but in that compact concentration under a single will which is manifestly intended by the word *regnum*, namely, ill will towards the *regnum Christi?* One thing is certainly plain: the unity in which everything in the concept *regnum mundi* is comprehended, is given as such only in antithesis to the *regnum Christi*. It is not a thing that can somehow be understood as a meaningful unity apart from this antithesis. The meaning of *regnum mundi* in the sense of the two kingdom doctrine cannot be defined independently of the *regnum Christi*. And this, too, is plain: the unity of the *regnum mundi* in its relation to the kingdom of Christ is not an undifferentiated unity. The fact that such a diversity of extremely different concepts can be employed synonymously to characterize the *regnum mundi* does not mean the complete washing out of all distinctions. But everything now depends on the correct understanding of the differentiating factor. The seemingly confused jumble of statements about the *regnum mundi* orders itself into two main coherent groups. Not, it is true, with the help of an existing dualism in the *regnum mundi* itself in the sense of different realms of subject or value. Rather, the *regnum mundi* as a whole in antithesis to the *regnum Christi* has to be regarded in a twofold way. We can also say: the *regnum mundi* as the claim of the world stands to the *regnum Christi* as the claim of Christ upon the world in a double relation—a contradictory one (of exclusiveness) and a contrasting one (of co-existence), or as we would prefer to say, a relationship of disagreement and a relationship of agreement. I prefer this way of expressing it because it interprets the relations as an event, and a linguistic event at that. We must therefore, in using the terms 'agree' (*entsprechen*) and 'disagree' (*widersprechen*), keep to the concrete meaning of the verb 'speak' (*sprechen*). This also safeguards us against the intrusion of an analogical view which takes its bearings on the comparison of two independent entities, and not—as the word 'agree' (*entsprechen*), which means speaking in response to another (*antwortendes Entgegensprechen*), indicates—on the event of two opposing poles making corresponding claims and entering into mutual relations.

VI

The relationship between the *regnum mundi* and *regnum Christi* is thus on the one hand an antithesis of disagreement, in which one excludes and denies the other. The *regnum mundi* is the negation of the *regnum Christi*. One cancels out the other. Co-existence between the two is out of the question. Here we have an irreconcilable Either-or in the sense of II Cor. 6.14 ff: 'What fellowship hath righteousness with unrighteousness? and what communion hath light with darkness? And what concord hath Christ with Belial? or what part hath he that believeth with an infidel? And what agreement hath the temple of God with idols?' The absolute incompatibility, the relation of contradiction, is in view when the *regnum mundi* is opposed to the *regnum Christi* as *regnum diaboli* or *civitas Babylonica*.

The phenomenon of irreconcilable disagreement has all too many parallels for it to appear strange to us. But it would be completely mistaking the nature of that contradictory relationship between the *regnum mundi* and *regnum Christi* if we were to understand it after the manner of mortal enmity between two earthly kingdoms. For the antithesis between the *regnum mundi* and *regnum Christi* differs from that both in the radicality and totality of the disagreement and in the certainty of repudiating the opponent as one who in truth is already annihilated. It is true that these symptoms of an antithesis that is to be understood in the eschatological sense can also be usurped in worldly conflicts. But if in face of that we must rightly maintain that to make merely relative antitheses absolute in this way is to do violence to reality and is therefore unreasonable, then the question certainly arises what right there can be for asserting an eschatological Either-or in history at all, and whether the understanding of the relationship between the *regnum mundi* and *regnum Christi* as an eschatological *contradictio* does not therefore pass beyond the sphere of what can be accounted for historically. Unless of course this understanding of the *regnum mundi* and *regnum Christi* in terms of contradiction is a thing we will venture to fight out in the sphere of the understanding of reality itself, as a way of deciding what is properly and ultimately to be claimed as real and what as inane. Johannes Heckel was undoubtedly right in his emphatic reminder that in interpreting the two kingdom doctrine the eschatological antithesis of the two kingdoms, i.e. their relationship of contradiction, requires to be noticed. Only, the problem of distinguishing the two kingdoms then has very much wider repercussions than can be seen in Heckel's con-

ception of the two kingdom doctrine—repercussions extending as far
as the ontological problem.

But now, there is just as little doubt on the other hand that the *regnum
mundi* and *regnum Christi* stand not only in a relationship of disagreement with each other, but also in a relationship of agreement, and thus
in an antithesis in which the one does not by any means cancel out the
other, but in fact even asserts it. In place of the absolute Either-or there
now comes a 'Both-and'—of such a kind, namely, that without prejudice to the difference between the two poles, the one belongs to the
other. The emphasis in the two kingdom doctrine usually lies so much
upon this relation of agreement that in the interests of undisturbed
compatibility even this agreement relationship is blunted and emascu-
lated into a meaningless juxtaposition of two separate realms fenced off
and removed from any possibility of conflict. The genuine meaning of
the relationship of agreement between the two kingdoms, however, is
shown by some of the pairs of terms by which Luther is often accustomed
to mark the distinction between the two kingdoms. The one *regnum*, he
says, is *terrenum*, the other *coeleste*, the one *temporale*, the other *aeternum*,
the one *carnale*, the other *spirituale*. This must not of course be understood as a relationship of disagreement. Heaven is not intended here to
mean the exclusive negation of earth, and just as little is eternity the
exclusive negation of time. And the same is true also, at least to a certain
extent, of spirit and flesh. Heaven and earth, eternity and time, spirit
and flesh are co-ordinated and associated with each other by the will
of God, they stand in a relation of response and responsibility, they have
as it were things to say to each other and to ask each other. And indeed
for this reason: that the relationship between God and the creature in
which they are comprehended is in essence (as distinct, that is, from its
perversion) a relationship not of disagreement but of agreement.

Admittedly these are in the first instance statements whose meaning
is open to question. We raised a moment ago the question whether the
understanding of the two kingdoms in terms of contradiction, and thus
the eschatological qualification of historical decision, is meaningful.
Now we are faced in this other context with the question whether a
relationship of agreement between the two kingdoms is meaningful
when it is interpreted in terms of the distinction between earth and
heaven, time and eternity. Can earth and heaven, time and eternity, even
world and God, be understood in any other way than in a relationship
of mutual contradiction? That is, can we seriously accept both together?
For what do 'heaven' and 'eternity' really mean if they are to be con-

ceived in an intelligible and convincing—which, however, means a necessary—relation of agreement with earth and time? Indeed, what does 'God' really mean if he is to be understood as distinct from the world and yet not as in contradiction to the world but rather as its Creator? The breadth and depth of the distinction between the two kingdoms which we have been trying to fathom assumes tremendous proportions. The problem of eschatology and the problem of creation now await discussion, and therewith the sense of speaking theologically at all. We are seemingly a long way from the usual questions of the two kingdom doctrine, but perhaps approaching the very point with which the two kingdom doctrine is really concerned.

VII

We find quite plainly in the two kingdom doctrine these two tendencies, as a result of which the various statements assemble themselves into competing groups. On the one side it is a question of the eschatological conflict between the divine and all that denies the divine, so that the victory of the one is the annihilation of the other. On the other side it is a question of preserving or restoring the relationship between Creator and creature, so that the vindication of the one is the glory of the other. These are completely familiar basic themes of the Christian faith. The difficulty seems to be merely that the usual two kingdom doctrine involves both in a most confusing way, instead of carefully separating the two groups of questions—perhaps even terminologically, by leaving to the concept of two 'kingdoms' the character of eschatological contradiction and reserving for the relationship of polar agreement the designation two 'orders' (*Regimente*). This terminological separation, it is true, has no convincing basis in Luther's own way of speaking. Yet that would be no essential hindrance.

From the material point of view, however, there is this much against it: in that way we evade the problem of the relation between eschatology and creation which is so disturbingly acute in the two kingdom doctrine. And there is the suspicion that in a separation of this kind both groups are abandoned to meaninglessness. It is a sign of bad theology when in the debate on the two kingdom doctrine one party fancies the eschatological perspective while the other hoists the flag of the ordinances of creation or providence. Creation and eschatology require to be thought together in theology and not merely held apart like the prelude and finale of a drama. That demands in some cases criticism of the traditional form both of the doctrine of creation and also of eschatology. All

the same, a sign of the problematical way in which the two belong together is provided by the far too little noticed tension *in* eschatology
between end and consummation. And although the doctrine of the two
orders allows relative justice to the ordinances of the world, yet it is by
no means related independently to creation and providence, but solely
in connexion with soteriology, and therefore also with eschatology, since
of course salvation radically understood is eschatological salvation.

If such a division of the two kingdom doctrine into a two order
doctrine is thus to be rejected, since both things must constantly be
present together, the relation of disagreement and the relation of agreement, then the twofoldness of the relation can be maintained only if one
of the two, the *regnum mundi* or the *regnum Christi*, has a double sense.
We can now take up again a point we made earlier. The cause of the
tension that comes up for discussion in the two kingdom doctrine we
saw to be the *regnum mundi* itself—and indeed not simply in its negative-
ness towards the kingdom of Christ, but in its own essential self-
contradiction. If, however, the antithesis between the two kingdoms is
not only one of disagreement, but also of agreement, then the peculiar
feature of the two kingdom doctrine—*viz.* this twofold relation between
the *regnum mundi* and *regnum Christi*—must be explained by the self-
contradiction of the *regnum mundi*. And if we do not grasp that twofold
relation and know how to deal with it, then neither shall we be able to
apply the two kingdom doctrine to the help of the world in its self-
contradiction and to prove its necessity for salvation.

VIII

But at this point we must certainly be careful, lest there should be a
short-circuit. We have now so to speak two high tension fields: the
regnum mundi itself, of which we have said that it is a self-contradiction,
and the relationship between *regnum mundi* and *regnum Christi*, which
we have seen to be a twofold relation and as such to be grounded in the
self-contradiction of the *regnum mundi*. But what is the nature of this
grounding link between the two fields of tension? One would expect a
simple equation in the sense of the two relations of contradiction and
agreement between the two kingdoms being related to the two sides of
the self-contradiction in the *regnum mundi*. That is how it is, too, if the
self-contradiction of the *regnum mundi* is rightly grasped, *viz.* as a contradiction between the creatureliness of the world and the autocratic
behaviour of a world that denies its being created. What we are designating as the self-contradiction of the creation, is thus primarily contra-

diction between creature and Creator. The creature which denies the Creator, thereby denies itself, although—indeed precisely because—it is concerned to assert itself against God. The structure of self-contradiction, it is true, seems to belong to the *regnum mundi* on its own, without regard to its relation to God, yet it is altogether only in view of the relation to God that it can be grasped as self-contradiction. The designation self-contradiction thus includes the assertion that the relation to God is not something which is tacked on to the reality of the world, but is the very thing which is truly the reality of the world. If, however, the *regnum Christi* is nothing else but the coming of the *regnum Dei*, then the relation of disagreement between the *regnum mundi* and *regnum Christi* is in the end the outbreak of the contradiction between the fallen creature and the Creator. And the relation of agreement between the *regnum mundi* and *regnum Christi* is the dawning of agreement between creature and Creator. The twofold relation between the *regnum mundi* and *regnum Christi* has thus to do with being a *peccator* and being *iustus*, since of course the *peccator* is the man who disagrees with the Creator and the *iustus* is the man who agrees with the Creator.

But now, the real meaning of *peccator* and *iustus* is constantly threatened with misunderstanding. For it is of no small consequence for the understanding of the two kingdom doctrine as a whole, but therefore also for the understanding of every part of it and every concept in it, whether we think within the sphere of the *regnum mundi* and according to its standards and accordingly interpret the *regnum Christi* after the manner of the *regnum mundi*, or whether we understand what the specific nature of the *regnum Christi* is as distinct from the *regnum mundi* and how that determines the peculiarity of the whole structure of the two kingdom doctrine. Thus it depends on whether the two kingdom doctrine is understood on terms of unbelief—and that means misunderstood—or whether it is understood on terms of faith. Or as Luther can also say, whether our understanding follows the *ratio*, which has its rightful place within the *regnum mundi*—for the *regnum mundi* is *regnum rationis*—or whether our understanding follows faith, which is the mark of the kingdom of Christ, for the *regnum Christi* is the *regnum fidei*. Or to put it a little differently again: it depends on whether the inner logic of the two kingdom doctrine is forced into the logic of the *regnum mundi*—and now we can say in place of that with astonishing synonymity: whether the interpretation is philosophical, metaphysical, moral, legal, political —or whether the logic proper to the two kingdom doctrine is maintained, and that means: the interpretation is theological. The whole struggle to understand the two kingdom doctrine comes to concentrate on the question, what is the real meaning of '*theologice*'. Indeed the whole intention of the two kingdom doctrine is to bring out clearly what is entrusted to theology, and preserve it from harm.

That seems to amount in the end to the decisive thing being whether the world is religiously understood or not, i.e. whether God is included in our thinking or not. But it is not a simple case of the two kingdom doctrine as the religious understanding of reality forming the antithesis to the monism maintained in one form or another by a-religious views of reality. Rather, according to Luther all religious ways of understanding the world also stand without distinction on the same level as what we have seen as philosophical, metaphysical, moral views and such like. Faith alone, taken strictly as *fides Christi*, is constitutive for the meaning of 'theological'. The decisive thing is not that God is spoken of, but that God is spoken of *theologically*, and that means *secundum fidem*. It is not the distinction of two kingdoms as such that is the characteristic feature of the two kingdom doctrine. *Mutatis mutandis* every view of reality that can be taken seriously can be claimed to be a two kingdom doctrine, a doctrine that calls for a decision. It depends whether the two kingdoms are distinguished *secundum fidem*.

Every view of the two kingdom doctrine which does not take its bearings on the nature of Christian faith ends up by dividing the *world* into two kingdoms. This appears to be a rough and ready characterization, but I think it touches the seat of the trouble, *viz.* the simple equation of the two kingdoms with the contradictoriness of the world. The theological alternatives are then only the metaphysical extension of the moral alternatives. Sin is then what is morally evil, righteousness before God what is morally good—in both cases, it may be, raised to a higher power by reference to a religious law which transcends the moral law. Now of course we, too, spoke of an equation in the sense of the relations of contradiction and agreement between the two kingdoms being related to the two sides of the self-contradiction in the *regnum mundi*. Yet we did not interpret this self-contradiction as a halving of the world, but in the sense that the world as a whole enters into contradiction with itself as creature. Sin, as theology understands it, is not one particular province. For the sinner everything becomes sin. And righteousness is likewise not one particular province. To the pure all things are pure.

Thus if we took the twofold relation of contradiction and agreement and connected it with the self-contradiction of the *regnum mundi*, then that did not mean: the *regnum Christi* contradicts the *regnum mundi* in *that* province in which the latter is evil, and there is agreement in *that* province of the *regnum mundi* which is good. But it means: the *regnum Christi* contradicts the *regnum mundi* as a whole, because the latter contradicts the created nature of the world. Yet the *regnum Christi* for that very reason confronts the *regnum mundi* in the form of responsive agreement. For the *regnum Christi* is indeed nothing else but the proclamation of the fact that the time of the self-contradiction of the *regnum mundi* has come to an end. The event of this responsive pronouncement, wherein the particular Word takes place on which the world as world depends, turns the *kingdom* of the world back again into mere world, world as God's creation. In the coming of this Word which agrees with the world as world, the world experiences the righteousness of God. For this is God's way of doing justice to the world—that he loves it, loves it creatively. The *regnum Christi* as the event of the *iustitia Dei* is and remains a word-event and therefore a faith-event. For that reason, however, until the final presence of the kingdom of God we are left with the distinction between the two kingdoms as a distinction between two modes of *iustitia*.

IX

Each of the two kingdoms has its *iustitia*: the one has *iustitia civilis*, the other *iustitia Christiana*. Thus it is not simply a contrast between *iniustitia* and *iustitia*. But neither is it one between some kind of modest, minumum *iustitia* and a maximum *iustitia* of those who are perfect (the way the Sermon on the Mount is misunderstood as a performance of voluntary extras or as a special law imposed on Christians; whereas it is surely, rightly understood, an encouragement to concrete faith). The two kinds of *iustitia* differ not in degree but qualitatively. The one is *iustitia legis, iustitia operum, iustitia activa, iustitia terrena*; the other is *iustitia Euangelii, iustitia fidei, iustitia passiva, iustitia coelestis*. The note of contradiction is not by any means now forgotten. The *iustitia* in the *regnum mundi* as *iustitia propria* is *iniustitia* before God. And the *iustitia fidei* as such can never be recognized in the *regnum mundi* as *iustitia*. If both are nevertheless to be called *iustitia*, then not in the same way but in a different one.

The distinction between the two modes of *iustitia* is determined by the distinction of different *fora* before which man is called to account, and before which he must answer for himself—and that, too, not merely some time some day, but in continual enquiry as to how he stands. Man

exists *coram mundo* and *coram Deo*. This fact of being addressed by
another party, of being dependent on an *extra se*, this openness of his
existence, is not something tacked on to his human nature, but constitutes his human nature as a nature called to responsibility. It is not a
case either of particular aspects among others. Everything that confronts
man, everything that befalls him, is involved in it. For this *coram*-
structure decides whether man is a self and a whole. The necessity of
the two kingdom doctrine depends on how far the *coram Deo* is binding
alongside of the *coram mundo* and in relation to it. For Luther it is not
an unverifiable assertion that the *coram Deo* belongs to human nature
in the same way as the *coram mundo* and at the very same time, but he
can point to elements in the structure of existence in which the distinction between the *coram Deo* and *coram mundo* can at all events be discussed. For man comes into view *coram mundo* in his *opus*, and is manifestly *coram Deo* as *persona* in the sense of the selfhood which is hidden
from the world and even from man himself, and which precedes all
opera as the ground of their origin and ultimately determines them. It is
true that Luther can also make a different use of the concept *persona*—
in the sense of mask. Then man is *persona* precisely *coram mundo*—as
the one who has to play a particular part, fill a particular position, just
as all creatures are called larvae of the divine will which conceals itself
within them. In this sense man is *coram Deo* anything but *persona*. For
with God there is no respect of persons. Then the concept *conscientia*
comes in as a description of man in his nakedness before God, stripped
of his *opera* and of the dignity of his position.

Do the two *fora* not now surely stand in competition with each other,
so that it must be decided whether man standing between God and the
world faces God with his back to the world or faces the world with his
back to God? For the concept *forum* involves not only being claimed,
but also receiving—at the least, receiving a judgment. And if we reflect
more deeply what it can mean to man for good and for ill to receive his
judgment, then we shall not be in such a hurry to weaken that statement
by adding 'only'. Rather, we shall realize that all receiving is connected
with this receiving, and that in the structure of the *forum* both things
become acute at the same time: having ourselves claimed, and receiving
ourselves. In the sense of thus having ourselves claimed and receiving
ourselves can the *coram mundo* and *coram Deo* exist side by side without
the result being an Either-or? It has certainly to be decided whether
man understands himself *coram mundo* or *coram Deo*, and that means,
where he receives himself from. Or rather, the conflict is already going

on continually, and by no means only in the form that man amid the claims made on him by the world forgets about God; but above all in the form that man gets the '*coram mundo*' and '*coram Deo*' hopelessly mixed up—he brings before the one *forum* what belongs before the other, presents the *opera* to God and surrenders himself as person, as conscience, to the world.

That of course already indicates that the Either-or presupposes the continual togetherness of the *coram mundo* and *coram Deo*. As man in expressing himself in *opera* does not cease to be *persona*, so too, precisely as one who exists *coram mundo*, he stands *coram Deo*. Even when in the qualified sense mentioned above he understands himself *coram mundo*, he does not cease to stand *coram Deo*, but stands *coram Deo* as one who understands himself not *coram Deo* but *coram mundo*. And conversely, by understanding himself *coram Deo*, man does not simply get rid of the *coram mundo*. He is made to feel very plainly that he still exists *coram mundo* and that the world judges differently from God. In the relationship of the *coram mundo* and the *coram Deo* to each other we thus meet again the structure of the two kingdom doctrine. In actual fact there is a contradiction here: 'For that which is highly esteemed among men is abomination in the sight of God' (Luke 16.15)—and *vice versa*. And indeed it is a contradiction which—one way or the other— no one can evade. The *absconditas sub contrario* is the basic structure of reality, given expression in the message of the Cross. Nonetheless, to the relation of contradiction there belongs also that of agreement. For rightly understood and rightly used, the *coram mundo* does not exclude the *coram Deo*, nor conversely does the *coram Deo* the *coram mundo*, but rather the one opens the way to the other. The man who truly stands *coram Deo* stands truly *coram mundo*. For he knows how to distinguish between what he has to expect from God and what he has to expect from the world; between what he has to thank God for and what he has to thank the world for; between what he owes to God and what he owes to the world. He knows how to distinguish between God and world.

For in certain respects it is in fact necessary to disregard the one *forum* where the other *forum* is concerned. *Coram mundo* we can and must know that the world is not God. And we should certainly beware of mixing God up with this *forum*, deifying the world or giving it a religious halo or even doing religious violence to it. *Coram mundo*, worldly behaviour is the proper thing. Caesar must be given no less, but no more either, than what is Caesar's. To be truly *coram mundo* means to let the world be world—not with the undertone of weary resignation which we usually give to that phrase, but in the sense of taking responsibility for the world, having proper dealings with the world, doing justice to it, i.e. giving it its due. Likewise, *vice versa*, it would have to be said in certain respects that *coram Deo* we have quite decidedly to disregard what counts *coram mundo*. For when it comes to the question of justification before God, then the only thing that counts is, that he is justified who does justice to God, i.e. lets God be God. In the one case we have to do with a partial justification—that of the *opera* —in the other case with the justification of the very person—with faith.

But this distinction is valid only in virtue of the closest association. For who can let the world be world in such a sober, matter-of-fact way? The freedom to do so comes of letting God be God. For we cannot truly let the world be world unless we truly let God be God. For that reason the *iustitia Christiana* as *iustitia coram Deo*, and indeed as *iustitia fidei*, opens the way to, and so makes possible, the *iustitia civilis* in its character of *iustitia coram mundo*, and indeed as *iustitia operum*. Yet this fundamental insight must at once be shielded against misunderstandings in three directions.

Firstly, it is usual to regard the relation between faith and works— and for that we can now also say, between what God does and what man does—in the first instance as a relationship between power and performance. Faith is supposed to give the power for works. This way of speaking requires to be very critically examined. The basic relation of faith and works is not the communication of power for works, but the communication of freedom for them—that is, freedom to do the works in their limitedness as works and therefore also in the limitedness of the powers that are at our disposal for them. Just as faith too does not, though it is easy to misunderstand it so, primarily receive the revelation of what is to be done; but faith gives the freedom to perceive the right, because faith assigns works to their due place.

A second misunderstanding is to suppose that faith does indeed make room for the *iustitia civilis* by inciting to it, yet also produces over and above it much higher works which far surpass the *iustitia civilis*. This misunderstanding is partly caused by the ineradicable tendency to adopt a working attitude even before God and therefore to set about special works *coram Deo*, and partly by the disastrously one-sided practice of letting the *iustitia coram mundo* take its cue from the political sphere and therefore from what can be compelled if necessary by force. That is certainly a standpoint which is highly significant for the worldliness of the world. But if we would grasp the basic theological sense of *iustitia civilis,* then we must ascribe to the *iustitia civilis* all works which can sensibly be done and are therefore right works. Even the man who is so unworldly as to give all his goods to the poor or to surrender his life in martyrdom remains, if it is rightly done (and that means if the man in question knows in faith what he is doing), within the sphere of the *iustitia civilis,* the *iustitia coram mundo*; i.e. he submits to the test of how far he is doing justice to the world by these works. For by works we can do justice only to the world, not to God. For that reason the criterion of works, precisely from the standpoint of the *iustitia civilis,* is love. In the realm of works there is no higher *iustitia* than the *iustitia civilis!* Yet for that very reason we should not imagine that with mere law-abidingness and bourgeois good conduct we have already done justice to the world and fulfilled all *iustitia civilis* in this basic sense.

A third misunderstanding is to suppose that without faith there is no *iustitia civilis* at all. Christian circles indeed are repeatedly haunted by the idea that an atheist is an immoral man and that if Christian colours do not justify an undertaking, then at least they certainly recommend it *a priori* as inspiring confidence. It is true that faith is the presupposition of the *iustitia civilis* in so far as it communicates the freedom to let the *iustitia civilis* be really only *iustitia civilis* and not to seek to derive somehow from works the justification of the person. But in spite of such misuse of the *iustitia civilis,* it can still *materialiter* very well be *iustitia civilis.* Where the *iustitia civilis* is concerned there is cause enough for believers to be shamed by non-believers, both as to discretion and as to readiness to make sacrifices. Over and above that, however, the freedom to matter-of-factness which is communicated in faith is a thing the world has to thank faith for, even without an immediate awareness of the connexion. That the idea of *iustitia civilis* has attained an isolated independence (which is admittedly wide open to falsification), is of course a major factor in the modern world. As Christians we do have ground for taking care that that is rightly understood, but hardly for seeking in principle to set it aside again. On the contrary, there are many reasons for the church to let the children of the world, who are often wiser in this respect also, remind it of the true meaning of the *iustitia civilis.*

X

Where the *iustitia fidei* gives freedom for true *iustitia operum,* so that in such *opera* of man the *opus Dei* takes place, that heralds the peace of the creation, the peace of the world at one with itself because it is at one with its Creator. With '*iustitia coram mundo*', however, it always remains doubtful whether it is at bottom *iustitia fidei*. It remains as such in the self-contradiction of the *regnum mundi*. And the *regnum Christi* remains a kingdom of the Word whose proper proclamation encounters the perdition of the *regnum mundi* at the point where that perdition has its source and develops its real virulence: in the heart, in the *conscientia* of man. The *conscientia* is the mathematical point at which the *regnum Christi* becomes one with a *regnum mundi* stripped of its power and freed from itself in order to be mere world. But as conscience, and that means as hearer, man remains dependent on the ἀκοὴ πίστεως, the faith-creating Word, whose truth is observed through the two kingdom doctrine, and by whose act alone the distinction of the two kingdoms takes place concretely.

XVII

THEOLOGICAL REFLEXIONS
ON CONSCIENCE

To Walter Gut on his 75th birthday

THE widespread antipathy towards the use of the concept conscience
in theology today is due on the one hand to a justified aversion to idealistic interpretations of conscience; on the other hand, however, it brings
about the suppression of problems which are felt to be embarrassing or
considered to be forbidden ground for the theologian. Nevertheless the
concept of conscience is of decisive importance for theology. I must
confine myself to a few reflexions on this subject, and shall first of all
(I) try from various standpoints to shed light on the theological relevance
of reflecting on the concept of conscience and then (II) examine particular aspects of the phenomenon of conscience.

I

Since theology has to do with what is ultimately valid and therefore
what is absolutely necessary and that means what is truly salutary, to
ask about the theological significance of conscience is to ask what speaking of conscience contributes towards interpreting the salutariness of
speaking of God. We could also say that it means asking about the
significance of the concept of conscience for the exposition of soteriology
—were it not that confusion is caused by the habit of understanding
soteriology as a mere part of theology, whereas, rightly understood,
speaking of God is in itself soteriological, i.e. communicates salvation.
Since my intention is not to reduce theology to soteriology (in the
customary sense), but to recall the real point of everything theology
says, I shall use the word 'theology' always in view of the soteriological
aim of the theological linguistic event and understand the term 'soteriology' in turn as a pointer to the specifically linguistic character of
theology. For teaching about God and teaching about salvation are
identical.

1. Reflecting on the concept of conscience should help towards a

clearer grasp of the *connexion between theology and language.* Let me give
three indications of how this connexion becomes a problem:

a. Theology places us inevitably in the midst of a collection of often
conflicting theories of salvation, and thus amid linguistic confusion.
Theories of salvation are complete linguistic units which severally bring
God, man and the world to expression[1] in different ways. Yet these
linguistic units are not carefully separated from each other and not
firmly closed towards each other. However much they certainly seek as
wholes to provoke conflict and decision, yet this relationship of contradiction is overlaid by manifold contacts between individual linguistic
elements. And thus—as always where there is linguistic variety—there
arises the problem of understanding and translation. That no doubt
suggests removing misunderstandings and opens up certain possibilities
of agreement. But the struggle with the problem of understanding does
not go on under the motto of settlement at any price. Theology indeed
has to take seriously the task of bringing out clearly the character of
decision that attaches to faith and unbelief, and thus of bringing their
relationship to expression as one of contradiction, making the antithesis
intelligible as such. The fundamental difficulty in the situation in which
we have to proclaim the Gospel today is, that the final alternative which
provides clarity is buried under so many unintelligible accretions that
confessionist pressing for a decision causes for the most part only misunderstanding and hinders the proper decision between faith and unbelief instead of furthering it. We therefore need a hermeneutics of
faith, which brings unbelief, too, to expression and thereby enables it
to be understood.

b. Theological language poses special problems in regard to its objectivity and verifiability. It does not have the character of substantiated
statement. It speaks of what is hidden, invisible, future. This aspect of
the linguistic problem is usually characterized by saying that theological
language is necessarily figurative, symbolic, mythological. Yet this outlook requires an immediate correction: theological language, whatever
way it may speak, speaks of what unconditionally concerns and conclusively affects man in the reality that concerns him, and thus it relates
to what concerns every man because it is given along with his existence.
For the language of theology as language of salvation relates to man as
man. If theology speaks of hidden, invisible, future things which elude
experience, yet it does so by referring in meaningful and intelligible ways
to the realm of human experience.

[1] Cf. my note on terms above, p. 294 note 1.—*Translator.*

c. Soteriological language addresses itself to man, seeks to be understood—more than that, seeks to communicate understanding, and thus seeks to be an event with an effect. Teaching about salvation, in that it is a word-event, has an inner connexion with the event of salvation itself. This connexion will be very differently understood in each particular case according to the structure of the particular theory of salvation. But it is of the essence of teaching about salvation that a connexion—possibly wholly indirect—is asserted between language and salvation, as indeed there is also a connexion between having nothing to say and perdition. The relation between salvation and language indicates the fundamental relation between human nature and language.

The conscience could now be the point where the nature of man's linguisticality comes to light. For the phenomenon of conscience is bound up both with the aspect of speaking and with that of hearing. What has here to come to expression and find a hearing is what concerns man in his selfhood, and therefore (since man's selfhood has the structure of being ahead of oneself) concerns him in regard to his future and hence conclusively and unconditionally. For the conscience has to do with the ground of the linguisticality of existence.

2. Reflecting on the concept of conscience should help towards the understanding of a basic characteristic of the Reformers' theology, *viz.* that salvation is communicated (in the full sense of appropriation) solely by word. The most astonishing thing about the Christian understanding of salvation as interpreted by the Reformers is this *identification of word-event and salvation-event.* If it is from preaching that the faith comes which alone justifies and is thus itself the gift of salvation, then that implies a singular understanding of the event of salvation as a linguistic event. What is the nature of salvation in the evangelical sense, if it is thus imparted solely by word, solely by faith? What sort of view of the cause of perdition is expressed in this wordly (*worthaft*)—i.e. word-bound (*am Wort haftend*)—view of salvation? What kind of understanding of word and language do we find here? And what is the nature of faith, indeed what is the nature of God, in the light of this understanding of 'word'?

When we reflect on the concept of conscience, these questions come to be further defined as follows:—What is the nature of man's linguisticality, that the perdition and salvation of man are decided by reference to it? What is man as one so dependent on the word-event? In what does perdition consist, if it is a lack or misuse of the proper word-event? In what does salvation consist if a single, mere word can put everything to rights and save? How does it come about that the decision on man is made in the conscience, so that he is written off, lost and dead when his conscience is written off, lost and dead, and he is raised, rescued and made alive to the extent that in his conscience he is raised, rescued and made alive? What is the nature of the word-event in which perdition and salvation come to expression and thereby to a decision? If we are taking our bearings from the conscience, then the distinction of the word-event into law and Gospel must become plain, and therewith also the real point of the traditional way of speaking of here and hereafter, of earth and heaven, of this world and the world to come, of the natural and the supernatural. From the theological point of view this way of speaking is rightly understood only in relation to the conscience. For the Gospel is the radical transposition of man which takes place in the conscience and by which he comes, as one under the law, to stand '*supra legem*'.[1] 'A Christian is'—in faith—'a free master of all things and no man's servant.' For that very reason it is true, as a consequence of this freedom, that 'a Christian is'—in love—'a bond-slave of all things and every man's servant.'[2] The distinction of the word-event into law and Gospel provides an understanding of reality which does not make reality separate into two strata, or cause an additional reality to be tacked on to that of the world. Rather, the issue is the truth of the one, single reality.

3. Reflecting on the concept of conscience should allow us to perceive rightly the *connexion between man, the world and God*. According to the customary view, speaking of conscience has a tendency towards individualistic isolation of man and withdrawal upon the inner life. It is true that 'conscience' means man as the bearer of a proper name, in his inexchangeable, individual selfhood—and that, too, in regard to the hidden roots of his actions, his 'inner nature', his 'heart' in the biblical sense. Yet that man is an individual in this sense is not to be understood in abstraction from the bonds of existence and the context of reality, but rather precisely as an interpretation of them. That we have to speak of an 'inner nature' of man is not meant to be an indication of a self-contained and independent 'inner world' alongside the 'outer world', but rather of the fact that man concerns himself with an 'outer world' and of the way in which he does so. If we follow that up, then we are led to the discovery that the only reason why man concerns himself with an outer world is, that his so-called inner nature is addressed in an

---

[1] For example *WA* 40/1, pp. 46.3 f, 47.1 and frequently elsewhere.
[2] *WA* 7, p. 21.1 ff.

essential and primary sense by what exists *extra se*, and thus that the outerness of the so-called outer world has another, and more radical outerness beyond it. Interpretation of the conscience is the very thing that could best contribute towards the overcoming of that superficial view of reality which sees things as complete in themselves and outwardly strung together. In the light of the connexion we have indicated between conscience and language it could therefore become plain that human nature, the world and God are not separate themes, but the dimensions of one single theme: the meaning of man, of the world and of God can be encountered and expressed only together.

In the light of the customary understanding of conscience the inclusion of the relation to God is the most likely to find general acceptance. To be sure, if conscience is viewed simply as the voice of God in man, then it does not by any means become sufficiently clear how the connexion between God and man is given in linguisticality. It would at all events have to be emphasized that what we are concerned with in conscience is not a legal code, not individual instructions on this or that, but man as a whole—and hence not an authority where morals are concerned, but the defining of man's place where the decision is made on his personal being that lies beyond morality. But above all, where conscience is concerned the relation of man to God would be spoken of in the right way only if the world were not left out in doing so. The concept of conscience sets God and man really in relation to each other only when the world is inseparably included as well. As also correspondingly the world in the strict sense can be spoken of only in relation to the conscience and therewith both to human nature and to God. The conscience would then have to be understood as the coming together, being present together, of man, the world and God.

The grasp of this structural connexion provides criteria for understanding. What is said of the world and God has to authenticate itself by showing that it is aimed at the conscience and therefore brings man to expression in his human nature. Talk of the world and God which did not concern the conscience would not be proper, at all events not theological, talk of the world and God, but at best scientific or metaphysical—whereby it can remain an open question whether such talk of the world and God can be meaningful at all. In the same way, however, the relation to the world is also the criterion of speaking properly of man and God—a criterion, too, that is also immediately involved precisely when we have an eye to the conscience.

In the light of these considerations we could venture to formulate the following propositions:—God—as a phenomenon, and that is precisely a way of saying as *Deus ABSCONDITUS*—is a phenomenon of conscience. But in the same way it is true that man is a phenomenon of conscience. Man does indeed meet us in manifold ways apart from the relation to conscience. Yet it is only in the relation to conscience that the human nature of man makes itself known in truth. Man is a matter of conscience in two senses: he *is* ultimately conscience, and he ultimately concerns the conscience. But the world, too, is a phenomenon of conscience. It is encountered as world only in the conscience of man. 'World' does not mean the so-called universe conceived in physical terms, nor the mere sum of all the separate individual experiences of reality; but the concept 'world' brings the whole of reality to expression as a question, and thereby points in a direction aimed at the conscience. For conscience is concerned with the whole, because it is concerned with the question of the finally valid. For that reason the question of the world as a total reality is a question that concerns the conscience, just as the question of man himself is also a question that affects the conscience. But these two things in turn cannot be separated from the fact that God appears as *the* question in the radical sense, the question as to the whole, as to the beginning and end. Only where God is encountered as a question of conscience are man and the world perceived to be a question of conscience.

The fact that man, the world and God thus belong together as phenomena of conscience implies further, that the mode of encountering man, the world and God is solely that of the word. If what man is as man confronts the conscience alone and can be experienced only as a claim on the conscience, then what man is as man can be communicable only as a word-event. The same is true of the world. The world as world in the full and final sense can encounter us only as a thing which concerns the conscience and therefore only as a word-event. But now we must take it further: man as a phenomenon of conscience and therefore as one who encounters us in word, is faith's concern. Likewise the world as a phenomenon of conscience and therefore as a thing that encounters us in word, is faith's concern. That of course is meaningful only in the context of what is said of God. For in contrast to man and the world, which can also very well be spoken of in part and which also encounter us in part and to that extent are by no means only phenomena of conscience, to speak of God is meaningful solely with an eye to the conscience. As the mode of God's encounter there can be no question of anything else but word. God is *the* absolute concern of faith. Since it is thus exclusively true only of God that he is a matter of conscience, that he encounters us in word and that he is faith's concern—therefore it is solely on that basis, and thus in a derivative way, that the same is true of man and the world. Only want of understanding can suspect the concentration upon conscience of turning theology into anthropology. To assert the togetherness of man, the world and God where conscience is concerned, is to assert the primacy of God.

There is still one final respect in which we have to consider the structural interconnexions of what is said of man, the world and God, with its centre in the concept of conscience. We have here at all events something that is not an object of experience, and therefore not completely given in the finished sense of the perfect tense. This aspect of eluding experience is positively characterized as the quality of being still to come, being future, having to be awaited. The meaning of the traditional statements about God's being invisible, not at our disposal, out of reach of experience, etc. comes to light only when we ask what is to be expected from God, what he pledges, what he promises. For the ground of the fact that God encounters us only in word is, that his encounter has purely the character of promise. Only so does it become plain how far God exclusively confronts the conscience. For the conscience, since it has to do with word, has to do with futurity and ultimate validity, with what has to be awaited, is still to come, but is yet already heralded and promised. The correlate which goes with that is of course the possibility of missing and losing the promise, and thus the experience of wrath. Since the conscience has to do with futurity, it has also in its negative mode to do precisely with the lack of a future, with death: so that the conscience that has become one with lack of a future and with death exercises fatal power itself, whereas the conscience that accepts the promise of a future is made alive and as such itself becomes a life-giver.

What is true of the futurity of God as a phenomenon of conscience, and of his consequently being out of reach of experience, is true *mutatis mutandis* also of man and the world as phenomena of conscience. Man is neither an object of experience to himself nor to others. Human nature is respected as personal being only when it is respected as a mystery that is out of reach of experience, incalculable, not at our disposal, i.e. when man is respected as man by being granted freedom, allowed a future, given a hearing, regarded with trust. This characteristic of mystery in human nature becomes all the greater in the relation of man to himself. As the being which has relations with itself, man in his selfhood questions and is questioned about his selfhood, has to account for his selfhood. Only as conscience can man be seen as *totus homo*, as *persona*. But he can be seen as such only in the word-event. For conscience is the event of being questioned and being challenged to respond, and thus the act of being responsible. The reason why personal being as a thing that does not lie open to experience has to do with futurity is, that a word-event is an event that waits for an answer and the answer in turn is a reaching out for a final, conclusive, unsurpassable word.

How far the quality of being out of reach of experience in the sense of futurity belongs also to the world, is a thing I would at least indicate by referring to Luther's interpretation of Rom. 8.19. Paul speaks of the earnest expectation of the creature. That gives Luther cause to emphasize the difference of theological from philosophical talk: 'The apostle philosophizes and thinks about reality differently from the philosophers and metaphysicians. For the philosophers fix their eyes only on the presence of things, so as to consider only their quiddities and qualities. But the apostle calls our gaze away from contemplating present things, away from their *essentia* and accidentals, and directs it to their futurity.'[1]

4. Reflecting on the concept of conscience should lead us to consider the *relation of morality and faith* as a fundamental theological problem. The concept of conscience is usually discussed as a basic concept in ethics, not in dogmatics. That means a disastrous foreshortening of the theological function of the concept of conscience, since it is the very concept in whose light the connexion between dogmatics and ethics should be thought through. This customary distinction of two disciplines in systematic theology points to the fact of two dimensions in the subject matter of theology, which together form a basic theological problem of extraordinary significance and are both alike rooted in the phenomenon of conscience. The nature of this dualism may be interpreted, say, by the customary division of the Decalogue into duties towards God and duties towards our neighbour, or in a somewhat different form by the distinction between *credenda* and *agenda*, between faith and love, or again by the distinction between teaching about God's doings and teaching about man's doings—which is related to, but not identical with, the distinction between Gospel and law. Now it is true that today the fundamental unity of dogmatics and ethics is being emphasized in

---

[1] *Aliter Apostolus de rebus philosophatur et sapit quam philosophi et metaphysici. Quia philosophi oculum ita in praesentiam rerum immergunt, ut solum quidditates et qualitates earum speculentur, Apostolus autem oculos nostros revocat ab intuitu rerum praesentium, ab essentia et accidentibus earum, et dirigit in eas, secundum quod futurae sunt* (*WA* 56, p. 371.2 ff).

justified criticism of naive juxtaposition or even mutual isolation. But it is a question whether the distinction which nevertheless still tenaciously persists is due merely to practical requirements and is of a purely technical kind, or whether it does not after all raise a fundamental problem for theology. For if ethics has to do with responsible action, i.e. with the works of man, then it has at all events also to do with what can and must happen *provisionally*, without reference to the faith in which we grasp the *ultimately valid*. That does not mean that these provisional things can be done in the right way as provisional things without reference to faith. But ethics has perforce (at least among other things!) to do with things whose claim to validity cannot be postponed until agreement is reached on the ultimately valid. What the theology of the Reformers designated the *primus usus legis* demands a relative distinction between dogmatics and ethics, which theology has to think through as the distinction of the two kingdoms—and which in regard to human nature itself can be interpreted with the help of the distinction between person and work. The concept of conscience, however, would be the point where it must become clear how far a sharp distinction has to be made between person and work and how far they belong inseparably together.

In order to define more closely the problem just touched upon, it would be necessary to enquire whether it is simply a case of the general problem of the relationship between religion and morality, and how the distinction between sacred and profane in turn is related to that. If we disregard for a moment the Christian view, then it would have to be emphasized that what primarily characterizes the religious outlook is the intermingling of the two aspects. Here there is in fact no sharp distinction at all between the 'moral' and the 'religious'. Rather, that is a thing which only arose in modern times as an expression of the emancipation from religion. Likewise the religious self-consciousness knows nothing 'purely profane' (in the modern sense); rather, everything stands in a relation to the holy, even if partly by way of separation or antithesis. On the other hand, this very intermingling presupposes an aspect of separation—the delimitation of the sacred realm and the relative independence of the profane. Two tendencies compete in a confusing way. On the one hand religion has the tendency to understand everything in religious ways, and therefore not to permit the distinction between religious and moral or, to give it a different emphasis, between 'spiritual' and 'worldly'. On the other hand, however, religion has precisely the tendency to separate between the holy and the profane.

The tendencies towards totality and towards particularity are combined in a peculiar way. It is part of the structure of the religious view of reality that the totalitarian and the particularizing tendencies exist side by side and condition each other.

If the Christian faith is understood as a form consistent with the basic structure of religion, then the result is understandably enough competition between two extreme views. Either we continue the totalitarian tendency of religion and maintain a totalitarian view of Christianity in the sense of a Christian religious outlook which seeks to Christianize everything. Or else we continue the particularizing tendency of religion and maintain a particularizing view of Christianity in the sense of a Christian religious outlook which separates itself from worldly things and withdraws upon the 'purely religious' or 'inner life'. Both views can be maintained with the passion of a Christian radicalism. For both have at bottom a legalistic streak in them. This is no accident. The basic structure of religion is—law. And it is precisely in the light of the nature of law that we are able to understand the co-existence of totalitarianism and particularism as two sides of the same thing.

But now, this interpretation of Christianity as the radicalized and perfected version of the basic structure of religion misses the decisive thing—the Gospel, and therewith the nature of faith. Through Jesus, i.e. through faith, the distinction of holy and profane has undergone a radical change, as a result of which the place of the intermingling of religion and morality has been taken by the very differently constructed relationship of faith and morality. It is true that here, too, we find a double tendency, which at first sight likewise appears to be a contradiction and on superficial examination gives the impression of being merely a modification within the framework of the basic structure of religion. On the one hand faith and morality in the Christian view belong together in so far as faith is not concerned with special religious works, but urges us to nothing else but what morality demands. The description of Christianity as the 'perfect moral religion' has something quite right about it. On the other hand faith as the Christian understands it is radically different from morality. It comes not from the law but from the Gospel, not by the power of man but by grace, is not the work of man but the work of God. Only the man who can distinguish in this way between faith and morality is a theologian. But this apparent contradiction between the unity of faith and morality on the one hand and the antithetical distinction of faith and morality on the other can be meaningfully interpreted only in view of the conscience.

II

To these pointers to the significance of theological reflexion on the concept of conscience I now add—likewise sketchily—a few remarks on the phenomenon of conscience.

1. The etymology of συνείδησις, on which the derived renderings 'conscientia' and 'conscience' are modelled, points to the fact that *the root of the phenomenon of conscience* lies in the basic ontological determination of man as the being whose relation to himself is that of joint cognizance. To call conscience an organ (even a vitally necessary organ) in man misses the basic fact that conscience is a matter of the coming to expression of man himself. Strictly man does not 'have' a conscience, but he is conscience. He is his own witness. The definition of man as ζῷον λόγον ἔχον could be bettered, or traced back to the ground of its truth, by saying—in allusion to the expression λόγον διδόναι (give account) or λόγον αἰτεῖν (require an account, call to account)—that man is the being who is answerable. As conscience man is call and answer at the same time. Hence in explaining the concept of conscience the distinction of subject and object is not applicable, since here the point at issue is the selfhood of man as identity of subject and object. For that reason it is likewise inappropriate to interpret conscience as an authority over against man. Without detriment to the question whether something standing over against man does not present itself in conscience, the first thing where the phenomenon of conscience is concerned is to grasp that the structure of human nature itself is confrontation. Conscience indeed both accuses and is also the very experience of being accused. Or in terms of the phrase about pangs of conscience, conscience as the thing in man that gives the pangs is surely man himself, but as man it is at the same time also what suffers the pangs. That indeed is also why it is a bad conscience not (as would be the case with a judicial authority) when it is mistaken, but rather when it reveals the truth— that is, when it rightly performs its warning and rebuking function and is thus to that extent a good conscience (i.e. one good at its job). Instead of speaking of an authority (*Instanz*), it would therefore be more appropriate to speak of the 'dissociation' (*Distanz*) which is given with conscience in human nature itself. Man experiences himself as one who is not identical with himself, but whose essence it is to be questioned about his identity with himself. Only in being thus questioned is his identity given.

That points us to the relation of conscience and time. The diastasis in temporal being as the present relation to past and future is the ground of the fact that man's identity is questionable, and consequently of the appearance of conscience. Man exists as one who is continually questioned as to what attitude he takes to himself in his own past and future, whether he identifies himself with himself, confesses to his past and decides for his future, and thus (though this of course is a secondary mode of the identification in question) whether he identifies himself with his deeds and his potentialities. This questionable nature of man's identity with himself, this identity which is never finally given and always demanded, constitutes the responsibility of man. To identify ourselves with our past deeds is to answer for them. To make a decision, and thus identify ourselves with our future possibilities, is likewise to answer for them. To identify ourselves with ourselves is to answer for ourselves. Thus existence is fundamentally word-event and can be answered for only in word-event.

This interpretation of conscience does not by any means leave the world out of account. On the contrary, it is only in relation to man as conscience that the world comes into view as world, i.e. not as something that is merely there, but as a thing to be answered for. The questionable nature of man's identity in time takes concrete form in the question as to his identification of himself with his being in the world and therefore in the question as to his responsibility for the world. Still less is it an atheistic interpretation of conscience, although it was spoken of in the first instance without speaking of God. If conscience constitutes the human nature of man, then it must surely be possible to reach a certain agreement about it which is based on the phenomenon itself and does not presuppose the acceptance of talk about God. It would be fundamentally wrong if the impression arose that conscience is a 'purely religious' matter which would disappear with the denial of God. Rather, conscience is the condition on which it becomes possible to understand what is meant by the word 'God'. In the interpretation of conscience it must become clear what we mean when we say 'God'. Certainly, the relation of 'coram seipso' which characterizes man as conscience is not simply already the 'coram Deo' —although the striking fact that man in his selfhood always faces towards a *forum*, towards something over against him, and even in his most private things has a certain tendency towards openness, raises the question what that may mean. Likewise the call of conscience as such is not by any means the voice of God, however much the peculiar constraint of its challenge and questioning certainly gives cause to think about what is happening here. Thus the fact of man's identity being open to question opens also the question of God. And indeed not least also in the sense that man can find himself asking how in spite of his constant non-identity with himself he yet remains upheld in that identity, in remaining questioned about it and summoned to it. However, God and conscience will not be related to each other in the right way by means of such reflexions, but rather by God's being spoken to the conscience. Only so do the locative statements '*in conscientia*' and '*coram Deo*' coincide. And it is only by God's being spoken to man that both things together—and indeed only in their togetherness—are truly answered for: the human nature of man and the divine nature of God.

If we venture to say that man is conscience, then we must embark on an ontological interpretation of conscience. But if it is true that conscience, at all events primarily, comes on the scene as a bad conscience and to speak of conscience is thus meaningful only in view of man's being at variance with himself (which is proclaimed to be a result of his being at variance with God), then—according to the traditional dogmatic view—it seems highly problematical to seek to present conscience as an ontological structure in the sphere of the question as to man's identity with himself. Is that not to understand the Fall as an ontological change in man and sin as man's nature? It is quite true that man can be spoken of ontologically only in a postlapsarian sense. Only so can the real sense of what theology says of the original state and the consummation become clear. To be sure, only when what theology customarily says of the original state and the consummation has passed through a serious crisis. For how can anything be *understood* as a state of unsoiled or perfect human nature, if it appears to run counter to what we can say ontologically of man, or at all events is averse to the possibility of being stated in ontological terms? Salvation in the theological sense is surely not the abrogation of human nature instead of the perfecting of man?—and thus only a carefully guarded statement about his end? This problem is so to speak the narrow way that leads to the right understanding of what the Christian message means by salvation—the eschatological nearness of God in time, and therewith the event that acts on the conscience by word: the word-event that sets man as a word-event to rights, the identification of man with himself in past and future, *fides* as *bona conscientia*.

2. So far we seem to have been speaking of conscience in an entirely formal way. The question arises as to *what is the content of the call of conscience*. Here of course it is important to free ourselves entirely from

the usual view of conscience as a codex of general truths and commands —that is, a law written in the heart, which is conceived as a sum of inborn ideas that by nature form part of the content of human consciousness. The law written in the heart is nothing else but the pure call and question of conscience, so to speak the question mark branded ineradicably upon man. But what is conscience's call, what does it ask about? It calls man himself, it asks about himself, it demands himself. Conscience makes no speeches. Heidegger gives a wholly proper interpretation: 'The call is not voiced in any way. It does not go the length of putting itself into words at all—and nevertheless remains anything but obscure and undefined. Conscience's mode of speaking is only and always that of silence. Therein it not only does not lose anything of its intelligibility, but also forces its own silentness on the being it calls and summons. The absence of a formulation of its call in words does not give the phenomenon the indefiniteness of a mysterious voice, but merely indicates that the understanding on the part of the person "called" must not cling to the expectation of information or such like.'[1]

The call of conscience receives its content by being heard, i.e. by man's taking up the challenge. Two things then contribute towards determining the content. First, the concrete situation in which the call of conscience takes place and to which it is related. Incidentally, it takes place only in relation to concrete situations, never in a general way. And second, everything in the way of training in understanding concrete situations which exists as a result of education in the widest sense and thus of participation in the history of language. This explains the historical definiteness of conscience. It is of course indeputably and inscrutably the conscience of the individual. It functions only in the individual, and only the individual as such can appeal to it. It is indeed the very *principium individuationis*. It brings into action only what concerns the individual, however much that may be something which relates to others and also concerns others or even all men. No one can be a substitute for conscience to someone else, however much he can rouse, sharpen and instruct the other's own conscience. To speak of a conscience above the individual level, such as a 'conscience of the nation' or 'world conscience' is therefore misleading, however important the conscience-stirring word-event may be which is sometimes meant by that. This individual determination of the conscience as always my own does not, however, exclude my participating in a general pattern

[1] M. Heidegger, *Sein und Zeit* I, 2nd ed. 1929, pp. 273 f [ET, *Being and Time*, 1962].

of conscience which according to the particular tradition concerned can
be of tough historical durability but can also, as it does today, find itself
in an acute crisis. In the light of the above understanding of conscience
it is certainly not permissible to speak, say, of a loss of conscience altogether today. Even so-called lack of conscience is only an aspect of the
fact that man is conscience. We must rather speak of a crisis of conscience which, in causing lack of any sense of direction and reducing
men to the dullness of the mass, betrays a failure to educate their
consciences. That of course sounds more harmless than the facts in
question really are. The contemporary crisis of conscience and the difficulties felt everywhere in the realm of language belong closely together.
The background is general loss of tradition and a fading sense of reality.
That serves to underline the responsibility in which these theological
reflexions also bear a part. They are an effort to learn the language
which affects the conscience and reaches to the point at which decisive
things happen and from which it is possible to set to work helpfully in
the contemporary world. We are clumsy beginners in this language
school. But we know the promise that a saving and healing Word is at
hand even amid the language difficulties of today. That is why we are
theologians and think humbly enough of ourselves but very highly of
our task.

But now, does what we have said of the content of the call of conscience not introduce a relativism which seems to contradict the absoluteness that belongs to the call of conscience? The important thing is,
that the seemingly formal character of the call of conscience should
nevertheless provide a material criterion which prevents conscience
from being separated from the question of truth and abandoned to
caprice. If the call of conscience is the question as to man's identity with
himself and as such the summons to him to be man, then it is the call
to stand on his own feet and therewith to responsibility—for only in
standing on my own feet am I responsible, and only as a responsible
being do I stand on my own feet. And it embraces both in one as the
call to truthfulness. For truth and freedom belong inseparably together.
This criterion is given in the call of conscience itself. For that reason
we can say with Luther, '*Conscientia Christo et Christus conscientiae*'.[1]
Because in Christ we are concerned with the Word in the absolute sense,
we are concerned in him with the very thing with which conscience is
concerned—truth and freedom. That is how it is put by the Johannine

[1] *WA* 8, p. 609.40 f.

Christ: 'If ye continue in my word, then are ye my disciples indeed; and ye shall know the truth, and the truth shall make you free. . . . Whosoever committeth sin is the servant of sin. . . . If the Son therefore shall make you free, ye shall be free indeed.'[1]

The interpretation of the Word of God in relation to conscience and of conscience in relation to the Word of God takes place in view of the bad conscience as the suicidal dividedness of man. Although conscience is the call to independence and responsibility, to truthfulness and therewith to freedom, yet it cannot confer all these things. Indeed, conscience cannot even make them conclusively intelligible as the things to which it really calls us. It calls upon man. But in calling upon man it really calls upon God as the One who alone can make man (i.e. conscience itself) true and free, because God alone can identify man as man, can make him one with himself, by reconciling him with God. For man's being at variance with himself is his being at variance with God. Hence for the salvation of man more must happen than always happens already through conscience one way or another. Conscience can do no more than define man as a divided being, hold him fast in his dividedness, his self-contradiction—hold him so completely fast that man does not even perceive the true ground of his self-contradiction but rather (hounded by conscience and therefore fleeing from conscience) veils it behind religions and world-views that are supposed to justify man and soothe his conscience. Even here conscience summons to truth. By driving the *homo peccator* more and more to *desperatio*, to *praesumptio*, or else to dullness and indifference, it makes man more and more his true self. Thus it brings him to his true self in so far as it drives him ever deeper into what he is—which of course means, into untrueness to himself, the power of which lies in the fact that it is not recognized as such. In this way conscience becomes a mistaken, captive conscience. And that, too, precisely also in the very place where man's self-contradiction seems to be obvious—in despair. The conscience which drives to despair is certainly true to the extent that it holds man fast to himself and drives him into the narrows of his own self; yet decidedly not true to the extent that it does not liberate, does not bring man into the open spaces (*Weite*='roominess', but can also='distance') of God—which is the same as to say into the nearness (*Nähe*) of God.

For that reason it is an illusion to suppose that a mere appeal to the conscience and sharpening of responsibility can bring deliverance today to man and consequently to the world. This illusion is created by the

[1] John 8.31 ff.

fact that man today appears primarily to be unconscientious and irresponsible, so that it seems there is everything to gain by a summons to conscientiousness and responsibility. Certainly there must be that too. The decisive help, however, if the crisis of conscience today is to be mastered, must come deeper down—with the communication of the truth that makes men free. It all depends on whether we are able today in ways that are convincing, that affect the conscience, i.e. liberate and make alive (and that includes salutary mortification!), to communicate the Gospel, i.e. the faith which is truly *bona conscientia*. Therein lies the greatness of our task: *Erigere et excitare conscientias nihil aliud est quam suscitare mortuos. Itaque Ecclesia plures vivificat per verbum vocale, quod habet, quam Christus ipse suo ministerio. Sicut inquit (Joh. 14.12): Qui credit in me opera quae ego facio, faciet, et maiora horum faciet.*[1]

[1] *WA* 44, p. 546.24 ff.

XVIII

DISCUSSION THESES FOR A COURSE OF INTRODUCTORY LECTURES ON THE STUDY OF THEOLOGY

1. On the Question of the Necessity of Theology

1. Theology is necessary for the observance of what is necessary for salvation, and is to that extent itself necessary for salvation.

2. Theology is necessary because what is necessary for salvation is a word-event.

3. Theology is necessary in order to answer for the self-evidence of the Word of God.

4. Theology is necessary as the hermeneutics (i.e. theory of understanding or theory of language) of faith.

5. Theology is necessary for the sake of the intellectual honesty of faith, i.e. in order that faith should be real faith.

6. Theology is necessary in order to call Christianity in question.

7. Theology is necessary in order to make preaching as hard for the preacher as it has to be.

8. Theology is necessary for the sake of the general intelligibility of our proclamation.

9. Theology is necessary in order that faith should not be spoken of abstractly.

10. Theology is necessary in order to hold our proclamation to the task of at once both agreeing and disagreeing with what has been handed down (*überliefert*) to us, and, coinciding with that, to agree or disagree with what we are exposed to (*ausgeliefert*).

11. Theology is necessary because man is by nature a fanatic.

12. Theology is necessary in order to protect the conscience from religious violation.

13. Theology is necessary for the defence of reason against unreasonableness.

14. Theology is necessary for the exercise of the distinction between faith and reason, faith and morality, faith and religion.

15. Theology is necessary in order to preserve the freedom which is essential to faith and identical with it.

16. Theology is necessary only to the extent that it makes itself superfluous and makes proclamation necessary.

2. On the Articulation of Theology

1. The man who wishes to study theology with success must radically break with the idea that theology is a conglomeration of separate groups of things and masses of material which are added together to form a whole. This view can lead only to a (manifest or hidden) catastrophe.

2. Theology is an indivisible whole because it has to do with one single, fundamentally simple thing—the Word of God which is not many things but one.

3. The articulation of theology into different fields of study is meaningful only if each partial concern can be understood as of such a kind that the whole is latent in it.

4. It must be grasped that what causes theology to be an indivisible whole and what causes it to be made up of different disciplines is one and the same thing—the event of the Word of God.

5. The basic structure of theology is given by the movement from past proclamation to present proclamation. Accordingly, the task of theology is directed on the one hand towards past proclamation—and indeed there is a threefold division in this, its historical reference: to the Old Testament as testimony to the provisional proclamation, to the New Testament as testimony to the conclusive proclamation, and to church history as testimony to the subsequent proclamation. And on the other hand it is directed towards present proclamation—and indeed there is a twofold reference in this, its systematic and normative task: to what is to be proclaimed (dogmatics) and to the process of proclamation (practical theology).

6. In contrast to the mistaken tendency towards division into independent tasks, we have to consider as the decisive point in this structural sketch how far the past proclamation demands present proclamation and present proclamation depends on past proclamation.

7. The division of theology into disciplines only acquired significance in modern times with the rise of the critical historical method and the tension between it and the normative, systematic approach. This tension is the only important problem in regard to the relationship of the theo-

logical disciplines to each other, but is so problematical that the unity of theology is threatened by it.

8. The earlier absence of this division of method in theology did not by any means guarantee automatically the correct grasp of the single whole of theology. Rather, the dogmatically constructed unity of theology was characterized both by the tendency to use force (e.g. allegorical interpretation, artificial harmonizing of the texts, doctrinarian foreshortening of reality, etc.) and by the summary stringing together of isolated factual truths.

9. The dogmatic positivism that turns theology after the model of jurisprudence into a legal code articulated in paragraphs (as a postulated future) is ultimately the same in structure as the historical positivism that turns theology after the model of descriptive natural science into a museum of established facts (as a substantiated past). The thing common to both is, that an untested view of reality misses the word-event with which theology has to do.

10. The rise of historical thinking and the virulence it brought to the division of theology into different disciplines is not, however, to be dismissed as merely replacing one danger (dogmatism) by another (historism). Apart from the possibility of a combination of both dangers (history as anti-theological dogmatism—dogmatics as pseudo-theological historism) we must consider above all how theology has been furthered by the historical method.

11. The historical part of theology's work holds us to the task of allowing past proclamation to be encountered in its own language without distortion, and precisely in that way becoming free to answer for the past proclamation in our own language in present proclamation.

12. Precisely because the historical part of the work calls the dogmatic part in question, but does not take its place, it is a challenge to pursue our theological studies in the tension between past and present proclamation, and thus by taking our bearings on the word-event.

13. The historical and systematic disciplines of theology do not stand each on their own feet, but are theological disciplines only in relation to each other. This mutual reference is not something accidental to them, but is grounded in their very nature. The historical task of theology, radically understood, contains within it the systematic theological approach, and *vice versa*.

14. The theological disciplines are one from the hermeneutic standpoint. The dualism of method in the competition between historical and systematic theology results from a faulty grasp of the hermeneutic

problem. The consideration which is now being given to hermeneutics serves towards the understanding of the unity of theology by overcoming the mutual isolation of the theological disciplines.

15. Nevertheless a division of the tasks of the theological disciplines (not merely in regard to the different historical fields, but also between historical and systematic theology) is a thing it remains impossible to abandon. But 'historical theology' is theology only to the extent that it bears a share also in the problem of systematic theology; and 'systematic theology' is theology only to the extent that it also shoulders the responsibility where history is concerned.

16. The fact of its reference to the word-event in past and present proclamation prescribes for theology its basic disciplines. It is fanaticism to seek to alter that by additions or subtractions. That way we can only miss the unity of theology. For only on the basis of a correct grasp of the unity can it be seen what can be adduced in theology at a given moment in a subsidiary (but never independent!) way for the carrying out of the hermeneutic task.

3. On the Question of the Bible

1. Holy scripture as the document of faith, i.e. as the testimony to the provisional and the conclusive proclamation of God, is *the* absolute source of present proclamation and therefore the authoritative text of theology.

2. The Bible must therefore be treated with the devotedness, thoroughness and conscientiousness that accord with its authority, i.e. its power to originate and further the coming of the Word of God and faith.

3. This conscientiousness demands the carrying out of every kind of study that can serve the coming to understanding of what the biblical text seeks to bring to understanding. The more biblical a text is, the more clearly it seeks to teach us to believe (not, to make us believe!).

4. Not although, but because we have to do in holy scripture with the Word of God, we have to give the most careful consideration in interpreting it to all the methods and expedients which are appropriate to a text transmitted by tradition. The exposition of the Bible as the most important of all books is in principle carried out in exactly the same way as the exposition of any other book.

5. When the theological significance of the Bible is made to provide (as happens in the doctrine of verbal inspiration) hermeneutic conclusions for the understanding of its origin and its structure as a text which

forbid the conscientious application of general principles of exposition, then that is a misguided, and therefore *de facto* false, respect for the Bible, and is a result of failure to understand the meaning of God's Word and of faith.

6. So-called biblical criticism stands only in seeming contradiction to the authority of the Bible. Rightly understood, it is in the realm of exegesis the way in which the authority of the Bible is brought out.

7. Criticism is an element of integration in the effort to understand the text. For the sake of what the biblical text seeks to bring to understanding, criticism is directed against everything that obstructs this hermeneutic function of the text. It is levelled in principle against distortion of the text—whether distortions in the form of the text resulting from the process of transmission, or distortions in the understanding of the text resulting from traditional prejudices, inappropriate systems of interpretation and unsuitable approaches to the problem, or distortions of the matter itself with which the text as a biblical text has to do, resulting from confusion in the linguistic medium of the text. The purpose of the critical historical method therefore lies ultimately in the interpreter's self-criticism in view of all the conceivable possibilities of deceiving himself as to the aim of the biblical text.

8. The text of holy scripture can open up to very different ways of approach. No angle is *a limine* forbidden, although considering the nature of the text questions from certain angles forbid themselves. And not every possible approach is really appropriate to the character of the text as a linguistic event. The question which is ultimately appropriate to the biblical text is, how it affects the conscience. The hermeneutic principle of proper exegesis of holy scripture is therefore man as conscience.

9. God's Word is the radical opposite of man's word from the standpoint whether the speaker is God, who alone is *verax*, or man, who is *mendax* (Rom. 3.4), and accordingly whether it is a life-giving or killing word-event. But from the standpoint of the manner of its encounter, God's Word as word is identical with the natural, human, spoken word.

10. The confessional statement, 'Scripture is the Word of God', can be rightly understood if the full breadth of the hermeneutic task is also included in the explanation of this way of speaking. But it is dangerously confusing, if the hermeneutic problem is left out of account. It cannot of course be corrected by asserting some form of intermingling of God's Word and man's word, but only by affirming that God's Word by its

very nature is not a written, once-upon-a-time word, but one that is orally spoken and happens. It is not the Bible text, but the proclamation, that is God's Word in the strict sense. In so far as the proclamation is dependent on the text, the exposition therefore serves towards the text proving itself a Bible text, i.e. becoming the source of God's Word.

4. *On the Study of Church History*

1. The study of church history is—because of the infinite abundance of material on the one hand, and because of the impression on the other hand that it seemingly contributes at best only indirectly to the perception of theological truth and the service of the proclamation—in danger of either being carried on in positivistic ways without any inner connexion with the questions of theology, and thus being felt to be superfluous ballast, or else of serving as a neutral field of study which is scientifically unassailable, closed to the troublesome theological problems that call for a decision, and therefore a way of escape from theology.

2. Special attention must be paid to the theological relevance of church history. If it is not correctly grasped, then that is fatal to the study not only of church history but of all the theological disciplines. The dissociation of theology from church history is a symptom and source of bad theology.

3. The question as to the theological significance of church history can be taken up only by embarking without reservations upon the study of church history and allowing it without reservations to relate itself to our theological interests.

4. The theological significance of church history lies in the very fact that it is not a direct source of theological knowledge. The service performed by the study of church history is the disturbance it causes. It makes a naive theological understanding of ourselves impossible and calls in question the sense of our own theological studies.

5. The salutary disturbance brought about in theology by church history consists in the fact that as history it is thoroughly unsystematic and as *church* history it combats the illusion that theology has to do only with theology.

6. The difficulty which church history causes is indicated already in the fact that the definition of what is meant by church history is very elastic. For the one church as an unambiguously demonstrable fact does not exist and never did exist. Plurality of churches, though, in the sense of mutually exclusive confessing churches, is inherently contradictory. A confessionalistically restricted view of church history, however, would

miss the real problem of church history. Church history confronts us with the problem of the self-contradiction of the church.

7. The problematical nature of the concept of the church must not mislead us into evading the difficulty of defining the nature of church history and escaping into the wide field of a history of Christian civilization or into the narrow field of a mere history of theology and dogma —however much both are also included in the task of church history. But the specifically distinguishing feature of church history must be seen in the event which—taking place as it does in human society and therefore producing definite sociological, institutional and linguistic formations and making use of them—makes the church its true self and maintains it as such.

8. The specifically theological question in regard to church history is, to what extent the phenomena of church history raise the question of the relation to Jesus Christ as the origin and ground of the church. The differentiations in church history then confront us from the theological point of view as differences of exposition, and indeed as partly necessary, partly culpable differentiations which cannot be judged from a neutral standpoint, but only in a theological decision. They do not allow of elucidation where their ultimate background is concerned, but rather confront us with a mystery—the mystery which, incidentally, in the form of the unintelligible, underlies all understanding.

9. The study of church history helps to bring us out of the conditionedness of our own historic situation and away from the narrowness and apparent self-evidence of our own spiritual outlook into the wide, but also alien, field, in which Christianity and the church exist in historic reality. Precisely the so-called non-theological factors in church history are important here, if we are to perceive both the corresponding non-theological factors in our own ecclesiastical and theological situation and also the necessary mutual interpenetration of the spiritual and the worldly and the problems of exposition which thereby become peculiarly acute.

10. The study of church history opens the way to the unsurpassed fundamental decisions on the understanding of the Christian faith and therewith to a study of theology which leads into the depths of ultimate questions, which helps us to understand our own background and the peculiarity of the present ecclesiastical and theological situation and assists us to inner freedom in face of the past, and which thus urges us to observe for ourselves our own theological responsibilities.

5. On Systematic Theology

1. It is in systematic theology—which, rightly understood, is an element in all theological disciplines and forms a special theological discipline only in the relatively distinct sense of enquiring explicitly into theology as a whole—that it comes to light whether theology still exists at all. If there were now only historical theology, there would be no theology any more.

2. The business of systematic theology is to consider the traditional testimony to faith as a thing to be answered for in the present. It does not say, 'This is how it was', but, 'This is how it is.'

3. Since theology is dependent on a text—and indeed not just any texts it likes, but a particular text—systematic theology would lose the character of theology the moment historical theology did so.

4. Just as preaching is certainly dependent on the text, yet its real aim is not to expound the text as a text, i.e. as testimony to a past word-event (although the latter is the absolutely necessary presupposition of the sermon), but is rather to expound with the help of the text the reality which presently concerns us, i.e. to bring it to expression in truth and so bring the text to execution as a present word-event—so likewise systematic theology stands at that hermeneutic point of transition from understanding the text to understanding by means of the text, whereby the text disappears as a text and leads to the freedom and authority of 'word', yet at the same time remains in existence as a text in order to preserve the freedom and authority of 'word'.

5. The nature of systematic theology can be defined only in the context of *the* word-event which in the name of Jesus brings God, and for that very reason also the world, to understanding by vindicating faith.

6. Systematic theology's nearness to proclamation is given with the factor they have in common—that they are concerned not with historical correctness, but with truth that opens up a future, truth with which the speaker identifies himself and with which he charges the person addressed.

7. The difference between systematic theology and proclamation consists in the fact that systematic theology uses critical reflexion to say in general, and to that extent abstract and improper, terms what attains to its proper truth only when it is said and heard in a concrete situation, yet for the sake of being vindicated in this concrete way must be exposed to the question of its theological vindicability.

8. In consequence of the relation between systematic theology and proclamation, the claims made by both on the man who embarks upon the one for the sake of the other are: not merely absolute intellectual honesty (which in view of the scientific character of theology is obvious at once), but also, because it is the point of the act of proclamation and must therefore likewise be decisive already in the working out of systematic theology, love to one's neighbour. Man does not exist for the sake of theology, but theology for the sake of man. The love of the subject, without which no act is rightly done, is in theology ultimately the love of our neighbour.

9. It is a fundamental misunderstanding to suppose that because of the 'sola scriptura' we can or must be content with biblical theology (in the historical sense) and confine the function of systematic theology to the mere ordering of the biblical *dicta probantia* according to the theological *Loci*. Rather, because of the 'sola scriptura', rightly understood, the systematic theologian must address himself to every text that is relevant to the coming of God's Word to the world: not only the texts of the church tradition, but also and particularly the texts which voice the world's opposition to God.

10. Systematic theology as a comprehensive assault on the task of theological hermeneutics is the language school of faith. Therefore two interacting methods are constitutive for it: to trace out the linguistic history of the Word of God (including the linguistic history of the opposition to it) and—guided thereby to the encounter with phenomena —to remain open in face of the reality which confronts us for new coming to expression of the Word of God, and that means for creative events in the realm of language.

11. The systematic aspect of systematic theology is not to be confused with the closed architectural structure of a theological doctrinal edifice, which may be useful on occasion, but is not to be overestimated and not without danger. Rather it is a question of grasping the coherence of the subject in two respects: on the one hand the coherence between faith and reality in the whole range of experience and in all the manifold ways of perceiving truth, on the other hand the coherence between the individual statements of faith as mere modifications of one single statement (not, however, as independent factors to be summed up together). Both forms of the question as to the coherence of theology coincide in this: that systematic theology is concerned with the question of what is absolutely necessary, and must therefore be studied with a constant eye to man in his sensitivity to the question

of what is absolutely necessary, i.e. with an eye to man as conscience.

12. Systematic theology, in order to fight out the battle of language with the proper freedom—calling in question and being called in question—requires certain guide-points in order to keep it to the theme of its text. The following propositions may provisionally serve to that end:

> Theology is the scientific coming to expression of the Word of God.
>
> Church doctrine is the coming to expression in confession of the Word of God.
>
> Proclamation is the coming into words of the Word of God.
>
> Revelation is the coming on the scene of the Word of God.
>
> Faith is the coming to its goal of the Word of God.
>
> God's Word is the coming of God.

INDEXES

INDEX OF BIBLICAL REFERENCES

INDEX OF NAMES

CPSIA information can be obtained at www.ICGtesting.com
Printed in the USA
BVOW021558270513

321623BV00007B/57/P